EIGHTH BOOK *of* JUNIOR AUTHORS AND ILLUSTRATORS

Edited by
Connie C. Rockman

The H.W. Wilson Company
New York • Dublin
2000

Biographical Reference Books and Databases from The H. W. Wilson Company

Wilson Biographies Plus Illustrated

American Reformers

Greek and Latin Authors 800 B.C.–A.D. 1000
European Authors 1000–1900
British Authors Before 1800
British Authors of the Nineteenth Century
American Authors 1600–1900
World Authors 1900–1950
World Authors 1950–1970
World Authors 1970–1975
World Authors 1975–1980
World Authors 1985–1990
World Authors 1990–1995
Spanish American Authors of the Twentieth Century

Junior Authors Electronic Edition
The Junior Book of Authors
More Junior Authors
Third Book of Junior Authors
Fourth Book of Junior Authors & Illustrators
Fifth Book of Junior Authors & Illustrators
Sixth Book of Junior Authors & Illustrators
Seventh Book of Junior Authors & Illustrators

Old Worlds to New

Great Composers: 1300–1900
Composers Since 1900
Composers Since 1900: First Supplement
Musicians Since 1900
American Songwriters
World Musicians

Nobel Prize Winners
Nobel Prize Winners: Supplements I & II

World Artists 1950–1980
World Artists 1980–1990

World Film Directors: Volumes I, II

Dedicated to my mother, Lillian Courtright, who introduced me to the joy of reading.

—Connie C. Rockman

International Standard Book Number 0-8242-0968-0

Library of Congress Cataloging-in-Publication Data

The eighth book of junior authors and illustrators / edited by Connie Rockman.
     p. cm.
  Includes biographical references and indexes.
  ISBN 0-8242-0968-0 (alk. paper) ·
  1. Children's literature—Bio-bibliography—Dictionaries. 2. Children's literature—Illustrations—Bio-bibliography—Dictionaries. I. Rockman, Connie.

PN1009.A1 E36 2000
809'.89282—dc21   99-086615

Contents

List of Authors and Illustrators

Preface

In the fall of 1997, *Life* magazine published a special issue commemorating significant events and discoveries of the last thousand years. Acknowledging that the year 2000 is an arbitrary number, the editors of *Life* nevertheless saw this grand, rounded date as an opportunity to reflect on the milestones of human thought and activity since the turn of the last millennium. Their one hundred groundbreaking events were organized in reverse order of importance. About halfway through this historic list, the editors placed "The Invention of Childhood," crediting the Moravian bishop Johan Amos Comenius (1592–1671) with first voicing the revolutionary thought that children need to play to learn, that they need affection as well as education in order to thrive.

Of all the millennium's social and technological revolutions, according to the *Life* editors, the most far-reaching was Johann Gutenberg's printing of the Bible in 1455, which eventually brought the written word to the masses. About one hundred years later, his invention made possible the printing of *Orbis Pictus*, a volume designed by that "inventor of childhood" Comenius to teach the young about the wonders of our world. Historians of children's literature consider *Orbis Pictus* to be the first true picture book for children, beginning a long and honorable tradition of excellent literature for young people.

The Junior Authors and Illustrators Series celebrates those people in our own century, the philosophical descendants of Johan Comenius, who believe that creating books of imagination, information, and fine illustration is an important way to contribute to society, as well as an agreeable and stimulating way to make a living. Within these pages you will meet authors and illustrators of picture books, novels, poetry, and nonfiction of all types.

Who are the authors and illustrators of children's books? They are ordinary people doing extraordinary work. Today they come from many cultural and ethnic traditions, which they share with us through their artistry, along with their innermost beliefs and dreams. To do their work they require discipline, solitude, attention to detail, and perseverance, as well as an abundance of talent. In this collection of sketches you will discover the unique background and experience each creator brings to the books you have come to know and love. You will learn how Jane Kurtz writes so eloquently and knowledgeably about Ethiopia; why Julius Lester, after years of retelling African American folktales, has added stories from the Jewish tradition to his repertoire; and who the model was for Linnea in Christina Björk's story of a visit to Monet's garden.

In the authors' and illustrators' own words, in most cases, children can learn the answers to questions that might intrigue them about their favorite writers and artists, while parents, teachers and librarians can find facts and anecdotes that will help them entice children to read more. Knowing about the creators of books can lead to a deeper understanding of their work and of the creative process in general. What were these artists' lives like when they were children? Who were the family members, teachers, friends, and pets that inspired their work? When did they first know they were destined for a career in children's books? Readers can learn these and many other truths about the creators of their favorite books in the Junior Authors and Illustrators Series.

History: *The Junior Book of Authors*, published in 1934, brought children's book authors to their audience of readers, both young and old. The first compilation of its kind, this volume contained short sketches of writers, often autobiographical and written in a conversational way, that gave the impression of a virtual visit with the author. Subsequent volumes have maintained this immediacy while adding more to the articles—editorial comments about the subjects' works, awards and prizes they have received, representative bibliographies, and suggestions for further research. The 1934 volume underwent a major revision in 1951, adding many newcomers to the field and dropping some early, well-known authors about whom information could readily be found in other sources. Since then six more volumes have been published in this series, all adding names of newly prominent contributors to the field.

Many changes have taken place in literature for young people in the years since this series began. The number of books published every year has grown enormously. Other biographical dictionaries on authors and illustrators have appeared, and a large body of critical writing has accumulated. Children's books have gained validity through literary research. Authors and artists from a wide variety of backgrounds have added cultural diversity to the field. Most recently, the Internet has created a new venue for research, and information on authors and illustrators is now accessible through online searching.

Scope: The Junior Authors and Illustrators Series provides a unique approach to biographical information. Every attempt is made to obtain a statement in the author's or artist's own words, offering the reader a feeling of "getting to know" each subject in an informal way. The editorial piece on each person points out information about his or her life and work that was not mentioned in the autobiography. The bibliographies are not meant to be complete (space constraints prohibit this) but are designed to give a representative sampling of each person's work. Important books that are out of print are included, as well as current titles. A list of suggested readings accompanies most of the sketches and is missing only for contributors who are too new on the scene to have accumulated research about their work. This book, used in conjunction with earlier volumes in the series, provides an excellent point of entry for young readers searching for information about their favorite writers and illustrators, as well as a treasure trove of insights for students of children's literature.

Method: The Editor compiled a voting list of names gleaned from annual lists of "Best Books," various awards in the field, and core lists developed by book wholesalers and librarians. Included on the list were people new to the field in the 1990s, as well as some authors of nonfiction whose books have been standard titles in library collections for many years. The list was sent to experts in children's literature, chosen to represent four parts of the country; they were asked to vote for the subjects they felt were most prominent in the literature today. The advisory committee consisted of Suzanne Hawley, Media Specialist, Laurel Oak Elementary School, Naples, Florida; Amy Kellman, Program Specialist, Carnegie Library of Pittsburgh, Pennsylvania; Cecilia McGowan, Youth Services Coordinator, Spokane Public Library, Washington; and Grace Ruth, Materials Selection Specialist, San Francisco Public Library, California. The authors and illustrators on the final list were then contacted through their most recent publisher and asked to contribute an autobiographical sketch, a photograph, and a signature. The paragraphs after each autobiography were written by the editor and a group of freelance researchers. Articles were contributed by Suzy Hawley, Amy Kellman, Sara Miller, Gail Ostrow, Peter Sieruta, Maeve Visser-Knoth, and Susan Halperin Weiss. Their dedication to tracking down information, verifying facts, and searching out awards was an inspiration to me throughout this process, and they all have my admiration and gratitude. After the editorial pieces were written, completed articles were sent to each author and artist for a final verification of facts.

New Features: The use of the Internet and online searching have expanded remarkably since the last volume in this series was published in 1996, but researching through the World Wide Web is still not as reliable as one might wish. Some authors and illustrators have created their own Web pages; others have had Web sites created for them by devoted fans; many have biographical sketches on publishers' Web sites; still others have a minimal Web presence or none at all. We have added Web site addresses to this volume with some trepidation, knowing how changeable such addresses can be, but at least they give the researcher some indication of how children's book creators are using the Internet to reach their readers in these still-early years of a new technology.

The option of e-mail made contacting many of the authors and illustrators easier and quicker than ever before. Some requested that we include their e-mail addresses in their entries. Of course, this information, along with Web site addresses, may change as people move and Internet service develops, but it does provide a new level of ongoing contact with authors and artists.

With regard to the issue of currency, for the first time in this series since the 1951 revision of *The Junior Book of Authors* we are including updated entries for persons who have appeared in earlier volumes. Of twenty subjects chosen from the first four volumes, fifteen responded enthusiastically with new information. Some chose to keep all or part of their original autobiography; others adapted it considerably to reflect changes in their lives. For each of these updated entries, the accompanying editorial essay indicates the importance of the person's contribution to twentieth century children's literature, and the representative bibliography lists significant works across the span of a long career. These articles are naturally longer than the others and include awards for lifetime achievement, rather than the many awards presented to individual titles. Future volumes in the series will include more of these revisions.

Other innovative features in this volume include a new one-column format, larger photographs, and the addition of book jacket art for many of the entries. A compilation of the major awards and honor lists cited in the articles provides the reader with more information about the professional journals and organizations that recognize excellence in children's books.

Acknowledgments: No work of this magnitude exists without the support and encouragement of many people behind the scenes. I am grateful to Judy O'Malley, editor of *Book Links* magazine, for involving me in the project in the beginning, when she was an editor at the H. W. Wilson Company. Anita Silvey graciously pointed me toward writers who had worked with her when she compiled *Children's Books and Their Creators*, and several of them worked with me as editors and excellent companions on this journey. Sally Holmes Holtze, editor of the 5th, 6th, and 7th books in the series, generously shared her files and advice to help me get started.

My thanks to Trev Jones and Luann Toth for an enjoyable afternoon of brainstorming and searching the database at the offices of *School Library Journal* for new names in the field, and to all the members of my New York–based book discussion group for their continued friendship and stimulation. The freelance editors who worked with me writing the third-person pieces, fact-checking and double-checking, made this an enjoyable collaborative effort all along. Their names are listed above, and they are the best.

I can never say enough about the cheerful help and willing support that my editors and I received from the marketing and editorial departments of all the publishing houses. They contacted authors, provided bibliographic information and biographical pamphlets, answered dozens of questions, and rounded up book jackets to illustrate the articles. In spite of mergers and reconfiguration at the top, the people who work directly in the publishing and marketing of children's books are a community of spirited, dedicated folks. Without them, this book would hardly exist.

The team at the H. W. Wilson Company made this project a joy. Thanks to Gray Young, Beth Levy, Norris Smith, and Jacquelene Latif for sharing my vision of a new look for the Junior Authors and Illustrators Series and for making it happen. For clerical help, kudos go to my ever-dependable helper and neighbor, Sarah Paoletta. For keeping me connected to what kids are *really* reading, my gratitude goes to The Borrowers Club of the Stratford Library. For technical assistance in my still-emerging computer skills, the next generation was always ready to help—thanks, Elena and Jon, for being there when your Mom needed you and for sharing my joy in literature from the beginning. And for his support, patience, and understanding, my husband, Joe Witkavitch, takes the prize.

Finally, I want to thank the contributors to this book who took time away from their own lives and livelihood to create the wonderful autobiographical statements you are about to enjoy. They have shared their talents with us in books of all kinds, and now each one also shares a window into his or her life so that we readers may know their books a little better than before.

Connie Rockman
Stratford, Connecticut
January 2000
connie.rock@snet.net

"I was born on January 3, 1938, in the outskirts of Camagüey, Cuba, in an old house which our neighbors believed was haunted. Every evening as we watched the sunset I listened to my grandmother's stories of the struggle for freedom, equality, and justice that had been carried on by the earlier inhabitants of that same house. Her ability to make history come alive for me planted the seed—that children can listen to very important topics if they are presented as a good story. Many of my books touch on issues like identity (*My Name Is María Isabel*), deciding by oneself what is right (*The Malachite Palace*), or finding ways to improve the world around us (*Jordi's Star*).

"I have also retold the folktales she told me (*The Rooster Who Went to His Uncle's Wedding, Half-Chicken*) and so, many years after her death, they became new gifts from her. But my grandmother was not the only storyteller in my childhood. Everyone in my family loved a story well told. My uncle Tony told family stories very vividly, making himself a part of the action . . . even if the story had happened before he entered the family by marrying my Aunt Lolita, or before he was born. No one could ever set the record straight. His telling was so convincing that he actually began to believe that he'd been there each time! My book *Where the Flame Trees Bloom* is a collection of real-life stories of my childhood and my relatives, part of this legacy of family storytelling.

"My father, instead, created each night a new chapter of an unending story of human beings in this planet. He was not concerned with the history of kings or well-known figures, but rather on how the common people, a step at a time, had developed civilizations. This combination of reality and fantasy delighted me. The fact that he created these stories just for me formed a most

Courtesy of Ann Duffy

Alma Flor Ada

January 3, 1938–

powerful bond between us. It also gave me the gift of fantasy to invent my own worlds (*The Unicorn of the West*) and the desire to sing the praise of those who make life every day, as in *Gathering the Sun*, my homage to the farmworkers.

"I was a rather quiet and observant child. I was lucky to be allowed long hours in nature by myself. A bird, a flower, or a leaf could fascinate me. I lived next to a river, a source of constant wonders: leaping frogs, funny tadpoles, skittish turtles that would disappear in the water at the slightest noise, dragonflies, egrets, cranes . . . they have all found a way into my writing, as in *Friend Frog*, because they are all so alive in my memory.

"Books were wonderful companions and their characters totally real to me. This is why I have enjoyed so much playing at writing letters between storybook characters in my picture books *Dear Peter Rabbit* and *Yours Truly, Goldilocks*.

"When we moved to town I discovered a world full of people. Every human feeling and thought seemed to exist around me, if I just listened and reflected enough. Little by little many of these people have also found their way into my books. Sometimes as real-life characters in my book of memories, *Under the Royal Palms*, sometimes as a character in a story, like Doña Josefa in *The Gold Coin*. I never believed I would be a writer—although as a teenager I thought I would be a journalist—and became a teacher instead. But my love for words, for books and creativity made it inevitable that I would become an author. The rewards of authoring books have been many: It has been the means to rescue many of the experiences of my life and share them with others. It has given me the opportunity to work collaboratively with my daughter, Rosa Zubizarreta, who has translated many of my publications, and above all it has allowed me to get to know many children and teachers throughout the world, perhaps even you. What a joy it is!"

> *"Every evening as we watched the sunset I listened to my grandmother's stories of the struggle for freedom, equality and justice."*

* * *

Not only is Alma Flor Ada a renowned author, but she is also well known as a translator, scholar, educator, storyteller, and advocate for bilingual and multicultural education. Her children's books have been published in Argentina, Colombia, Mexico, Peru, Spain, and the United States. She is the recipient of Argentina's Marta Salotti Gold Medal Award for *Encaje de Piedra* (*Stone Lace*), an intriguing mystery set in Spain during the Middle Ages. She received a Christopher Award for *The Gold Coin*, a tale set in a South American country, that invites readers to explore the true nature of wealth. A number of her books have been selected as Notable Trade Books in the Field of Social Studies—*The Lizard and the Sun*, *Gathering the Sun*, *Under the Royal Palms*, *The Gold Coin*, and *My Name Is María Isabel*. *Dear Peter Rabbit* won a Parents' Choice Honor Award. In 2000

Ada received the Pura Belpré Award for her memoir *Under the Royal Palms: A Childhood in Cuba*.

Ada has studied and taught in Spain, Peru, and the United States. She earned an undergraduate degree from Universidad Complutense de Madrid in Spain in 1959 and moved to Peru, where she completed her master's degree and doctorate at Pontificia Universidad Catolica del Peru. She is currently a professor of multicultural education at the University of San Francisco; she also works in schools with teachers, children, and parents. She has received numerous awards for research, including the University of San Francisco Distinguished Research Award from the School of Education in 1984. In the following year, she received the University of San Francisco's Outstanding Teacher Award.

Alma Flor Ada is the mother of four and grandmother of eight. She says that her children inspire some of her best writing. She takes great pleasure in the fact that her daughter Rosa collaborates with her and translates and edits many of her books.

SELECTED WORKS: *The Song of the Teeny Tiny Mosquito*, illus. by Vivi Escriva, 1989; *The Gold Coin*, illus. by Neil Waldman, 1991; *How the Rainbow Came to Be*, illus. by Vivi Escriva, 1991; *The Rooster Who Went to His Uncle's Wedding*, illus. by Kathleen Kuchera, 1993; *My Name Is María Isabel*, illus. by K. Dyble Thompson, 1993; *The Unicorn of the West*, illus. by Abigail Pizer, 1994; *Dear Peter Rabbit*, illus. by Leslie Tryon, 1994; *Mediopollito / Half-Chicken*, illus. by Kim Howard, 1995; *Jordi's Star*, illus. by Susan Gaber, 1996; *The Lizard and the Sun / La Lagartija y el Sol*, 1997; *Gathering the Sun: An Alphabet in Spanish and English*, illus. by Simon Silva, 1997; *Where the Flame Trees Bloom*, illus. by Antonia Martorell, 1998; *The Malachite Palace*, illus. by Leonid Gore, 1998; *Yours Truly, Goldilocks*, illus. by Leslie Tryon, 1998; *Under the Royal Palms: A Childhood in Cuba*, 1998; *The Three Golden Oranges*, illus. by Reg Cartwright, 1999.

Courtesy of Simon & Schuster Children's Publishing Division

SUGGESTED READING: *Contemporary Authors*, vol. 123, 1988; Day, Frances Ann. *Latina and Latino Voices in Literature for Children and Young Adults*, 1997; *Something About the Author*, vol. 43, 1986; vol. 84, 1996. Periodicals—Ada, Alma

Flor, "From Flame Trees and Royal Palms to Manzanitas and Madronnes," *CMLEA Journal*, Spring 1992.

WEB SITE: *www.penguinputnam.com/catalog/yreader/authors*

Courtesy of Alexander Limont

Lloyd Alexander

January 30, 1924–

"Writers are supposed to have colorful imaginations; but I could never have imagined the joy I would find in writing for young people. At one point, I could never have imagined becoming any kind of writer at all. Born in Philadelphia, Pennsylvania, and hoping, from the age of fifteen, to be a poet, I had even tried to memorize (unsuccessfully) every poem in every anthology I could find; a hungry reader, I also devoured Dickens, Shakespeare, Mark Twain, Victor Hugo, fairy tales, mythology, and whatever else came to hand. At sixteen, graduating from high school, I announced my literary intentions to my parents. They assured me there was no brisk commercial demand for poets and very vigorously urged me to forget about writing and do something sensible with my life.

"My parents couldn't afford sending me to college, but they did find me a job as a bank messenger. I found the job a disaster. A poet toiling away in some earthbound financial wasteland? I spent my nights reading and writing and spent my days being miserable. Eventually, I saved enough money for a year at a local college, but I soon dropped out, disappointed, for I wanted to learn more than what was being taught. In World War II, I joined the Army—amazed that such a large organization should be at a loss what to do with a would-be poet. I became an artilleryman, a cymbal player in the band, a first-aid man, and, finally, a staff sergeant in combat intelligence in France and Germany. Later, I was attached to a counter-intelligence unit in Paris.

"After the war, I stayed in Paris and went to the Sorbonne. At the same time, I met—and married—a Parisian girl, Janine; in 1946 we came back to the United States, where I set about being a writer. Turning from poetry, I wrote novel after novel. The only difficulty: no one would publish them. And rightly so, for they were the worst ever perpetrated. Writers, like everyone else, have to buy groceries, so I worked at whatever I found: advertising copywriter, cartoonist, layout artist, and associate editor for a local industrial magazine. It took seven years, rejection slip after rejection slip, before my first novel was published.

"During the next ten years, I wrote a variety of books for adults. For reasons I still don't quite understand, I felt an over-powering urge to attempt a book for young people. My first fantasy for children, *Time Cat*, led me to create my own mythical world in what would become the Chronicles of Prydain. Writing for young people turned out to be the most creative and liberating experience of my life.

"What I discovered, joyously and suprisingly: In books for young people, I was able to express my own deepest feelings far more than I could ever do in writing for adults. Most of my books have been in the form of fantasy; but fantasy, for me, is merely one of the many ways to deal with our own here-and-now reality: our relationships, problems, and often anguishing dilemmas. Writing realism or fantasy, my concerns are the same: how we learn to be genuine human beings.

"This has been, I realize, a very sketchy autobiography and one that is still an ongoing process. Even when we discover, each of us, what it is that we love best to do, it's not an ending, only a beginning. As for writers, their truest autobiography is in the books they write. Every work is, I believe, an aspect of the writer himself and his own personal vision. This, really, is all that any writer can offer—along with the hope that he will offer it well."

* * *

Stationed briefly in Wales with a U.S. Army combat intelligence unit during World War II, Lloyd Alexander found himself captured by the wild beauty and ancient folklore of the country, recalling his boyhood enjoyment of the tales of King Arthur. Twenty years later, while working on his first fantasy book for children, *Time Cat*, Alexander researched a chapter on Celtic Britain and decided to expand it into a series of stories, which became The Chronicles of Prydain. One of the more compelling fantasy worlds in literature, Prydain is a medieval land about the size of Wales. *The Book of Three* begins the story of Taran, an impetuous Assistant Pig-Keeper who longs for heroic adventure. Through the next four volumes (*The Black Cauldron*, *The Castle of Llyr*, *Taran Wanderer*, and *The High King*), Taran's encounters with warriors, enchanters, talking beasts, and magical devices show him growing into manhood through a series of adventures that test his courage and heart and teach him wisdom. With characters and events loosely based on *The Mabinogion*, an ancient cycle of Welsh tales, the Prydain chronicles are distinctively Alexander's own mix of heroism and humor. *The Black Cauldron* was designated as a Newbery Honor Book in 1966 and *The High King* was awarded the Newbery Medal in 1969.

> *"Every work is, I believe, an aspect of the writer himself and his own personal vision. This, really, is all that any writer can offer . . . along with the hope that he will offer it well."*

Alexander's picaresque novel about a wandering musician, *The Marvelous Misadventures of Sebastian*, won the National Book Award for children's books in 1970. His Westmark trilogy (*Westmark*, *The Kestrel*, and *The Beggar Queen*) is set in an imaginary European kingdom and constitutes a searching study of power politics, the brutality of war, and the effect of both on the human spirit. *Westmark* was the winner of the 1982 American Book Award for children's literature. Another, lighter, series—beginning with *The Illyrian Adventure*—chronicles the escapades of Vesper Holly, a dashing young woman who is regularly called upon to foil villains and right wrongs, sometimes in her home town of Philadelphia but more often in exotic locales.

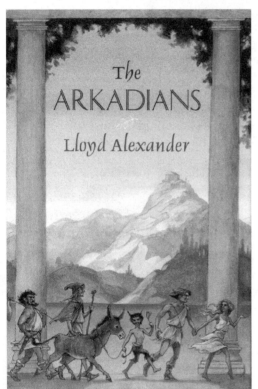

Courtesy of Penguin Putnam

Reminiscent of old-time serials, the Vesper Holly books feature cliff-hanger plots and tongue-in-cheek humor.

Alexander's later quest-fantasies— *The Remarkable Journey of Prince Jen*, set in China and inspired by novels of the Ming and Ch'ing dynasties; *The Iron Ring*, set in India and loosely based upon episodes of the *Mahabharata*; and *The Arkadians*, arising out of his love for the Greek myths—are all full of humor, adventure, and highly expressive characters.

Though not as well known as his novels, Alexander's picture book texts have pleased many readers over the years. Two short tales of Prydain were published in picture book format in the 1960s (*Coll and His White Pig* and *The Truthful Harp*) and a modern fable, *The King's Fountain*, was powerfully illustrated by Ezra Jack Keats in 1971. A droll story that Alexander had written years before, *The Fortune-tellers*, found its way into print in 1992 with striking illustrations by Trina Schart Hyman and captured the *Boston Globe–Horn Book* Award for picture books in 1993.

Alexander's novels and picture books have consistently appeared on the "best" lists for children's books throughout the years. In 1986 he was awarded the Regina Medal by the Catholic Library Association for the body of his work, and in 1984 he received the Swedish Golden Cat prize for his contributions to children's literature. In 1999 the entire Prydain series was reissued, with pronunciation guides for the Welsh names, and a new edition of *The Foundling* was expanded to include the texts of the picture-book stories about Prydain.

An avid amateur violinist, Alexander has often woven music themes and musician characters into his stories. His fondness for cats is evident in the many and various feline characters throughout his books. Lloyd Alexander lives in Drexel Hill, Pennsylvania, with his wife, Janine.

Courtesy of Henry Holt & Co.

SELECTED WORKS: *Border Hawk*, 1958; *The Flagship Hope: Aaron Lopez*, 1960; *Time Cat: The Remarkable Journeys of Jason and Gareth*, illus. by Bill Sokol, 1963; *The Book of Three*, 1964; *The Black Cauldron*, 1965; *Coll and His White Pig*, illus. by Evaline Ness, 1965; *The Castle of Llyr*, 1966; *Taran Wanderer*, 1967; *The Truthful Harp*, illus. by Evaline Ness, 1967; *The High King*, 1968; *The Marvelous Misadventures of Sebastian*, 1970; *The King's Fountain*, illus. by Ezra Jack Keats, 1971; *The Four Donkeys*, illus. by Lester Abrams, 1972; *The Foundling and Other Tales of Prydain*, illus. by Margot Zemach, 1973; *The Cat Who Wished to Be a Man*, 1973; *The Wizard in the Tree*, illus. by Laszlo Kubinyi, 1975; *The Town Cats and Other Tales*, illus. by Laszlo Kubinyi, 1977; *The First Two Lives of Lukas-Kasha*, 1978; *Westmark*, 1981; *The Kestrel*, 1982; *The Beggar Queen*, 1984; *The Illyrian Adventure*, 1986; *The El Dorado Adventure*, 1987; *The Drackenberg Adventure*, 1988; *The Jedera Adventure*, 1989; *The Philadelphia Adventure*, 1990; *The Remarkable Journey of Prince Jen*, 1991; *The Fortune-tellers*, illus. by Trina Schart Hyman, 1992; *The Arkadians*, 1995; *The House Gobbaleen*, illus. by Diane Goode, 1995; *The Iron Ring*, 1997; *Gypsy Rizka*, 1999.

SUGGESTED READING: Alexander, Lloyd. *And Let the Credit Go*, 1955; Alexander, Lloyd. *Janine Is French*, 1959; *Children's Literature Review*, vol. 1, 1976; vol. 5, 1983; vol. 48, 1998; *Contemporary Authors*, New Revision Series, vol. 55, 1997; *Contemporary Literary Criticism*, vol 35, 1985; *Dictionary of Literary Biography*, vol 52, 1986; Hipple, Ted, ed. *Writers for Young Adults*, 1997; Jacobs, James and Tunnell, Michael O. *Lloyd Alexander: A Bio-bibliography*, 1991; May, Jill P. *Lloyd Alexander*, 1991; Pendergast, Sara, ed. *St. James Guide to Children's Writers*, 5th ed., 1999; Silvey, Anita, ed. *Children's Books and Their Creators*, 1995; *Something About the Author*, vol. 3, 1972; vol. 49, 1987; vol. 81, 1995;

Something About the Author Autobiography Series, vol. 19, 1995; Tunnell, Michael O. *The Prydain Companion: A Reference Guide to Lloyd Alexander's Prydain Chronicles*, 1989. Periodicals—Alexander, Lloyd, "American Book Award Acceptance Speech," *The Horn Book*, October 1982; Alexander, Lloyd, "Fantasy and the Human Condition," *New Advocate*, Spring 1988; Alexander, Lloyd, "The Flat-Heeled Muse," *The Horn Book*, April 1965; Alexander, Lloyd, "Newbery Acceptance Speech," *The Horn Book*, August 1969; Alexander, Lloyd, "Wishful Thinking—or Hopeful Dreaming?" *The Horn Book*, August 1968; Tunnell, Michael O., "Fantasy at Its Best: Alexander's Chronicles of Prydain," *Children's Literature in Education*, December 1990; Tunnell, Michael O., "An Interview with Lloyd Alexander," *New Advocate*, Spring 1989.

WEB SITE: *www.penguinputnam.com/catalog/yreader/authors*

An earlier profile of Lloyd Alexander appeared in *Third Book of Junior Authors* (1972).

Jennifer Armstrong

May 12, 1961–

"I always was a liar. I was born that way. I'm not malicious or anything, just fond of embellishment. And really, isn't the story usually better when it's augmented by fascinating details and episodes? I was, as they say, an imaginative child. I played well with others, sure—my nursery school report card will bear me out—but I was very happy alone, spinning out my own fantasies. It amused me. It made my world large.

"Perhaps my parents did not realize they should be so on guard about my moral education; I did not discriminate between making up stories for myself and fobbing them off on other people as the truth. And here's the kicker: I was good. Mostly, people didn't suspect I was lying, because a) I was very sweet, and b) I threw in just enough truthfulness to make my lies credible. So I never had to suffer the shame of being chased off the playground by classmates screaming 'Liar, liar, pants on fire!' Perhaps I should have; it would have served as a much-needed corrective. But as I grew older, my lies became more and more sophisticated, and I delighted in testing my powers: Just how big a whopper could I tell and still be believed?

"Fortunately, I had long since begun making up stories *as* stories. I graduated from being an imaginative child to being a creative student. I wrote poetry. I wrote plays. I knew I was a storyteller. It didn't take long for me to realize I was a *Writer*. And with that realization came (thank goodness!) my belated moral development. I stopped telling lies and concentrated on writing fiction. But still, as any confirmed liar will tell you, I become enraged when I'm accused of prevaricating.

"Inasmuch as fiction is *made up*, some people think it's not true. 'I only like true books,' I've heard some students say as they head for the nonfiction stacks. They're suspicious and wary around novels: novels just aren't trustworthy. But I consider it the duty of a fiction writer to write what is truthful, whether the events described in the story ever happened or not.

"Unlike many children's book authors, I don't mine the ore of my own childhood for novels. I spend a lot of time reading history, and when I hit upon an intriguing event or set of circumstances, I begin the what-if game. What if a girl lived on the prairie in a sod house and her mother was withdrawn, but someone gave them a canary? What if an Irish immigrant got caught up in the American Civil War and had to assign her allegiance? And when I'm answering these what-if questions, I try to be truthful: I believe this is what *would* happen if . . . .

"It's important to me that readers feel my books are honest. Because I'm not a liar. I just make up stories. There's a difference.

"I will mention briefly how I work, because people always seem to be curious about the nuts and bolts of a writer's day. I do extensive prep work for my novels: lots of research, lots of notes, lots of outlining, lots of plans, lots of lists. Then, when I know what I'm working with, I sit down at the computer and write it. That's it, pretty much. Five to ten pages a day, and eventually you get to write THE END. (Of course, it's doesn't really happen *quite* like that, but doesn't it sound better that way?)"

Courtesy of Phil Haggerty

*　*　*

Jennifer Armstrong was born in Waltham, Massachusetts, and, with the exception of one year spent living in Switzerland with her family, grew up in South Salem, New York. After receiving her B.A. from Smith College in 1983, she began working as an assistant editor at Cloverdale Press, a packager of fiction paperback series. Soon she was ghostwriting some of the books herself. As "Julia Winfield," she contributed to the Sweet Dreams series. As "Kate William" she wrote for Sweet Valley High. Ultimately, she wrote the first several dozen volumes in the Sweet Valley Kids series.

Jennifer Armstrong has also written paperback series under her own name, including the four-volume Pets, Inc. series and the Wild Rose Inn sequence of historical romances, which trace an American family through several generations. However, she is best known for her hardcover fiction and picture books. Her first novel, *Steal Away*, was an ALA Notable Children's Book and Best Book for Young Adults. It was also named a Golden Kite Honor Book by the Society of Children's Book Writers and Illustrators. Armstrong's picture books *Hugh Can Do* and *Chin Yu Min and the Ginger Cat* were also cited as ALA Notable Children's Books. *The Dreams of Mairhe Mehan* was named a 1997 Children's Book of Distinction by the *Hungry Mind Review* and received a Blue Ribbon citation from the *Bulletin of the Center for Children's Books*. In 1999, *Shipwreck at the Bottom of the World* was named an ALA Notable Children's Book and received the Orbis Pictus Award from the National Council of Teachers of English for the best nonfiction book for children. *In My Hands*, the memoir of Irene Gut Opdyke, as told by Jennifer Armstrong, was named one of the top ten of ALA's Best Books for Young Adults in 2000.

The author and her husband live in Saratoga Springs, New York.

SELECTED WORKS: *The Puppy Project*, 1990; *Steal Away*, 1992; *Hugh Can Do*, illus. by Kimberly Bulcken Root, 1992; *Chin Yu Min and the Ginger Cat*, illus. by Mary Grandpré, 1993; *Bridie of the Wild Rose Inn*, 1994; *Black-eyed Susan*, 1995; *King Crow*, illus. by Eric Rohmann, 1995; *Wan Hu Is in the Stars*, illus. by Barry Root, 1995; *The Dreams of Mairhe Mehan*, 1996; *Patrick Doyle Is Full of Blarney*, illus. by Krista Brauckmann-Towns, 1996; *Mary Mehan Awake*, 1997; *Audubon*, 1998; *Shipwreck at the Bottom of the World: The Extraordinary True Story of Shackleton and the Endurance*, 1998; *Pierre's Dream*, illus. by Susan Gaber, 1999; *In My Hands: Memories of a Holocaust Rescuer*, by Irene Gut Opdyke with Jennifer Armstrong, 1999.

SUGGESTED READING: *Contemporary Authors*, New Revision Series, vol. 67, 1998; *Something About the Author*, vol. 77, 1994; *Something About the Author Autobiography Series*, vol. 24, 1997.

SHIPWRECK AT THE BOTTOM OF THE WORLD

Courtesy of Random House

"When I was growing up, books were something you fooled with occasionally when things were quiet. That wasn't often in a family of four boys. Mom read to us when we were little. Dad always had a thick Reader's Digest Condensed Books volume open on his chest as he napped in front of the TV. I seldom saw Mom read for herself, but I know she did. Sometimes in the night I would go to her bedside for some reason. Dad would be snoring. Mom's small light would be on and she would be just closing a book, ready to see what I needed. They never talked to us about their books. Reading just happened quietly, in the background.

"I was in fifth grade in my hometown of Elmira, New York, when Dad lost his factory job. Soon after, my brothers and I learned we were moving to Florida. Wow! Beaches and swimming and sunshine and beaches!!! With a job lined up, Dad drove us to Gainesville, Florida, which I learned later is as far from beaches as you can get and still be in Florida (almost).

Courtesy of Carol Arnold

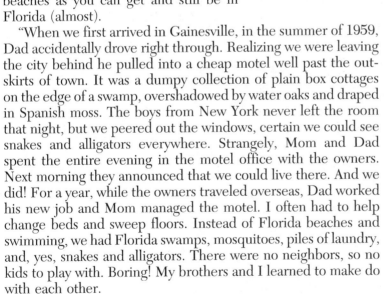

Tedd Arnold

January 20, 1949–

"When we first arrived in Gainesville, in the summer of 1959, Dad accidentally drove right through. Realizing we were leaving the city behind he pulled into a cheap motel well past the outskirts of town. It was a dumpy collection of plain box cottages on the edge of a swamp, overshadowed by water oaks and draped in Spanish moss. The boys from New York never left the room that night, but we peered out the windows, certain we could see snakes and alligators everywhere. Strangely, Mom and Dad spent the entire evening in the motel office with the owners. Next morning they announced that we could live there. And we did! For a year, while the owners traveled overseas, Dad worked his new job and Mom managed the motel. I often had to help change beds and sweep floors. Instead of Florida beaches and swimming, we had Florida swamps, mosquitoes, piles of laundry, and, yes, snakes and alligators. There were no neighbors, so no kids to play with. Boring! My brothers and I learned to make do with each other.

"Except for school, I seldom got into Gainesville. But soon a pattern set in that would help to shape my future as an artist and author. Each Sunday after church, we stopped downtown at Mike's Bookstore and Newsstand. While Dad bought his pipe tobacco and Sunday paper, I discovered *Mad* magazine and paperback science fiction. Then Mom found the public library. On Saturday mornings she would drop the kids there and go shopping. (You could do that back then.) I read about Charles Lindbergh and western cowboys. I checked out books on card games and magic tricks. And I wore out the library's 'how to draw' books.

"Often I feel that, as parents, we don't provide time for our children to discover themselves naturally. We fill their schedules with activities. But some self-discovery can only come from an ample supply of free time. We shouldn't be afraid to let our children experience boredom. Let them work through to the other side of boredom, where creativity resides. During that year of isolation in a Florida swamp, two of my biggest treats involved going into town for books. Don't get me wrong. We lived very active, outdoor lives and learned about Florida from the inside out. And I will never forget the bizarre mix of people that checked into the motel. Nevertheless, I had huge chunks of boring free time. Much of it I filled with *Mad*-inspired cartooning and books. Looking back, I see it was my childhood drawing and reading that put me on the path to becoming an artist and author."

> *"Looking back, I see it was my childhood drawing and reading that put me on the path to becoming an artist and author."*

* * *

Born on January 20, 1949, in Elmira, New York, Tedd Arnold moved with his family to Gainesville, Florida, at age ten. His first art lessons in an abandoned dentist's office over the Happy Hour Pool Hall eventually led to a fine arts degree from the University of Florida. He married Carol Clark on August 15, 1971, and they started their family in Tallahassee, where Tedd worked as a commercial illustrator. For three years he owned and directed a graphic design studio. Carol, a kindergarten teacher, brought Tedd's attention to children's books. He was attracted to their colorful pages and the way the words and pictures played with each other, much like the captioned cartoons he had drawn when he was young. He started writing stories that he thought would be fun to illustrate and began submitting his ideas and artwork to publishers. For six years, he received only rejection slips in return. During that time, Tedd moved his family to New York City, where he worked as a book designer for a large publisher.

The Arnolds' first son, Walter, and their aging apartment building in Yonkers inspired Tedd Arnold's breakthrough picture book, *No Jumping on the Bed!* Later Walter inspired *Parts* when he lost his first tooth. Once Tedd Arnold's dream of publishing his own picture books came true, it freed him from his "day job" routine. He and his family moved back to Elmira, where he now writes and illustrates children's books full-time. The Arnolds' second son, William, stars in *No More Water in the Tub!*, a sequel to *No Jumping on the Bed!*.

Axle Annie, the story of an unstoppable school bus driver, illustrated by Tedd Arnold from Robin Pulver's text, was named a 1999 Smithsonian Notable Book for Children.

SELECTED WORKS WRITTEN AND ILLUSTRATED: *No Jumping on the Bed!*, 1987; *Ollie Forgot*, 1988; *Mother Goose's Words of Wit and Wisdom: A Book of Months*, 1990; *The Signmaker's Assistant*, 1992; *Green Wilma*, 1993; *No More Water in the Tub!* 1995; *Five Ugly Monsters*, 1995; *Parts*, 1997; *Huggly Gets Dressed*, 1997; *Huggly Takes a Bath*, 1998; *Huggly and the Toy Monster*, 1998.

SELECTED WORKS ILLUSTRATED: *My Working Mom*, by Peter Glassman, 1994; *Inside a Barn in the Country*, by Alyssa Capucilli, 1995; *Tracks*, by David Galef, 1996; *My Dog Never Says Please*, by Suzanne Williams, 1997; *Axle Annie*, by Robin Pulver, 1999.

SUGGESTED READING: *Contemporary Authors*, vol. 137, 1992; Cummins, Julie. *Children's Book Illustration and Design*, vol. 2, 1998; *Something About the Author*, vol. 69, 1992. Periodicals—*Growing Point*, July 1989; Kuby, Patricia, "Learning About Environmental Print Through Picture Books," *Early Childhood Education Journal*, Fall 1996; *Language Arts*, April 1988; *New Yorker*, November 30, 1987; *Times Literary Supplement*, April 7, 1989.

WEB SITE: *www.teddarnold.com*

Mary Jane Auch

(owk)

November 21, 1938–

"I was born in Mineola, New York, and raised in Rochester. The thought of becoming a writer never occurred to me; when I was in school, we never had visits from authors and illustrators. If I had known there was such a job as book author and illustrator, I would have picked my future career by first grade.

"I loved books and read every book I could get my hands on, and I had loved to draw from the time I was able to hold a pencil or crayon. I studied art through high school and went on to become an art major at Skidmore College. After graduation, I headed for New York City to seek fame and fortune, but after a year of designing prints for men's pajamas, I decided I wanted to do something more 'meaningful' with my life. I enrolled in the Occupational Therapy program at Columbia University, which led to some wonderful years of working in a children's hospital near Hartford, Connecticut.

"My husband, Herm, and I were married in 1967 and within a few years had produced a son and daughter and moved from the city to a small farm, complete with chickens, ducks, and geese. Armed with a huge collection of *Mother Earth News* and absolutely no practical experience, I tackled farm life with gusto, gaining much comedy material for books I still didn't know I would write.

"As our children grew older, I began to look for work in my original field of art. I had a few strange jobs: designing a billboard for a local politician, and, like Jenna's mother in *Mom Is Dating Weird Wayne*, a brief stint as 'zit zapper' at a school picture factory. Then I started illustrating for Pennywhistle Press, a national children's newspaper, and this rekindled my interest in illustrating children's books.

"In the summer of 1984, some friends suggested that I join them for a week-long children's writing workshop. I tried to write a picture book manuscript, but instead found myself writing a middle grade novel. When our instructor, Natalie Babbitt, told of starting out as an artist and finding she could paint better pictures with words, something clicked inside my head. At the age of forty-six, I finally knew what I wanted to be when I grew up!

"I started sending my manuscripts to publishers, writing four full-length novels before I sold the first one, *The Witching of Ben Wagner*. Then I sold a second book to another publisher that same week. It had taken two years and thirteen rejections, but I had finally reached my goal!

"I continued writing books for older kids and abandoned my dream of illustrating for a while. Then, after nine books, I wrote and illustrated *The Easter Egg Farm*. This set in motion a series of picture books featuring poultry involved in the arts.

"We have now become a family of artists. Both my daughter, Kat, and my son, Ian, work in graphic design; and Herm, who works as a graphic artist for the *Rochester Democrat & Chronicle*, has just made his first venture into children's books by illustrating one of my recent titles, *I Was a Third Grade Science Project*."

Courtesy of Mary Jane Auch

Mary Jane Auch

*   *   *

Mary Jane Auch, who lives in Ontario, New York, is a popular author whose books consistently appear on state award lists, voted on by children. *Cry Uncle!* was nominated for Missouri's Mark Twain Award, the Virginia Young Readers Award, the Utah Children's Book Award, and Tennessee's Volunteer State

Book Award. *Glass Slippers Give You Blisters* was nominated for the Indian Paintbrush Book Award in Wyoming, the Pacific Northwest Young Readers' Choice Award, Oklahoma's Sequoyah Children's Book Award, and state prizes in Virginia, Florida, Utah, and West Virginia. *Kidnapping Kevin Kowalski* was a nominee for both the Florida Sunshine State Young Reader's Award and the Mark Twain Award in Missouri.

Her first effort as an author-illustrator, *The Easter Egg Farm*, was named an IRA/CBC Children's Choice book, and won both the North Dakota Flicker Tale Children's Book Award and the "Little Archer" designation from Wisconsin's Golden Archer Awards. Among her other self-illustrated books, *Hen Lake* was nominated for the Black-Eyed Susan Picture Book Award in Maryland and the Young Readers Award in Virginia, and *Peeping Beauty* appeared on Tennessee's Volunteer State Book Award nomination list. *I Was a Third Grade Science Project* was listed for the Texas Bluebonnet Award, while *Journey to Nowhere* appeared on the Hoosier Award nomination list.

A number of Auch's titles have been Junior Library Guild selections in recent years. Mary Jane Auch visits schools to discuss her work and has been a writing instructor in the Children's Publishing and Writing Institute at Vassar College.

"It had taken two years and thirteen rejections, but I had finally reached my goal."

SELECTED WORKS WRITTEN: *The Witching of Ben Wagner*, 1987; *Cry Uncle!*, 1987; *Pick of the Litter*, 1988; *Mom Is Dating Weird Wayne*, 1988; *Glass Slippers Give You Blisters*, 1989; *A Sudden Change of Family*, 1990; *Kidnapping Kevin Kowalski*, 1990; *Seven Long Years until College*, 1991; *Out of Step*, 1992; *Bird Dogs Can't Fly*, 1993; *The Latchkey Dog*, illus. by Cat Bowman Smith, 1994; *Dumbstruck*, 1994; *Journey to Nowhere*, 1996; *Frozen Summer*, 1998; *I Was a Third Grade Science Project*, illus. by Herm Auch, 1998.

SELECTED WORKS WRITTEN AND ILLUSTRATED: *The Easter Egg Farm*, 1992; *Peeping Beauty*, 1993; *Monster Brother*, 1994; *Hen Lake*, 1995; *Eggs Mark the Spot*, 1996; *Bantam of the Opera*, 1997; *The Nutquacker*, 1999.

"Growing up on a small farm in what is now suburban Washington, D.C., I had the best of two worlds. On the one hand, I lived surrounded by gardens, fields, and woods. I spent hours on a pony exploring what was then still a rural area. On the other hand, we lived within thirty minutes of Washington and its wealth of museums and other cultural opportunities. I spent many hours in the National Gallery, the Museum of Natural History, and other parts of the Smithsonian.

"I developed an interest in art at an early age. In the fourth grade, I did my first linoleum cut; it was, not surprisingly, a Christmas card with the word NOEL carved below the image. Un-

Mary Azarian

December 8, 1940–

fortunately, I didn't realize that the image would reverse when it was printed and wound up with a card that proclaimed LEON. Oh well, a valuable lesson. After forty-plus years of making woodcut prints I have developed the ability to read and write upside down and backwards with complete ease, an obscure skill to say the least.

"In college, I majored in art and studied printmaking with Leonard Baskin. After graduating, my husband, Tom, and I moved to Vermont with the intention of establishing a small subsistence farm, complete with a cow, a flock of chickens, a team of work horses, and a big garden. It soon became obvious that a source of income was necessary, and I found myself teaching in a small one-room school, grades one through eight. This was an exciting and challenging time in my life.

"After a few years of teaching, I decided to launch a printmaking studio, partly so that I could work at home and partly to pursue my love of carving wood blocks. The business grew, and eventually I designed a set of alphabet posters that were printed and distributed to all Vermont classrooms, kindergarten through third grade. I thought these posters would make an ideal children's book and scheduled a trip to the big city—New York—to see if I could find a publisher. No one was in the least interested, and I returned to Vermont and forgot about book illustration.

"About a year after my unproductive trip to New York, I got a phone call from Boston publisher David Godine. It seemed he had heard about the woodcut alphabet and wanted to take a look at it. He decided to publish it and this became my first children's book, *A Farmer's Alphabet*. So, I guess you'd have to say that I got into children's book illustration through a lucky accident of fate.

Courtesy of Mary Azarian

"I especially like illustrating books because it gives me the chance to work on something new. Since my principal business involves running a printmaking studio, I spend a lot of time printing and coloring blocks that I have carved long ago. It is straight production work and can become quite boring. The prospect of a new book fills me with creative energy. It was, needless to say, very exciting to learn that I had won the Caldecott Award for *Snowflake Bentley*. It is an honor that I never even dreamed of.

"I now live on a small 'farm' near Montpelier, the capitol of Vermont. My house is surrounded by flower and vegetable gardens, although the cow, horses, and chickens are but a memory."

* * *

Born in Washington, D.C., Mary Azarian grew up in nearby Virginia. She attended Smith College, where she received a bachelor's degree in art. Since 1967, she has been a freelance printmaker and illustrator. A career breakthrough occurred when the Vermont Council on the Arts awarded her a grant to develop artwork with a state theme. The resulting alphabet posters depicted images of rural Vermont and served as the basis of her first children's book, *A Farmer's Alphabet*, which was nominated for the American Book Award in 1981.

Azarian uses Japanese tools and a specially prepared wood from that country to create her prints. The initial design is done in ink and marker directly on the wood surface, then the surrounding areas are cut away. The raised lines that remain form the backward image that will be printed. Oil-based ink is rolled across this woodblock, which is then fitted into a printing press that the artist operates by hand. Acrylic paint is often added to the print to provide color detail. Some of the woodblocks are printed thousands of times, producing posters to be sold across the country; others are designed for political and social organizations.

SNOWFLAKE BENTLEY

Jacqueline Briggs Martin
Illustrated by Mary Azarian

Houghton Mifflin Company Boston

Courtesy of Houghton Mifflin

Increasingly, Azarian's woodcuts are created specifically for book illustration, an avocation that culminated in her winning the 1999 Caldecott Medal for *Snowflake Bentley*, a biography of an independent scientist written by Jacqueline Briggs Martin. *Snowflake Bentley* was also a *Booklist* Editor's Choice, a *Bulletin of the Center for Children's Books* Blue Ribbon selection, and an Outstanding Science Trade Book for Children.

The parents of three adult sons, the illustrator and her musician husband, Tom, live in Calais, Vermont.

SELECTED WORKS ILLUSTRATED: *The Man Who Lived Alone*, by Donald Hall, 1984; *A Symphony for the Sheep*, by C. M. Millen, 1996; *Barn Cat*, by Carol P. Saul, 1998; *Faraway Summer*, by Johanna Hurwitz, 1998; *Snowflake Bentley*, by Jacqueline Briggs Martin, 1998; *Sea Gifts*, by George Shannon, 2000.

SELECTED WORKS WRITTEN AND ILLUSTRATED: *A Farmer's Alphabet*, 1981; *The Tale of John Barleycorn*, 1982.

SUGGESTED READING: *Contemporary Authors*, vol. 118. Periodicals—Azarian, Mary, "Caldecott Acceptance Speech," *The Horn Book*, July/August, 1999; *Booklist*, June 1 & 15, 1999.

Courtesy of Alan Baker

Alan Baker

November 14, 1951–

"When I first started school, I had a real difficulty in concentrating. I remember one sunny afternoon, sitting in class while the teacher droned on about something. I was miles away. The next thing I knew, we had been handed out pieces of paper and were expected to write something . . . what, I had no idea! Feeling panic rising in me, I decided my only option was to copy from the boy sitting next to me. Rather mindlessly I carefully copied everything he wrote, not really taking any of it in. Unfortunately, I did my job too well, and copied his name down as well as everything else. When the teacher arrived at my desk, she was furious and accused me of copying. I denied it, of course, even after she had asked me my name and then made me read out the name at the top of my paper. I was told to erase the writing and start again. Unfortunately, I had forgotten to bring in my eraser and was, by now, far too frightened to explain this to the teacher. The boy next to me, quite understandably, did not want to lend me his, so I ended up tearing a piece of rubber from the sole of one of my shoes and attempted to rub out my words. As you can imagine, the result was a terrible mess. The more I tried to correct it, the worse it became, finally ending with a hole in my paper . . . a good starting point for a picture book!

"I originally started life studying science. Being an academic subject, it was thought much more likely to result in a solid, secure career. Although I had a real interest in science, my heart was not in it. One summer, like a lot of people of my generation, I took the hippie trail to India. I hitchhiked across Europe, through Turkey, Iran, etc., sleeping rough all the way. After several unfortunate incidents, I ended up penniless in Afghanistan, suffering from dysentery. I didn't even have the money to buy my visa back into Iran. I ended up illegally crossing the border one night via the desert that separates the two countries. A couple weeks later I was smuggled out of Iran in the back of a truck. In Turkey I jumped aboard a ship and, after a series of adventures, eventually got home. Looking back, I was lucky to have survived. That particular trip gave me a lot of time to think about my future. I decided that I must choose the path in life that would make me happy. Even if I failed, at least I would have tried. I had made money on the way home by drawing people's portraits. It was enough money to feed myself. As soon as I arrived back in England, I applied for art school. I was lucky to get in at such short notice, but I did, and I gave it everything I could. I was determined to make a career of it. I loved art school; it opened up a whole new world for me. I still love the subject and wouldn't want to do anything else!"

* * *

After attending Croydon Technical College for two years, Alan Baker shifted his professional goals to a career in art, ultimately graduating from the University of Brighton Art College with a first-class honors degree in art and design. Since 1976 he has worked as a freelance illustrator in the fields of advertising, packaging, and publishing. His first book for children, *Benjamin and the Box*, had its origins in art school, as part of an examination project. Several volumes about Benjamin the hamster followed, including *Benjamin's Book*. This story, in which the hamster accidentally makes a mark on a piece of white paper and then can't erase it, had its beginnings in the real-life incident Baker describes in the autobiography above.

"I decided that I must choose the path in life that would make me happy."

In addition to writing and illustrating his own books, Baker has provided the artwork for texts written by authors as diverse as Rudyard Kipling, Philippa Pearce, Michael Rosen, Anita Ganeri, and Canadian songwriter Joni Mitchell. Baker's illustrations for Mitchell's song "Both Sides Now" featured two caterpillars along with a variety of other insects and won an award as Best Children's Bug Book from Y.E.S., the Young Entomologists' Society. Other awards and honors include several citations for his advertising illustrations, an IRA/CBC Children's Choice Award for *White Rabbit's Colour Book*, and another IRA/CBC Children's Choice for *Grey Rabbit's Odd One Out*. *Benjamin and the Box* was featured on children's television shows broadcast in the United States, Canada, Great Britain, and Norway.

Alan Baker lives in East Sussex, England, and shares his love of art by visiting schools to talk with young readers and by serving as a visiting lecturer at Brighton University and Northbrook College.

SELECTED WORKS WRITTEN AND ILLUSTRATED: *Benjamin and the Box*, 1977; *Benjamin Bounces Back*, 1978; *Benjamin's Dreadful Dream*, 1980; *Benjamin's Book*, 1982; *A Fairyland Alphabet*, 1984; *Benjamin's Portrait*, 1986; *One Naughty Boy*, 1989; *Goodnight William*, 1990; *Two Tiny Mice*, 1990; *Benjamin's Balloon*, 1990; *Where's Mouse*, 1992; *Black and White Rabbit's ABC*, 1994; *Brown Rabbit's Shape Book*, 1994; *Grey Rabbit's 1 2 3*, 1994; *White Rabbit's Colour Book*, 1994; *Grey Rabbit's Odd One Out*, 1995; *Mouse's Christmas*, 1996; *I Thought I Heard—*, 1996; *Mouse's Halloween*, 1997; *Look Who Lives in the Rainforest*, 1998; *Look Who Lives in the Desert*, 1999; *Look Who Lives in the Arctic*, 1999.

SELECTED WORKS ILLUSTRATED: *The Battle of Bubble and Squeak*, by Philippa Pearce, 1978; *The Butterfly That Stamped*, by Rudyard Kipling, 1982; *Hairy Tales and Nursery Rhymes*, by Michael Rosen, 1985; *The Odyssey*, adapted by Robin Lister, 1987; *Mike and Lottie*, by Verna Wilkins, 1988; *The Story of King Arthur*, retold by Robin Lister, 1988; *Wordspells*, by Judith Nicholls, 1988; *What on Earth? Poems with a Conservation Theme*, by Judith Nicholls, 1989; *Mini-Beasties*, by Michael Rosen, 1991; *Both Sides Now*, by Joni Mitchell, 1992; *Dragons and Monsters*, by Anita Ganeri, 1996; *Animal Homes*, by Debbie Martin, 1999.

SUGGESTED READING: *Contemporary Authors*, New Revision Series, vol. 68, 1998; Peppin, Brigid and Lucy Micklethwait. *Book Illustrators of the Twentieth Century*, 1984; *Something About the Author*, vol. 93, 1997.

T. A. Barron

March 26, 1952–

"For me, writing is exploring. Whether it's the surprising connections among people, the wondrous patterns of nature, or the mysterious wellsprings of the spirit—the universe beckons. I love to explore it, whether by foot or by pen.

"Writing is both the most joyous—and the most agonizing—labor I know. And it is by far the best way to travel—in our world or any other. Ever since my youth on a ranch in Colorado, I've felt passionate about nature—and about writing. (I even published my own magazine when I was a kid, called 'The Idiot's Odyssey,' which sold about five copies an issue—including the ones bought by my parents.) I kept writing during my college years at Princeton and during my time as a Rhodes Scholar at Oxford, England. (My major field of study was the hiking trails of Scotland!) During that time at Oxford, I composed stories and poems while hiking in the Scottish highlands; while sitting beneath the boughs of an English oak I named Merlin's Tree; while backpacking through Asia, Africa, and the Arctic; and while participating in a traditional roof thatching in Japan. Even during my years helping to manage a fast-growing business in New York

City, my writing continued. In all those years, I often rose before dawn just to write.

"Finally, I followed my dream to write full time. In 1990, I moved back to Colorado and started writing in the attic of my home, with the help of my wife, Currie, and our five young children. So I still often get up before dawn to write—but now I can keep going after breakfast.

"I have written three novels about an intrepid (but vulnerable) young heroine named Kate Prancer Gordon. These books—*The Ancient One*, *The Merlin Effect*, and *Heartlight*—are sometimes called The Kate Adventures. I became fascinated by Merlin, the greatest enchanter of all times and the mentor to King Arthur, and the secrets of his lost youth. I wanted to add another, new dimension to the lore of this enduring figure. This will be a five-book epic; so far *The Lost Years of Merlin*, *Seven Songs of Merlin*, *Fires of Merlin*, and *The Mirror of Merlin* have been published, and Book 5 is in the works. Why am I spending almost a decade writing about Merlin? Because he is much, much more than a great wizard. His story is, in truth, a metaphor—for the idea that all of us, no matter how weak or confused, have a magical person down inside, just waiting to be discovered.

"*To Walk in Wilderness* is the story of my month-long trek in a magnificent Colorado wilderness area, and *Rocky Mountain National Park: A One Hundred Year Perspective* celebrates the vision of a great conservationist, Enos Mills, and the park he bequeathed to us all. In creating both of these nature books, I was joined by a marvelous nature photographer, John Fielder."

Courtesy of Currie Barron

* * *

T. A. (Tom) Barron was born in New England and spent part of his childhood on a ranch in Colorado. He received his bachelor's degree from Princeton University and then studied as a Rhodes Scholar at Oxford University. He married Currie Cabot and worked for a number of years in business in New York City—as president of a venture capital firm, chairman of the board of the major U.S. importer of Swiss Army knives, and developer of a national child-care operation and a new environmental testing business—before deciding to put writing first in

Courtesy of Penguin Putnam Books

his professional life. He and Currie now live in Colorado with their five children and enjoy hiking the wilderness trails near their home.

Many of Barron's novels involve quests of mythical proportions that emphasize the vital importance of nature and the cycle of life. In *The Ancient One*, for example, Kate travels 500 years back in time in order to meet a mysterious Indian tribe and to help a sacred forest survive its enemies, past and present. The *New York Times Book Review* called this book "august and compelling."

The Ancient One was named an IRA/CBC Young Adult Choice book, a New York Public Library Book for the Teen Age, and a *VOYA* Best of the Year. *The Lost Years of Merlin* was named an ALA Best Book for Young Adults and was included on New York Public Library's Books for the Teen Age list. *The Fires of Merlin* was a *VOYA* Best of the Year, and *The Seven Songs of Merlin* was an IRA/CBC Young Adult Choice book.

In addition to his fantasy cycles and nature books, Barron has recently begun to write stories for younger children. His first picture book, *Where Is Grandpa?*, features illustrations by Chris K. Soentpiet. He is also working on a book of autobiographical essays.

SELECTED WORKS: *Heartlight*, 1990; *The Ancient One*, 1992; *To Walk in Wilderness*, 1993; *The Merlin Effect*, 1994; *Rocky Mountain National Park: A One Hundred Year Perspective*, 1995; *The Lost Years of Merlin*, 1996; *The Seven Songs of Merlin*, 1997; *The Fires of Merlin*, 1998; *The Mirror of Merlin*, 1999; *Where Is Grandpa?* illus. by Chris Soentpiet, 2000.

SUGGESTED READING: *Contemporary Authors*, vol. 150, 1996; *Something About the Author*, vol. 83, 1996. Periodicals— Barron, T. A., "A Place for Love: The Story Behind *Where Is Grandpa?*," *Book Links*, March 2000; Beers, Kylene, "Fantasy and Realism: Two Topics, One Author," *Journal of Adolescent and Adult Literacy*, April 1998; Beers, Kylene, "An Interview with T. A. Barron," *Emergency Librarian*, March/April 1997; Cox, Ruth, "Fantastical Flights of Fantasy" *Emergency Librarian*, March/April 1998; "The Lost Years of Merlin

Series," *Book Links*, January 1998; "T. A. Barron: Glowing like a Crystal," *School Library Media Activities*, June 1995.

WEB SITE: *www.tabarron.com*

"I was born at 11 A.M., a most reasonable time, my mother often said, and when the nurse put me in my mother's arms for the first time I had both a nasty case of the hiccups and no discernible forehead (it's since grown in). I've always believed in comic entrances.

"As I grew up in River Forest, Illinois, in the 1950s, I seem to remember an early fascination with things that were funny. I thought that people who could make other people laugh were terribly fortunate. While my friends made their career plans, declaring they would become doctors, nurses, and lawyers, inwardly I knew that I wanted to be involved somehow in comedy.

"This, however, was a difficult concept to get across in first grade. But I had a mother with a great comic sense (she was a high school English teacher) and a grandmother who was a funny professional storyteller—so I figured the right genes were in there somewhere, although I didn't always laugh at what my friends laughed at and they rarely giggled at my jokes. That, and the fact that I was overweight and very tall, all made me feel quite different when I was growing up—a bit like a water buffalo at a tea party.

Courtesy of Evan Bauer

Joan Bauer

July 12, 1951–

"My grandmother, whom I called Nana, had the biggest influence on me creatively. She taught me the importance of stories and laughter. She never said, 'Now I'm going to tell you a funny story'; she'd just tell a story, and the humor would naturally flow from it because of who she was and how she and her characters saw the world. She showed me the difference between derisive laughter that hurts others and laughter that comes from the heart. She showed me, too, that stories help us understand ourselves at a deep level. She was a keen observer of people.

"I kept a diary as a child, was always penning stories and poems. I played the flute heartily, taught myself the guitar, and wrote folk songs. For years I wanted to become a comedienne, then a comedy writer. I was a voracious reader too, and can still remember the dark wood and the green leather chairs of the

River Forest Public Library, can hear my shoes tapping on the stairs going down to the children's room, can feel my fingers sliding across rows and rows of books, looking through the card catalogues that seemed to house everything that anyone would ever need to know about in the entire world.

"My parents divorced when I was only eight years old, and I was devastated at the loss of my father. I pull from that memory regularly as a writer. Every book I have written so far has dealt with complex father issues of one kind or another. My father was an alcoholic, and the pain of that was a shadow that followed me for years. I attempted to address that pain in *Rules of the Road*. It was a very healing book for me. I didn't understand it at the time, but I was living out the theme that I try to carry into all of my writing: adversity, if we let it, will make us stronger.

"In my twenties, I had a successful career in sales and advertising with the *Chicago Tribune*, McGraw-Hill, and *Parade* magazine. I met my husband, Evan, a computer engineer, while I was on vacation. Our courtship was simple. He asked me to dance; I said no. We got married five months later, in August 1981. But I was not happy in advertising sales, and I had a few ulcers to prove it. With Evan's loving support, I decided to try my hand at professional writing. I wish I could say that everything started falling into place, but it was a slow, slow build, writing newspaper and magazine articles for not much money. My daughter Jean was born in July of 1982. She had the soul of a writer even as a baby. I can remember sitting at my typewriter (I didn't have a computer back then) writing away with Jean on a blanket on the floor next to me. If my writing was bad that day, I'd tear that page out of the typewriter and hand it to her. 'Bad paper,' I'd say, and Jean would rip the paper in shreds with her little hands.

"I had moved from journalism to screenwriting when one of the biggest challenges of my life occurred. I was in a serious auto accident which injured my neck and back severely and required neurosurgery. It was a long road back to wholeness, but during that time I wrote *Squashed*, my first young adult novel. The humor in that story kept me going.

"Over the years, I have come to understand how deeply I need to laugh. It's like oxygen to me. My best times as a writer are when I'm working on a book and laughing while I'm writing. Then I know I've got something."

"I seem to remember an early fascination with things that were funny. I thought that people who could make other people laugh were terribly fortunate."

✳   ✳   ✳

Joan Bauer was born and grew up in River Forest, Illinois. After high school she worked in a variety of waitressing and office jobs. At the *Chicago Tribune* she began working in classified ads and moved on to becoming advertising manager for the Lifestyles section. Her career in sales continued at McGraw-Hill

Publishers and *Parade* magazine. After her marriage she lived briefly in Los Angeles and Washington, D.C., before settling in southwestern Connecticut. Taking courses in screenwriting at the New School in New York City led Bauer to writing for film and television, a discipline she credits with developing her ear for dialogue. A Master Class in Fiction Writing at New York University gave her feedback from fellow students as well as the professor.

Bauer was chosen by *Publishers Weekly* as one of the top new writers for young people in 1992. Her first novel, *Squashed,* the funny story of an overweight teenage girl who attempts to grow the biggest pumpkin in Iowa, won the Delacorte Prize for a First Young Adult Novel and was a *School Library Journal* Best Book of 1992. *Squashed, Thwonk,* and *Rules of the Road* were ABA Pick of the Lists selections and Junior Library Guild choices and were cited in the New York Public Library's Books for the Teen Age. *Sticks,* Bauer's first novel for middle-grade readers, was a Junior Library Guild selection. *Thwonk* and *Rules of the Road* were both cited in the ALA Top Ten Best Books for Young Adults. *Rules of the Road,* the funny and poignant story of a teenage super-saleswoman who struggles with her father's alcoholism and her grandmother's senility, won the prestigious *Los Angeles Times* Book Prize in the newly created YA Fiction category in 1999 and also received a Golden Kite Award. Patty Campbell, one of the judges for the *L.A. Times* award, stated in a *Horn Book* magazine article that this novel demonstrated "the power and sweetness of laughing with—not at—the pain of the human struggle to grow up."

Joan Bauer lives with her husband and daughter in Darien, Connecticut. In addition to writing, she enjoys cooking, as well as hiking with her family in the Adirondacks, the setting for her novel *Backwater*.

SELECTED WORKS: *Squashed,* 1992; *Thwonk,* 1995; *Sticks,* 1996; *Rules of the Road,* 1998; *Backwater,* 1999.

SUGGESTED READING: Hipple, Ted, ed. *Writers for Young Adults,* 1997. Periodicals—Bauer, Joan, "Humor, Seriously," *ALAN Review,* Winter 1996; Campbell, Patty, "Funny Girls," *The Horn Book,* May/June 1999; "Sticks: Between the Lines," *Book Links,* July 1997.

June Behrens

April 25, 1925–

"My need to write started in elementary school, but it was not until I was almost forty that I became a published writer. From then until now I have done what I most wanted to do—write books for children. My career as a writer actually started in the fifth grade. Our teacher, Mrs. Otis, loved books, and that love spilled over into the classroom and touched those of us who adored her. I wrote my first book, about my horse

Bess, for Mrs. Otis. I illustrated it with cut-outs from magazines and a black-and-white snapshot of Bess and me. Mrs. Otis said it was one of her favorite stories. Many years later I did another book, *Looking at Horses*, and I thought about Mrs. Otis when the book came back from the printer.

"In high school I worked on the newspaper and edited the yearbook. In college, my interest in writing took second place to my career goals, but I still took time to edit the University of California yearbook.

"As a young teacher, I was thrilled with the prospect of teaching children to read and write. My students became writers as they wrote about themselves, their families, their ideas and feelings and experiences. It was an exciting part of our school day.

Courtesy of Sears Studio

"Once, when we were studying about an obscure California Indian tribe, I could find no materials suitable for child reference. I researched available adult texts and wrote a book my class could read. It was a very satisfying project and one that eventually led to my second career. As a teacher, I often looked for books on a given subject only to find that they had not yet been written. That was my cue. Many of the books I write grow out of this need, and I will not be able to tap the full resources of my 'idea file' in my lifetime.

"Through playwriting and scripting media programs, I have introduced my readers to other forms of communication. Writing plays and watching children turn into actors is one of my most rewarding writing experiences.

"Whatever the form of written expression—manuscripts, plays, or film scripts—my greatest joy comes from knowing that my work has provided entertainment and learning experiences for children.

"After many years of writing, I am still plugging away, excited by the research for nonfiction writing. My computer is 'magical' and a constant source of amazement."

✳   ✳   ✳

June Behrens was born, raised, and educated in California, where she has lived continuously except for periods of study and teaching in Germany and London and overseas travel with her husband. She received her B.A. in 1947 from the University of

California, Santa Barbara, and her M.A. in 1961 from the University of Southern California. She has also done graduate work at the University of California, Los Angeles; the University of Maryland (Overseas Program); and the University of London.

Behrens began her educational career teaching elementary school in California (1947–1954), overseas (1954–1956), and back in California (1956–1963). She was a vice-principal in Los Angeles in 1966, when she became a reading specialist for the city schools. In 1979 Behrens received the distinguished Achievement Award in Education from the University of California, Santa Barbara.

Behrens is a member of the National Education Association, the American Association of University Women, the California Teachers' Association, the Authors Guild, the International Reading Association, Delta Kappa Gamma, the National Association for Education of Young Children, the California Writers Guild, the Southern California Council on Literature for Children and Young People, and Reading Specialists of California.

Her writing career began in 1965 with *Soo Ling Finds a Way*, which was a Junior Literary Guild Selection. She writes prolifically in various forms—children's nonfiction, picture books, plays, and film scripts—and covers topics ranging from animals and ecology to ethnic and holiday traditions, history, and the lives of famous people. Her work includes a number of series: Picture-Story Biography, Fine Art, Childhood Awareness, Economic Transportation and Trade, All American, Holiday Plays, and I Can Be. Many of Behrens's books are also published in Spanish.

"My career as a writer actually started in the fifth grade. Our teacher, Mrs. Otis, loved books, and that love spilled over into the classroom and touched those of us who adored her."

SELECTED WORKS: *Soo Ling Finds a Way*, 1965; *Earth Is Home: The Pollution Story*, 1971; *Look at the Forest Animals*, 1974; *Whalewatch!* 1978; *Ronald Reagan, All American*, 1981; *Gung Hay Fat Choy*, 1982; *Puedo Ser Astronauta/I Can Be an Astronaut*, 1984; *Sally Ride, Astronaut: An American First*, 1986; *Passover*, 1987; *Juliette Low*, 1988; *Dolphins!* 1989; *Sharks!* 1990; *Barbara Bush: 1st Lady of Literacy*, 1990; *Fiesta!* 1991; *Powwow*, 1994; *King! The Man and His Dream: A Play*, with Pauline Brower, 1996; *Flag for a New Country: The Betsy Ross Story*, 1996; *Missions of the Central Coast*, 1997; *Snake . . . and Amy-Tsosie: The Navajo Sandpainting Story*, 1997.

SUGGESTED READING: *Contemporary Authors*, New Revision Series, vol. 24, 1988; *Something About the Author*, vol. 19. 1980.

E-MAIL: *yorkho@aol.com*

Courtesy of Sarah Bial

Raymond Bial

November 5, 1948–

"My work as a writer and a photographer has grown out of my love for the farms and small towns of America. I spent several joyous years of my childhood in a small town in Indiana, and I vividly recall bicycling around the neighborhood, swimming at the municipal pool, and stopping for ice cream at the local hotspot. Later our family moved to a farm in Michigan. I missed my hometown, yet I loved taking care of the livestock and exploring the woods, marshes, and fields. The moment I walked out of the house I was truly outside in the light and weather. The land was bursting with wildlife, and I became the delighted naturalist. I was thrilled to be alive, deeply experiencing the world around me.

"When I was thirteen our family moved back to Illinois. It was many years later, after attending college and moving to a city on the East Coast, that I realized how deeply I missed the country. On a visit home, I drove the back roads, swaying with the pitch of the road, absorbing the subtleties of light, the fields brilliant with snow and the sky so phenomenally blue, and made my first photograph—of a barn riddled by wind—and several others. These scenes were so remarkably lovely, beyond words, that I had to find some way of sharing my feelings about them with others.

"Thereafter, on every visit home, I sought to capture the vanishing rural landscape, making photographs of fence posts stacked in a woodlot, of gas pumps in front of a grocery store, of a broken café window. I came to appreciate the ability of light and shadow to evoke a distinctive mood. My photographs were meant to be art, with significant content, not just because they were carefully made, but because they evoked profound feelings. The plains swept relentlessly in every direction, with scarcely a lull for a stream, or a rise for a line of trees to interrupt the eye. The sky appeared to overwhelm the land and I seemed to be the least significant object on the horizon. Yet I was captivated by the velvety black fields, dappled with troughs of snow, and the height of the sky. I often say that photography and writing 'happened to me.' I didn't consciously decide to become a creative person. I had long harbored a quiet wish to become an author, but in my early twenties I was suddenly overwhelmed with a compelling need to write and make photographs.

"I have since published many photo-essays for children, which are intended to be lovely as well as useful. For many of the books I have returned to rural subjects and lately, historical and cultural topics. Just as when I was young, I love to be outside, making photographs, capturing that heightened sense of feeling for people, places, and everyday objects. I believe that adults as well as children should live fully, not only in their minds, but also through their senses.

"My wife Linda and I inhabit an old house in a midwestern town with our three children: Anna, Sarah, and Luke. Above all else, I love being a husband and father. For me, the only thing better than being a child is to grow up and raise children. In making photoessays, I now draw upon experiences with my children as well as youthful memories. I write my books at home in the midst of my family. We also blend photography assignments with vacations so that we can be together as a family. Who could ask for anything more?"

*   *   *

Raymond Bial was born on November 5, 1948, in Danville, Illinois. His parents were Marion, an Air Force officer, and Catherine, a medical secretary. He attended the University of Illinois, where he earned a bachelor of science degree with honors in 1970 and an M.S. degree in 1979. On August 25, 1979, he married Linda LaPuma.

Other than being a devoted husband and father, Bial's greatest interests revolve around outdoor pursuits. He loves to be outside and free. He enjoys gardening, fishing, hiking, and travel. Bial was named the Historian of the Year, Champaign County, Illinois, in 1984. In 1991 *Corn Belt Harvest* was named an Outstanding Science Trade Book for Children. *Amish Home* was named an ALA Notable Children's Book in 1994 and received a Parents' Choice Award in 1995. *Portrait of a Farm Family* received the Ohio Farm Bureau award in 1996 as "the most distinguished contribution to American literature for children with an agricultural theme." *One-Room School* was chosen as a Junior Library Guild selection. Many of Bial's books have been named Notable Trade Books in the Field of Social Studies. He lives with his family in Urbana, Illinois.

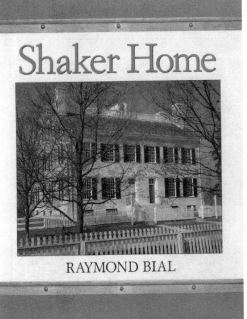

Shaker Home

RAYMOND BIAL

Courtesy of Houghton Mifflin

SELECTED WORKS: *Corn Belt Harvest*, 1991; *County Fair*, 1992; *Amish Home*, 1993; *Frontier Home*, 1993; *Shaker Home*, 1994; *Portrait of a Farm Family*, 1995; *The Underground Railroad*, 1995; *With Needle and Thread: A Book About Quilts*, 1996; *Where Lincoln Walked*, 1997; *The Strength of These Arms: Life in the Slave Quarters*, 1997; *Mist over the Mountains: Appalachia and Its People*, 1997; *The Fresh Grave and Other Ghostly Stories*, 1998; *Cajun Home*, 1998; *One-Room School*, 1999; *The Cherokee*, 1999; *The Iroquois*, 1999; *The Navajo*, 1999; *The Sioux*, 1999; *The Comanche*, 2000.

SUGGESTED READING: *Contemporary Authors*, vol. 143, 1994; *Something About the Author*, vol. 76, 1994. Periodicals— "On Writing *Amish Home*," *Book Links*, January 1996; *Instructor*, September 1997.

WEB SITE: *www.raybial.com*

Courtesy of Debbie Birdseye

Tom Birdseye

July 13, 1951–

"I grew up in North Carolina and Kentucky, an ardent fan of anything that smacked of sports, crawdads, mud balls, forts in the woods, secret codes, bicycles without fenders, chocolate pie, and snow. I was, however, decidedly uninterested in writing—or any academic aspect of school, for that matter—never imagining that I would someday become a published author.

"Writing was a difficult process for me. Everything seemed to get in the way: from being left-handed (my cursive slanted the wrong direction), to my poor spelling skills (*i* before *e* except after what?); from punctuation woes (to comma or not to comma, that is the question), to a lack of ideas. I had no clue how writers dreamed up those stories. What I was able to write generally came back from the teacher with so much red ink on it that it looked like it had been in a car wreck. Not once did I get a comment on the top of the page saying, 'Nice job!' or 'How creative!' My teachers meant well, of course. I'm sure they thought they were helping me learn by pointing out each and every error I made. But back then I didn't see it that way. To me, all the red ink translated into a message that rang loud and clear in my mind: 'You are not a writer.'

"And yet a writer is just what I've become. As a character named Ora Mae Cotton in my picture book *Airmail to the Moon* says, 'Life, it seems, is full of who'd-a-thought-its.' This turn-around didn't come like a miraculous bolt out of the blue, however. It was only after many years of frustration that I lucked onto two Oregon writers who had an instinctive knack for teaching. From them I learned that although undeniably important, writing mechanics alone don't make a story. (After all, who has ever gone running to a friend, book in hand, exclaiming, 'You've got to read this one! It's got the most incredible spelling and punctuation!') Concentrate on the story, they told me. It is a journey into the realm of the heart. Keep your eyes fixed on that road, then deal with the other stuff later.

"With their help, I began to see how I could turn the material of my life into the material of a story, fictionalizing to my heart's content, as long as I conveyed emotional truth. They urged me to carry a small notebook, to be on the lookout for things to jot down: the funny, telling, or poignant glimpses of life that are too often overlooked, ordinary people who would make good characters, memories of my childhood triggered by what I might see and hear, the wonderfully wise things people will say at the most unexpected moments.

"Feedback was honest, but always constructive. Support for my efforts was unwavering. No pom-pom waving throng of cheerleaders could have been more encouraging. And slowly, very slowly, I began to think of myself as a writer, to believe in myself as a writer, to write. Now writing is an undeniable part of who I am. True, I still labor at it, wrestling with the spelling beast and punctuation monster—writing and rewriting, then rewriting some more, until I glean my best. But the process has become more one of pleasure than of pain. I love doing it, and I love sharing it with others. The boy who couldn't imagine himself a writer, now can't imagine himself anything else.

"I was born in Durham, North Carolina. I attended the University of Kentucky and Western Kentucky University, but by no stretch of the imagination have I learned even one-thousandth of what I'd love to know. Currently I live in Corvallis, Oregon, with my wife, Debbie; two daughters, Kelsey and Amy; and my cat, Emma Bark Birdseye. When not writing or doing school visits, I enjoy mountain climbing, hiking, skiing, canoeing, camping, mountain biking, jogging, get-togethers with friends, and (of course) writing."

"The boy who couldn't imagine himself a writer, now can't imagine himself anything else."

*   *   *

Tom Birdseye is a teacher and a writer of children's books who hasn't forgotten what it's like to be a kid or a student. He knows the issues children and adolescents struggle with, he knows what's fun and what isn't, and he has managed to keep a bit of silliness in his humor that amuses readers of all ages. Birdseye is also a storyteller, able to create immediate, believable situations and characters who speak exactly as you would expect them to—he has an ear for a good story and an open heart for the people whose stories he tells.

Birdseye attended the University of Kentucky and Western Kentucky University, where he earned a B.A. in Mass Communication in 1974 and a B.A. in Elementary Education in 1977. He has taught elementary school in Oregon and Idaho, and English in Japan. As an author he travels all over the country making presentations about the writing process to public schools, libraries, universities, and various educational groups. He not only teaches children about the joys of reading and writing their own stories, he also teaches educators how to excite even the most reluctant reader or writer to explore and create. He is a member of the Authors Guild, the Authors League of America, and the Society of Children's Book Writers and Illustrators.

Birdseye's first book, *I'm Going to Be Famous*, received award nominations in three states; was published in the U.K., New Zealand, and Holland; and is also available on tape. *Airmail to the Moon* was an IRA/CBC Children's Choice book in 1989, as was *A Regular Flood of Mishap* in 1995. *A Song of Stars* was named a Notable Children's Trade Book in the Field of Social Studies. *Tucker* was placed on the "Best of 1990" list by the Society of School Librarians International. Birdseye's 1993 retelling of an Appalachian folktale, *Soap! Soap! Don't Forget the Soap!*, received four state Picture Book Awards. *Under Our Skin: Kids Talk About Race* was a Notable Children's Trade Book in the Field of Social Studies. Birdseye's works have consistently been included on lists for award books in states throughout America.

SELECTED WORKS: *I'm Going to Be Famous*, 1986; *Airmail to the Moon*, illus. by Stephen Gammell, 1988; *A Song of Stars*, illus. by Ju Hong Chin, 1990; *Tucker*, 1990; *Waiting for Baby*, illus. by Loreen Leedy, 1991; *Soap! Soap! Don't Forget the Soap! An Appalachian Folktale*, illus. by Andrew Glass, 1993; *Just Call Me Stupid*, 1993; *A Kid's Guide to Building Forts*, illus. by Bill Klein, 1993; *A Regular Flood of Mishap*, illus. by Megan Lloyd, 1994; *She'll Be Comin' Round the Mountain*, with Debbie Holsclaw Birdseye, illus. by Andrew Glass, 1994; *Tarantula Shoes*, 1995; *What I Believe: Kids Talk About Faith*, with Debbie Holsclaw Birdseye, photos by Robert Crum, 1996; *Under Our Skin: Kids Talk About Race*, with Debbie Holsclaw Birdseye, photos by Robert Crum, 1997.

SUGGESTED READING: *Contemporary Authors*, vol. 133, 1991; *Something About the Author*, vol. 66, 1991; vol. 98, 1998. Periodicals—"From a Frozen Sea," *New Advocate*, Fall 1996.

WEB SITE: *www.tombirdseye.com*

"I was born in 1938 in Stockholm, Sweden, and I have been living there ever since. I love this city, built on some small islands between Lake Mälaren and the sea. It's a city with lots of water and trees and a lot of nature all around it. I lived and went to school on the island Kungsholmen, just like my good friend and illustrator Lena Anderson, but our school was so big that we never met.

"I was the only child, and every night my father told me a story he had invented, often about my teddy bear, Nalle, and my toy monkey, Jakob, who flew away on my bed-carpet during the night. Dad read aloud many good books for Mum and me, e.g., *Pippi*, *Pooh*, *Nils Holgersson*. He also taught me to go to the library to find still more books. He took me often to museums and the opera; he was keen on culture, my dad.

"He was also interested in botany. We biked around in Sweden collecting wildflowers to examine and press. We also made a family magazine together. He was good at drawing, educated as a graphic designer, but he worked all his life as a principal assistant secretary at an office of the state, safer than being an artist.

"I often stayed with some nice uncles and aunts when my mother was ill with multiple sclerosis. My aunts also told me stories about Nalle and Jakob, whom they knew very well. My uncles were amateur botanists and birdwatchers, and we were often out in the woods together. One of my uncles even took me on a trip to Venice and told me a lot of its secrets.

"Writing was my best subject in school except for gymnastics. I was an eager letter-writer. I corresponded with aunts, uncles, cousins, and lots of friends. I even wrote to Tove Jansson, the author of my favorite books about the Moomintrolls in Moomin Valley, books where I first discovered the richness of the language (I tried to copy her); her books were quite different from Enid Blyton's scanty choice of words. And Tove did answer my letter! Three pages about why I shouldn't buy a live monkey!

"When school was over I cried; we had had so much fun together, what to do now? I studied art history at the University for a while, but then I decided to become a graphic designer, just like my boyfriend. Dad thought it a good idea. That took three years. As holiday work I did layout at a ladies' magazine, and

Courtesy of Orjan Bjorkdahl/Pressens Bild

Christina Björk

(byork)

July 27, 1938–

that's where I first met Lena Anderson. We got to be very good friends. This was in 1958.

"I continued with the layout work at different magazines, and soon Lena and I worked at the same magazine again. We both married, and our families each bought a row house in the same street. Lena got a little baby from Korea, whom she called Nicolina, Nico for short. I didn't want to have any babies.

"Later I took a degree in political science. Then I worked at a leftist magazine. There I started a children's page, and I also began to write articles of my own. Suddenly I slipped on a banana-skin into children's TV. I made documentaries, and I also wrote stories, which Lena illustrated. Suddenly we had made thirty-four stories, one every week. And some of these stories became books.

"Now both Lena and I were freelancers, and that was much more fun. We had a working studio together, a small ex–tobacco shop. Among other projects, I was the editor of the children's page in Sweden's biggest morning paper. There Lena and I invented Linnea in 1976. She looks a bit like Nico, who, from an early age, was very interested in planting and flowers and gardens.

"Some publishers wanted us to make a book about Linnea. We chose one publisher and started. We planted and planted; the little shop was filled with jars. We had to try everything out before we wrote about it. I can assure you, only a fraction of it ended up in the book, *Linnea's Windowsill Garden*.

"We made a lot of other books, articles, TV programs, and another Linnea book, *Linnea's Almanac*, that took some years. During these years, I visited Paris and a big wonderful Monet exhibition there in 1980. I brought home books and found out that Monet was Lena's favorite artist too. How to be able to work with Monet for a living? As soon as the almanac was ready, we allowed ourselves to apply for scholarships to go to Giverny. And we got one each! We took Nico with us to Paris. We went to all the museums and several times to Monet's garden in Giverny.

"We didn't dare to tell our publisher what we were working with; art wasn't a subject for kids at that time. We didn't tell them until we had made a dummy of the whole book. As graphic designers we always do the layout even before we draw and write. The publisher said, 'Hmm . . . a narrow subject for kids . . . looks sweet . . . the other Linnea books sold OK . . . perhaps people won't notice the difference . . . so . . . . . yes.'

"It took five years and many trips to Paris before the book was ready: *Linnea in Monet's Garden*. I even studied French for two months in Paris to be able to get through all the French books about Monet. Everything Linnea experiences in the book is true. Lena, Nico, and I experienced every bit of it: Hotel Esmeralda, the picnic, Monet's relative that we met in the garden. He even invited us to his home to go through his boxes of family photos

> *"We didn't dare to tell our publisher what we were working with; art wasn't a subject for kids at that time."*

from Monet's time. Some are in the book. Many years have passed, but Linnea is still with us. She gets letters and calls from all over the world. We try to answer them all. We made a film about her, but no more books.

"I have just finished a book about Venice together with Inga-Karin Eriksson, *Vendela in Venice*. It's about the four golden horses in St Mark's Basilica and their thrilling history, that my uncle told me about when I was a child. I am now a member of the Swedish Children's Book Academy. We try to encourage parents and grandparents and secretaries of state and headmasters to spoil children with books. That's what my father did. Books give you a language to think with, and they train your sense of empathy. Yes, thank you Dad! *Tack Pappa!*"

* * *

Christina Björk is a Swedish graphic designer and independent filmmaker as well as an award-winning author of children's books. Educated at the Graphic Institute of Stockholm, she worked for many years in magazine layout and editing and as an art director. Björk is best known in the United States for her books about Linnea, created in collaboration with Lena Anderson, who provided the illustrations. While *Linnea in Monet's Garden* was the third book in the series in Sweden, it was the first to appear in America, in 1986. It was an immediate success, being named an American Booksellers Association Pick of the Lists, appearing on *Publishers Weekly*'s Children's Bestsellers list, and receiving a Parents' Choice Award. *Linnea's Windowsill Garden* was published in America in 1987, nearly ten years after its Swedish debut, and was cited as an ALA Notable Children's Book and an ABA Pick of the Lists. *Linnea's Almanac* soon followed, with its variety of activities for every month of the year. Björk has been awarded the German Children's Book Prize twice, as well as the Astrid Lindgren Prize in her native country.

Linnea in Monet's Garden has now been translated into more than twenty languages and made into a film by the author/illustrator team (writing, directing, and producing) that has won international awards. Linnea dolls are available to accompany the books, another indication of the title character's enduring popularity. After the *Linnea* projects, Björk (together with Maria Brännström) made a puppet animation film, *Teddies and People*, about her childhood teddy bears, and a book about them, *Big Bear's Book*. Published in Sweden in 1988 and in America in 1993, and told from the point of view of Big Bear, the book draws on the author's memories to re-create scenes from her childhood.

Among the children's books read to Björk by her father was *Alice's Adventures in Wonderland*, and that inspired her lifelong interest in Lewis Carroll and the real Alice, Alice Liddell. Per-

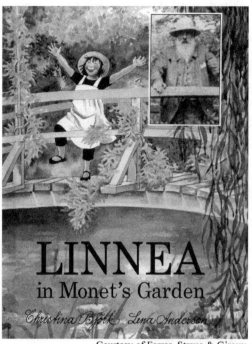

LINNEA
in Monet's Garden

Christina Björk Lena Anderson

Courtesy of Farrar, Straus & Giroux

haps Björk's experiences in childhood with her own uncles helped her identify with Alice's relationship to Charles Dodgson. Together with illustrator Inga-Karin Eriksson, she spent four years researching the story behind the *Alice* books, often in Oxford, England. The result was *The Other Alice* (published in England as *The Story of Alice in Her Oxford Wonderland*). Björk is active in the Lewis Carroll Society and has made friends throughout the world as a result of her study of Carroll's works.

In recent years Christina Björk has taken advanced training for multimedia production at the Swedish Industrial Society and the Film School of Denmark. She is working on a CD-ROM adaptation of *The Other Alice*. *Vendela in Venice*, translated by Patricia Crampton, received an Honor Book citation in 2000 for the Mildred Batchelder Award.

SELECTED WORKS: (Original Swedish titles and dates appear in parentheses) *Linnea in Monet's Garden*, illus. by Lena Anderson, 1986 (*Linnea i Maalarens Trädgaard*, 1985); *Linnea's Windowsill Garden*, illus. by Lena Anderson, 1987 (*Linnea Planterar Karnor*, 1978); *Linnea's Almanac*, illus. by Lena Anderson, 1987 (*Linneas AArsbok*, 1982); *Elliott's Extraordinary Cookbook*, illus. by Lena Anderson, 1991 (*Linus bakar och lagar*, 1980); *Big Bear's Book*, 1993 (*Store-Nalles Bok*, 1988); *The Other Alice*, illus. by Inga-Karin Eriksson, 1993 (*Sagan om Alice i Verkligheten*, 1993); *Vendela in Venice*, illus. by Inga-Karin Eriksson, 1999 (*Lavendel i Venedig*, 1999).

SUGGESTED READING: *Children's Literature Review*, vol. 22, 1991; *Contemporary Authors*, vol. 135, 1992; *Something About the Author*, vol. 67, 1992; vol. 99, 1999. Periodicals— "Alice," *Library Talk*, March/April 1994; Rhoades, Jane, "Visiting Monet's Garden," *Teaching PreK–8*, November/December 1992; "Talking with Christina Björk," *Book Links*, May 1995.

"I am a child of suburbia. I was born and grew up in Elizabeth, New Jersey. I walked two blocks to my elementary school and came home for lunch every day. The walk to school was an adventure because when I was very young I was afraid of dogs. On most days my friend, Barry, and I walked together. He helped me feel more secure.

"Along with my fears I always had a lot of imagination. My husband tells me I have too much, but I say a writer can never have too much imagination. From the time I was ten I'd bounce my pink rubber 'spaldeen' ball against the side of our brick house for hours while I made up stories inside my head. I never told anyone about my stories, and I never wrote them down, but from the time I can remember they were there. I was never bored because I had my stories to keep me company.

"The most memorable years of my childhood were the two I spent in Miami Beach. My older brother had been sick and the doctor suggested we spend the winter someplace warm and sunny. So off we went to Miami Beach, to live in a tiny apartment in a pink stucco building with a goldfish pond in the courtyard. My brother and I slept on day-beds in the living room and my mother and grandmother shared a Murphy bed in the alcove. I missed my father terribly. He was a dentist in New Jersey and could fly down to see us just once a month. But I loved the freedom I had in Miami Beach. I could play outside until dark every night, roller-skate to music at Flamingo Park, and go to the beach every weekend. Even my anxious and overprotective mother seemed more relaxed in Florida. My most autobiographical book, *Starring Sally J. Freedman as Herself*, is about those two years. It's one of my favorites, and I hope to turn it into a musical play someday.

"Back in New Jersey, I went to the only all-girls public high school in the state. We complained a lot about being separated from the boys, but I'm not so sure it wasn't a good experience. We ran the school! I was co–feature editor of the newspaper with my best friend, Mary Sullivan. I sang with the chorus, danced in the modern dance troupe, tried out for every school play, and had great fun with my friends. How much did I learn at that school? Not enough. Only one or two teachers encouraged us to think for ourselves, which I consider the most important part of any education. Only a few challenged us intellectual-

Courtesy of Peter Simon

Judy Blume (signature)

Judy Blume

February 12, 1938–

ly. Those are the teachers I remember best, the ones I respect most.

"I went to college with two goals: to become an elementary school teacher and to find a husband. That's what was expected of most young women back then. I married John Blume, a young lawyer, at the end of my junior year and our daughter, Randy, was born a year and a half later, in 1961. By the time I was twenty-five I had two small children (our son, Larry, was born in 1963). I had a degree in education, but I never taught. I lived in a house in suburban New Jersey in a neighborhood not that different from the one in which I grew up. I loved my little children, but I wasn't really happy. Something was missing from my life—an outlet for my creative energy.

"I always shudder when someone asks how I started to write children's books, because the truth is, I'm not sure. I used to make up rhyming stories while doing the dinner dishes, daydreaming about becoming the next Dr. Seuss. Then I took a course at New York University in writing for children, and while I believe that no one can teach you how to write, I needed professional encouragement (especially after two years of rejection letters) and found it in that class. When the semester ended, I signed up and took the course again. Before that session ended I'd sold several stories to magazines, my first picture book was accepted for publication, and I'd written most of what would become my first middle grade novel, *Iggie's House*. But it was the publication of *Are You There God? It's Me, Margaret* (my third book) that made me feel I might actually become a writer. *Margaret*'s popularity over the years has proved to me that while the way we live may have changed, what's deep inside us hasn't.

> "Margaret's popularity over the years has proved to me that while the way we live may have changed, what's deep inside us hasn't."

"That was the beginning of what's been a long and exciting adventure. Writing changed my life forever. It may have even saved it. Every writer who connects with her readers is grateful. But I am especially grateful to have the most loyal and loving readers any writer could ever wish for."

* * *

Judy Blume's books have made publishing history since the appearance in 1970 of *Are You There God? It's Me, Margaret*, one of the first novels to deal frankly with the issues of early adolescence. The immense popularity of this book, and of subsequent Blume novels that centered on real issues in her readers' lives, has made Blume one of the best-loved authors of this century. Her books have won over ninety awards, many of them decided by children themselves, in the U.S. and abroad.

Born Judy Sussman, the author grew up in suburban New Jersey. She received her B.S. in education from New York University in 1961. She has lived in a variety of places, all providing background for her writing. *Tiger Eyes*, for example, is set in New

Mexico, where she lived for seven years. Her marriage to John Blume ended in divorce. In 1987 Judy Blume married George Cooper, a writer of nonfiction (and also the designer of her Web page). The couple have three grown children (Judy's daughter Randy and son Larry from her first marriage, and George's daughter Amanda) and one grandchild. They live in Key West, Florida, and spend summers on the island of Martha's Vineyard. In 1999 Judy's daughter Randy, a pilot, dedicated her first book, *Crazy in the Cockpit*, to her mother.

Judy Blume has now written twenty-two books, all of them still in print, including three bestselling novels for adults. Over 70 million copies of her books have been sold worldwide, translated into 26 languages. Blume has written for young children (*Tales of a Fourth Grade Nothing, Superfudge, Fudge-a-mania*), middle-grade children (*Blubber, It's Not the End of the World, Just as Long as We're Together*, etc.) and young adults (*Tiger Eyes, Forever*). The Fudge books have been adapted for TV, and she is currently at work on other TV adaptations of her novels.

Courtesy of E.P. Dutton

Over the years, because many of her books deal in a straightforward manner with sexual awakening and other controversial topics, Blume has been a target for censors. This has led her to become an active spokesperson for intellectual freedom and to work with organizations such as the National Coalition Against Censorship. She has also taken leadership roles in the Authors Guild and the Society of Children's Book Writers and Illustrators and is a founder of The Kids Fund, an educational and charitable organization established in 1981, supported by royalties from several of her books. She has most recently edited *Places I Never Meant to Be*, a collection of original stories by other writers whose works have been censored or challenged in various ways.

Are You There God? It's Me, Margaret was included on the *New York Times* list of Outstanding Books of the Year in 1970, the first of many citations for Blume's books. In 1996 she received the Margaret A. Edwards Award for Lifetime Achievement from the American Library Association. It is this award and the many, many children's choice awards she has won over the years that are the most important to her.

Courtesy of Bradbury Press

SELECTED WORKS: *The One in the Middle Is the Green Kangaroo*, 1969 (rev. ed. 1981 illus. by Amy Aitken; rev. ed. 1991 illus. by Irene Trivas); *Iggie's House*, 1970; *Are You There God? It's Me, Margaret*, 1970; *Then Again, Maybe I Won't*, 1971; *Freckle Juice*, illus. by Sonia O. Lisker, 1971; *Tales of a Fourth Grade Nothing*, 1972; *Otherwise Known as Sheila the Great*, 1972; *It's Not the End of the World*, 1972; *Deenie*, 1973; *Blubber*, 1974; *Forever*, 1975; *Starring Sally J. Freedman as Herself*, 1977; *Superfudge*, 1980; *Tiger Eyes*, 1981; *The Pain and the Great One*, illus. by Irene Trivas, 1984; (as editor) *Letters to Judy: What Your Kids Wish They Could Tell You*, 1986; *Just as Long as We're Together*, 1987; *Fudge-a-mania*, 1990; *Here's to You, Rachel Robinson*, 1993; (as editor) *Places I Never Meant to Be*, 1999.

SUGGESTED READING: *Authors and Artists for Young Adults*, vol. 3, 1990; *Children's Literature Review*, vol. 15, 1988; Collier, Laurie and Joyce Nakamura, eds. *Major Authors and Illustrators for Children and Young Adults*, 1993; *Contemporary Authors*, New Revision Series, vol. 66, 1998; *Contemporary Literary Criticism*, vol. 30, 1984; *Dictionary of Literary Biography*, vol. 52, 1986; Hipple, Ted, ed. *Writers for Young Adults*, 1997; Pendergast, Sara, ed. *St. James Guide to Children's Writers*, 5th edition, 1999; Silvey, Anita, ed. *Children's Books and Their Creators*, 1995; *Something About the Author*, vol. 2, 1971; vol. 31, 1983; vol. 79, 1995; Weidt, Mary Ann, *Presenting Judy Blume*, 1989; Wheeler, Jill. *Judy Blume*, 1996. Periodicals—*American Libraries*, June/July 1999; *New Yorker*, December 13, 1993; *Newsday*, June 2, 1998; Oppenheimer, Mark, "Why Judy Blume Endures," *New York Times Book Review*, November 16, 1997; Sutton, Roger, "Forever . . . Yours: An Interview," *School Library Journal*, June 1996; *Voice of Youth Advocates*, December 1993.

WEB SITE: *www.judyblume.com*

An earlier profile of Judy Blume appeared in *Fourth Book of Junior Authors* (1978).

"For as long as I can remember, I have loved writing. There was something very 'grown up' about it. My father, a Naval officer, wrote. My mother, an unpublished poet, wrote. Even my brother, who is ten years my senior, wrote. Granted, the writing my father and brother did was either job- or school-related. But I didn't know that. I knew only that everyone would hunch over their desks or the kitchen table writing, and I wanted to do it too.

"My parents would often read aloud to my brother and me—my mother's poetry or letters to and from family and friends. I was always amazed that such riveting tales could come out of a pencil, pen, or typewriter. No doubt these examples set the stage for my own first attempts at writing stories. I learned to treasure paper and pencils even before I knew how to form the 26 letters of the alphabet, or words. My scibbles would become notes to Papa, my mother's father, or they might be poetry or stories of my own invention. My family made all the appropriate noises, and Papa even wrote back to me!

"Writing is what I did as a kid. When I was seven, my brother joined the Air Force and I knew exactly what to do: Write a letter to him. 'Dear Wayne,' it began. 'Since I have nothing to do, I thought I would write. Since I have nothing to say, I guess I will close.' It was of little importance to me that he hadn't actually left yet. It was an excuse to write!

"Born in St. Petersburg, Florida, I was blessed, I think, to have spent a significant portion of my first five years on Alaska's Kodiak Island, for at that time there was no television in the Alaskan frontier. Books, our imaginations, and family activities provided our entertainment. They also planted the seeds of a fertile imagination, an interest in nature, and an appreciation of individual or small-group activities, all of which can be seen in the books I've written.

"In 1967 I was graduated from high school and began college. When I announced to my parents that I thought I wanted to be a writer, my father said, 'Real people don't become writers. Real people get jobs.' It was probably sound advice, given the fact that I was too shy to share my creative writing with anyone outside the family. So I studied British literature and became a teacher of writing instead. Still, the desire to write and publish burned deeply, and eventually I began submitting my work for publica-

Courtesy of Michael Hartung

Larry Dane Brimner

November 5, 1949–

tion. Some of my earliest published work was poetry, for which I was paid in 'complimentary copies' of the journals in which the poems appeared. (Suddenly my father's advice became crystal clear!) During this time, I began to read children's books and decided they were the kinds of books I wanted to write. So I taught school by day and wrote children's stories, articles, and books by night. And I collected rejections. Hundreds of them. I sent one article on children's fitness to every major children's magazine at the time, and all rejected it. I was one discouraged critter! Even so, something told me to send it out one more time. On a lark, I changed the title to 'How to Stay Fit in Your Spare Time' and submitted it to *Modern Maturity*, a magazine for people over fifty. They sent me a check for $100—the first money I ever earned for something I'd written. This was the validation I needed to keep writing.

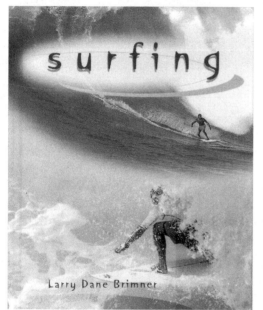

Courtesy of Grolier

"After that, I wrote 'grown-up' articles for *Sunset*, *San Diego Home/Garden*, *California Highway Patrolman*, the *Seattle Post-Intelligencer*, and many other magazines and newspapers before finally landing a children's story in a magazine. A nonfiction book was accepted shortly after that. Then another. Then a picture book. Then a chapter book. I've lost track now of how many books I've written or am contracted to write, but I love doing what I do—playing with those 26 letters of the alphabet, and with words."

* * *

Larry Dane Brimner was born in St. Petersburg, Florida, and has lived most of his life in California. He received his B.A degree in 1971 and his M.A. degree in 1981, both from San Diego State University. From 1974 to 1984, he was a writing teacher at Central Union High School in El Centro, California. He then went on to lecture at San Diego State University from 1984 to 1991. He has been a freelance writer since 1985. He is a member of the International Reading Association, the Authors Guild, the Society of Children's Book Writers and Illustrators, and the Southern California Council of Literature for Children and Young People. Brimner is also affiliated with the Sierra Club and AmFar (AIDS research).

In 1988, *BMX Freestyle* received a Children's Choice Award from the International Reading Association. *Country Bear's Good Neighbor* was named a 1988 Pick of the Lists by the American Booksellers Association. *Animals That Hibernate* was included on the Best Children's Science Book List—1991 compiled by *Science Books and Films*. *A Migrant Family* was designated a 1992 Notable Trade Book in the Field of Social Studies. In 1995, *Max and Felix* was a nominee for the Kentucky Bluegrass Award, and both *Voices from the Camps* and *Being Different* were cited by the New York Public Library in its annual list, Books for the Teen Age. *Merry Christmas, Old Armadillo* was included in the Alabama Emphasis on Reading List for 1995 and 1996, as well as the Kansas State Reading Circle for 1996 and 1997. *E-mail*, *The World Wide Web*, and *Polar Mammals* were included on *Science Books and Films'* "Outstanding Science Book List—1997." In 1998 *Snowboarding* was named a Children's Choice book by the International Reading Association.

SELECTED WORKS: *BMX Freestyle*, 1987; *Country Bear's Good Neighbor*, 1988; *Snowboarding*, 1989/1997; *Animals That Hibernate*, 1991; *A Migrant Family*, 1992; *Unusual Friendships: Symbiosis in the Animal World*, 1993; *Max and Felix*, 1993; *Voices From the Camps: Internment of Japanese Americans during World War II*, 1994; *Being Different: Lambda Youths Speak Out*, 1995; *Merry Christmas, Old Armadillo*, 1995; *Polar Mammals*, 1996; *E-mail*, 1997; *The World Wide Web*, 1997; *What Good Is a Tree?*, 1998; *Nana's Hog*, 1998; *Raindrops*, 1999; *Cowboy Up!*, 1999.

SUGGESTED READING: *Something About the Author*, vol. 79, 1995. Periodicals—*The California Reader*, Fall 1997.

WEB SITE: *www.brimner.com*

"I wrote my first story in second grade. It was not in any way good, but (like Dr. Johnson's dancing dog) I received praise from teachers and parents for having done it at all. This was a dangerous lesson to learn. The next few years produced a steady stream of stories (all full of dangling from cliffs and rising floodwaters, whatever I'd seen in a movie) which were trotted out to impress the grown-ups.

"In high school, I learned it could also impress girls. This was an even more intoxicating discovery. No more adventure. Humor was now the keynote. My fellow high-schoolers, being forced to write a story or poem, would dredge up the deepest anguish of the teenaged soul. So I wrote wacky parodies and made girls laugh.

"At the same time, I discovered acting. This was a great release for me, acting out someone else's life and making lots of people laugh, not just the one reading my rough-typed manuscript. And it impressed girls. So writing subsided as I pursued the immediate gratification of bright lights and applause.

William J. Brooke

November 28, 1946–

"Many years later, the dream of a Broadway career had faded, but I still regularly performed with various Gilbert & Sullivan groups (I've played thirty different roles in the repertory over the years) and small opera companies, and I still wrote, but I hadn't submitted a manuscript in years. A composer friend, with whom I had written some modestly successful musical revues, asked if I would write a narration for an American equivalent to *Peter and the Wolf*, a folk tale with musical interludes and underscoring. It was to be for percussion ensemble, so I thought Paul Bunyan might be a natural. Then I started reading about Paul Bunyan and realized that he was basically a shill for the lumber industry and how good it is for mankind to wreak devastating changes on the environment. This didn't appeal to me, so I kept looking in my book of folk tales and the name Johnny Appleseed struck me.

Courtesy of William J. Brooke

"Here was America the grower, the great contrast with Paul Bunyan as America the chopper, and I wondered what the two would have to say to each other. So I wrote the story, put them together and let them work it out. My composer friend let the project lapse, and another couple of years went by. Then I ran across the story again and was surprised at how good it was. ('This author writes just the way I like!') So I submitted it around as a children's book. Six rejections came before Harper & Row wrote a nice letter saying they liked it but it was too slight for a book and they didn't want a whole book of Paul Bunyan stories, so if I could think of something else let them know. I took a look at other folk and fairy tales and tried to apply the same 'what if?' technique to answer questions that I personally had about the stories. This became my first book, *A Telling of the Tales*.

"And suddenly, much to my surprise, I was a children's book author. My writing grows from my theatrical background. The biggest job of creating a character onstage is finding business for him, the gestures and actions that delineate who he is and what he's feeling. For my written characters, I try to act them out, finding movements and gestures and improvising dialogue. I am happiest with my stories when the characters just talk to each other; I am unhappiest when I have to shovel through too much plot or description.

"On some level, I'm still writing and acting to impress people. But more and more I feel the responsibility of being true to the character. The act of creation is a lonely one; in writing, there's just me and the computer. When the book finally comes out, I feel almost no connection with it because the actual time of creation is two or three years in the past. In acting, what happens in performance is the playing out of what you have discovered, but the real act of creation happens in rehearsals with only one or two other people involved. So I suppose I've found some higher commitment as I've grown older, and I find my gratification in those private little moments of truth and beauty and joy.

"Besides, I've already impressed my girl. She's Lynne, my wife. We met on-stage twenty-five years ago, and she's reason enough."

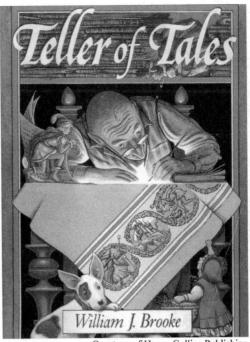

Courtesy of HarperCollins Publishing

* * *

Born in Washington, D.C., the son of Jim and Merney Brooke, William Brooke went to the College of William and Mary, graduating with a B.A. in 1968. He received his M.A. from the University of North Carolina at Chapel Hill in 1971. He acted extensively in high school and college, working for three years in *The Common Glory*, an outdoor summer drama, and helped run a dinner theater for two years. He was employed by the Metropolitan Opera in New York City from 1973 to 1987, and married Lynne Kiernan Greene on May 7, 1975. In New York he performed leading roles with all the major Gilbert and Sullivan companies as well as singing in opera, and he is the author of plays and musical revues produced off-Broadway in New York and in other cities. His humorous collections of "fractured" fairy tales have delighted readers with their word play and clever plot twists. *A Telling of the Tales* was named an ALA Notable Children's Book in 1991.

SELECTED WORKS: *Operantics: Fun and Games for the Opera Buff*, 1986; *A Telling of the Tales*, 1990; *Untold Tales*, 1992; *Teller of Tales*, 1994; *A Brush with Magic: Based on a Traditional Chinese Story*, illus. by Michael Koelsch, 1995; *A Is for Aarrgh!*, 1999.

SUGGESTED READING: *Contemporary Authors*, vol. 134, 1992.

E-MAIL: *billbrooke@aol.com*

Courtesy of Visage Studio

Don Brown

October 4, 1949–

"At the start, I wasn't a good reader. I struggled miserably with Dick & Jane stories. Look. Look at Dick. Look at Dick run. Look. Look at Don. Look at Don fail. Soon I was expected to read whole books; I dutifully borrowed one after another from the school library, never finished any of them, and lied to my teacher about my progress. She knew the truth, and I knew she knew and, well, I cried a lot.

"It was an unhappy routine that nearly became habit until I met Sitting Bull, an acquaintance made through an extraordinary biography. This book was no bland stew of consonants and vowels but a feast of imagination; I devoured it and was hungry for more. Books became part of my diet, and I could honestly report consuming biographies, novels, mysteries, and adventures. I even read the five newspapers my parents had delivered to our home: three 'mornings' and two 'afternoons.' I was addicted to the comic strips and actively followed forty. I loved the quirky line drawings and the dramatic black-and-white graphics.

"My fascination with cartooning led me to *Up Front*, Bill Mauldin's World War II memoir. Mauldin, a self-taught cartoonist for the Army newspaper *Stars & Stripes*, captured the heartbreak and humor of ordinary soldiers fighting in Europe. Willy and Joe, Mauldin's cartoon GIs, defined a generation and won a Pulitzer Prize for their creator. I desperately wanted to be Bill Mauldin. Assuring myself that to be Bill Mauldin I had to draw like him, I armed myself with poster paper, India ink, and pen and sat for hours copying his work. Eventually I realized there was no longer a war in Europe and the position of Bill Mauldin had already been filled. I was also tired of copying only him. I trained my relentless plagiarism elsewhere and copied the wonderful work of Bruce Stark, Mort Drucker, Paul Coker, Edward Sorel, Oliphant, Ralph Steadman, Shel Silverstein, Henrich Kley, and Ronald Searle. They taught me how to draw, and I owe them everything.

"Of course, books and drawing were a backdrop to the larger drama of growing up. I went to school, made friends, played sports, teased girls, watched TV, and bedeviled my parents. In other words, I was no different than the other millions of Baby Boom boys. College came and went, leaving me with a degree in history but no clear notion of what I should do with my life.

I worked as movie theater manager, professional clam digger, and waiter.

"By chance I met an art director who revealed the world of magazine and advertising illustration. Despite my ignorance of publishing and absence of formal art training, I decided to become a professional illustrator. Stubbornness carried me past my handicaps, and I've drawn pictures for a living for nearly twenty years.

"I married and had two beautiful girls. I started writing kids' history books when I had difficulty finding stories about real people—especially heroic women—to read to my daughters. The girls, Sheahan and Corey, now review my works-in-progress. I am working on my fourth book and thrilled at the prospect of doing others.

"Maybe I'll write one about Sitting Bull."

* * *

Don Brown was born on October 4, 1949, in Rockville Center, New York. He graduated from St. Lawrence University in 1971 with a B.A. degree in History and Government. He began working as a freelance illustrator in 1980, and his work has appeared in many magazines, including *Business Week*, *Diversion*, *Scholastic*, and *PC Week*. Brown has done extensive work in illustration for both corporations and advertising agencies. He has also worked in the computer industry, constructing Web sites for the Internet, and at Ehrlich Multimedia, where he created CD-ROMs for children. Several of the animations he directed were selected for their excellence in *PRINT Magazine*'s 1995 Digital Art Annual.

In the mid-1980s Brown became involved in the world of children's publishing, contributing articles to *Cobblestone*, a history magazine for children. His work has since been incorporated into the teaching curricula in several states. His first book for children, *Ruth Law Thrills a Nation*, was immediately recognized as a fresh and important contribution to children's literature. This picture-book biography of Ruth Law, which focuses on her record-setting flight from Chicago to New York, was featured as a *Reading Rainbow*/PBS selection. It was an American Booksellers Association Pick of the Lists and a Notable Children's Trade Book in the Field of Social Studies as well. *Ruth Law Thrills a Nation* was also selected for the Parents Prize by *Parents* magazine and included in the list "*Book Links* Salutes a Few Good Books" by *Book Links* magazine in 1993. *Alice Ramsey's Grand Adventure* received the Authors Award from the Antique Automobile Club of America. Brown's third book, *One Giant Leap: The Story of Neil Armstrong*, was listed among the New York Public Library's 100 Titles for Reading and Sharing and received a Parents' Choice Gold Award. The Society of Illus-

> *"I started writing kids' history books when I had difficulty finding stories about real people— especially heroic women—to read to my daughters."*

trators included his artwork in a show highlighting the best in children's book illustration in 1994.

SELECTED WORKS WRITTEN AND ILLUSTRATED: *Ruth Law Thrills a Nation*, 1993; *Alice Ramsey's Grand Adventure*, 1997; *One Giant Leap: The Story of Neil Armstrong*, 1998; *Rare Treasure: Mary Anning and Her Remarkable Discoveries*, 1999.

SUGGESTED READING: "Adventurers and Accomplishments," *School Library Journal*, December 1996; "Children's Books: Triumphs," *Reading Teacher*, December 1998/January 1999.

Courtesy of John Pflug

Joseph Bruchac

(BROO-shack)

October 16, 1942–

"I was raised by my mother's parents in the rural New York town of Greenfield Center. The story of how I was raised by a college-graduate grandmother of *Mayflower* ancestry and a functionally illiterate, dark-skinned grandfather became one of the books I'm proudest of having written, an autobiography called *Bowman's Store*.

"Because we lived in the country, I didn't play much with other children. I was buried in my grandmother's books half the time and outside with my grandfather in the woods and fields the other half. But that's not completely true. My grandparents ran a general store named after my grandfather, Jesse Bowman. We lived in that store more than in the adjoining house. My childhood memories always circle back to Bowman's store—the gas pumps with big glass globes on top making them look like aliens from outer space, the jingly cash register they let me use to make change, the shelves of groceries and penny candy, the stove people sat around at night telling tales.

"Hearing those stories about the things people in the town did and said, sometimes a song or a fiddle tune from the Adirondack woods—for Grampa Jesse had been a logger—stirred my imagination. It made me want to tell stories too. Mostly stories about animals back them. My earliest ambition, carried through high school and my first year of college at Cornell University, was to be a naturalist and write about the outdoors.

"A creative writing course changed all that. Swept away by poetry, I changed my major to English. That disappointed my wife-to-be, Carol. She'd hoped we'd live in a National Park, somewhere far from the places we'd known. But I was hooked now on being a poet. I did so well I won a writing fellowship to Syracuse University. And, after Syracuse, Carol and I did go to someplace much further away than any National Park. We went to West Africa.

"Three years of volunteer teaching in Ghana showed me a great deal about traditional community. I'll never forget the warmth and beauty and depth of Ewe culture. But Africa also taught me about myself and my own country. For one, it gave me the perspective to see the Abenaki Indian heritage that had been set aside by the generations before me. Returning to America in 1969, I began to work intensively on learning and sharing that heritage.

"My wife, our new son, James, and I moved in with my grandfather in the same house where I was raised. Far as I'd gone, I'd circled back to where it all began. Such nearby Native elders as Swift Eagle and Maurice Dennis became my friends and teachers. (A poem of mine called 'Birdfoot's Grampa,' now included in more than sixty anthologies, is based on an experience with Swift Eagle.) I wrote and taught at Skidmore College while Carol and I ran a small press publishing books by African, American Indian, and Asian American poets.

"After our second son, Jesse, was born, I began to tell and then write down some of the Native stories I'd learned. These stories turned into my first collection for young people, *Turkey Brother and Other Iroquois Stories*. I think it can truly be said that my sons turned me into a storyteller and writer for young people.

"Today, Carol and I still live in that house in Greenfield Center where I was raised. Our two sons are grown. They're both storytellers and writers. Sometimes we perform together, singing traditional Abenaki songs and telling stories. One recent book, *When the Chenoo Howls*, was co-authored with Jim—remembering the monster stories I told when they were kids. Another circle completed. Looking back at it all, those circles that became my life as a writer fit together in more ways than I ever could have imagined."

"Looking back at it all, those circles that became my life as a writer fit together in more ways than I ever could have imagined."

* * *

Joseph Bruchac is a poet, a writer, an editor and publisher, a performer, a teacher, and, most of all, a storyteller. Part Abenaki Indian (the Abenaki are an Algonquian people of the eastern woodlands), Bruchac has been telling and performing Native American stories for over twenty-five years. Exploring his own multicultural heritage led him to collect Native legends, folktales, and stories from many tribes. Whether he is translating and retelling traditional Native tales, creating poems and text for picture books, or combining Native American culture with contemporary stories, Joseph Bruchac's books celebrate family, nature, and the spirituality and wisdom of the Native American tradition.

Bruchac earned a B.A. from Cornell University, an M.A. in Literature and Creative Writing from Syracuse University, and a Ph.D. in Comparative Literature from the Union Institute of Ohio. His teaching experience includes three years in West Africa and eight years directing a writing program for Skidmore College inside a maximum-security prison.

Bruchac's career as a writer/storyteller at correctional facilities, hospitals, libraries, Indian Schools, Native American Institutes, and universities began in the early 1970s and continues to this day. He has been a featured storyteller at numerous festivals, including the British Storytelling Festival, the Stone Soup Festival, and the National Storytelling Festival in Jonesborough, Tennessee, and a writer/storyteller-in-residence in various academic settings. He also participates in workshops, poetry readings, and storytelling programs at museums, universities, and festivals.

With his wife Carol, Bruchac owns and manages the Greenfield Review Press, a small publishing firm; he also directs the Greenfield Review Literary Center. His poems, articles, translations, and folk stories have appeared in over 500 magazines and are represented in over 100 anthologies. In addition to creating original works, Bruchac has edited more than fifteen Native American and multicultural anthologies, including *The Light from Another Country: Poetry from American Prisons* (1984).

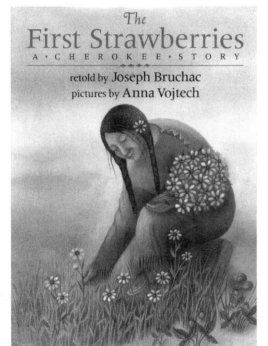

Courtesy of Dial Books

Joseph Bruchac was a Rockefeller Humanities Fellow and an NEA Poetry Writing Fellow. *The Story of the Milky Way* won a *Scientific American* Young Readers Book Award and was an Aesop Award Accolade book. *The Boy Who Lived with the Bears* received a *Boston Globe–Horn Book* Honor Award and was an ALA Notable Children's Book, as was *A Boy Called Slow*, Bruchac's picture book account of the boyhood of Sitting Bull. *Dog People* won the Patterson Children's Writing Award. Many of his books have been cited as Notable Trade Books in the Field of Social Studies, including his autobiographical *Bowman's Store*. In 1996 Joseph Bruchac received the Knickerbocker Award for Juvenile Literature from the New York State Library Association, and in 1998 he was honored with the David McCord Children's Literature citation for the body of his work. The Native Writers' Circle of The Americas presented him its Lifetime Achievement Award in 1999.

SELECTED WORKS: *Turkey Brother and Other Iroquois Folk Tales*, 1975; *Keepers of the Earth*, with Michael Caduto, 1988; *Thirteen Moons on Turtle's Back*, with Jonathan London, illus. by Thomas Locker, 1992; *Fox Song*, illus. by Paul Morin, 1993; *The First Strawberries: A Cherokee Story*, illus. by Anna Vojtech, 1993; *The Story of the Milky Way*, with Gayle Ross, illus. by Virginia Stroud, 1995; *A Boy Called Slow*, illus. by Rocco Baviera, 1995; *The Boy Who Lived with the Bears and Other Iroquois Stories*, 1995; *Dog People: Native Dog Stories*, illus. by Murv Jacob, 1996; *Four Ancestors*, 1996; *Tell Me a Tale: A Book about Storytelling*, 1997; *Between Earth & Sky: Legends of Native American Sacred Places*, illus. by Thomas Locker, 1997; *Eagle's Song*, illus. by Dan Andreasen, 1997; *Lasting Echoes: An Oral History of Native American People*, illus. by Paul Morin, 1997; *The Arrow Over the Door*, 1998; *Heart of a Chief*, 1998; *Pushing Up the Sky: Seven Native American Plays for Children*, illus. by Teresa Flavin, 2000.

SUGGESTED READING: Bruchac, Joseph. *Bowman's Store: A Journey to Myself*, 1997; *Children's Literature Review*, vol. 46, 1998; *Contemporary Authors*, New Revision Series, vol. 47, 1995; *The Native North American Almanac*, 1994; *Native North American Literature*, 1994; Pendergast, Sara, ed. *St. James Guide to Children's Writers*, 5th ed., 1999; Riley, Patricia, ed. *Growing Up Native American: An Anthology*, 1993; Silvey, Anita, ed. *Children's Books and Their Creators*, 1995; *Something About the Author*, vol. 42, 1985; vol. 89, 1997.

"I grew up in Salt Lake City, the youngest of five children. It was my good fortune, among many things, to grow up in a household where books were important. My mother didn't often have time for her own reading, but we knew that she loved books. It seemed to me that we had some of the most wonderful books on the shelf—big and small, with lots of colored pictures, or the big book of bedtime stories. I remember sitting on my mother's lap as she read to me, or listened to me read. Some of the books that are clearest in my memory are the ones she would sometimes read to us when we were traveling. The whole family would be packed into a tiny motor home, and we would lie in

Caralyn M. Buehner

(BEE-ner)

May 20, 1963–

our beds at night while Mom read to us from the light of a little propane lantern that we called 'Hump.'

"For a time when I was young, all four of us girls slept in one basement bedroom. I remember my oldest sister reading aloud to us from the P. G. Wodehouse series about the unflappable Jeeves. I know that there was much that I didn't understand since I was so much younger than the older girls. But because they were convulsed in laughter, so was I. The unfolding of a story was exquisite, and I loved books from the time I can remember.

"I loved going to the library; the wonderful smell and feel of a stack of books to take home and savor. At home I would curl up by the furnace vent or in the big corner chair with a snack and a book, and be content for hours. Often I just couldn't quit, and I'd go to bed and read under the covers with a flashlight. I read the books my older sisters read. One of my sisters worked at the library at the local university. She took me to work with her once when I was about eleven, sat me in a cubicle with some good books, and let me read for hours while she worked. I had a bag of sunflower seeds—and a great time. I was exposed to some of the world's greatest literature—and probably some of its worst—and felt as if I had lived a thousand lives as well as my own.

"In my junior high and high school years I never went anywhere without a book. I was also discovering other wonderful interests. I loved my classes in history and geography and social studies. I took classes in Latin and drama and dance. I made constant use of the skills I picked up in reading, but had no desire to write.

Courtesy of the Buehners

"I met Mark Buehner in college. He introduced me to a fascinating world of color and shape, where a whole story can be told in a single picture. It is always with a sense of awe that I watch the emergence of the artwork. A few years after we married and moved to New York, Mark illustrated his first children's books. He encouraged me to write and was the catalyst for our first book, *The Escape of Marvin the Ape*. Since then we've written four more books together and plan to do many more. The challenge for me always is to write a story that is meaningful to me and is complemented by his artwork and talent.

"Mark and I now live in Salt Lake City with our six children. My time spent writing is ludicrously limited, but there is always time to read! I love being with my family and living close to my parents and siblings. We have a rare closeness. I am often at school—my children's or someone else's. I also enjoy the time I spend working with the children in my church. Mostly, though, I am a 'mom at home' and find that my deepest joys and richest emotions, whether they emerge fully in my writing or not, are those that envelop me in the day-to-day routines of my homelife. What I hope to do in my writing is to package that sense of real life—the fun, the love, the silliness—for any child to savor."

*　*　*

Although born in St. George, Utah, Caralyn Morris Buehner has spent most of her life in Salt Lake City, surrounded by her family. Caralyn and her sisters and mother still spend every Thursday together, often having lunch and talking about books. Caralyn Morris met Mark Buehner at the University of Utah and they married in 1983. Both had grown up in large families, and now they have a growing family of their own. One of Caralyn's greatest pleasures is keeping scrapbooks on her children's lives, filled with the funny things they say, the pictures they draw, and other wonderful mementos. She also loves to read aloud to her children and has found that reading aloud helps to hone her own sense of story and pacing as she writes. Her husband claims that she "devours books, and lots of them. She has a critical eye for writing, and it comes out in her own writing."

A Job for Wittilda was an IRA/CBC Children's Choice in 1994 and won the Utah Children's Choice award in 1997. *It's a Spoon, Not a Shovel* was cited on the New York Public Library's annual list, 100 Titles for Reading and Sharing, in 1995 and won the Utah Children's Informational Book Award for 1997–98. *Fanny's Dream* was named an ALA Notable Children's Book and won a Parents' Choice Award and a *Boston Globe–Horn Book* Honor Award in the picture book category.

SELECTED WORKS: (all illus. by Mark Buehner) *The Escape of Marvin the Ape*, 1990; *A Job for Wittilda*, 1993; *It's a Spoon, Not a Shovel*, 1995; *Fanny's Dream*, 1996; *I Did It, I'm Sorry*, 1998.

SUGGESTED READING: *Something About the Author*, vol. 104, 1999.

E-MAIL: *carab467@aol.com*

Mark Buehner

(BEE-ner)

July 20, 1959–

"My older sisters tell me that I learned to walk by holding a pencil in my hand; I expect it gave me the illusion of balance, and perhaps it still does. Certainly I have always been influenced by the visual world around me—the atmosphere of a room, pictures in a book, and nature itself.

"I grew up in a lively home, the youngest of seven children. One of my early memories is of my dad drawing pictures to entertain me in church. When I got a little bigger I did what most children do—draw pictures on pages to staple them together to make a little book—but I had no idea that what I was doing would eventually become my line of work. It was a natural part of my routine to come home from school and pull out the pencils, paper, and watercolors.

"My childhood was a magical time of play. I had a sandbox, which I practically lived in until I was twelve. Happiness to me was a truckload of fresh sand, and my parents kept me in good supply. My neighborhood friends and I used to play for hours in the box imagining all kinds of fun things. At first we were content to dig with kitchen spoons. Eventually the sandbox became somewhat of a swimming hole; we would fill the box with water, making dinosaur islands and floating boats. We used to contemplate deep subjects while we were digging, such as What if we dig all the way to China? We came a little closer to that realization after seeing the movie *The Great Escape*, and turned in our spoons for army shovels. We started digging trenches, which we covered with plywood and then dirt, so we could relive the movie for ourselves. After that we decided to build a fort, using the sandbox for a foundation. The fort became a makeshift shack when we put a roof on it, which spawned the idea of turning the hut into a restaurant and selling pizza. We cooked up some frozen pizza and discussed the idea as we ate it—in the hut. But someone else took the 'pizza hut' idea a bit farther than we did.

"In grade school my artwork was often praised. I had one friend who was king of the neighborhood, very athletic and tough. I remember him saying to me once, 'I'm better than you at everything, except art.' That encouraged me more! I remember poring over picture book illustrations. I particularly latched onto one small book called *Pierre*, by Maurice Sendak. I couldn't read as well as some of the other children, but I could read *Pierre*; I even memorized it.

"In high school I started taking art more seriously and began taking classes outside of school. I took my first oil painting class when I was sixteen, and found it to be a method I preferred. I still work mostly in oils. I studied landscape painting and some of the techniques of the old masters. When I went on to college, I majored in illustration. All through college I waffled from fine art and a more painterly look, to commercial art and a more whimsical look. Following my graduation in 1985 my wife and I moved to New York City, where we lived for four and a half years. It was while living in New York that I made a decided shift in style and had the opportunity to illustrate my first children's book, *The Adventures of Taxi Dog*, by Debra and Sal Barracca, and the other books soon followed.

"I now live in Salt Lake City with my wife and six children. I have a built-in test group to try out new stories and illustrations for approval. One of the wonderful things about illustrating children's books is the tremendous creative freedom that I have, and the endless potential for imagination. I want every book that I illustrate to be quality, with pictures that appeal to both children and adults, and that can be read over and over again with something new to discover every time."

* * *

Mark Buehner was born and raised in Salt Lake City. He graduated from Utah State University, where he met his wife, Caralyn. The Buehners have collaborated on five picture books to date, with Caralyn writing the text and Mark illustrating. Buehner finds his children's informal comments about his illustrations extremely helpful. His children often let him know what will or won't work for the other children who will be reading the book after it is published. He also keeps in mind that adults may be reading the books aloud to children; they are an important part of his audience as well.

The Buehners recently bought an old house, and Mark is learning a whole new trade, snaking drains and meeting the demands of an ancient boiler and antique wiring. He has come to appreciate the luxury of owning state-of-the-art tools (like cordless drills). When not busy with his work, his growing family, and the house, he loves puttering around in his yard and dabbling in interior design.

Courtesy of Dial Books for Young Readers

The Adventures of Taxi Dog was given a Parents' Choice Award, chosen as a Reading Rainbow Feature Selection, and selected for a *Parenting* magazine Reading Magic Award. *Maxi, the Hero* was chosen by *Parents* magazine as a Best Children's Book in 1991. *Harvey Potter's Balloon Farm*, *Fanny's Dream*, and *My Life with the Wave* were all named ALA Notable Children's Books, and *Fanny's Dream* received a *Boston Globe–Horn Book* Honor Award as well. *Harvey Potter's Balloon Farm* won children's choice awards in Maryland and Kentucky. *My*

Life with the Wave received a Cuffie Award from *Publishers Weekly* and a Silver Award at the Society of Illustrators' Original Art exhibition in 1997. See the article on Caralyn Buehner for additional awards.

SELECTED WORKS ILLUSTRATED: *The Adventures of Taxi Dog*, by Debra and Sal Barracca, 1990; *Maxi, the Hero*, by Debra and Sal Barracca, 1991; *The Escape of Marvin the Ape*, by Caralyn Buehner, 1992; *A Job for Wittilda*, by Caralyn Buehner, 1993; *Harvey Potter's Balloon Farm*, by Jerdine Nolen, 1994; *It's a Spoon, Not a Shovel*, by Caralyn Buehner, 1995; *Fanny's Dream*, by Caralyn Buehner, 1996; *My Life with the Wave*, by Catherine Cowan, 1997; *I Did It, I'm Sorry*, by Caralyn Buehner, 1998; *I Am the Cat*, by Alice Schertle, 1999; *My Monster Mama Loves Me So*, by Laura Leuck, 1999.

SUGGESTED READING: Cummins, Julie. *Children's Book Illustration and Design*, vol. 2, 1998; *Something About the Author*, vol. 104, 1999.

Clyde Robert Bulla

(BULL-uh)

January 9, 1914–

"I was born on a farm near the little town of King City, Missouri. I learned to read and write in a one-room country school. As soon as I discovered words and what they meant and what they could be made to mean, my path was set. I was going to be a writer.

"Long before I should have, I started sending my stories to magazines. For years my life was writing, mailing out manuscripts, getting them back with rejection slips. But when I was twenty, the tide turned. I made my first sale. More sales followed. In those Depression years, the checks were welcome. But I was realizing that while I knew I wanted to be a writer, I didn't know what kind of writer I wanted to be. I wasn't happy with my magazine stories. I switched to novels and wrote three or four. Only one was published, and that was a failure.

"I began to look for work that would support me while I learned to be a writer. I moved to my home town and went to work on the weekly newspaper. Mostly I ran the linotype and helped the printer. Much later I wrote a column called 'People and Places.'

"My best friend was a teacher in Louisiana with the romantic name of Emma Celeste Thibodaux. We hadn't met—we never met—but she had read some of my published work and written to me. She had written stories for children. She thought this was something I might do.

"I didn't want to write for children. I didn't know how. The children's books I had read hadn't appealed to me. I told her I had no ideas. She gave me one. It didn't appeal to me either, but because she was my best friend and I didn't want to disappoint her, I wrote a book, *The Donkey Cart*, based on her idea. She urged me to send it out. I sent it to my agent, who promptly sent it back.

"Years passed. Em Celeste met a famous author and illustrator of children's books who was doing research in Louisiana. Her name was Lois Lenski. 'If only you could get to know her!' wrote Em Celeste. 'Why don't you write to her?' For the first time I was a little impatient with my friend. What was I to this famous author-illustrator?

"And one day a letter came from Lois Lenski! 'Em Celeste has been sending me your newspaper columns. Judging from these, I think you might be able to write for children. She tells me you have written a children's book. Could I see it?' I sent her *The Donkey Cart*. She showed it to Elizabeth Riley, juvenile editor of the Thomas Y. Crowell Company. After I had completely rewritten it and thrown out a couple of chapters, it was accepted.

"The book came out in style, with illustrations by Lois Lenski. I liked it—all but the story. Who was going to read about the mild adventures of a mild boy and girl? I was amazed when Elizabeth Riley asked me for another book.

"I had grown up in the neighborhood of St. Joseph, Missouri, where the Pony Express started in 1860. I thought young readers might be interested in a story about the men who had carried mail across the West on horseback. I began to see it as an exciting story, with plot and character. I would keep it simple and clear. It might be different from any other children's book!

"*Riding the Pony Express* was published, and again I was disappointed. It fell short of my hopes and expectations. I began to learn that no book would ever be the wonderful work I planned. But I

Courtesy of Clyde Robert Bulla

had found the kind of writing I wanted to do—the kind I was meant to do. Now, more than fifty years and seventy-odd books later, I am as sure of this as ever."

* * *

The son of Julian and Sara Bulla, Clyde Robert Bulla was born January 9, 1914, on a farm near King City, Missouri. He had two older sisters and a brother. He describes himself as being largely self-educated with a special passion for opera, music, painting, history, and travel. In his autobiography, *A Grain of Wheat*, Bulla tells of his determination to become a writer, a storyteller. Though his family didn't encourage his hopes, he knew at a young age that writing was what he wanted to do and persevered, as many of his characters do in their own adventures.

Bulla has said that he never forgets how difficult reading was for some of his classmates. He has tried to make his own books easy to read but complex enough in content to interest older children as well as younger ones. Known for his ability to create close-knit, strong, fast-moving plots and for simple, direct language that conveys an innate understanding of children's feelings and needs, Bulla has had a special impact on middle grade readers over the years.

Bulla researches thoroughly before writing his historical novels. *A Lion to Guard Us* provides a vivid picture of the hardships endured by early settlers, as the three Freebold children make a perilous voyage across the Atlantic to join their father in squalid, fever-ridden Jamestown. The boy in *Charlie's House* makes the same crossing about a hundred years later, though not by choice. Kidnapped off the streets of London, he is sold as an indentured servant in America, where he has so few rights that his master can use him as a stake in a card game. But Charlie is determined to have a life of his own; he escapes and eventually prospers. Bulla's contemporary stories include *Shoeshine Girl*, about a tough ten-year-old who apprentices herself to an elderly shoeshine man and learns to value something besides money, and *The Chalk Box Kid*, in which a boy's talent for drawing helps him cope with sudden changes after his father loses his job.

> *"As soon as I discovered words and what they meant and what they could be made to mean, my path was set. I was going to be a writer."*

As well as being a prolific writer of children's fiction, Bulla has written nonfiction and composed music for children's songbooks and plays. A talented amateur painter and a better-than-amateur musician, he has composed songs for his own books and has also set Lois Lenski's poems to music. His accounts of opera plots (in three books, plus a fourth on Gilbert and Sullivan) are clear and concise. Los Angeles has been his home for many years, and he has been an active member of the Authors Guild and the Society of Children's Book Writers and Illustrators.

Winner of the George G. Stone Center for Children's Books Award in 1968, *Squanto, Friend of the White Men* received a Boys' Clubs of America Gold Medal in 1955. *Benito* was cited as an outstanding juvenile book by the Authors Club of Los Angeles, and in 1971 Bulla received a Christopher Award for *Pocahontas and the Strangers*. *Shoeshine Girl* garnered many awards, including a 1976 Southern California Council on Children's Literature Award, the Charlie May Simon Award, the Sequoyah Children's Book Award and the South Carolina Children's Book Award. *A Lion to Guard Us* was cited as a 1982 Notable Children's Trade Book in the Field of Social Studies. *The Chalk Box Kid* was an ALA Notable Children's Book.

SELECTED WORKS: *The Donkey Cart*, illus. by Lois Lenski, 1946; *Riding the Pony Express*, illus. by Grace Paull, 1948; *Song of St. Francis*, illus. by Valenti Angelo, 1952; *Eagle Feather*, illus. by Tom Two Arrows, 1953, 1994; *Squanto, Friend of the White Men*, illus. by Peter Burchard, 1954; *Poppy Seeds*, illus. by Jean Charlot, 1955, 1994; *The Sword in the Tree*, illus. by Paul Galdone, 1956 (illus. by Bruce Bowles, 2000); *Ghost Town Treasure*, illus. by Don Freeman, 1957, 1994; *Pirate's Promise*, illus. by Peter Burchard, 1958; *Stories of Favorite Operas*, illus. by Robert Galster, 1959; *The Valentine Cat*, illus. by Leonard Weisgard, 1959, 1994; *Three Dollar Mule*, illus. by Paul Lantz, 1960, 1994; *Benito*, illus. by Valenti Angelo, 1961; *The Ring and the Fire: Stories from Wagner's Niebelung Operas*, 1962; *What Makes a Shadow*, illus. by Adrienne Adams, 1962 (illus. by June Otani, 1994); *Viking Adventure*, illus. by Douglas Gorsline, 1963; *More Stories from Famous Operas*, 1965; *White Bird*, illus. by Leonard Weisgard, 1966 (illus. by Donald Cook, 1990); *The Ghost of Windy Hill*, illus. by Don Bolognese, 1968; *Stories of Gilbert and Sullivan Operas*, illus. by James & Ruth McCrea, 1968; *The Moon Singer*, illus. by Trina Schart Hyman, 1969; *Pocahontas and the Strangers*, illus. by Peter Burchard, 1971; *Open the Door and See All the People*, illus. by Wendy Watson, 1972; *Shoeshine Girl*, illus. by Leigh Grant, 1975 (illus. by Jim Burke, 2000); *The Beast of Lor*, illus. by Ruth Sanderson, 1977; *Conquista!* (with Michael Syson), illus. by Ronald Himler, 1978; *Daniel's Duck*, illus. by Joan Sandin, 1979; *Last Look*, illus. by Emily Arnold McCully, 1979, 1995; *My Friend the Monster*, illus. by Michele Chessare, 1980; *A Lion to Guard Us*, illus. by Michele Chessare, 1981; *Dandelion Hill*, illus. by Bruce Degen, 1982; *Charlie's House*, illus. by Arthur Dorros, 1983 (illus. by Teresa Flavin, 1993); *The Chalk Box Kid*, illus. by Thomas B. Allen, 1987; *Place for Angels*, illus. by Julia Noonan, 1995; *The Paint Brush Kid*, illus. by Ellen Beier, 1999.

SUGGESTED READING: Bulla, Clyde Robert. *A Grain of Wheat: A Writer Begins*, 1985; Collier, Laurie and Joyce Nakamura, eds. *Major Authors and Illustrators for Children and Young Adults*, 1993; *Contemporary Authors*, New Revision Series,

Courtesy of HarperCollins Publishers

vol 40, 1993; Pendergast, Sara, ed. *St. James Guide to Children's Writers*, 1999; Roginski, James W. *Behind the Covers*, vol. 2, 1989; Silvey, Anita, ed. *Children's Books and Their Creators*, 1995; *Something About the Author*, vol. 2, 1971; vol. 41, 1985; vol. 91, 1997; *Something About the Author Autobiography Series*, vol. 6, 1988.

An earlier profile of Clyde Robert Bulla appeared in *More Junior Authors*, 1963.

Courtesy of John Sheldon

Michael Caduto

December 20, 1955–

"When I was a child my friends and I often visited Goose Pond, where we caught frogs, turtles, and other fascinating creatures. I loved animals. My best friend was our dog—an enormous German Shepherd named Tiny. Tiny was a kindred spirit, a true friend who was sensitive and intelligent. It seemed natural to believe that Tiny had a soul. But I was taught in Sunday school that only people had souls, and you could not get into heaven without one. I knew heaven would be a lonely place without Tiny, and I wondered what kind of heaven wouldn't allow dogs.

"As I grew up in Warwick, Rhode Island, my surroundings changed from farm and forest to a noisy, crowded suburb. Nearly every place I loved was clearcut, bulldozed, and paved. I was sad, stunned and angry to see how easily ponds and marshes were filled, developed, and forgotten. Ironically, Goose Pond was saved because it lay beneath a major power line.

"Some of my first poems, songs, stories, and illustrations were about people and nature. Being shy, I loved hiking out to Billygoat Bluff; taking quiet moments to sit and craft my words so they expressed the meanings and feelings I wanted to convey. I had some excellent teachers who encouraged my writing, especially Mr. Russell Thomas in fifth grade and Mr. Richard Fucci in my senior year of high school—the year I wrote my first songs.

"The first writing I ever had published was a letter to the editor of the *Warwick Beacon*, that told people how they could become involved in a national effort to save wetlands and clean up our waterways. While I attended the University of Rhode Island, I wrote editorials for the college newspaper, *The Good 5 Cent*

Cigar. After graduating I worked as the land manager for the Audubon Society of Rhode Island. Gradually I was drawn into teaching children and adults, helping them to understand and care for the Earth. I wrote several nature articles for the Audubon newsletter and started writing for regional newspapers and national magazines.

"In 1981, after completing graduate school at the University of Michigan, I moved to Vermont to teach at a nature center. There I discovered the wisdom of Vermont's native people, the Abenaki Indians. From individuals, written records, and stories, I learned about the Earth ways of the Abenaki and other Native Americans. At the same time I discovered that the ancient mystic traditions of all the world's religions are deeply rooted in Earth, the Creator's work.

"In January of 1984, I struck out on my own to offer educational programs and performances of storytelling and music under the name P.E.A.C.E., Programs for Environmental Awareness and Cultural Exchange. It was then that I discovered the joy of storytelling. At the same time, I began writing several books, including a book of Native American stories co-authored with Joseph Bruchac, combined with nature information and activities for children. Eventually the book was published as *Keepers of the Earth*. During the next ten years, I co-authored many more books in the Keepers series. More recently, in *Earth Tales from Around the World* and *The Crimson Elf: Italian Tales of Wisdom*, I wrote original retellings of folk tales and fairy tales. I have written several picture books for children also.

Courtesy of Fulcrum Publishing

"All of my creative energies are engaged while writing, speaking, and storytelling, playing music and sharing ecological and educational knowledge and spiritual connections with others. My job as writer, storyteller, and educator is perfect for sharing this energy. The appreciation that I receive shows me that life is truly a circle of giving and receiving. Every one of us has strong roots and our own amazing story to tell. I want to help children and adults find the voice with which to tell their own stories. May the collective experience of our living stories be a heartfelt and wondrous journey!"

*　*　*

Michael Caduto was born on December 20, 1955, in Providence, Rhode Island, to Ralph and Esther Caduto. He received a B.S. degree (with highest distinction) in Natural Resources from the University of Rhode Island in 1978 and an M.S. degree (summa cum laude) in Natural Resources/Environmental Education from the University of Michigan in 1981. In 1984 he founded P.E.A.C.E., Programs for Environmental Awareness and Cultural Exchange, to promote understanding, awareness, appreciation, and stewardship as the basis for building a harmonious relationship between people and the Earth and among the various cultures of North America. Fortunately, Caduto's vocation and his other interests blend nicely. When he's not creating stories, songs, and speeches, or pursuing his interest in human spirituality, he enjoys contra dancing, bicycling, swimming, travel, and puns. He married Marie Levesque in September of 1990.

Keepers of the Animals was chosen by the American Booksellers Association as a 1991 Pick of the Lists and won a 1992 Choice Award in the collections category from the Association of Children's Booksellers. *Keepers of the Earth* was an ALA Notable Book for Children, and *Keepers of the Night* was named to the ALA Best Books for Young Adults list. *Earth Tales from Around the World* was awarded a 1997 Aesop Prize by the Children's Folklore Section of the American Folklore Society, as well as the 1998 *Skipping Stones* Honor Award for excellence as a teaching resource in multicultural and nature awareness. In 1998 "The Land of Eternal Life," one of the stories in *The Crimson Elf: Italian Tales of Wisdom*, received a *Storytelling World* Honor Award as a "most tellable tale" from a published collection. Caduto received the New England Regional Environmental Educator Award in 1992.

SELECTED WORKS: *Keepers of the Earth: Native American Stories and Environmental Activities for Children*, with Joseph Bruchac, 1988; *Keepers of the Animals: Native American Stories and Wildlife Activities for Children*, with Joseph Bruchac, 1991; *Keepers of the Night: Native American Stories and Nocturnal Activities for Children*, with Joseph Bruchac, 1994; *Keepers of Life: Discovering Plants through Native American Stories and Earth Activities for Children*, with Joseph Bruchac, 1994 ; *Earth Tales from Around the World*, 1997; *The Crimson Elf: Italian Tales of Wisdom*, 1998; *Remains Unknown: The Final Journey of the Human Spirit*, 1999.

SUGGESTED READING: *Contemporary Authors*, vol. 153, 1997; *Something About the Author*, vol. 103, 1999. Periodicals— "There's Science in That Story," *Instructor*, March 1994.

"Growing up, I had no idea I would someday become a writer. Writing programs in schools were very different from the good programs of today. I wrote as little as possible, feeling discouraged—demolished—by the red and blue pencil marks made on my efforts.

"I do remember that I always loved books. Even as a young child, I read every word and number on the copyright page—I still do. I loved the sounds of words and the wonderful ways they could be put together to make a story, a poem, a joke, a song. I loved the places books could take me—from the room I shared with my brother in a Brooklyn apartment to a cabin of a beloved grandfather in the Swiss Alps, or to the circus, or the rodeo. I remember reading a Western after school one day and my mother calling me to dinner. I made believe I didn't hear her because I didn't want to fall off my horse!

"As I grew older, I knew I wanted to work with children and decided to become an early childhood teacher. It was while getting my Master's Degree in Education that I fell into writing. I took a children's literature course with an inspiring professor, which led me—with great trepidation—to sign up for a course called 'Writing for Children.' There were no red and blue pencil marks, and my very first story was published in *Humpty Dumpty* magazine.

"I went on to become an early childhood teacher and had the pleasure of reading to children and discovering which books captivated them. When budget cuts left me looking for work, I became a children's book editor and had the pleasure of seeing how a book is made. Now I have the pleasure of being a writer. I'm surrounded by books and, while I'm not in a classroom, I'm still closely connected to children.

"Before I begin a book, I always ask myself the same question: What will this book give to a child? Will it be a love of language? A feeling of being valued? A trip to a new place? An introduction to numbers or letters? A belly laugh to ease a difficult growing-up day? When I am satisfied with the answer, I begin to write.

"I am lucky. I am a writer of children's books. I get to put my heart into my work. I get to go back and remember being a child. I get to create books—gifts—for children every day."

Courtesy of Justin Sutcliffe

Stephanie Calmenson

November 28, 1952–

* * *

Stephanie Calmenson was born in Brooklyn and has lived all her life in and around New York City. She earned a B.A. in Education from Brooklyn College and an M.A. in Early Childhood Education from New York University. After a brief teaching career, she entered the publishing world, where she worked as an editor and then as an editorial director until the early 1980s, when she became a full-time author of children's books. Calmenson is a member of PEN, the Authors Guild, the Society of Children's Book Writers and Illustrators, the American Society of Composers, the Academy of American Poets, and the Delta Society.

Calmenson has written a wide variety of books for children: picture books; counting, rhyming, humor, and activity books; easy readers; and nonfiction. She is especially known for her humorous books. She also enjoys writing about dogs: her own dog was profiled in her book *Rosie: A Visiting Dog's Story*, a Junior Library Guild Selection that *Smithsonian* magazine called "one of the outstanding nonfiction titles of the year." *My Dog's the Best*, a beginning reader's book, was followed by *Shaggy, Waggy Dogs (and Others)*, a book that advises readers on getting—or not getting—canine pets of their own.

In addition to her solo publications, Calmenson writes books with co-author Joanna Cole, including the popular Gator Girls series and volumes of jokes, games, and tongue twisters. She also has written features and stories for magazines and contributes to textbooks, workbooks, and teacher guides.

Dinner at the Panda Palace, a counting poem, was a PBS Storytime Selection. *Marigold and Grandma on the Town, It Begins with an A, Six Sick Sheep: 101 Tongue Twisters, The Gator Girls*, and *Rockin' Reptiles* were all named Pick of the Lists titles by the American Booksellers Association. *The Gator Girls* was chosen for New York Public Library's annual list, 100 Titles for Reading and Sharing. *Rockin' Reptiles, Hotter Than a Hot Dog!* and *Walt Disney's Alice's Tea Party* (written under the pseudonym Lyn Calder) were named as IRA/CBC Children's Choices.

SELECTED WORKS WRITTEN: *The Principal's New Clothes*, illus. by Denise Brunkus, 1989; *What Am I? Very First Riddles*, illus. by Karen Gundersheimer, 1989; *Dinner at the Panda Palace*, illus. by Nadine Bernard Westcott, 1991; *Walt Disney's Alice's Tea Party* (as Lyn Calder), illus. by Jesse Clay and David Pacheco, 1992; *Zip, Whiz, Zoom!* illus. by Dorothy Stott, 1992; *Six Sick Sheep: 101 Tongue Twisters*, with Joanna Cole, illus. by Alan Tiegreen, 1993; *It Begins With an A*, illus. by Marisabina Russo, 1994; *Rosie: A Visiting Dog's Story*, photos by Justin Sutcliffe, 1994; *Marigold and Grandma on the Town*, illus. by Mary Chalmers, 1994; *Hotter Than a Hot*

Dog!, illus. by Elivia Savadier, 1994; *The Gator Girls*, with Joanna Cole, illus. by Lynn Munsinger, 1995; *Bug in a Rug: Reading Fun for Just-Beginners*, with Joanna Cole, illus. by Alan Tiegreen, 1996; *Engine, Engine, Number Nine*, illus. by Paul Meisel, 1997; *Rockin' Reptiles*, with Joanna Cole, illus. by Lynn Munsinger, 1997; *My Dog's the Best*, illus. by Marcy D. Ramsey, 1997; *The Teeny Tiny Teacher*, illus. by Denis Roche,1998; *Shaggy, Waggy Dogs (and Others)*, illus. by Justin Sutcliffe, 1998; *Get Well, Gators!*, with Joanna Cole, illus. by Lynn Munsinger, 1998; *Gator Halloween*, with Joanna Cole, illus. by Lynn Munsinger, 1999; *Fun on the Run: Travel Games and Songs*, with Joanna Cole, illus. by Alan Tiegreen, 1999.

SELECTED WORKS EDITED: *Ready . . . Set . . . Read!: The Beginning Reader's Treasury*, with Joanna Cole, illus. by Chris Demarest, 1990; *Miss Mary Mack and Other Children's Street Rhymes*, with Joanna Cole, illus. by Alan Tiegreen, 1990.

SUGGESTED READING: *Contemporary Authors*, vol. 107, 1983; *Contemporary Authors*, New Revision Series, vol. 24, 1988; *Something About the Author*, vol. 37, 1985; vol. 51, 1988; vol. 84, 1996.

Janell Cannon

November 3, 1957–

"I grew up in Minnesota in the suburbs. Looking back on this place, I would describe it as a very typical middle-class neighborhood. But when I was a four-year-old, I would sit in the front and listen to the world. The hissing of the distant freeways was to me the sound of a great ocean. I imagined we lived on an island among many islands, and on each of them, I saw factories and forests and all sorts of things as my mind gave me a bird's-eye view. I have no idea where I came up with this stuff, but I was always daydreaming. 'She's in a trance again,' my parents would say.

"Close by our house was an old natural pond teeming with life. My brothers, sister, and I often went there to explore. We found turtles, frogs, salamanders, snakes, as well as insects and fish of many sorts. We would bring salamanders home and feed them bits of hamburger. I became fascinated with nature by studying all these wonderful creatures. None of them were scary to me, and I felt they were all beautifully designed.

"My parents were readers, and the house was full of books. Every Sunday, my dad would stay in bed late and read the newspaper. It was a ritual to sit around the piles of papers and hang out. Before I could read, I imitated my parents by holding the paper open and gazing into its pages. I remember having absolutely no idea what any of those little symbols meant. I couldn't wait to learn how to decipher them.

"Grade school was so much fun. I enjoyed my teachers and learned quickly how to read. I was always doodling in class, however, and sometimes got into trouble. Once a teacher held up my doodled-up paper in front of the class and said, 'Somebody forgot to put her name on her paper, but we all know who she is, don't we?'

"Life took a big turn when I was twelve. My parents were the first on the block to get a divorce, and our family had to work through all of the emotional and financial difficulties that come with it. By junior high, I was socially awkward, had little interest in school, and became even more of a daydreamer. I escaped into my drawing and painting and journalized my thoughts and

Courtesy of Dawn Mamikunian

dreams. All through high school, I carried a big sketchbook that completely covered a desktop. I drew in class if the teacher became repetitive or when the class was out of control. I got lots of practice. Some teachers noticed my work and asked me to illustrate newsletters, and some even bought my drawings. This encouraged me to keep up the drawing habit.

"I left Minnesota when I graduated from high school and traveled west. I ended up in Southern California, where I worked all sorts of odd jobs, lived in crazy, low-rent places, and learned to survive on almost nothing. I sought out and got more and more work as an artist and eventually landed a full-time job in a graphics department in a library. It was the perfect job for me. I loved promoting the library through my art. I had worked there for twelve years when I began to feel I needed a change. On weekends and after work, I began to draw a series of pictures that soon developed into the story of Stellaluna, a fruit bat. I purposely chose a creature that many people feared and disliked, hoping I could show it in a more positive light.

"I submitted the finished piece to an agent and, much to my surprise, *Stellaluna* was soon published and doing well. I left my job and now I work full time on my books. I continue to choose unpopular animals as heroes in my stories and thoroughly enjoy doing the research it takes to draw my characters correctly. I surf the Internet, scour the library, talk to scientists, and visit my local zoo to gather information. Often I sit back and marvel at my good fortune. Here I am—after all these years still studying critters, daydreaming, and drawing—and making a living at it!"

Courtesy of Harcourt Brace & Company

*   *   *

Janell Cannon was born in St. Paul, Minnesota, and grew up in Eagle, a suburb of Minneapolis. She began drawing in earliest childhood and loved black Bic pens. She was left-handed and often doodled through her classes, dragging the side of her left hand across the art work as she drew. As a result, she walked around for most of her school years with an ink-blackened left hand. When she was eighteen, she left home to work in Yellowstone National Park for a summer, visited Colorado and Arizona, traveled up to the Bay Area and down the California Coast. She traveled until she ran out of money. Finally, in Leucadia, she took a job in a greenhouse. Cannon, who has no formal art training, actually starts her stories with the pictures. "I keep drawing and I watch what happens, and I catch up later with my writing." Working from her home studio in California, which she shares with a cat and a parrot, she champions misunderstood creatures in her books. Her love for bats, spiders, Komodo dragons, and snakes inspired her to create unusual (and unusually successful) summer reading programs at her public library. Cannon won the prestigious John Cotton Dana Award from the American Library Association for her summer reading program "Supervet." Much of what she has learned about the various animals comes from articles and photographs in *National Geographic*. Her mission is to write stories about these animals that will transform young people's fear into informed affection. "Fruit bats don't drink blood and won't get caught in your hair. I hope to show them in a positive light so that they might be given more respect," she says. Her first book, *Stellaluna*, received the ABBY Award in 1994; members of the American Booksellers Association give that award to the titles they have most enjoyed selling during the previous year.

SELECTED WORKS: *Stellaluna*, 1993; *Trupp: A Fuzzhead Tale*, 1995; *Verdi*, 1997.

SUGGESTED READING: *Something About the Author*, vol. 78, 1994.

Courtesy of Wolfgang Dietrich

Eric Carle

June 25, 1929–

"I was born in Syracuse, New York. There I went to kindergarten. I remember large sheets of paper, colorful paints, and big brushes. Every morning I set off to kindergarten with great enthusiasm. When I was six years old, my parents returned to their homeland and relatives in Germany. There I went to school. I remember that we children were given small sheets of paper, a hard pencil, a ruler, an eraser, and a warning not to make any mistakes. My enthusiasm for school was considerably reduced.

"As a six-year-old boy I had the doubtful privilege of going to school twice, of learning two languages, of coping with two cultures, and adapting myself to two societies. The messages I received during that period of my life were somewhat confused.

"I went to school in Germany until I was sixteen. I disliked most of my education with the exception of a wonderful art teacher and a kind and gentle librarian.

"I was ten years old when World War II broke out. My father (and best friend) was drafted into the German army. He did not return home until I was eighteen years old. I had missed him especially while he was in a POW camp in Russia from 1945 to 1947.

"From 1946 to 1950 I spent four happy and influential years at the Akademie der Bildenden Künste in Stuttgart, Germany. For the first time I felt my horizons expanding and the love for making pictures carrying me on.

"From 1950 to 1952 I designed posters for the United States Information Center in Stuttgart. Then I returned to New York and started to work as a graphic designer for the *New York Times*. I was drafted into the U.S. Army the same year and returned to the *Times* after my discharge in 1954. In 1956 I became an art director for a pharmaceutical advertising agency, but I began losing interest in advertising and in 1963 quit my job in order to freelance as an illustrator.

"In the late 1960s, several publishing houses asked me to illustrate material for first readers, and I found myself becoming deeply involved in these assignments. I felt something of my own past stirring in me. An unresolved part of my own education needed reworking, and I began to make books—books for myself, books for the child in me, books I had yearned for. I became my own teacher—but this time an understanding one.

"After I had illustrated several books for other authors, one day I was punching holes in a stack of paper. Looking at the holes, I thought of a bookworm. Later, after working some more on the idea with my editor, the bookworm became a caterpillar. And that was the beginning of *The Very Hungry Caterpillar*.

"My pictures are collages. I didn't invent the collage. Artists like Picasso and Matisse and children's book artists like Leo Lionni, Ezra Jack Keats and Lois Ehlert have made collages. I begin with plain tissue paper and paint it with different colors, using acrylic paint. Sometimes I paint on a piece of carpet, sponge, or burlap and then use that like a stamp on my tissue papers to create different textures.

"After these papers have dried I store them in color-coded drawers. Let's say I want to create a caterpillar. I cut out a circle for the head from a red tissue paper and many ovals for the body from green tissue papers; and then I paste them with wallpaper glue onto an illustration board to make the picture. Lately I have been experimenting with laying out the pages on a computer, and this has made me aware of other possibilities for using computers. It is my next 'terra incognita,' my unexplored territory.

"Since 1968 I have illustrated and written seventy books. *The Very Hungry Caterpillar* has been translated into thirty languages, and many of my other books have also been translated. As a child I did not have any children's books aside from a Mickey Mouse and a Flash Gordon book in the United States and a *Max und Moritz* and *Struwwelpeter* book in Germany. As an adult I am in the midst of writing and illustrating books for children in all parts of the world. I hope that the children have as much fun looking at my books as I have doing them."

"After I had illustrated several books for other authors, one day I was punching holes in a stack of paper. Looking at the holes, I thought of a bookworm. Later, after working some more on the idea with my editor, the bookworm became a caterpillar. . . ."

* * *

When Eric Carle was a small boy living in a suburb of Stuttgart, Germany, his father would take him on Sunday morning walks through the nearby woods and meadows. He would lift a stone or peel back the bark of a tree to show his son the living creatures underneath, explaining about their life cycles before carefully putting the creatures back into their homes. As an adult artist, Carle now echoes that respect for the natural world in his books for children.

In 1952 when Carle moved to New York, it was Leo Lionni (then art director of *Fortune* magazine and later a highly successful picture-book artist) who helped him get his first job. In the mid-1960s Bill Martin Jr. saw a poster of a red lobster that Carle had designed and asked him to illustrate *Brown Bear, Brown Bear, What Do You See?* Carle had also provided illustrations for an historical cookbook, *Red-Flannel Hash and Shoo-Fly Pie*, and the editor of that book, Ann Beneduce, asked to see some of his own ideas. The result was the first book that he both wrote and illustrated, *1, 2, 3 to the Zoo*, a counting book that features groups of animals on their way to the zoo in open railroad cars.

One year later, Carle produced *The Very Hungry Caterpillar*, his ground-breaking book in concept and design. This story, which follows the transformation of a caterpillar into a butterfly, has become one of the most successful children's books of all time, selling, to date, over fourteen million copies worldwide.

Carle's books usually feature animals or insects and are rendered distinctive by the use of collage, bold design, bright colors, and Carle's creative use of textures and page features to enhance the story. In *The Very Hungry Caterpillar*, the voracious insect literally eats his way through the various foods pictured, with holes appearing throughout the pages to represent the caterpillar's path. *The Grouchy Ladybug*, in which a bad-tempered ladybug recklessly challenges a number of insects and animals, features pages that get progressively bigger as the ladybug encounters ever larger creatures. *Papa, Please Get the Moon for Me* presents pages that fold upwards and outwards as the moon changes in size. *The Very Quiet Cricket* includes a microchip that creates the sound of a cricket chirping as the last page is turned. Carle's books are interactive and involve children's active participation in the story.

While innovations in design are a mark of Carle's work, he himself attributes much of the popularity of his works to their ability to speak to children. "The success of my books is not in the characters or the words or the colors, but in the simple, simple feelings," Carle said in an interview that appeared in the *New York Times*, April 14, 1994. "I remember that as a child, I always felt I would never grow up and be big and articulate and intelligent. *Caterpillar* is a book of hope: you, too, can grow up and grow wings."

From the beginning, Carle's books received critical recognition as well as popular acclaim. In 1970 *1, 2, 3 to the Zoo* captured the German Children's Book Prize and also the First Prize for Picture Books at the International Children's Book Fair in Bologna. *The Very Hungry Caterpillar* was named one of the ten best illustrated books of the year in 1969 by the *New York Times* and was the recipient of an American Institute of Graphics Award. It also received the 1975 Nakamori Reader's Prize in Japan and a Brooklyn Museum Art Books for Children Citation and was a California Reading Initiative title. *Do You Want to Be My Friend?*, an ALA Notable Children's Book and an Honor Book in the *Book World* Children's Spring Book Festival for 1971, won the First Prize for Picture Books at Bologna in 1972. *The Very Busy Spider* was an ALA Notable Children's Book and named to "best" lists of the decade as well as the year. *The Very Quiet Cricket* was cited on New York Public Library's list of 100 Titles for Reading and Sharing in 1990 and won the Buckeye Book Award in Ohio. *The Very Lonely Firefly* was an IRA/CBC Children's Choice and a Child Study Association Children's Book of the Year.

In 1989 Carle received a Silver Medal from the City of Milan, Italy, for *The Very Quiet Cricket.* He was presented with the University of Southern Mississippi Medallion for outstanding contributions in the field of children's literature in 1997 and in 1999 received the Regina Medal from the Catholic Library Association for his "continued distinguished contribution to children's literature."

Eric Carle has two children, Cirsten and Rolf, from his marriage to Dorothea Wohlenberg. He and his second wife, Barbara Morrison, were married in 1973 and currently live in western Massachusetts.

Courtesy of HarperCollins Publishers

SELECTED WORKS WRITTEN AND ILLUSTRATED: *1, 2, 3 to the Zoo*, 1968; *The Very Hungry Caterpillar*, 1969; *Pancakes, Pancakes!*, 1970; *The Tiny Seed*, 1970; *Do You Want to Be My Friend?*, 1971; *The Secret Birthday Message*, 1972; *Rooster's Off to See the World*, 1972; *The Very Long Tail*, 1972; *The Very Long Train*, 1972; *Walter the Baker*, 1972; *Have You Seen My Cat?*, 1973; *I See a Song*, 1973; *All About Arthur*, 1974; *The Mixed-Up Chameleon*, 1975; *Eric Carle's*

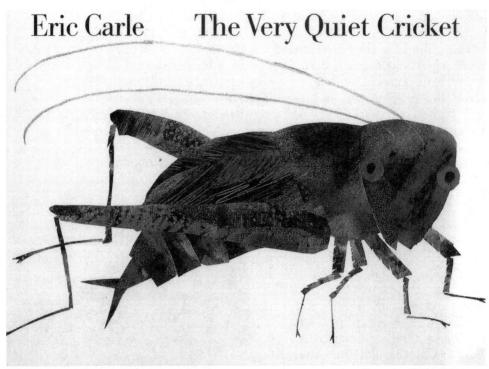

Eric Carle   The Very Quiet Cricket

Courtesy of Penguin Putnam

Storybook: Seven Tales by the Brothers Grimm, 1976; *The Grouchy Ladybug,* 1977; *Seven Stories by Hans Christian Andersen,* 1978; *Watch Out! A Giant!,* 1978; *Twelve Tales from Aesop: Retold and Illustrated,* 1980; *The Honeybee and the Robber,* 1981; *What's for Lunch?,* 1982; *Catch the Ball,* 1982; *Let's Paint a Rainbow,* 1982; *The Very Busy Spider,* 1984; *Papa, Please Get the Moon for Me,* 1986; *All Around Us,* 1986; *A House for Hermit Crab,* 1987; *The Very Quiet Cricket,* 1990; *Draw Me a Star,* 1992; *Today Is Monday,* 1993; *My Apron,* 1994; *The Very Lonely Firefly,* 1995; *Little Cloud,* 1996; *From Head to Toe,* 1997; *Flora and Tiger: 19 Very Short Stories from My Life,* 1997; *Hello Red Fox,* 1998; *You Can Make a Collage,* 1998; *The Very Clumsy Click Beetle,* 1999.

SELECTED WORKS ILLUSTRATED: *Red-Flannel Hash and Shoo-Fly Pie: American Regional Foods and Festivals,* by Lila Perl, 1965; *Brown Bear, Brown Bear, What Do You See?,* by Bill Martin, Jr., 1967; *Tales of Nimipoo,* by Eleanor B. Hardy, 1970; *The Boastful Fisherman,* by William Knowlton, 1970; *The Feathered Ones and Furry,* 1971; *The Scarecrow Clock,* by George Mendoza, 1971; *Do Bears Have Mothers, Too?,* by Aileen Fisher, 1973; *Why Noah Chose the Dove,* by Isaac Bashevis Singer, 1974; *The Hole in the Dike,* by Norma

Green, 1975; *Otter Nonsense,* by Norton Juster, 1982; *The Greedy Python,* by Richard Buckley, 1985; *The Mountain that Loved a Bird,* by Alice McLerran, 1985; *The Foolish Tortoise,* by Richard Buckley, 1985; *All in a Day,* comp. by Mitsumasa Anno, 1986; *The Lamb and the Butterfly,* by Arnold Sundgaard, 1988; *Animals Animals,* 1989; *Polar Bear, Polar Bear, What Do You Hear?,* by Bill Martin, Jr., 1991; *Dragons Dragons,* comp. by Laura Whipple, 1991.

SUGGESTED READING: Carle, Eric. *The Art of Eric Carle,* 1996; Collier, Laurie and Joyce Nakamura, eds. *Major Authors and Illustrators for Children and Young Adults,* 1993; *Contemporary Authors,* First Revision, vols. 25–28, 1977; *Contemporary Authors,* New Revision Series, vol. 10, 1983; Pendergast, Sara, ed. *St. James Guide to Children's Writers,* 5th ed., 1999; Silvey, Anita, ed. *Children's Books and Their Creators,* 1995; *Something About the Author,* vol. 4, 1973; vol. 65, 1991. Periodicals—Glassman, Miriam, "In the Studio with Eric Carle," *Publishers Weekly,* August 29, 1994; *Language Arts,* April 1977; Lewis, Valerie and Leslie Cefali, "Meet the Author: Eric Carle," *Instructor,* October 1993; *New York Times,* April 14, 1994; Williams, Elaine, "Spread Your Wings and Fly," *Times Educational Supplement,* May 28, 1999.

WEB SITE: *www.eric-carle.com*

An earlier profile of Eric Carle appeared in *Fourth Book of Junior Authors and Illustrators,* 1978. Eric Carle's name and signature logotype are trademarks of Eric Carle.

Nancy L. Carlson

October 10, 1953–

"**N**ot many people know in kindergarten what they want to do with the rest of their life, and even fewer stick with those early dreams. But I was determined from the age of five to be an artist. I would sit on my bed and draw for hours on end. In those early drawings I told stories about popular girls I knew and girls who rode horses. I began creating characters and telling stories through my drawings. I always felt the need to communicate something through my art.

"Growing up I was surrounded by an outgoing family. My parents read to my brother and my sister and me every night. I loved to read comic books as a child, and they certainly influenced my style of drawing and use of color. Although when I started drawing stories as a child, I used an ordinary pencil. I didn't use colored pencils or paints like you find in the brightly colored drawings of my books today. In fact, I didn't use color until I was an adult! However, I was still getting lots of practice, and that is important for a young artist.

"After graduating from art school, my first job was dusting children's books and helping customers in the gift shop at the Walker Art Center in Minneapolis. I became fascinated with the books. I started to send my own sketches to a local publisher, but it took a year of persistent contact and two assignments illustrating other writers' work before I was ready to produce my own book, *Harriet's Recital*. My first draft of *Harriet's Recital* was 80 pages long. The words appeared in balloons out of the characters' mouths, like in comic books. I had a lot to learn about writing books for young children, including the fact that they are typically no longer than 32 pages.

"Inspiration for the characters in the books I have published comes from childhood friends and neighbors. Loudmouth George, the boastful bunny, was inspired by a boy in my school whose white hair reminded me of a rabbit. He was always bragging and getting into trouble, just like George. Louanne Pig is based on another childhood friend, who was an only child like Louanne. The experiences of a neighbor I once had inspired the character of Arnie, the mouse-loving cat who wears glasses.

Courtesy of Peter Beck

"And then there's Harriet. Everything that happens to Harriet happened to me when I was a child—from Harriet's stage fright to learning to share Halloween candy to Harriet's interest in baseball. My own dog, Dame, was the model for drawing Harriet. My three children, as well as our two dogs, cat, and guinea pig, all provide me with ideas for my books today. The underlying theme in all my books is helping kids to feel good about themselves."

*   *   *

Nancy Carlson was born in Minneapolis, Minnesota. Her excellent recall of childhood situations and ability to deliver a message with light-hearted humor have resulted in a body of work for early readers that delights children and adults alike. Carlson attended the University of Minnesota at Duluth and the Sante Fe Workshop of Contemporary Art, and received her B.F.A. degree from Minneapolis College of Art and Design in 1976. She presented one-person shows at her college in 1975 and 1976, and since 1980 has exhibited in a variety of venues in the Midwest, as well as in New York City. She has received awards from the Northshore Arts Festival, from Women in International Design, and from the Minneapolis Graphic Design Association, among others.

In addition to her illustrated books, Carlson has written and produced children's plays; she also designs T-shirts, caps, and posters, which are marketed by her family business, McCool Unlimited, Inc. Married in 1979 to Barry McCool, a graphic designer, she lives in Bloomington, Minnesota, with her husband and their three children—Kelly, Patrick, and Michael.

Louanne Pig in the Talent Show received a Parents' Choice Award in 1985, and *Sit Still!* was named an IRA/CBC Children's Choice book in 1996. Three of Carlson's books have been chosen as *Reading Rainbow* review books: *Loudmouth George and the Sixth-Grade Bully*, *Harriet's Recital*, and *Louanne Pig in Making the Team*. *It's Going to Be Perfect* was a Book-of-the-Month Club selection. *Louanne Pig in Making the Team*, *Loudmouth George and the Sixth-Grade Bully*, and *Louanne Pig in the Talent Show* have been adapted for the stage as musicals, and all the Harriet, Loudmouth George, and Louanne Pig books have been issued additionally in book-and-cassette sets for lively read-alongs.

Courtesy of Lerner Publishing Group

SELECTED WORKS WRITTEN AND ILLUSTRATED: *Harriet's Recital*, 1982; *Harriet and Walt*, 1982; *Harriet and the Roller Coaster*, 1982; *Harriet and the Garden*, 1982; *Harriet's Halloween Candy*, 1982; *Loudmouth George and the New Neighbors*, 1983; *Loudmouth George and the Cornet*, 1983; *Loudmouth George and the Big Race*, 1983; *Loudmouth George and the Sixth-Grade Bully*, 1983; *Loudmouth George and the Fishing Trip*, 1983; *Bunnies and Their Hobbies*, 1984; *Louanne Pig in the Talent Show*, 1985; *Louanne Pig in the Perfect Family*, 1985; *Louanne Pig in the Mysterious Valentine*, 1985; *Louanne Pig in the Witch Lady*, 1985; *Louanne Pig in Making the Team*, 1985; *Arnie and the Stolen Markers*, 1987; *I Like Me!*, 1988; *Arnie and the New Kid*, 1990; *What if It Never Stops Raining?*, 1992; *Life Is Fun!*, 1993; *How to Lose All of Your Friends*, 1994; *Arnie and the Skateboard Gang*, 1995; *Sit Still!*, 1996; *ABC, I Like Me!*, 1997; *Snowden*, 1997; *It's Going to Be Perfect*, 1998; *Look Out Kindergarten, Here I Come!*, 1999.

SELECTED WORKS ILLUSTRATED: *Halloween*, by Joyce Ressel, 1980; *Egyptian Boats*, by Joyce Ressel, 1981; *Baby and the Bear*, by Susan Pearson, 1987; *When Baby Went to Bed*, by Susan Pearson, 1987; *Watch Out for Those Weirdos*, by Rufus Klein, 1990; *Lenore's Big Break*, by Susan Pearson, 1992; *The Masked Maverick*, by Jacqueline K. Ogburg, 1994; *What to Do When a Bug Climbs in Your Mouth and Other Poems to Drive You Buggy*, by Rick Walton, 1995.

SUGGESTED READING: *Contemporary Authors*, vol. 110, 1984; *Contemporary Authors*, New Revision Series, vol. 57, 1997; *Something About the Author*, vol. 45, 1986; vol. 56, 1989; vol. 90, 1997.

WEB SITE: *www.nancycarlson.com*

Courtesy of Allen Whitney Chocolate

Debbi Chocolate

January 25, 1954–

"For as far back as I can remember I've had a book in my hands. In fact, I can't remember a time as a child when I wasn't reading, painting, drawing, or writing. Even as a child I had a passion for color, movement, and drama. It runs in the family. My grandmother danced in stage shows and my grandfather was a musician. My grandparents met in vaudeville, fell in love, and the rest is history.

"Being raised in the theater, my mother was always fond of books and the arts. She taught me to read when I was only three. By the age of five I discovered comic books. Comic books changed my life. From that moment on, I joined forces with Flash Gordon in his perilous adventures on the planet Mongo. Along with Dr. Zarkov, the blonde crusader and I would protect the clay people from the villainous emperor, Ming the Merciless.

"Perhaps because of my background, I always felt I would do something in the arts when I grew up. I wrote my first real story when I was about six. I don't remember what the story was about. But I do recall vividly my mother proudly reading it to neighbors who made their way to our flat in Chicago's crowded East Garfield Park. And I recollect the tender expressions on my neighbors' faces as they listened. It was an early lesson for me in how the written word could be used to touch people's hearts.

"When I turned eight, my mother bought me my first oil paint set. At that time, I thought I would become a painter. In between painting and music came my love of movies. I was nine years old when my mother bought me an eight-millimeter film projector. On Saturday afternoons in late autumn and early winter, when the weather was too cold for my friends and me to play outside, I'd set up folding chairs in my basement, pop popcorn, and sell tickets to my 'movie theater' to all the kids in the neighborhood. Even though I showed the same movies each Saturday, my friends didn't seem to mind. They kept coming back every week.

"I turned into quite a musician by the age of thirteen. In high school I was the only girl in the band who played trumpet. As I grew older, I found myself writing stories more often than I found myself painting, playing music, or showing movies to my friends. After finishing high school I went to Spelman College in Atlanta, Georgia, where I met teachers who encouraged my writing. I wrote stories every spare moment I could get. Upon graduating from Spelman, I was awarded a fellowship to the creative writing program at Brown University. That's when I knew I was finally on my way to becoming a professional writer.

Courtesy of Scholastic, Inc.

"Much of what I write about in my books comes from memories of my own childhood. Some of what happens in *A Very Special Kwanzaa* really happened to me—learning to stand up to the school bully and becoming best friends with someone for the very first time. When I finished writing this book, it took me quite a while to get back to writing. I felt I could never care about another character the way I had cared about Charlie Potter.

"Whenever I visit schools, kids always ask if Debbi Chocolate is my real name. I always answer by saying, 'I'm married to Robert Chocolate and I have two boys, Bobby and Allen Chocolate.' My family plays an important role in my work. The father in *A Very Special Kwanzaa* thinks and talks and acts just like Mr. Chocolate. *The Piano Man* is based on my grandparents and their lives in the theater. And Allen, my youngest son, who is a promising visual artist, sometimes helps me visualize scenes in my stories by sketching them out in his art book.

"I like writing books for children. It gives me the chance to share my vision of life's hope, its beauty, and its promise."

* * *

After receiving her Master's degree from Brown University in 1978, Deborah Newton Chocolate worked for twelve years as a children's book editor at Riverside Publishing in Chicago. She has also been a college English instructor, a storyteller at African Arts festivals, and a writing workshop leader for the Oak Park, Illinois, public schools. Three of her books that deal with African American themes—*My First Kwanzaa Book*, *A Very Special Kwanzaa*, and *Kente Colors*—have been Book-of-the-Month Club selections.

Among her other honors are a Parents' Choice Award for *Talk, Talk: An Ashanti Legend*, and an American Booksellers Association Pick of the Lists designation for *Imani in the Belly*. *On the Day I Was Born* was cited as a Notable Trade Book in the Field of Social Studies. *Kente Colors* won a *Parenting Magazine* Reading Magic Award, and *The Piano Man* received the 1999 Coretta Scott King/John Steptoe Award for new talent. *The Piano Man* was also named a Notable Trade Book in the Field of Social Studies.

Debbi Chocolate is a member of the Children's Reading Roundtable of Chicago and resides in Wheaton, Illinois, with her family.

SELECTED WORKS: *Kwanzaa*, illus. by Melodye Rosales, 1990; *My First Kwanzaa Book*, illus. by Cal Massey, 1992; *NEATE: To the Rescue!*, 1992; *Spider and the Sky God: An Akan Legend*, illus by Dave Albers, 1992; *Talk, Talk: An Ashanti Legend*, illus. by Dave Albers, 1993; *Imani in the Belly*, illus. by Alex Boies, 1994; *Elizabeth's Wish* (*NEATE* series, Book 2), 1994; *On the Day I Was Born*, illus. by Melodye Rosales, 1995; *A Very Special Kwanzaa*, 1996; *Kente Colors*, illus. by John Ward, 1996; *The Piano Man*, illus. by Eric Velasquez, 1998.

SUGGESTED READING: *Contemporary Authors*, vol. 161, 1998; *Something About the Author*, vol. 96, 1998.

Sook Nyul Choi

January 10, 1937–

"When I was a little girl in Korea, I often sat reading by candlelight. One night, as I watched the flame of the candle shine and dance, I was inspired to write a poém about it. Proud of my first work of poetry, I showed it excitedly to my mother and expected that she would want to save it in a special place. She read it and told me it was beautiful, but that I would have to burn it. The Japanese, who occupied Korea at the time, did not permit Koreans to write or even read Korean. If my poem were found, our whole family would be severely punished, she explained. As I burned my poem, trying to memorize it before it was destroyed, I was filled with a great yearning for the day when I would be allowed to write and to express my feelings and share them with others.

"For many years, during the Japanese and Russian Occupations, I would have to keep my thoughts pent up inside of me. Finally, in 1947, after my family escaped to Seoul, South Korea, I experienced freedom—the freedom to learn, to explore, and, at last, to write. My friends and I went on hiking trips and wrote poems about the beauty of nature. The most magical experience of all was when some of our poems were published—for everyone to see—in the Sunday children's section of the Seoul newspaper.

"But the bliss was short-lived. The Korean War broke out and lasted for three years. The devastation and sadness overwhelmed me. I felt helpless. I no longer wrote poems. My mother tried to teach me to find comfort in seeing a different kind of beauty—the beauty and resilience of the human spirit as everyone persevered and kept alive their hopes and dreams for better days.

"When the war ended, Mother hoped I would begin to write again. But I had set my sights on learning English and attending college in America. Once I arrived in the States, my studies and my work to pay my tuition left me no time to write. Immediately after graduation, I began to teach school in New York City, and got married, and had two children. Though I often thought about all I had learned from Mother and wanted to write a book about my experiences growing up in Korea, I had no time.

Courtesy of Lovella Beres

"One cold Friday morning, in February of 1980, my husband died suddenly. My full, orderly life was thrown into turmoil as I struggled to find a way to provide for my two young girls. I had to leave the teaching I loved and enter the business world to run my husband's orphaned company. His sudden death made me realize how important it was for me to begin writing at once instead of continuing to put it off.

"Each day after a long day working at my husband's company, I would come home and write. Although it was painful to return to the memories of my life growing up in occupied and war-torn Korea, I was determined to write the stories that had been bottled up inside me for so long.

"In my first novel, *Year of Impossible Goodbyes,* I wrote the story of my family's enduring the Japanese and subsequent Russian Occupations, and how we eventually escaped to freedom in the South. When the book was published, it was enormously rewarding to hear from so many readers who asked to know more about the characters in my book. As a result, I wrote two sequels, *Echoes of the White Giraffe* and *Gathering of Pearls.* In all my novels, I write in the first person because I want to share my feelings, experiences, thoughts, and visions with my readers as if they are my close friends.

"I also wrote three picture books. These were inspired by my experiences as a long-time teacher and as a mother. Often our feelings are so delicate, confusing, and complex that it helps to write and speak about them honestly. I believe it brings us a bit closer to each other and makes us realize how we are so much alike in our fears, insecurities, hopes, and dreams.

Courtesy of Houghton Mifflin

"I love writing, but now and then I get discouraged because it's hard to keep at it. But I know how happy I am to read a good book, and it encourages me to keep working, hoping that my writing will bring some joy, comfort, and happiness to my readers.

Sook Nyul Choi was born on January 10, 1937, in Pyongyang, Korea, and spent her childhood in a country torn apart by war. She came to the United States to attend college and graduated from Manhattanville College with a B.A. in European History. She worked as an elementary and high school teacher in New York, married, and raised two daughters. She began writing her first novel while running her husband's import/export business.

Year of Impossible Goodbyes was greeted with immediate accolades when it appeared in 1991. This essentially autobiographical novel received the Judy Lopez Award from the Women's National Book Association and a Blue Ribbon citation from the *Bulletin of the Center for Children's Books* in 1991. It was also chosen as an ALA Notable Children's Book and a Best Book for Young Adults and was cited in New York Public Library's Best Books for the Teen Age in 1992. In the same year the Cambridge (Massachusetts) YWCA gave Sook Nyul Choi the Women of

Achievement Award. *Gathering of Pearls*, which brings the heroine of *Impossible Goodbyes* to the United States, was selected for New York Public Library's Books for the Teen Age in 1995. The picture book *Halmoni and the Picnic* was chosen as a *Reading Rainbow* review book in 1994. Sook Nyul Choi's books have been widely anthologized in educational reading series and have appeared on numerous state reading award master lists.

SELECTED WORKS: *Year of Impossible Goodbyes*, 1991; *Echoes of the White Giraffe*, 1993; *Halmoni and the Picnic*, illus. by Karen Dugan, 1993; *Gathering of Pearls*, 1994; *Yunmi and Halmoni's Trip*, illus. by Karen Dugan, 1997; *The Best Older Sister*, 1997.

SUGGESTED READING: *Children's Literature Review*, vol. 53, 1999; Davidson, Cathy N. and others, eds. *The Oxford Companion to Women's Writing in the United States*, 1995; *Perspectives on Literary Research and Practice*, 44th Yearbook of the National Reading Conference, 1995; *Something About the Author*, vol. 73, 1993. Periodicals— "Flying Starts," *Publishers Weekly*, Dec. 20, 1991.

WEB SITE: *www.scils.rutgers.edu/special/kay/choi.html*

Beverly Cleary

1916–

"When I was a little girl named Beverly Bunn, I lived on a farm outside of Yamhill, Oregon, where I followed my mother around pleading, 'Tell me a story. Tell me a story.' Finally, because she was worn out by my whining and because she was lonely for books herself, she started a small library in a lodge room upstairs over a bank. 'There is entirely too much gossip in Yamhill,' she said. 'People should read.' Books shipped from the State Library were shelved in a donated china cabinet. Saturday afternoons Mother acted as librarian while I sat in a slippery leather chair listening to the patrons' unstoppable gossip and looking forward to evening when Mother would read to me from one of these books. *More English Fairy Tales*, edited by Joseph Jacobs, was my favorite.

"When I was six years old we moved to Portland, where I was awed by the beauty of the downtown public library and stunned by the size of the boys and girls room. Shelves and shelves of books, all for children! (I would have been even more stunned if I had known that room would someday bear my name.) Every two weeks Mother and I traveled by streetcar to the library for books.

"I looked forward to starting school, but unfortunately the transition from a carefree life on a farm to a city classroom of forty children (yes, really!) was too much. The teacher was harsh, I had had little contact with other children, and I was ill much of that dreadful year. I begged to stay home from school and wept when my anxious mother tried to help me with reading. Fortunately a beautiful, kind second-grade teacher soothed my fears and taught me to read, but by then I was disillusioned. I no longer wanted to read, and no one could make me. So there!

"Mother, horrified at the thought of an illiterate daughter, continued to read aloud. I recall enjoying *The Blue Bird* by Maurice Maeterlinck and *The Princess and the Goblin* by George MacDonald. She also supplied easy books, which I sulkily ignored until one rainy Sunday afternoon when I was so bored I looked at the pictures in *The Dutch Twins* by Lucy Fitch Perkins and discovered that in spite of myself I was actually reading and enjoying what I read. That moment changed my life. I became a reader and tried to read all the books on the children's side of our branch library. I read, enjoyed, and was disappointed because I could not find what I wanted to read most of all—books about the sort of children who lived in my neighborhood. Maybe someday I could write what I longed to read.

Courtesy of Alan McEwen, 1999

Beverly Cleary

"After graduation from University of California at Berkeley and the School of Librarianship at the University of Washington, I became Children's Librarian in Yakima, Washington, where I soon discovered boys had trouble finding what they wanted to read. 'Books about kids like us,' one of them said. Again, I thought maybe someday . . . .

"Someday held marriage to Clarence Cleary in California, followed by World War II, when I put aside thoughts of writing to become the librarian in the Oakland Army Hospital. After the war we bought a house in the Berkeley hills where we found a pile of typing paper in the linen closet. An omen! The time had come. With memories of the boys in Yakima in mind I sat down to write a book of six stories about a boy named Henry for readers who were ready for chapter books. In reading over the manuscript I discovered that all the characters appeared to be only children, so I added a little sister named Ramona and allowed her a paragraph or two. *Henry Huggins*, my first attempt at writing outside of school assignments, was the result of that attempt. I sent the book off to the editor of Morrow Junior Books, who accepted it. Suddenly I was, as children were to say, a 'real live author.'

"Books followed about Henry, Ellen Tebbits, and Otis Spofford. I also became the mother of twins but continued to write about Henry. Ramona walked into the stories and in her determined way demanded attention until she got it in *Ramona the Pest*. The first Ramona story was followed by seven books telling of her journey through school in the neighborhood in which I had grown up, a neighborhood of modest houses, lawns, churches, and a nearby park.

"When our son was in fourth grade he became disgusted with books, reading, and school. I understood how my mother had felt. He wanted, he said, to read about motorcycles. About that time, on a trip to England, he woke up in the night with a fever. The town was locked up for the night and no aspirin was available until dawn, when the hotel porter found a package at the local bus station. It had been an anxious night. While our son recovered we bought him miniature cars and a little motorcycle which he ran up and down the stripes of his bedspread creating a fantasy of his own. This was the inspiration for *The Mouse and the Motorcycle*, which he read and pronounced a good book, sweet words to the mother of a nonreader and the beginning of a trilogy about Ralph, the (mostly) intrepid mouse.

"Other books were written at the suggestion of readers. A group of junior high school girls asked, 'Why don't you write like you write, only for our age?' *Fifteen* was the result, followed by three more novels of young love set in the 1940s. *Dear Mr. Henshaw* and *Strider* were written at the request of two boys, unknown to one another, who asked for a book about a boy whose parents were divorced.

"Two volumes of autobiography, *A Girl from Yamhill* and *My Own Two Feet*, came about because I wanted to tell young readers what life was like in safer, simpler, less-prosperous times, so different from today. In this computer age I still write in longhand on yellow paper. Then I type what I have written in my bad typing, revise it, retype it, and take it to a good typist. As much as I dislike typing, I feel that I have had an exceptionally happy career and am grateful for the enthusiasm with which my stories have been received."

". . . I could not find what I wanted to read most of all— books about the sort of children who lived in my neighborhood."

* * *

Beverly Cleary has written for all ages, ranging from picture books to teen novels, but it is her books for eight- to twelve-year-olds that have won her the greatest critical and popular acclaim. Her characters are normal, average children who face many of the challenges that any child growing up will encounter, making it easy for her readers to identify with them. Most importantly, her stories are told with large doses of humor, the kind of humor she found missing in the books that were available in her own growing years. Her first book, *Henry Huggins*, recounting Henry's efforts to smuggle a dog he has found onto a bus and bring him home for keeps, was an immediate success. The plot is episodic in nature, with each chapter telling a distinct story. Cleary followed this book with a number of others about Henry and his friends in their Portland, Oregon, neighborhood.

A pair of sisters introduced in the Henry books, Beezus and Ramona Quimby, became the main characters in *Beezus and Ramona*, published in 1955. In this book, Cleary examines the somewhat ambivalent relationship between nine-year-old Beezus and her younger sister, the spirited and mischievous Ramona. Ramona immediately became one of Cleary's most popular characters, and later stories followed her adventures, including two that were designated Newbery Honor books, *Ramona and Her Father* and *Ramona Quimby, Age 8*. In the newest Ramona story, *Ramona's World*, the intrepid heroine is approaching the age of ten—"zeroteen," she calls it—and is dealing with the ups and downs of fourth grade as well as a new baby in the family.

Courtesy of William Morrow & Co., Inc.

The stories of Ralph S. Mouse, beginning with *The Mouse and the Motorcycle* in 1965, show another side of Cleary's ability to capture her readers' imaginations. This trilogy of stories about the adventures of a boy and a talking mouse speaks directly to the rich fantasy life that is so much a part of childhood.

In *Dear Mr. Henshaw* Cleary introduced Leigh Botts, who is struggling with his parents' divorce and making efforts to adjust to life in a new neighborhood. Written in the first person and unfolding through Leigh's journal entries and letters to his favorite author, Mr. Henshaw, this story won the 1984 Newbery Medal for its moving, sometimes humorous, account of a boy's growth through difficult emotional times.

Cleary's books have consistently appeared on many best-of-the-year lists, and she has a wide and loyal readership that now spans several generations. Among her many honors, in 1975 Beverly Cleary was presented with the Laura Ingalls Wilder Award for her substantial and lasting contribution to literature for children.

SELECTED WORKS: *Henry Huggins*, illus. by Louis Darling, 1950; *Ellen Tebbits*, illus. by Louis Darling, 1951; *Henry and Beezus*, illus. by Louis Darling, 1952; *Otis Spofford*, illus. by Louis Darling, 1953; *Henry and Ribsy*, illus. by Louis Darling, 1954; *Beezus and Ramona*, illus. by Louis Darling, 1955; *Fifteen*, illus. by Joe and Beth Krush, 1956; *Henry and the Paper Route*, illus. by Louis Darling, 1957; *Jean and Johnny*, illus. by Joe and Beth Krush, 1959; *Henry and the Clubhouse*, illus. by Louis Darling, 1962; *Sister of the Bride*, 1963; *Ribsy*, illus. by Louis Darling, 1964; *The Mouse and the Motorcycle*, illus. by Louis Darling, 1965; *Mitch and Amy*, illus. by Bob Marstall, 1967; *Ramona the Pest*, illus. by Louis Darling, 1968; *Runaway Ralph*, illus. by Louis Darling, 1970; *Socks*, illus. by Beatrice Darwin, 1973; *Ramona the Brave*, illus. by Alan Tiegreen, 1975; *Ramona and Her Father*, illus. by Alan Tiegreen, 1977; *Ramona and Her Mother*, illus. by Alan Tiegreen, 1979; *Ramona Quimby, Age 8*, illus. by Alan Tiegreen, 1981; *Ralph S. Mouse*, illus. by Paul O. Zelinsky, 1982; *Dear Mr. Henshaw*, illus. by Paul O. Zelinsky, 1983; *Ramona Forever*, illus. by Alan Tiegreen, 1984; *Lucky Chuck*, illus. by J. Winslow Higginbottom, 1984; *A Girl from Yamhill: A Memoir*, 1988; *Muggie Maggie*, illus. by Kay Life, 1990; *Strider*, illus. by Paul O. Zelinsky, 1991; *Petey's Bedtime Story*, illus. by David Small, 1993; *My Own Two Feet*, 1995; *The Hullabaloo ABC*, illus. by Ted Rand, 1998; *Ramona's World*, illus. by Alan Tiegreen, 1999.

SUGGESTED READING: *Children's Literature Review*, vol. 2, 1976; vol. 8, 1985; Collier, Laurie, and Joyce Nakamura, eds. *Major Authors and Illustrators for Children and Young Adults*, vol. 2, 1993; *Contemporary Authors*, New Revision Series, vol. 66, 1998; *Dictionary of Literary Biography*, vol. 52, 1986; Pendergast, Sara, ed. *St. James Guide to Children's Writers*, 5th ed., 1999; Pflieger, Pat. *Beverly Cleary*, Twayne's Author Series, 1991; Silvey, Anita, ed. *Children's Books and Their Creators*, 1995; *Something About the Author*, vol. 79, 1995; *Something About the Author Autobiography Series*, vol. 20, 1995. Periodicals—Cooper, Ilene, "The Booklist Interviews: Beverly Cleary," *Booklist*, October 15, 1998; Klass, Perri, "To Think That It Happened on Klickitat Street," *New York Times Book Review*, Nov. 12, 1995.

An earlier profile of Beverly Cleary appeared in *More Junior Authors* (1963).

Courtesy of Andrew Clements

Andrew Clements

May 29, 1949–

"I still enjoy my childhood every day, and I have my mom and dad, Doris and Bill Clements, to thank for that. Growing up in New Jersey and then Illinois, I really had no ideas about being a writer. To be a reader was more than enough. I loved books, and my parents and teachers and school librarians kept me well supplied. I can recall reading particularly stirring bits from Jack London or Robert Louis Stevenson, or especially funny parts from *Winnie the Pooh* or *Charlotte's Web*, and saying to myself, 'I wish I had written that!' So I'm certain there's a link between reading good books and becoming a writer. I don't know a single writer who wasn't a good reader first.

"When I was a high school senior, my English teacher, Mrs. Bernice Rappell, taught us about parody and then made the class write some. I wrote a piece called 'Lynndonne the White Knight,' a parody of a heroic poem that skewered President Lyndon Johnson. Mrs. Rappell thought it was hilarious. As she handed it back, she said, 'You know, this really ought to be published.' She was the first person who'd ever suggested that my writing might be appealing to people other than my family and teachers.

"During college I wrote a lot, mostly poems and song lyrics. And somewhere along the line I began to feel pretty confident that I was a better-than-average writer. Often professors would comment that my papers were enjoyable to read, and I was accepted into a 'by invitation only' creative writing course. I was an English major and read great books and plays and poetry for about three years solid. That immersion in classic literature tuned up my ear and gave me a taste for words and language and well-crafted plots.

"Before *Frindle*, I had only written picture books. I love the compactness of the picture book form and the discipline required to write one—like pouring ten gallons of ideas into a teacup. The transition to longer fiction didn't come easily. In fact, I first wrote *Frindle* as a picture book—the entire plot and all the characters compressed into a three-page story called 'Nick's New Word.' Four different editors each said, 'Fun idea, but don't you think it should be a short chapter book instead?' I finally agreed and, as I expanded the idea, paragraphs or even sentences in the picture book text became whole chapters in the novel. It was a great learning process, and as I keep writing both picture books and chapter books, the learning continues.

"That's the fun of it all. The only thing I like better is being married to my wife, Rebecca, and working together to give our four boys the kind of happy memories we each enjoy.

"I talked with a fourth-grade boy who had read *Frindle*, and he asked, 'How come you write for children?' The short answer is that I like kids. The longer answer includes the fact that I taught fourth grade for two years, eighth-grade English for three years, and then high school English for two years. I loved those moments when I would be reading a story with a class, and everyone would be involved in the plot and immersed in the character's adventure. The talk and ideas that flowed from reading good books was nothing short of wonderful. I guess at heart I'm still a teacher. When a kid reads a book, the writer has his or her full attention—and any teacher will tell you that that's worth a lot. It's a privilege to be able to write stories that may become part of another's childhood, and I'm grateful for it."

* * *

Born in Camden, New Jersey, Andrew Clements attended Northwestern University in Evanston, Illinois, and received an M.A. in teaching from National-Louis University, also in Evanston. After seven years of teaching school, he went to work for the Keller Graduate School of Management, as director of their Chicago Center. He has held many jobs in publishing, beginning as an editor at Allen D. Bragdon Publishers, a book packaging firm in New York. He also worked as a sales manager and marketing manager at Alphabet Press; later, when this company was known as Picture Book Studio, he served as its vice president and editorial director. In recent years he has been a full-time writer of children's books, though he has also done freelance work, editing, translating, and consulting for various publishers, including Houghton Mifflin, North-South Books, Encyclopedia Britannica, and Jim Henson Productions.

Clements's many picture book texts were well-received by young readers and critics, but his breakthrough book was the middle-grade novel *Frindle*. This comic war of words between a student and his teacher has won numerous honors, including a 1997 Christopher Award. It was selected as a Parents' Choice honor book and appeared on the *Horn Book*'s annual Fanfare list. *Frindle* has been nominated for more than thirty-five children's choice awards across the United States, from Maine to Hawaii, and the book has won many of these awards, including the Georgia Children's Book Award, the Sasquatch Children's Book Award, the Massachusetts Children's Book Award, the Rhode Island Children's Book Award, the William Allen White Children's Book Award, the Great Stone Face Book Award, the

"That immersion in classic literature tuned up my ear and gave me a taste for words and language and well-crafted plots."

Maud Hart Lovelace Award, and the Rebecca Caudill Young Readers Award. *The Landry News* was named a *School Library Journal* Best Book and received a Parents' Choice Award in 1999.

Clements has served on the Executive Board of Directors of the Children's Book Council and continues to speak as an author and literacy advocate at schools, conventions, and seminars. He lives with his family in Massachusetts.

SELECTED WORKS WRITTEN: *Big Al*, illus. by Yoshi, 1988; *Santa's Secret Helper*, 1990; *Temple Cat*, illus. by Kate Kiesler, 1991; *Billy and the Bad Teacher*, illus. by Elivia Savadier, 1992; *Who Owns the Cow?*, illus. by Joan Landis, 1995; *A Dog's Best Friend*, 1995; *Frindle*, 1996; *Bright Christmas: An Angel Remembers*, illus. by Kate Kiesler, 1996; *Double Trouble in Walla Walla*, illus. by Sal Murdocca, 1997; *Life in the Desert* (Earth Awareness series), 1998; *The Landry News*, illus. by Sal Murdocca, 1999.

SELECTED WORKS TRANSLATED: *The Christmas Teddy Bear*, by Ivan Gantschev, 1992; *The Midnight Play*, by Kveta Pacovska, 1993.

SUGGESTED READING: *Something About the Author*, vol. 104, 1999.

Carolyn Coman

October 28, 1951–

"Writing stories is my way of getting to the heart of the matter—whatever matter it is that I am trying to see clearly. To improve my vision I often and instinctively imagine from a child's perspective—because I trust that perspective to be innocent, fresh, and remarkably strong, unfettered by the vast preconceptions of adulthood. I'm a big fan of children; I deeply respect how much they bear with strength, resilience, and humor. They surprise me, too—their responses to situations, the way they use language, what they make of the world around them. And being surprised is a key reason to keep writing, and reading, and, for that matter, living.

"Saying what I mean to has always been important to me. I moved a lot growing up—Chicago; Washington, D.C.; Connecticut; Indiana; New Jersey—and I went to a bunch of different schools. I was shy then and am shy now. But my writing isn't shy.

"I always cared more about writing than I did other subjects in school. When I wrote my first complete story in fourth grade (about Mrs. Easter Bunny delivering all the eggs because Mr. Easter Bunny overslept), I learned that getting it right— choosing the exact word, pacing it so that it sounded good inside my head, saying what I cared about—made me oblivious to how long it took or how many times I had to do it over, or whatever else I was supposed to be doing.

"Even though I knew writing mattered more to me than almost anything, I spent a lot of time trying to hide from it. I was scared that I wouldn't be good enough. I tried to fool myself into thinking I could do other work that I could love just as much. I went to college and studied different subjects, and I became a hand bookbinder and made beautiful books. I taught some, I wrote articles, I edited other people's books, but nothing—nothing—satisfied except writing my own short stories and novels. Now I know better than to try and do anything else. When you're lucky enough to have a passion for something, the least you can do is follow it.

"I mostly write about emotional journeys that people make getting from one place in the heart to another. Much of what I write about is interior—a geography/landscape that calls to me much more than a lot of outward plot twists and adventure. I'm probably unusually satisfied by small and quiet moments. I try to let the story take me where it needs to go—even if it leads me to places that are dark. Then my job is to find the light. I am often guided by visual images—arresting sights—that nudge the story forward. I believe in starting with what's given and going from there. So much of writing takes place in a cave. It's essential to stumble forward feelingly.

"It would never occur to me to write differently or somehow 'less' because children read my stories. If anything, that audience holds me to the edge. Kids cut to the chase, and so must I. (My daughter, Anna, is one of my most valued and important readers and critics. She said to me once, after listening to a chapter-in-progress, 'Mom, do you have any idea how boring this is?' So much for trying to get away with murder.)

Courtesy of Kim Pickard

"I never think about trying to write 'for' children, just of them. That's plenty, that's a ton: to try and do justice to the experience, the emotional journey of a particular child at a particular moment.

"My editor said a wise thing: that I seemed to be more interested in discovery than in recognition. Maybe I am."

*   *   *

After receiving a B.A. from Hampshire College in 1974, Carolyn Coman went on to apprentice with Arno Werner, Master Bookbinder in Pittsfield, Massachusetts. She worked in her own bindery and then in partnership with Nancy Southworth until 1982. She has taught writing at Harvard Summer School, Harvard Extension, in the public schools of Newburyport (Mass.), and at the University of New Hampshire Summer Writing Program. The National Book Foundation brought her to New York City as a visiting author, and she has lectured at numerous education conferences and taught in schools around the country. She is a faculty member of the M.F.A. Writing for Children Program of Vermont College, Norwich University.

Tell Me Everything, Coman's first novel, was named an ALA Notable Children's Book and included in New York Public Library's 100 Ttiles for Reading and Sharing. Coman received a Newbery Honor Award for *What Jamie Saw*, which was also named a National Book Award Finalist, an ALA Notable Children's Book, a *Booklist* Editors' Choice, and a *Bulletin of the Center for Children's Books* Blue Ribbon Book, and was listed additionally on the New York Public Library's 100 Titles for Reading and Sharing. She won a Short Story Prize from the Poets & Writers Exchange Program in 1990, as well as the Massachusetts Artists' Foundation Fiction Award in 1985.

Coman lives in South Hampton, N.H. She has two children, Anna and David.

SELECTED WORKS: *Tell Me Everything*, 1993; *What Jamie Saw*, 1995; *Bee and Jacky*, 1998.

SUGGESTED READING: Coman, Carolyn. "Thoughts on Creating Character" in Ralph Fletcher, *Live Writing*, 1999; Jenkins, Carol Brennan. *The Allure of Authors: Author Studies in the Elementary Classroom*, 1999.

WEB SITE: *www.frontstreetbooks.com*

Courtesy of Front Street Books, Inc.

"I grew up in Old Greenwich, Connecticut. It has a wonderful library: you walk into a rotunda with double white marble stairs which you climb to a sun-bright room with statues and portraits. The children's room used to be on the left. It was dark and gloomy and wonderful, a true rainy-day hideout. Later I graduated to the Young Adult Room. It shared space with Reference, and for years I read encyclopedias as well as novels. I wanted to read every single book in the YA collection and used to fill out index cards for each book I read to have my own author/title/subject/opinion card catalog! I wish I still had that. It would be fun, now that I'm a YA author too, to read what I said about the books I loved then.

"I had a wonderful sixth-grade teacher. The walls of his classroom were covered with charts of really good adjectives and adverbs and even prepositions. Mr. Albert made us write many short stories. He'd hand out covers of the *New Yorker* to use as a springboard for the plot. I was the one in the class who never stopped writing.

Courtesy of Saybrook Studio

Caroline B. Cooney

May 10, 1947–

"I took piano lessons and began accompanying the school choirs when I was in sixth grade. My father was Superintendent of Sunday Schools at the Congregational Church, and one day the minister called and said I had to play the organ; it was an emergency. That organ was the most thrilling magnificent instrument I had ever imagined. I've been a church organist for many years. Next to books, I love Bach and organ music best.

"I still play piano for fun, and accompany the middle-school choirs in my town. I'm a soprano and have perfect pitch, a really cool thing to be born with. Right now I sing in two choirs, but sometimes I'm in three.

"I love books. I love reading, borrowing, buying, shelving, and writing them. I can't go more than a week without visiting at least two libraries and a bookstore. A few years ago I covered one entire room with bookshelves and painted it all fire engine red and indigo blue. It holds hundreds of books, and they look like jewels against these colors.

"I read everything. At the library I go to New Books and read travel and essays and economics and birding and autobiography and especially history. My first eight books (not one of which was ever published) were set in ancient Rome, and I am always reading at least one book about the ancient Mediterranean. (I tend to read many books at once, and I keep little book depositories for every bed, chair, and sofa.) At the bookstore I just wander, awestruck by how much there is and how much I want to read it all. Although I write fiction, for my own reading I'm more attracted to nonfiction. I do love mysteries—I like action. I like the good guys to win.

"Writing comes easily to me. I enjoy most stages. I write three books a year, so I'm always daydreaming about a distant one, plotting the next, halfway through writing the current story, and probably re-writing one I thought was finished. Having an editor is like having your own personal life-long English teacher. No matter how well you write, she thinks you can do better and mails the story back to be improved.

THE COMPANION TO *WHATEVER HAPPENED TO JANIE?*

the FACE on the MILK CARTON

·········· CAROLINE B. COONEY

Courtesy of BDD Books

"Many of my ideas came from one of my three children: Louisa became an EMT at sixteen and inspired *Flight #116 Is Down*. Harold wanted to live abroad, so we went to London, which led to *The Terrorist*. Once I forced Sayre to be in beauty contests so I could get background information for *Twenty Pageants Later*.

"*The Face on the Milk Carton* was entirely fiction. I was shocked to see a homemade missing-child poster in an airport and read that the child had been missing for fifteen years! Nobody could recognize her from her toddler photograph . . . unless, of course, she recognizes herself. I did not expect to write a sequel to this book. It was a book about worry, and I wanted my readers to go on worrying. But for me and for my readers, it became very intense, and I found I had many more things to say about what happened to Janie. So now there are two more books, and I am planning a fourth!

"My newest book, *Burning Up*, is based upon a fire in which my junior high music teacher lost his home. Nothing in my book happened in real life, and yet there's memory in it: my own seventh and eighth grade is there. It's the first time I've really used my own childhood for a story, although the time travel books (*Both Sides of Time*, *Out of Time*, *Prisoner of Time*) really take place in Old Greenwich, at its beach, Tod's Point.

"My children are grown up and now I get to lead two lives. In the first, I'm at home—writing, reading, singing in choirs, walking on the beach, practicing music, gardening. Very quiet.

Very small-town. In the second, I'm traveling all over the country on school visits or speaking at conventions. It's a great way to see America. I love to meet my readers. I love to get on the plane and go to a new place and find out who cares about kids and books.

"There are lots of advantages to being a writer. Here's my coolest: my daughter Sayre's husband, Mark, has a race car. I'm the sponsor, and so the name of our car is *The Face on the Milk Carton*. We have a reproduction of the book cover on the hood!

"If you want to be a writer, start now. Nothing is more fun. Let me hear from you!"

* * *

Caroline Bruce Cooney is one of the most popular authors writing for teenagers today. Born in Geneva, New York, and raised in Old Greenwich, Connecticut, she attended Indiana University, Massachusetts General Hospital School of Nursing, and the University of Connecticut. Her writing began as a diversion from raising her children. She was successful in selling short stories to magazines such as *Seventeen* and *American Girl*, so she tried her hand at writing a novel for teenagers.

Cooney's first and second books for young readers, *Safe as the Grave* and *The Paper Caper*, were chosen as Junior Library Guild selections. A novel she wrote for adults, *Rear View Mirror*, was made into a television movie in 1984, but Cooney's attention has remained focused on writing for teenagers. Her many romance and suspense novels have gained an avid readership. Critics have especially praised her books that deal realistically with teen issues while weaving romantic themes with a suspenseful plot. *The Face on the Milk Carton* was an IRA/CBC Children's Choice book and an ALA Recommended Book for Reluctant Readers. This suspenseful and psychologically taut story of a girl who was kidnapped as a toddler was continued in *Whatever Happened to Janie?*, cited as an ALA Best Book for Young Adults and a Notable Trade Book in the Field of Social Studies, and *The Voice on the Radio*.

What Child Is This? and *Driver's Ed* were both named ALA Best Books for Young Adults. *Driver's Ed* was also cited as an ALA Quick Pick for Reluctant Readers and a *Booklist* Editors' Choice.

Caroline Cooney lives in Westbrook, Connecticut.

SELECTED WORKS: *Safe as the Grave*, illus. by Gail Owens, 1979; *Rear View Mirror* (for adults), 1980; *The Paper Caper*, illus. by Gail Owens, 1981; *An April Love Story*, 1981; *He Loves Me Not*, 1982; *I'm Not Your Other Half*, 1984; *Nice Girls Don't*, 1984; *Rumors*, 1985; *Don't Blame the Music*, 1986; *Among Friends*, 1987; *Saying Yes*, 1987; *The Rah Rah Girl,*

1987; *Summer Nights*, 1988; *The Fog*, 1989; *The Face on the Milk Carton*, 1990; *The Cheerleader*, 1991; *Flight #116 Is Down*, 1992; *Whatever Happened to Janie?*, 1993; *Driver's Ed*, 1994; *Flash Fire*, 1995; *Both Sides of Time*, 1995; *Out of Time*, 1995; *Prisoner of Time*, 1996; *The Terrorist*, 1996; *The Voice on the Radio*, 1996; *What Child Is This? A Christmas Story*, 1997; *Wanted!*, 1997; *Burning Up*, 1999; *Tune in Anytime*, 1999; *What Janie Found*, 2000.

SUGGESTED READING: *Authors and Artists for Young Adults*, vol. 5, 1991; Collier, Laurie and Joyce Nakamura, eds. *Major Authors and Illustrators for Children and Young Adults*, 1993; *Contemporary Authors*, vol. 97–100, 1981; *Contemporary Authors*, New Revision Series, vol. 37, 1992; Drew, Bernard. *The 100 Most Popular Young Adult Authors*, rev. ed., 1997; Gallo, Donald R., ed. *Speaking for Ourselves, Too*, 1993; Hipple, Ted, ed., *Writers for Young Adults*, 1997; Pendergast, Tom, ed. *St. James Guide to Young Adult Writers*, 2nd ed., 1999. Periodicals—*ALAN Review*, Winter 1994; Nathan, Paul, "Another Problem Kid," *Publishers Weekly*, April 10, 1995.

Ilene Cooper

March 10, 1948–

"I was a reader when I was a child, but not a writer. I read after I was supposed to be asleep from the light in the hall closet. When my mother caught me, she would say, 'You'll ruin your eyes, reading in the dark like that,' but, in fact, I'm one of the few people I know who doesn't wear glasses.

"One reason I didn't write much was because of a particular teacher I had. Actually, I had her in several grades, and she didn't much like me. My work was often sloppy, and I didn't pay much attention to spelling. Even though my compositions were among the most imaginative in the class, I always got graded down because of spelling and neatness. Since she didn't praise me for what was good about my writing, only criticizing me for what was bad, I never thought of myself as being good at writing until much later in life. Ironically, in my job as a magazine editor (in addition to writing children's books, I have a full-time career at a magazine called *Booklist*) I spend a lot of my time correcting other people's grammar and spelling.

"It wasn't until I was ready for college that I decided I wanted to major in journalism. I was very interested in current events and politics, so I thought I might like to write about that. I went to the University of Missouri, which had an excellent journalism school. The college students ran the newspapers and television station for the city of Columbia, Missouri, where the school is located, so it was real hands-on experience.

"I worked in television for a while, but in my twenties I became ill with a stomach ailment called Crohn's Disease. I decided journalism was too exhausting a profession, so I went to library school and became a children's librarian. I loved being around children's books, especially some of my old favorites like the Betsy-Tacy series, *Ballet Shoes*, and *All-of-a-Kind Family*. I have always liked books in series. It made me happy to know after I finished one book about favorite characters, there was another one waiting.

"In the years I spent working in the library, I looked at lots of children's books and began to think perhaps I could write one. My very first book was a biography of Susan B. Anthony, an early fighter for women's rights. After that, I began to write fiction and used many of the things that happened to me as a child in my books. The teacher with whom I had so many run-ins would recognize herself in my book, *The Winning of Miss Lynn Ryan*. After writing lots of fiction, I have recently gone back to where I started—nonfiction. My book *The Dead Sea Scrolls* tells the story of biblical documents hidden in a cave for two thousand years. Now I am working on a book about the boyhood of President John F. Kennedy. I find that writing fiction has helped me become a better nonfiction writer because I know how to tell a story. That's what nonfiction should be—a great story that just happens to be true."

Courtesy of Ilene Cooper

* * *

Ilene Cooper received her Master of Library Science degree from Rosary College in River Forest, Illinois, and worked for eight years as a children's librarian at the Winnetka Public Library in Winnetka, Illinois. She has also been active in television, writing scripts for the public broadcasting series American Playhouse and the CBS sitcom *The Jeffersons*, as well as serving as a consultant to ABC Afterschool Specials. She has been the children's book editor at *Booklist* magazine since 1985.

Cooper's love of the series genre as a reader is evident in her work as a writer. She is the author of four separate series: the Frances in the Fourth Grade series; the Holiday Five series, which centers on a group of friends as they celebrate Thanksgiving, Valentine's Day, and other holidays; the Kids from Kennedy Middle School series, about boys and girls and their school relationships; and the Hollywood Wars series, concerning teenage rivalry on the set of a long-running television program.

The Dead Sea Scrolls—Cooper's first nonfiction book in many years—was cited as a Notable Trade Book in the Field of Social Studies. The *Chicago Tribune* selected two of Cooper's works as Best Books: *Buddy Love—Now on Video* and *The Dead Sea Scrolls*. *Choosing Sides* was named an IRA/CBC Children's Choice book.

Ilene Cooper lives in the Chicago area and is a member of the Society of Children's Book Writers and Illustrators.

SELECTED WORKS: *Susan B. Anthony*, 1982; *The Winning of Miss Lynn Ryan*, 1987; *Queen of the Sixth Grade*, 1988; *Choosing Sides*, 1990; *Mean Streak*, 1991; *The New, Improved Gretchen Hubbard*, 1992; *Frances Takes a Chance*, 1991; *Frances Dances*, 1991; *Frances Four-Eyes*, 1992; *Frances and Friends*, 1992; *Lights, Camera, Attitude*, 1993; *My Co-star, My Enemy*, 1993; *Seeing Red*, 1993; *Trouble in Paradise*, 1993; *Trick or Trouble*, 1994; *The Worst Noel*, 1995; *Stupid Cupid*, 1995; *Buddy Love—Now on Video*, 1995; *Star Spangled Summer*, 1996; *No Thanks Thanksgiving*, 1996; *I'll See You in My Dreams*, 1997; *The Dead Sea Scrolls*, 1997.

SUGGESTED READING: *Contemporary Authors*, vol. 163, 1998; *Something About the Author*, vol. 66, 1991; vol. 97, 1998. Periodicals—"The Dead Sea Scrolls," *Book Links*, May 1997.

Susan Cooper

May 23, 1935–

"Like my books, I'm mostly English, partly Welsh. I had two homes in Britain: one in Buckinghamshire, where I was born and raised, and the other in Aberdovey, North Wales, my grandmother's village, where my parents lived their last twenty years.

"I discovered I was a writer when I was about eight. Life was noisy at the time, being punctuated by World War II bombs, but we paid no great attention, my younger brother Rod and I. (He's a writer too: very funny thrillers.) It was only twenty-five years later that the bombs echoed again, in an autobiographical book I wrote called *Dawn of Fear*.

"From high school I went to Oxford, took a degree in English, and edited the university newspaper. Then I became a reporter and feature-writer for the *Sunday Times* in London and had a wonderful time exploring odd corners of life for seven years. In my spare time—sitting on the floor of my apartment, with pen and paper, scribbling—I wrote an adult novel and my first children's book, *Over Sea, Under Stone*. Then, to everyone's astonishment, I married an American with three teenage children and moved to Massachusetts.

"In intervals of coping with the teenagers, I had two children of my own (Jonathan, born 1966, and Katharine, born 1967) and wrote three more adult books. But nothing could quite blot out my homesickness, which was possibly the reason for my discovering that *Over Sea, Under Stone* was in fact the first of five books in a sequence of fantasies called The Dark Is Rising. So I spent several years writing the other four books, living in two worlds at once. Physically, I was in Massachusetts, or in the little holiday house we built on an island called Great Camanoe, in the British Virgin Islands. But inside my head, while I was writing, I was in England or Wales.

"I've lived in the United States now for longer than I lived in Britain, though I haven't yet managed to write about it. I'm getting closer: *The Boggart*, published in 1993, was set mostly in Toronto—though I then went backwards and set its sequel, *The Boggart and the Monster*, entirely in Scotland. But the next book, *King of Shadows*, begins in Massachusetts! I have to admit, however, that it then crosses the Atlantic to London—as do I, briefly, once or twice a year.

Courtesy of Jeffrey Hornstein

"When Kate and Jonathan were aged thirteen and fourteen, their father and I were divorced, which was hard for everybody. We lived in Cambridge, Mass., for a long time, and I wrote for the theater and television, between books, as well as providing poems, songs, and short plays for *The Christmas Revels,* a celebration of the winter solstice which is now performed simultaneously in cities all over the U.S.

"Now Jonathan and Kate are grown up and married, and I'm remarried too, to the actor Hume Cronyn. We live in Connecticut, in a house with a large garden and a small fishpond, containing four chubby goldfish named Alpha, Bravo, Charlie, and Delta. We had Echo, too, but he died of heatstroke last summer.

"I'm still writing, of course. I have a computer now; indeed I even have a home page, designed by a young Englishman, at *http://missy.shef.ac.uk/~emp94ms/*. But when I start the first draft of a book, you'll still find me sitting on the floor with pen and paper, scribbling . . . ."

✳ ✳ ✳

Susan Cooper grew up in the small town of Burnham, about twenty miles from London. After secondary school she attended Oxford University, taking classes from C. S. Lewis and J.R.R. Tolkien, among others, and graduated with a degree in language and literature. It was in response to a contest for the best story in the tradition of E. Nesbit's classic tales of family adventure that Cooper wrote her first work for young readers, *Over Sea, Under Stone*. For the background of this story, Cooper drew on memories of Cornwall and on her knowledge of Celtic legends. In 1963 she married an American scientist, Nicholas Grant, who was teaching at the Massachusetts Institute of Technology; they made their home in Winchester, Massachusetts.

Feeling homesick for Britain, Cooper wrote a book for adults, *Behind the Golden Curtain*, about the differences between British and American life and then a biography of J. B. Priestley, an older British author and dramatist famous for the robust "Englishness" of many of his stories. She also wrote, for young adults, an autobiographical novel, *Dawn of Fear*, which was included on the *Horn Book* honor list. In the meantime Cooper had been inspired (while cross-country skiing in the wake of a blizzard) to begin a new novel, which she soon realized would constitute a return to the mythological world of *Over Sea, Under Stone*. She sketched out the entire course of the series of five books, down to the last page of the last book, before going back to finish volume two.

The Dark Is Rising opens with Will Stanton's discovery, on the snowy morning of his eleventh birthday, that he is one of the Old Ones, a combatant in the immemorial contest between the Light and the Dark. The novel was highly praised, won the *Boston Globe–Horn Book* Award for fiction, and was named a Newbery Honor Book in America and Carnegie Award Honor Book in England. The series continued with *Greenwitch*, *The Grey King*, and *Silver on the Tree*, following Will Stanton and characters from the first volume through a series of high adventures leading up to a culminating battle between the forces of Dark and Light. *The Grey King* won the Newbery Medal in 1976. Both *The Grey King* and *Silver on the Tree* received the Welsh Tir na N'og award for the best English-language book set in Wales. The series as a whole has been praised for its breathtaking imaginative sweep and convincing evocation of a landscape steeped in ancient lore.

Courtesy of Simon & Schuster Children's Publishing Division

Through much of the 1980s, Cooper was absorbed in writing scripts for stage and television in collaboration with the actor Hume Cronyn. They received Emmy nominations for two of their productions, *Foxfire* and *The Dollmaker*; the latter also won a Christopher award, a Writers' Guild of America award, and the Humanitas Prize. Cooper continued her writing for children with three picture-book retellings of Celtic folktales— *The Silver Cow, The Selkie Girl*, and *Tam Lin*—all with watercolor illustrations by Warwick Hutton. An earlier picture book, *Jethro and the Jumbie*, introduced a different fantasy character from the author's Caribbean Island vacation home. In 1993 she captured the imaginations of fantasy readers again with *The Boggart*, about a mischievous sprite who is accidently transported from an ancestral Scottish castle to bustling Toronto. A highly inventive combination of old magic and modern technology, *The Boggart* was followed by a sequel which also involves Scotland's most famous monster, from the depths of Loch Ness.

Courtesy of Simon & Schuster Children's Publishing Division

King of Shadows, published in 1999, returns to Cooper's native England and its heritage, evoked through time travel. Here an American boy, visiting London with a troupe of young actors, finds himself at the Globe Theatre in 1599, with a role to play in Shakespeare's life as well as his latest production. This richly descriptive and emotional story was named to the *Horn Book*'s Fanfare, *Booklist*'s Editors' Choice, and ALA's Best Books for Young Adults.

A collection of Cooper's essays and speeches over the years, *Dream and Wishes*, published in 1996, provides further background on the author's use of fantasy elements, metaphor, and life experience in her writing.

SELECTED WORKS: *Over Sea, Under Stone*, 1966; *Dawn of Fear*, 1970; *The Dark Is Rising*, 1973; *Greenwitch*, 1974; *The Grey King*, 1975; *Silver on the Tree*, 1977; *Jethro and the Jumbie*, illus. by Ashley Bryan, 1979; *The Silver Cow*, illus. by Warwick Hutton, 1983; *Seaward*, 1983; *The Selkie Girl*, illus. by Warwick Hutton, 1986; *Matthew's Dragon*, illus. by Joseph A. Smith, 1991; *Tam Lin*, illus. by Warwick Hutton, 1991; *The Boggart*, 1993; *Danny and the Kings*, illus. by Joseph A.

Smith, 1993; *The Boggart and the Monster*, 1997; *King of Shadows*, 1999.

SUGGESTED READING: *Children's Literature Review*, vol. 4, 1982; Collier, Laurie and Joyce Nakamura, eds. *Major Authors and Illustrators for Children and Young Adults*, 1993; *Contemporary Authors*, New Revision Series, vol. 63, 1998; Cooper, Susan, *Dreams and Wishes: Essays on Writing for Children*, 1996; Cooper, Susan. Comments in *Innocence & Experience: Essays and Conversations on Children's Literature*, ed. by Barbara Harrison and Gregory Maguire, 1987; *Dictionary of Literary Biography*, vol. 161, 1996; Drew, Bernard A. *The 100 Most Popular Young Adult Authors*, 1996; Silvey, Anita, ed. *Children's Books and Their Creators*, 1995; *Something About the Author*, vol. 4, 1973; vol. 64, 1991; vol. 104, 1999. Periodicals—*Christian Science Monitor*, May 12, 1976; Cooper, Susan, "Newbery Acceptance Speech," *The Horn Book*, August 1976.

WEB SITE: *missy.shef.ac.uk/~emp94ms/*

An earlier profile of Susan Cooper appeared in *Fourth Book of Junior Authors and Illustrators*, 1978.

Lucy Cousins

February 10, 1964–

Lucy Elizabeth Cousins, the author/illustrator of the immensely popular Maisy books, was born in Reading, England. Her favorite books when she was a child were the Lucy and Tom stories by Shirley Hughes. Her brother's name is Tom, and the drawings reminded her of her own home. She also enjoyed *Babar*, the Little Tim stories by Edward Ardizzone, and the picture books of Dick Bruna and Richard Scarry.

Cousins took a foundation course at Canterbury Art College and received her B.A. degree with honors in graphic design from Brighton Polytechnic. While studying at Brighton, she took some courses in illustration from Raymond Briggs, the well-known illustrator of *The Snowman* and many other picture books. She did postgraduate work at the Royal College of Art from 1986 to 1988, and one of her instructors there was another renowned British illustrator, Quentin Blake.

While she was a student at the Royal College, Cousins submitted one of her school projects—a small black-and-white book about a penguin—to a competition sponsored by Macmillan UK The book won second prize in the competition and became her first published children's book, *Portly's Hat*. It was named a runner-up for the 1989 Bologna Graphics Prize, and Lucy Cousins's career was off to a running start.

The following year Cousins illustrated a collection of nursery rhymes, *The Little Dog Laughed*, which was named to *School Library Journal's* Best Books list, New York Public Library's 100

Titles for Reading and Sharing, and CCBC Choices. Critics cited the carefree humor and vibrant forms of her illustrations. In this book she first used the bright, bold colors that were to become one of her stylistic trademarks.

Since her college days Lucy Cousins had had an idea for an interactive book with pull-tabs and flaps. She experimented with various animal characters—a cat, a polar bear, and others—but it was a mouse that caught her attention in her experimental drawings. The name Maisy came from poring over baby-name books, looking for one that would suit the character perfectly. The endearing mouse/child made her debut in *Maisy Goes to Bed* and *Maisy Goes Swimming*, both published in 1990, and be-came an overnight success. Many more Maisy books have followed. Pre-schoolers enjoy the interactive qualities of these books, the simplicity of the de-sign, the bright colors, and the reflection of their own daily lives. Children can take part in Maisy's routines—bedtime rituals, going to the playground, starting school, and changing clothes—through the movable features on each page.

Critics also loved Maisy. *Maisy Goes Swimming* won a Special Mention in the 1992 Bologna Graphics Prize and a Mention in the Bologna Critici in Erba Prize. *Maisy's House* captured the Bolo-gna Ragazzi Nonfiction Prize in 1997. While she is best known for the Maisy stories, Cousins has achieved critical ac-claim for other titles as well. *Noah's Ark*, her own retelling of the Biblical story, was cited in 1993 as a *Horn Book* Fan-fare title. In *ZaZa's Baby Brother*, named a CCBC Choice, Cousins creat-ed a zebra toddler who feels she is being displaced by her baby brother; this book was also highly commended for the Na-tional Art Illustration Award in England.

Courtesy of Lucy Cousins

Lucy Cousins

Always attuned to the young child's world, Cousins created her first books even before she had children of her own. Now that she is a mother, she is often inspired by her experiences as a parent. She has four children and has said that the insights they give her are like having a market research team in her own home. *ZaZa's Baby Brother* was written after the birth of her second child, Oliver, and is dedicated to him and his older sister, Josie. The twins, born in 1996, are named Rufus and Ben.

In 1999 the Maisy stories became a popular animated TV series in Britain and in America. As simple and unassuming as the books, the TV shows and accompanying merchandise have captured a wide audience for the unique mouse character with her exuberant and playful personality. Translated into nearly twenty languages, Maisy has become one of the best-loved characters in children's literature, recognized throughout the world.

Lucy Cousins and her family live in Petersfield, Hampshire, England, in a house surrounded by farmland.

SELECTED WORKS WRITTEN AND ILLUSTRATED: *Portly's Hat*, 1989; *The Little Dog Laughed and Other Nursery Rhymes*, 1990; *Maisy Goes Swimming*, 1990; *Maisy Goes to Bed*, 1990; *Country Animals*, 1990; *Farm Animals*, 1990; *Garden Animals*, 1990; *Pet Animals*, 1990; *What Can Rabbit Hear?*, 1991; *What Can Rabbit See?*, 1991; *Maisy Goes to School*, 1992; *Maisy Goes to the Playground*, 1992; *Noah's Ark*, 1993; *Maisy's ABC*, 1995; *My Toys*, 1995; *Maisy's Pop-up Playhouse*, 1995; *ZaZa's Baby Brother*, 1995; *Humpty Dumpty and Other Nursery Rhymes*, 1996; *Jack and Jill and Other Nursery Rhymes*, 1996; *Katy Cat and Beaky Boo*, 1996; *Maisy's Colors*, 1997; *Count with Maisy*, 1997; *Little Miss Muffet and Other Nursery Rhymes*, 1997; *Wee Willie Winkie and Other Nursery Rhymes*, 1997; *What Can Pinky Hear?*, 1997; *Happy Birthday, Maisy*, 1998; *Maisy at the Farm*, 1998; *Maisy Dresses Up*, 1999; *What Can Pinky See?*, 1999; *Where Is Maisy?*, 1999; *Where Is Maisy's Panda?*, 1999; *Maisy's Pool*, 1999; *Maisy Makes Gingerbread*, 1999; *Maisy's Bedtime*, 1999; *Maisy Takes a Bath*, 2000.

Courtesy of Candlewick Press

SUGGESTED READING: Silvey, Anita, ed. *Children's Books and Their Creators*, 1995. Periodicals—Handleman, David, "Quiet as a Mouse," *TV Guide*, April 24–30, 1999; Logan, Claudia, "The Fresh Vision of Lucy Cousins," *Publishers Weekly*, March 1, 1991.

"Most people are in their twenties when they discover what they want to do in life. I was almost forty. Let me explain.

"I come from a very artistic family, something that has its advantages but is also quite intimidating. Particularly awe-inspiring were my grandfather, father, and brother—stage designer, art director for films, and designer/illustrator respectively, and all wonderful wood engravers. Leaving school at sixteen, I felt unable to compete with all this talent and did not pursue a career in the graphic arts. Instead I became apprenticed to a commercial photographic studio in Central London. Drawing, I decided, would be for myself alone.

"After some years, I left and started my own photographic studio, still working for magazines and advertising but also taking portraits, which I preferred. I continued drawing for my own pleasure but still with no confidence.

"My son was born in 1965. It was while buying books for him that I came across *Where the Wild Things Are* by Maurice Sendak. Through that book, I realized just how exciting illustrating for children might be, and began to experiment with ideas, working in the evenings after my son had gone to bed.

"Eventually, in 1970, at the advice of a new friend (the writer Sarah Hayes), I showed some drawings and an unfinished story to Marni Hodgkin, children's book editor at Macmillan Publishers. She encouraged me to complete the story, but in the meantime gave me another book to illustrate. My own story was never finished, but my career as an illustrator had begun.

"I was born in London. Just before World War II, my mother, brother, and I moved to a tiny thatched cottage in the country to be safe from the bombs. My father had to stay in London. A lot of images from this country life go into my illustrations, especially in the Angelina books. It was a time when life moved a little slower. We lived near a farm where huge carthorses pulled the hay carts. The corn was cut and bound into sheaves that looked beautiful standing in rows in the fields; the old threshing machines are now museum pieces. We had washing water only if my brother or I pumped it into the tank from the pond in the garden. The pond was full of newts, and once a tiny one came through the tap into the bath. Drinking water had to be fetched in churns on a little cart from the main tap at the end of the lane,

Courtesy of Richard Duggan

Helen Craig

August 30, 1934–

another of our jobs. There was no electricity, just paraffin lamps and candles. Cooking was done on a paraffin stove or the range. Open fires in an enormous hearth and candlelight are things I will never forget. There was no refrigerator: we had ice cream only when it snowed. (My mother mixed clean snow with chocolate custard!)

"During the war, we didn't have many children's books, just those that had belonged to our parents, but I realize now just how much they meant to me. As a child, I would almost enter the pictures and become so absorbed that I would wait, expecting the figures to move.

"Now that I'm an illustrator myself, I try to make my pictures live for the children who look at them, as those other pictures did for me when I was a child. Inspiration comes from many sources. The Angelina books are full of images from my childhood. The design for *The Town Mouse and the Country Mouse* titles were inspired by the work of Winsor McCay and my love of the comic book format. The four *This Is the Bear* books feature the teddy bear I never had during the austerity of the war.

Courtesy of Candlewick Press

"Every illustrator always wants to produce beautiful pictures, but for me the most important element is to make the characters communicate with each other. I hope I manage to do this."

Helen Craig has worked in an advertising agency and as a photographer, sculptor, potter, and restorer of Chinese wallpaper in addition to illustrating over fifty books for children. She has written a number of these herself, including four Susie and Alfred titles. However, she is best known in the United States as the illustrator of the Angelina series written by Katharine Holabird, a serendipitous partnership that began in 1983 and has resulted in nine titles to date. There are more Angelina books planned, as well as animated films; the series has also spun off a Craig-designed doll. *Angelina Ballerina* received 1985's Kentucky Blue Grass Award; *Angelina's Christmas* was selected as one of the Child Study Association's Children's Books of the Year in 1987; and *Angelina's Birthday* won a category award in the 1990 British Book Design and Production exhibition, at which Craig was invited to exhibit two other titles as well. Other well-known books include *This Is the Bear* and its sequels, authored by Sarah Hayes; *This Is the Bear and the Bad*

Little Girl was named a 1995 American Booksellers Asociation Pick of the Lists. Craig was short-listed for England's prestigious Smarties Book Prize in 1992 for her retelling of *The Town Mouse and the Country Mouse*. She also received an award from the Society of Illustrators in 1977 for the concertina fold-out she created for *The Mouse House ABC*.

Helen Craig lives in the town of Aylesbury in England.

SELECTED WORKS WRITTEN AND ILLUSTRATED: *The Mouse House ABC*, 1978; *The Knight, the Princess, and the Dragon*, 1985; *The Night of the Paper Bag Monsters*, 1985, 1994; *A Welcome for Annie*, 1986; *The Town Mouse and the Country Mouse*, 1992; *I See the Moon and the Moon Sees Me: Helen Craig's Book of Nursery Rhymes*, 1992; *Charlie and Tyler at the Seashore*, 1995.

SELECTED WORKS ILLUSTRATED: *Angelina Ballerina*, by Katharine Holabird, 1983; *Angelina and the Princess*, by Katharine Holabird, 1984; *Angelina at the Fair*, by Katharine Holabird, 1985; *Angelina's Christmas*, by Katharine Holabird, 1985; *This Is the Bear*, by Sarah Hayes, 1986; *Angelina on Stage*, by Katharine Holabird, 1986; *Angelina and Alice*, by Katharine Holabird, 1987; *Alexander and the Dragon*, by Katharine Holabird, 1988; *Angelina's Birthday Surprise*, by Katharine Holabird, 1989; *Alexander and the Magic Boat*, by Katharine Holabird, 1990; *The Pumpkin Man and the Crafty Creeper*, by Margaret Mahy, 1990 (1991); *Angelina's Baby Sister*, by Katharine Holabird, 1991; *Angelina Ice Skates*, by Katharine Holabird, 1993; *This Is the Bear and the Bad Little Girl*, by Sarah Hayes, 1995; *One Windy Wednesday*, by Phyllis Root, 1996; *The Bunny Who Found Easter*, by Charlotte Zolotow, 1998; *Turnover Tuesday*, by Phyllis Root, 1998.

SUGGESTED READING: *Contemporary Authors*, vol. 117, 1986; *Contemporary Authors*, New Revision Series, vol. 68, 1998; Silvey, Anita, ed. *Children's Books and Their Creators*, 1995; *Something About the Author*, vol. 46, 1986, vol. 49, 1987; vol. 94, 1998.

Christopher Paul Curtis

1954–

"I give a lot of the credit for my writing career to my wife, Kaysandra. She had more faith in my ability to write than I did. She translated this faith into action by giving me a year off work to write. I spent mornings and afternoons of that year in the children's section of the public library working on a book that became *The Watsons Go to Birmingham—1963*.

"Another strong influencing factor in my writing was the thirteen years I spent working in Flint, Michigan's Fisher Body Plant Number 1 immediately after graduating from high school. My job was hanging doors, and I still have nightmares about the numbing repetitiveness of the work, but I believe it helped me become a writer. It helped me develop the discipline to write daily.

"My friend and I used to 'double up' on the assembly line. That means we would each hang thirty doors in a row instead of doing every other one, which allowed us each a half hour off every hour. I discovered this way if I spent my half hour off the line writing, time would fly by for me, the days weren't as long and tedious. This constant writing served as a sort of apprenticeship and helped me gain a flexibility and confidence in my ability to write that otherwise would never have developed.

"I often tell students that the best practice for writing is to do it at every opportunity. Many times young people feel that writing is, or should be, the result of a consultation with some mysterious, hard-to-find muse. I don't think so, I think in many ways writing is much like learning a second language or playing a sport or mastering a musical instrument: the more you do it, the better you become at it. That's why I think keeping a daily journal should be high on the list of priorities for every young writer.

"Both of my published novels, *The Watsons Go to Birmingham—1963* and *Bud, Not Buddy*, are set in my hometown of Flint, Michigan, as are the third and fourth books I am currently working on. Flint is a fascinating city; in many ways it's emblematic of many of the so-called Rust Belt American towns; it has had tremendous booms and terrifying busts. It is rich in history and fertile ground for a writer. When I'm asked why all of my stories have taken place in Flint, I answer why not? There are so many untold stories there. And that is true of every city and town."

Courtesy of Curtis Photographic

* * *

Christopher Paul Curtis was born and has spent most of his life in Flint, Michigan. He worked from 1972 to 1985 in the Fisher Body Plant, attending Flint's branch of the University of Michigan by taking classes after work or during the periods when the factory was closed. He received his B.A. in 1996. Curtis's dedication to writing has been greatly influenced by family—his wife, who urged him to take the time off to write; his son Steven, who typed his handwritten pages into the computer every night; and his daughter Cydney, who wrote the lyrics for a song that appears in his second book. Entered in a national writing contest, Christopher Curtis's first novel came to the attention of Wendy Lamb, an editor at Delacorte. Although the novel did not fit the guidelines of the contest, Delacorte decided to publish it.

The Watsons Go To Birmingham— 1963 made a stunning debut in the children's book field. It received the 1996 Newbery and Coretta Scott King Honor Book Awards and was cited as an ALA Notable Children's Book, an ALA Best Book for Young Adults, and a Notable Trade Book in the Field of Social Studies. In addition, it was listed among the *New York Times*'s Best 100 Books of 1996 (the only young adult novel on that list), named to all the "best" lists in children's book review journals, nominated for 27 state award reading lists, and translated into 11 foreign languages. Whoopi Goldberg has bought the rights to turn the novel into a motion picture. An honor that Curtis is especially proud of is the Golden Kite Award, given by the Society of Children's Book Writers

Courtesy of BDD Books

and Illustrators and voted on by other authors. "To be recognized by your peers is the greatest feeling," he has said, "If I had known writing was going to be this much fun and this rewarding I would have started decades ago!"

Curtis's second novel, *Bud, Not Buddy*, the story of an irrepressible young orphan who sets out during the Great Depression to find his father, won the 2000 Newbery Award and the Coretta Scott King Award. It was the first book to be honored with both of these prestigious awards. *Bud, Not Buddy* was also a Junior Library Guild selection, an ALA Notable Children's Book, a Best Book for Young Adults, and a *School Library Journal* Best Book of the Year, in addition to winning a Parents' Choice Gold Award in 1999.

Christopher Paul Curtis and his family currently live in Windsor, Ontario, Canada.

SELECTED WORKS: *The Watsons Go to Birmingham—1963*, 1995; *Bud, Not Buddy*, 1999.

SUGGESTED READING: *Biography Today: Author Series*, vol. 4, 1998; *Contemporary Authors*, vol. 159, 1998; *Something About the Author*, vol. 93, 1997.

Courtesy of John Massimino

Doug Cushman

May 4, 1953–

"My mother tells this story: many years ago, while reading some bedtime stories, I asked, 'Who makes the pictures in books?' 'The person who draws the pictures is called an illustrator,' my mother answered. 'That's what I'm going be when I grow up,' I said. I don't remember this incident, but I know I've always been fascinated by pictures. Ever since I learned how to hold a pencil, I've been drawing pictures. I wrote and illustrated my first books at age eight, creating such memorable characters as Space Cat and Danny Dog.

"I spent the first thirteen years of my life in Springfield and Columbus, Ohio. I moved with my family to Connecticut, where, in junior high and high school, I wrote and illustrated original comic books (lampooning my teachers), selling them to my classmates for a nickel. In my senior year I wrote and drew political cartoons for the local newspaper, the *Waterbury American*. This was a great job because it gave me a taste of what a freelance life would be like: getting an assignment, working under a deadline, delivering artwork on time, and seeing the final result published (and seeing all the mistakes). I would use these skills for the rest of my life.

"In 1971 I attended the Paier School of Art. In my book illustration class, under the direction of author/illustrator Leonard Everett Fisher, I realized what a picture book could really be. I learned it's not just a series of pictures with some words underneath. A picture book is a very physical object. That's very important to me when I'm working on one. The size, feel, touch, and even smell of a book are part of the entire picture-book experience.

"After I graduated from Paier, I began freelancing right away, grabbing any job I could, which included filmstrip art, insurance brochures, and toy package illustration. In 1977 I was fortunate to be apprenticed to author/illustrator Mercer Mayer. He helped me fine-tune some of my book illustration skills and taught me some of the fine points of working with clients and editors. In

1978 I illustrated my first book. I've been illustrating books ever since.

"I think with pencils and paints. I fill sketchbooks with doodles, ideas, and scenarios. I need to physically see the character and the environment. The words come later. I'm after a mood. To me, a picture book is like a piece of music. If one thinks of music as organized noise, then a picture book is the organization of scattered words and images. It must work on many levels. I have to see the character on the page before I can write about him or her.

"I love mysteries. I was always looking for good mystery books when I was growing up. Besides the classics, Sherlock Holmes and such, I couldn't find anything I liked, especially in the picture-book format. So I decided I would write and illustrate something I wanted when I was that age.

"I now live in Northern California among mountains, rivers, and digger pines. I live with a yellow Lab and a cat (who are as lazy as can be). I like cooking and kayaking. I love traveling and talking to kids about reading and writing. I can't think of a better way to spend a life: talking, drawing, and writing books."

Courtesy of HarperCollins Publishers

* * *

Doug Cushman was born in Springfield, Ohio, the son of Donald E. and Juney I. Cushman. His earliest memories of books were of the bookmobile arriving on his street every other week or so. He pored over every book his mother would let him check out, absorbing every detail. Sometimes he even copied the pictures on a pad of notebook paper. After his graduation from Paier College of Art, he became an instructor there during 1980 and taught at Southern Connecticut State University during 1981.

Traveling is one of Cushman's greatest pleasures. On a trip to Kenya he collected a wealth of material that he hopes to use in his stories. He made many paintings of the land and the Masai people. One of his most enjoyable moments was sitting one evening with his guide, a Kamba tribesman, and sharing folktales from their respective countries.

Cushman's awards and honors include *Aunt Eater Loves a Mystery* being chosen as a *Reading Rainbow* Review Book. *The Mystery of King Karfu* received the National Cartoonists Society 1996 Reuben Award for Magazine and Book Illustration and was named a National Council of Teachers of English 1996 Notable Trade Book in the Language Arts.

SELECTED WORKS WRITTEN AND ILLUSTRATED: *Aunt Eater Loves a Mystery*, 1987; *Camp Big Paw*, 1990; *Aunt Eater's Mystery Vacation*, 1992; *ABC Mystery*, 1993; *Mouse and Mole and a Year-Round Garden*, 1994; *Mouse and Mole and the Christmas Walk*, 1994; *Mouse and Mole and the All-Weather Train Ride*, 1995; *Aunt Eater's Mystery Christmas*, 1995; *The Mystery of King Karfu*, 1996; *Aunt Eater's Mystery Halloween*, 1998; *The Mystery of the Monkey's Maze*, 1999.

SELECTED WORKS ILLUSTRATED: *Halloween Mice*, by Bethany Roberts, 1995; *Valentine Mice*, by Bethany Roberts, 1998.

SUGGESTED READING: *Contemporary Authors*, vol. 117, 1986; *Contemporary Authors*, New Revision Series, vol. 54, 1997; *Something About the Author*, vol. 65, 1991; vol. 101, 1999.

WEB SITE: *www.doug-cushman.com*

Jane Cutler

September 24, 1936–

"I've been a writer all my life. By this I mean, I can't remember a time that I wasn't 'writing'—making up pretend games to play with a friend that involved characters and dialogue and a plot; imagining stories when I was alone and using pebbles and stones as characters, or pillows in my bed at night.

"Even after I learned to write on the page, I kept writing in my head too. Dawdling on the way home from school, I would become lost in the story I was telling myself and would play all the different parts aloud. This drew inquiring looks from ladies out walking the dog or pruning the hedge. I didn't care. But I haven't really answered the question, have I? How, why, did I become a writer?

"Usually I'm not stumped by questions. Usually I have answers. But when someone asks me to explain my writing self, I feel exactly the way I did when Mrs. Fulbright and Miss Rudloff and Miss Noonan asked us to write an essay called: 'What I Did over My Summer Vacation.' What exactly did I do during those long, lazy, school-free months? And when or how or why did I become a writer?

"Fate?

"Luck?

"Circumstances beyond my control?

"All of the above?

"Look, here's how it was: my mother was sick and confined. She hungered for news of the outside world. And she didn't want to have it delivered in the shape of a headline. She wanted a complete story, with plenty of details and enough drama to make it worth waiting all day long for. Every day after school, my mother met me at the door, her face alight with expectation. 'What happened at school today?' she'd ask.

"Nobody had to tell me, an only child perfectly attuned to the needs of both my parents, that the story of a lively and dramatic day was what my mother longed to hear. And, since the routine and repetition of the average school day never made much of a tale, I quickly understood that I would have to exaggerate and embellish. I would have to lie. So I did. And it was easy.

"I knew what made a good story, after all. I listened, rapt, to fairy tales dramatized on *Let's Pretend* on the radio every Saturday morning. I knew that the stories people wanted to hear had heroes and heroines, and that the heroes and heroines had difficulties, and that because of cunning and courage and good fortune, they overcame their difficulties and lived happily ever after.

"So that was the sort of story I told my mother. In every one of those stories, I was the heroine. I had difficulties, and I resolved them. I was steadfast, brave, resourceful—and lucky. I made mistakes, of course, because that added to the drama of the narrative. But at the end, things always came right.

"Lying to my mother—that's how I got to be a writer, I think. Or maybe not. Maybe it was Fate.

"Since then, I've done many different kinds of writing. I churned out sentimental verses—no two alike—for Mother's Day cards for nearly everyone in my class one year. I was always the reporter from my grade for the school newspaper. And then I was the editor. I wrote a short story about racial prejudice when I was in high school and won a prize. After that, I wrote poems about Spring and Death. I wrote single-spaced ten-page letters every week to a friend who was living in Paris. I wrote book reports and term papers and speeches and exams and a talent show.

"Eventually I finished school, joined the ranks of the employed, and wrote for wages. My childhood history of lying came in handy right away: I wrote advertising copy and public relations

Courtesy of Judy Steinhart

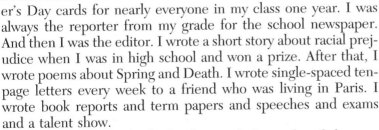

releases. Then I went straight: I wrote encyclopedias and textbooks. I was still writing when I got married and had children. But after awhile, I was too busy. Or I thought I was. And I went back to writing only in my head.

"In the normal amount of time, the children grew up, and I had plenty of time again. I drew a deep breath and looked around. What did I want to do next? I wanted to write! So off I went to graduate school, where I learned to write short stories. Some of them were published in literary journals and others in slick magazines. And I worked as an editor, as a literary agent, and as a writing teacher, too. Finally one day when I wasn't paying attention, I sat down and wrote a story for children. I liked doing it so much, I wrote another.

"All the stories I've written since then have been for children. All the books I've written and all the books I plan to write are children's books. They have characters and plots and dialogue and difficulties and conclusions. And they all have a lot in common with the lies I told my mother. Except for one lucky, added thing: now they're often funny. And if someone were to ask me, 'Say, how did you learn to write funny?,' that's a question I'd be able to answer quick as a wink. 'It was pure luck,' I'd tell them. 'I am just plain lucky.' And that would be the truth."

"I drew a deep breath and looked around. What did I want to do next? I wanted to write!"

Jane Cutler was born in the Bronx, New York, and grew up in Clayton, Missouri, a suburb of St. Louis. She received a B.S. in English from Northwestern University in 1958 and an M.A. from San Francisco State University in 1982. She began her career as an editor for Consolidated Publications writing articles for a children's encyclopedia about many topics, including children's books, authors, and Native Americans. Her editing career also involved developing some of the first "hi-lo" reading materials, intended for struggling middle-grade readers.

Jane Cutler began writing short stories as a graduate student in Creative Writing. Her short fiction for adults has been published in many literary quarterlies and magazines, including *Epoch*, *North American Review*, and *Redbook*. In 1982 Cutler received the Herbert Wilner Award for Short Fiction presented annually for the best short story by a San Francisco State graduate student, and in 1987 she won the PEN prize for short fiction. She has taught short story writing and children's writing at San Francisco State University and the University of California Extension in San Francisco.

Her first novel for children, *Family Dinner*, was well reviewed and was included on the West Virginia Children's Book Award Master Reading List in 1994. *My Wartime Summers* was cited as a Notable Children's Trade Book in the Field of Social Studies in the same year. *Darcy and Gran Don't Like Babies* was included in *School Library Journal*'s list of Best Books in 1993 and was a finalist for the Bay Area Book Reviewers Award in 1994. *Darcy and Gran Don't Like Babies* was also a *Reading Rainbow*/PBS selection and a *Horn Book* Fanfare book in 1993. *The Song of the Molimo* was among the Best Children's Books of the Year selected by the Children's Book Committee at Bank Street College of Education, and *The Cello of Mr. O* was named a *Booklist* Editors' Choice.

SELECTED WORKS: *Family Dinner*, 1991; *No Dogs Allowed*, 1992; *Darcy and Gran Don't Like Babies*, 1993; *My Wartime Summers*, 1994; *Rats!*, 1996; *Mr. Carey's Garden*, 1996; *Spaceman*, 1997; *The Song of the Molimo*, 1998; *The Cello of Mr. O*, 1999; *'Gator Aid*, 1999.

SUGGESTED READING: *Contemporary Authors*, vol. 142. 1994; *Something About the Author*, vol. 75, 1994.

WEB SITE:
www.geocities.com/~janecutler

Courtesy of Farrar, Straus & Giroux

"If eleven years ago someone had told me my name would be listed on one of *Publishers Weekly*'s bestseller lists I would have said, 'You're crazy!' But, much to my amazement, that was true for the better part of two years.

"I was born on May 18, 1959, in Morganfield, Kentucky, and grew up in the small town of Henderson, Kentucky, which is along the Ohio River. My mother was a teacher and my father was a model-maker. I was a tomboy and played baseball a lot with my two brothers. I was a water-skier and even performed in ski shows. I played basketball and was a cheerleader in junior high school. I went to Henderson County Senior High School and then to Western Kentucky University.

"After I graduated from the University in 1980 with a degree in Elementary Education, I returned for my master's degree in Library Science. I taught first grade the five years before our son Nathan was born in 1986. After his birth, I became a librarian at the Sayre School in Lexington, Kentucky, where Marcia Jones also worked. I was the librarian and surrounded by books. We started writing together after saying what a lot of people say: 'I

Debbie Dadey

May 18, 1959–

could write a children's book as good as that one.' Of course, we found out that it's not as easy as it seemed.

"We wrote like crazy for two years, sending out manuscript after manuscript. After a hard day of teaching kids with spring fever, we jokingly said we needed to be a monster teacher to get kids to pay attention to us. From that joke sprang our first book sale, *Vampires Don't Wear Polka Dots*, which we sent unsolicited to Scholastic.

"I worked as a librarian at Sayre while my husband finished his doctorate in Pharmaceutical Sciences at the University of Kentucky in Lexington. During that time I also co-taught a writing class at the University of Kentucky. After my husband finished school we moved close to Dallas, Texas, where we lived for two years. It was there that our daughter, Rebekah (Becky) was born and I became a full-time writer and taught writing at Southern Methodist University. From Dallas we went to California, where we lived for only eight months. Now we're in Illinois, near Chicago. Our family has increased. We have a new son named Alex and a dog named Bailey and a gerbil. Now I'm a full-time writer and mom."

Courtesy of Sears

*   *   *

Debbie Dadey and Marcia Jones, the writing team behind the best-selling Adventures of the Bailey School Kids series, have something in common with the grown-ups who work at the Bailey School. Although they aren't vampires, gremlins, or elves, they're teachers—and once both worked at the same elementary school in Lexington, Kentucky. Marcia was a reading teacher and Debbie was the head librarian when they decided they wanted to write for children. The two wrote every day while the students were eating lunch. Now that Debbie and Marcia no longer live near one another, how do they continue to collaborate? "We use the hot-potato method of writing," they explained. "We start with a brief outline. Then we take turns writing chapters. We send them to each other using the fax machine and e-mail. When the other person has the story, we say it's her 'hot potato.'"

Dadey gets her ideas from everywhere, including the newspaper, her children, and fan letters. She lives with her family in Aurora, Illinois.

SELECTED WORKS: *Shooting Star: Annie Oakley, the Legend*, 1997; *Will Rogers: Larger Than Life*, 1999; The Adventures of the Bailey School Kids (with Marcia Thornton Jones—for a complete list visit the Bailey Kids Web Site): *Vampires Don't Wear Polka Dots*, 1990; *Leprechauns Don't Play Basketball*, 1992; *Unicorns Don't Give Sleigh Rides*, 1997; *Mrs. Jeepers in Outer Space*, 1999; Triplet Trouble series (with Marcia Thornton Jones—for a complete list visit the Bailey Kids Web Site): *Triplet Trouble and the Talent Show Mess*, 1995; *Triplet Trouble and the Runaway Reindeer*, 1995; *Triplet Trouble and the Field Day Disaster*, 1996; *Triplet Trouble and the Class Trip*, 1997; Bailey City Monsters (with Marcia Thornton Jones—for a complete list visit the Bailey Kids Web Site): *The Monsters Next Door*, 1997; *Kilmer's Pet Monster*, 1998; *Vampire Trouble*, 1999; *Spooky Spells*, 1999.

Courtesy of Scholastic, Inc.

SUGGESTED READING: *Something About the Author*, vol. 73, 1993.

WEB SITES: *www.baileykids.com* and *www.scholastic.com*

For a statement by Marcia Thornton Jones, Dadey's co-author, see her entry in this volume.

Marguerite Davol

July 2, 1928–

"My writing career developed slowly—after years of teaching, years of reading anything and everything. In fact, writing children's books is my second career, albeit a successful and highly satisfying one.

"I grew up in an Illinois farming community surrounded by flat lands and flat speech. They were Depression years and my parents struggled to feed and clothe four children. We had few toys and no money for extras. But we had a large lawn and garden by a river, fruit trees to climb, an old barn to explore. And we had books bought during better times.

"I was the third child, shy, a loner. My sisters and brother were too old or too young to be my playmates, so my childhood was spent perched in a tree, hiding in the barn or attic, under my bed—reading! Reading dreadful Victorian morality tracts, fairy tales, turn-of-the-century romances, boys' adventure series, and comics. After devouring the children's books in our town library, I consumed shelves of murder mysteries, romances, bestsellers, even pop psychology. The world of books was much more real to me than my day-to-day life!

"Even though I loved to read and loved using words, I never thought about writing my own stories while growing up. I envy writers who are inspired by their storytelling family members. Mine were mostly stolid, silent, second-generation German farmers, not storytellers. Only late in life did I discover storytelling, a strong influence on my writing today.

"Through the years I continued to read and read. At Colorado University, I married Stephen Davol, a psychologist, who also read and read, as did our three children. Then, when my youngest started school, I 'fell' into teaching preschoolers in the laboratory school at Mount Holyoke College. This was the perfect career for me. For twenty-five years I lived in the creative and highly imaginative world of four-year-olds. Reading to them, I learned what characterizes a good picture book—its rhythm, tone and texture, the characters, the story itself. Preschoolers are uninhibited critics. You know when a book succeeds—or doesn't. What an ideal apprenticeship for writing children's books!

"But why did I quit teaching to become an author? In 1982 my husband died. Our children had graduated from college and I was alone. What should I do with the rest of my life? I couldn't teach forever! The next spring, I attended a children's literature conference. Hearing Jane Yolen, Jane Dyer, and Patricia MacLachlan, among others, talk about their work, I decided that was what I wanted to do—write children's books.

Courtesy of Ellen Augarten

"I had the intense desire, perhaps the talent, but I had to learn the art, the craft of writing. So I taught half-time and attended conferences, workshops, college courses, and became immersed in children's books. I also discovered the world of storytellers. Fascinated, I listened and learned from their performances, acquiring my own family of storytellers. And I wrote and wrote—novels, poetry, and picture-book texts. Finally, a manuscript, *The Heart of the Wood*, was accepted. And in 1992, with *Black, White, Just Right!* under contract, I reluctantly retired from teaching.

"Writing often comes from our life experiences. My son married a Kenyan, so my grandchildren are 'black, white, just right!' But my other books are not about my family. Instead, these original creation tales, pourquoi stories, folk tales, and tall tales were written because of my love of reading and storytelling. Using some tiny seed of an idea gleaned from traditional tales I've read or heard storytellers perform, I create oral tales to tell, then turn them into picture book manuscripts—it's always a subtle process.

"Today I am married to a most supportive husband, Robert Greenberg. We live in Massachusetts and New Hampshire and travel widely. I still write and write. I've discovered that I can think anywhere, from Iceland to Antarctica. Stories go on and on in my head, sometimes for weeks before I ever pick up a pen. And I continue to write from my rich world of reading books, teaching young children, and storytelling."

* * *

Marguerite W. Davol had a long and successful career in education before turning her efforts to full-time writing in the 1980s. Born in East Peoria, Illinois, she attended the University of Colorado, where she received her B.A. in 1951, and did graduate work at both Kansas State University and the University of Rochester. She first taught at the Rocky Ford Junior High School in Colorado, 1952–1953, and then taught preschool at the Gorse Child Study Center at Mount Holyoke College from 1964 to 1992.

Courtesy of Simon & Schuster Children's Publishing Division

Davol is a member of the national and New England chapters of the Society of Children's Book Writers and Illustrators, the Authors Guild, the League for the Advancement of New England Storytelling, and the National Storytelling Association.

The Paper Dragon, illustrated by Robert Sabuda, won the 1997 Golden Kite Award for picture book text and illustration; the following year it was named an ALA Notable Children's Book, a Parents' Choice Honor Book, and a Notable Children's Book in the Field of Social Studies. Both *Batwings and the Curtain of Night* and *The Paper Dragon* were ABA Pick of the Lists selections.

SELECTED WORKS: "Flesh and Blood" in *Werewolves*, 1988; *The Heart of the Wood*, illus. by Sheila Hamanaka, 1992; *Black, White, Just Right!*, illus. by Irene Trivas, 1993; *Papa Alonzo Leatherby: A Collection of Tall Tales from the Best Storyteller in Carroll County*, 1995; *How Snake Got His Hiss: An Original Tale*, illus. by Mercedes McDonald, 1996; *Batwings and the Curtain of Night*, illus. by Mary Grandpré, 1997; *The Paper Dragon*, illus. by Robert Sabuda, 1997; *The Loudest, Fastest, Best Drummer in Kansas*, illus. by Cat Bowman Smith, 2000.

SUGGESTED READING: *Something About the Author*, vol. 82, 1995.

Courtesy of Cynthia Del Conte

Lulu Delacre

December 20, 1957–

"I was born in Puerto Rico to Argentinean parents, the middle child in a family of three daughters. Growing up in the island was a fun-filled experience, where climbing up a tamarindo tree with a friend to eat its fruit was as commonplace as hunting for tiny brown lizards. I used to gently open their mouths and hang them from my earlobes as earrings!

"My earliest recollections of drawing—I must have been five then—go back to my grandmother's house. My grandma, Elena, was from Uruguay. She baby-sat my sister and me, in the second floor apartment of an old pink house, while my parents taught at the University of Puerto Rico. She would give me white sheets of paper on which I would draw as I lay on the floor of her bedroom and listened to classical music. I don't remember her ever throwing away one of my pictures. She kept them neatly stacked in a corner of her closet in a pile that one day grew as tall as I was.

"I had my first formal art training when I was ten in Buenos Aires, Argentina, where we lived for a year while my father was on sabbatical. One of my mother's closest friends, who was a fine artist and gave painting lessons, encouraged me to join her class. She was the first of several instructors who taught me to draw from real life, and it was with her that I first learned the immense joy of being able to create.

"By the time I entered the Fine Arts department of the University of Puerto Rico, I knew I wanted a career in art. Later on I was accepted into L'École Supérieure d'Arts Graphiques in

Paris, France. And after I had finished my thesis, an audiovisual project illustrating Saint-Saëns' *Carnival of the Animals*, I knew I wanted to become an illustrator of children's books.

"In 1980 I got married and came to live in the United States with the clear goal of breaking into the children's book publishing field. Two years later I took a Greyhound bus from Ayer, Massachusetts, to New York City, with two portfolios under my arm. The Monday I arrived I had twenty-two appointments scheduled with children's book editors and art directors. By Friday afternoon I had my first assignment.

"The fact that I became a writer took me by surprise. Somehow my creative energy was harnessed into the process of writing when I discovered I could invent my own characters. It is a draining task to achieve a certain standard in both manuscript and art. But since early on I've enjoyed a challenge, as well as the learning that takes place while attaining a goal.

"The birth of my daughters made me want to create books inspired by the heritage I love and deeply respect. Books that celebrate the rich folklore and colorful traditions I was nurtured on. Books that tap into deep-rooted memories that I share with so many other Latinos. Books to be cherished by children like my daughters, born in the United States to Latino parents. Books that might broaden the horizons of non-Latino children as well, expanding their vision of the world.

"It is with great pleasure that I have seen these books succeed. I've measured their success in the proud smiles of many Latino children as they join hands with their schoolmates and myself, in the game song of 'Arroz con leche.' Or as we all sing *vejigante* chants behind paper masks when recreating a *carnaval*.

"Through the years I've seen myself evolve from illustrator to picture-book author, from reteller to short story writer, from watercolorist to oil painter. There are always obstacles when you seek creative change, but with a good dose of persistence most of them can be surmounted.

"And I love what I do."

*   *   *

Lulu Delacre was born on December 20, 1957, in Rio Piedras, Puerto Rico. Marta Orzabal, Lulu's mother, taught French and French culture at the University of Puerto Rico and provided her daughter, as well as her students, with insight into the importance of one's heritage. Lulu's father, Georges Carlos Delacre, a professor of philosophy at the same university, was an avid reader who kept thousands of English, Spanish, and French books in his personal library. It was a rare moment when he was not reading, and Lulu "loved to be in his library surrounded by floor-to-ceiling bookcases."

"The birth of my daughters made me want to create books inspired by the heritage I love and deeply respect. . . Books that tap into deep-rooted memories that I share with so many other Latinos."

Lulu Delacre spent 1976–1977 at the University of Puerto Rico in the Fine Arts Department. In 1977 she was accepted into the prestigious five-year program at L'École Supérieure d' Arts Graphiques in Paris, France. Due to the excellence of her portfolio, she was allowed to enter as a third-year student. The next year she received a full merit scholarship for the final two years of the program. In 1980 she married Arturo Betancourt, a doctor serving in the U.S. Army. They now live with their two daughters, Veronica and Alicia, in Silver Spring, Maryland, where Delacre enjoys gardening, cooking, and baking when she's not writing or illustrating.

Lulu Delacre's illustrations for *The Bossy Gallito / El Gallo de Bodas: A Traditional Cuban Folktale* earned a 1996 Pura Belpré Honor Book award. The bilingual *Bossy Gallito* was also a Notable Children's Trade Book in the Field of Social Studies and an American Booksellers Association Pick of the Lists. *Vejigantes Masquerade* was also chosen as an ABA Pick of the Lists. In addition it received a 1993 Américas Award and was named a Notable Children's Trade Book in Language Arts by the National Council of Teachers of English. *Golden Tales: Myths, Legends and Folktales from Latin America* was a Cooperative Children's Book Center Choice Book in 1996.

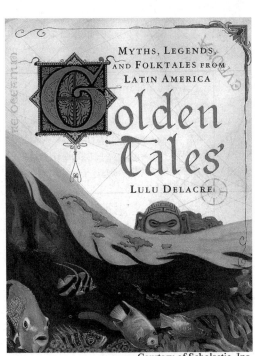

Courtesy of Scholastic, Inc.

SELECTED WORKS WRITTEN AND ILLUSTRATED: *Arroz con Leche: Popular Songs and Rhymes from Latin America*, 1989; *Las Navidades: Popular Christmas Songs from Latin America*, 1990; *Vejigantes Masquerade*, 1993; *Golden Tales: Myths, Legends and Folktales from Latin America*, 1996; *De Oro y Esmeraldas: Mitos, Leyendas y Cuentos Populares de Latinoamérica*, 1996; *Salsa Stories*, 2000.

SELECTED WORKS ILLUSTRATED: *The Bossy Gallito / El Gallo de Bodas: A Traditional Cuban Folktale*, by Lucía M. González, 1994; *Los Zapaticos de Rosa*, by José Martí, 1997; *Señor Cat's Romance and Other Favorite Stories from Latin America*, by Lucía M. González, 1997.

SUGGESTED READING: Day, Frances Ann. *Latina and Latino Voices in Literature*, 1997; Harns, Violet, ed. *Multicultural Children's Literature*, 1992; Kovacs, Deborah and James Preller. *Meet the Authors and Illustrators*, vol. 2, 1993;

Manna, Anthony L. and Carolyn S. Brodie. *Art and Story: The Role of Illustration in Multicultural Literature for Youth*, 1997; *Something About the Author*, vol. 36, 1984.

"I was about eight or nine years old at the time. I was reading my first Hardy Boys and Tom Swift books, and my reaction to them was 'oh boy, writing books—that's the life for me!' I've not changed my mind one bit in all the time since. Over the years, I've written for magazines and newspapers, but I still find the writing of books to be the most exciting and satisfying job of all. In large part, this is due to my feelings on seeing any book. I love the look and feel of the thing—its dust jacket, its thickness, its weight, the printing down its spine. It always has a look of completeness. Then, just as I get ready to look inside, it holds out the promise of something wonderful to come. Finally, there is the book's lasting quality. Newspapers and magazines all too frequently disappear in hardly any time at all, taking their writing with them. But a book can last for years—for lifetimes if it has something truly valuable to say.

"I've spent my adult life writing books because of these feelings. I began with the publication of a young people's biography of Louis Pasteur and have now written more than 100 books about sports and recreation, science, medicine, the law, current socio-economic problems, the environment, folklore, and history. My books are all nonfiction because I learned early on that this is the area in which I am most interested and for which I am best suited. I write for four audiences: adults, young adults, children, and young people with reading difficulties.

"Nonfiction poses a number of challenges for the writer, and I enjoy meeting them all. Obviously, it first requires a great deal of research, which involves reading all sorts of material and talking to or corresponding with people in the field being studied. In a nutshell, it adds up to an education in the topic. Second, there's the problem of arranging the various aspects of the subject in their proper order—an order that is different for each book. Then comes the job of presenting the subject in the most interesting way possible—as a story with lots of drama in it—and as simply and clearly as possible.

Courtesy of Russ Booth

Edward F. Dolan

Edward Dolan

February 10, 1924–

Courtesy of Millbrook Press, Inc.

"I was born in Oakland, California, but my family took me to Los Angeles when I was two years old. I spent my boyhood there, graduating from Loyola High School and finally leaving during World War II when I enlisted in the army. I spent three years with the 101st Airborne Division in England, France, Belgium, Germany, and Austria. While in England, I met and married a young Londoner. We were together until her death in 1997, just two months before our 52nd wedding anniversary. We shared a son and a daughter—both now long grown and married—and three grandchildren."

* * *

Edward F. Dolan has been writing since he was twelve and published his first story at sixteen. Born in Oakland, California, Dolan attended the Universities of Southern California and San Francisco, as well as San Francisco State. He has worked as a reporter, communications teacher, publications director, and freelance writer for radio and television. He has written or co-authored over 100 nonfiction books that cover a broad range of historical and contemporary topics, including sports, the environment, science, law, drugs, and gun control.

Many of Dolan's books have been cited as Children's Books of the Year by the Child Study Association: *The Camera*; *Kyle Rote, Jr.*; *The Bermuda Triangle*; *Great Mysteries of the Air*; *Anti-Semitism*; *Our Poisoned Sky*; *The American Revolution*; and *Your Privacy*. *Disaster 1906: The San Francisco Earthquake and Fire* was a selection of the Junior Literary Guild, as was *Your Privacy*. *How to Leave Home—and Make Everybody Like It* and *Adolf Hitler* were both chosen as American Library Association Best Books for Young Adults. *The American Revolution* was cited as a Notable Trade Book in the Field of Social Studies.

SELECTED WORKS: *The Camera*, 1965; *Disaster 1906: The San Francisco Earthquake and Fire*, 1967; *Amnesty: The American Puzzle*, 1976; *How to Leave Home—and Make Everybody Like It*, 1977; *Our Poisoned Sky*, 1991; *Child Abuse*, rev. ed., 1992; *Adolf Hitler: A Portrait in Tyranny*, 1981; *Protect Your Legal Rights: A Handbook for Teenagers*, 1983; *The Simon and Schuster Sports Question and Answer Book*, 1984; *Drugs in Sports*, rev. ed., 1992; *America After Vietnam: Legacies of a Hated War*, 1994; *America in World War II* series, 1991–94; *Your Privacy: Protecting It in a Nosy World*, 1995; *Illiteracy in America*, 1995; *The American Revolution: How We Fought the War of Independence*, 1995; *America in World War I*, 1996; *Our Poisoned Waters*, 1997; *The American Civil War: A House Divided*, 1997; *America in the Korean War*, 1998.

SUGGESTED READING: *Contemporary Authors*, New Revision Series, vol. 68, 1998; *Something About the Author*, vol. 31, 1983; vol. 45, 1986; vol. 94, 1998.

"When I am doing my children's show at a school or a library, there are always one or two children who come up at the end of the session and ask me, 'When did you start to draw?' Of course I can't remember when I didn't draw, but I think it first really occurred to me that I wanted to be a cartoonist when I was in the fourth grade. I remember that that was when I first began to decorate my school papers with funny little drawings. By the time I was in the sixth grade, some of my teachers would let me decorate the drawing boards with cartoons about the subjects we were studying.

"From the time I was ten years old until I was sixteen, I was a newspaper boy. After getting up at five on Sunday mornings to deliver the Sunday editions, all the paperboys would meet at a local diner for their breakfast. I would spend hours on those Sunday mornings, filling notebooks with my drawings of wild comic strips that I created.

"By the time I went to college I was determined to become a cartoonist. It was a shock to find that in the colleges prior to World War II, there were no courses in graphic arts, illustration, or design. 'Fine Art' was the course. I did all the required courses—life drawing, watercolor, oil painting, sculpture, art history, etc.—but on each and every piece of art was always a little figure or two making a humorous aside on that piece of art. Humor had already become a part of my life.

"During WWII I was lucky enough to become a cartoonist for the army. I worked for many army publications: *Yank, Stars & Stripes, Army Talks*, and *Overseas Woman*, a magazine for

Courtesy of Fabian

Roy Doty

September 10, 1922–

Wacs, nurses, and Red Cross workers. I also worked on the side for the *London Daily Mail* and for the first issues of *Elle*. I was stationed in Paris for two years.

"When the war was over I came to New York and immediately began freelancing. I began working for magazines, newspapers, and advertising agencies, and in 1948 wrote and illustrated my first book. I'm still doing the same today, fifty-three years later.

"Being in Paris for over two years changed all my ideas about cartooning. I did not do a comic strip, or gags, or editorial cartoons—I illustrated serious articles with a touch of humor. I became something new at that time, a humorous illustrator. I'm considered by the profession as an illustrator; but at heart, like the fourth-grader I once was, I'm a cartoonist.

"I have never held a job. I've always worked for myself—and like the dream I had in the fourth grade, I have always been a cartoonist. It is truly wonderful to be able to do all your life what you dreamed of doing as a child. Many young people want to be singers, musicians, writers, dancers, artists, and cartoonists and so few get to achieve their goal. I did.

"I can only hope that the girls and boys who come up to talk to me at my school shows get the chance to do what I did."

Roy Doty has enjoyed a steady and distinguished career for more than fifty years doing what he loves to do—drawing humorous illustrations and cartoons. Born in Chicago, Doty attended

Courtesy of Roy Doty

the Columbus College of Art and Design. One of his earliest cartoon series, "Wordless Workshop," continues to be published in *Family Handyman* magazine after four decades. From 1968 to 1971, Doty wrote and illustrated "Laugh-In," a daily and Sunday comic strip based on the popular television show of those years; it appeared in over 700 newspapers. Recent comic strips include "Patent Nonsense," a salute to silly inventions, and "Sandy's World," a panel feature about golfing. Doty has been named Illustrator of the Year six times by the National Cartoonists Society. He has also won numerous awards for his advertising work; his illustrations have been used to promote cars, insurance companies, bottled water, and juices, among other products. In addition, he has designed Christmas cards and posters and contributed artwork to the *New York Times*, *Newsweek*, *Business Week*, *Fortune*, and many sports magazines.

Children have long been familiar with Doty's illustrations. He wrote and illustrated numerous joke and riddle books in the 1970s and provided the artwork for a wide variety of nonfiction books by such authors as Norma Klein, Rhoda Blumberg, and Alvin and Virginia Silverstein. He is perhaps best known to young readers as the illustrator of Judy Blume's perennially popular *Tales of a Fourth Grade Nothing*.

Doty co-created *The Adventures of Danny Dee*, a daily children's television show which ran for three years. A longtime supporter of public libraries, he designed a mascot figure for the Ferguson Library in Stamford, Connecticut—a green and yellow bookworm named "Fergie"—and for years he has presented cartooning workshops for children in schools and libraries. His marriage to the writer Jean Slaughter Doty ended in divorce in 1981. The father of four grown children and two stepchildren, Roy Doty lives with his present wife in Norwalk, Connecticut.

SELECTED WORKS WRITTEN AND ILLUSTRATED: *Puns, Gags, Quips, and Riddles: A Collection of Dreadful Jokes*, 1974; *Q's Are Weird O's: More Puns, Gags, Quips, and Riddles*, 1975; *Where Are You Going with That Tree?*, 1976; *Where Are You Going with That Oil?*, 1976; *Gunga, Your Din-Din Is Ready: Son of Puns, Gags, Quips, and Riddles*, 1976; *Pinocchio Was Nosey: Grandson of Puns, Gags, Quips, and Riddles*, 1977; *The Incredible Television Machine*, with Lee Polk, 1977; *Where Are You Going with That Coal?*, with Leonard Maar, 1977; *Where Are You Going with That Energy?*, with Leonard Maar, 1977; *Old One-Eye Meets His Match*, 1978; *King Midas Has a Gilt Complex*, 1979; *Tinkerbell Is a Ding-a-Ling*, 1980; *Fleet of Nursery Rhymes*, 1991; *Wonderful Circus Parade*, 1991.

SELECTED WORKS ILLUSTRATED: *Tales of a Fourth Grade Nothing*, by Judy Blume, 1972; *Girls Can Be Anything*, by Norma Klein, 1973; *Take Tarts as Tarts Is Passing*, by Eleanor S. Clymer, 1974; *No Pushing, No Ducking: Safety in the Water*, by Barbara Rinkoff, 1974; *Hamburgers—and Ice Cream for Dessert*, by Eleanor S. Clymer, 1974; *Life with Working Parents*, with Esther R. Hautzig, 1976; *Itch, Sniffle, and Sneeze*, by Alvin Silverstein, 1978; *How Sports Came to Be*, by Don L. Wulffson, 1980; *The First Travel Guide to the Moon*, by Rhoda Blumberg, 1980; *How to Be School Smart: Secrets of Successful Schoolwork*, by Elizabeth James and Carol Barkin, 1988; *Balloons: Building & Experimenting with Inflatable Toys*, by Bernie Zubrowski, 1990; *Jobs for Kids*, by Elizabeth James and Carol Barkin, 1990; *Extraordinary Stories: Behind the Inventions of Ordinary Things*, by Don L.

Wulffson, 1991; *Making Waves: Finding Out About Rhythmic Motion*, by Bernie Zubrowski, 1994; *Listen to the Trees: Jews & the Earth*, by Molly Cone, 1995; *Shadow Play: Making Pictures with Light & Lenses*, by Bernie Zubrowski, 1995; *Soda Science: Designing & Testing Soft Drinks*, by Bernie Zubrowski, 1997.

SUGGESTED READING: *Contemporary Authors*, New Revision Series, vol. 8, 1983; *Something About the Author*, vol. 28, 1982.

WEB SITES: *www.themews.com/doty* and *www.reuben.org/doty*

Courtesy of Susan Walsh

Sharon M. Draper

August 21, 1948–

"Ever since I was a little girl, I have loved three things—reading, writing, and school. My mother read to me long before I could walk or talk and continued to do so long after I started school. I became a voracious reader, gobbling up books by the dozens each week at our local library. By the time I was eleven, I had read just about every single book on the children's side of the library and was given a special pass to check out adult books. By the time I finished high school, I had read most of those as well. So of course when I went to college, I majored in language, literature, and composition.

"At the time, I didn't know that the knowledge and ideas gained from all that reading would become the knowledge base for my writing years later. When I write now, the words gallop from my fingers, sometimes faster than my conscious thoughts, and always faster than my fingers can write or type. Writing is thrilling and exhilarating.

"When I wrote my first book, I sent it to 25 publishing companies and got 24 rejection notices in a row. But persistence is powerful, and *Tears of a Tiger*, which is now used in schools all over the country, was finally published. Later, *Forged by Fire*, its sequel, and the three books in the Ziggy and the Black Dinosaurs series were published. I wrote those books for students. I wanted to write books that young people could relate to, and could enjoy, and that their teachers could use to help them read and discuss. I receive letters from young people all over who say that my books have made a difference in their lives.

That's so very meaningful to me because I am teaching through my writing.

"I teach. That is what I do. That defines the essence of my existence. Whether through my writing, or through direct contact with my students in the classroom, I love to teach. I believe in creativity and spontaneity; in flexibility and enthusiasm; and my classroom is relaxed, refreshing, and rewarding for my students. I enjoy what I do, which encourages my students to enjoy themselves as well while they learn.

"When I was selected as the National Teacher of the Year, all of my dreams became a reality. To be honored and recognized as the representative for the three million teachers in this country is an awesome responsibility and a wonderful opportunity. I was privileged to travel all over the country speaking to students, educators, and learners about the magic of dreams and the power of education. I learned to dream through reading, learned to create dreams through writing, and learned to develop dreamers through teaching. I shall always be a dreamer."

✳ ✳ ✳

Sharon Draper is a teacher who has expanded her classroom to include thousands of students and teachers and parents all over the country by writing books that appeal to today's young readers. Combining over twenty-five years of teaching adolescents with her love of reading and writing, Draper crafts compelling stories about the challenges facing today's young people.

Draper was born in Ohio and has lived there all of her life. She earned her B.A. from Pepperdine University and her M.A. from Miami University in Oxford, Ohio. Draper has been teaching junior and senior high school since 1972 and has been honored many times for her outstanding teaching, culminating in her selection as the National Teacher of the Year in 1997. She has been an active member of many professional educational associations and has contributed to a variety of journals in the field.

Beginning with her first short story, "One Small Touch," in 1990, which won first prize in an *Ebony* magazine literary contest, Sharon Draper's work has been recognized for its excellence. Her first book, *Tears of a Tiger*, received the 1995 ALA/Coretta Scott King Genesis Award, was named an ALA Best Book for Young Adults, and was cited as a Notable Trade Book in the Field of Social Studies. In 1997, its sequel, *Forged by Fire*, won the Coretta Scott King Award and a Parents' Choice Award and was named an ALA Best Book for Young Adults. Both *Tears of a Tiger* and *Forged by Fire* were named to New York Public Library's Books for the Teen Age. In addition to her books for children and young adults, Sharon Draper also writes poetry and short stories for literary magazines.

SELECTED WORKS: *Tears of a Tiger*, 1994; *Ziggy and the Black Dinosaurs*, illus. by James Ransome, 1994; *Lost in the Tunnel of Time*, illus. by Michael Bryant, 1996; *Forged by Fire*, 1997; *Shadows of Caesar's Creek*, 1997; *Romiette and Julio*, 1999.

SUGGESTED READING: *Children's Literature Review*, vol. 57, 2000; *Something About the Author*, vol. 98, 1998. Periodicals—*Biography Today*, April 1999; Hendershot, Judy, "A Conversation with Sharon Draper," *Reading Teacher*, April 1999.

Courtesy of Bill Duffey

Betsy Duffey

February 6, 1953–

"I used to get in trouble in grade school—for reading. There was something irresistible about books to me; the things that happened in books always seemed more interesting than my real world of freeze tag and jump rope in Morgantown, West Virginia. My favorite books were biographies. Like most writers I know, I have always been interested in people. I like to try to figure out how people think and what they are going to do next. I love to hear how people talk and what they care about.

"I was quiet as a child. I have always liked to listen more than I like to talk. I think that's why I am a writer. If I pay enough attention and listen hard enough to a person, I begin to see beyond the words to the feelings and the truth.

"When I was young I didn't plan to be a writer. My mother, Betsy Byars, is a writer and I knew firsthand what that meant. You sat at a desk for hours and typed and typed and typed. It didn't seem very exciting. I wanted a job that did not take place in a bedroom, a job that required clothes like a business suit or a white lab coat.

"My mother's writing was a part of my childhood. I have early memories of watching my mother at the typewriter, of reading her manuscripts, of sharing the excitement when a book was accepted for publication, and of seeing her stories become books. She often asked me to critique a manuscript by placing an arrow in the margin pointing to the spot where I lost interest. I learned to edit at a young age.

"When it was time for me to choose a career I decided on medical technology. I loved science, and I got to wear that white lab coat. My favorite job title was given to me when my husband,

Bill, and I lived in Ankara, Turkey, and I worked at a Turkish hospital: Grand Supreme Supervisor and Expert Specialist. It was the pinnacle of my career as a scientist.

"When my children were born I stayed home to raise them and read to them. I began to get ideas for books of my own, and when those ideas came, I knew what to do. I sat at a desk for hours and typed and typed and typed, and I discovered it was exciting after all. Most of my ideas come from my own children and the things that they do. When Charles invented a food-fight catapult at Young Inventors Camp, I wrote *The Gadget War*. When we were housebreaking our dog, Chester, I wrote *A Boy in the Doghouse*. When we moved, I wrote *Hey, New Kid!*.

"When I create characters I usually start with their appearances. The physical features come from people I know. All the feelings of the character come from me. All of my characters are a little bit me. I have Cody's imagination, Lucky's optimism, Booker's love of words.

"When I was growing up in West Virginia, my family ate every meal together—breakfast, lunch, and dinner. What I remember most about those meals is laughter. There was no problem so big that we couldn't solve it around that table with love and humor. Most of the laughter came from the stories that we told each other. They usually started with phrases like: 'You won't believe what happened to me,' or 'That's nothing, I . . . .' Sharing stories helps people feel better about their own problems.

"I write only in the mornings when my kids are in school. In the afternoons I spend time with them, carpooling them to sports and church activities. My favorite thing to do in my spare time has not changed since I was a child—reading."

illustrated by Fiona Dunbar

Courtesy of BDD Books

*　*　*

Betsy Duffey was born on February 6, 1953, in Anderson, South Carolina, to Edward Ford and Betsy Byars, the well-known children's writer. She spent her childhood in Morgantown, West Virginia, in a house filled with books. She graduated from Clemson University with a B.S. in 1975 and married William Duffey, Jr., an attorney. During the first years of their marriage Betsy Duffey worked as a scientist, but after her children were born she stayed home to raise them.

In 1989 her older son, Charles, who had always loved books, completed the first grade and stopped reading. Duffey searched the library for the right book for him—but everything she found that might interest him was too hard for him to read. She decided to write a book for him. She knew what he wanted—"a book with the look of a novel, driven with action, but with a simple vocabulary and sentence style." As a volunteer at her son's school, she worked with a group that talked with kids about problems and how to solve them, and one of the children mentioned feeling sad because her classmates would never choose her to play on their soccer teams. Duffey, having experienced the same thing as a child, sat down to write *The Math Wiz*. Her children and her dog Chester have inspired other books. "After watching fifteen hours of Little League baseball practices a week one spring, I knew I had two choices—write a baseball book or lose my mind." *Lucky in Left Field* was the result. She finds her ideas everywhere, and things the Duffey family do together find their way into her books. Besides reading during those precious moments she has to herself, Betsy Duffey likes to work in her garden and to make quilts.

A Boy in the Doghouse was an ABA Pick of the Lists and a Junior Literary Guild selection. *Lucky in Left Field* received a Pick of the Lists citation, and *The Math Wiz* was a pick of the year for the Federation of Children's Book Groups. *How to Be Cool in Third Grade* won an IRA/CBC Parents' and Children's Choice Award in 1994.

SELECTED WORKS: *The Gadget War*, illus. by Janet Wilson, 1991; *A Boy in the Doghouse*, illus. by Leslie Morrill, 1991; *Lucky in Left Field*, illus. by Leslie Morrill, 1992; *The Math Wiz*, illus. by Janet Wilson, 1992; *How to be Cool in Third Grade*, illus. by Janet Wilson, 1993; *Coaster*, 1994; *Camp Knock, Knock*, illus. by Fiona Dunbar, 1996; *Hey, New Kid!*, illus by Ellen Thompson, 1996; *The Camp Knock, Knock Mystery*, illus. by Fiona Dunbar, 1997; *Utterly Yours, Booker Jones*, 1997; *Virtual Cody*, illus. by Ellen Thompson, 1997; *Cody's Secret Admirer*, illus. by Ellen Thompson, 1998; *Spotlight on Cody!*, illus. by Ellen Thompson, 1998; *Alien for Rent*, 1999; *Cody Unplugged*, illus. by Ellen Thompson, 1999.

SUGGESTED READING: *Something About the Author*, vol. 80, 1995.

"I was born in New York City and grew up there, the oldest of four children. Both my parents were and are great readers, and we children were always plentifully supplied with books. My introduction to the world of literature was a satisfying one from the start, for my parents seemed to enjoy reading to me as much as I enjoyed being read to. And no stories have made such an impression on me as those I was exposed to as a child. Doctor Dolittle was my first major hero; I yearned passionately to be able to talk to animals as he did. My next role models were Nancy Drew, whose lifestyle I still envy, and Harriet the Spy. Harriet's exploits prompted me, at age eleven, to start following pedestrians around my neighborhood, taking notes on their every 'suspicious' move. I think I owe Harriet my first conscious awareness of the act of writing as important and meaningful work. I'm sure if I could read my spy notes now, they'd look utterly bland, but at the time, writing them seemed thrilling.

Courtesy of Sidney Harris

Kate Duke

August 1, 1956–

"At about the same time that I began to think I might want to be a writer like Harriet, I also discovered I could draw. In fact, I recall the exact moment of revelation: in art class one day, the picture of a dog that I was copying from a how-to-draw book came out looking pretty much like a dog. No such thing had ever happened before! I remember being quite surprised by this new development, not to say stunned, and pleased.

"After I grew up, left school, and floundered around for a long while, I started taking art classes in New York, and after a few years produced the dummy that became my first published book. I never went to art school for a formal course of training, which I have sometimes regretted. However, things have turned out all right as it is. I live now with my husband, who's also self-employed, in a house large enough to allow us separate studio space. When deadlines are tight, I work every day from early morning to early afternoon. When my schedule allows it, I give myself weekends off to do assorted non-book projects, or, sometimes, to do nothing at all, which can be most refreshing.

"And since writing and illustrating are solitary pursuits, I try to make a point of getting out into the real world once a day, even if it's just to go buy a loaf of bread. A little human contact is important to keeping one's equilibrium. One of my great pleasures is visiting schools and talking to children about what I do.

These occasions are a chance to get in touch with my books' intended audience and to recharge my memories of what it was like to be a child. I don't have children of my own, so it's good to be able to interact with them once in awhile. I'm always cheered and inspired by their energy and imagination. Plus, they laugh at my jokes!"

*   *   *

Kate Duke made a promising debut as a children's book author-illustrator. Her first picture book, *The Guinea Pig ABC*, received critical acclaim with a *Boston Globe–Horn Book* Honor Book Award, a Parents' Choice Award, and an IRA/CBC Children's Choice Award. It was also a *Booklist* Editors' Choice and a Junior Library Guild selection. The guinea pigs returned in her second book, *Guinea Pigs Far and Near*, to explore and demonstrate spatial relations. This book was also chosen as a Junior Library Guild selection.

The rhyming text and colorful illustrations of *Seven Froggies Went to School* were recognized with another IRA/CBC Children's Choice Award and selection by the Junior Library Guild. A third IRA/CBC Children's Choice Award went to *It's Too Noisy!*, with text by Joanna Cole. *Aunt Isabel Tells a Good One*, in addition to being an IRA/CBC Children's Choice, was chosen as a Children's Book of the Year by the Bank Street Child Study Children's Book Committee. It was heard on the radio series *Mrs. Bush's Story Hour* and shown on the public television series *Kino's Storytime*.

> "One of my great pleasures is visiting schools and talking to children about what I do."

Four titles issued in the Guinea Pig Board Book series (*Bedtime*, *What Bounces?*, *Clean-up Day*, and *Playground*) were cited by *Publishers Weekly* as among the year's best, while another guinea pig story, *What Would a Guinea Pig Do?*, was an ABA Pick of the Lists. With a text by Barbara Baker, *One Saturday Morning* appeared on *School Library Journal*'s Best Books list, received a Parents' Choice Award, and was a Junior Library Guild selection.

A member of the Society of Children's Book Writers and Illustrators, PEN, and the Authors League of America, Duke lives in New Haven, Connecticut, with her husband, cartoonist Sidney Harris. When not busy creating books, she enjoys gardening, reading, and visiting schools to lecture and discuss her career as a writer and illustrator.

SELECTED WORKS WRITTEN AND ILLUSTRATED: *The Guinea Pig ABC*, 1983; *Guinea Pigs Far and Near*, 1984; *Seven Froggies Went to School*, 1985; *Bedtime*, 1986; *What Bounces?*, 1986; *The Playground*, 1986; *Clean-up Day*, 1986; *What Would a Guinea Pig Do?*, 1988; *Roseberry's Great Escape*, 1990; *Aunt Isabel Tells a Good One*, 1992; *If You Walk Down This Road*,

1993; *Aunt Isabel Makes Trouble*, 1996; *Archaeologists Dig for Clues*, 1996; *One Guinea Pig Is Not Enough*, 1998.

SELECTED WORKS ILLUSTRATED: *Tingalayo*, by Raffi, 1989; *It's Too Noisy!*, by Joanna Cole, 1989; *Don't Tell the Whole World*, by Joanna Cole, 1989; *Good News!*, by Barbara Brenner, 1991; *Let's Go Dinosaur Tracking!*, by Miriam Schlein, 1991; *Show-and-Tell Frog*, by Joanne Oppenheim, 1993; *One Saturday Morning*, by Barbara Baker, 1995; *Mr. Garbage*, by William H. Hooks, 1996; *Mr. Big Brother*, by William H. Hooks, 1999; *One Saturday Afternoon*, by Barbara Baker, 1999.

SUGGESTED READING: *Children's Literature Review*, vol. 51, 1999; *Something About the Author*, vol. 90, 1997.

"It is no surprise to me that I ended up as a children's book illustrator. My parents met in art school—my mother majoring in fashion design, my father in illustration. As the child of two artists, I have always been making things. As far back as I can remember we have been a family of 'makers.' When I was very young we made greeting cards and holiday presents. I graduated to sewing, as my mother taught me the pleasures of fabrics. In high school, I experimented with batik, silversmithing, felt, and fur puppets. I sold many of these creations at craft fairs to earn money. My father led me through silk-screening, building a boat, and making leather sandals. I also earned money using a hand printing press from the nineteenth century, setting type for tickets to school dances. That's a far cry from the laptop computer that I am using to write this essay.

"We worked on drawing, my father and I, through several summers of high school. Every day, up in his studio, from 9 to 12. I spent most of the time drawing *Vogue* magazine covers, until my father, out of frustration, made me draw a portrait of Bobby Orr, a popular Boston Bruins hockey player. I developed skill, but not a love of drawing. My father had six or seven years of training in art school; he seemed determined to teach it all to me on those hot summer mornings.

Courtesy of Rebecca Emberley

Rebecca Emberley

June 12, 1958–

"It must have been during this time period that I started making pictures with cut paper. I still have some of these exercises. Left over from trying to assemble a portfolio for art school, they are the roots of the artwork I do today for children's books. I took pleasure in the bright colors and the forgiving nature of the medium. With drawing I was often hesitant to begin, to commit that first stroke to paper. It would usually result in a lot of erasing. I took to drawing on tracing vellum, in part for the depth and smoothness of the cool grey paper, but mostly for the ease of erasure. With painting or markers it was worse. Once the first stroke was made, it could not be taken back. It glared up at me saying, 'a little to the left.' But using cut paper enabled the placement of the elements to be rearranged before making the final image! This knowledge allowed me to make swift, sure decisions, translating my visions in wild and abstract ways. Later in my career I would come to love the paper itself, the look and feel of it. Reminiscent of fabrics, it felt familiar—more like making something, as I had been doing all my life.

"Those early pictures prepared for my portfolio are all that remains of my quest for art school. I never went. I was too restless. I imagined becoming a fashion designer (oh, oh, a lot more drawing) and a graphic designer. In my late teens and early twenties, I worked for my father doing color separations on his series of drawing books. Often my brother and I also did the steps leading up to the finished drawing provided by my father. It was exacting, tedious work. I decided that if I could do this, I could do a book of my own, and that is how I became a children's book illustrator. At twenty-one, too young and stupid to think I couldn't do it, I just did it! That was *Drawing with Numbers and Letters*, a variation on my father's drawing books and the only book I have illustrated in line drawing.

"I didn't do another book for a long time. I had not taken into account the isolation that inevitably occurs when producing a book. I just wasn't ready for that. I went off to work in the restaurant business, which afforded me the social interaction I was missing, but left me without a focus to do art work. Six years later, when my daughter was born, I wanted to be at home with her, and I started doing color separations for my father again— perhaps the last book separated by hand, since this is now done by computers. A few months later we moved to Colorado, and I found some of my old collages when I unpacked. Inspired by my daughter's fascination with a painting by Rousseau entitled *The Dream*, which featured animals hidden in the jungle vegetation, I created two concept books called *Jungle Sounds* and *City Sounds*. I was thrilled at the ease with which I was able to create large, colorful pictures.

"I have never looked back. After seven concept books, I had an idea for a story book and I wrote *Three Cool Kids*. I find the writing much more difficult than the illustrating. Both of these

"As the child of two artists, I have always been making things. As far back as I can remember we have been a family of 'makers.'"

crafts require that you put yourself on the line each and every time, exposing a little piece of your soul. There are parts of me in all my work. Sometimes you can see them clearly and sometimes you have to look really hard, but they're there.

"I have always loved to read. I can still remember my first trip to the library. I was shocked that they would let me borrow all those great books! We spent many long summers on a sailboat, and reading sustained me. Through good times and bad, books are always there for me. I read to my daughter when she was young. I volunteered in the library of her elementary school. The best part of that job was story-time; I loved listening to the librarian read out loud. I read all kinds of books: fiction, nonfiction, mysteries, poetry, biographies. I take them on vacation and in the car. I take them to bed and into the bathtub. I just love books.

Courtesy of Little, Brown & Co.

"So, I am pretty sure that I am in the right place. I don't know if I will continue to illustrate picture books forever, but I will always be an artist and I will always have books in my life. I am currently working on a series of bilingual board books, and my next project may be something very different for older children."

*   *   *

Rebecca Emberley's parents, Ed and Barbara Emberley, are the author/illustrator team who created the Caldecott Award–winning *Drummer Hoff* in 1967; her father is also well known for his series of books about learning to draw. Her younger brother, Michael, is also a children's book illustrator, but Rebecca Emberley has found her own niche in this creative family and the children's book world with her bright and inventive cut-paper illustrations.

Well suited to concept books for the very young, this style of illustration works equally well in complementing a narrative story. In *Three Cool Kids*, an upbeat adaptation of the folktale "The Three Billy Goats Gruff," Emberley used materials of different textures to create visual variety and a three-dimensional effect—corrugated cardboard forms the horns of the goats, sinewy string suggests the whiskers of the rat, and a variety of colored papers brighten the background. Adapting her collage techniques to match each story, Emberley explores the effects they create. Her bilingual book *My House / Mi Casa* received a Parents' Choice Gold Award.

Rebecca Emberley lives with her husband and daughter in Newburyport, Massachusetts.

SELECTED WORKS: *Drawing with Numbers and Letters*, with Ed Emberley, 1981; *Jungle Sounds*, 1989; *City Sounds*, 1989; *Taking a Walk / Caminando*, 1990; *Rebecca Emberley's Cut-Ups*, 1992; *Let's Go: A Book in Two Languages / Vamos: Un Libro en Dos Lenguas*, 1993; *My Day: A Book in Two Languages / Mi Dia: Un Libro en Dos Lenguas*, 1993; *My House: A Book in Two Languages / Mi Casa: Un Libro en Dos Lenguas*, 1993; *Three Cool Kids*, 1995; *My Mother's Secret Life*, 1998; *Three: An Emberley Family Scrapbook*, with Ed and Michael Emberley, 1998; *My Colors / Mis Colores*, 2000; *My Numbers / Mis Numeros*, 2000; *My Opposites / Mis Opuestos*, 2000; *My Shapes / Mis Formas*, 2000.

Barbara Juster Esbensen

April 28, 1925–
October 25, 1996

B arbara Juster Esbensen was a versatile and accomplished author of books of poetry, books about animals, and folktales for children. Born in Madison, Wisconsin, she graduated from the University of Wisconsin in 1947. Although she trained in art, Esbensen knew that she also wanted to be a writer from the time she was fourteen. That was the year she presented an appreciative English teacher with a poem she had written in response to the Russian invasion of Finland.

Esbensen taught art and creative writing for many years before her first book of poetry, *Swing Around the Sun*, was published in 1965. Then for a time she devoted herself to raising her six children, her second collection of poems not appearing until 1984. After that, many books followed.

She became well known for her poetry and was the tenth recipient of the National Council of Teachers of English Award for Excellence in Poetry for Children in 1994, an award that recognizes the body of a poet's work. She received the 1996 Lee Bennett Hopkins Poetry Award for *Dance with Me*, and NCTE's Teachers' Choice Award for *Words with Wrinkled Knees: Animal Poems* in 1987. *Who Shrank My Grandmother's House?* was an ALA Notable Children's Book and an NCTE Notable Trade Book in the Language Arts.

Barbara Esbensen brought her poet's eye to many other projects, including a series of informational books about animals, such as *Great Northern Diver: The Loon* and *Playful Slider: The North American River Otter*, which was named an Outstanding Science Trade Book for Children. Her book on the great horned owl, *Tiger with Wings*, was cited as an ALA Notable Children's Book. She also adapted folklore for children. Her version of an Ojibway tale, *The Star Maiden*, won an NCTE Teachers' Choice Award in 1988 and was named a finalist for the Minnesota Book award. *Ladder to the Sky: How the Gift of Healing Came to the Ojibway Nation* was selected as a Notable Trade Book in the Field of Social Studies. Esbensen's last book of poetry, *Echoes for the Eye: Poems to Celebrate Patterns in Nature*, received the Elizabeth Burr Award for Best 1996 Children's Book published by a native of Wisconsin and was named an Outstanding Science Trade Book for Children, an IRA/CBC Teachers' Choice, and an NCTE Notable Children's Book in the Language Arts.

Courtesy of HarperCollins Publishers

In addition to her own books of poetry, Esbensen had poems included in anthologies by such distinguished compilers as Myra Cohn Livingston (*Valentine Poems, Halloween Poems, Thanksgiving Poems*, and *Poems for Jewish Holidays*), Caroline Feller Bauer (*Windy Day: Stories and Poems*), and Bobbye S. Goldstein (*Bear in Mind*). Esbensen enjoyed writing and traveling, making author appearances before audiences of writers and children alike.

Always warm and enthusiastic, Esbensen was devoted to encouraging a new generation of poets, in the same way as her beloved English teacher inspired her so long ago. Through her books of poetry, nature, and legend, and her volume for teachers, *A Celebration of Bees: Helping Children Write Poetry*, she was able to do just that. Barbara Juster Esbensen died in 1996 at the age of seventy-one.

SELECTED WORKS: *Swing Around the Sun*, 1965; *Cold Stars and Fireflies*, illus. by Susan Bonners, 1984; *Words with Wrinkled Knees: Animal Poems*, illus. by John Stadler, 1986; *The Star Maiden: An Ojibway Tale*, illus. by Helen K. Davie, 1988; *Ladder to the Sky: How the Gift of Healing Came to the*

Ojibway Nation, illus. by Helen K. Davie, 1989; *Great Northern Diver: The Loon*, illus. by Mary Barrett Brown, 1990; *Tiger with Wings: The Great Horned Owl*, illus. by Mary Barrett Brown, 1991; *Who Shrank My Grandmother's House?*, illus. by Eric Beddows, 1992; *Playful Slider: The North American River Otter*, illus. by Mary Barrett Brown, 1993; *Sponges Are Skeletons*, illus. by Holly Keller, 1993; *The Dream Mouse*, illus. by Judith Mitchell, 1994; *The Great Buffalo Race: How the Buffalo Got Its Hump: A Seneca Tale*, illus. by Helen K. Davie, 1994; *Baby Whales Drink Milk*, illus. by Lambert Davis, 1994; *Dance with Me*, illus. by Megan Lloyd, 1995; *The Dream Mouse: A Lullaby Tale from Old Latvia*, illus. by Judith Mitchell, 1995; *Echoes for the Eye: Poems to Celebrate Patterns in Nature*, illus. by Helen K. Davie, 1996; *A Celebration of Bees: Helping Children Write Poetry*, 1996 (reissue); *Swift as the Wind: The Cheetah*, illus. by Jean Cassells, 1996; *Jumping Day*, illus. by Maryann Cocca-Leffler, 1999.

SUGGESTED READING: *Contemporary Authors*, vol. 134, 1992; *Something About the Author*, vol. 53, 1988; vol. 62, 1990; vol. 97, 1998. Periodicals—Greenlaw, M. J., "Profile: Barbara Esbensen," *Language Arts*, November 1994; Rasmussen, J. B., "Author Profile: Barbara Juster Esbensen," *Reading Teacher*, November 1994; *Saint Paul Pioneer Press*, October 28, 1996 (obituary).

Margery Facklam

September 6, 1927–

"When I was very young, I never thought of being a writer, although one summer I did write neighborhood news for the 'Junior Journal,' which my brother sold for two cents a copy. My mother and my aunts were avid readers, and one of the things I remember best was taking the trolley car downtown with them on Saturday to get a week's worth of books at the big stone library, which had turrets that made it seem like a castle.

"I was born in Buffalo, New York, and grew up in a suburb called Eggertsville, surrounded by open fields where we played and found all sorts of animals. I was the kind of kid who loved science and kept a snake in the bedroom I shared with my sister. (Unfortunately, she didn't like snakes.) My brother had rescued an injured opossum he called Luis, and a crow named Joey, and a skunk, who was there too short a time to have a name. But we always had a few turtles or salamanders or crayfish.

"From the time I was seven or eight until I was fourteen, I spent almost every Saturday at the Buffalo Museum of Science, where I belonged to clubs and took classes. My favorite class on reptiles led to a summer job in the reptile house at the Buffalo Zoo when I was in high school. The zoo's director was Marlin Perkins, who later started the first wildlife TV program, *Wild*

Kingdom. When Mr. Perkins heard that the theme of our high school water follies was the circus, he loaned me a beautiful six-foot indigo snake to use in my part as a snake charmer. I did not charm my teacher, who had assumed I was going to use a fake snake.

"I loved to read about explorers, especially Roy Chapman Andrews, who discovered the first dinosaur eggs in Mongolia's Gobi desert in 1923, and I longed to become an explorer too. But I went to the University of Buffalo, where I earned my tuition by taking care of a colony of porcupines and other animals for the biology department. Soon after I received my bachelor's degree in biology, I married Howard Facklam, and we raised a family—four sons and one daughter. During those years, I began to write as a hobby and surprised myself by selling my first book, *Whistle for Danger.* It was the story of two kids who worked in a zoo reptile house. I didn't know it at the time, but I had followed the rule to 'write what you know.' Now I realize that the rule really is, 'write about things that fascinate you, because you can always find out what you don't know.'

Courtesy of Lawrence Photography

"When our oldest son began to look at colleges, I took a 'real' job at the Buffalo Museum of Science, but I continued to write part-time. Later I worked at the Aquarium of Niagara Falls and then at the Buffalo Zoo. Each of these places gave me new things to write about. I wrote *Frozen Snakes and Dinosaur Bones* to show children the most exciting parts of a museum, which they don't see on tours—the labs and workrooms where exhibits are built. I wrote *Wild Animals, Gentle Women* after a teacher asked me to talk to her class about women scientists. There were so many women to choose from that I finally focused on women who studied animals, such as Dian Fossey, Jane Goodall, Eugenie Clark, and others.

"I have written fiction but I really love nonfiction, although I wish there was a better word for a true story. Digging up the facts is fun. The hardest part is weaving a good story from the facts. Revising is like laying cement. When cement is poured, it's a lumpy mess until someone smoothes it to a fine finish. There's nothing more satisfying to a writer than smoothing out lumpy sentences.

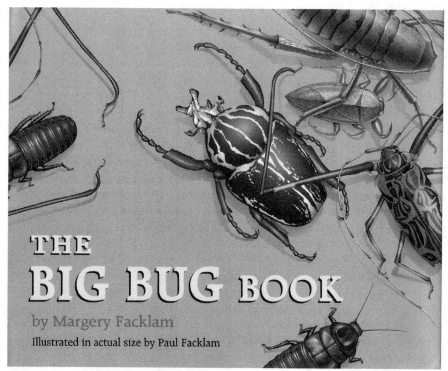

Courtesy of Little, Brown & Co.

"Nonfiction writing has allowed me to become an armchair explorer with an occasional adventure. Researching one book gave me a berth on a research ship around the Galapagos Islands, and material for another book. But my biggest adventure was following the trail of Roy Chapman Andrews to the Flaming Cliffs of the Gobi Desert, where the first dinosaur eggs were discovered, and then writing about my favorite explorer in *Tracking Dinosaurs in the Gobi*. I wouldn't trade writing for anyone's job."

* * *

Margery Facklam's fascination with the animal kingdom and her spirit of adventure (she once ate insect treats at a museum reception), combined with a background in science education, make her a writer whose books stimulate appreciation of the natural world. Facklam received her B.A. from the University of Buffalo in 1947 and her M.S. from the State University of New York at Buffalo in 1976. In addition to teaching and working as an educator at museums and zoos, she has been an instructor at the Institute of Children's Literature (Redding Ridge, Conn.) and at the Vassar Summer Institute of Publishing (Poughkeepsie, N.Y.); a staff member at the Highlights Institute in Chautauqua, New York; and a teacher at the Cape Cod Writers' Workshop in Massachusetts.

Writing informative and captivating science books for children is often a family effort for the Facklams. With her husband, Howard, Margery wrote *Spare Parts for People* and a number of books for the Invader and Nature's Disasters series. Their son Paul has illustrated several of her books, and in 1992 Facklam and her daughter, Margaret Thomas, co-wrote *The Kids' World Almanac of Amazing Facts About Numbers, Math and Money*.

The excellence of Facklam's work has been widely recognized. Over the years, many of her books have been named Outstanding Science Trade Books for Children. Her novel for young adults, *The Trouble with Mothers*, was chosen as a Recommended Book for Reluctant Young Adult Readers in 1990. *Spare Parts for People* and *The Kids' World Almanac of Amazing Facts . . .* were cited by the New York Public Library as Best Books for the Teen Age; *And Then There Was One* and *What Does the Crow Know* were included in *School Library Journal*'s Best Books of the Year. *The Big Bug Book* was named an ALA Children's Notable Book in 1995 and won New Jersey's Garden State Children's Choice Award for nonfiction in 1997. An award Margery Facklam is especially proud of is the one she received in 1998: the Eva L. Gordon Award, given by the American Nature Study Society to an author of science books for children "whose work is of the highest standards in readability, accuracy, joyousness, and understanding of interrelationships while encouraging children to make their own scientific observations."

SELECTED WORKS: *Whistle for Danger*, 1962; *Behind These Doors: Science Museum Makers*, 1968; *Wild Animals, Gentle Women*, 1978; *Changes in the Wind: Earth's Shifting Climate*, with Howard Facklam, illus. by Paul Facklam, 1986; *Spare Parts for People*, with Howard Facklam, illus. by Paul Facklam, 1987; *Do Not Disturb: The Mysteries of Hibernation and Sleep*, illus. by Pamela Johnson, 1989; *The Trouble with Mothers*, 1989; *And Then There Was One: The Mysteries of Animal Extinction*, illus. by Pamela Johnson, 1990; *Bees Dance and Whales Sing: The Mysteries of Animal Communication*, illus. by Pamela Johnson, 1992; *The Kids' World Almanac of Amazing Facts about Numbers, Math and Money*, with Margaret Thomas, 1992; *What Does the Crow Know? The Mysteries of Animal Intelligence*, illus. by Pamela Johnson, 1993; *The Big Bug Book*, illus. by Paul Facklam, 1994; *Creepy Crawly Caterpillars*, illus. by Paul Facklam, 1996; *Only a Star*, illus. by Nancy Carpenter, 1996; *Bugs for Lunch*, illus. by Sylvia Long, 1999.

SUGGESTED READING: *Contemporary Authors*, New Revision Series, vol. 48, 1995; *Something About the Author*, vol. 20, 1980; vol. 85, 1996.

Courtesy of Tom Feelings

Tom Feelings

May 19, 1933–

"I was born and raised in the Bedford-Stuyvesant section of Brooklyn, New York. Since childhood I have been interested in drawing and painting.

"I attended the George Westinghouse Vocational High School, where I majored in art, and received upon graduation a scholarship to the School of Visual Arts, which I attended for two years before entering the U.S. Air Force in 1953.

"I was stationed in London, England, where I worked those four years in the Graphics Division as staff illustrator. I returned to the United States in 1957 and resumed studies at the School of Visual Arts.

"In 1958 I created a comic strip series, 'Tommy Traveler in the World of Negro History', which I wrote and illustrated for the (now defunct) *New York Age* until 1959. I created this series out of an old desire I had as a child to know more about the history of my people. It was reissued in 1991 as *Tommy Traveler in the World of Black History*.

"From 1959 to 1964 I worked as a freelance artist. My first subjects were the Black people of my community, whom I drew on the streets, in homes, bars, poolrooms—anywhere I found them. My first published works drawn from life appeared in the *Liberator*, a Black monthly magazine, where my work received wide exposure in the Black community; also in *Freedomways*, a Black quarterly. I also received some exposure through the magazines *Look*, *Harper's*, and *Pageant*. I was one of the illustrators for the Negro Heritage Library, its volumes *Profiles of Negro Womanhood* and *Reader for Young People*.

"My field of graphic concentration has been the Black peoples of the world, a subject that I feel deserves much fuller illustrative exploration than the neglect it has received. In September 1961 I went to the South, where I drew the people of the Black rural communities of New Orleans. Some of the drawings were used in *Look* magazine's feature article, 'The Negro in the U.S.,' and the *Reporter*'s depiction of 'Images of the South.'

"In 1964 I left the United States for West Africa, stopping in Dakar, Senegal, for one month. There I put on a one-man show of works done of the Black people of New York, the South, and of Senegal. I then went on to Ghana, where I worked for two years for the Ghana Government Publishing House, illustrating the *African Review*, a monthly magazine, and local newspapers. My life in Ghana was one of the most meaningful and rewarding experiences of my life: feeling the warmth and pride of the people, and seeing real Black power—living in a country where every facet of the nation's operations is manned by Black people. The children I drew had the faces I had seen here, except that the Ghanaian children reflected a glow of happiness and security I had for so long wanted to see in the Black children I drew in America.

"I returned to the United States in 1966 to find that the Black community all over the country was far more enlightened and demanding of change; among those changes was a demand for more representational literature and images of themselves. Because of the demands, the various heads of media, including the publishing world, were pressed to produce more literature of relevance to the Black public.

"As I stated earlier, it had always been my desire that Black children see images of themselves in books which were positive and honest, so I embarked on the field of children's book illustration. The books for children which I have illustrated since 1966 deal with African culture and African-American themes. They are the books I wanted to have when I was a child, and could never find.

"In 1972 I went to Guyana, a former British colony in South America, to head the Guyanese Ministry of Education's newly created children's book project and to train young illustrators. Since returning to the United States in 1974, I have applied myself to paintings and illustrations that will appeal to Black people across the generations. I was strongly affected many years ago by a conversation I had with an eight-year-old girl. I tried to explain to her that my drawings were of 'pretty little Black children, like you.' The girl replied, 'Ain't nothin' Black pretty.' I have dedicated my career to showing that child and people like her that there is tremendous beauty in Black people and power in Black experience."

"My life in Ghana was one of the most meaningful and rewarding experiences of my life: feeling the warmth and pride of the people, and seeing real Black power—living in a country where every facet of the nation's operations is manned by Black people."

*   *   *

Tom Feelings's artistic talents were developed at an early age. Growing up in Brooklyn, he was encouraged by an art teacher at the Wynn Center to draw from the life around him, and throughout his distinguished career he has focused on the African-American experience and its roots in African culture. In 1996 he received an honorary doctorate degree from the School of Visual Arts in New York City in recognition of his illustrious career.

The two years Tom Feelings spent in Ghana had a profound influence on his art. In the early 1960s, at the start of his career, the civil rights movement was stirring the consciousness of the American nation, and the young artist began to feel overwhelmed by the sorrow, anger, and pain of the struggle. His decision to go to Africa, to a country that was in the forefront of the fight for African independence, was based on a desire to find the roots of joy in Black experience and to heighten his own sense of identity. The result was growth and change in his art, that included rhythmic lines of motion, a brightness in his black-and-white work, and colors that were more vivid and alive.

His first wide recognition in children's books came when he illustrated *To Be a Slave* by Julius Lester, named a Newbery Honor Book in 1969 and winner of a Lewis Carroll Shelf Award in 1970. In this intense work, Feelings brought that luminous quality his art had gained in Ghana to bear upon a somber era in American history. In 1972 he became the first African-American artist to win a Caldecott Honor Award with his illustrations for *Moja Means One*, a counting book written by his wife, Muriel. This groundbreaking picture book explained the numbers in Swahili, the language spoken by millions of people in East Africa, and introduced American children to the rich cultural features of African life. The artwork for a companion volume, *Jambo Means Hello*, won a second Caldecott Honor in 1975, as well as capturing the 1974 *Boston Globe–Horn Book* Award for illustration.

In the 1980s Tom Feelings continued to expand on the themes he had developed in his early books. His autobiographical book, *Black Pilgrimage*, made his mission clear to young readers and chronicled his sojourn in Africa. He received the Coretta Scott King Award for the art in *Something on My Mind*, a book of poems by Nikki Grimes, and a Coretta Scott King Honor Award for his illustrations for *Daydreamers*, by Eloise Greenfield. Both books were also ALA Notable Children's Books. In *Daydreamers*, Feelings made a conscious effort to appeal to adult readers as well as children, aiming for a multigenerational readership. This appeal to all ages was even more pronounced in *Soul Looks Back in Wonder*, with flowing, full-color paintings illustrating the writings of great poets, including Maya Angelou, Margaret Walker, and Langston Hughes. This vibrant collection received the Coretta Scott King Award for illustration in 1994.

In 1995 Tom Feelings published his most ambitious work, *The Middle Passage: White Ships/Black Cargo*, which won the Coretta Scott King Award for illustration and was an ALA Notable Children's Book. A masterpiece nearly twenty years in the making, the book opens with an account by Feelings of his own search for his African roots. In the words of Paule Marshall, he termed this search a "psychological and spiritual journey" into the past in order to "shape a future that reflects you." An intro-

TOM FEELINGS
SOUL LOOKS BACK
IN WONDER

Courtesy of Dial Books

ductory overview of the four centuries of the slave trade by the eminent historian Dr. John Henrik Clarke creates a context for the remarkable paintings that make up the body of the book—sixty-four pages of wordless narrative depicting the journey of slave ships from Africa to the Caribbean and North America. Illustrated in Feelings's trademark style of understated tones ranging from cream to charcoal to black, the book shows the terror and horror of the slave trade in graphic detail. Into this powerful visual journey Feelings put all the emotion of a people torn from their homeland and the sorrow of their unrealized dreams in the present. He has stated that he intended this work to be not depressing but uplifting, inspiring pride in a people who could endure such hardships and survive triumphantly.

In 1989 Tom Feelings moved to Columbia, South Carolina, to teach book illustration at the University of South Carolina. He has two children, Zamani and Kamili, from his marriage to Muriel Feelings, which ended in divorce in 1974. In 1992 he married Diane Johnson, and their daughter Niani was born in 1994. Feelings retired from teaching at the university in 1995.

SELECTED WORKS WRITTEN AND ILLUSTRATED: *Black Pilgrimage*, 1972; *Tommy Traveler in the World of Black History*, 1991; *The Middle Passage: White Ships/Black Cargo*, 1995.

SELECTED WORKS ILLUSTRATED: *Bola and the Oba's Drummers*, by Letta Schatz, 1967; *When the Stones Were Soft: East African Fireside Tales*, by Eleanor Heady, 1968; *To Be a Slave*, ed. by Julius Lester, 1968; *Song of the Empty Bottles*, by Osmond Molarsky, 1968; *Tuesday Elephant*, by Nancy Garfield, 1968; *Tales of Temba: Traditional African Stories*, by Kathleen Arnot, 1969; *Black Folktales*, by Julius Lester, 1969; *A Quiet Place*, by Rose Blue, 1969; *African Crafts*, by Jane Kerina, 1970; *Zamani Goes to Market*, by Muriel Feelings, 1970; *Moja Means One: A Swahili Counting Book*, by Muriel Feelings, 1971; *Jambo Means Hello: A Swahili Alphabet Book*, by Muriel Feelings, 1974; *Something on My Mind*, by Nikki Grimes, 1978; *Daydreamers*, by Eloise Greenfield, 1981; *Black Child*, by Joyce Carol Thomas, 1981; *Now Sheba Sings the Song*, by Maya Angelou, 1987; *Soul Looks Back in Wonder*, by various poets, 1993.

SUGGESTED READING: *Black Writers*, vol. 1, 1989; *Children's Literature Review*, vol. 5, 1983; vol. 58, 2000; Collier, Laurie, and Joyce Nakamura, eds. *Major Authors and Illustrators for Children and Young Adults*, 1993; *Contemporary Authors*, New Revision Series, vol. 25, 1988; Cummings, Pat, ed. *Talking with Artists*, 1992; Harrison, Barbara, and Gregory Maguire, eds. *Origins of Story: On Writing for Children*, 1999; Hopkins, Lee Bennett, ed. *Books Are by People*, 1969; Silvey, Anita, ed. *Children's Books and Their Creators*, 1995; *Something About the Author*, vol. 8, 1976; vol. 69, 1992; *Something About the Author Autobiography Series*, vol. 19, 1995. Periodicals—Bishop, Rudine Sims, "Tom Feelings and the Middle Passage," *The Horn Book*, July/August 1996; Feelings, Tom, "The Artist at Work," *The Horn Book*, November/December 1985; Ingalls, Zoe, "Images of Slavery," *Chronicle of Higher Education*, February 16, 1996; Steele, Vincent, "Tom Feelings: A Black Arts Movement," *African American Review*, Spring 1998.

An earlier profile of Tom Feelings appeared in *Third Book of Junior Authors* (Wilson, 1963).

Carol Fenner

September 30, 1929–

"Reading was as natural as eating in our house. My mother is the only person I ever knew who laughed out loud (and nearly fell off the bed) reading one of Shakespeare's comedies. 'It was probably *As You Like It*,' she said when I recently asked which play. 'That's the funniest.' My father had a chair he read in every evening. Books were reward and respite as well as entertainment. They connected us to the world. My mother read to us, in a voice filled with mystery, Mother Goose rhymes, the poetry of Milne, Eugene Field, and from *A Child's Garden of Verses*. My father read us *Sherlock Holmes*. One evening, getting ready for bed, my sister, Faith, asked him if he was going to read us some more of 'The Hound of the Basketballs.'

"Long before I went to school, I decided I would be a poet. I remember sitting in a vast field of grass and sun and dandelions and being filled with such an excess of pleasure and happiness that I couldn't contain it. I needed to say something. Name something. Words came into my mind. I said them over and over to myself. I was four or five and couldn't write yet. I ran to my mother with a poem dancing in my head. She wrote it down, careful to keep every word. After that, my mother wrote down all my gems until I learned to write them down myself. She says I would come in from playing and tell her, 'I feel a poem coming on.'

"I have a happy memory of my father from about this time. My sister and I are being pulled in a wagon by our father. The lawn is bumpy and the wagon leaps and lurches. My father runs. We shriek and giggle with excitement and plea-sure. My father sings out: 'Rumbly, tum-bly! Tangerino! Beanerino!' We squeal the words out after him. The tiger song from my first book, *Tigers in the Cellar*, called on this memory:

> Rumbly tumbly,
>   pull my toes.
> Rumbly tumbly,
>   rub my nose.
> Cobwebs on
>   the currant jelly.
> Scratch my ears
>   and tickle my belly.

Courtesy of Jiles B. Williams

"We had a magic aunt, my father's sister. Phyllis Fenner was a librarian and a well-known anthologist of short stories for children. She wrote two highly ac-claimed books about reading: *Proof of the Pudding* and *Our Library*, and she reviewed books for the *New York Times*. Phyllis sent many books for birthdays and Christmas and 'just for fun.' Whenever Phyl visited us, she would tell us unforgettable fairy tales drenched with her own excitement and pleasure. The joy in cadence and word shape, the way words color each other, was a gift from both my Aunt Phyl and my mother. I love the way words rub up against each other, clash and support and change each other. I love the shapes they make on the page and in my mind. I love reading aloud.

"When I was twenty, I moved to New York City to seek my fortune. I thought I would study art but became enthralled with the theater. I studied acting and anything related to it—voice and speech, fencing and dance. I performed in off-Broadway plays and in summer stock, did a little television. I wrote lengthy biographies for all of the characters I played, exploring their persona. And all the time I read—working my way through a lot of English, Spanish, German, French, and Russian classics—prose and poetry, plays, too, since the theater had seized me.

"My aunt Phyllis worried that I was off track, that I would be a jack of all trades. I have never regretted those years with the theater or any of the side roads I explored so eagerly. All I learned along the way has given me greater insight and control in my writing than had I stayed in the well-tended old gardens."

Courtesy of Simon & Schuster Children's Publishing Division

* * *

Born in Hornell, New York, Carol Fenner spent her childhood years in Almond, N.Y., but also lived in Shelton, Connecticut, and Brooklyn, N.Y., before returning to Almond, where she graduated from high school. After moving to New York City, she studied acting at the Herbert Berghof School of Drama and Curt Conway's Acting School, and modern dance at the New Dance Group and Irving Burton School. During her early entertainment career, she performed with the New Century Dancers and played small television roles in such series as *The Defenders* and *Naked City*. She later worked for *McCall's* magazine and, later still, served as the assistant to the director of public relations for the Girl Scouts of the USA.

Fenner's first published work, *Tigers in the Cellar*, was an ALA Notable Children's Book. *Gorilla, Gorilla* was also an ALA Notable Children's Book and a Library of Congress Book of the Year in addition to receiving both a Christopher Award for nonfiction and an Outstanding Science Trade Book for Children citation from the National Science Teachers Association. *The Skates of Uncle Richard* was a runner-up for the Coretta Scott King Freedom Award and was adapted for a television movie. *Randall's Wall* was named to master lists for readers' choice awards in ten states and won the Maryland Children's Choice Book Award.

Yolonda's Genius, the inventive story of a girl who is convinced her brother is a musical prodigy, received a Newbery Honor Book award and was named an ALA Notable Children's Book. It was also cited in the New York Public Library's 100 Titles for Reading and Sharing and in *Book Links* magazine's A Few Good Books. *The King of Dragons*, a poignant story about a boy living in an abandoned town hall, won the Paterson Prize for Books for Young People and was named a Notable Trade Book in the Field of Social Studies as well as a Notable Children's Book in the Language Arts.

Married in 1965 to Jiles B. Williams, a U.S. Air Force career officer, Fenner traveled extensively with her husband throughout the Far East and lived for two years in the Philippines. Since 1968 the couple has resided in Battle Creek, Michigan. Some of their interests, which include horseback riding, tennis, dancing, and listening to live jazz and blues, have been incorporated into Fenner's novels.

SELECTED WORKS WRITTEN: *Gorilla, Gorilla*, 1973; *The Skates of Uncle Richard*, 1978; *A Summer of Horses*, 1989; *Randall's Wall*, 1991; *Yolonda's Genius*, 1995; *The King of Dragons*, 1998.

SELECTED WORKS WRITTEN AND ILLUSTRATED: *Tigers in the Cellar*, 1963; *Christmas Tree on the Mountain*, 1966; *Lagalag, the Wanderer*, 1968.

SUGGESTED READING: *Contemporary Authors*, New Revision Series, vol. 57, 1997; *Something About the Author*, vol. 89, 1997; *Something About the Author Autobiography Series*, vol. 24, 1997.

E-MAIL: *fenwms@iserv.net*

"I was given the gift of life on June 24, 1924. My art career began two years later when I tried to improve a watercolor my father was creating. Three years after that I drew a faithful portrait of a willing uncle. No one seemed too suprised at the time, least of all my father. He was a marine and civil engineer—the greatest engineering draftsman that ever lived—who would have preferred to have been gifted as an artist rather than as a designer of ships. He could also recite most of *Caesar's Gallic Wars* and *The Rime of the Ancient Mariner* from memory just to remind us all that he had a taste for literature and meaningful history. My mother filled in the gaps by readings from *Aesop's Fables*, *A Child's Garden of Verses*, and, over a two-year period, nearly every article in *Compton's Picture Encyclopedia* in alphabetic order, usually at bedtime, or on rainy days in my front hall closet 'studio.' In any event, my father created for me a looseleaf 'how to draw this and that' book. By the time I was ready for

Leonard Everett Fisher

June 24, 1924–

more formal schooling I already knew simple perspective, human figure proportions, what asteroids were, all about howler monkeys, and how to draw rowboats. When I was seven I won my first award in the Wanamaker Art Competition for New York City School Children. I had submitted a picture of a Pilgrim shooting a turkey. The following year I was enrolled in the art classes of the Heckscher Foundation and began the long, hard process of more dispassionate instruction.

"My apprenticeship continued through a variety of schools and artists until 1942, when I enlisted in the United States Army. I went to war and came out alive in 1946. This was my second gift of life, and I made the most of it at Yale University's School of Art, where I became an educated craftsman. Shortly thereafter, I was sent to Europe as a Winchester Fellow and Pulitzer Scholar. I had spent the first twenty-six years of my life preparing for that trip. I remained spellbound through it all. I knew what I had seen as no pleasure-bent tourist could imagine and as no casually trained artist or amateur could understand. It was a humbling artistic experience.

Courtesy of Leonard Everett Fisher

"I needed a new perspective and reassurance. I experimented for a while and then, in 1951, I took a job as an assistant to a muralist. My credentials were two murals painted during the war and Yale's long reputation for graduating wall painters. However, I quit at the end of the first week to accept an appointment as dean of the Whitney School of Art in New Haven. Several months later I found Margery Meskin. This was my third gift of life. We were married in December 1952. Meanwhile, I had had a one-man show in Manhattan and my paintings were beginning to turn up in various exhibitions. But by the time Julie, Susan, and James were born I had left the school, put aside my paintbrush, and turned to the illustration of children's books. It seemed the natural way of celebrating their arrival. Now, some forty-four years and six grandchildren later, I still think it was the natural thing to do.

"Since 1955 I have illustrated books of all types; I even added a new dimension when I began to write in 1960. This diversification is a reflection of my interest in everything that goes on in this world. I continue to paint, illustrate, and write with ever-increasing zest. But more important, the images that I produce—whether they be paintings, illustrations, or designs for

United States postage stamps (there have been ten)—all stem from my creative passions. And if my images seem uncompromising and nondecorative, it is because of my own belief in the indomitable human spirit. I try to move my audiences toward this conviction with honest rendering and simple arrangements rather than with complicated, vacant designs."

* * *

Leonard Everett Fisher's illustrated books for young readers number over 260, about 80 of them also written by him. His paintings and illustrations have been included in numerous exhibitions, in a career spanning more than fifty years, and his books are known throughout the world. Born in the Bronx and raised in Brooklyn, he began his formal art training at the age of eight in Manhattan. During the Second World War, Fisher served as a topographer in the tactical mapping of major invasions and campaigns in both Europe and the Pacific. After the war he enrolled in the Yale Art School, receiving his B.F.A. in 1949 and M.F.A. in 1950. He was a graduate teaching fellow and won a Pulitzer painting scholarship.

Fisher's book illustration career began in 1955 with *The Exploits of Xenophon* and soon encompassed fiction, nonfiction, book jackets, and textbooks. In 1961 he published the first book that he had both written and illustrated, a book about fire engines, and in 1962 his first picture book story appeared—*A Head Full of Hats*. Ten years later he began writing fiction for teenagers with *The Death of Evening Star*, a powerfully evocative story of whaling days.

Throughout his career Fisher's books have been recognized for their excellence and have often appeared on lists of recommended titles. His first major critical success was *Casey at the Bat*, named one of the ten best-illustrated children's books of the year in 1964 by the *New York Times Book Review*. Three of his pictures originally created for children's books were incorporated into a mural for the Washington Monument. The Fifth International Book Fair in Bologna, Italy, awarded him its Graphics Prize for Juvenile Books in 1968. *A Russian Farewell*, about the immigration of a family from the Ukraine to the United States in the early days of the twentieth century, won the National Jewish Book Award for Children's Literature in 1981. Fisher won a Christopher Medal in illustration in 1980 for *All Times, All Peoples* by Milton Meltzer. He received the 1979 University of Southern Mississippi Medallion, the 1981 Regina Medal from the Catholic Library Association, and the Kerlan Award from the University of Minnesota in 1991, all for the body of his work. In 1995 he was selected as Arbuthnot Lecturer by the American Library Association.

"If my images seem uncompromising and non-decorative, it is because of my own belief in the indomitable human spirit."

While Fisher has illustrated and written books in a wide variety of genres and styles, his greatest contributions to children's literature have been his illustrated nonfiction books in the fields of history and mythology. The Colonial Craftsmen series, which he wrote and illustrated between 1964 and 1976, expresses his respect for early American craftsmen and describes the painstaking techniques of tradesmen and artisans of the Colonial era. The series is widely used in classrooms and is currently being reissued. A series about nineteenth-century America, starting with *The Factories* in 1979, examines institutions of that era in remarkable detail. Fisher's historical writing has extended to other cultures, and his depictions of ancient mythological figures from around the world are vigorous and vivid. In the succinct style of his writing and the brilliant technical work of his illustrations, Fisher brings history to life for readers of all ages.

In addition to his book art, Fisher has designed filmstrips, posters, and U.S. postage stamps; he has been a frequent contributor to *Cricket* and *Ladybug* magazines as well as educational journals. His paintings have been seen in many exhibitions and are in collections of the Museum of American Illustration, the Smithsonian Institution, and numerous New York galleries. He lives with his wife, Margery, in Westport, Connecticut.

Courtesy of Marshall Cavendish

SELECTED WORKS WRITTEN AND ILLUSTRATED: *Pumpers, Boilers, Hooks and Ladders,* 1961; *Pushers, Spads, Jennies and Jets,* 1961; *A Head Full of Hats,* 1962; *The Glassmakers,* 1964, 1987, 1995; *The Silversmiths,* 1964, 1995; *The Printers,* 1965, 1987, 2000; *The Papermakers,* 1965; *The Wigmakers,* 1965, 2000; *The Hatters,* 1965; *The Weavers,* 1966, 1998; *The Tanners,* 1966, 1987; *The Cabinetmakers,* 1966, 1987, 1995; *The Shoemakers,* 1967, 1998; *The Schoolmasters,* 1967, 1995; *The Peddlers,* 1968, 1998; *The Doctors,* 1968, 1995; *The Potters,* 1969; *The Limners,* 1969, 2000; *The Architects,* 1970, 2000; *Two if by Sea,* 1970; *The Death of Evening Star,* 1972; *The Homemakers,* 1973, 1998; *The Warlock of Westfall,* 1974; *Across the Sea from Galway,* 1975; *Sweeney's Ghost,* 1975; *The Blacksmiths,* 1976, 2000; *Letters from Italy,* 1977; *Noonan,* 1978; *Alphabet Art: Thirteen ABCs from Around the World,* 1978; *The Railroads,* 1979; *The Factories,* 1979; *The Hospitals,* 1980; *The Sports,* 1980; *A*

Russian Farewell, 1980; The
Newspapers, 1981; Storm at the Jetty,
1981; The Seven Days of Creation,
1981; The Unions, 1982; Number Art,
1982; Star Signs, 1983; The Schools,
1983; Boxes! Boxes!, 1984; The
Olympians, 1984; The Statue of
Liberty, 1985; The Great Wall of
China, 1986; Ellis Island, 1986;
Calendar Art, 1987; The Tower of
London, 1987; The Alamo, 1987; Look
Around: A Book about Shapes, 1987;
Monticello, 1988; Pyramid of the Sun,
Pyramid of the Moon, 1988; Theseus
and the Minotaur, 1988; The Wailing
Wall, 1989; The White House, 1989;
Prince Henry the Navigator, 1990;
Jason and the Golden Fleece, 1990;
The Oregon Trail, 1990; The ABC
Exhibit, 1991; Sailboat Lost, 1991;
Cyclops, 1991; Galileo, 1992; Tracks
Across America: The Story of the
American Railroad, 1825–1900, 1992;
David and Goliath, 1993; Gutenberg,

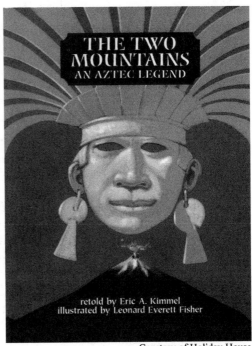

Courtesy of Holiday House

1993; Kinderdike, 1994; Marie Curie, 1994; Moses, 1995;
Gandhi, 1995; Niagara Falls, 1996; William Tell, 1996;
Anasazi, 1997; The Gods and Goddesses of Ancient Egypt,
1997; The Jetty Chronicles, 1997; To Bigotry, No Sanction /
To Persecution, No Assistance, 1998; The Gods and Goddesses
of the Ancient Maya, 1999; Alexander Graham Bell, 1999.

SELECTED WORKS ILLUSTRATED: The Exploits of Xenophon, by
Geoffrey Household, 1955; The First Book of the American
Revolution, by Richard B. Morris, 1956 (revised 1985); The
First Book of American History, by Henry Steele Commager,
1957; Mike Fink, by James C. Bowman, 1957; Energy and
Power, by Robert Irving, 1958; David's Campaign Buttons, by
Catherine Wooley, 1959; Paul Bunyan, by Maurice Dolbier,
1959; America Is Born, by Gerald W. Johnson, 1959; America
Moves Forward, by Gerald W. Johnson, 1960; America Grows
Up, by Gerald W. Johnson, 1960; The Man Without a
Country, by Edward Everett Hale, 1960; The Golden Hind,
by Edith Thacher Hurd, 1960; Vasco Nuñez de Balboa, by E.
G. Sterne, 1961; A Horse Named Justin Morgan, by Harold
Felton, 1962; The Supreme Court, by Gerald W. Johnson,
1962; The Presidency, by Gerald W. Johnson, 1962; But Not
Our Daddy, by Margery Meskin Fisher, 1962; The Congress,
by Gerald W. Johnson, 1963; Casey at the Bat, by Ernest L.
Thayer, 1964; Archimedes, by Martin Gardner, 1965; Rebel

Sea Raider, by John T. Foster,1965; *Forgotten by Time*, by Robert Silverberg, 1966; *The Legend of Sleepy Hollow*, by Washington Irving, 1966; *Rip Van Winkle*, by Washingon Irving, 1966; *Journey with Jonah*, by Madeleine L'Engle, 1967; *The Great Stone Face and Other Stories*, by Nathaniel Hawthorne, 1967; *The Founding of the Republic*, by Richard B. Morris, 1968 (revised 1985); *The Luck of Roaring Camp*, by Bret Harte, 1968; *The Wicked City*, by Isaac Bashevis Singer, 1972; *The Journey of the Grey Whale*, by Gladys Conklin, 1974; *All Times, All Peoples: A World History of Slavery*, by Milton Meltzer, 1980; *A Circle of Seasons*, by Myra Cohn Livingston, 1982; *Sky Songs*, by Myra Cohn Livingston, 1984; *Celebrations*, by Myra Cohn Livingston, 1985; *Sea Songs*, by Myra Cohn Livingston, 1986; *Earth Songs*, by Myra Cohn Livingston, 1986; *Space Songs*, by Myra Cohn Livingston, 1988; *Up in the Air*, by Myra Cohn Livingston, 1989; *Little Frog's Song*, by Alice Schertle, 1992; *The Spotted Pony*, by Eric Kimmel, 1992; *The Three Princes*, by Eric Kimmel, 1994; *Festivals*, by Myra Cohn Livingston, 1996; *The Two Mountains: An Aztec Legend*, by Eric Kimmel, 2000.

SUGGESTED READING: *Children's Literature Review*, vol. 18, 1989; Collier, Laurie and Joyce Nakamura, eds. *Major Authors and Illustrators for Children and Young Adults*, 1993; *Contemporary Authors*, New Revision Series, vol. 37, 1992; Cummins, Julie. *Children's Book Illustration and Design*, vol. 1, 1992; *Dictionary of Literary Biography*, vol. 61, 1987; *Leonard Everett Fisher: A Life of Art*, University of Connecticut, 1997; Pendergast, Sara, ed. *St. James Guide to Children's Writers*, 5th ed., 1999; Silvey, Anita, ed. *Children's Books and Their Creators*, 1995; *Something About the Author*, vol. 4, 1973; vol. 34, 1984; vol. 73, 1993; *Something About the Author Autobiography Series*, vol. 1, 1986. Periodicals— Fisher, Leonard Everett, "Censorship and the Arts," *ALAN Review*, Fall 1993; Fisher, L. E., "The Craft and Creed of Leonard Everett Fisher," *North Light*, July/August, 1973; Fisher, L. E., "Creative Rights and American Destiny," *Language Arts*, March 1982; Fisher, L. E., "From Xenophon to Gutenberg," *The New Advocate*, June, 1997; Fisher, L. E., "My Life in the Arts," *Catholic Library World*, July/August 1971; Fisher, L. E., "On the Fiction of Nonfiction," *Five Owls*, 1988; Zvirin, Stephanie, "The *Booklist* Interview: Leonard Everett Fisher," *Booklist*, November 15, 1993.

WEB SITE: *www.bergenstein.com/SCBWI/fisher/fisher.htm*

An earlier profile of Leonard Everett Fisher appeared in *Third Book of Junior Authors* (1972).

"I grew up as the oldest of nine children. And my parents were each one of eight children, so we always had tons of relatives around. I grew up swimming in stories. I got them from my grandparents; I heard them from my wild Irish uncles; I traded them with friends and cousins. And I read them in books.

"Books really opened my eyes. I started reading sports stories and then branched off into everything else. As a kid I'd finish reading the stories of Edgar Allen Poe or *The Call of the Wild* by Jack London and would say to myself: 'Man! Wouldn't it be unbelievable if I could write a book that would affect other people even half as much as this book affected me!'

"These books taught me the power of words. In school I was lucky enough to have a few teachers who gave me the space and encouragement that allowed me to keep writing. When I didn't get that encouragement, I wrote secretly in notebooks. I wrote for myself.

Courtesy of Jay Paul

Ralph Fletcher

March 17, 1953–

"In college I participated in two foreign study programs, first in Tonga in the South Pacific and later in Sierra Leone, West Africa. Travel has always been a passion of mine. After college I traveled around the world as a tour leader. Wherever I went I paid attention, and I used my notebook to jot down strange facts, local slang, insights, and impressions.

"When I was twenty-one, my brother Bob (age seventeen) was killed in a car accident. This tragedy had a huge impact on my whole family. The death of my brother stirred up a hornet's nest of emotions inside me—anger, grief, guilt. I needed some kind of container to hold all those feelings. It was around that time that I started writing poetry. Poems appealed to me because they were short and intense—they aimed straight for the heart. For years my friends and family held a big poetry reading around the end of the year. These were BYOP parties: Bring Your Own Poem. We sat in a big circle listening and reading poetry far into the night.

"Earning a master's degree in fiction writing from Columbia University, I got to work with some wonderful writers (Richard Price, Gail Godwin, Edmund White) who left a mark on me. I began working in New York City classrooms as part of the Teachers College Writing Project. I lugged a big bag of books from class to class and shared them with students to spark their

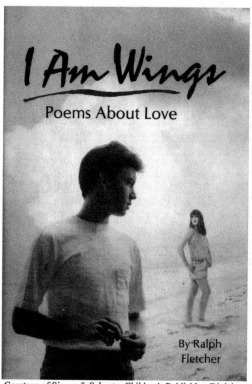

I Am Wings
Poems About Love

By Ralph
Fletcher

Courtesy of Simon & Schuster Children's Publishing Division

writing. I didn't plan it, but I fell in love with books by William Steig, Cynthia Rylant, Katherine Paterson, Gary Soto, John Steptoe, and others. I decided to try writing for young readers. But it would take several years and many rejection letters before my first book (*I Am Wings: Poems About Love*) got published.

"I have since published novels, poetry collections, nonfiction, books for teachers, and picture books. Most writers specialize in one particular kind of writing. Not me. I find that each form comes with its own particular pleasures and challenges.

"I am married now, with four terrific sons who astonish me with their energy, humor, intensity (and appetites!). I'm lucky to have them around me. I know that I am a far better writer because of them.

"I have a special interest in young writers. I believe that every kid—even a five- or six-year-old—can learn to write! I want to do whatever I can to nourish the talents of young writers. I enjoy visiting schools, talking with young readers and writers. But I've also learned that I need more solitude than most people so I can listen to the words and lines and characters' voices inside me.

"If I could have chosen it, what would have been the perfect career for me? Playing center field for the Boston Red Sox, of course! But becoming a writer is also a dream that has come true. I love to write. I love getting up every morning and mucking around in sentences, playing with stories, trying to build my city of words."

* * *

Ralph Fletcher was born in Plymouth, Massachusetts, and grew up in Marshfield, Massachusetts; Winnetka, Illinois; and West Islip, New York. He graduated Magna Cum Laude from Dartmouth College in 1975.

His collection *I Am Wings: Poems About Love* was selected as an ALA Best Book for Young Adults and a *School Library Journal* Best Book of 1994 and received an IRA/CBC Children's Choice Award. One of the few authors consistently publishing book-length poetry collections for young people, Fletcher has received critical acclaim for the range and diversity of his style and subject matter. He has written about teenage romance, nature, and changing family dynamics. The death of Fletcher's younger brother was the catalyst for his first novel, *Fig Pudding*, which was named an ALA Notable Children's Book and won the Virginia Reading Association Award as an outstanding middle grade novel. His second novel, *Spider Boy*, and his collection of poems *Relatively Speaking* were both selected for New York Public Library's annual list, 100 Titles for Reading and Sharing.

In addition to poetry and fiction, the author has published a number of inspirational nonfiction volumes for both young writers and their teachers. Books aimed at children include *A Writer's Notebook: Unlocking the Writer Within You*, *A Kid's Guide to Writing*, and *Live Writing: Breathing Life into Your Words*. For adults he has written the bestselling *What a Writer Needs* and, with JoAnn Portalupi, *Craft Lessons: Teaching Writing K–8*.

Ralph Fletcher lives with his wife and four sons in Durham, New Hampshire.

SELECTED WORKS: *Water Planet: Poems About Water*, 1991; *I Am Wings: Poems About Love*, photos by Joe Baker, 1994; *Fig Pudding*, illus. by Arthur Howard, 1995; *Buried Alive: The Elements of Love*, photos by Andrew Moore, 1996; *Spider Boy*, 1997; *A Writer's Notebook: Unlocking the Writer Within You*, 1996; *Ordinary Things: Poems from a Walk in Early Spring*, illus. by Walter Lyon Krudop, 1997; *Twilight Comes Twice*, illus. by Kate A. Kiesler, 1997; *Flying Solo*, 1998; *Room Enough for Love*, (combined texts of *I Am Wings* and *Buried Alive*), 1998; *Relatively Speaking: Poems about Family*, 1999; *Live Writing: Breathing Life into Your Words*, 1999.

SUGGESTED READING: *Something About the Author*, vol. 105, 1999.

WEB SITE: *www.ralphfletcher.com*

Dennis Brindell Fradin

December 20, 1945–

"I was born in 1945 in Chicago. I remember as a child being in love with the world: the smell of nearby Lake Michigan, the sight of sunlight streaming in through my window, the sounds of neighbors' laundry flapping on the clotheslines between the apartments. I was a daydreamy, absent-minded child. My favorite times in grade school were when we finished our work for the day and could spend the last hour of the day reading our library books—not just the stories but also the insignias of the publishers on the title pages and the dates when the books were published. Also, there was nothing quite like the smell of an old library book that had been taken out many times. I haven't changed a bit in the half century since. Few things excite me as much as taking out a book from 1865 from the university library.

"By the time I was in second grade I was making up little stories that I convinced my mother to type. I liked the look of the typed stories as much as I liked the stories themselves. By the age of seven I was pretty sure that I wanted to be an author when I grew up, but I must admit that over the next few years I also wanted to be an archaeologist, baseball player, and astronomer at various times.

"As a freshman in high school, I wrote a science fiction story called 'The First Ten Thousand Years' about a man who gets stuck in a time machine between the past, present, and future. My English teacher told me it was the best story he had ever read by a freshman and led me to think I could become a writer.

Courtesy of Judith Bloom Fradin

Two years later, I showed a few of my stories to another English teacher and he advised me to forget about becoming an author. I realized then that if I wanted to become an author I would have to toughen up and not let myself get destroyed by other people's opinions.

"My first story was published in 1964 in *Ingenue*, a girls' magazine. It was called 'Judy Is the Best,' and was about my girlfriend. In the summer of that year my family went to New York City on a vacation and copies of the magazine were piled five feet high at the newsstand in Penn Station. Wow! To be eighteen years old and to see your story in a real magazine! Nothing can ever equal that moment. I was paid $25 for the story and I married the real Judy just before we graduated from college, and we now have three grown children: Tony, Diana, and Mike. Tony and his wife, April, just made us first-time grandparents with the birth of Aaron.

"I taught for twelve years after college while trying to become an author. The old expression that 'you can't see the nose in front of your face' applied to me. I was writing adult stories but not selling them. Yet at the same time I was making up children's stories and entertaining my second-grade students with them, without realizing I might be cut out to be a children's author. Finally I typed up some of my children's stories and sent them out. They were rejected, but the editor at Children's Press, Fran Dyka, liked them enough to ask me to try writing a book about Illinois. She liked the Illinois book so much that she asked me to write about the other 49 states. I have now written two sets of States books, and have co-authored a number of them with my wife, Judy.

More books followed for Children's Press and other publishers, and in recent years I have branched out to writing books for teenagers. I should mention, though, that I am one of the most rejected authors of the universe. One of my stories, 'Cara,' was turned down thirty-six times before it was accepted and published as a picture book.

"My hobbies are astronomy and baseball. I have a six-inch telescope with which my family and I observe the sky, and every Sunday that the weather allows I play baseball with my friends, and often my sons. I have been a Pony League baseball coach in my hometown for the past nine years. I write several hours a day, virtually every day of the year, and love and need it so much that I couldn't picture life without writing."

* * *

Dennis Fradin was born on December 20, 1945, in Chicago, Illinois, to Myron and Selma Fradin. Just before he graduated from Northwestern University in 1967, on March 19, he married Judith Bloom, the inspiration for his first published story. The Fradins live in Evanston, Illinois, and have three grown children and one grandchild.

Although Fradin had a few stories published in magazines during his college years, it wasn't until his late twenties that he began to realize his dream of becoming a writer. He published several picture books and more stories, but found his true niche in writing nonfiction for children. He is the author of over one hundred books, on a wide variety of topics. He was first known as a "states book" author, writing text for the Children's Press series In Words and Pictures and later for another series, From Sea to Shining Sea. Some of these titles were co-authored with his wife, Judith. He also wrote the Thirteen Colonies series, used widely by students researching Colonial America. By now the topics he has written about include disasters, astronomy, the earth, holidays, explorers, history, and Native Americans, to name a few. Some of his work has been translated into Spanish.

Courtesy of Simon & Schuster Children's Publishing Division

Dennis Fradin has taken on a variety of age levels as well as a wide range of topics. His contributions to the Children's Press New True series were designed for beginning readers, while his more recent, highly praised nonfiction titles were written for young adults. *The Planet Hunters: The Search for Other Worlds* received a *VOYA* award as one of the best nonfiction books of the year and was named an ALA Best Book for Young Adults in 1998.

SELECTED WORKS: *Illinois in Words and Pictures*, 1976 (and subsequent titles in the series); *Astronomy* (New True Books), 1983; *The Flag of the United States* (New True Books), 1988; *King Philip: Indian Leader*, 1990; *The Connecticut Colony*, 1990 (and others in the Thirteen Colonies series); *Amerigo Vespucci*, 1991; *The Niña, the Pinta, and the Santa Maria*, 1991; *Hiawatha: Messenger of Peace*, 1992; *Alabama*, 1993 (and others in the From Sea to Shining Sea series); *Christmas*, 1990 (and others in the Best Holiday Books series); *"We Have Conquered Pain": The Discovery of Anesthesia*, 1996; *Airplanes* (New True Books), 1997; *The Planet Hunters: The Search for Other Worlds*, 1997; *Searching for Alien Life: Is Anyone Out There?*, 1997; *Samuel Adams: The Father of American Independence*, 1998; *Sacagawea: The Journey to the West*, 1998; *Is There Life on Mars?*, 1999; *Ida B. Wells: Mother of the Civil Rights Movement*, with Judith Bloom Fradin, 2000.

SUGGESTED READING: *Contemporary Authors*, New Revison Series, vol. 50, 1996; *Something About the Author*, vol. 29, 1982; vol. 90, 1997; Wyatt, Flora, et. al. *Popular Nonfiction Authors for Children*, 1998.

Suzanne Freeman

September 4, 1950–

"When I was growing up, my family moved often, rarely living in the same house for more than two years. We changed neighborhoods, schools, states, sometimes even countries. But, from anywhere, we would always come back to Tennessee, to my grandmother's house in Murfreesboro. As soon as we opened the car door, I'd smell the familiar mix of spearmint and gravel dust along the driveway and—that fast—I would have my bearings. I was home again. This was the place I counted on for the simple mystery of its being unchanging and true.

"I spent many summers at my grandmother's house, and it was so hot there that, if we weren't at the town swimming pool, I would usually find a shady place and a book and lie around reading. I read whatever I could find, from my grandmother's childhood books, which seemed mostly to be romantic stories involving brave orphans, to my cousins' comic books about superheroes. When I ran out of things to read, I started writing stories of my own, but I was too embarrassed to read them to anybody. I hid them away in a drawer. It didn't really cross my mind then that I could ever be a real writer.

"As I went through high school, though, I found myself drawn more and more to books and writing. I decided when I went to college that I would major in journalism. In my first newspaper job, on a small daily paper in Virginia, I didn't get to do much actual writing—only headlines for the news articles. But after a year or so I took over a feature writing position, and I loved that—writing stories about people and their families and the things they had accomplished in their lives.

"The only trouble was that sometimes I wished I didn't have to stick to just telling the truth. I'd think how much better a story I could tell if I could just make up my own ending or change the facts even a little bit. But, of course, that's exactly what you cannot do in journalism and that's why I began to think about trying to write fiction.

"I put off the idea of writing a novel for many years, though. I was married and raising two children and I was writing book reviews for a number of newspapers and, besides, I didn't have any idea how to write a novel. Where would I start? What would I say?

"My luckiest instinct when I finally made myself sit down and get to work was that I decided to use my grandmother's house in Tennessee as the setting for my book. I had come up with an idea of a character—a grieving, willful, and often difficult young girl named Mia, a displaced child whose parents are missing at sea—but I hadn't quite figured out what would happen in her life, or where her story would go. When I set Mia down in my grandmother's house, I knew more about her. I knew she would see the thin slant of sunlight across the kitchen table, the pattern of knotholes in the pine-paneled back bedroom, the dust motes flying when she beat her fist against the back of the scratchy red sofa. I knew she'd hear the low, steady hum of the refrigerator and

Courtesy of Colleen McCallion

Suzanne Freeman

taste the chlorine flavor of the water that came out of the kitchen tap. Because I knew all of these details, I knew a lot about the life that Mia and her aunt and her sisters were living there. I began to understand what had to happen in the next chapter and the next.

"Now as I work on my next novel, I think about what I learned from writing that first one: that in fiction you can indeed make things up and change facts, but, somehow, you still end up telling the truth that was there all along."

The Cuckoo's Child

by Suzanne Freeman

Courtesy of William Morrow & Co., Inc.

* * *

Like Mia Veery of *The Cuckoo's Child*, Suzanne Freeman spent a year living in Beirut, while her father taught there at the American University. After graduating from Boston University, she became a book reviewer for the *Boston Globe*, *Ms.*, *USA Today*, and the *Washington Post*. She now lives in Manchester, Massachusetts, with her husband and two children, and "as soon as the other members of my family go off each morning, to work or to school or to summer camp, I go to my desk [to write]."

The Cuckoo's Child made a stunning debut as a first novel in 1996 and was named to *School Library Journal*'s Best Books, the *Bulletin of the Center for Children's Books* Blue Ribbon list, and the *Horn Book*'s Fanfare as well as being cited as both an ALA Best Books for Young Adults and an ALA Notable Children's Books. Freeman is currently at work on a second novel featuring a character from *The Cuckoo's Child*.

SELECTED WORKS: *The Cuckoo's Child*, 1996.

SUGGESTED READING: Comerford, Lynda, "Suzanne Freeman," *Publishers Weekly*, July 1, 1996; Hurst, Carol Otis, "New Novels," *Teaching PreK–8*, March 1996.

Jean Fritz

November 16, 1915–

"As an only child, I spent more time with story characters than with real people and I learned early that words could get me where I wanted to go, which was simply some place else, especially America. I was born and grew up in China—an experience I am now very grateful for, but at the time it seemed far away from what was my real home in America. I had never been there.

"We came back to America in 1928, when I was thirteen, and ever since I have been trying to dig down to my roots. Studying American history and writing about it makes me feel more and more that I am taking possession of America—all of it. One of my first books was *The Cabin Faced West*, the story of my great-great-grandmother, a pioneer in western Pennsylvania. The most exciting scene in the book is when George Washington, in Pennsylvania on business, takes dinner with the Hamiltons in their log cabin. Of course there would have been conversation, but what did George say? I felt uncomfortable putting words in his mouth, but unless I let him sit mute, I'd have to invent the conversation.

"Later, as I began writing biographies, I determined not to make up anything, including conversation. I tell children that if they see quotation marks, they can be sure there is a source for them.

"Not only do I love getting to know the people I am writing about, I love doing the research to find out about them. Often I have research adventures. When I visited the site of John Hancock's house, I came upon bricks that were used in his house or on his property. They were eighteenth-century bricks, and I was assured that they were among the original ones. When I went home that day, I had a John Hancock brick with me; it sits proudly in front of my fireplace.

"As part of my research on the Lost Colony, I have been to Cape Hatteras to watch an archaeologist dig for clues. When a sixteenth-century ring was recovered, I rejoiced as if I had been the Lost Colonist who had spent the last five hundred years looking for that ring."

Courtesy of Jean Fritz

* * *

Jean Guttery Fritz was born in Hankow, China, and spent her childhood there while her father, a minister, worked for the YMCA. Returning to America, Fritz's family spent time in Washington, Pennsylvania, with relatives before moving to Hartford, Connecticut, where she graduated from high school. After receiving her A.B. degree from Wheaton College in 1937, Fritz worked at the Silver Burdett textbook company in New York as a research assistant. She married Michael Fritz in 1941, just before the United States entered World War II. Though Michael was in the service, he served in radio intelligence on the West Coast, and Jean was able to stay with him. Their son David was born in San Francisco during this time. They returned to New York after the war, and their daughter Andrea was born there in 1947.

Writing has always been an important part of Jean Fritz's life. While her children were small, she did freelance editing and ghostwriting for textbooks and wrote many stories of her own, collecting many rejection slips. When the family moved to Dobbs Ferry, New York, in 1951, Fritz discovered that the library did not have a children's room. She volunteered to lead a weekly story hour and was soon hired by the library to establish a children's area. For the next two years she immersed herself in children's books, reading ten or twenty a week, to build the library collection, and she credits this experience with helping her develop her own sense of story.

During this time her stories began to appear in children's magazines. She had several picture book texts accepted and published her first full-length novel, *121 Pudding Street*. Her first real success came with the historical fiction book *The Cabin Faced West*, based on a family story about her grandmother's grandmother, Ann Hamilton. Several more novels followed, but when Fritz ventured into the territory of historical biography, she found a very special niche for herself in children's literature. *And Then What Happened, Paul Revere?* was published in 1973, the first of five biographies by Fritz to be named Outstanding Book of the Year by the *New York Times*; two others became *Boston Globe–Horn Book* Award Honor Books, in 1974 and 1976.

Courtesy of Penguin Putnam

The humorous titles of her so-called "question biographies" (*Why Don't You Get a Horse, Sam Adams?*; *What's the Big Idea, Ben Franklin?*, etc.) offer a clue to Jean Fritz's success in getting children interested in reading about history. By concentrating on the human quirks of her famous subjects, such as Samuel Adams's aversion to horseback riding, she brings her characters to life with humorous touches, all discovered through meticulous research. Profusely illustrated by fine artists who accentuate the humor and human interest of these narratives, Fritz's biographies for middle grade readers have been immensely popular.

Jean Fritz has likened her work to that of a reporter, "looking for clues, connecting facts, digging under the surface." Her longer biographies, written for older elementary and middle-school students, continued her unique approach to history and brought her further accolades. She received a *Boston Globe–Horn Book* Honor Award for *Stonewall* in 1980 and was twice awarded the *Boston Globe–Horn Book* Nonfiction Award: in 1984 for *The Double Life of Pocahontas* and in 1990 for *The Great Little Madison*. The Madison biography also captured the Orbis Pictus Award.

Nearly thirty years after she started publishing children's books, Jean Fritz wrote about her own childhood in *Homesick: My Own Story* to share with young readers the sense of longing she felt growing up far from her "real home" in America. Though it is a memoir, *Homesick* was classified as fiction because Fritz shaped the story to make the narrative flow smoothly. Published in 1982, it received the prestigious American Book Award, a Newbery Honor Book Award and a Boston Globe–Horn Book Honor citation for fiction. After writing *Homesick* Fritz felt that it was time to visit her childhood home, so fifty-five years after leaving China, she returned, accompanied by her husband. This journey is described in *China Homecoming*.

In addition to her own writing, Fritz has been an inspiration to other authors. As the founder and instructor of the Jean Fritz Writers' Workshops in Katonah, New York, from 1962 to 1970 she provided a place for many aspiring writers to learn their craft. In 1985 she was awarded the Regina Medal by the Catholic Library Association, and the following year she was presented the prestigious Laura Ingalls Wilder Award by the American Library Association for the body of her work. Jean Fritz continues to create lively and informative biographies; most recently she has added Harriet Beecher Stowe, Lafayette, and Elizabeth Cady Stanton to the list of historical figures who have been given new life between the pages of her books.

Courtesy of Penguin Putnam

SELECTED WORKS: *121 Pudding Street*, illus. by Sophia, 1955; *The Animals of Dr. Schweitzer*, illus. by Douglas Howland, 1958; *The Cabin Faced West*, illus. by Feodor Rojankovsky, 1958; *Brady*, illus. by Lynd Ward, 1960; *I, Adam*, illus. by Peter Burchard, 1963; *Early Thunder*, illus. by Lynd Ward, 1967; *George Washington's Breakfast*, illus. by Paul Galdone, 1969; *And Then What Happened, Paul Revere?*, illus. by Margot Tomes, 1973; *Why Don't You Get a Horse, Sam Adams?*, illus. by Trina Schart Hyman, 1974; *Where Was Patrick Henry on the 29th of May?*, illus. by Margot Tomes, 1975; *Who's That Stepping on Plymouth Rock?*, illus. by J. B. Handelsman, 1975; *Will You Sign Here, John Hancock?*, illus.

by Trina Schart Hyman, 1976; *What's the Big Idea, Ben Franklin?*, illus. by Margot Tomes, 1976; *Can't You Make Them Behave, King George?*, illus. by Tomie de Paola, 1977; *Brendan the Navigator*, illus. by Enrico Arno, 1979; *Stonewall*, illus. by Stephen Gammell, 1979; *Where Do You Think You're Going, Christopher Colombus?*, illus. by Margot Tomes, 1980; *The Man Who Loved Books*, illus. by Trina Schart Hyman, 1981; *Traitor, the Case of Benedict Arnold*, illus. by John Andrew, 1981; *The Good Giants and the Bad Pukwudgies*, illus. by Tomie de Paola, 1982; *Homesick: My Own Story*, 1982; *The Double Life of Pocahontas*, illus. by Ed Young, 1983; *China Homecoming*, photos by Mike Fritz, 1985; *Make Way for Sam Houston!*, illus. by Elise Primavera, 1986; *Shh! We're Writing the Constitution*, illus. by Tomie de Paola, 1987; *China's Long March: 6,000 Miles of Danger*, illus. by Yang Zhr Cheng, 1988; *The Great Little Madison*, 1989; *Bully for You, Teddy Roosevelt*, illus. by Mike Wimmer, 1991; *The Great Adventure of Christopher Columbus: a Pop-up Book*, illus. by Tomie de Paola, 1992; *George Washington's Mother*, illus. by DyAnne DiSalvo-Ryan, 1992; *Surprising Myself*, 1992; *The World in 1492* (with others), illus. by Stefano Vitale, 1992; *Just a Few Words, Mr. Lincoln: The Story of the Gettysburg Address*, illus. by Charles Robinson, 1993; *Around the World in a Hundred Years: From Henry the Navigator to Magellan*, illus. by Anthony Bacon Venti, 1994; *Harriet Beecher Stowe and the Beecher Preachers*, 1994; *You Want Women to Vote, Lizzie Stanton?*, illus. by DyAnne DiSalvo-Ryan, 1997; *Why Not, Lafayette?*, illus. by Ronald Himler, 1999.

SUGGESTED READING: *Children's Literature Review*, vol. 14, 1988; *Contemporary Authors*, New Revision Series, vol. 37, 1992; *Dictionary of Literary Biography*, vol. 52, 1986; Hostetler, Elizabeth. *Jean Fritz: A Critical Biography*, 1981; Pendergast, Sara, ed. *St. James Guide to Children's Writers*, 5th ed., 1999; Silvey, Anita, ed. *Children's Books and Their Creators*, 1995; *Something About the Author*, vol. 1, 1971; vol. 29, 1982; vol. 72, 1993; *Something About the Author Autobiography Series*, vol. 2, 1986. Periodicals—Fritz, Jean, "Acceptance Speech for the *Boston Globe–Horn Book* Award," *Horn Book*, January/February 1985, 1991; Fritz, Jean, "Laura Ingalls Wilder Acceptance Speech," *Horn Book*, July/August 1986; Hakim, Joy, "The History Connection: It's the Real Thing," *School Library Journal*, May 1994; "Kudos to Jean Fritz," *Booklist*, April 15, 1990; Scales, Pat, "Jean Fritz's *You Want Women to Vote, Lizzie Stanton?*" *Book Links*, July 1996.

An earlier profile of Jean Fritz appeared in *Third Book of Junior Authors* (1972).

"When I was five, my older brother came home crying from his first-grade class because the teacher had punished him for speaking Spanish. This incident was very confusing, because according to my parents we were going to have fun in school. The experience caused much discussion between my parents and their friends, whose children were also experiencing the same treatment. Even though it had been seven years since my father and other Mexican Americans had returned from military service during World War II, things had not changed very much in Texas, and now their children were becoming of school age and the discrimination continued.

"My parents decided that from then on we would practice speaking only in English and not both languages as we had been doing. I did not understand the distinction between the two languages, and many times my parents spoke in both languages in spite of their decision.

Courtesy of Marvin Collins

CARMEN LOMAS GARZA

Carmen Lomas Garza

September 1948–

"My first-grade teacher was a bit more compassionate and explained that we spoke two languages. She demonstrated this by bringing from her bedroom a huge fluffy pillow with colorful embroidery and said that the name we knew for it, 'almohada,' was Spanish and 'pillow' was English. I knew and used both words.

"Knowing the difference between the two languages did not save me from using Spanish in the classrooms and on the school grounds, so I too suffered many physical and emotional punishments. Each time I spoke English I was ridiculed for my accent and made to feel ashamed. At the time when most children start to realize that there is an immense outside world and communication is an important vehicle toward becoming a part of that world, I was struggling with my ability to communicate in two languages.

"The struggle continued in high school. We could take classes in Latin, French, or Spanish, but the Mexican American students were not allowed to speak Spanish in other classrooms or in the halls. Other students could practice their new Spanish words while walking down the halls, yet Mexican American students could expect punishment for doing the same. I graduated from high school confused, depressed, introverted, and quite angry.

"The Chicano Movement for civil rights of the late sixties and early seventies clarified some of that confusion, started the slow process of self-healing, and provided a format to vent some of that anger. I had decided at the age of thirteen to become an artist, so when I was in college the Chicano Movement nourished that goal and gave me back my voice.

"The anger, pride, and self-healing came out as Chicano art. My goal was to start with my earliest recollections of my life and validate each event or incident by depicting it in a visual art format. I needed to re-celebrate each special event or re-examine each unusual happening. We Chicano artists have been doing Chicano art for Mexican Americans but also for others to see who we are as a people. If you see our heart and humanity through our art, we hope that you will accept and appreciate our culture. In my work, I give you a piece of my heart."

* * *

"My goal was to start with my earliest recollections of my life and validate each event or incident by depicting it in a visual art format."

Carmen Lomas Garza was raised in Kingsville, Texas, a small community not far from the Mexican border. She is the second of five children and knew from the age of thirteen that she wanted to be an artist. Her whole family supported her dream, but her mother was her real inspiration. "She made up our beds to sleep in and have regular dreams, but she also laid out the bed for our dreams of the future," Garza has written. Her mother created *loteria tablas*, which resemble bingo cards but include depictions of little figures, using pen and ink and watercolor. Her grandmother also made drawings, which she used as patterns for her embroidery.

Garza took her first art classes in high school and earned her master's degree in 1980 from San Francisco State University. In college she became involved with the Chicano movement, an effort for political reform and cultural recognition for Mexican Americans and others of Latino ancestry.

Garza's paintings focus on the joyful memories of everyday life with her family and friends in the close-knit Mexican American community of Kingsville. In her books, *Family Pictures / Cuadros de Familia* and *In My Family / En Mi Familia*, she paints detailed stories of her life in a deceptively simple, childlike style. She decided to use this style during her senior year at Texas Arts and Industry University (now Texas A & I) in Kingsville. In a recent interview Garza explained that "very deliberately, after having learned all the principles of art and the Renaissance elements of art and all the academic stuff, I chose to drop some of those concerns and do my artwork as simple and as direct as possible. . . . Nobody else was doing anything that dealt with just the ordinary everyday life, and that's what I wanted to concentrate on."

Both *Family Pictures / Cuadros de Familia* and *In My Family / En Mi Familia* were named Honor Books for the Pura Belpré Award in 1996 and 1998, respectively. Both books were also cited on the CCBC Choices list in their years of publication. In 2000 Carmen Lomas Garza received the Pura Belpré Award for *Magic Windows / Ventanas Magicas*.

Garza continues to work in variety of artistic media, primarily painting and printmaking. Her work is displayed in public galleries and private collections throughout California and Texas. At present she resides in San Francisco, California.

SELECTED WORKS: *Family Pictures / Cuadros de Familia*, 1990; *In My Family / En Mi Familia*, 1996; *Magic Windows / Ventanas Magicas*, 1999; *Making Magic Windows: Creating Picado/Cut-Paper Art with Carmen Lomas Garza*, 1999.

SUGGESTED READING: Day, Frances Ann. *Latina and Latino Voices in Literature for Children and Teenagers*, 1997; Garza, Carmen Lomas. *A Piece of My Heart / Pedacito de Mi Corazón: The Art of Carmen Lomas Garza*, 1994; Telgen, Diane and Jim Kamp, eds. *Latinas! Women of Achievement*, 1996; Telgen, Diane, ed. *Notable Hispanic American Women*, 1993. Periodicals—Easton, Jennifer, *Artpapers*, May/June 1994.

Parts of the autobiographical statement above first appeared in Carmen Lomas Garza's *A Piece of My Heart / Pedacito de Mi Corazón* (New York: The New Press, 1994).

Kathlyn Gay

March 4, 1930–

"Writing has long been a way of life for me, and I began putting words on paper at age ten or eleven, writing stories and plays for my own amusement and amazement and also writing articles as co-editor for an elementary school newspaper. Through all my growing-up years I hoped to be a professional writer, but I thought journalism, advertising, or public relations would be my career. Instead I found that writing nonfiction for children, teenagers, and adults was more satisfying, and through the years I've been especially challenged to write informative material about difficult topics in a way that will interest and entertain readers.

"I did not begin writing professionally until after I finished college and was married. In fact, I wrote my first article (published in a travel magazine) in the hospital on the day my daughter, Karen, was born in 1957. When I learned that I had sold that feature story for a grand total of $15, I was 'hooked' and seriously began writing for publication while trying to raise a family and work part-time at a variety of jobs. My husband Art, an elementary school teacher and administrator, helped out with child care and household chores so that I could have a few hours each day at the typewriter—a small portable one at first and then an electric typewriter. Now, of course, I use a computer, and I've gone through five of them.

"After that first article was sold—and with lots of rejections in between the published pieces—I was able to write and sell hundreds of magazine articles, some short stories and plays, and nearly a hundred books on a myriad of topics over the last forty years. I feel that one of the great advantages of writing nonfiction is being able to enjoy a lifetime of learning—and get paid for it, too! I especially enjoy interviewing people and traveling around the United States to do research in libraries and museums and at historical sites. I also like taking photographs for some of my books. For the past few years a great deal of my research has also been done via the World Wide Web and e-mail.

"Our family has lived in different parts of the United States, which I think is helpful for any writer. Our first home was in Barrington, Illinois. Then we moved to Ventura, California, living there for six years. Back in the Midwest we lived in Elkhart, Indiana, for thirty-six years, and in 1996 we moved to my hometown, Zion, Illinois, to help care for my mother, who was ninety-four in 1998. In Zion, which was founded by a religious group and which I wrote about in *Communes and Cults* (1997), I set up my office in my old room where I used to write as a kid. Now we are living in New Port Richey, Florida, in a villa near my daughter and her husband.

Courtesy of Kathlyn Gay

"Perhaps one of the most rewarding aspects of my writing career in recent years has been collaborating with my sons Martin and Douglas and daughter Karen on various books. Marty, our eldest, lives in Port Townsend, Washington, and we have collaborated via e-mail on at least a dozen nonfiction books. The latest of our collaborations is an encyclopedia on anarchy and anarchists. Most of my nonfiction work focuses on social, political, and environmental issues, history, and communication. With the help of Doug, who lives in Wheaton, Illinois, I produced *The Not-So-Minor Leagues* (about minor league baseball) and with the help of Karen and her husband, Dean Hamilton, in Florida I wrote about food rituals and customs. In short, we've become a family of writers, and some of our combined efforts are described on my homepage on the Internet."

*   *   *

Kathlyn Gay was born in Zion, Illinois, on March 4, 1930, to Kenneth and Beatrice McGarrahan. While attending Northern Illinois University she met fellow student Arthur L. Gay, and they married on August 28, 1948. The Gays have lived in Illinois and California and now live in Florida, but their longest stay was in Elkhart, Indiana. There they took part in amateur theater productions, political campaigns, civil rights activities, and innovative school programs.

Married to an educator and working so closely with schools and their programs, Kathlyn Gay started out as a writer of textbooks; soon, however, she entered the nonfiction trade book field. The topics she chooses are of current concern and are often studied in America's schools. *Acid Rain* in 1983 and *Silent Killers* in 1988 were selected as Outstanding Science Trade Books and as Notable Books in the Field of Social Studies. *Caution—This May Be an Advertisement, Caretakers of the Earth, Getting Your Message Across, Pregnancy,* and *Keep the Buttered Side Up* were each selected for the New York Public Library's annual Books for the Teen Age list. With her son Martin she has written a series of American history books— *Voices from the Past*—which re-create war experiences through documents and letters.

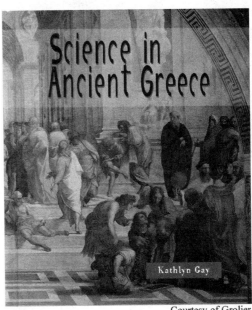

Courtesy of Grolier

SELECTED WORKS: *Acid Rain*, 1983; *The Greenhouse Effect*, 1986; *Silent Killers*, 1988; *Changing Families*, 1987; *Garbage and Recycling*, 1991; *Caution—This May Be an Advertisement: A Teen Guide to Advertising*, 1992; *Getting Your Message Across*, 1993; *Caretakers of the Earth*, 1993; *Pregnancy: Private Decisions, Public Debates*, 1994; *Pollution and the Powerless: The Movement for Environmental Justice*, 1994; *Church and State: Government and Religion in the United States*, 1994; *Keep the Buttered Side Up: Food Superstitions from Around the World*, 1995; *The Information Superhighway*, with Martin Gay, 1995; *I Am Who I Am: Speaking Out about Multiracial Identity*, 1995; *The Not-So-Minor Leagues*, with Douglas Gay, 1996; *Communes and Cults*, 1997; *Neo-Nazis: The Growing Threat*,

1997; *After the Shooting Stops: The Aftermath of War*, with Martin Gay, 1998; *Who's Running the Nation? How Corporate Power Threatens Democracy*, 1998.

SUGGESTED READING: *Contemporary Authors*, New Revision Series, vol. 50, 1996; *Something About the Author*, vol. 9, 1976.

WEB SITE: *http//ourworld.compuserve.com/homepages/Kathy*

Courtesy of Ellan Young

Jean Craighead George

Jean Craighead George

July 2, 1919–

"I can remember very clearly being six and deciding that when I grew up I would become an illustrator, a writer, a dancer, a poet, and mother. I thought I would take up listening to music, swimming, and ice-skating as hobbies. My parents thought this an ambitious program. However, they went along with it, and to further these careers they sent me to dancing school, provided me with a desk for writing, a winter home where ice occasionally formed on the Chesapeake and Ohio Canal, and a summer home with a swimming creek. In this family house was a piano, and Aunt Peg provided the music I loved.

"The painting I had to take care of myself. I spent hours at this, lying on the floor with my cousin, Paula, drawing or creating dream people and landscapes in watercolors. I continued all these interests at Penn State University, adding to them science and politics. Finally a professor said to me, 'Jean, you can't do all of these things well. You will have to decide what you really want to do.' I settled on two careers—painting and writing—but kept all the others as hobbies.

"I had much to paint and write about. All through my childhood my parents took my brothers, Frank and John, and me into the wilderness along the Potomac River outside Washington, D.C., where I was born. Dad, a naturalist, taught us the trees, flowers, birds, and insects and how to find and harvest wild foods for lunch and dinner. Frank and John, today the national experts on grizzly bears, were the first falconers in the United States and gave me a falcon to train. Each night I would write about what I saw and did. My diaries piled up.

"After college I was a reporter for the International News Service and the *Washington Post*. Journalism was exciting. I met senators, diplomats, and the President of the United States, Franklin Delano Roosevelt.

"But my heart belonged to the wilderness, and when I met John George, my brothers' college roommate and a graduate student in natural history, I married him. He was in the Navy at the time, on a destroyer in the North Atlantic. At the end of World War II we went off to Michigan University to finish his doctorate. To understand the natural world better we lived in a tent in a beautiful beech-maple forest on his study area. It was there I truly came to understand the beauty and complexity of the natural world.

"And then I became a mother. Twig (and that's her real name) was born. We left the tent and moved to Poughkeepsie, N.Y., where I found being a mother was the most satisfying of all careers. Craig was born two years later and four years after Craig came Luke. I brought wild pets in from the wilderness for the children to learn about—great horned owls, screech owls, weasels, raccoons, orphaned birds—and wrote about first the animals themselves and finally my children interacting with animals. I kept on writing and illustrating, for this is what I did well because I loved it.

"*My Side of the Mountain*, the story of my childhood with Dad, Frank, and John, was written while the children napped and slept at night. It was then a Newbery Honor Book in 1960.

"The way to write books, I was discovering, was to pack up the kids and the car and travel to waterfalls and mountains to study the animals that dwelled there, to do things and come home and write about them. Children hopping in and out of the house was no problem.

"We moved to Chappaqua, N.Y., in 1957 when John took a job with the Bronx Zoo. I have been here ever since. I am in the beautiful eastern hardwood forest, near the publishers in New York City with airways and highways to the wilderness not far from my door.

"John's path and mine grew apart and we were divorced in 1964. I wrote nature articles for *Reader's Digest* and continued to write books, both adult and children's. I traveled. I took the three kids with me to camp on tundras, in high mountains, on the prairie. The things that interested them became books.

"I read a great deal and joined scientists in the field and in their labs. And then I read about the wolves. I took Luke and journeyed to Barrow, Alaska, where scientists were studying the behavior and social life of the gray wolf, *Canis lupus*. I studied and watched, then went south to Denali National Park, where Luke and I lay on our bellies watching a wild pack of wolves. I came home to write *Julie of the Wolves*. Now I knew that my writing required research, wild pets, and going to the places I

"All through my childhood my parents took my brothers, Frank and John, and me into the wilderness along the Potomac River outside Washington, D.C. . . . "

was writing about. I wrote and published. Better artists than I were my illustrators.

"Twig, Craig, and Luke went off to colleges and universities, and—became naturalists. They also caught the love of writing. Twig has published three children's books, *A Dolphin Named Bob*, *Swimming with Sharks*, and *Jellies*. Craig studies bowhead whales in Alaska and writes for scientific journals, and Luke is a professor at Humboldt College in California. He writes for obscure but distinguished scientific journals. We are all deeply connected by our early love of the outdoors. The connection was made deeper with the arrival of five grandchildren: Twig's Rebecca and Katie, Craig's Luke and Sam, and Luke's Hunter. They all go camping, canoeing, hiking, and walking with their parents. Once a year we travel together to some wilderness: Maine, Hawaii, the rain forests of Belize, the reef world of Little Cayman.

"And now it is 1999. *My Side of the Mountain* and *Julie of the Wolves* have turned into trilogies. I have just completed my 81st book, *Frightful's Mountain*. It is told from the peregrine's point of view. I am delighting in doing picture books with that fabulous artist Wendell Minor: books like *Everglades*, *Arctic Son*, and *Morning, Noon, and Night*.

"As if bringing my childhood dreams full circle, I am now working on a film and musical version of *Julie of the Wolves* with composer Chris Kubie. I am not dancing or ice-skating, but I write letters to my congressmen trying to pass environmental protection bills and that makes me a sort of politician for this day and age."

*   *   *

Throughout her career, Jean Craighead George has been renowned for integrating scientific knowledge and a love of nature into her stories for young readers. She received her B.A. degree from Pennsylvania State University in 1941 and in 1968 was named Woman of the Year by that institution. George was a reporter for the *Washington Post* and *Pageant* magazine and a roving editor and nature writer for *Reader's Digest* before she became a full-time author. Over the years she and her children have raised 173 wild pets, eventually returning them to nature; the chronicle of those many creatures can be found in her book *The Tarantula in My Purse* (1996). In 1982 she wrote an autobiography titled *Journey Inward* about her childhood, marriage, divorce, career, and her adjustment to being alone after her children had grown up. She continues to travel and explore and goes on hikes regularly.

George's first books were animal biographies, co-authored with her husband, John, and based in many cases on actual experiences with the animals. In 1956 she and her husband won the

Aurianne Award for best nature writing with *Dipper of Copper Creek*. But her greatest recognition came when she started writing books on her own. *My Side of the Mountain*, written as the diary of Sam Gribley, a young boy who leaves New York City to live in the Catskill Mountains for a year, received a Newbery Honor Book award in 1960. Sam writes detailed observations of the wildlife, plants, and the changing seasons around him while discovering the importance of courage and his own relationship to nature. The book was highly praised and has since become a favorite for several generations of young readers.

In 1973 *Julie of the Wolves* won the Newbery Medal; it was also a National Book Award finalist, received the German Youth Literature Prize, and (in its Dutch language edition) captured the Silver Skate Award. The riveting tale of a young girl who gets lost on the Alaskan tundra and survives by being adopted into a wolf pack, this book has become a modern classic. Only a few years after its publication, *Julie of the Wolves* was selected by the Children's Literature Association as one of the ten best American children's books in the past 200 years. Both *My Side of the Mountain* and *Julie of the Wolves* are fine examples of how George weaves together many elements—scientific facts about animals and plants, the importance of living in balance with nature, an understanding of cultures and the difficulties of growing up—to form gripping and believable tales.

JEAN CRAIGHEAD GEORGE

JULIE *of the* WOLVES

CELEBRATING THE 25TH ANNIVERSARY

Courtesy of HarperCollins Publishers

Jean George is an active researcher of her books, and many of the events in them are based on her own experiences. Her nonfiction is often as exciting to read as her adventure stories. In the One Day series, written in the 1980s and re-released with new illustrations in the 1990s, George focused on a different habitat in each book—the tundra, the desert, the prairie, etc. Her Thirteen Moons series, in which each book focuses on a different animal and its behavior during one of the thirteen moons of the year, was also re-released in the early 1990s.

Twenty years after her Newbery Award for *Julie of the Wolves*, Jean George published a sequel, *Julie*, that tells the story of Julie's return to the Eskimo community and her adjustment to living with people again. *Julie's Wolf Pack* appeared in 1997. Sam's story was also continued in *On the Far Side of the Mountain* in 1990. The third book, *Frightful's Mountain*, is told from the point of view of the falcon, as the third book in the Julie series is from the wolves' perspective. George's ability to empathize with animals of all kinds informs both her fiction and nonfiction. In *Animals Who Have Won Our Hearts* in 1994 she introduced her readers to ten real-life animals with amazing stories—Koko, a gorilla who learned sign language, and Sugar, a cat who traveled from Oklahoma to California to rejoin her human family, among others.

Jean Craighead George has received the Kerlan Award from the University of Minnesota, the de Grummond Award from the University of Southern Mississippi, and the Knickerbocker Award in New York—all for her body of work. The Washington Irving Award from the Westchester (N.Y.) Library Association in 1991 was presented to *On the Far Side of the Mountain*. Her books have consistently appeared on "Best" lists and the compiled lists of important books in the fields of social studies and science. Whether writing fiction, nonfiction, or picture books, she has succeeded in bringing the natural world vividly to life for readers of all ages.

SELECTED WORKS WRITTEN: *Summer of the Falcon*, 1962; *Gull Number 737*, 1964; *Moon of the Bears*, illus. by Mac Shepard, 1967, illus. by Ron Parker, 1993; *Moon of the Owls*, illus. by Jean Zallinger, 1967, illus. by Wendell Minor, 1993; *Coyote in Manhattan*, illus. by John Kaufmann, 1968; *Moon of the Wild Pigs*, illus. by Peter Parnall, 1968, illus. by Paul Mirocha, 1992; *Moon of the Alligators*, illus. by Adrina Zanazanian, 1969, illus. by Michael Rothman, 1991; *Moon of the Deer*, illus. by Jean Zallinger, 1969, illus. by Sal Catalano, 1992; *Moon of the Gray Wolves*, illus. by Lorence Bjorklund, 1969, illus. by Sal Catalano, 1991; *All upon a Stone*, illus. by Don Bolognese, 1971; *Who Really Killed Cock Robin?*, 1971; *Julie of the Wolves*, illus. by John Schoenherr, 1972, 1997; *All upon a Sidewalk*, illus. by Don Bolognese, 1974; *Hook a Fish, Catch a Mountain*, 1975; *The Wentletrap Trap*, illus. by Symeon Shimin, 1978; *Cry of the Crow*, 1980; *Wild, Wild Cookbook*, 1982; *Talking Earth*, 1983; *One Day in the Desert*, illus. by Fred Brenner, 1983; *One Day in the Alpine Tundra*, illus. by Walter Gaffney-Kessell, 1984; *One Day in the Prairie*, illus. by Bob Marstall, 1986; *Water Sky*, 1987; *One Day in the Woods*, illus. by Gary Allen, 1988; *The Shark Beneath the Reef*, 1989; *One Day in the Tropical Rain Forest*, 1990; *Missing 'Gator of Gumbo Limbo*, 1992; *The Fire Bug Connection*, 1993; *Animals Who Have Won Our Hearts*, 1994; *Julie*, illus. by Wendell Minor, 1994; *To Climb a Waterfall*, illus. by Thomas Locker, 1995; *Everglades*, illus. by Wendell Minor, 1995; *There's an Owl in the Shower*, illus. by Christine Merrill, 1995; *Acorn Pancakes, Dandelion Salad, and 38 other Wild Recipes*, illus. by Paul Mirocha, 1995; *Julie's Wolf Pack*, illus. by Wendell Minor, 1997; *Look to the North: A Wolf Pup Diary*, illus. by Lucia Washburn, 1997; *Arctic Son*, illus. by Wendell Minor, 1997; *Dear Katie, the Volcano Is a Girl*, illus. by Daniel Powers, 1998; *Rhino Romp*, illus. by Stacey Schuett, 1998; *Morning, Noon, and Night*, illus. by Wendell Minor, 1999; *Snow Bear*, illus. by Wendell Minor, 1999.

SELECTED WORKS WRITTEN AND ILLUSTRATED: *Vulpes, the Red Fox*, 1948, 1996; *Vision, the Mink*, 1949; *Masked Prowler, the Story of a Raccoon*, 1950; *Bubo, the Great Horned Owl*, 1954; *Dipper of Copper Creek*, 1956, 1996; *Hole in the Tree*, 1957; *Snow Tracks*, 1958; *My Side of the Mountain*, 1959; *Beastly Inventions*, 1970; *On the Far Side of the Mountain*, 1990; *The Tarantula in My Purse, and 172 Other Wild Pets*, 1996; *Frightful's Mountain*, 1999.

SUGGESTED READING: *Authors and Artists for Young Adults*, vol. 8, 1992; *Children's Literature Review*, vol. 1, 1976; *Contemporary Authors*, New Revision Series, vol. 25, 1988; *Dictionary of Literary Biography*, vol. 52, 1986; Drew, Bernard. *The 100 Most Popular Young Adult Authors*, 1997; Gallo, Don, ed. *Speaking for Ourselves*, 1997; George, Jean Craighead. *Journey Inward*, 1982; Graham, Paula W. *Speaking of Journals*, 1999; Hipple, Ted, ed. *Writers for Young Adults*, 1997; Kutzer, M. Daphne and Emmanuel S. Nelson, eds. *Writers of Multicultural Fiction for Young Adults*, 1996; McElmeel, Sharon. *100 Most Popular Children's Authors*, 1999; Silvey, Anita, ed. *Children's Books and Their Creators*, 1995; *Something About the Author*, vol. 2, 1971; vol. 68, 1992. Periodicals—"On Writing *Everglades*," *Book Links*, September 1995; Williams, Karen, "Talking with Wolves, Then Writing About Them," *Christian Science Monitor*, September 25, 1997; Winarski, Diane, "The Dynamic Environment of Jean Craighead George," *Teaching PreK–8*, May 1994.

WEB SITE: *www.jeancraigheadgeorge.com*

An earlier profile of Jean Craighead George appeared in *More Junior Authors* (1963).

Adèle Geras

March 15, 1944–

"I was born in 1944. When I was six years old and at school in Nigeria, I told my schoolfriends I was born in Jerusalem, and they didn't believe me. 'Jerusalem's in heaven,' they said, but it isn't, and I was born there. We traveled to many different countries when I was a girl, because my father worked for the British Colonial Service and he was posted to places like North Borneo and The Gambia. When I was eleven, I was sent to boarding school in England and enjoyed my time there a lot. I'm an only child, and here, suddenly, was an enormous number of sisters . . . .

"After school, I studied French and Spanish at Oxford and graduated in 1966 from St. Hilda's College.

"All through my childhood and youth, I had a very clear idea of what I wanted to be when I grew up. I was going to be a STAR: something between Barbra Streisand and Judy Garland. In college I spent most of my time on stage in one performance after another, and stardom didn't look like a long shot. But then I married and moved with my husband to Manchester, and there were no job opportunities for stars anywhere. So I became a teacher . . . well, it *did* provide me with a captive audience . . . and I taught French for four years, until my first daughter was born, in 1971.

"In 1973 I went in for a competition. I love competitions and always think I'm going to win, right up to the day the results come out. A newspaper was offering a large amount of money, and, like most people who've never tried it, I thought that writing a children's story had to be simplicity itself. I didn't win the competition, but I hadn't written a story since I was twelve, and I enjoyed the process so much that I thought: this is huge fun and certainly a lot easier than working!

"I still think it's fun. It's about pretending. It's like having a big box of dressing-up clothes in the corner of the room and deciding every day who I'm going to be. What about a fat black cat who knows everything? Or a grandmother, telling stories to her grandchild? Or a teenager in love? It's tremendously liberating to do exactly what you want to do. You can travel through time and space, change yourself and everything around you, rearrange the world to your satisfaction, and all without moving out of your chair.

Courtesy of Della Batchelor

"I like writing about cats, relationships, memory, families, love, ghosts, and places that are interesting in some way. I like writing sad books and funny ones, but funny ones are harder. I don't really write about my family, but I borrow bits and pieces of people I know and use them to make characters up, rather like those heads-bodies-legs books that little kids enjoy. My teachers from long ago are a rich source of material and sometimes, I put them in exactly as they were. I've done this in The Egerton Hall Trilogy.

"I love reading, talking, eating, going to the movies and the theater, and knitting. I have two mottoes. One is from Isak Dinesen: 'Write a little every day without hope and without despair,' and the other is from Kaffe Fassett (a knitting designer): 'If in doubt, add twenty more colors.'"

* * *

Adèle Geras, whose last name begins with a hard *g* and rhymes with *terrace*, was born March 15, 1944 in Jerusalem, Palestine (now Israel), to Laurence and Leah Weston. She spent her childhood accompanying her father on his assignments for the British Colonial Service, and her experiences during that time have had a great influence on her writings. In 1966, a year after graduating with a B.A. from St. Hilda's College, Oxford, she married Norman Geras, a lecturer and writer. That year she acted in London in the play *Four Degrees Over*. From 1968 through 1971 she taught French at Fairfield High School, Droylsden, Lancashire, England. Since then she has focused her energies on her family—her husband and their two daughters—and on writing.

Geras writes short stories and picture books for young children as well as fiction for older readers. In 1991 she received the Sydney Taylor Award for *My Grandmother's Stories: A Collection of Jewish Folktales* and in 1994 the National Jewish Book Council Award for *Golden Windows and Other Stories of Jerusalem*. Her books have been translated into several languages, including Dutch and German.

"I like writing about cats, relationships, memory, families, love, ghosts, and places that are interesting in some way."

SELECTED WORKS: *Tea at Mrs. Manderby's*, 1976; *Apricots at Midnight and Other Stories from a Patchwork Quilt*, 1977; *Voyage*, 1983 (reissued, 1999); *Snapshots of Paradise: Love Stories*, 1984; *My Grandmother's Stories: A Collection of Jewish Folktales*, illus. by Jael Jordan, 1990; The Egerton Hall Trilogy: (*The Tower Room*, 1990; *Watching the Roses*, 1991; *Pictures of the Night*, 1993); *Golden Windows and Other Stories of Jerusalem*, 1993; *A Lane to the Land of the Dead*, 1994; *Little Swan*, illus. by Johanna Westerman, 1995; *Beauty and the Beast and Other Stories*, illus. by Louise Brierley, 1996; *The Fabulous Fantoras, Book One: Family Files*, illus. by Eric Brace, 1998; *The Random House Book of Opera Stories*, illus. by various artists, 1998; *silent snow secret snow*, 1998; *The Fabulous Fantoras, Book Two: Family Photographs*, illus. by Eric Brace, 1999.

SUGGESTED READING: *Contemporary Authors*, New Revision Series, vol. 19, 1987; vol. 52, 1996; *Something About the Author*, vol. 23, 1981; vol. 87, 1996; *Something About the Author Autobiography Series*, vol. 21, 1996. Periodicals— "Cooking with Books," *Children's Literature in Education*, March 1993.

Courtesy of Jose L. Gonzalez

Lucía M. González

December 13, 1957–

"I was born in Caimito del Guayaval, a very small town in the province of Havana, Cuba. The year after my birth marked the triumph of the Cuban Revolution. I still remember the day the bearded revolutionaries came to my town. I must have been about three years old when my grandmother carried me in her arms fighting the crowds and tossed me in the arms of the tallest one of the bearded giants. Fidel Castro, her beloved leader, gave me a kiss on my forehead and a tiny Cuban flag. This event stands out as one of the earliest memories of my childhood.

"Back then, very few people had television in their houses, particularly in the countryside, where many did not even have electricity. The adults sat outside in their big rocking chairs conversing with the neighbors or the passersby. We, the children in the block, hunted *cocuyos*, or fireflies, played games, and listened to stories. Our favorite nights were when my *Tía Abuela* Nena, my Great Aunt Nena, came to stay with us. She taught us many games and told us the most wonderful stories. *Tía* Nena did not know how to write and read, but she knew all the stories in the world, and especially all the family stories from long ago. She was a natural storyteller, the keeper of the memories, who enchanted all of us with her tales. I always begged her to repeat my favorite stories. I never forgot those stories, or her special way of telling them.

"In 1965 my parents, who never shared the rest of the family's devotion to the Revolution, decided to leave Cuba and come to the United States. I, like many children whose parents choose to migrate, was heartbroken. We left Cuba and came to Miami, Florida, on August 4, 1970. The first two years in this country were not easy. I was terribly homesick and did not know a word of English. It was also my first year in junior high! It was then that I became an avid reader. The school librarian pointed me

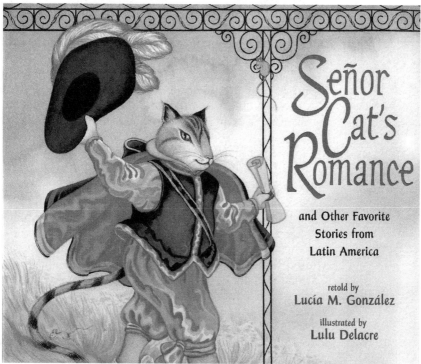

Señor
Cat's
Romance

and Other Favorite
Stories from
Latin America

retold by
Lucía M. González

illustrated by
Lulu Delacre

Courtesy of Scholastic, Inc.

to a hidden shelf where she kept a small collection of Spanish books. After the first month, I had read all 25 titles in the section. I re-read them many times during that year. I also read comic books and magazines my parents brought from the Spanish market.

"During my first year in high school we moved to an all-Cuban neighborhood. The school there had an English as a Second Language Program and a wonderful library. By then, reading had become my preferred pastime. I also enjoyed writing poetry and long essays. The public library became my favorite hideaway.

"I studied history at the University of California in Santa Barbara. After many travels I returned to Miami and got a position in the children's department at a small public library. I fell in love with children's literature and folklore and re-discovered the art of storytelling. It was then that I started writing, adapting, and telling in English the stories told to me in Spanish by *Tía Abuela* Nena in Cuba. It gave me great pleasure to recollect and retell the adventures of some of my favorite characters, such as the bossy rooster on the way to the wedding of his uncle the parrot, the little cockroach Martina marrying Pérez the Mouse, or the Little Half-Chick on his way to Madrid to meet the king. I realized how important it was for me to keep those stories alive and to pass them on to our children growing up in the United States.

"One day I received a call from a big publisher. They were looking for Cuban-American stories to include in the anthology *From Sea to Shining Sea: A Treasury of American Folklore*, compiled by Amy Cohn and published by Scholastic in 1993. They selected two of my stories for publication in the anthology. They liked the story of the bossy little rooster very much and published it as a picture book. Illustrated by Lulu Delacre, *The Bossy Gallito* became my first book. Currently I am working on a collection of scary tales from the oral tradition of the Hispanic Caribbean.

"I love being a writer and researching my stories. I am very grateful that I have the opportunity to reach so many children and leave them with these stories."

* * *

When she was twelve years old, Lucía Martínez came to the United States with her older sister, Nieves, and their parents, Caridad and José Martínez. During her final year at university she wrote a paper on Venezuela and decided that she would spend a month in that country after graduation. The month turned into a year, and she returned to Miami with a husband, José Luis González. Lucía and José continue to live in Miami with their children, Anna and José Antonio.

González began her career in library service for children with the Miami Dade Public Library System in 1987, receiving her M.A. degree in Library and Information Science at the University of South Florida in 1991. Soon she began to translate her Great Aunt Nena's wonderful stories into English with an American flavor and shared them with the children in the library. She has been active throughout her library career in promoting diversity and cultural integration, and she has been a speaker at many educational and library conferences.

The Bossy Gallito won honorable mention for the 1996 Pura Belpré Award for text and illustrations and was cited on the New York Public Library's 100 Titles for Reading and Sharing and the CCBC Choices lists. Lucía González is still working in the Miami Dade Library System. However, she has moved to a smaller branch that is closer to home so she can ride her bike to and from work and spend more time writing.

SELECTED WORKS: "Juan Bobo and the Buñuelos" and "El Gallo de Bodas / The Rooster on the Way to the Wedding," in *From Sea to Shining Sea: A Treasury of American Folklore and Folk Songs*, comp. by Amy Cohn, 1993; *The Bossy Gallito / El Gallo de Bodas: A Traditional Cuban Folktale*, illus. by Lulu Delacre, 1994; *Señor Cat's Romance*, illus. by Lulu Delacre, 1997.

SUGGESTED READING: Santiago, Fabiola, "Stories in Their Own Image," *Miami Herald*, October 18, 1996.

Libba Moore Gray was born Elizabeth Hobson Francis in Roanoke, Virginia. The second of four children, Gray had one older sister, Nancy, and a younger sister and brother, Suzanne and Michael. From the beginning she was precocious, with a commanding and theatrical personality—a very determined child who loved being the center of attention. There was little money for presents in the Francis household, so when she was about thirteen she composed a heart-wrenching letter and sent it in to a radio contest, hoping to win a Sparkle Plenty doll for her younger sister Suzanne. Her essay was so poignant she won the prize, and at that moment, she said later, she saw the power of words.

In high school Gray studied dance and acting. Her creativity was encouraged and nurtured by her dance and drama teachers, and their importance in her life influenced her decision, later, to become a teacher herself. By working at many odd jobs, she managed to save enough money to go to college, but after two years she left school to marry her first husband, Eldon Moore, in 1957 and become a minister's wife. The marriage ended in divorce twenty-five years later, and in 1986 she married Robert Gray, a television news anchor.

Libba Moore Gray

March 3, 1937–June 3, 1995

While her four children were small, Gray worked on her dream of earning a B.A. at Carson Newman College in Jefferson City, Tennessee. She graduated cum laude in 1973 at the age of thirty-six, with a double major in theater and English. She taught kindergarten for a time and then went on to teach high school English and drama for twenty years. Gray was a very creative teacher, who encouraged her students to keep journals and explore their own creative gifts, and to read the classics with imagination and enthusiasm. When she taught Shakespeare, for example, she acted out all the parts. She didn't just read *Macbeth*, she *became* Macbeth, in full costume. Deeply involved with her students, she coached the mime team, taught drama, and sponsored the school literary magazine. She kept a rocking chair in her classroom and read aloud to her students while sitting there. Over the years, her students wrote all over that chair. After her death, the school named the high school theater the Libba Moore Gray Theatre.

Gray was talented across many of the arts. She wrote all her life. She loved classical music and was a competent pianist—her mother was also a pianist and an organist. She loved drama and performed in many theaters in the Knoxville area, playing major female roles: Kate in *The Taming of the Shrew*, Regina in *The Little Foxes*, Mame in *Auntie Mame*, and Queen Eleanor in *The Lion in Winter*. She was a liturgical (interpretative) dancer in the Methodist Church. Looking back, family members say she was destined to become an actress and a writer. "My mother wrote anywhere and everywhere," recalls her daughter Amy Morton. "She wrote on bulletins in church while Daddy preached his heart out, and later on the backs of phone books and magazines in doctors' offices. She kept paper and pencil by her bed always—in case she awoke with an idea or a phrase that needed writing down. She would take her coffee out on the porch and write and write."

Gray's poems appeared in small literary magazines across the South. A number were included in the anthology *All Around Us: Poems from the Valley*, which was published in 1996 and dedicated to her memory. In the preface to the book, Don Williams (a journalist whose six-month series on Gray's battle with cancer in the *Knoxville News–Sentinel* won him Tennessee's top journalism award in 1995) wrote: "In the end I was reduced to cataloging this woman who had been so many women—wife, mother, grandmother, actress, teacher, dancer, children's author, cancer-fighter, poet—above all, perhaps, she was a poet."

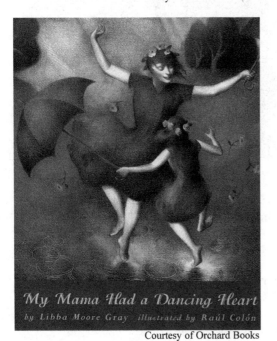

My Mama Had a Dancing Heart
by Libba Moore Gray illustrated by Raúl Colón

Courtesy of Orchard Books

When she first became ill, Gray quit drama and dance and began writing children's books full-time. Her talent as a writer and the subjects she chose— mothers and children, parental love and influence, diversity, the healing power of music—combined to produce stories of exceptional quality. Their tone and language are lyrical—ranging from the hissing words used in *Small Green Snake* to the rhythmic prose of *Fenton's Leap* to the music-like phrasing of *Little Lil and the Swing-Singing Sax*.

Gray wrote and published five books in little more than a year after being diagnosed with breast cancer. She went on to write four more, three of which were published after her death in 1995. Many of the stories are either autobiographical or derived from the experiences of her immediate family. Gray did have a nanny named Willie Rudd and an uncle who played jazz; her battle with cancer is seen in *Miss Tizzy* and again in *Little Black Truck*; her daughter Rachel's story about a frog and her own childhood distress over having to wear glasses led to *Fenton's Leap*; her love of dancing and her daughter Amy's career as a ballerina are beautifully expressed in *My Mama Had a Dancing Heart*; and her love of music, interest in Appalachian history and culture, and a family fiddle handed down through several generations all influenced *When Uncle Took the Fiddle*.

While Gray wrote only nine books during her brief career as a children's author, a number of them have been recognized for their excellence with awards and starred reviews. The bittersweet *Dear Willie Rudd* was cited as a Notable Trade Book in the Field of Social Studies as well as an American Booksellers Pick of the Lists. *My Mama Had a Dancing Heart*, with lovingly rendered song-like text accompanied by Raúl Colón's dreamy pictures of mother and daughter dancing through the seasons, was an ALA Notable Children's Book, a *Booklist* Editors' Choice, and a *New York Times Book Review* Best Illustrated Book for 1995. *Is There Room on the Feather Bed?* was an IRA/CBC Children's Choice. *Small Green Snake* and *My Mama Had a Dancing Heart* were named to the New York Public Library's list, 100 Titles for Reading and Sharing.

Gray was given a posthumous lifetime achievement award by the Tennessee Arts Council in 1999. The Knoxville Writers' Guild now awards an annual Libba Moore Gray Poetry Prize. Gray's children's book manuscripts and color proofs for her published works have been donated to the archives of Emory & Henry College, a small Methodist arts school in Emory, Virginia, which Gray attended for two years.

Each of Libba Moore Gray's children has carried on her creative spirit. Amy is owner and artistic director of the Van Metre School of Dance and the driving force behind the Appalachian Ballet Company. Mike is in the corporate world but composes music in his spare time. David is a graduate of Ringling Brothers Clown College and is a comedian in a theater in Tennessee. Rachel and her husband own and operate the Miss Tizzy Day School in Louisville, Tennessee, where the emphasis is on creative growth for all students.

SELECTED WORKS: *Dear Willie Rudd*, illus. by Peter M. Fiore, 1993; *Miss Tizzy*, illus. by Jada Rowland, 1993; *Small Green Snake*, illus. by Holly Meade, 1994; *Fenton's Leap*, illus. by Jo-Ellen Bosson, 1994; *Little Black Truck*, illus. by Elizabeth Sayles, 1994; *My Mama Had a Dancing Heart*, illus. by Raúl Colón, 1995; *Little Lil and the Swing-Singing Sax*, illus. by Lisa Cohen, 1996; *Is There Room on the Feather Bed?*, illus. by Nadine Bernard Westcott, 1997; *When Uncle Took the Fiddle*, illus. by Lloyd Bloom, 1999.

SUGGESTED READING: *Something About the Author*, vol. 83, 1996.

Courtesy of Russ Hodge

Adele Griffin

July 29, 1970–

"As the oldest child growing up in a house of boys, two brothers and two stepbrothers, I often sought peace and order in the counter-reality of my doll house. This was no ordinary doll house; after my mother helped me build it from a kit, gluing down its balsa wood floors, hinging its shutters and doors, and painting it lemonade yellow, the process of furnishing the house into an idealized home—for paper doll sisters Lavinia, Odette, Vanessa, and Skye—was left up to my powers of improvisation. While I coveted the doll furniture sold in crafts shops, it was prohibitively expensive, not to mention intimidating in its 'don't touch' delicacy. And so I became something of a 'borrower,' scavenging my larger house for any unusual items that would fit into my smaller one.

"Wrapping paper was pasted to the walls, a crocheted doily became a parlor rug, a drink coaster balanced on a spool of thread made a perfect coffee table. Aluminum foil could be reinforced with shirt cardboard to become a full-length mirror, and it was a wonderful day when my mother decided to recover the living room couch. Discarded fabric swatches instantly were draped and folded into new curtains and bedspreads for all.

"Of course my paper dolls fell in love with their surrounding splendor and often praised the house lavishly and loudly to one another. But when they were not validating my choices in interior design, the sisters were preoccupied with high-energy dramas that might best be described as *Wuthering Heights* meets *General Hospital*. Every afternoon brought a new intrigue; there were rivalries and celebrations, secrets and tragedies, and occasionally the odd Kleenex-tissue ghost roamed the corridors. It wasn't long before I began to jot ongoing plots into a pocket notebook, just so that I could keep track of what was happening.

"Eventually, I outgrew my doll house (or, rather, was shamed into giving it up by a friend who informed me that eighth grade was much too old for such whimsy) and became preoccupied by the very real dramatic business of being a teenager. But there were days when I missed making up stories and settings for my beloved surrogate paper sisters, and sometimes I pulled them out of shoe box storage, just to check in on them.

"After I finished school and left my parents' home to make a new one in New York City, I began working for a children's book publishing house. The editorial staff encouraged delving back into the classics, as well as appreciating books by new voices. Whatever the choice, there was no such thing as being 'too old' for any book. Whimsy prevailed. The natural progression, from helping to edit other writers' books to writing my own, was compounded by a fascination with rediscovering the books of my youth, through which I seemed able to access personal memories of that stored-away, younger self.

"Today, as I take my place at my desk and prepare for an afternoon of writing, I feel that I have reclaimed a piece of my past. In creating a story and an imaginary world, I am reminded of the breathless excitement of those hours spent behind my doll house. The stage is assembled from bits and pieces, the act unfolds, and the characters' voices provide the authenticity. Writing books has become, for me, a means to reclaim that old pleasure—storytelling—and a wonderful way once again to transform and render paper characters into a vivid and viable drama."

Courtesy of Hyperion Books

*   *   *

Adele Griffin entered the field of children's fiction at an early age and has published an impressive array of novels within a brief number of years. Born in Philadelphia, she attended the Agnes Irwin School in Rosemont, Pennsylvania, and graduated from the University of Pennsylvania in 1993. After college she went to work as an editorial assistant at Macmillan for a short time before moving to Hyperion Books in 1994. In the spring of 1996 Griffin joined the editorial department at Clarion Books, and since the end of 1997 she has worked part-time for Clarion to allow more time for her own writing.

Although not autobiographical, her first novel, *Rainy Season*, is set in Panama, a country that Griffin visited as a teenager. *Sons of Liberty* was one of five finalists for the 1997 National Book Award in the category of children's books. *Sons of Liberty* and *The Other Shepards* were both named ALA Best Books for Young Adults and nominated for the Dorothy Canfield Fisher Award. *The Other Shepards*, a story about a troubled New York

family touched, it is hinted, by the supernatural, was also selected as a *School Library Journal* Best Book of 1998, a *Bulletin of
the Center for Children's Books* Blue Ribbon title, a *Booklist* Editors' Choice, and an ALA Notable Children's Book. *Split Just
Right* was named to New York Public Library's list, 100 Titles
for Reading and Sharing.

The author and her husband, Erich Mauff, live in New York
City.

SELECTED WORKS: *Rainy Season*, 1996; *Split Just Right*, 1997;
Sons of Liberty, 1997; *The Other Shepards*, 1998; *Dive*, 1999.

SUGGESTED READING: *Something About the Author*, vol. 105,
1999. Periodicals—*Publishers Weekly*, December 16, 1996.

Courtesy of Joelle Petit Adkins

Nikki Grimes

October 20, 1950–

"'Writers are a dime a dozen,' my
mother used to say, but I never believed her. I believed that each
writer was one of a kind, and so was I.

"I began writing when I was six years
old, and I was immediately drawn to poetry. The challenge of painting a picture
or telling a story in only a few words in-
trigued me, and so I filled one spiral
notebook after another with verse.
Sometimes my teachers would catch me
staring out the classroom window form-
ing lines of a poem in my head when I
was supposed to be paying attention to
a lesson in math or science.

"English was my best subject, and in
high school I jumped at the chance to
work on the literary journal. One of my
teachers, Evelyn Wexler, was particularly encouraging, as were my father and
my sister. Each of them, in their own
way, fueled my dreams of being an author. I especially remember my father
taking me to the home of author John
Oliver Killens, who presented me with
my first autographed book. He signed it
'to a fellow writer.' When I read those
words, I nearly burst!

"During the political turmoil of the
1960s, I wrote a lot of protest poetry about racism in America
and I read it aloud in coffeehouses around New York City. At
twenty, I published a chapbook of some of the poems and called
it simply 'Poems by . . . .' This was before the days of desktop
publishing! I sold the book through local bookstores and at my

poetry readings. I printed a thousand copies and they all sold out. I think I have two copies left.

"Later, in college, I studied prose and fiction and tried my hand at essay writing, which I enjoyed. Meanwhile, I published my poetry in literary journals like *Callaloo, Obsidian,* and the *Greenfield Review*. I graduated with a minor in African languages and went to Tanzania, East Africa, for a year to research Swahili literature. Memories of that year found their way into the book *Is It Far to Zanzibar?*

"On my return to the U.S. in 1975, I began freelancing as an arts journalist, reviewing art shows and off-Broadway plays and writing profiles of actors and musicians for periodicals such as the *Amsterdam News, Ms.,* and *Essence* magazine. This was great work for me because I loved theater and, as a critic, I got in for free! Sometimes I'd see four plays in one week.

"One day, a story inspired by my own childhood began to bubble up in me, and I realized I had the makings of a children's book. I knew very little about children's literature, or who published it. To learn, I began reading books for the Children's Book Review service and the Council on Interracial Books for Children. I learned a lot from reading and reviewing children's books—including the best publisher for submitting my own manuscript. That publisher was Dial and they brought out my first book, the mid-grade novel *Growin'*.

"I moved around a great deal when I was growing up, living with a variety of guardians, in a variety of homes, including foster homes, and they're all reflected in my books. I've lived in two-parent homes like Danitra, and in single-parent homes like Zuri. Two years living with my sister provided the stories for *Jazmin's Notebook,* while six years with my mother inspired the poems in *A Dime a Dozen*. I lost my father just as Pump did in *Growin'*, and I based *Meet Danitra Brown* on a real-life friendship that continues still today. Even when the narratives I write are not historically true, they're always emotionally true. In other words, I write about feelings I've felt, fears I've wrestled with, dreams that have filled my imagination.

"Why do I write? Because I have to. Because stories rise up in me demanding to be told, and I obey. I feel fortunate that the people I share my stories with seem to enjoy and learn from them."

> *"One day, a story inspired by my own childhood began to bubble up."*

❋   ❋   ❋

Born in Harlem, Nikki Grimes has lived in nearly every borough of New York City, a fact that is reflected in the urban settings of her stories and poems. Raised mostly by relatives and foster parents, in a variety of family settings, Grimes remembers books as her "soul's delight" in youth, but she has also said that too few of the books she enjoyed then contained African

MEET
DANITRA
BROWN

NIKKI GRIMES
ILLUSTRATED BY
FLOYD COOPER

Courtesy of William Morrow & Co., Inc.

American characters or dealt with problems like those she faced, as a child from a dysfunctional home. Her goal has been to write about children who look and feel just as she did when she was growing up.

After graduating from college, Grimes received a Ford Foundation grant for research in Tanzania in 1974–1975. She has traveled widely, and lived for six years in Sweden. She has worked as a talent coordinator for BlackAfrica Promotions, a writing instructor at various universities, a documentary photographer, a library assistant, a radio scriptwriter and producer, a translator, and a writer and editor at Disney Studios before concentrating on her own freelance writing full-time.

Grimes's first book for young readers received recognition immediately. The Child Study Association named *Growin'* to its Best Books of the Year list, and Bank Street College presented it with a Children's Book of the Year Award. *Come Sunday*, *Meet Danitra Brown*, and *Something on My Mind* have all been designated as ALA Notable Children's Books. *Something on My Mind* and *Meet Danitra Brown* were named Coretta Scott King Honor Books. *Meet Danitra Brown*, *"C" Is for City*, and *My Man Blue* were all included on New York Public Library's list, 100 Titles for Reading and Sharing, and *A Dime a Dozen* was a Junior Library Guild Selection. Grimes's novel of growing up, *Jazmin's Notebook*, received another Coretta Scott King Honor award and was named a *Booklist* Editors' Choice, a Bank Street College Book of the Year, and a New York Public Library Book for the Teen Age. *Aneesa Lee and the Weaver's Gift* received a Parents' Choice Gold Award in 1999, and *My Man Blue* was a *Booklist* Editors' Choice.

Nikki Grimes continues to be a strong voice in African American literature, creating poetry and stories for all ages. In April of 1999 she had the honor of presenting her poetry at the Library of Congress. She makes her home in Corona, California.

SELECTED WORKS: *Growin'*, illus. by Charles Lilly, 1977; *Something on My Mind*, illus. by Tom Feelings, 1978; *Oh, Bother! Someone's Baby-Sitting*, illus. by Sue DiCicco, 1991; *Oh, Bother! Someone's Fighting*, illus. by Darrell Baker, 1991; *Malcolm X: A Force for Change*, 1992; *From a Child's Heart*, illus. by Brenda Joysmith, 1993; *Meet Danitra Brown*, illus. by

Floyd Cooper, 1994; *"C" Is for City*, illus. by Pat Cummings, 1995; *Come Sunday*, illus. by Michael Bryant, 1996; *Wild, Wild Hair*, illus. by George Ford, 1996; *It's Raining Laughter*, photos by Myles Pinkney, 1997; *Jazmin's Notebook*, 1997; *A Dime a Dozen*, illus. by Angelo, 1998; *Aneesa Lee and the Weaver's Gift*, illus. by Ashley Bryan, 1999; *Hopscotch Love: A Family Treasury of Poems*, illus. by Melodye Rosales, 1999; *My Man Blue*, illus. by Jerome Lagarrigue, 1999; *At Break of Day*, illus. by Paul Morin, 1999; *Is It Far to Zanzibar?*, illus. by Betsy Lewin, 2000.

SUGGESTED READING: *Children's Literature Review*, vol. 42, 1997; *Contemporary Authors*, New Revision Series, vol. 60, 1998; Givens, Archie, ed. *Strong Souls Singing: African American Books for Our Daughters and Our Sisters*, 1998; Hopkins, Lee Bennett. *Pass the Poetry, Please*, 3rd edition, 1998; Rand, Donna, et. al. *Black Books Galore*, 1998; Rollock, Barbara T., ed. *Black Authors and Illustrators of Children's Books*, 1988; *Something About the Author*, vol. 93, 1997. Periodicals—Grimes, Nikki, "Reading (and Writing) on a Dare," *Book Links*, September 1999; Grimes, Nikki, The Power of Poetry," *Book Links*, March 2000.

Susan Guevara

(gay-VAH-rah)

January 27, 1956–

" **A** s a kid I loved to be outdoors, building forts in the waist-high field grass at the end of my street. I loved having tea parties with my cat, Smokey, on the huge redwood stump that was my fort in the Santa Cruz mountains. And I loved strange and exotic-sounding words. Once a garbled phrase tripped off my five-year-old tongue and my mother said, 'What was that?' 'French, I think,' I said. It was not French. But it felt like French.

"During the school year I lived in the same house for eighteen years in the suburbs of the San Francisco Bay Area. I still remember the way the sunlight fell in the rooms and in the patio. My first memory is of being almost two and having the powerful pleasure of a bath in the kitchen sink. In the sink, I was almost as tall as my mother. I was taller than my seven-year-old sister. The water was warm and the sink a perfect fit. (I love being in water to this very day and have swum the length of the Golden Gate Bridge twice and the distance to Alcatraz Island twice.)

"All my extracurricular interests were encouraged by my parents. They always found ways for me to have new and different experiences. I took lots of music lessons over the years—piano, viola, flute, guitar. I took riding lessons and oil painting lessons and karate lessons. But doing anything truly well eluded me. Finishing anything was an impossible task.

"During my eleventh summer my family toured Europe in a VW camper. Magic and mystery abounded. I heard languages that bit and spit, clipped and clopped, zheed and zhawd. I ate french-fried octopus and snails in butter, and hot rolls with a middle of cheese. I saw real castles along the Rhine where Grimm's stories incarnated before my imagining eyes. I saw a magical fellow, little and quick. He scuttled into the Black Forest trees. I drew a doodle of him in my diary and wrote, 'It all really gives me an urge to write . . . .' (Picture books were what I had in mind.)

"At twenty-seven, and after several unfocused semesters at various junior colleges, I decided to follow that urge I felt on the Rhine River. I would learn to draw first, and then I would learn to write. I attended Oregon College of Art in Ashland, the San Francisco Academy of Art, and the Royal Academy of Fine Arts in Mechelen, Belgium. Remy Van Sluys, an 83-year-old Flemish impressionist painter on the outskirts of Antwerp, was my mentor. From February to June in 1986 I worked with him in an intensive independent study; he taught me how the light must 'faire une promenade sur le tableau' [go for a walk across the picture]. Finally, at the age of thirty-two, I received my B.F.A. in illustration from the Academy of Art College in San Francisco. I completed something! It was exhilarating. And not only did I complete a degree program but I also had a picture-book dummy from my last semester's independent study. My first book, *Emmett's Snowball* by Ned Miller, was published by Henry Holt one year later.

Courtesy of Michael E. Kozlowski

"Now, ten years since, I've completed nine books and am working on my tenth and eleventh. Each project brings its particular challenges and forces me to grow. A recent picture book, *Chato's Kitchen* by Gary Soto, is now in its eighth printing. Along with some flattering reviews and various awards, it received the first Pura Belpré Award for illustration and the first Tomás Rivera Award.

"Book illustration has me up to my eyebrows in challenges. None of my books has emerged in the same style. Since each story is unique to its setting and characters, it seems reasonable to reflect that uniqueness in the pictures. I use palette, technique, and style, often in ways I've never tried before, to accomplish this end. In this way, illustrating books is truly a journey for me, fraught with danger, excitement, and release.

"Now that I'm well into my apprenticeship years with illustration, the time seems right to begin formal training in writing. And so the small steps begin. Dreams are made real by taking baby steps. Taking baby steps is made possible by believing baby steps are good enough. Enjoying baby steps is probably the real dream come true.

"My day-to-day life is spent living and working in an old cabin in the Sierra Nevada mountains. All sorts of music from opera to Zappa plays on the boom box. The lake across the street is for swimming in the short glorious summers and skiing in the long snowy winters. All this I'm blessed to share with my dear friends and neighbors and K-9 perfection: my dog, Don Diego Felipe Briones Ramirez Guevara."

* * *

Susan Guevara's illustrations have appeared in textbooks for elementary schools, children's magazines such as *Cricket* and *Ladybug*, and greeting cards, as well as picture books and a few chapter books. She received her B.F.A. in 1988 and has concentrated on art for children ever since. In each book she uses a different style and technique, depending on the author's meaning. The most important ingredient for the success of each book, Guevara feels, is emotional empathy—if she can feel what the author is trying to convey, then she can illustrate it. Often her work requires research; for a current project she traveled to Michoacán in the mountains of Mexico to gather background and firsthand information on butterflies.

Courtesy of Penguin Putnam

Guevara's illustrations have a vitality and humor that appeal to children and adults alike. The expressive characters and amusing details in her art for Gary Soto's *Chato's Kitchen* brought her much praise from reviewers. In addition to the Pura Belpré and Tomás Rivera awards, *Chato's Kitchen* received Honorable Mention for the Américas Award and was named an ALA Notable Children's Book, a Child Study Committee Children's Book of the Year, a CCBC Choice Book, and a Parents' Choice Honor Book. Guevara speaks at schools, libraries, and conferences across the country about the craft of bookmaking. She is a periodic guest lecturer at the Academy of Art College in San Francisco, and her work has appeared in a number of exhibitions, including the Society of Illustrators Original Art Show in New York.

Living in an old cabin at the top of Donner Summit in the Sierra Nevada mountains where the snow in winter can sometimes reach the second-story windows, Guevara says her dining-room window is her entertainment center. Flocking to her bird feeders are also squirrels, deer mice, ermine and even an occasional bear. She keeps an Audubon field guide and the Sierra Club western forests book near the window to identify creatures, thus making her window "interactive."

SELECTED WORKS ILLUSTRATED: *Emmett's Snowball*, by Ned Miller, 1990; *The Class with the Summer Birthdays*, by Dian Curtis Regan, 1991; *I Have an Aunt on Marlborough Street*, by Kathryn Lasky, 1992; *The Boardwalk Princess*, by Arthur Levine, 1993; *The King's Commissioners*, by Aileen Friedman, 1995; *Chato's Kitchen*, by Gary Soto, 1995; *Favorite Fairy Tales Told in Italy*, by Virginia Haviland, 1996; *My Daughter, My Son, the Eagle, the Dove: An Aztec Chant*, by Ana Castillo, 2000; *Chato and the Party Animals*, by Gary Soto, 2000; *Not One Damsel in Distress: World Folktales for Strong Girls*, by Jane Yolen, 2000.

SUGGESTED READING: "Chato's Kitchen," *Book Links*, January 1996; Guevera, Susan, "Pura Belpré Award Acceptance Speech for Illustration 1995," *Journal of Youth Services*, Spring 1997.

Jessie Haas

July 27, 1959–

"I grew up on a small Vermont farm, where I trained my own horse. We raised all our fruits, vegetables, meat, and eggs. The farm equipment was two generations old; the way of life harked back a hundred years. That finds its way into my stories all the time, especially the picture books like *Mowing* and *Sugaring*. I want people to remember this, even if only in books.

"I always loved to read, horse stories as first choice. At college I learned to love Jane Austen and Anthony Trollope and wondered if I could write a horse story that embraced these literary standards. In Austen's *Emma* you weren't supposed to admire the heroine at first. Could I write a horse story with a naughty, willful horse instead of a Noble Steed, and a heroine with faults like my own?

"I'd used writing as a refuge from loneliness since seventh grade, and through high school always kept a long story going, another world to escape into. Junior year at Wellesley my best friends went on exchange programs. I took a semester off, worked in a motel laundry, and wrote *Keeping Barney*. My advisor suggested I send the book to Susan Hirschman, a former student of hers, now head of Greenwillow Books. *Keeping Barney* was rejected with many useful suggestions. I took them, made the revisions, and the book was accepted a month before I graduated.

"That same month I married Michael Daley, and three years later we built a tiny cabin just uphill from my parents' cow pasture. We had one room, no insulation, no phone, no plumbing, no electricity—and no mortgage. That gave us freedom to pursue our interests without having to get 'real' jobs.

"That freedom was crucial, because I had written my first book accidentally. I didn't know how to structure a novel and had to go through an apprenticeship, making mistakes and learning from them. That period lasted for nearly ten years before I hit my stride.

"Many of my books are horse stories. In my life and in my stories, horses make things happen. My horse Josey gave me the Beware books and *Safe Horse, Safe Rider*. She's bucked me off, dragged me, trampled me, cured my carpal tunnel, and helped me make a living. Atherton gave me *A Horse like Barney* and *Unbroken*, and got me into politics. I'm glad to give horse stories back to the world, because horse stories have given me so much enjoyment. But they're more than 'just' horse stories: they're about everything else in the world too.

"I dwell inside a novel for days at a time. It's almost a crazy way to live. I still have the impression that I've hurt my hands recently and that they've healed very well. That's because Harry Gibson in *Unbroken* hurt her hands, and I spent a long time feeling what that was like.

"I try to create and then step into a world in which even the minor characters are real people. I don't do this systematically—I don't do anything systematically. I usually throw myself, via the central character, into a situation and then start looking around. Who is that person over there? What does she think about what's happening, and what does she say? What's the weather like here?

Courtesy of June T. Campbell

"This doesn't happen all at once. It takes months of thinking and refining over and over until every part of the story rings a pure note. I want to make the words transparent, so the page becomes an open window. I hope to pass along, through my stories, the joy and strength that others have given to me."

Beware the Mare
by JESSIE HAAS

pictures by
MARTHA HAAS

Courtesy of William Morrow & Co., Inc.

* * *

Katherine Jessie Haas was born in Westminster, Vermont, graduated from Wellesley College in 1981 with a degree in English, and now lives in rural Putney, where she continues to enjoy many of her childhood interests, such as horseback riding and working with animals. Although writing is her main focus, she has worked part-time jobs at a yarn mill, a village store, and a vegetable stand. She is also active in social causes—campaigning for a national health care plan, delivering Meals-on-Wheels, and belonging to groups such as the New England Coalition on Nuclear Pollution and the Vermont Consumers Campaign for Health.

Her first book, *Keeping Barney*, appeared on the voting lists for the Dorothy Canfield Fisher Award, the Volunteer State Award, and Australia's Northwest Territories Award. *Uncle Daney's Way* was nominated for the Bluebonnet Award, the Mark Twain Award, the South Carolina Children's Book Award, and the Dorothy Canfield Fisher Award. *Busybody Brandy*, *No Foal Yet*, and *Clean House*, three books for preschoolers and early readers, were named Pick of the Lists titles by the American Booksellers Association. *Clean House* and *Sugaring* were Child Study Association Children's Books of the Year, and *Sugaring* was named a Notable Children's Trade Book in the Field of Social Studies.

Haas's popular stories about a mare named Beware have been nominated for many state awards. The original, *Beware the Mare*, was named a Pick of the Lists title by the ABA; later the Bank Street College Child Study Association chose *Be Well, Beware* as a Children's Book of the Year. Haas herself illustrated the fourth book in the series, *Beware and Stogie*, with sketches at the opening of each chapter. Her latest novel, *Unbroken*, received a Parents' Choice Gold Award and was named one of *School Library Journal*'s Best Books of the year.

SELECTED WORKS: *Keeping Barney*, 1982; *The Sixth Sense and Other Stories*,1988; *Skipping School*, 1992; *A Horse like Barney*, 1993; *Beware the Mare*, 1993; *Busybody Brandy*, illus. by Yossi Abolafia, 1994; *Mowing*, illus. by Joseph A. Smith, 1994; *Uncle Daney's Way*, 1994; *A Blue for Beware*, 1995; *No Foal Yet*, illus. by Joseph A. Smith, 1995; *Be Well,*

Beware, 1996; *Sugaring*, illus. by Joseph A. Smith, 1996; *Clean House*, illus. by Yossi Abolafia, 1996; *Westminster West*, 1997; *Beware and Stogie*, 1998; *Fire! My Parents' Story*, 1998; *Unbroken*, 1999.

SUGGESTED READING: *Contemporary Authors*, vol. 114, 1985; *Something About the Author*, vol. 98, 1998.

"**M**y parents have always hated to write. Though they're both perfectly capable of it, they view writing even a letter as akin to torture. So they were stunned when I decided I wanted to be a writer.

"'You want to do *what?*' they asked. 'When you don't have to?'

"But even if they didn't pass down a love of commas and semicolons and the struggle to find the right word, my parents did give me a love of books and stories. I can remember my mother apologizing, 'Oh, I meant to clean house today, but I just had to see how this book ended.' I can remember my father looking up from some historical novel and telling the rest of us, 'Listen to this. When Simon Kenton came to Ohio . . . .' They were busy people—there were four of us kids to take care of, my father was trying to establish his own farm, and for a while my mother was his only help; once all of us kids were in school she went back to work as a nurse. So the message they gave us was clear: no matter how busy you are, books are worth finding time for. They're fun.

"And it wasn't just my parents. My grandfather was always recommending science fiction books to my brothers—books I read too, because I didn't want my brothers making fun of me for not knowing who Robert Heinlein or Isaac Asimov was. My grandmother on the other side was full of stories that had been passed down through the family for generations. One of my ancestors supposedly threw rose petals in front of George Washington's horse; another was kidnapped. Even my grandmother doubted the truth of some of the stories, but they were worth passing on anyhow.

Courtesy of Summit Photographics

Margaret Peterson Haddix

Margaret Peterson Haddix

April 9, 1964–

"Given that mix of influences—science fiction and family history—it's no wonder I can't seem to write books that are easily categorized.

"But even as I was sure that I wanted to write books, I also believed it was probably an unattainable goal for a farm girl from Washington Court House, Ohio. I'd read the author's bios on the jackets of the books I checked out from the library. Authors, I knew, were always from New York, London, Los Angeles—important places.

"So when I went off to college, I hedged my bets and majored in both journalism and creative writing, and then took a series of newspaper jobs in the summers and after college. Journalism was a great experience for an aspiring novelist. I interviewed politicians and homeless people, celebrities and people who asked, 'Why would anyone be interested in me?' even as they launched into fascinating tales. I wasn't just an Ohio farm girl anymore; I was a farm girl who'd been entrusted with lots of people's life stories.

Courtesy of Simon & Schuster Children's Publishing Division

"In the meantime, I also got married. When my husband, Doug, got a job in a city that held little opportunity for me, we agreed: it was time for me to start writing books. Looking back, I'm stunned at what a gamble that was, having me work only part-time, devoting the rest of my time to fiction. For two years it seemed like a particularly stupid gamble. I'm grateful that my husband stayed supportive, even as I collected rejection letter after rejection letter.

"My first two books sold just as we were starting a family. So I'm also grateful that our children, Meredith and Connor, mostly coordinated their naps, giving me time to work on subsequent books. Sometimes I really should have used their naptimes for naps of my own, so I only wrote what was exciting enough to keep me awake.

"Now that my kids are past naps, my criteria haven't changed that much. I know I have to write a story when the story keeps me awake at night, teases at the back of my brain all day, just won't let me go.

"And that's why I became a writer."

*   *   *

Margaret Peterson grew up on a farm near Washington Court House, Ohio, and received her B.A. in creative writing and journalism from Miami University of Ohio in 1986. She worked as a copy editor on the Fort Wayne *Journal-Gazette* in Indiana and then as a reporter for the *Indianapolis News*; in 1987 she married another reporter, Doug Haddix. When they moved to Danville, Illinois, four years later, after Doug had accepted a new job as a newspaper editor, Margaret decided it was time to pursue her dream of writing fiction as well as fact. Taking a series of temporary and part-time jobs, such as teaching at a community college, she drew on stories she had heard as a reporter to try her hand at writing novels.

Haddix's first book, *Running Out of Time*, had its genesis in a news story she had once written about a restored historic village. The innovative plot, about an historic restoration in which many of the inhabitants believe they are actually living in the 1840s, made this book a favorite of young readers immediately. It was a Junior Library Guild Selection, an American Booksellers Association Pick of the Lists, an ALA Best Book for Young Adults, a Quick Pick for Reluctant YA Readers, and a Notable Trade Book in the Field of Social Studies. *Running Out of Time* also won children's choice awards in Maryland, Arizona, and Oklahoma.

Her next four novels were all chosen as ALA Best Books for Young Adults, a remarkable record for a new author. *Don't You Dare Read This, Mrs. Dunphrey* grew out of another newspaper assignment, one for which Haddix had talked to more than a dozen neglected and abused young people. Their stories remained with her and became embodied in Tish, an angry, tough-talking, and deeply frightened teen, trying to hold her life together in spite of parental neglect. This book was also an IRA Children's Book Award winner and a Quick Pick for Reluctant Young Adult Readers. *Leaving Fishers* was cited as a New York Public Library Book for the Teen Age and an ABA Pick of the Lists. *Among the Hidden* was among the Top Ten of ALA's Best Books for Young Adults.

Margaret Peterson Haddix currently makes her home in Powell, Ohio, with her husband and their two children.

SELECTED WORKS: *Running Out of Time*, 1995; *Don't You Dare Read This, Mrs. Dunphrey*, 1996; *Leaving Fishers*, 1997; *Among the Hidden*, 1998; *Just Ella*, 1999.

SUGGESTED READING: *Contemporary Authors*, vol. 159, 1998; *Something About the Author*, vol. 94, 1998.

Courtesy of Mary Landry Decker

Wendy Anderson Halperin

April 10, 1952–

"I was born in Illinois, among fields and fields of corn. The land was forever flat and the sky was everywhere. There were four children in my family, three girls and one boy, and we played with each other.

"Aside from making clothes for a crawfish for a 4-H show, my earliest memory of creativity was with acrylic paint and rocks. We would collect rocks on the shores of Lake Michigan, then take them to our kitchen table where we would all sit around and paint them. Some would have simple designs, others would actually look like something. For example, a rock might resemble a car, so the rock would be transformed into a car with headlights, etc. We then sold them at the local art fair.

"I discovered figure drawing when I was fourteen, attending Oxbow, the Art Institute of Chicago's summer school in Saugatuck, Michigan. I loved it. It helped me discover that drawing wasn't just something you learned but something you felt. Because figure drawing has time limitations (30-second or 5-minute poses), it forces you into the spontaneous, or the moment when your hand just does it. Leonardo da Vinci said, 'It's not enough to draw a person, you have to draw the state of mind of that person.' This sums up how I feel about drawing people and my goals in drawing.

"I worked in New York City for a while. There, ideas were the important thing. I learned, for example, that one problem has many solutions, and I discovered the forms that ideas, day-dreams, night dreams, or mind-wandering thoughts might take. As a result, I am sensitive to that moment when an idea pops into my head.

"One day I got the idea that I wanted to stop drawing cartoons and draw and paint things and people that looked real—with shadows, expressions, relationships, environments, and land-scapes. That challenge has been keeping me busy and inspired for twenty years. I continue to have a love and curiosity for that endeavor.

"My life enters into my books as if I were reading a mystery. I never know how, who, when, or why things and people enter my drawings. It is not calculated—it is mysteriously woven. Drawing has affected my observations of the world. I see things I can draw and can remember. Then I weave them into pictures.

I see things that technically I can't draw but would like to, thus I'm inspired to figure it out. I go to other artists' paintings and drawings for help.

"My mother is an artist—an abstract sculptor—and has given me her honesty every day of my life. She has played an important role in pointing out my weaknesses and strengths. Artistically we are very different, yet somehow we share an artistic dialogue and inspire each other. My children, sisters, nieces and nephews are all involved in the arts (theater, music, writing, or visual), so our summers together have inspired circuses, musicals, improvisational theater, and basically dress-up clothes all over the house and yard. I believe that creativity is contagious.

"I love to teach children how to draw people, and I hope to inspire others to draw, as so many artists have inspired me."

Courtesy of Orchard Books

*　*　*

Wendy Halperin's signature style is a full-page frame surrounding a series of smaller scenes that enhance and expand upon the story.

Halperin grew up in the Midwest. She attended Syracuse University in upstate New York and then went on to study art at the Pratt Institute in New York City, the California College of Arts and Crafts, and the American Academy in Chicago. She also studied privately with the artist David Hardy in California. She worked as an advertising agency art director in Chicago and New York before turning to fine art painting in 1980. In the late 1980s, she began leading art workshops for students at elementary schools and local art centers, as well as drawing workshops for teachers, librarians, and educators.

Halperin received an Honorable Mention, Palette & Chisel Award, in 1985 and a Best of Show Award from the South Haven Center for the Arts in 1990. Her paintings have been exhibited at the Art Institute of Chicago Sales and Rental Gallery, the Kalamazoo Institute of Arts, and the Works Gallery in New York City. Her work is also displayed in the permanent Grosse Pointe (Michigan) Library Collection.

The Lampfish of Twill was a *New York Times* Notable Book of the Year, an American Booksellers Assocation Pick of the Lists, a *Boston Globe* Best Book of the Year, and a Bank Street

College Children's Book of the Year. *Hunting the White Cow* was a *School Library Journal* Best Book of the Year, an ALA Notable Children's Book, a Marion Vannett Ridgway Memorial Award honor book, and an NCTE Notable Children's Book in the Language Arts. It was listed as well among the New York Public Library's annual 100 Titles for Reading and Sharing. *Homeplace* was named a Best Book of the Year by *School Library Journal* and was a Junior Library Guild selection; it was also placed on the New York Public Library's 100 Titles list. Halperin's book about her children's business ventures, *Once upon a Company,* was likewise cited by the New York Public Library and was named a Notable Trade Book in the Field of Social Studies.

SELECTED WORKS WRITTEN AND ILLUSTRATED: *Once upon a Company: A True Story,* 1998.

SELECTED WORKS TRANSLATED AND ILLUSTRATED: *When Chickens Grow Teeth,* by Guy De Maupassant, 1996.

SELECTED WORKS ILLUSTRATED: *The Lampfish of Twill,* by Janet Taylor Lisle, 1991; *Hunting the White Cow,* by Tres Seymour, 1993; *Homeplace,* by Anne Shelby, 1995; *A White Heron,* by Sarah Orne Jewett, 1997; *In Aunt Lucy's Kitchen* (The Cobble Street Cousins, Book 1), by Cynthia Rylant, 1998; *A Little Shopping* (The Cobble Street Cousins, Book 2), by Cynthia Rylant, 1998; *Sophie and Rose,* by Kathryn Lasky, 1998; *Special Gifts* (The Cobble Street Cousins, Book 3), by Cynthia Rylant, 1999; *Some Good News* (The Cobble Street Cousins, Book 4), by Cynthia Rylant, 1999; *The Full-Belly Bowl,* by Jim Aylesworth, 1999.

SUGGESTED READING: Cummins, Julie, *Children's Book Illustration and Design,* vol. 2, 1998; *Something About the Author,* vol. 80, 1995.

WEB SITE: *www.parrett.net/halperin*

Joyce Hansen

October 18, 1942–

"I was born in the Bronx, a borough of New York City, on October 18, 1942. I grew up with two younger brothers who have appeared in several of my books and stories as one pesty baby brother. A number of the characters in my stories are based on family members. We had a large extended family with many interesting 'characters.' I was also very much touched by the stories my mother told to my brothers and me of her childhood in Charleston, South Carolina, and the stories my father told us of his boyhood in the Caribbean. My father, who was a photographer and historian in his own right, told interesting tales with his camera. My parents' narratives provided the inspiration for several of my own stories and novels.

"I've always loved books, words, talk, and stories. My mother was my first teacher and introduced me to books even before I knew how to read. I remember begging her to read *Alice in Wonderland* to me over and over, and she did. How I loved that story, and recall wishing that I knew how to read so that I could read it to myself. At a very young age, books were important to me because they took me to many grand and exciting places, far beyond the Bronx (not that I didn't like the Bronx).

"I talked and read my way through elementary and middle school (it was called junior high school in my day) and day-dreamed through high school—except in English and History and Stenography. One of the daydreams was that I would like to be a writer, for I still loved books. But dreams have to be supported with a real job and a regular salary.

"When I graduated from high school in 1960, I worked as a secretary in an of-fice and a few years later, attended col-lege at night. I also read extensively dur-ing this period as I tried to develop my writing skills. The civil rights movement and the concurrent activities of African American scholars, writers, playwrights, performing and visual artists whose works were finally getting the attention they deserved, influenced me deeply; however, it would be a long time before I became a published writer.

"In 1973 I accepted a teaching posi-tion and remained a public school teach-er for the next twenty-two years. My first class as a new teacher consisted of a feisty group of seventh graders who be-came known throughout Stitt Junior High School as Hansen's Huns. When I began writing my first children's book in 1978, I found the Huns creeping be-tween the lines, pushing their way into

Courtesy of Austin Hansen

Joyce Hansen

my story. I gave in to them. The book became *The Gift Giver* and was published in 1980. I'd also finally found my writer's voice and realized that the combination of my own childhood memories coupled with the many wonderful children whose lives I shared as their teacher would be my central theme, my primary focus as a writer.

"When I wrote my second and third novels I had changed teaching positions and taught reading to special education stu-dents in a facility for high school–age youngsters. *Home Boy* is the story of a troubled young man, and *Yellow Bird and Me*, a sequel to *The Gift Giver*, is about a student who has reading problems. I was, at the time, teaching both types of students. My subsequent books have been historical fiction and nonfiction, growing out of my interest in history in general, with a focus on American history and the experience of African Americans. But I even wrote my historical books with my students in mind. There is nothing I enjoy more than bringing life and human emotions to the facts and figures of history. I try to tell interesting and honest stories about our country's past that will help young readers appreciate the importance of historical knowledge—stories that will give them strength and encouragement as they make their own journeys through life and create their own personal histories.

Courtesy of Scholastic, Inc.

"I retired from teaching in 1995 and now live outside of Columbia, South Carolina, with my husband, Matthew Nelson. We were married in 1982. I write full-time; however, I still enjoy meeting and talking with young people, who continue to be my inspiration. And I will always be thankful to Hansen's Huns—the students who helped me to find my writer's voice."

*   *   *

Joyce Hansen graduated from high school in 1960 and worked at several secretarial jobs before going back to school in earnest in 1968. She graduated from Pace University in 1972, working full-time and going to school at night, and received her master's degree from New York University in 1978. Family life formed the backbone of her growing years, and she has said she learned from her father "to see the beauty and poetry in the everyday scenes and the 'just plain folks' he captured in his photographs."

That sensibility is evident in her writings. Joyce Hansen's books are notable for strong characterization: they carry messages of courage and hope in the face of struggle and emphasize the importance of family as well as the necessity of taking personal responsibility.

Hansen's early novels—realistic works in contemporary settings—explore friendship, the pressures of urban life, and the problems of young people like those she taught at school. *Yellow Bird and Me*, about a girl's friendship with a talented dyslexic boy, received a Parents' Choice Award in 1986. Hansen's first historical novels (*Which Way Freedom* and its sequel, *Out from*

This Place, both ALA Notable Books) were set during the Civil War period. *I Thought My Soul Would Rise and Fly*, an entry in Scholastic's popular Dear America series, is set during the Reconstruction Era. *The Captive* tells the story of Kofi, captured in West Africa and sold into the slave trade, and of his escape and eventual career as a free black sailor. *The Captive* received the 1995 Children's Book Award from the Africa Studies Association. *Which Way Freedom, The Captive, I Thought My Soul Would Rise and Fly*, and *Breaking Ground, Breaking Silence* all received Coretta Scott King Honor Book Awards in their respective years. *Women of Hope* and *Breaking Ground, Breaking Silence* were chosen as Notable Trade Books in the Field of Social Studies. *The Heart Calls Home* continues the story of Obi and Easter, characters in *Which Way Freedom?*, and was chosen as a Junior Library Guild selection in spring 2000.

SELECTED WORKS: *The Gift Giver*, 1980; *Home Boy*, 1982; *Yellow Bird and Me*, 1986; *Which Way Freedom?*, 1986; *Out from This Place*, 1988; *Between Two Fires: Black Soldiers in the Civil War*, 1993; *The Captive*, 1994; *I Thought My Soul Would Rise and Fly: The Reconstruction Era Diary of Patsy*, 1997; *Women of Hope: African Americans Who Made a Difference*, 1998; *Breaking Ground, Breaking Silence: The Story of New York's African Burial Ground*, with Gary McGowan, 1998; *The Heart Calls Home*, 1999.

SUGGESTED READING: *Children's Literature Review*, vol. 21, 1990; Collier, Laurie and Joyce Nakamura, eds. *Major Authors and Illustrators for Children and Young Adults*, 1993; *Contemporary Authors*, vol. 105, 1982; *Contemporary Authors*, New Revision Series, vol. 43, 1994; Malinowski, Sharon, ed. *Black Writers 2*, 1993; Pendergast, Sara, ed. *St. James Guide to Children's Writers*, 5th ed., 1999; Rollock, Barbara. *Black Authors and Illustrators of Children's Books*, 2nd ed., 1992; *Something About the Author*, vol. 39, 1985; vol. 46, 1987; vol. 101, 1999; *Something About the Author Autobiography Series*, vol. 15, 1993. Periodicals— *Book Report*, March/April 1997; *Interracial Books for Children Bulletin*, vol. 15, no. 4, 1984.

Cheryl Harness

July 6, 1951–

"I'm the oldest of a family of seven children, which can be a pretty rambunctious proposition. Being a crabby sort of kid, I liked the peaceful, solitary business of reading books, drawing pictures, and making fussy little sculptures out of dime-store clay, rather than 'playing well with others.'

"Although I was born in California—on the 6th of July, 1951—I grew up in the Queen City of the Trails: Independence, Missouri, and thereabouts. We moved around a lot. My favorite books were, besides the encyclopedia, the Betsy-Tacy series by

Maud Hart Lovelace. Her idyllic girlhood in pre-WWI Minnesota and Laura Ingalls Wilder's more rugged experiences were constants. Wherever we lived, whatever was going on in the real world, Betsy was safe in Deep Valley. Pa was playing the fiddle.

"I certainly did not think I would be a writer when I grew up. My first ambition, when I was eight, was to be a puppeteer. Drawing was what I seemed to be pretty good at—but being an artist? Who knew of, who ever heard of anyone making a living at that? So, in time-honored fashion, I went to college to be an art teacher. After all, I had my best time in art class. Didn't I know how shockingly putrid I would be as a twenty-year-old student teacher, every day in a classroom full of young people? Well, I found out.

Courtesy of Laura Sturman

"So I found work as a portrait artist, sitting by a roller coaster in an amusement park. Very good training, I later discovered, for drawing all those folks in my books. I worked as a short-order cook for a while and painted a mural once, on a restaurant wall in exchange for two bucks an hour and all I could eat. Then I worked as an artist at Hallmark's 'social expression' factory, designed and stitched needlework kits in California, and worked for years happily painting flowers, pink-cheeked children, and teddy bears for a greeting card company in Colorado Springs, Colorado. But when I went to bookstores, which was all the time, I was more and more taken by the illustrations I saw in the children's books. I adored the illustrators of the Golden Age: N. C. Wyeth, Jessie Wilcox Smith, and Maxfield Parrish. Could anything be more beautiful? I didn't see how. And there were Lois Lenski and Garth Williams who'd illustrated my old friends, Maud's and Laura's, books. I loved Trina Schart Hyman's illustrations too.

"Inside the fortress of children's books, people were painting wonderful things. How did one scale the walls? I found a tiny advertisement in the back of a magazine: Uri Shulevitz was going to teach a children's book workshop in Oneonta, New York. Just writer a letter. And if he likes it, send money. Find out.

"I went to Oneonta in the summer of 1984. Mr. Shulevitz, the best of teachers, tore my first story to tatters and suggested I take samples of my pictures to New York. I screwed up my courage and went there the next spring. This led to my illustrating the jacket of *Constance*, by Patricia Clapp, a story about a Pilgrim girl. Every evening and weekend, after I got home from my greeting card job, I worked on my illustrations for, eventually, nine books. And I worked on stories of my own until I, at last, wrote and illustrated two fiction books: *The Windchild* and *The Queen with Bees in Her Hair*. They, perhaps, may be found on the remainder tables or in your local library.

"I quit my day job at the end of the 1980s. I was still doing greeting cards freelance, but I began work on *Three Young Pilgrims*. I thought: tell a real-life story, then surround the story with pictures and information about the time and place. Then the book could be an introduction to the Pilgrims, or the Revolutionary War (*Young John Quincy*), or the settling of the continent (*The Amazing Impossible Erie Canal* and *They're Off! The Story of the Pony Express*). Nowadays I research, write, illustrate, and talk about my nonfiction books full-time. I go to classrooms around the country, sometimes in period costume. Who'd a' thought it would be such fun?

"Some might think history's boring. The people in it, except for us, are gone. Long ago. Far away. Black and white. Dusty and dead. Luckily, my job is to imagine away the years between us here in the *now*, and the others back in the *then*. They were living out their stories, not knowing how they would end. Just like us. I go where they lived, read about them, then tell their stories clearly. I paint the pictures and try my best to show what that lost world looked like.

"A girl leans her arm on the splintery railing of a ship called the *Mayflower*. The wind is cold and smells of the salty sea. She has no idea that way off in the unimaginable future, people will read about her. She's history—right then. Just like us—right now."

"My job is to imagine away the years between us here in the now, and the others back in the then. They were living out their stories, not knowing how they would end. Just like us."

* * *

Cheryl Harness was born in California, but her parents' roots were deep in Missouri soil, both their families having settled there in the nineteenth century. The Harnesses moved back to Independence when Cheryl was one year old. After receiving her B.S. in Art Education from Central Missouri State University in 1983, she worked at a variety of jobs, all related to art. When she settled on children's book illustration as a career choice, she illustrated nine books by other authors before finding her signature style in writing and drawing. Her own books depict eras, events, and characters in American history with a distinctive voice and colorful, detailed, and historically accurate illustration. They are widely used in social studies classes to introduce children to various historical periods through a personal approach.

Courtesy of Simon & Schuster Children's Publishing Division

Young John Quincy, The Amazing Impossible Erie Canal, and *They're Off!* were all cited as Pick of the Lists titles by the American Booksellers Association. *Erie Canal* was also noted in *Book Links* magazine's A Few Good Books. *Ghosts of the White House* was named one of the Society of School Librarians International 1998 Honor Books. Harness's books have often been cited as Notable Trade Books in the Field of Social Studies, titles so honored including *Papa's Christmas Gift*, *Young Abe Lincoln*, and *Mark Twain and the Queens of the Mississippi*.

Cheryl Harness lives in a little white house at the end of a lane in Independence, Missouri, with Irene the cat, Ruby the basset hound, and Maude the Scottie. Both dogs have served as models for her books, and Maude, of course, is named after Maud Hart Lovelace.

SELECTED WORKS WRITTEN: *Midnight in the Cemetery*, illus. by Robin Brickman, 1999.

SELECTED WORKS WRITTEN AND ILLUSTRATED: *The Windchild*, 1991; *Three Young Pilgrims*, 1992; *The Queen with Bees in Her Hair*, 1993; *Young John Quincy*, 1994; *The Amazing Impossible Erie Canal*, 1995; *Papa's Christmas Gift: Around the World on the Night Before Christmas*, 1995; *They're Off! The Story of the Pony Express*, 1996; *Young Abe Lincoln: The Frontier Days, 1809–1837*, 1996; *Abe Lincoln Goes to*

Washington, 1837–1865, 1997; *Ghosts of the White House*, 1998; *Mark Twain and the Queens of the Mississippi*, 1998; *Young Teddy Roosevelt*, 1998; *Ghosts of the 20th Century*, 1999.

SELECTED WORKS ILLUSTRATED: *Grandpa's Slide Show*, by Deborah Gould, 1987; *Fudge*, by Charlotte Graeber, 1987; *Gus Wanders Off*, by Alice Schertle, 1988; *Aaron's Shirt*, by Deborah Gould, 1989; *Under the Moon*, by Joanne Ryder, 1989; *The Night Before Christmas*, by Clement C. Moore, 1990.

"**I** was born in a small mining village in county Durham, England. My father was a coal miner at the time, and my mother a very talented housewife who designed and made dresses. She also took photographs with a simple Kodak Brownie and developed them herself.

Courtesy of The Bay

Ted Harrison

August 28, 1926–

"My twin sister and I were brought up with much love and care—during the Great Depression, so we relied on our imaginations to create games and stories for entertainment. My geography teacher fired my imagination with stories of lands far away, and the local cinema proved to be a wondrous opening to other worlds. The character Frank Buck went exploring in a series called Bring 'em Back Alive, while my hero, Ronald Coleman, visited exotic Shangri-La in the movie *Lost Horizon*. All this illuminated my mind.

"One month after my thirteenth birthday Britain declared war on Nazi Germany, so my teenage years were spent aiding the war effort by working on the land and giving public service as a Boy Scout. At grammar school I studied German, and as Heinkel bombers flew over our heads, we sang German folk songs in the air-raid shelter. I was editor of our German class magazine and also its illustrator, so 'Wöchentliche Nachrichten' [Weekly News] was my first illustration assignment.

"My parents bought us an encyclopedia, which I devoured with relish. I read the volumes from cover to cover and learned many stories: Aesop's Fables, the Brothers Grimm, and Shakespeare became my companions. I give thanks today that there was no television to limit my reading and my imagination.

"Later I entered art school and finally joined the British Army Intelligence Corps, where I served in India, Egypt, Kenya, Uganda, and Somaliland. Now I was like Ronald Coleman, seeing the world and gaining knowledge of other peoples and cultures, which continues to enrich my life.

"After teaching in England, I became an art teacher in an Army School in Malaysia for five years before moving to Te Kauwhata in New Zealand, where I taught English, history, and art to Maori students. Here I began including Maori design features into my own work.

"Finally my wife Nicky and son Charles accompanied me to Canada. After teaching on a reservation in Northern Alberta, I wrote my first reading book for Cree children, incorporating aspects of their culture. This marked the beginning of my writing career, and when I moved to Carcross in the Yukon, my painting underwent a complete transformation from academic to abstract realism. It was as if all my travel experiences had gone to form a colorful personal style.

"My picture book *O Canada!* is a personal tribute to the land that for thirty years has inspired and nourished my writing and painting. I now live within sight of the Olympic Mountains of Washington State, and from my vantage point in Victoria, B.C., there is a host of new experiences to write and illustrate."

THE
CREMATION OF SAM M'GEE
by ROBERT W. SERVICE

paintings by TED HARRISON
Courtesy of William Morrow & Co., Inc.

*　*　*

Ted Harrison is an artist whose work is collected by both corporations and individuals but who is perhaps best appreciated by the readers of his finely illustrated picture books about northern life and its landscapes. He was born Edward Hardy Harrison in England and raised and educated there; he has both a Design and an Art Teacher's Diploma. During his military service, he traveled to the Middle East and Africa, afterward teaching art in Malaysia and New Zealand.

In 1968 he moved with his family to Canada, settling in the Yukon and becoming a Canadian citizen in 1973. He continued teaching art to both schoolchildren and adults until 1979, when he turned all his attention to writing and illustrating books.

Harrison's illustrated edition of Robert W. Service's poem *The Cremation of Sam McGee* was an ALA Notable Children's Book and a *New York Times* Best Illustrated Book in 1987. In the same year Harrison was named a Member of the Order of Canada in recognition of his contributions to his adopted country. His tribute book *O Canada!* was short-listed for the Canadian Elizabeth Mrazik-Cleaver Picture Book Award in 1992. He is a member of the Writers Union of Canada and the National Society of Art Education (U.K.). He has received honorary doctorates from Athabasca University in Alberta and the University of Victoria, British Columbia. He is also an Honorary Admiral, HMCS Whitehorse.

Harrison's work has been featured in five documentary films and was displayed at the Yukon Pavilion at Expo 86. His illustrations from *Children of the Yukon* were shown at the International Children's Book Exhibition in Bologna in 1978, and in 1985 his illustrations from *A Northern Alphabet* and *Children of the Yukon* were exhibited at the Biennale of Illustration in Bratislava.

SELECTED WORKS WRITTEN AND ILLUSTRATED: *Children of the Yukon*, 1977; *The Last Horizon: Paintings & Stories of an Artist's Life in the Yukon*, 1980; *A Northern Alphabet*, 1982; *The Blue Raven*, 1989; *O Canada!*, 1992.

SELECTED WORKS ILLUSTRATED: *The Cremation of Sam McGee*, by Robert W. Service, 1987; *The Shooting of Dan McGrew*, by Robert W. Service, 1988.

SUGGESTED READING: *Contemporary Authors*, vol. 116, 1986; *Contemporary Authors*, New Revision Series, vol. 39, 1992; Roberts, Joyce. *Using Picture Books with Older Students: Book 2*, 1995; Silvey, Anita, ed. *Children's Books and Their Creators*, 1995; *Something About the Author*, vol. 56, 1989; *The World of Ted Harrison*, 1966 (Exhibition Catalog). Periodicals—"Author and Illustrator Portraits: Monica Hughes and Ted Harrison, the Canadian Creators of ICBD 1990 (International Children's Book Day)," *Bookbird*, February 1990; Jobe, Ronald, "Beyond Munsch: Canadian Literature for Children and Young People," *Reading Teacher*, April 1992.

Selina Hastings

1945–

"The greatest influence in my life as a writer was undoubtedly my mother. Under her maiden name, Margaret Lane, she wrote novels and biographies, as well as being a regular reviewer of books in the press. Our house was always full of books—new books, old books, parcels of books coming in for review (and often going straight out again to the nearest charity bookstall). Some of these books were by my parents' friends, many of whom were writers and publishers, so my sister and I became accustomed at meals to hearing talk of authors and their newest work, good, bad, and indifferent. On Sunday afternoons my mother would read aloud from Grimm and Hans Andersen, from E. Nesbit and later from *David Copperfield* and *Great Expectations*.

"We lived in London and both of us were sent to St. Paul's, a day school for girls which placed great emphasis on the importance of academic achievement. Although the down side of this (from our point of view) was far too much homework, the up side was an exceptionally well-stocked school library, which we were encouraged to use as much as we liked. Here, totally absorbed, I made my way through the wordy novels of Rider Haggard, Harrison Ainsworth, Alexandre Dumas, and other nineteenth-century worthies which you would probably have to pay me to read now!

"After school I went on to Oxford University, where I read English Language and Literature. Although I moaned and groaned about the hardships of having to learn Anglo-Saxon—it seemed so unfair that those studying French or Spanish could spend months in France or Spain perfecting their languages, but who spoke Anglo-Saxon?—I came to love the poems and stories, such as *Beowulf*, *The Seafarer*, and *The Wanderer*; and later when Middle English was added to the menu, I fell wholly under the spell of Chaucer and the mysterious unidentified poet of *Sir Gawain and the Green Knight*.

Courtesy of Jerry Bauer

"In my last year at Oxford I made friends with a flamboyant figure then just beginning on a soon-to-be-abandoned academic career. Sebastian Walker was a brilliant and eccentric character who stood out from his contemporaries by his dandified taste in clothes and his brilliance as a cook. (The first time I met him was at a birthday dinner he gave for a colleague at which the *pièce de résistance* was a gluttonously rich chocolate cake which had taken eleven hours to construct.)

"Abandoning academe, Sebastian went into publishing and soon set up his own imprint publishing children's books. One of his young illustrators had completed a series of pictures for *Sir Gawain*, and Sebastian asked me if I would do a retelling of the poem to go with the pictures. I jumped at the chance and enjoyed it so much that a long series for Walker Books followed, including my own personal favorite, a retelling of some of *The Canterbury Tales*.

"Since then I have written two adult biographies and am working on a third, but I still consider my irregular return journeys to this rich literary field some of my most rewarding work, evoking as it does not only my entranced discoveries as a student but the happy hours of reading aloud when I was a child."

* * *

After attending the St. Paul's Girls' School and St. Hugh's College, Oxford, Selina Hastings commenced her career as a writer. She worked at the *Daily Telegraph* for fourteen years and served as the literary editor of the English periodical *Harper's and the Queen*. Her first book, *Sir Gawain and the Green Knight*, was illustrated by Juan Wijngaard, who received the Kate Greenaway Medal for his work. The author and illustrator collaborated again on *Sir Gawain and the Loathly Lady*. Many of Hastings's children's books are adaptations of classic works, including *The Canterbury Tales*, *Peter and the Wolf*, and *Reynard, the Fox*.

Courtesy of Mulberry Books

The Children's Illustrated Bible was a major success, selling over 100,000 copies in the United States in its first year of publication. Hastings has provided the text for other volumes with religious themes, including *Noah's Ark*, *David and Goliath*, and *The Miracles of Jesus*. These retellings of Bible stories are illustrated with photographs and maps and contain factual material on history and geography, along with other pertinent information that supplements and buttresses the texts.

Selina Hastings's adult biographies of Nancy Mitford, Evelyn Waugh, and Rosamund Lehmann have been favorably reviewed, and she has served as a jurist for Great Britain's prestigious Booker Award for literary excellence. She currently lives in London.

SELECTED WORKS: *Sir Gawain and the Green Knight*, illus. by Juan Wijngaard, 1981; *Sir Gawain and the Loathly Lady*, illus. by Juan Wijngaard, 1985; *Peter and the Wolf*, illus. by Reg Cartwright, 1987; *The Singing Ringing Tree*, illus. by Louise Brierly, 1988; *The Canterbury Tales*, illus. by Reg Cartwright, 1988; *The Man Who Wanted to Live Forever*, illus. by Reg Cartwright, 1988; *Reynard, the Fox*, illus. by Graham Percy, 1990; *The Firebird*, illus. by Reg Cartwright; 1991; *The Children's Illustrated Bible*, illus. by Eric Thomas and Amy Burch, 1994; *David and Goliath, and Other Bible Stories*, 1994; *Noah's Ark, and Other Bible Stories*, 1994; *The Birth of Jesus, and Other Bible Stories*, 1996; *The Miracles of Jesus, and Other Bible Stories*, 1996; *The Illustrated Jewish Bible for Children*, illus. by Eric Thomas and Amy Burch, 1997.

Courtesy of Michael Hays

Michael Hays

June 21, 1956–

"I love to sing really loud while pounding out a rhythm on my guitar. Feeling that sound vibrating in my head and tickling my toes is pure joy. When all the troubles of the world are closing in, singing helps me feel strong and whole. My picture book *Abiyoyo*, by Pete Seeger, comes with a song in it. Pete loves to gather together big groups of people and get them all singing.

"From my early days these threads of inspiration weave through my life. In 1957, when I was one year old, I heard Pete Seeger's songs and his sparkling banjo playing on the family hi-fi: folk songs, union songs, and civil rights spirituals like 'Eyes on the Prize.' That year my parents met Martin Luther King Jr. at a friend's house. Throughout my childhood the Religious Society of Friends (Quakers) taught me practical applications for nonviolent social action. As I grew up, I saw a world filled with social struggle: war and peace, racism and civil rights, materialism and the life of the spirit.

"One scene from my childhood illustrates the times. In 1969 my whole family joined a big war protest in Washington, D.C. After countless speeches, Pete Seeger got up on the stage and led all 600,000 of us, arms swaying in the air, singing in unison 'All we are saying is give peace a chance' for 15 minutes. Years later, Pete told me that this was a peak moment in his life.

"Both my parents were teachers, and they emphasized academic achievement. My older brother and sister got straight A's. (I have a younger sister too.) Unlike the rest of my family, I excelled in the world of art. Early on, the artwork of Leo and Diane Dillon caught my attention. I spent hours examining the lithographs and woodcuts of M. C. Escher. Without really knowing where I might specialize, I followed my interests in art to Rhode Island School of Design. At RISD I met artists who shifted my focus to children's books. Freshman year, I roomed with David Wiesner (eighteen years later he published his book *Tuesday*). My instructors included children's book illustrators Chris Van Allsburg (*Jumanji* and *The Polar Express*) and David Macaulay (*Cathedral* and *The Way Things Work*). They all opened my eyes to the unexplored possibilities of the picture book.

"After receiving my B.F.A. in Illustration, in the one full-time position I ever held, I was hired as a computer graphics artist. I still keep my computer skills up to date, but I use traditional media when I illustrate books. Ironically, while producing computer graphics for General Electric (a scary giant of a company), I drew my first sketches of Abiyoyo. I contacted Pete Seeger directly, years before a publisher became involved, and began working with him on a picture-book adaptation of his story/song 'Abiyoyo.'

"In 1981 my freelance illustration career began when Margaret McElderry hired me to illustrate a young-adult book jacket. At last count, my artwork appears on dozens of book jackets and in eighteen picture books. Many of my books (begining with *Abiyoyo*) have featured African American characters. Over the years I've had a chance to illustrate stories from many cultures around the world. Still, it seems to me that stories written by Black authors or involving Black characters have brought out the best in my art.

"My work now involves many teaching roles as well. I network with other illustrators in the Graphic Artists Guild,

Courtesy of Simon & Schuster Children's Publishing Division

and together we organize professional education programs focusing on copyright issues, contract negotiation, and the impact of electronic media. I enjoy exploring my illustration process with elementary school students too. It's fun to leave behind my quiet little art studio and talk to 200 kids all at once. I lead them on a photographic tour of my studio and explain the tools and materials I use. After a performance of 'Abiyoyo' (I sing too), I reconstruct my illustration process from thumbnail sketches through rough drawings, photographic reference, layouts, comps, and finished paintings. Picture books present an endless creative challenge. I feel I have only scratched the surface. In particular, I want to explore a synthesis of music and illustration."

* * *

Michael Hays was born in Iowa City, Iowa, but spent most of his growing years in Pittsburgh, Pennsylvania, where his father served as chairman of the history department at the University of Pittsburgh. Between high school and college Hays attended Trailside County School, now know as the Audubon Expedition Institute. Along with a group of twenty students and three teachers, he traveled across the United States, camping and backpacking, studying natural history and environmental sciences, and playing folk music. In 1979 he received his B.F.A. in Illustration from the Rhode Island School of Design and was hired by General Electric as a computer graphics artist at their offices in Norwalk, Connecticut. In the early 1980s Hays "pounded the sidewalk" in New York, taking his artwork to some twenty publishers before receiving his first assignment to illustrate a book jacket. Moving to the Chicago area in 1988, he helped establish a new chapter of the Graphic Artists Guild and started teaching children's book illustration and other art classes at Columbia College.

Abiyoyo was named one of *Redbook Magazine*'s top ten picture books in 1986 and was also a featured book on *Reading Rainbow*. *The Gold Cadillac*, for which Hays created the illustrations, won a 1987 Christopher Award.

SELECTED WORKS ILLUSTRATED: *Abiyoyo: Based on a South African Lullaby & Folk Story*, by Pete Seeger, 1986; *The Gold Cadillac*, by Mildred Taylor, 1987; *A Birthday for Blue*, by Kerry Lydon, 1989; *The Tin Heart*, by Karen Ackerman, 1990; *Hello, Tree!* by Joanne Ryder, 1991; *Jonathan and His Mommy*, by Irene Smalls, 1992; *The Three Wishes*, by Lucille Clifton, 1992; *The Storm*, by W. Nikola-Lisa, 1993; *The Hundredth Name*, by Shulamith Levey Oppenheim, 1995; *Jackie Robinson*, by Kenneth Rudeen, 1996; *Pedro and the Monkey*, by Robert D. San Souci, 1996; *Because You're Lucky*, by Irene Smalls, 1997; *Kevin and His Dad*, by Irene Smalls-Hector, 1999; *The History of Counting*, by Denise Schmandt-Besserat, 1999.

Karen Hesse

(hess)

August 29, 1952–

"**I**'m not certain when I realized I wasn't like my friends. But from an early age it felt right to keep my inner world a secret. As a result people thought of me as shy; I was an observer of life more than a full-fledged participant.

"My elementary school was an easy walk from home. After classes let out, I would swing on the playground for hours, watching my feet rise into the sky, then fall away again. I felt so big, so powerful, blotting out the sun with my saddle-shoed feet. My friend Joey accompanied me on walks to Cylburn Park where nature abounded within the crowded city limits. Sometimes Joey and I would sit on the stoop outside his house and he would quiz me on the passing cars. He knew every model, every make. I couldn't tell a Ford from a Chevy, a coupe from a sedan.

"I caught lightning bugs in glass jars, participated in talent shows with my girlfriends, and cooled off on stifling summer afternoons in my plastic wading pool. In the airless closet of my bedroom I wrote poetry. Day after day I poured my heart out onto pages of notebook paper.

"In college I majored in theater, anthropology, psychology, and English. I graduated in 1975, and in 1976 my husband, my two cats, and I took six months and tent-camped across the country, visiting most of America's national parks. We met people everywhere we stopped. I fell in love with the land and the many people living across it. My husband and I ended up in Brattleboro, Vermont, at the end of our cross-country journey. I knew as soon as we crossed the Connecticut River from New Hampshire into Vermont that I'd come home. I found work, joined a writing group, gave birth to two children, and learned how to survive endless weeks of sub-zero temperatures and great tunnels of dazzling snow. When I began reading children's literature to my daughters, I felt I'd discovered at last the key to releasing my secret inner world. In 1991, with the publication of my first book, *Wish on a Unicorn*, a lifetime of bottling up my imagination ended.

Courtesy of Scholastic, Inc.

"In the forty-six years I've observed my surroundings and the people within them, I've discovered how painful life can be, and how joyous it can be as well. How fortunate I am, not only to live my own life, but to spend my days recording what it's like to live someone else's—someone from another culture, another economic strata, another belief system, another time.

"I haunt bookstores, conduct interviews, comb the shelves of libraries, read articles, study, probe, and sift. I listen to public radio and public television. Every day I absorb mountains of details, most of which are quite interesting. But every now and then something totally captivates me, breaks my heart, takes my breath away. Those are the details that become my books.

"Whether I'm revisiting in my mind Joey on the stoop back in Baltimore city (*Lester's Dog*) or staring down river at Vermont Yankee Nuclear Power Plant (*Phoenix Rising*), whether I'm poking around inside the parish house which once was an emergency hospital (*A Time of Angels*) or sitting beside the tank of a recently widowed dolphin (*The Music of Dolphins*), I don't keep my inner world a secret any more, and these days that feels completely right."

*　　*　　*

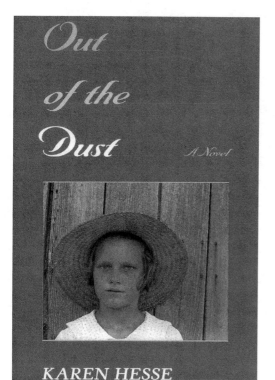

Courtesy of Scholastic, Inc.

Karen Hesse was born and raised in Baltimore, Maryland. She attended Towson State College and graduated from the University of Maryland. Many of her jobs have been related to books and reading; she has been a proofreader and a typesetter, and has worked in a library.

From the publication of her first book in 1991, Hesse's career has been distinguished by the extraordinary number of national honors she has received. *Wish on a Unicorn* was selected as a Children's Book of Distinction by the *Hungry Mind Review*. *Letters from Rifka* won a Christopher Medal and was named an American Library Association Best Book for Young Adults, an ALA Notable Children's Book, and a *School Library Journal* Best Book of the Year. *Sable* was also an *SLJ* Best Book. *Phoenix Rising* was cited as an ALA Best Book for Young Adults, an ALA Notable Children's Book, and an *SLJ* Best Book. *The Music of Dolphins* was an ALA Best Book for Young Adults and made the annual "best" lists of *School Library Journal* and *Publishers Weekly*, in addition to being named a 1996 Golden Kite Honor Book by the Society of Children's Book Writers and Illustrators. *Out of the Dust*, an historical novel written in free verse, won the 1998 Newbery Medal and the Scott O'Dell Award, was named an ALA Best Book for Young Adults and an ALA Notable Children's Book, and won year-end honors from *Publishers Weekly*, *School Library Journal*, and *Booklist*.

Karen Hesse lives with her husband and two daughters in Brattleboro, Vermont. She has served on the boards of a school district and a public library, been affiliated with the hospice movement, and led the Southern Vermont chapter of the Society of Children's Book Writers and Illustrators.

SELECTED WORKS: *Wish on a Unicorn*, 1991; *Letters from Rifka*, 1992; *Lavender*, 1993; *Poppy's Chair*, 1993; *Lester's Dog*, 1993; *Phoenix Rising*, 1994; *Sable*, 1994; *A Time of Angels*, 1995; *The Music of Dolphins*, 1996; *Out of the Dust*, 1997; *Just Juice*, 1998; *Come On, Rain!*, illus. by Jon J. Muth, 1999; *A Light in the Storm: The Civil War Diary of Amelia Martin, Fenwick Island, Delaware, 1861*, 1999.

SUGGESTED READING: *Authors and Artists for Young Adults*, vol. 27, 1999; *Children's Literature Review*, vol. 54, 1999; *Contemporary Authors*, vol. 168, 1999; *Something About the Author*, vol. 74, 1993; vol. 103, 1999; *Something About the Author Autobiography Series*, vol. 25, 1998. Periodicals— Bryant, Ellen, "Honoring the Complexities of Our Lives: An Interview with Karen Hesse," *Voices from the Middle*, April 1997; Hesse, Karen, "Newbery Acceptance Speech," *The Horn Book*, July/August 1998; *Publishers Weekly*, Feb. 8, 1999.

Will Hillenbrand

May 31, 1960–

"I have lived almost all my life in Cincinnati, Ohio, where I grew up surrounded by the stories in my neighborhood. My parents owned a barber shop, where I listened to conversations that seemed to me to be stories about adult life. When I wasn't at the shop, I spent hours at baseball games, sharing the stories about the teams and players that make up the mythology of baseball. My grandmother lived nearby, and my three brothers and I would keep her company during thunderstorms while she told us stories about her earlier life on a farm. Although I regularly visited the nearby library, there weren't many books at our house. But we had an encyclopedia from which my father read aloud 'The Night Before Christmas' each year, and I remember the sound of his voice giving life to the words as I conjured pictures in my mind.

"Drawing was how I captured the stories I heard. My older brother sketched cartoons and I began by copying him. I drew mostly at the kitchen table, but also used my crayons on stairwell walls. My early pictures still decorate the basement of my mother's house.

"My first art class was as a sophomore in high school. I was sure everyone else was more talented and experienced, but I discovered that all those years of listening and drawing had given me a good eye for putting ideas together as pictures. After high school I went on to art school, even though my father was worried that I wouldn't be able to make a living. When I graduated, I found work in advertising but, after a class in picture book art, I decided to try my hand at illustrating children's literature. Now it is my full-time work. I spend a lot of time in schools sharing my picture books and how I create them. I think it's important for children to enjoy the process of art and not worry too much about the finished product.

"When I approach a story, I think of myself as a choreographer giving movement to a score or a movie director bringing a script to life. I read the story many times just to let the wonder of it wash over me and feel it stretch and deepen in my imagination. I really work in three worlds at once: the world of the imagination, the world of myth, and the physical world. Children seem to live comfortably in all three of these worlds. Successful illustrations link these worlds together to give a visual voice to the written story.

Courtesy of D. Altman Fleischer

"As I begin to draw, I try to keep the child's viewpoint foremost in my mind. For each book, I keep a large binder of my sketches, and each one has a child's drawing tucked inside to remind me that a child's imagination is the starting and ending point for my art. My studio shelves are lined with Chinese marionettes, stuffed toys, and clay animals to help me with ideas for my drawings. My wife, Jane, and son, Ian, provide inspiration too.

"I begin with pencil sketches, then scan some of them into my computer to experiment with size, line, and shading. I also use the computer for page composition, but I still like to add the color by hand.

"My favorite illustrators are Maurice Sendak, Arnold Lobel, and E. H. Shepard. I am fascinated with Sendak's way of costuming and parading his characters across a stage and with Shepard's and Lobel's animal characters, who are fully individual yet true to their animal natures. They seem like children, vulnerable yet independent and wholly themselves. They exemplify how something that seems simple, like a picture book, can be infused with all the wonderful complexities of life. And that's what I try to do."

✳   ✳   ✳

Sometimes mysterious, often funny, and always highly original, Will Hillenbrand's illustrations are magical and dramatic depictions of the worlds described in children's literature, ranging from the everyday to the exotic and fantastic. Working in oils or

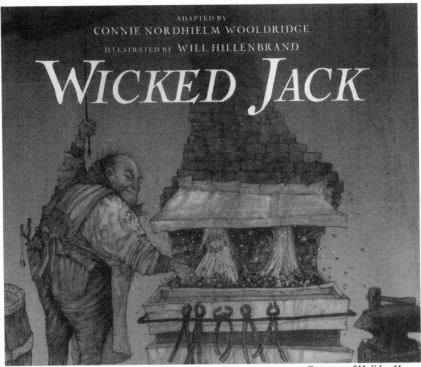

Courtesy of Holiday House

oil pastels, Hillenbrand uses texture and layering, along with color and contrast, to bring each story to life.

After high school Hillenbrand attended the Art Academy of Cincinnati, earning a B.F.A. in 1982. He then began a career in commercial art. In 1990, he was awarded a gold medal from the National Society of Illustrators for his National Collegiate Rowing Championship poster. After a course in picture-book art at Ohio State University, he turned his attention to illustrating children's books, which he has been doing full-time since 1989.

In 1995, *Wicked Jack* was named a *School Library Journal* Best Book and a Blue Ribbon Book by the *Bulletin of the Center for Children's Books*. It also received the Irma S. and James H. Black Award in 1996 from the Bank Street College of Education and was a Children's Book Award winner in North Carolina in 1997. *The Golden Sandal* was a Notable Children's Trade Book in the Field of Social Studies in 1999.

SELECTED WORKS ILLUSTRATED: *Awfully Short for the Fourth Grade*, by Elvira Woodruff, 1989; *Traveling to Tondo*, by Verna Aardema, 1991; *Go Ask Giorgio*, by Patricia Wittmann, 1992; *Asher and the Capmakers*, by Eric A. Kimmel, 1993; *The King Who Tried to Fry an Egg on His Head: A Russian Tale*, by Mirra Ginsburg, 1994; *Wicked Jack*, by Connie N. Wooldridge, 1995; *Coyote and the Firestick: A Northwest*

Coast Indian Legend, by Barbara D. Goldin, 1996; *Counting Crocodiles*, by Judy Sierra, 1997; *The Golden Sandal: A Middle Eastern Cinderella Story*, by Rebecca Hickox, 1998; *The Biggest, Best Snowman*, by Margery Cuyler, 1998; *The Last Snake in Ireland: A Story About St. Patrick*, by Sheila MacGill Callahan, 1999; *Down by the Station* (traditional), 1999; *Andy and Tamika*, by David Adler, 1999.

SUGGESTED READING: *Something About the Author*, vol. 84, 1996.

Courtesy of Copper Coast

Ron Hirschi

May 18, 1948–

"I grew up at the edge of the sea. That I was lucky to be able to row about as I pleased at a very young age, watching seals and whales and fishing for salmon, escaped me at the time. I thought everyone had their own rowboat and that orcas were a part of every child's life.

"Those early experiences filled me with love and curiosity about fish, eagles, whales, and other sea life. Then too, the surrounding forests were filled with their own attractions, and I spent many days hiking, hunting, or fishing in the woodlands of western Washington. Since my family was rather poor, one of my 'jobs' was to supply the table with fresh fish and game.

"Writing about all of this never occurred to me when I was young. But I did have a keen interest in natural science, fostered by experience and a very kind grandfather, who helped me learn how to watch nature. I also credit my cousin, Tom Rice, for prompting me to learn to identify the small, shoreline animals many people never even see. He is the best kind of naturalist—one who loves the world and shares knowledge with others in a generous way. His guidance is a major reason why I entered college soon after high school.

"After college and two years of graduate school, I accepted a job with a state agency and worked for several years as a wildlife biologist. During one research project, I was looking into the impact of logging on stream habitat. At that time, timber companies were clear-cutting Washington forests at a rapid rate, then clearing, and even burning, right up to the edge of rivers and streams. The result was devastating to water quality, including the near-extinction of several salmon stocks in the Pacific Northwest. Seeing the destruction of the forests and rivers firsthand, I became concerned that my young daughter, Nichol, might not get to see the fish, wildlife, and natural landscapes I had always taken so much for granted as a child.

"I wrote my first book after coming home one night from a clear-cut forest along the Hoh River. I was saddened by the sight of the devastated forest and imagined things might be different if fish lived in trees. My book, 'A Trout in Every Tree,' was never published. But the effort to teach about nature and my interest in children's books had begun. Most of my books are about animals and nature. And much of my associated work is integrated with these books in some way. I visit schools around the country, working with students and teachers on environmental projects. We have restored wetlands, created outdoor learning centers, and studied streams as part of water quality work.

"I also help to restore salmon populations, most recently as a biologist for the Jamestown S'Klallam Indian Tribe. One of my books, *Seya's Song*, includes S'Klallam language and the simple story of the life of the salmon, which is held in such high regard by the native people of the Northwest Coast.

"When I am not writing or working with fish, I am either with my family, walking our Labradors, or fishing. After living in Montana for five years, my wife, Brenda, and I have returned home to Washington, where we live near our daughter, Nichol, and her husband, Bert—and, once again, near the sea."

I wrote my first book after coming home one night from a clear-cut forest along the Hoh River.

* * *

Ron Hirschi is a biologist, naturalist, and conservationist whose nonfiction writing entertains and educates children and young adults about the natural world and its inhabitants. Born in Bremerton in the state of Washington, he attended the University of Washington, where he received his B.S. degree in 1974 and performed graduate research in wildlife ecology from 1974 to 1976. He worked as a biologist for the Washington Game Department of Seattle from 1976 to 1981. During 1984–85, he worked as a counselor in the North Kitsap Schools Indian education program in Poulsbo, Washington. Since 1988, he has worked as a biologist with the S'Klallam Indian Tribe in Jamestown, Washington, and for the Jefferson County Planning Department as a biologist helping to protect critical habitat for salmon. Hirschi spends a great deal of time visiting schools, often helping with nature projects, including the creation of wetland habitats.

In 1986 *Headgear* and *One Day on Pika's Peak* were chosen by the Child Study Association as Children's Books of the Year. *Headgear, City Geese, A Time for Babies, Who Lives in the Forest?*, and *What Is a Bird?* have all been selected as Outstanding Science Trade Books for Children. *Seya's Song* was the recipient of a Washington Governor's Writer Award in 1992. Two of the books in Hirschi's Discover My World series were included on the John Burroughs List of Nature Books for Young Readers: *Winter* in 1990 and *Summer* in 1991. *Spring* (1990) was also a featured selection of PBS's *Reading Rainbow*. *People of Salmon and Cedar* was selected as a Notable Children's Trade Book in the Field of Social Studies for 1997 by NCSS/CBC. In 1994 *A Time for Babies* was selected for the NSTA/CBC Outstanding Science Trade Book list.

SELECTED WORKS: *Headgear*, 1986; *One Day on Pika's Peak*, 1986; *City Geese*, 1987; *What Is a Bird*, 1987; *Who Lives in the Forest?*, 1987; *What Is a Horse*, 1989; *Winter*, 1990; *Discover My World: Ocean*, 1991; *Loon Lake*, 1991; *Summer*, 1991; *Seya's Song*, 1992; *A Time for Babies*, 1993; *A Time for Sleeping*, 1993; *Save Our Wetlands*, 1994; *Turtle's Day*, 1994; *Dance with Me*, 1995; *People of Salmon and Cedar*, 1995; *Faces in the Mountains*, 1997.

SUGGESTED READING: *Contemporary Authors*, vol. 120, 1987; *Contemporary Authors*, New Revision Series, vol. 68, 1998; *Something About the Author*, vol. 56, 1989; vol. 95, 1998; Wyatt, Flora, et.al. *Popular Nonfiction Authors for Children*, 1998. Periodicals—Allen, Raymond, "Ron Hirschi: He Finds Excitement in a Handful of Dirt," *Teaching PreK–8*, February 1994.

Katharine Holabird

January 23, 1948–

"I was born in Cambridge, Massachusetts, in 1948, the second in a boisterous tribe of four daughters. We were born close together and remained great companions through all the adventures and scrapes of our childhood. We danced and painted together when we were small, shared a passion for horses when we grew big enough to ride, quarrelled over make-up and boyfriends as teenagers, and remained fiercely loyal.

"We moved to Chicago when I was four. On Sundays we went to a formal lunch with Grandmother Holabird, a formidable matriarch who adored opera and ballet. Invitations to the ballet with Grandmother were thrilling events. I'll never forget the excitement of seeing real ballerinas flying across the stage. We couldn't wait to get home, dress ourselves up as the dying swan or the Sleeping Beauty, and do our own ecstatic ballets.

"Our side of the family was known to be unconventional. Everyone was an artist of one kind or another, and we scribbled and danced and painted with utter abandon. My parents met while doing plays together at the university, and when I was little they were both very involved with the theater. My father was a director and set designer for a time, and although my mother gave up a promising career on the stage when she had four daughters, she understood how to make her life a kind of exuberant theater and always entertained us with her contagious humor. Our father loved painting and once took us down to the basement, handed out paints and brushes, and encouraged us to decorate everything in sight.

"At school I was always willing to read a book or write essays about anything under the sun, but math was a grim struggle, even though my father patiently tried to help me. Fortunately I had some wonderful allies on the teaching staff, and their smiles and encouraging words inspired me to continue my love of writing despite my deplorable grades in math.

"Both our parents read aloud when we were young, and we loved listening to them read wonderful stories like *The Wizard of Oz* series, *Huckleberry Finn*, the legends of King Arthur, and Grimm's fairy tales. I read everything I could about animals, and adored *Charlotte's Web* and a mouse called Stuart Little.

"In 1965 I went to Bennington College in Vermont, where I studied creative writing with Bernard Malamud, read novels day and night, wrote madly, and joined modern dance classes. After graduation I worked on the *Bennington Review*, until the chance to visit Rome during a particularly frozen January changed my life. Once in Italy, I was determined to stay and learn Italian, and eventually extended my visit to three years. There I met my half-Italian husband, Michael Haggiag, who showed me how beautiful the Italian language, and Italy, could be.

"In 1973 we moved to England, where Michael started a small publishing company while I taught nursery school and did some freelance writing. Two daughters were born, and our growing family inspired us to buy a house and settle down in our adopted country.

Courtesy of Ms. Bridie Bonas

"Helen Craig and I became friends in London when my children were still very young. Helen had already been published and asked me if I could write a children's story for her to illustrate. At the time my eldest daughter was a four-year-old prima ballerina, permanently outfitted in a pink tutu, fairy wings, and ballet slippers. I recognized Tara's balletomania as strikingly similar to my own dreams of grandeur at her age and decided I must write about our shared passion for dancing in the limelight. In this way, the impulsive, theatrical character of Angelina

Ballerina was born while Tara and her little sister, Alexandra, waltzed around me in the kitchen.

"The first edition was published in 1983. The following year our U.S. editor, Carol Southern, encouraged me to write another Angelina story. I wrote *Angelina and the Princess* and realized that Angelina really had a life of her own. When our son was born, I began to explore another imaginary world. There were friendly dragons and flying supermen hiding under the furniture, and I was generously invited to join the perilous expeditions setting out daily from Adam's bedroom.

"Writing about childhood has been a great adventure, and continues to enthrall me. I am very fortunate to work with a gifted illustrator like Helen Craig, and wish that all children's writers could enjoy such a wonderful collaboration with an accomplished artist. I will always be indebted to Angelina's original publishing team—my husband, Michael, and Carol Southern—and am very thankful for my three spirited sisters, my lovely children, and the natural gift for singing and dancing of children all over the world."

"The chance to visit Rome during a particularly frozen January changed my life."

After graduating from Bennington College in Vermont, Katharine Holabird worked as a journalist, a television presenter in Italy, and a nursery school teacher in London. Her collaborations with Helen Craig include two Little Mouse books and two Alexander books, in addition to the nine stories in the Angelina series. In 1985 *Angelina Ballerina* won the Kentucky Bluegrass Award, and in 1987 *Angelina's Christmas* was named one of the Child Study Association's Children's Books of the Year. *Angelina and the Princess*, *Angelina at the Fair*, and *Angelina's Christmas* were all cited as ALA Notable Children's Books. The nine original Angelina books are now being re-launched by HIT Entertainment in London, with four new picture books planned. An animation series is also in development, along with a high-profile licensing program. Katharine Holabird lives with her family in London, England.

SELECTED WORKS: (all illus. by Helen Craig) *The Little Mouse ABC*, 1983; *Angelina Ballerina*, 1983; *Angelina and the Princess*, 1984; *Angelina at the Fair*, 1985; *Angelina's Christmas*, 1985; *Angelina on Stage*, 1986; *Angelina and Alice*, 1987; *Alexander and the Dragon*, 1988; *Angelina's Birthday Surprise*, 1989; *Alexander and the Magic Boat*, 1990; *Angelina's Baby Sister*, 1991; *Angelina Ice Skates*, 1993.

SUGGESTED READING: *Something About the Author*, vol. 62, 1990.

Thomas Hoobler writes:

"My father was a printer, and letters and words have always been part of my life. I started working in Dad's shop—bagging newly-printed calendars—when I was five and got my first job as a proofreader when I was ten.

"Having a printer in the family allowed me to publish a school newspaper in the eighth grade, giving me my first chance to see my work in print. If economic considerations permitted, I'd still be my own publisher, for I've never had a better one. I started to learn the limits of free speech when I was fired as editor of my high school newspaper. A similar experience happened in college, when the editors of the student weekly fired me because I disagreed with their political views.

"In both high school and college, I was fortunate to have teachers who encouraged me to think I had talent as a writer. After working for a year on a small magazine, I went to the Writers' Workshop program at the University of

Courtesy of Ellen Hoobler

Iowa. A teacher there—who would one day be a famous novelist—told me that nobody could teach you to write. (Maybe he meant nobody could teach me to write.)

"Taking that to heart, I went home to Cincinnati, where I taught school for four years. These were the years of the Vietnam War, and I figured it was better to teach than to be drafted. It gave me time to work on what I hoped would be the great American novel. Looking back on it, I realize I would have been better off—as a writer—going to Vietnam.

"In 1971 I came to New York with a manuscript. I learned the realities of the publishing business when I took the book to Delacorte, which had published the novels of my University of Iowa teacher. When an editor asked me to describe my work, I said it was a literary novel. The immediate reply was a slightly horrified, 'Oh, we don't publish literary novels.'

"Moving to New York did change my life in an unforeseen way. The first night I was there I met the person who would become my wife and co-author of (so far) more than seventy books."

Dorothy Hoobler continues:

"My stereo had been stolen that day, and I hadn't even paid for it yet. Nothing consoles me like classical music, so I brought some records to the apartment of friends. As it turned out, they

Thomas and Dorothy Hoobler

Thomas Hoobler:
1941–
Dorothy Hoobler:
1940–

had invited Tom to come stay with them until he could get a start in New York. By the end of the evening we were bridge partners, and by the end of the year we were married.

"I had no thought of a writing career but was making a living as an editor for a textbook publisher. Since childhood, I have been a passionate reader for whom books are an obsession. That was the first thing Tom and I discovered we had in common. A friend of mine was editing a series of small books for a Macmillan reading series. She asked if I would be interested in writing some. They wanted biographies and I had always admired Margaret Mead, so I called her office and she agreed to let me interview her. Tom helped me to turn the tape of that meeting into a book, and our collaboration was born. We also did a short work of fiction about a girl living on the frontier in the nineteenth century.

"Other books followed. We met Phyllis Jackson, who was one of the top agents in New York. She suggested that we concentrate on books for young adults, a term that was new to us. In short order, Phyllis found an editor who liked our work. Our career was launched. Since then we have written both nonfiction, primarily history, and historical fiction. To me, the most enjoyable part of any project is the research. I have a chance to make a living doing what I love most: reading and learning."

Courtesy of Ellen Hoobler

* * *

Over the years of their personal and professional partnership, now in its third decade, Dorothy and Thomas Hoobler have published dozens of well-received nonfiction books for young readers, as well as several historical novels. Dorothy Hoobler was born in Philadelphia. She received an undergraduate degree in history from Wells College and a M.A. in American History from New York University. Thomas Hoobler, born in Cincinnati, majored in English at the University of Notre Dame and received a master's degree in education from Xavier University in Cincinnati. The Hooblers have both worked as editors of textbooks and as supervising editors for book developers. In addition, Thomas has been a magazine editor and Dorothy a genealogist.

From early on, many of their books were selected for awards and honors. *Photographing History: The Career of Mathew Brady* was chosen as a Notable Trade Book in the Field of Social Studies, named a Book of Outstanding Merit by the Children's Book Committee at Bank Street College, and listed as a Book for the Teen Age by the New York Public Library. *The Trenches: Fighting on the Western Front During World War I* was selected by *School Library Journal* as one of the Best Books of the Year in 1978. The National Council of Teachers of Social Studies and Children's Book Council chose *Your Right to Privacy* for their list of recommended children's books on the Constitution. *Vietnam: Why We Fought* received Honorable Mention for the Virginia Library Association Jefferson Cup, was named a Notable Trade Book in the Field of Social Studies, and appeared on ALA's Best of the Best for Children list. *Showa: The Age of Hirohito* also received recognition as a Notable Trade Book in the Field of Social Studies.

The Hooblers' ambitious multivolume works of history have been among their most honored. Images Across the Ages, an illustrated series containing biographical sketches of famous international figures, appeared on the New York Public Library's Books for the Teen Age list. The ten-volume American Family Album series uses first-person narratives, original documents, and photographs to trace the immigrant experiences of various ethnic groups, including African Americans, Mexican Americans, and Japanese Americans. Among many other awards, these books received honors from the Commonweal/National Conference of Christians and Jews, the National Council of Teachers of English, the New York Public Library, the American Council of Teachers, and the National Council of Teachers of Social Studies. Individual volumes in the series also received three Parents' Choice Awards.

The Hooblers' historical fiction has been praised as well. The first four volumes in their Her Story series were all chosen by the American Booksellers Association for its Pick of the Lists. *The Ghost in the Tokaido Inn* was named to ALA's Best Books for Young Adults in 2000. The Hooblers have written for *Boys' Life* and *National Geographic World* magazines. They have also written books on gardening for adults and a number of social studies textbooks. Their works have appeared in British, Spanish, Czech, Polish, Italian, and Norwegian editions.

The parents of a grown daughter, Dorothy and Thomas Hoobler reside in New York City.

SELECTED WORKS: *Margaret Mead: A Life in Science*, 1974; *Frontier Diary*, 1975; *An Album of World War I*, 1976; *Photographing History: The Career of Mathew Brady*, 1977; *The Trenches: Fighting on the Western Front in World War I*, 1978; *An Album of the Seventies*, 1982; *The Voyages of*

Captain Cook, 1983; *Stalin*, 1985; *Your Right to Privacy*, 1986; *Nelson and Winnie Mandela*, 1987; *Drugs and Crime*, 1988; *George Washington*, 1990; *Showa: The Age of Hirohito*, 1990; *Vietnam: Why We Fought*, 1990; *The Sign-Painter's Secret*, 1991; *Next Stop: Freedom*, 1991; *Treasure in the Stream*, 1991; *Aloha Means Come Back*, 1991; *Vanished: The Fact or Fiction Files*, 1991; *Lost Civilizations: The Fact or Fiction Files*, 1992; *Mandela: The Man, the Struggle, the Triumph*, 1992; *The Trail on Which They Wept*, 1992; *A Promise at the Alamo*, 1992; *Confucianism*, 1993; *African Portraits*, Images Across the Ages series, 1993 (first of eight titles); *The Chinese American Family Album*, American Family Album series, 1994 (first of ten titles); *Julie Meyer: The Story of a Wagon Train Girl*, 1997; *Florence Robinson: The Story of a Jazz Age Girl*, 1997; *Priscilla Foster: The Story of a Salem Girl*, 1997; *Sally Bradford: The Story of a Rebel Girl*, 1997; *Real American Girls Tell Their Own Stories*, 1999; *The Ghost in the Tokaido Inn*, 1999.

SUGGESTED READING: *Contemporary Authors*, New Revision series, vol. 27, 1989; vol. 53, 1997; *Something About the Author*, vol. 28, 1982. Periodicals—Hoobler, Dorothy and Thomas, "Writing History for Young People, *School Library Journal*, January 1992.

E-MAIL: *TandDHoob@aol.com*

Cheryl Willis Hudson

April 7, 1948–

"I became a book creator and publisher as a direct result of my experiences of literally making books and bulletin boards as a child. I was born and raised in Portsmouth, Virginia, where my mother was a schoolteacher and my father was the district manager of a Black-owned insurance agency. Through the years, I helped my mother check and grade her pupils' homework papers (editing) and created classroom bulletin boards (design and art direction). Sometimes on Saturdays I'd go to the office with my father and pretend to 'take care of business.' While he reviewed ledgers and added long rows of figures on his adding machine, I'd amuse myself by drawing cartoons on the chalkboard and making up success stories. Both my parents loved the written and spoken word, and that appreciation has fueled my own love of words and images.

"When I looked in my elementary school textbooks and didn't see images of Black children or families on the pages, I instinctively knew that there was something 'missing in the picture.' Our books were pretty drab and uninviting by today's graphic design standards. To relieve the boredom and to compensate for the void, I'd doodle, add charts, tables, and maps, and make elaborate book report covers—anything to liven things up. That made reading and writing fun!

"The highlight of the school year always came during February when I helped to create 'Negro History Week' bulletin board displays. Teams of students competed with those from other classes in our all-Black school for the most outstanding design. That gave all of us a chance to recognize and identify African American heroes and sheroes on a large scale and in positive, creative ways.

"In spite of what was missing in them, I still loved books. My favorite place was the library. Following high school, I attended Oberlin College, where I filled every moment of extra time reading from the stacks of its wonderful library. I majored in sociology but took courses in studio art, art history, and African American studies.

"Following college, I took a summer course in publishing procedures at Radcliffe College in Cambridge, Massachusetts, and decided my career would be in publishing. I became an art editor at Houghton Mifflin Company and met the illustrator Jerry Pinkney. I later moved to New York, where I worked as a graphic designer for the school textbook division of Macmillan. During the early 1970s, I joined a group called Black Creators for Children, where I met illustrators Tom Feelings and George Ford and a handful of writers, designers, and editors who were attempting to establish a philosophy and increase the presence of Black creators in the publishing industry.

Courtesy of Cheryl and Wade Hudson

Wade Hudson

Cheryl Willis Hudson

"During this time my husband, Wade, and I developed a number of ideas and prototypes for children's books, which were rejected by a long list of publishers. Following a series of jobs with large publishing companies, trade book packagers, and various freelance assignments creating books for other people, Wade and I took the plunge and decided to create and publish our own book. *The Afro-Bets ABC Book* was the first of a number of projects we eventually collaborated on from concept through bound book.

"What began as a personal journey of my own to get the most out of books in the classroom has ended in a professional career and mission to add to the body of quality literature for children. The establishment of our company, Just Us Books, has become a vehicle to make our dreams a reality for others who share similar experiences and our vision."

* * *

Cheryl Willis Hudson is an author, designer, and publisher of quality literature with an African American focus. She received her B.A. degree from Oberlin College and did postgraduate work at Northeastern University while beginning her career in graphic design and art direction in publishing houses. In 1972 she married Wade Hudson. After many years of working in the publishing industry and trying to sell her own projects and ideas for books about African Americans, she combined forces with her husband to create the publishing company Just Us Books.

The first title published by Just Us Books was one that Cheryl Hudson had been trying to sell for several years, her own *Afro-Bets ABC*. Characters in this book and its companion volume, *Afro-Bets 123*, were based on the Hudsons' own children, Katura and Stephan. More picture books for young children followed, along with compilations of African American songs and stories. In 1997 the *Horn Book* magazine honored a joint compilation of Wade and Cheryl Willis Hudson's, *In Praise of Our Fathers and Our Mothers*, with a featured review. This anthology brings together writings and illustrations of nearly four dozen African American creators of children's books, work that honors the fathers, mothers, and extended families of these creative people. A significant contribution, this family album reaches across generations and cultural boundaries to celebrate shared values and strong spirit.

The Hudsons live and work in East Orange, New Jersey. Their daughter, Katura, edited her first book with Just Us Books in 1999, *Afro-Bets Quotes for Kids: Words for Kids to Live By*. Their son, Stephan, is a high school senior.

> "What began as a personal journey of my own to get the most out of books in the classroom has ended in a professional career . . ."

SELECTED WORKS: *Afro-Bets ABC Book*, 1987; *Afro-Bets 123 Book*, 1988; *Bright Eyes, Brown Skin*, with Bernette Ford, illus. by George Ford, 1990; *How Sweet the Sound: African-American Songs for Children*, comp. with Wade Hudson, illus. by Floyd Cooper, 1995; *Hold Christmas in Your Heart*, comp. with various illus., 1995; What-a-Baby! series: *Good Morning Baby, Good Night Baby, Animal Sounds for Baby*, and *Let's Count Baby*, illus. by George Ford, 1995–1997; *Many Colors of Mother Goose*; illus. by Ken Brown, Mark Cochran, Cathy Johnson, 1997; *Kids' Book of Wisdom: Quotes from the African American Tradition*, comp. with Wade Hudson, 1997; *In Praise of Our Fathers and Our Mothers: A Black Family Treasury by Outstanding Authors and Artists*, ed. with Wade Hudson, 1997; *Glo Goes Shopping*, illus. by Cathy Johnson, 1999.

SUGGESTED READING: *Something About the Author*, vol. 81, 1995. Periodicals—"Book Publishers' Bet on Black Children Pays Off," *Emerge*, October 1996; *Horn Book*, March/April 1997.

WEB SITE: *www.justusbooks.com*

Wade Hudson

October 23, 1946–

"I grew up in a small town in Louisiana during the 1950s and 1960s. Mansfield was as segregated as any town or city in the South at that time. African Americans lived on one side of town, and white people lived on the other side. They were two different towns, really. They may well have been two different worlds.

"We had no public library in our part of town. The textbooks in our school and the few books that were in our school library were selected by and large by the people from that 'other part of town.' The books had virtually nothing in them about Black people. The implication was that Black people had done hardly anything important. They hadn't made any significant contributions to the world, as Europeans had. Some textbooks even attempted to prove why we hadn't made any contributions.

"The message was clear and the intention certain. Books produced to 'educate' were not only being used to train and inform, but also to maintain segregation and white supremacy.

"I can remember two 'Black' books in our school library. There may have been a few others, but these two I remember. They were biographies of George Washington Carver and Booker T. Washington. I read them over and over. The important contemporary Black authors—James Baldwin, Ralph Ellison, W.E.B. DuBois, Gwendolyn Brooks, Zora Neale Hurston, and Langston Hughes—did not exist for me. Nor did they exist for many other African Americans who found themselves in a similar situation.

"But I felt, even at an early age, that there was much more to Black people than could be found in the books I was able to get my hands on. I knew, even though I couldn't prove it, that we had to have a history . . . a history full of good deeds as well as bad ones, just as other peoples who have populated our world. It just didn't seem reasonable to me that millions of people who had lived for centuries (I did not know then that African history went back *thousands* of years) had virtually nothing to show for their long stay on earth. Something was wrong somewhere.

"Many times my grandfather would captivate me with his intriguing stories about my aunts, uncles, and cousins. My mother would hold sessions for hours talking about relatives and the interesting, funny, and crazy things they had done. Some of these stories would make excellent books, I thought. But why weren't there any books with stories like these in them?

"When I was ten years old, I decided I was going to do some something about the 'situation.' I was going to write and publish my own book. And I did! I wrote it in pencil, stapled the pages together, and emblazoned the title on the front page in big, bold letters. It was a story about a little boy who found a sum of money and made his family rich. Of course, the little boy was me, and the family was my own.

"At the time, I didn't know what book publishing was all about. Nor did I really understand the writing process. I just thought that there should be something written about the people I saw every day, something that others could read. Our stories had to be told. That mission led me to become a writer, and subsequently, a publisher. Still viable, that mission continues to motivate me and continues to motivate many other Black writers I now know exist."

* * *

Wade Hudson was born and raised in Mansfield, Louisiana, in the heart of the segregated South. He attended Southern University in Baton Rouge, 1964–1968, and in the late 1960s and early 1970s he worked for a number of civil rights organizations. Through the years he has had a variety of jobs as a news reporter, a sportswriter, and a public relations specialist.

IN PRAISE OF
OUR FATHERS AND
OUR MOTHERS
A Black Family Treasury
by Outstanding Authors and Artists

Compiled by Wade Hudson and Cheryl Willis Hudson

Courtesy of Just Us Books

In 1987 Hudson and his wife, Cheryl Willis Hudson, combined his public relations experience and her graphic arts background, along with their shared love of writing, to establish Just Us Books, Inc. The company was designed from the start to publish books by and about African Americans, with an emphasis on making those books available for the general market. The Hudsons' good business sense and ability to recruit fine writers and illustrators, in addition to their own creative talents, have made Just Us Books one of the leading publishers of Black interest materials for young people. The Hudsons are well known for publishing books by some of the leading African American writers in the field: Eleanora E. Tate, Mari Evans, and Sharon M. Draper, among others.

Wade and Cheryl Hudson live and work in East Orange, New Jersey. They have two children, Katura and Stephan.

SELECTED WORKS: *Afro-Bets Book of Black Heroes from A to Z*, with Valerie Wilson Wesley, 1989; *Jamal's Busy Day*, illus. by George Ford, 1991; *Afro-Bets Kids: I'm Gonna Be!*, illus. by Culverson Blair, 1992; *I Love My Family*, illus. by Cal Massey, 1993; *Pass It On: African-American Poetry for Children*, illus. by Floyd Cooper, 1993; *How Sweet the Sound:*

African-American Songs for Children, comp. with Cheryl Willis Hudson, illus. by Floyd Cooper, 1995; *Great Black Heroes: Five Notable Inventors*, illus. by Ron Garnett, 1995; *Great Black Heroes: Five Brave Explorers*, illus. by Ron Garnett, 1995; *The Kids' Book of Wisdom: Quotes from the African American Tradition*, ed. with Cheryl Willis Hudson, 1996; *In Praise of Our Fathers and Our Mothers: A Black Family Treasury by Outstanding Authors and Artists*, ed. with Cheryl Willis Hudson, 1997; *NEATE: Book #3 Anthony's Big Surprise*, 1998; *Robo's Favorite Places*, illus. by Cathy Johnson, 1999.

SUGGESTED READING: *Black Writers*, vol. 2; *Contemporary Authors*, vol. 142, 1994; *Something About the Author*, vol. 74, 1993. Periodicals—"Book Publishers' Bet on Black Children Pays Off," *Emerge*, October 1996; *Horn Book*, March/April 1997.

WEB SITE: *www.justusbooks.com*

Trina Schart Hyman

April 8, 1939–

"I was born in Philadelphia, Pennsylvania. My mother was a gingery, independent, capable lady with red hair, and my father was a quiet, funny man who liked to go fishing and play the accordion. I grew up in a little village north of the city. There was a beautiful farm across the road from our house, and acres of woods and streams and backyards all around. I also had a little sister who soon grew up to be six feet tall and wise and beautiful, but we were usually good friends in spite of that. I had a very nice childhood, and I enjoyed myself very much most of the time. I liked best to be under the kitchen table with the dog, and for one whole year I really believed that I was Red Riding Hood—but my family never seemed to mind, so I grew up weird but encouraged.

"After I graduated from public school I went to the Philadelphia Museum of Art to learn to be an illustrator, which is what I had in mind to do since I was about six. I had a lovely time in art school, and Henry C. Pitz was my favorite teacher.

"In 1959 I married my friend Harris Hyman and we lived in Boston for a year, where I went to the Boston Museum School and learned about etching and lithography and printmaking. Then we went to Stockholm so that Harris could learn statistics, and I went to the Swedish State Art School for a year. At the end of that year I went looking for work and met Astrid Lindgren, who was the children's book editor who gave me my first real illustration job. It took me two months to read the book (it was in Swedish) and two weeks to illustrate it.

"Then Harris and I took a 3000-mile bicycle trip through southern Sweden, Denmark, Norway, and England. We arrived back in the States with fifty-six cents between us. I had illustrated my first book, learned Swedish, and found out how to pedal a bicycle up huge mountains and then carry it down on my back. We lived in Boston for the next five years. After a very discouraging year of pounding the pavements in New York and Boston with my portfolio, I finally got to illustrate a Little Golden Book. Gradually I got more work. In 1963 I did my first picture book, for Houghton Mifflin, and also had a baby. The baby turned out to be a very articulate and strong-minded little girl, who is now thirty-six years old and my severest critic, as well as my most supportive collaborator. Her name is Katrin. The picture book turned out to be rather dreadful, but I learned a lot from it.

"In 1967 Harris and I got a divorce and I moved to New Hampshire along with Katrin, my friend Nancie, her twin daughters Clea and Gaby, five cats, and two parakeets. We all lived very happily in a little stone house on the banks of a big river with a working farm next door and the mountains all around. I wrote my first children's book during that winter and fell in love with the countryside. The long snowy winters are good weather for working hard—and I worked very hard indeed! I started to illustrate books at the rate of eight or nine a year.

Courtesy of Jean K. Aull

"Slowly but surely over the years to come I illustrated over 150 children's books of all sorts. Some of them won awards and some of the best of them got ignored. In 1971 we moved to a rambling 170-year-old wooden farmhouse with fourteen rooms and big old falling-down barns, not too far from the little stone house. It has cobwebs in the corners, mice in the attic, shelves full of books, pictures on all the walls, and big old sugar maple trees in the front lawn. It has a pond and a pasture and some woods and fields with cows all around.

"This is the house where I still live with my partner, Jean, two dogs, three cats, five sheep, and a donkey. Jean is a teacher and the director of Open Fields School. My daughter Katrin, her husband Eugene, and their two sons, Michou and Xavier, live just across the river in Vermont. We like to get together and do things like invite friends to come over, cook meals and eat them, dance to music, look at movies, talk about interesting stuff, play games, read books, and watch the world go by."

＊　＊　＊

Trina Schart Hyman is one of the foremost artists illustrating folk and fairy tales today. Besides the picture books for which she is most famous, her drawings and paintings have also graced many children's novels, poetry anthologies, story collections, and even a few cookbooks since her career began in the mid-1960s. Citing Howard Pyle, Arthur Rackham, and N. C. Wyeth as early influences on her art, Hyman roots her fanciful tales in a convincingly real world and makes her characters look like people we might know. Her princesses are vibrant young women; her princes look intelligent and caring as well as handsome; her witches and wicked queens embody the transforming emotions of jealousy and hatred rather than simply equating evil with ugliness; her fairies and elves resemble playful, mischievous children; her goblins and dragons are some of the scariest ever conceived. The settings of these fairy tales are also rooted in reality, with every detail in the drawings researched and meticulously rendered. Decorative borders often incorporate a folk motif or a pattern from nature to fit the mood of these age-old stories.

Hyman has written the texts for several of her picture books, including her own adaptations of *Little Red Riding Hood* and *Sleeping Beauty*. Her fable of a journey and the five senses, *How Six Found Christmas*, is about finding the most important elements in any holiday. Her profusely illustrated autobiography, *Self Portrait: Trina Schart Hyman*, gives a rare insight into the development of the illustrator and is at once informative and accessible to young readers. Whether illustrating her own texts or those written by others, Hyman uses the story as a starting point. Matching color, tone, and energy of line to the intent of the text, her art often extends the narrative beyond the written word. The vitality in her characters' facial expressions, gestures, and body language and the atmospheric colors of her palette underscore the mood of each story. Her line drawings and full-color paintings for such classic novels as *A Christmas Carol* and *Peter Pan* have breathed new life into old favorites. Writers as varied as Kathryn Lasky, Susan Cooper, and Karen Cushman have had their fiction enhanced by Hyman's jacket art and interior drawings.

Early recognition for her talent came when her picture-book version of Howard Pyle's story *King Stork* won the prestigious *Boston Globe–Horn Book* Award in 1973. Two later works were named Honor Books for this same award—*All in Free but Janey* and *On to Widecombe Fair* — and then in 1992 Hyman received the award again for *The Fortune-Tellers*, a story written by Lloyd Alexander in the style of a traditional tale. The American Library Association has cited her books three times for Caldecott Honor Awards: in 1984 for *Little Red Riding Hood*, in 1990 for *Hershel and the Hanukkah Goblins*, and in 2000 for *A Child's Calendar*.

"I liked best to be under the kitchen table with the dog, and for one whole year I really believed that I was Red Riding Hood."

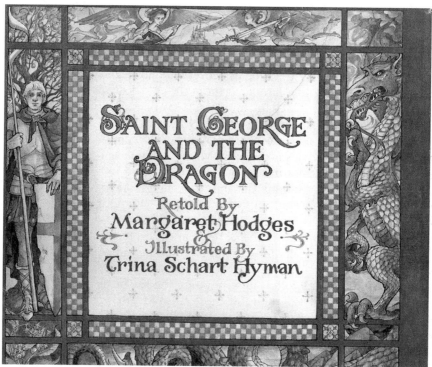

Courtesy of Little, Brown & Co.

Little Red Riding Hood also received the Golden Kite Illustration Award from the Society of Children's Book Writers and Illustrators, and *The Canterbury Tales* was a runner-up for the 1989 Golden Kite Illustration Award. In addition to these, many of her other titles have been designated ALA Notable Children's Books and appeared on the "best of the year" lists in major journals.

In 1985 Trina Schart Hyman received the Caldecott Medal for *Saint George and the Dragon*, a medieval legend from England retold by Margaret Hodges. This book incorporates many of the hallmarks of her artistic technique: a romantic atmosphere, paintings suffused with light, text enclosed by borders, meticulous research of the period, and strong characterization (including a remarkably fierce dragon). Each page of illustration is enclosed in a window-like border, giving a sense of looking back in time to experience the story. The text pages are surrounded by borders of flowers indigenous to medieval England.

From 1972 to 1979 Hyman served as the art director for the children's literary magazine *Cricket*. This gave her an opportunity to seek out and recruit other artists to illustrate the many fine stories for children that would be included in the magazine and to create her own pen-and-ink drawings of insect characters cavorting in the margins of each issue. Her sure eye for matching text with illustration helped the magazine get off to a good start with an excellence that continues to this day. Hyman has received awards from Keene State College in New Hampshire and Drexel University in Philadelphia for the body of her work.

Hyman's daughter, Katrin, spent several years in the Peace Corps in North Africa, where she met and married Eugene Tchana, a native of Cameroon. Sketching and painting the landscape and people while visiting in Cameroon gave Hyman the idea of setting her award-winning illustrations for *The Fortune-Tellers* in that richly varied culture. Katrin, Eugene, and their two sons take center stage in the award-winning illustrations for John Updike's *A Child's Calendar*, depicting every month of the year in the Vermont/New Hampshire countryside where they now make their home. Showing the magic in everyday life as well as the human side of the fantastic has been Trina Schart Hyman's ongoing contribution to the world of children's books.

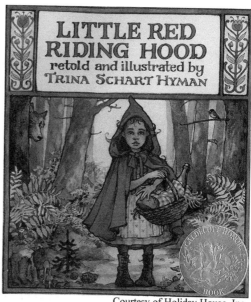

Courtesy of Holiday House, Inc.

SELECTED WORKS WRITTEN AND ILLUSTRATED: *How Six Found Christmas*, 1969, reissued 1991; *The Sleeping Beauty*, retold, 1977, 2000; *Self-Portrait: Trina Schart Hyman*, 1981; *Little Red Riding Hood*, retold, 1983; *A Little Alphabet*, 1980, 1993.

SELECTED WORKS ILLUSTRATED: *Joy to the World: Christmas Legends*, by Ruth Sawyer, 1964; *Dragon Stew*, by Tom McGowen, 1965; *Favorite Fairy Tales Told in Czechoslovakia*, by Virginia Haviland, 1966; *Epaminondas*, by Eve Merriam, 1968; *All in Free but Janey*, by Elizabeth Johnson, 1968; *The Moon Singer*, by Clyde Robert Bulla, 1969; *The Pumpkin Giant*, by Ellin Greene, 1970; *The Walking Stones*, by Mollie Hunter, 1970; *Let's Steal the Moon*, by Blanche Serwer, 1970, 1987; *The Bread Book*, by Carolyn Meyer, 1971; *Listen, Children, Listen*, by Myra Cohn Livingston, 1972; *The Wanderers*, by Elizabeth Coatsworth, 1972; *The Bad Times of Irma Baumlein*, by Carol Ryrie Brink, 1972; *King Stork*, by Howard Pyle, 1973; *Caddie Woodlawn*, by Carol Ryrie Brink, 1973; *Clever Cooks*, by Ellin Greene, 1973; *Joanna Runs Away*, by Phyllis LaFarge, 1973; *Snow White*, trans. by Paul Heins, 1974, 2000; *Why Don't You Get a Horse, Sam Adams?*, by Jean Fritz, 1974; *Greedy Mariani and Other Folktales of the Antilles*, by Dorothy S. Carter, 1974; *Two Queens of Heaven*, by Doris Gates, 1974; *Magic in the Mist*, by Margaret M. Kimmel, 1975; *Star Mother's Youngest Child*, by Louise Moeri, 1975; *The Quitting Deal*, by Tobi Tobias, 1975; *Will You Sign Here, John Hancock?*, by Jean Fritz, 1976; *Jane, Wishing*, by Tobi Tobias, 1977; *On to Widecombe Fair*, by Patricia Lee Gauch, 1978; *How Does It Feel to Be Old?*, by Norma Farber, 1979; *Tight Times*, by Barbara Shook Hazen, 1979; *Peter Pan*, by James M. Barrie, 1980; *Fairy Poems*, by Daisy Wallace, 1980; *The Night Journey*, by Kathryn Lasky, 1981; *Rapunzel*, retold by Barbara Rogasky, 1982; *A Christmas Carol*, by Charles Dickens, 1983; *Saint George and the Dragon*, by Margaret Hodges, 1984; *Christmas Poems*, ed. by Myra Cohn Livingston, 1984; *A Child's Christmas in Wales*, by Dylan Thomas, 1985; *The Water of Life: A Tale from the Brothers Grimm*, retold by Barbara Rogasky, 1986; *Cat Poems*, ed. by Myra Cohn Livingston, 1987; *The Canterbury Tales*, retold by Barbara Cohen, 1988; *A Connecticut Yankee in King Arthur's Court*, by Mark Twain, 1988; *Hershel and the Hanukkah Goblins*, by Eric Kimmel, 1989; *Swan Lake*, retold by Margot Fonteyn, 1989; *The Kitchen Knight*, by Margaret Hodges, 1990; *The Fortune-Tellers*, by Lloyd Alexander, 1992; *Iron John*, retold by Eric Kimmel, 1994; *Winter Poems*, ed. by Barbara Rogasky, 1994; *The Adventures of Hershel of Ostropol*, by Eric Kimmel, 1995; *Haunts*, by Angela Shelf Medearis, 1996; *Comus*, by Margaret Hodges, 1996; *The Golem*, by Barbara Rogasky, 1996; *Bearskin*, by Howard Pyle, 1997; *A Child's Calendar*, by John Updike, 1999; *The Serpent Slayer and Other Stories*, by Katrin Tchana, 2000.

SUGGESTED READING: *Children's Literature Review*, vol. 50, 1999; Collier, Laurie and Joyce Nakamura, eds. *Major Authors and Illustrators for Children and Young Adults*, 1993; *Contemporary Authors*, New Revision Series, vol. 70, 1999; Cummins, Julie, ed. *Children's Book Illustration and Design*, vol. 1, 1992; *Dictionary of Literary Biography*, vol. 61, 1987; Pendergast, Sara, ed. *St. James Guide to Children's Books*, 5th edition, 1999; Silvey, Anita, ed. *Children's Books and Their Creators*, 1995; *Something About the Author*, vol. 7, 1975; vol. 46, 1986; vol. 95, 1998. Periodicals—Brodie, Carolyn, "Trina Schart Hyman: Gifted Creator," *School Library Media Activities Monthly*, January 1999; Evans, Dilys, "The Art of Trina Schart Hyman in *Comus* and *The Golem*," *Book Links*, March 1997; Hearn, Michael Patrick, "The 'Ubiquitous' Trina Schart Hyman," *American Artist*, May 1979; Hyman, Trina Schart, "Acceptance Speech for the *Boston Globe–Horn Book Award*," *The Horn Book*, January/February 1994; Hyman, Trina Schart, "Acceptance Speech for the Caldecott Award," *The Horn Book*, July/August 1985.

An earlier profile of Trina Schart Hyman appeared in *Fourth Book of Junior Authors and Illustrators* (1978).

"I was born in Buffalo, New York, and lived there until I left to attend university in 1967. As a child, I did a limited amount of creative writing on my own. I had two poems published at the age of ten in a city-wide magazine of writing by schoolchildren. I read constantly, selecting books haphazardly from my parents' and the public library's shelves. In fifth grade, for example, along with *The Wind in the Willows*, I read Shakespeare's *Romeo and Juliet* and *The Tempest*, plus *Lorna Doone* and *The Caine Mutiny*. As now, poetry affected me more profoundly than any other genre. At age ten, I memorized Coleridge's 'Kubla Khan' while reading it for the first time.

"Probably the greatest childhood influence on my writing was my reading and re-reading, over a period of years, of *Little Women*. I would finish the last page and immediately start over at the first. The story became a kind of life plan for me, although I didn't realize that until a few years ago. Like Alcott's semi-autobiographical heroine Jo, I grew up to marry a kindly, professorial man with an unpronounceable name, to raise a passel of kids in the country, and to combine careers in educational program development and children's book writing. This experience has taught me to respect the long-term influence a children's book may have on its readers.

"I studied English literature in my undergraduate years at the University of Michigan and in a year of graduate study at the State University of New York in Buffalo. I also studied French, Russian, Latin, and American literature during these years. I have always been especially interested in nineteenth-century novels and poetry. My most serious focus has been on the romantic poets of England and France, in particular Keats and Yeats. Only as an adult have I begun to read extensively in children's literature, often experiencing a book for the first time while reading it to my children."

Courtesy of Anne Isaacs

Anne Isaacs

March 2, 1949–

*   *   *

Anne Isaacs received her B.A. from the University of Michigan in 1971 and her M.S. in 1975. In 1978 she married Samuel Koplowicz, a media producer, and they now have three children—Jordan, Amy, and Sarah. Writing is Isaacs's second profession: she held a series of positions in the field of environmental education before becoming a writer in the mid-1980s.

The imaginative tall tale *Swamp Angel*, illustrated by Paul O. Zelinsky, was Isaacs's first children's book and was named a Caldecott Honor Book, a *Boston Globe–Horn Book* Honor Book, an ALA Notable Children's Book, and a Notable Trade Book in the Field of Social Studies. *Swamp Angel* was also cited as one of the year's Ten Best Illustrated Books by the *New York Times* and included on all the other "best of year" lists as well. Since this stunning debut, Anne Isaacs has published *Treehouse Tales,* a humorous collection of stories about children on a homestead in western Pennsylvania in the early 1880s, and *Cat up a Tree,* an illustrated cycle of poems for older readers. Both of these were cited in the New York Public Library's annual list, 100 Titles for Reading and Sharing. Her novel, *Torn Thread,* tells the story of her mother-in-law's experiences in a Nazi labor camp in Czechoslovakia.

SELECTED WORKS: *Swamp Angel*, illus. by Paul O. Zelinsky, 1994; *Treehouse Tales*, illus. by Lloyd Bloom, 1997; *Cat up a Tree: A Story in Poems*, illus. by Stephen MacKey, 1998; *Torn Thread*, 2000.

SUGGESTED READING: *Contemporary Authors*, vol. 155, 1997; *Something About the Author*, vol. 90, 1997; *Who's Who in America*, 54th edition. Periodicals—Lewis, Valerie, "Meet the Author: Anne Isaacs," *Instructor*, March 1995.

Nina Jaffe

October 10, 1952–

"I grew up in New York City, in a neighborhood near East Harlem where people from many different countries had come to live and work. My own parents were born in the United States, but my grandparents emigrated from the Jewish communities of Russia, Poland, and Lithuania. Growing up in the 1950s and '60s, I heard people around me speaking many different languages—Spanish, Russian, French, Yiddish.

"As a child, I especially loved reading folktales and myths. Even as a teenager, I would return to the collections of fairy tales and folktales at the public library near my home. When I read a collection of Russian folktales or Turkish fairy tales, I felt that I was being given a gift of insight, a window into other peoples' culture, history, and world view. Once, in my senior year in high school, I turned to my friend Stacey Andreatos and said, 'Would you like to hear a story?' She agreed, and so I told her 'The Tinder Box,' by Hans Christian Andersen. After I had finished, Stacey called another friend over and said, 'Nina, tell us another one.' Then I understood that stories were important, not only to read but to tell, and that people, even friends my own age, wanted to hear them.

"I attended Wesleyan University, where I played and studied with master musicians from Ghana, South India, Indonesia, and other parts of the world. I also learned that music and storytelling were a vital part of many peoples' way of life and were integrally woven into their rituals, beliefs, and life passages. I slowly began to practice my craft—telling stories for children in schools and libraries. It seemed natural to incorporate the songs and rhythms I was learning with the stories. Travels to Israel, Puerto Rico, and the Dominican Republic also gave me a chance to study music—and languages: Spanish and Hebrew. I've played the guitar and piano since childhood. My favorite instruments to play are hand drums, especially percussion styles from West Africa, the Caribbean, and the Middle East. Even when I write, I often think of songs or music to go with the stories.

"After college, I pursued a master's degree in Bilingual Education and became a teacher. My work as a writer began after my son, Louis, was born. Some book publishers were interested in my stories from the Jewish tradition, and by that time I knew many stories. My first book, *The Three Riddles*, was published in 1989, and it is still one of my favorites to share in performance. It is the story of a wise girl, named Rachel, and how she solved some difficult riddles and saved her family. It is always fascinating to discover that different versions of a story like this are told all over the world.

"By now I have written more than twelve books—some picture books, some story collections, and a biography of Harold Courlander, a great folklorist and storyteller. I also teach courses in storytelling, music and folklore to graduate students at Bank Street College of Education in New York City. For me, storytelling and story writing are a way of connecting, of passing on wisdom, knowledge, and understanding that have been part of human history and civilization for many centuries. These stories come through my own voice, my own imagination, but they are also part of other people's lives and histories. It's wonderful to think that stories will continue to be told and retold, as I put them into written form."

Courtesy of Nancy Adler

*　*　*

Nina Jaffe graduated from Wesleyan University in 1976 with a B.A. in World Music. After graduation she concentrated on performing and studied Afro-Caribbean music, which led to her role as a co-founder of an Afro-Caribbean women's music group called Retumba. At that time Jaffe was also a storyteller-in-residence in the New York City public schools. Her travels in Puerto Rico launched her fieldwork towards a M.S.Ed. in Bilingual Special Education from the Bank Street College of Education, where she is currently on the graduate faculty as a specialist in storytelling, folklore, and music. The fact that she is fluent in French, Hebrew, and Spanish allows her to work with original sources. In 1993, with funding from the National Endowment for the Arts, she co-founded the Center for Folk Arts in Education with City Lore: The New York Center for Urban Folk Culture.

Nina Jaffe & Steve Zeitlin THE COW OF NO COLOR

Riddle Stories and Justice Tales from Around the World

Pictures by Whitney Sherman

Courtesy of Henry Holt & Co.

Her skill as a storyteller was recognized in 1992 when she received the Adele and Robert S. Blank Creative Jewish Arts Award, sponsored by the Stephen Wise Synagogue in New York City. Her interest in stories and music from many cultures led to a special invitation in December 1998 to be the first representative of the United States at an International Story Festival held in Tenerife in the Canary Islands, where all the stories were told in Spanish. The books Nina Jaffe has published reflect her interests in stories and music of the world.

Jaffe received the 1996 Prix VersAelles, sponsored by the Family League in Brussels, Belgium, for the French edition of *While Standing on One Foot: Puzzle Stories and Wisdom Tales from the Jewish Tradition*, which was also given an Anne Izard Storytellers Choice Award. Her biography, *A Voice for the People: The Life and Work of Harold Courlander*, received an Anne Izard Storytellers Choice Award in 1998 and was a 1997 Smithsonian Notable Book Selection. *The Mysterious Visitor: Stories of the Prophet Elijah* was a *Bulletin for the Center of Children's Books* Blue Ribbon title and won a Sydney Taylor Award, as did *The Uninvited Guest and Other Jewish Holiday Tales*. *Patakín: World Tales of Drums and Drummers* was cited by New York Public Library as a Best Book for the Teen Age. The Bank Street Child Study Children's Book Committee named *Older Brother, Younger Brother: A Korean*

Folktale the 1996 Book of the Year. *The Cow of No Color* was chosen as a Junior Library Guild Selection for 1998.

Nina Jaffe lives in New York City with her husband, Bob, and their son, Louis.

SELECTED WORKS: *The Three Riddles: A Jewish Folktale*, illus. by Bryna Waldman, 1989; *Canto Saquito! Sing, Little Sack: A Folktale from Puerto Rico*, illus. by Ray Cruz, 1993; *In the Month of Kislev: A Story for Hanukkah*, illus. by Louise August, 1992; *The Uninvited Guest and Other Jewish Holiday Tales*, illus. by Elivia Savadier, 1993; *While Standing on One Foot: Puzzle Stories and Wisdom Tales from the Jewish Tradition*, with Steve Zeitlin, illus. by John Segal, 1993; *Patakín: World Tales of Drums and Drummers*, illus. by Ellen Eagle, 1994; *Older Brother, Younger Brother: A Korean Folktale*, illus. by Wenhai Ma, 1995; *The Golden Flower: A Taino Myth from Puerto Rico*, illus. by Enrique Sanchez, 1996; *The Mysterious Visitor: Stories of the Prophet Elijah*, illus. by Elivia Savadier, 1997; *A Voice for the People: The Life and Work of Harold Courlander*, 1997; *The Cow of No Color: Riddle Stories and Justice Tales from World Traditions*, with Steve Zeitlin, illus. by Whitney Sherman, 1998; *The Way Meat Loves Salt: A Cinderella Tale from the Jewish Tradition*, illus. by Louise August, 1998.

SUGGESTED READING: *Book Links*, July 1999; *Five Owls*, May/June 1999; *The Republican Journal*, Belfast, Maine, August 21, 1997; *The Resident* (Queens, New York), October 1997; *School Library Journal*, September 1996.

WEB SITE: www.bnkst.edu/jaffestory

E-MAIL: *njaffe@bnkst.edu*

Steve Jenkins

March 31, 1952–

"I was born in Hickory, North Carolina, in 1952. My father was a scientist and college physics professor and my mom stayed home and raised my younger brother and me. We moved often while my father pursued his various degrees and teaching opportunities. I lived in Panama and Raleigh, North Carolina, during my pre-school years, spent first grade in Charlottesville, Virginia, and second and third grades in Denver, Colorado. I attended fourth through eighth grades in Wichita, Kansas, and went back to North Carolina to finish my education, first high school and then the School of Design at North Carolina State University in Raleigh.

"I was interested in natural science, as many kids are, and collected all sorts of interesting specimens. In Virginia we lived in the country and I collected lizards, turtles, and mice and a variety of insects. They lived in glass jars and cages in my room. When we moved to Colorado I began collecting rocks and fossils and became interested in geology and paleontology. I made notebooks with drawings of specimens and information about where they were collected, their hardness, color, and so on. In Kansas I graduated to chemistry and had a few close calls mixing substances over a gas burner.

"All along, I liked to draw and paint but assumed that I would be a scientist of one sort or another. It wasn't until late in high school when I met some people who were students at the School of Design that I decided to try design school. They looked like they were having a lot more fun than the physics or chemistry students. I loved design. Don Ensign was the teacher who showed me that many of the things that appealed to me about science—the importance of process, the combination of logical structure and intuition—are part of design as well. I realized that it's much easier to actually do design than science. Doing science often requires equipment and funding that are dependent on a bureaucratic organization. I received my B.A. from the School of Design at North Carolina State University in Raleigh in 1974 and my M.A. in 1976. It was there that I met Robin Page, who would become my partner in life and business. In 1978 Robin and I moved to New York City to pursue design careers. I had a chance to work with some of the best designers in New York at a top firm, Chermayeff & Geismar. I stayed there three and a half years before leaving in 1982 to start my own studio with Robin. We have done design work for a number of large and small companies, including American Express, AT&T, Banana Republic, Calvin Klein, Doubleday, the *New York Times* and the National Audubon Society.

Courtesy of Laura Lyons

"I sort of backed into children's book writing and illustration. While working on a book design project for Stewart, Tabori & Chang, I suggested to the editor that I also illustrate the books we were designing and she agreed. Shortly thereafter, I submitted a proposal to Ticknor & Fields, a Houghton Mifflin imprint, for a book of animal superstitions. It was accepted, and my career as an author/illustrator was launched. In 1994 we moved to Boulder, Colorado. We loved (and hated) New York but needed more space and a change of pace. Our daughter, Page, was born in 1986, followed in two years by Alec. Jamie arrived nine years later. The questions they've asked have

Courtesy of Houghton Mifflin

been the source of most of my book ideas. The books have been getting a little 'older' as the children have grown up. I'm a lucky man. Writing and illustrating children's books about the natural sciences has unified my two lifelong interests in the most rewarding way."

* * *

Steve Jenkins's interest in both science and art was encouraged by his father, a physicist and physics professor. Not only did Steve collect animal specimens when he was a boy, but he also memorized the periodic table of elements, the geologic periods, and the hardness scale. Ivan Chermayeff was also an important influence on Jenkins, who calls him "a great designer with a very broad education and a refreshing faith in the intelligence of his audience. He's a wonderful collage artist."

Steve Jenkins has become well known for his own brilliant cut-paper collage illustrations in books for children of all ages. Three of his books—*Elephants Swim, What Do You Do When Something Wants to Eat You?* and *Biggest, Strongest, Fastest*— have been named Outstanding Science Trade Books. *Biggest, Strongest, Fastest* also won the 1998 Washington Children's Choice Picture Book Award and the 1998 *Print* magazine Regional Design Competition. *Big and Little* won a 1997 *Scientific American* Young Readers Book Award and was named one of *School Library Journal*'s Best Books of the Year. *This Big Sky* was selected as a Notable Trade Book in the Field of Social Studies and named to the New York Public Library's 100 Titles for Reading and Sharing. *Hottest, Coldest, Highest, Deepest* was awarded an Orbis Pictus Honor Book citation, and *The Top of the World: Climbing Mount Everest* won the 1999 *Boston Globe–Horn Book Award* for nonfiction and was named an ALA Notable Children's Book.

Jenkins continues to work in corporate design with his wife, Robin Page, in addition to writing and illustrating books. During his few free moments he likes to ski, read, and run. He has also practiced martial arts for nearly ten years.

SELECTED WORKS WRITTEN AND ILLUSTRATED: *Biggest, Strongest, Fastest*, 1995; *Looking Down*, 1995; *Big and Little*, 1996; *What Do You Do When Something Wants to Eat You?*, 1997; *Hottest, Coldest, Highest, Deepest*, 1998; *The Top of the World: Climbing Mount Everest*, 1999.

SELECTED WORKS ILLUSTRATED: *My Dad*, by Janet Horowitz & Kathy Faggella, 1991; *Cock-a-Doodle Doo! What Does It Sound Like to You?*, by Marc Robinson, 1992; *Elephants Swim*, by Linda Riley, 1995; *Animal Dads*, by Sneed B. Collard III, 1997; *This Big Sky*, by Pat Mora, 1998; *Making Animal Babies*, by Sneed B. Collard III, 2000.

Dolores Johnson

February 1949–

"I was twelve years old when I began my first attempt at writing. It was 1961, in my hometown of New Britain, Connecticut. My parents had given me a typewriter for Christmas, and I figured I could teach myself to type by writing the Great American Novel. Despite the fact that I sat at that typewriter for what seemed like hours, that novel never got written. I didn't know what to write. I think it's ironic that I now make my living by writing stories about what it was like to be twelve years old.

"It seems I was more inclined to illustrate the Great American Picture Book. I loved to draw and decided to go to art school at Boston University when I graduated from high school. I wasn't the most practical thinker at that time, so I majored in sculpture. When I graduated from college, I took a job as a secretary because it was the only job for which I was qualified. Eventually I started working at advertising agencies as a production artist and production manager. A production artist is the person who puts the art and text of ads and books together so that they can be printed. The production manager sets the deadlines and submits the artwork, that the production artist has created, to printers.

"I was very frustrated working in advertising, and so I often worked at home at night on more creative projects. I made pottery and stained glass windows and began painting in watercolors. Soon I took classes in children's book illustration and writing and started to submit my work to publishers.

"My first published illustrations were for a book titled *Jenny*, a series of poems from the point of view of a six-year-old girl, written by Beth P. Wilson. I became successful at writing when I started telling stories about things that happened to me as a child. The first book that I wrote and illustrated that was published was *What Will Mommy Do When I'm at School?* The book is about a girl who hates to leave her mother home alone while she goes off to school for the first time. The fun that I had with my mother when she and I were home alone before I went to school prompted the writing of this book.

"The next book that I wrote and illustrated, *What Kind of Baby-Sitter Is This?*, is the story of a little boy who hates to be left with baby-sitters. I hated to be left with baby-sitters when I was a child. *The Best Bug to Be*, the story of a little girl who wants to star in her school play, was written because I remembered how nervous I was when I performed in church and school plays. Other books I wrote and illustrated are *Your Dad Was Just Like You*, *Grandma's Hands*, and *My Mom Is My Show-and-Tell*, stories about contemporary children dealing with their roles in the family. I also illustrated similar stories for other authors, such as *Big Meeting*, written by Dee Paler Woodtor, and *Calvin's Christmas Wish*, written by Calvin Miles.

Courtesy of Elizabeth King

"I have also written a biography, *Bessie Coleman: She Dared to Fly*, and two historical fiction books about slavery, *Now Let Me Fly: The Story of a Slave Family* and *Seminole Diary: Remembrances of a Slave*. The last two titles show how families were destroyed by slavery. Even when I'm writing about history, I'm writing about families."

* * *

Dolores Johnson grew up in New Britain, Connecticut. She knew early on that she could draw but didn't think she could be an artist because the family already had an artist, her older brother Bill, who seemed to be out of her league. Billy ate, drank, and breathed art. Although Dolores liked to draw, she liked other things as well—sewing, knitting, and reading. But she followed her big brother to art school and graduated with a B.F.A. from the Boston University School of the Arts in 1971.

After graduation, Johnson moved from the East Coast to the West Coast and found work as a part-time production artist in a Los Angeles television station. In 1977 she got a job in the art department of a mail-order company, Sunset House, and worked there as the production manager for four years. She became restless with her work and started submitting manuscripts and illustrations to publishers. It took five years, but she was finally awarded a contract to illustrate her first picture book, *Jenny*.

Now Let Me Fly and *Seminole Diary* were both named Notable Children's Books in the Field of Social Studies. Johnson has taught children's book writing and illustrating at Los Angeles Southwest College Continuing Education, the Art Center College of Design in Pasadena, and Otis College of Art and Design in Los Angeles.

" I became successful at writing when I started telling stories about things that happened to me as a child."

SELECTED WORKS WRITTEN AND ILLUSTRATED: *What Will Mommy Do When I'm at School?*, 1990; *What Kind of Baby-Sitter Is This?*, 1991; *The Best Bug to Be*, 1992; *Your Dad Was Just Like You*, 1993; *Now Let Me Fly: The Story of a Slave Family*, 1993; *Papa's Stories*, 1994; *Seminole Diary: Remembrances of a Slave*, 1994; *The Children's Book of Kwanzaa: A Guide to Celebrating the Holiday*, 1996; *Bessie Coleman: She Dared to Fly*, 1996; *Grandma's Hands*, 1998; *My Mom Is My Show-and-Tell*, 1999.

SELECTED WORKS ILLUSTRATED: *Jenny*, by Beth P. Wilson, 1990; *Calvin's Christmas Wish*, by Calvin Miles, 1993; *Big Meeting*, by Dee Woodtor, 1996.

SUGGESTED READING: *Contemporary Authors*, vol. 137, 1992; *Something About the Author*, vol. 69, 1992.

Stephen T. Johnson

May 29, 1964–

"I grew up in Lawrence, Kansas, where my parents taught French and French literature at the University of Kansas. France was a big part of our lives and we lived there for several years, returning for periodic summer visits. For our long stays of a year or more, we would pack up the Country Squire station wagon with our trunks and bags and head east to New York. There we would leave our car with my grandparents on Long Island. Then we would journey across the Atlantic on board the

QE II, leaving the glorious skyscrapers of New York City behind, and six days later we were in France—pure excitement!

"The time spent in France, including my junior year in college, played an important role in developing my interest in art, reading, and communicating. My interests and passion for collecting flourished with such finds as prehistoric fossils, Gallo-Roman pottery, and even a French bayonette from World War I. Stamps, seashells, coins, anything with rust on it—all were ardently collected and displayed, turning my bedrooms into mini-museums. The colors, patterns, and surface textures of my various collected items are analogous to the colors and textures in urban settings that I now find visually captivating. Coupled with my parents' love of travel and exploring cities, I suppose it was only natural for me to eventually see letters and numbers in various urban shapes, culminating in my books *Alphabet City* and *City by Numbers*.

"My years growing up in Lawrence, Kansas, were equally important. Our home was always filled with books and art. Many of my favorite books were the art books of my grandfather, John Theodore Johnson, who was a professional artist. His paintings adorned just about every wall in our house. Although I never knew him, his paintings and in particular his early academic drawings, executed in the 1920s, had a profound influence on my growth as an artist. As I do today, I loved to pore over books in my father's library, public libraries, and bookstores, then bask in my new discoveries. How the books feel in my hands, the weight, the smell, the binding are still of great importance to me.

"In 1987 I graduated from the University of Kansas with a B.F.A. degree in Painting and Illustration. That fall I

Courtesy of Stephen T. Johnson

moved to New York City to try my hand at the precarious business of freelance illustration. I have been illustrating ever since, creating artwork for magazines, books, CD covers, and the like. Three years after the move to New York I illustrated my first book, *The Samurai's Daughter,* by Robert San Souci. With this book I was introduced to the world of children's books and was instantly taken by the vast dedication and enthusiasm of this industry, exemplified by my editors, art directors, and all the many talented people behind the scenes. I quickly became passionate about making books, too. For me the essence of picture book–

making is creative freedom. I am very fortunate to have support and guidance from my wonderfully insightful editors —Paula Wiseman, Regina Hayes, and Anne Schwartz—who allow me to grow and develop artistically while helping me retain the passion and spirit of what made me tick as a young boy. I am grateful to be working in the rich and inspiring world of children's books."

* * *

Stephen T. Johnson lived in his birthplace of Madison, Wisconsin, for only three months before his parents moved to Princeton, New Jersey. When he was four years old, in 1968, the family moved to Lawrence, Kansas, where Stephen grew up.

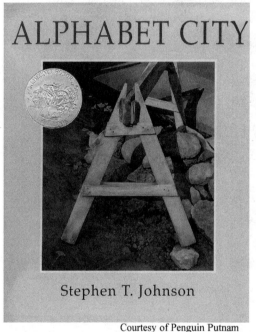

ALPHABET CITY

Stephen T. Johnson

Courtesy of Penguin Putnam

Frequent trips to France were highlights of his childhood, and in 1984–1985 he spent his junior year in college at the Université de Bordeaux and at the Conservatoire des Beaux-Arts in Bordeaux, France.

Johnson's work has been the subject of many group and solo exhibitions, beginning in his student days at the University of Kansas. In 1986 he won Best of Show in an Annual Student Scholarship Competition at the Art and Design Gallery of the University, an honor that he credits with helping him gain confidence in his work. In 1989 the Locust Gallery in Lawrence, Kansas, staged an exhibit entitled "Three Generations of Johnsons" featuring Stephen's work along with that of his grandfather, John Theodore Johnson, and his father, John Theodore Johnson, Jr.; in 1998 Stephen's work was again shown alongside his father's in "Drawing from Life: Drawings, Paintings, Illustrations of Ted and Stephen Johnson." As early as 1991, when he was only twenty-seven, Stephen Johnson had a solo exhibition at Moorhead (Minnesota) State University. Examples of his work were included in The Society of Illustrators Traveling Exhibition in 1994.

The Samurai's Daughter was an IRA Teachers' Choice and a Notable Children's Trade Book in the Field of Social Studies. *Alphabet City*, a book Johnson developed on his own and published in 1995, brought him his greatest recognition as an illustrator. Composed of very realistic pictures of city scenes, each incorporating a letter of the alphabet (Z, for instance, is part of a zig-zag fire escape; M is traced by the arches of the Brooklyn

Bridge), *Alphabet City* was praised for its originality and the excellence of its design. Besides receiving a Caldecott Honor Book Award, it was a *New York Times* Best Illustrated Book and an ALA Notable Children's Book and was included on other lists of distinction. A companion volume, *City by Numbers* (1998), covering the integers from 1 to 21, was also well received. *Hoops*, with a free-verse text by Robert Burleigh and Johnson's drawings of basketball players in motion, was named an ALA Notable Children's Book in 1998 and included among best books of the year by both *Booklist* magazine and *School Library Journal*.

Stephen Johnson and his wife, Debbie Goldberg Johnson, met during their student days at Kansas University. They were married August 12, 1995, and their daughter Sophia Gabrielle was born in 1998. They live in Brooklyn, New York.

SELECTED WORKS WRITTEN AND ILLUSTRATED: *Alphabet City*, 1995; *City by Numbers*, 1998; *My Little Red Toolbox*, 1999.

SELECTED WORKS ILLUSTRATED: *The Samurai's Daughter*, by Robert D. San Souci, 1992; *The Nutcracker Ballet*, by Melissa Hayden, 1992; *The Snow Wife*, by Robert D. San Souci, 1993; *A Christmas Carol*, by Charles Dickens, adapted by Donna Martin, 1993; *When Solomon Was King*, by Sheila MacGill-Callahan, 1995; *The Tie Man's Miracle*, by Steven Schnur, 1995; *The Girl Who Wanted a Song*, by Steve Sanfield, 1996; *Hoops*, by Robert Burleigh, 1997; *Love as Strong as Ginger*, by Lenore Look, 1999.

SUGGESTED READING: Cummins, Julie, ed. *Children's Book Illustration and Design*, vol. II, 1998; *Something About the Author*, vol. 84, 1996. Periodicals— "Hooked on Seeing in a Different Way to Make Picture Books: Stephen T. Johnson," *School Library Media Activities Monthly*, April 1997; "Out of Misty Dreams: The Enchanted Art of Stephen T. Johnson," *Realms of Fantasy Magazine*, October 1995.

"I am convinced that I was the luckiest kid in the world. I grew up in Lexington, Kentucky, with the best family a kid could ever want.

"I was born on July 15, 1958, in Joliet, Illinois, the youngest of three children. My father, Robert Thornton, worked for the government, and by the time I was five we had moved to Silver Spring, Maryland, and then to Lexington, Kentucky. My mother, Thelma Kuhljuergen Thornton, was the epitome of what a good mom should be. Together, my parents provided a safe haven in which I thrived.

"My favorite childhood memories include playing in our backyard on steamy summer days. We had a big backyard surrounded by dense hedges. The backyard was my playground and I let my

**Marcia
Thornton Jones**

July 15, 1958–

imagination turn it into kingdoms, or circuses, or the horse ranches of the wild, wild west. I would rather race barefoot across the backyard than be curled up with a book, but there are a few books that remain my favorites. I especially enjoyed *Henry Huggins* by Beverly Cleary, and I'll never forget sobbing as I turned the last page of *The Yearling* by Marjorie Kinnan Rawlings.

"I wasn't a storyteller as a child. I was a daydreamer. No one encouraged me to turn my daydreams into stories. I did try my hand at poetry as a sixth-grader. My mother thought my poem was good enough to send to *Good Housekeeping* magazine. It became my first rejection!

Courtesy of Tom Barnett

Marcia Thornton Jones

"I graduated from the University of Kentucky in 1980 with a teaching degree and attended Georgetown College. Still, nobody encouraged me to develop my writing skills. The only writing I was asked to do was research papers, and even those were a challenge since I was never taught how to write That's why I was a nervous wreck when I found myself in Dr. Helen Reed's class. Dr. Reed was notorious for demanding excellence of her graduate students, and she required her students to write a paper every week. I thought, for sure, that I was doomed. I was so scared to look at my first graded paper that I waited until I was in the safety of my car before lifting the cover sheet. Sure enough, red marking pen littered the pages. I took a deep breath and looked closely at Dr. Reed's comments. I couldn't believe it. Her comments were not negative at all. They were merely her responses to my words like, 'I hadn't thought of that,' or 'Good point.' There wasn't a negative word on that entire paper. Dr. Reed was the first teacher that ever responded to my written words as if they had value. After that, I signed up for every course Dr. Reed taught. I credit Dr. Reed with giving me the courage—and the desire—to write.

"I earned my master's degree in Education from Georgetown College in 1986. I continued teaching during the day, and I worked in a bookstore in the evenings and during the weekends. I found myself shelving books, wondering about the people that wrote all those words. I wondered what it would be like to have my name on the cover of a book. Soon after that, I was talking to the librarian of the school where I taught. We both admitted a secret desire of seeing our names on the cover of a book. The librarian, Debbie Dadey, looked at me and asked, 'What's stopping us from trying?' I couldn't think of a single thing. The next day we started writing during our twenty-minute lunch break. I've been writing ever since!"

*   *   *

The first book in the Adventures of the Bailey School Kids series came to life in 1988. After a bad day at school, when her students didn't want to behave, Marcia Jones told Debbie Dadey, the librarian at the Sayre School in Lexington, Kentucky, that she'd have to sprout horns, blow smoke out of her nose, and grow ten feet tall to get the kids to pay attention! That sounded funny, so they decided to write *Vampires Don't Wear Polka Dots*, a story about a teacher who might be a monster. The book was published in 1990 and cited that year as a CBC/IRA Children's Choice selection. Since then Jones and Dadey have co-authored many more titles in the Bailey School Kids series and have launched two other popular series, Bailey City Monsters and Triplet Trouble.

Marcia Jones has been an elementary school teacher for nineteen years. She's taught first grade, third grade, reading, writing, computer skills, and gifted/talented students. She won the Sayre School Short Award honoring excellence in teaching in 1986. She has also taught adult writing courses for the University of Kentucky and Lexington Community College.

"I wasn't a storyteller as a child. I was a daydreamer."

Jones founded the Lexington writing critique group Writers, Ink. She is currently teaching gifted and talented students in Lexington, Kentucky, where she lives with her husband, Steve, and their kittens, Tazz and Purrl. However, her writing partner, Debbie Dadey, has moved to Illinois. How do they continue to collaborate? "We use the hot potato method of writing," they explained. "We start with a brief outline. Then we take turns writing chapters. We send them to each other using fax machine and e-mail. When the other person has the story, we say it's her 'hot potato.'"

Writing, teaching, and visiting schools to talk about her books all keep Jones busy, but when she has free time she likes to read, go for long walks, watch movies, and have fun with her husband and their cats.

SELECTED WORKS: *Godzilla Ate My Homework*, 1997; The Adventures of the Bailey School Kids (with Debbie Dadey—for a complete list visit the Bailey Kids Web site): *Vampires Don't Wear Polka Dots*, 1990; *Leprechauns Don't Play Basketball*, 1992; *Unicorns Don't Give Sleigh Rides*, 1997; *Mrs. Jeepers in Outer Space*, 1999; *The Bride of Frankenstein Doesn't Bake Cookies*, 2000; Triplet Trouble series (with

Debbie Dadey—for a complete list visit the Bailey Kids Web site): *Triplet Trouble and the Talent Show Mess*, 1995; *Triplet Trouble and the Runaway Reindeer*, 1995; *Triplet Trouble and the Field Day Disaster*, 1996; *Triplet Trouble and the Class Trip*, 1997; Bailey City Monsters (with Debbie Dadey—for a complete list visit the Bailey Kids Web site): *The Monsters Next Door*, 1997; *Kilmer's Pet Monster*, 1998; *Vampire Trouble*, 1999; *Spooky Spells*, 1999.

SUGGESTED READING: *Something About the Author*, vol. 73, 1993.

WEB SITES: *www.baileykids.com* and *www.scholastic.com*

For a statement by Debbie Dadey, Marcia Thornton Jones's co-author, see her entry in this volume.

Courtesy of Sue Karas

G. Brian Karas

September 27, 1957–

"**M**y career in art had a humble beginning. I was in kindergarten. We had just finished a study on Native Americans. I was inspired. Our teacher gave us an unprecedented one whole week to create something of our own choice. I immediately set out with an ambitious plan: a life-sized three-dimensional teepee. It didn't matter that I had never attempted 3-D before, I thought. I was wrong. I labored and sweated for the entire week over something I was unable to do and was too . . . something—afraid? proud? . . . to ask for help. At the end of the week, surrounded by truly awesome projects my classmates had constructed, with nothing to show for my week's worth of work, I hastily drew a three-inch teepee on white paper and cut it out. Maybe she wouldn't notice its modest size, I hoped. She did, and pointed out to the entire class how some people can manage to waste a great amount of time, when others work so hard. I was crushed. Great intentions sometimes have sad endings.

"I resurrected my stature as a serious artist in the first grade. I drew caricatures. Mostly of my teacher, who found them, and found them most unflattering. My classmates, however, thought they were brilliant. I had gained their respect. I had become 'the class artist.' Through my school years, my projects began to improve in merit. I moved on to stage sets, snowflakes for holiday windows, and posters for the walls. I was very impressed with the artwork of Charles Schulz. I thought of the 'Peanuts' characters as close friends and liked their subtle humor. I managed to do a very good rendition of Schulz's work. And I enjoyed that more than anything I had done before. I also read a great deal and had an interest in writing. At one point I was selected to be part of a creative writing class in a different school system, an experience that freed my creativity in a way I hadn't known before.

"At home I was not encouraged to pursue art as a profession. So I didn't take seriously the notion of being an artist until late into my senior year in high school. When it became clear that I had no real direction to go in, I felt like I was adrift. I couldn't find anyplace where I fit. It was at that time I found a person who changed the course of my life: my art teacher. I enrolled in her class. She took a special interest in me and my work. I think she saw that I had the talent but lacked the confidence, drive, and support to apply to art schools. She encouraged me to apply to the school she had once taught in, and began to help me pull together a portfolio.

"I knew from the first day of art school that there was no other choice for me. This was it, a place where I fit. I had the good fortune of having many fine teachers, some of whom were working in the field of children's book publishing. In a way, there was never a question in my mind of what to do in the field of art. There was never a defining moment when I said, I want to be a children's book artist. I just was.

"I've illustrated over fifty books for children, two of which I also wrote. I can still say that there is never a question of what I should do. This is what I do, and it comes very naturally to me. Not that I don't struggle with it or that it doesn't present a challenge, or that I can't continue to grow as an artist. Because I do, and it does, and I can. But what doesn't exist is a question of my purpose. Aside from watching my children grow, creating books for children is the most gratifying and worthwhile thing I can do."

Courtesy of HarperCollins Publishers

✳   ✳   ✳

G. Brian Karas was born in Milford, Connecticut. After graduating from the Paier School of Art with highest honors, he went to work as a greeting card artist at Hallmark Cards in Kansas

City, Missouri. Three years later he moved to New York City and began freelancing as a commercial illustrator. His first illustrated book was published in 1983 and he has since illustrated more than fifty books for children.

Karas's first book as author-illustrator, *Home on the Bayou: A Cowboy's Story*, received a *Boston Globe–Horn Book* Honor Book award. *Saving Sweetness* was a Capitol Choices Noteworthy Book for Children, received a *Bulletin of the Center for Children's Books* Blue Ribbon, and was a *School Library Journal* Best Book. It also was listed in New York Public Library's annual 100 Titles for Reading and Sharing and in the ABA's Pick of the Lists. *Truman's Aunt Farm*, *Elevator Dreams*, and *Sleepless Beauty* were also included in Pick of the Lists. *Like Butter on Pancakes* was a *School Library Journal* Best Book of 1995. *On the Trail with Miss Pace* was a *Smithsonian Magazine* Notable Children's Book of 1995. *I Know an Old Lady* received a Parents' Choice Honor and was a *Booklist* Editors' Choice.

G. Brian Karas lives with his family in Rhinebeck, New York.

SELECTED WORKS WRITTEN AND ILLUSTRATED: *I Know an Old Lady* (adapted), 1994; *Home on the Bayou: A Cowboy's Story*, 1996; *The Windy Day*, 1998; *Bebe's Bad Dream*, 2000.

SELECTED WORKS ILLUSTRATED: *Squeaky Shoes*, by Morgan Matthews, 1986; *If You're Not Here, Please Raise Your Hand: Poems About School*, by Kalli Dakos, 1990; *The Best Teacher in the World*, by Robin Pulver, 1991; *Nobody's Mother Is in Second Grade*, by Robin Pulver, 1992; *Truman's Aunt Farm*, by Jama K. Rattigan, 1994; *Cinder-Elly*, by Frances Minters, 1994; *Like Butter on Pancakes*, by Jonathan London, 1995; *On the Trail with Miss Pace*, by Sharon Phillips Denslow, 1995; *Sid and Sam*, by Nola Buck, 1995; *Give Me Half!*, by Stuart J. Murphy, 1996; *Mr. Carey's Garden*, by Jane Cutler, 1996; *Sleepless Beauty*, by Frances Minters, 1996; *The Spider Who Created the World*, by Amy MacDonald, 1996; *Saving Sweetness*, by Diane Stanley, 1996; *Bootsie Barker Ballerina*, by Barbara Bottner, 1997; *Elevator Magic*, by Stuart J. Murphy, 1997; *Puddles*, by Jonathan London, 1997; *In the Hush of the Evening*, by Nancy P. Graff, 1998; *Raising Sweetness*, by Diane Stanley, 1999; *I Like Bugs*, by Margaret Wise Brown, 1999; *The Bone Keeper*, by Megan McDonald, 1999; *The Seals on the Bus*, by Lenny Hart, 2000.

SUGGESTED READING: Cummins, Julie, ed. *Children's Book Illustration and Design*, vol. 2, 1998.

WEB SITE: *www.gbriankaras.com*

"I began my writing career at the age of ten when I had my own newspaper. It was the 'Dog Newspaper,' with news of all the dogs in my neighborhood. Each week, I interviewed everyone who had a dog to find out what interesting things the pet had done. The 'Dog Newspaper' went out of business because in every issue, *my* dog got the whole front page and the other dogs only got short articles on the back side. After awhile, the other kids were tired of reading about B.J. and wouldn't buy my paper.

"The most unusual event of my life happened when I was in seventh grade: a severe case of polio paralyzed me from the neck down. I nearly died, and my parents were told I would never walk again. I spent nine months in hospitals, and had my thirteenth birthday in a wheelchair, but I learned to walk and have been able to lead a nearly normal life. My memories of that year became my autobiography, *Small Steps: The Year I Got Polio.*

Courtesy of Carl Kehret

Peg Kehret

November 11, 1936–

"Because my weakened muscles made it hard for me to participate in sports, my extracurricular activities in high school consisted of writing for the school newspaper and yearbook, and helping with school plays. I began to dream of becoming a writer.

"After one year at the University of Minnesota, I got married. My husband, Carl, and I moved to California, where we spent the next fifteen years. I wrote radio commercials and some two-character sketches that Carl and I performed with an amateur theater group, but mostly I enjoyed being a mom.

"In 1970 we moved to Washington State where I began writing plays and magazine articles. For the first time, I submitted my writing for publication— and quickly got rejected. Undaunted, I continued to write, and to get rejected. I finally sold a short magazine piece and was paid five dollars for it. I was as thrilled as if it had been five million. In the next ten years I published one-act plays and collections of skits, full-length plays, adult nonfiction books, and hundreds of magazine stories.

Then I was asked to write a book of monologues for student actors, a request that changed my life. As soon as I began writing from a young person's point of view, I knew I had found my true voice as a writer. When *Winning Monologs for Young Actors* was

Courtesy of Penguin Putnam

finished, I wrote a mystery for kids and I've been doing books for young people ever since.

"I volunteer at the Humane Society, and I am a vegetarian for humane reasons. Although I no longer feature my own pets in everything I write, I often have animals in my stories.

"I try to put unusual information in every book. My research has included visiting a volcano, getting hypnotized, camping where bald eagles fish for salmon, and flying to San Francisco to attend a baseball game.

"My life is truly a dream-come-true. My husband and I both work at home and we love our work. Our two children grew up to be our friends and married wonderful people. We have four fun grandchildren, plus a dog and two cats. From our log house in the forest, we often see black-tail deer, elk, rabbits, and other wildlife. Every day I wake up eager to go into my office and work on the next book."

*   *   *

Peg Kehret was born in LaCrosse, Wisconsin, and now lives in Washington State. Her plays have been performed across the country, and her published works include the paperback Frightmares series and many hardcover novels of mystery and suspense for middle-grade and young adult readers.

Kehret's books have been nominated for student choice awards in more than half the fifty states and have won in Nebraska, Iowa, Oklahoma, New Mexico, Vermont, Indiana, Missouri, Minnesota, and West Virginia. *Terror at the Zoo* won the 1995 Pacific Northwest Library Association Award, conferred by young readers from British Columbia, Alberta, Alaska, Idaho, Montana, Oregon, and Washington. She has also received national recognition for several titles. *Danger at the Fair* was on the ALA Quick Picks for Reluctant Young Adult Readers list in 1996. *Cages* and *The Winner* were also ALA Recommended Books for Reluctant Young Adult Readers. *Cages, Danger at the Fair, Terror at the Zoo, Earthquake Terror, Deadly Stranger,* and *Sisters, Long Ago* were all IRA/CBC Children's Choices. *Small Steps: The Year I Got Polio* was an ALA Notable Children's Book and was cited as one of the Top Ten Quick Picks for Reluctant Young Adult Readers; it also won the 1996 Golden

Kite Award for nonfiction from the Society of Children's Book Writers and Illustrators. For the entire body of her work, Peg Kehret received the Pacific Northwest Writers Conference Achievement Award.

The author gives speeches at schools and libraries across the nation, traveling to her destinations via motor home with her husband and their pets.

SELECTED WORKS: *Winning Monologs for Young Actors*, 1986; *Deadly Stranger*, 1987; *The Winner*, 1988; *Sisters, Long Ago*, 1990; *Cages*, 1991; *Terror at the Zoo*, 1992; *Danger at the Fair*, 1995; *Cat Burglar on the Prowl*, 1995; *Earthquake Terror*, 1996; *Shelter Dogs: Amazing Stories of Adopted Strays*, 1999.

SUGGESTED READING: Kehret, Peg. *Small Steps: The Year I Got Polio*, 1996; *Something About the Author*, vol. 73, 1993; vol. 108, 1999.

WEB SITE: *users.owt.com/kehretbp/*

True Kelley

February 25, 1946–

"I had the good fortune to be born into a quirky and funny family. My parents were both professional artists. When I was about four I published my first illustrated story (about chickens) in *Child Life* magazine. It was very helpful that my dad was the art director there.

"My brother, Mark, and I grew up on an old farm in Hampton Falls, N.H. We played in a big old barn that I later used in my book, *The Mystery of the Stranger in the Barn*. We were surrounded by woods, fields, swamps, and brooks and quite a few animals—chickens, ducks, turkeys, a horse, dogs, and we even had twelve barn cats at one time. Since our parents were artists, we had loads of art supplies around and were encouraged to use them. But after seeing how hard my parents worked, I was sure being an artist was not something I wanted to do. I thought being a teacher or a writer might be easier.

"In 1964 I went to the University of New Hampshire, and by the time I graduated I had changed my major eight times. Finally I settled on Elementary Education. I did my practice teaching in a sixth-grade classroom and loved the kids but not the hours. I started getting the idea that teaching might not be easier than being an artist after all. Fortunately, I was accepted at the Rhode Island School of Design and things began to fall into place. I learned how to be an illustrator and I met Steven Lindblom. After two years at Rhode Island School of Design, I cautiously entered the field of commercial art in Boston. I hung around my dad's studio, which he shared with Jerry Pinkney. Jerry doesn't know it, but he was a huge inspiration. I loved (and still do) his drawings, design, and, above all, his color. I began my career trying to duplicate his colors and using the same materials that he did. It was a pale imitation, but a beginning. At the same time, I was trying to imitate my father's style. Dad was a master of expressive and humorous drawing. I fear I'll never achieve his facility.

"My first illustration jobs were for advertising, but I really wanted to illustrate children's books. Little Brown hired me to illustrate my first book, *I Saw a Purple Cow*, a book of projects for kids. By then Steve and I were living in Boston with Jub, the cat. We traveled as much as we could on a very low budget. The first trip was by Vincent motorcycle all over Europe, followed by trips to Turkey, India, and the Caribbean.

Courtesy of Steven Lindblom

True Kelley

"Soon after, Steve and I moved to my old hometown, Hampton Falls, and built a house. In 1978 we collaborated on a book, *The Mouses' Terrible Christmas*. What a feeling it was when I held that first published book in my hands! Over sixty books later I still get that feeling! Several years later we moved to Henniker, N.H. I timed the move perfectly. I was pregnant and couldn't lift boxes or move furniture. A month later our daughter, Jada, was born. She has been an inspiration for many of my books. In fact, I often use my old photo albums for reference.

"While we lived in Henniker, Steve designed and built our solar gothic house on a hilltop in Warner, N.H. I stayed home with our daughter and worked on various educational publishing projects. I also began working on nonfiction books for children that required lots of research, which I love to do. It's fun to try to jazz up a nonfiction book with some silliness. We still live in Warner, a great town with lots to do. I played on a softball team. My friend Eliza and I organize a yearly canoe-camping trip. I often bicycle around town and on logging roads and snowmobile trails near my house. In winter we cross- country ski on those same trails. I like to go camping and birdwatching and still like to travel. I play the piano, in my fashion. My downhill skiing skills are a bit rusty lately, as are my softball skills. Of course, I spend lots of time drawing, painting, and writing. And, I love the Boston Red Sox!

"I spend most days sitting at my desk working on something enjoyable with my music blaring away. I can look out my studio window and see the mountains and sometimes a deer—or even a moose—in the field. It is great to work at home in a place like this!"

* * *

True (Adelaide) Kelley was born in Cambridge, Massachusetts, to Mark and Adelaide Kelley. Her father was an illustrator and her mother, whose maiden name was True, is an artist. True Kelley graduated from the University of New Hampshire in 1968 and studied at the Rhode Island School of Design from 1968 to 1971. Kelley is a member of the Society of Children's Book Writers and Illustrators, the Authors Guild, the Audubon Society, the New Hampshire Writers' Project, and the Society for Protection of New Hampshire Forests.

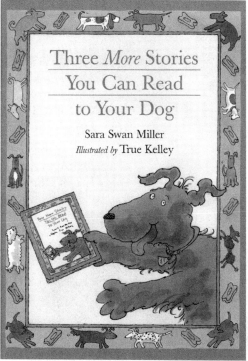

Courtesy of Houghton Mifflin

A *Valentine for Fuzzboom* was an IRA Children's Choice in 1982. *What the Moon Is Like* was named an Outstanding Science Trade Book for Children in 1987. *I've Got Chicken Pox* was on the Bank Street College Child Study Book Committee's 1995 list of Children's Books of the Year. In 1995 *Three Stories You Can Read to Your Dog* made the New York Public Library's list, 100 Titles for Reading and Sharing, and the American Booksellers Association's Pick of the Lists; it was also a Parents' Choice Honor Book. In 1997 a Parents' Choice Award was given to *Stay! Keeper's Story*, written by Lois Lowry and illustrated by Kelley.

SELECTED WORKS WRITTEN AND ILLUSTRATED: *The Mouses's Terrible Christmas* (with Steve Lindblom), 1978; *The Mouses's Terrible Halloween* (with Steve Lindblom), 1980; *A Valentine for Fuzzboom*, 1981; *The Mystery of the Stranger in the Barn*, 1986; *Look, Baby! Listen, Baby! Do, Baby!*, 1987; *I've Got Chicken Pox*, 1994.

SELECTED WORKS ILLUSTRATED: *I Saw a Purple Cow*, by Ann Cole et. al., 1972; *Sun Dogs and Shooting Stars*, by Franklyn Branley, 1980; *Shivers and Goose Bumps*, by Franklyn Branley, 1984; *Cuts, Breaks, Bruises, and Burns*, by Joanna Cole, 1985; *What the Moon Is Like*, by Franklyn Branley 1987, 2000; *The Skeleton Inside You*, by Philip Balestrino, 1989; *Roller Skates!*, by Stephanie Calmenson, 1992; *The*

Spider on the Floor, by Raffi, 1993; *How to Read Your Mother's Mind*, by James Deem, 1994; *What Makes a Magnet*, by Franklyn Branley, 1996; *Three Stories You Can Read to Your Dog*, by Sara Swan Miller, 1995; *Don't Try This at Home*, by Vicki Cobb and Kathy Darling, 1998; *Floating in Space*, by Franklyn Branley, 1998; *Day by Day a Week Goes Round*, by Carol Diggory Shields, 1998; *Baseball Buddies*, by Jean Marzollo, 1998; *Three More Stories You Can Read to Your Dog*, by Sara Swan Miller, 2000.

SUGGESTED READING: *Contemporary Authors*, vol. 105, 1982; *Contemporary Authors*, New Revision Series, vol. 23, 1988; vol. 47, 1995; *Something About the Author*, vol. 39, 1985; vol. 41, 1985; vol. 92, 1997.

Courtesy of Paul F. Roediger

Patrice Kindl

Patrice Kindl

October 16, 1951–

"I was born in the evening hours of October 16, 1951. Much to the amazement of the assembled doctors and nurses, it was discovered that I had entered the world fiercely clutching in my tiny fists an even tinier book. A novel, or so I have been told.

"My mother, heavily drugged, as women giving birth were in those days, stirred feebly and muttered, just loud enough for everyone present to hear: 'Put down that book this instant, young lady, and go outside and play.'

"None of the above, other than the first sentence, is true. Oh, it's true enough that I read a great deal as a child and that my mother waged a heroic but ultimately unsuccessful campaign to get me to do something, anything, that did not involve deciphering the alphabet in a prone position, but that bit about me reading novels in the womb is sheer fantasy on my part. After all, there would hardly be enough light to make out the text of even an Easy Reader; I really doubt I would be up to perusing Proust or Dostoevsky under the circumstances.

"However, I am a novelist and cannot resist embellishing a dull tale just a little bit. Or lying, if you prefer to call it that. That's what they *did* call it when I was a child. Now that I'm grown-up it's an art form and they pay me to do it. Just another bit of evidence that being middle-aged is infinitely superior to being young.

"Mind you, I very much enjoy writing about and for young adults, as my ten- to-fourteen-year-old readers are called, but I certainly wouldn't want to *be* one again. Goodness, what a thought! Writers choose to write about characters whose lives are interesting and full of conflict, because where else would you get the plot? Personally, I like my life without a plot; it's much more restful.

"Undoubtedly, the single most important influence on my writing has not been any living being, but rather an inanimate object, albeit a very large one. It was 6 Pleasant St., Ballston Spa, New York, a tottering great white elephant of a house, a Queen Anne Victorian in a time when Victorian houses were most decidedly out of fashion. To me it was a whole country, with highlands and lowlands, caverns and mountaintops. There were secret places and deserted rooms and little winding stairs. There was so much empty space! I now own a fourteen-room Greek revival. It's far too large for my family of three. But do I care? No, I do not; I love it. I am a person with a strong need for privacy, and in my muddled way I feel that owning rooms I do not enter every day somehow gives me a spiritual cushion of sorts. It is for me the ultimate luxury.

"I am interested in secrets, in hidden things, in mystery. My old home had all of that, as well as a satisfyingly sinister appearance. When, at age ten, I was whisked away to suburbia, I was heartbroken. For years I wandered in the wilderness of practical, compact houses in good school districts. But now at last in middle age I live in a big old house with creaking floorboards, a haunted closet, peculiar little rooms with no apparent purpose, and a huge stone cistern in the basement that looks exactly like a crypt. After many years I am at home again."

> "I am interested in secrets, in hidden things, in mystery. My old home had all of that, as well as a satisfyingly sinister appearance."

* * *

Patrice Kindl was born in Alplaus, New York, and spent her formative years in Ballston Spa, New York. She attended Webster College in St. Louis, Missouri, before moving to New York City, intent on becoming an actress. Despite one or two roles in television commercials, she spent most of her time waitressing and eventually returned to her hometown and found employment as a secretary. Her volunteer activities include working as a rape crisis counselor, serving as group coordinator for the Rape Crisis Service of Schenectady, and raising and training Capuchin monkeys to assist quadriplegics as part of the Helping Hands Program.

Kindl's first novel, *Owl in Love*, made an impressive debut, garnering a number of prizes and honors. A mixture of the fantastic and the familiar (the story deals with a teenage were-owl), it was named an ALA Notable Children's Book and a Best Book for Reluctant Young Adult Readers, and it made the 1993 "best books" lists of both *School Library Journal* and the *Bulletin of the Center for Children's Books*. In addition, it was selected as a Golden Kite Honor Book in fiction by the Society of Children's Book Writers and Illustrators. *Owl in Love* also won the Mythopoeic Fantasy Award in the children's book category. Her second book, *The Woman in the Wall*, was named an ALA Best Book for Young Adults and included in the Blue Ribbon list of the *Bulletin of the Center for Children's Books* as well as the New York Public Library's Books for the Teen Age.

Patrice Kindl lives with her husband and son in Middleburgh, New York, where she enjoys reading and "painting, wallpapering, and otherwise propping up" her elderly house.

SELECTED WORKS: *Owl in Love*, 1993; *The Woman in the Wall*, 1997.

SUGGESTED READING: *Contemporary Authors*, vol. 149, 1996; *Something About the Author*, vol. 82, 1995. Periodicals— "Patrice Kindl," *Publishers Weekly*, December 20, 1993; "Raising Monkeys with a Mission," *Good Housekeeping*, June 1995.

Natalie Kinsey-Warnock

November 2, 1956–

"My sister, three brothers, and I grew up on a Vermont dairy farm in a region known as the Northeast Kingdom, where my Scottish ancestors settled almost two hundred years ago. Our lives revolved around our church, our community, and the hard work of farming. Along with milking and feeding the animals each morning and evening, there was the work of each season: maple sugaring, plowing, picking stone, planting, haying, corn-cutting, harvest, cutting wood. While my parents' lives were consumed by farming and providing for their children, they managed to pass on much more to us. My mother, a teacher, instilled in us a love of books, and reading, and a curiosity about everything, while my father, besides being an excellent athlete, has always been a student of history, especially American history, the presidents, and baseball. They also encouraged our interest in the natural world, whether it was identifying birds, trees, and wildflowers, or pointing out constellations on a starry night. My book *As Long as There Are Mountains* is based on my childhood and my love of the farm, the land, and the Northeast Kingdom.

"The Kingdom is hard country, a hard place to make a living, but a wonderful place to live. My husband, Tom, and I have worked many years building our timber-frame house in these hills. We make syrup from our maple trees each spring, and we've planted an orchard of old apple varieties. We enjoy many sports together on the dirt roads and trails here. I am an athlete, naturalist, artist, and writer. I run five to ten miles each morning, cross-country ski, mountain bike, Rollerblade, swim, windsurf, kayak, canoe, rockclimb, and play tennis. I am an outdoorswoman, enjoying hiking, astronomy, birdwatching, and creating watercolor and pastel paintings of wildflowers, birds, and landscapes. I love animals and have rescued most of my pets: three horses, seven cats, and six dogs. I love history, especially the Civil War. I am learning to play the bagpipes.

"My first children's book, *The Canada Geese Quilt*, grew out of my love and admiration for my grandmother, Helen Urie Rowell, and a special quilt we made together. My grandmother began quilting in her sixties and made 250 quilts. I designed several of them, including the quilt that inspired the book. I show these quilts in the schools I visit, and I encourage students to look for the stories in their own families. Two of my true family stories are *Wilderness Cat* and *The Bear That Heard Crying*, which is an amazing story of my great-great-great-great-great aunt, who was lost in the woods in 1783 when she was three years old, and the bear who took care of her. Every family has stories that are too good to be forgotten, stories that need to be written down and told and passed on to the next generations. I am currently working on over thirty books, most of them based on family stories. My sister, Helen, is the family genealogist; I have such fun researching town histories and walking old cemeteries with her, to find the stories. I feel my family's history will provide me with enough stories for a lifetime of writing."

Courtesy of Tom Warnock

*   *   *

In the 1930s, Senator George Aiken invented the term "The Northeast Kingdom" to describe the remote, mountainous area of Vermont where Natalie Kinsey-Warnock's ancestors lived, and where the author herself was raised and still resides today. She attended Johnson State College and graduated with a double major in arts and sports medicine. Before becoming a full-time writer, she worked for five years as an energy auditor for the University of Vermont Extension Service and another five years as an Elderhostel director and cross-country ski instructor at the Craftsbury Sports Center. She played field hockey for thirteen years on the national level and has coached numerous high school athletics, including basketball and track. She has also developed a local reputation for rescuing animals. "I feel that it's one of my missions in life to help as many animals as I can," says

Kinsey-Warnock, who has both adopted strays and stepped in to rescue pets and livestock from abusive or negligent owners.

Her first book, *The Canada Geese Quilt*, was selected as an ALA Notable Children's Book and won the Joan Fassler Memorial Book Award from the Association for Children's Health. The Bank Street College chose both *The Wild Horses of Sweetbriar* and *The Night the Bells Rang* as Children's Books of the Year. The latter title was also an American Booksellers Association Pick of the Lists in 1991. *Fiddler of the Northern Lights* was named a National Trade Book in the Field of Social Studies. In 1997 Natalie Kinsey-Warnock received the New England Book Award.

SELECTED WORKS: *The Canada Geese Quilt*, illus. by Leslie Bowman, 1988; *The Wild Horses of Sweetbriar*, illus. by Ted Rand, 1990; *The Night the Bells Rang*, illus. by Leslie Bowman, 1991; *Wilderness Cat*, illus. by Mark Graham, 1992; *The Bear That Heard Crying*, with Helen Kinsey, illus. by Ted Rand, 1993; *When Spring Comes*, illus. by Stacey Schuett, 1993; *On a Starry Night*, illus. by David McPhail, 1994; *The Fiddler of the Northern Lights*, illus. by Leslie Bowman, 1996; *As Long as There Are Mountains*, 1997; *Sweet Memories Still*, illus. by Lurie Harden, 1997; *The Language of Loons*, 1998; *The Summer of Stanley*, illus. by Brian Gates, 1998.

SUGGESTED READING: *Something About the Author*, vol. 71, 1993.

Satoshi Kitamura

June 11, 1956–

"There is an old photograph of my brother and me sitting at opposite sides of the table, drawing with crayons with our heads bent to our papers. It was taken in our dining room under the dim light. We are wearing identical stripey shirts, and my brother is drawing with his left hand and I with my right. We almost look like mirror images of each other, except that my brother is bigger. He must have been six years old and I was three or four.

"Almost forty years have passed and we both grew out of the stripey shirts long ago, but are still drawing. My brother paints and sculpts. I illustrate books.

"Back then, occasionally I drew from life, but most of the time my drawings were about the things I imagined: airplanes, cars, machines, and monsters. I would spend hours filling a sheet of paper with pencil lines every night. During the day, if we were not playing baseball, spinning tops, or disturbing ants' nests, the neighborhood kids and I used to draw on the pavement with chalk. Come to think of it now, it was a marvelous way to draw. We drew like cavemen. Our canvas was constantly walked on by the pedestrians, driven on by cars and bikes, and in the end washed out by rain. The little masterpieces were lost forever, but none of us cared and went on drawing all over again.

"I carried a lump of clay in my pocket. When I had no one to play with, I sat on the stone steps, pulled the clay out, and made dinosaurs from the good old (original) Godzilla films. The clay gathered dust from the constant use outdoors and was not very sticky. I could keep it in my pocket without a wrapper.

"There were books on art in our house. I remember a book of Leonardo da Vinci and Raphael paintings and the one with Van Gogh's postman on the cover. I liked looking at paintings as much as reading comic books. My brother started to paint like a post-impressionist, and we often went to art exhibitions. The first one I went to was Pierre Bonnard's. I was nine or ten years old.

"During my early teens, I became interested in modern art, graphic art, music (the Beatles and Ornette Coleman), and literature. Still, I never considered myself to be an artist. I didn't know what I wanted to be. When I was nineteen, I was offered a job illustrating at a magazine. I worked as an illustrator for advertising and periodicals for the next few years. In the end I was bored by drawing for other people all the time and decided to pack up and leave my native country for a while.

"I arrived in England in the summer of 1979. I spent the first year learning English and wandering about London. Being handicapped in language was an interesting experience. I was frustrated by the failure in communication all the time, and the frustration made me draw more and think intensely about how to draw, as if that were my only means of communication. As I did so, I felt I was getting to the essentials beneath the cultural and linguistic differences. It turned out to be a useful lesson for writing and illustrating picture books later on.

Courtesy of Motoko Matsuda

Satoshi

"One day during the next summer, I was lying in bed daydreaming when I came up with a story about a boy who cracked his head hitting an octopus egg. (I didn't know then that an octopus egg had a soft shell.) I got out of bed to write the story down, together with illustrations. When I finished, I made photocopies and sent them to publishers. After visiting a dozen publishing houses, I came across Andersen Press, and my career began."

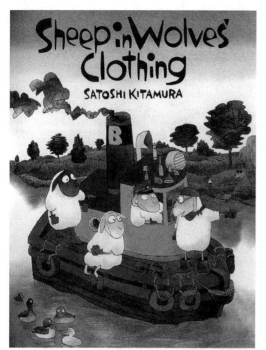

Courtesy of Farrar, Straus & Giroux

* * *

Satoshi Kitamura was born in Tokyo, Japan. After working as a commercial artist and greeting-card designer in Japan, he moved to London permanently in 1983. His rich, humorous style was noticed from the very start, and the first book he illustrated, *Angry Arthur*, written by Hiawyn Oram, received the 1983 Mother Goose Award for "the most exciting newcomer to British children's book illustration" and the Japan Picture Book Award, Special Prize for Foreign Books. *Ned and the Joybaloo* and *A Boy Wants a Dinosaur*, both by Oram, were named to the *New York Times* Notable Children's Books of the Year lists, as was his own *What's Inside?*, which was also named an IRA Teachers' Choice for 1985. *When Sheep Cannot Sleep* won an award from the New York Academy of Sciences, as well as a Parents' Choice Award for illustration in 1987. *Sheep in Wolves' Clothing* was a *Child* magazine Best Book of the Year, as were the titles in Kitamura's board book series: *Cat Is Sleepy, Dog Is Thirsty, Duck Is Dirty*, and *Squirrel Is Hungry*. This series was also named to the *Parents* magazine Best Books of the Year list, the Children's Literature Choice List, and the American Booksellers Association Pick of the Lists. Another board book, *Bath-Time for Boots*, was also cited in ABA's Pick of the Lists.

SELECTED WORKS WRITTEN AND ILLUSTRATED: *What's Inside?*, 1985; *Lilly Takes a Walk*, 1987; *Captain Toby*, 1987; *When Sheep Cannot Sleep*, 1988; *UFO Diary*, 1989; *From Acorn to Zoo and Everything in Between in Alphabetical Order*, 1992; *Sheep in Wolves' Clothing*, 1996; *Squirrel Is Hungry*, 1996; *Duck Is Dirty*, 1996; *Dog Is Thirsty*, 1996; *Cat Is Sleepy*, 1996; *Goldfish Hide-And-Seek*, 1997; *Bath-Time for Boots*, 1998; *A Friend for Boots*, 1998.

SELECTED WORKS ILLUSTRATED: *Angry Arthur*, by Hiawyn Oram, 1982; *Ned and the Joybaloo*, by Hiawyn Oram, 1983; *A Boy Wants a Dinosaur*, by Hiawyn Oram, 1985; *My Friend, Mr. Morris*, by Pat Tomson, 1995; *In the Attic*, by Hiawyn Oram, 1984; *Fly with the Birds*, by Richard Edwards, 1995.

SUGGESTED READING: *Contemporary Authors*, vol. 165, 1998; *Something About the Author*, vol. 62, 1990; vol. 98, 1998.

Sheila Solomon Klass

November 6, 1927–

"Fiction has always offered me pleasure and escape. I was a Depression child, born November 6, 1927, to an Orthodox Jewish family in Brooklyn, New York. Chubby, nearsighted, and unathletic, I delighted in reading and then in making up stories in my head. Which is what a writer does! This, incidentally, was the only entertainment my family could afford.

"In elementary school, I had my first publication, a limerick which appeared in *Pen & Ink*, P.S. 16's magazine:

> Mrs. Astorbilt once had a poodle,
> She fed him on apple strudel.
>   He became temperamental,
>   Wouldn't eat beans or lentils,
> So they shot him right through the noodle.

"The joy and excitement of seeing my words in print set me to writing poems and essays and stories. And I've never stopped.

"Soon after, I had a second literary triumph; I entered the Stuhmer's Pumpernickel Company contest, which required finishing the sentence, 'I like Stuhmer's Pumpernickel because . . . .' Money was the first prize, but I won a consolation prize, a two-pound pumpernickel, which I claimed at the corner grocer's and carried home in my arms unwrapped, for all the neighbors to admire. My family ate thick slices of brown bread slathered with butter in celebration. They were incredibly proud of me, and I was in ecstasy. That pumpernickel was my Nobel Prize!

"All through my school years—in P.S. 16, Eastern District High School, Brooklyn College—I wrote for the newspapers and magazines: feature stories, humor columns, and news. I particularly enjoy writing humor; terrible puns are my specialty. Both my graduate degrees were earned in the State University of Iowa's Writers' Workshop.

"Since I came from a poor family—and I liked to eat—I knew very early that I would have to earn my own living. Happily, I became a teacher and to this day I have combined my two interests: I teach and I write.

"Though I started out writing only adult fiction, during a difficult time in my life I turned to a new genre and wrote a juvenile novel, *Nobody Knows Me in Miami*, based somewhat on my own childhood. Like much of my fiction, it starts from some real occurrence which is then altered by imagination.

"I enjoyed my time in *Miami* so much, I followed it immediately with a young adult novel, *To See My Mother Dance*, and just kept going. Since then I've written about children and young adults who are often in difficult situations, and whose resourcefulness and courage and wit see them through.

"Recently, I became fascinated by the life story of Annie Oakley, the world's best sharpshooter of her time, so I tried my hand at a historical novel. Researching and then writing this book, *A Shooting Star*, was so gratifying I turned to another historical figure—Louisa May Alcott—and wrote *Louey in Paradise*, about the strange summer when Louisa was ten and the Alcotts moved onto 'Fruitlands,' a communal farm where everyone was equal, vegetarian, selfless and spiritual, and money was unnecessary.

"For many years, as part of the School Volunteer Program, I have been visiting New York public schools regularly to read my work and talk to students about writing. They are always eager to learn, and I get useful criticism of my books.

Courtesy of Morton Klass

Sheila Solomon Klass

"Best of all, my enthusiasm about writing has been inherited by my three grown children, all of whom are professional writers. My daughter Perri Klass, a pediatrician, is a novelist and writer of nonfiction. My son, David Klass, is a screenwriter (*Kiss the Girls*) and has written many young adult novels, and my youngest child, Judy Klass, is a playwright, poet, and the author of *The Cry of the Onlies*, a Star Trek novel.

"This delights me; they, too, know there is no higher calling."

*   *   *

After receiving her M.A. and M.F.A. degrees from the Univeristy of Iowa, Sheila Solomon Klass began her teaching career at a Harlem junior high school in the early 1950s. A hiatus from the classroom was devoted to raising her growing family as they lived in locations as diverse as Trinidad and India. In 1965 she joined Manhattan Community College as an assistant professor of English, and she continues to teach there today as a professor.

Although she has published adult novels and short stories and has seen her plays produced on stage, she is best known for her middle-grade and young adult fiction. The New Jersey Institute of Technology bestowed its children's literature award on two of her titles, *Alive and Starting Over* and *The Bennington Stitch*. The American Library Association selected *Rhino* as a 1993 Recommended Book for Reluctant Young Adult Readers.

The author and her husband live in New York City and enjoy traveling.

SELECTED WORKS: *Nobody Knows Me in Miami*, 1981; *To See My Mother Dance*, 1981; *Alive and Starting Over*, 1983; *The Bennington Stitch*, 1985; *Page Four*, 1986; *Credit-Card Carol*, 1989; *Kool Ada*, 1991; *Rhino*, 1993; *Next Stop: Nowhere*, 1995; *A Shooting Star*, 1996; *The Uncivil War*, 1997.

SUGGESTED READING: *Contemporary Authors*, New Revision Series, vol. 13, 1984; vol. 37, 1992; *Something About the Author*, vol. 45, 1986; vol. 99, 1999; *Something About the Author Autobiography Series*, vol. 26, 1998.

"I wrote a twenty-page poem when I was in the fourth grade and from that point on I wanted to be a writer. That was quite a few years before creative writing was even part of any school curriculum and I was writing when I was supposed to be doing my math assignment like everyone else in my class. The fact that my teacher, Mrs. Liebling (who later was to become a star in my *Annie Bananie* chapter books) caught me writing and encouraged me to keep on going was my saving grace. I was terrible at math and most other subjects besides lunch; I had an eye defect that had me looking like a little Cyclops, and I came from a family where everybody was highly creative in the arts so I felt the pressure was on for me to find something I could excel in too. There were three musicians in my family and my parents wanted me to be a musician too. Despite the fact that I loved music and had perfect pitch, I wanted nothing to do with it. I needed to be different from the herd. Writing was it for me.

Courtesy of Mary Ann Halpin

Leah Komaiko

June 1, 1954–

"Writing was my anchor and main interest throughout college, where I had the opportunity to study with a few remarkable poets and novelists. I thought I was going to become a serious poet 'when I grew up' and I was on a devoted path to find what is called 'the writer's voice.' My search took me from my home in Chicago to Los Angeles to New York and back to L.A. with a few smaller-city stops in between and a marriage and plenty of chaos and jobs ranging from the film business to door-to-door sandwich sales. In the background, always lurking, was a desire to write for kids.

"I finally found my voice in the venue of children's books, and all that music I rebelled against as a child was right there waiting for me to incorporate it into my writing. I often tell kids I visit in the schools they might as well do what their parents tell them to do now, because they're just going to end up doing it one way or another sooner or later. They always think that's funny.

"I have written eighteen books for kids, fourteen in rhyme with different rhythms and musical beats. I have written four chapter books based on my first published picture book, *Annie Bananie*, illustrated by Laura Cornell. The chapter books are based on my own childhood. I wrote these books when I was beginning to go through another phase of a continuous midlife crisis where I feared I had to 'grow up' because it wasn't okay to be my age and still writing for kids. In the chapter books, there is a character/heroine named Grandma Gert, who is the living and mildly less angry version of my own grandmother. I loved writing about a senior citizen who could still save the day.

Courtesy of BDD Books

"As I was completing these books, I found myself 'adopting' a 95-year-old woman who lived in a retirement hotel and had no other visitors, and I am just completing a book about her and my fears of aging, which is my first book for adults.

"I am grateful now for all the music and the humor and the expression and activity of writing, which keeps me involved in the real world and off the streets. I am far less fearful about growing old and having to grow up since I am certain now I wouldn't know a grown-up if I saw one. I just hope life keeps allowing me to write for children—children of all ages."

* * *

Born and raised in Chicago, Leah Komaiko studied poetry at the University of Utah, where she received a Bachelor of Arts degree. All her picture books are written in rhyme, and they usually celebrate friendship, family relationships, and the special connections between the young and the elderly. Komaiko visits schools as a speaker and has appeared on children's television programs to share her books with young readers. She read the texts of *Earl's Too Cool for Me* and *Annie Bananie* on the PBS

Storytime series, and her book *I Like the Music* was featured on *Reading Rainbow*.

A Million Moms and Mine was commissioned by Liz Claiborne, Inc. This story of kids with working moms was written and illustrated by Komaiko and twenty Chicago grade-school children; royalties from the book went to the Harold Washington Library Center in Chicago and Reading Is Fundamental, an organization that promotes reading for children.

Leah Komaiko is a member of the Society of Children's Book Writers and Illustrators and currently lives in California.

SELECTED WORKS: *Annie Bananie*, illus. by Laura Cornell, 1987; *I Like the Music*, illus. by Barbara Westman, 1987; *Earl's Too Cool for Me*, illus. by Laura Cornell, 1988; *My Perfect Neighborhood*, illustrated by Barbara Westman, 1990; *Where Can Daniel Be?*, illus. by Denys Cazet, 1992; *A Million Moms and Mine*, 1992; *Leonora O'Grady*, illus. by Laura Cornell, 1992; *Aunt Elaine Does the Dance from Spain*, illus. by Petra Mathers, 1992; *Shoe Shine Shirley*, illus. by Franz Spohn, 1993; *Broadway Banjo Bill*, illus. by Franz Spohn, 1993; *Great-Aunt Ida and Her Great Dane, Doc*, illus. by Steve Schindler, 1994; *Just My Dad and Me*, illus. by Jeffrey Greene, 1995; *Fritzi Fox Flew in from Florida*, illus. by Thatcher Hurd, 1995; *On Sally Perry's Farm*, illus. by Cat Bowman Smith, 1996; *Annie Bananie Moves to Barry Avenue*, illus. by Abby Carter, 1996; *Annie Bananie: Best Friends to the End*, illus. by Abby Carter, 1997; *Annie Bananie and the People's Court*, illus. by Abby Carter, 1998; *Annie Bananie and the Pain Sisters*, illus. by Abby Carter, 1998.

SUGGESTED READING: *Contemporary Authors*, vol. 164, 1998; Komaiko, Leah. *Am I Old Yet?: The Story of Two Women, Generations Apart, Growing Up and Growing Young in a Timeless Friendship*, 1999; *Something About the Author*, vol. 97, 1998. Periodicals—*Publishers Weekly*, December 25, 1987.

E. L. Konigsburg

February 10, 1930–

"Although I was born in New York City, I did most of my growing up in small towns in Pennsylvania. My mother and father were business people, and I am the middle of three daughters. I graduated from high school in Farrell, Pennsylvania, and then worked as a bookkeeper in a wholesale meat plant. One of the owners had a brother, David Konigsburg, who would sometimes visit the office.

"Having saved enough money to start college, I entered Carnegie Institute of Technology (now called Carnegie Mellon University) in Pittsburgh. At the time David was a graduate student of psychology at the University of Pittsburgh and taking courses in testing. I was subject #14 for the Stanford-Binet and subject

#8 for the Wechsler I.Q. Tests. I graduated with honors; and David Konigsburg married me. (I had played it safe and refused to take the Rorschach.)

"At the time I wanted to be a chemist, so I worked in a laboratory and went to graduate school at the University of Pittsburgh. After David received his doctorate and moved us to Jacksonville, Florida, I taught science at a private girls' school. I began to suspect that chemistry was not my field when I became more interested in what was going on inside my students' heads than what was going on inside the test tubes. I finished teaching a few weeks before my son Paul was born. Then came Laurie, and then Ross.

Courtesy of Simon & Schuster

E. L. Konigsburg

"We moved from Florida into the metropolitan New York area, and I took art lessons on Saturdays at the Art Students League. When Ross started kindergarten, I started writing. I wanted to tell about the suburban kids, comfortable-uncomfortable kids, that I had taught once and that I was raising now. The ideas for my books come from people I know and what happens to them. From places I've been and what happens to me, and from things I read. *Jennifer, Hecate, Macbeth, William McKinley, and Me, Elizabeth* was based upon what happened when my daughter was the newcomer to our apartment house in Port Chester, New York.

"One day I read in the newspaper that the Metropolitan Museum of Art in New York City had purchased a statue for $225. Even though they did not know who had sculpted it, they suspected it had been done by someone famous in the Italian Renaissance. They knew they had an enormous bargain. (The real statue is *not* an angel, and it was *not* sculpted by Michelangelo. It is called *Bust of a Lady*).

"The summer after that article appeared in the paper, our family took a trip to Yellowstone Park. I decided that we should have a picnic in the park. After buying salami and bread, chocolate milk and paper cups, paper plates and napkins, and potato chips and pickles, we got into the car and drove and drove but could not find a picnic table. So when we came to a clearing in the woods, I suggested that we eat there. We all crouched slightly above the ground and spread out our meal. Then the complaints began. The chocolate milk was getting warm, and there were ants all over everything, and the sun was melting the icing on the cupcakes. This was hardly roughing it, and yet my small group could think of nothing but the discomfort.

"What, I wondered, would my children do if they ever decided to leave home? Where, I wondered, would they go? At the very least, they would want all the comforts of home, and they would probably want a few dashes of elegance as well. They would certainly never consider any place less elegant than the Metropolitan Museum of Art. And then, I thought, while they were there, perhaps they could discover the secret of the mysterious bargain statue, and in doing so, they could also learn a much more important secret—how to be different on the inside, where it counts.

"Winning the Newbery Medal for *Mixed-up Files* gave me the courage to write about unusual people in unusual places—people like Eleanor of Aquitaine in *A Proud Taste for Scarlet and Miniver* and Leonardo da Vinci in *The Second Mrs. Giaconda*. Readers let me know they like books that have more to them than meets the eye. Had they not let me know that, I never would have written *The View from Saturday*.

"I had started writing a story about a young man named Ethan Potter who boards a school bus the first day of sixth grade. The bus takes an unexpected turn, and a strangely dressed young man boards and sits down next to Ethan. He introduces himself as Julian and explains that his father is about to open a bed and breakfast inn—a *B and B*. At that point, I left my desk and took a walk along the beach. (By this time we had moved back to Florida.)

"When I write a book, I more or less start a movie in my head, and there I was doing a re-run of what I had written. When I got to where Julian was telling Ethan about the B and B, I remembered that I had a story in my files—my mixed-up files—about a young man named Noah whose mother insists that he write his grandparents a bread-and-butter letter, a *B and B* letter. That made me remember another short story I had about a dog named Ginger that plays the part of Sandy in the play *Annie*. And that led me to another story about an Academic Bowl team.

"Before I had finished my walk, I realized that all those short stories were united by a single theme. Taken together, they reinforced one another, and the whole became more than the sum of the parts. I knew that kids would love meeting one character and then two and three and four, and I also knew—because I had learned it from them—that they would think that fitting all the stories together was part of the adventure.

"Now that my children are grown up I sometimes use my grandchildren as inspiration to write picture books for younger children. I live on the beach in North Florida and when I am not writing I love to draw and paint, to read and walk along the beach, and I also love going to the movies. I have never returned

"I began to suspect that chemistry was not my field when I became more interested in what was going on inside my students' heads than what was going on inside the test tubes."

to the chemistry lab, but all the years I spent there were not wasted. I learned useful things: to use the materials at hand, to have a point of view, to distill."

* * *

Elaine Lobl Konigsburg made a remarkable debut in children's books by winning the Newbery Award for her second book, *From the Mixed-up Files of Mrs. Basil E. Frankweiler*, while her first book, *Jennifer, Hecate, Macbeth, William McKinley, and Me, Elizabeth*, took Newbery Honors in the same year, 1968. *From the Mixed-up Files* also won a Lewis Carroll Shelf Award in 1968 and the William Allen White Children's Book Award in 1970. Nearly thirty years later, Konigsburg received a second Newbery Medal for *The View from Saturday*, and in the intervening years she published a long list of books notable for their quirky characters and inventive plots.

Courtesy of Simon & Schuster Children's Publishing Division

It is fitting that the plot of Konigsburg's first Newbery winner revolves around a statue that may have been sculpted by Michaelangelo, for in many ways she is a bit of a Renaissance person herself. A scientist by training, she took art classes for a hobby and eventually illustrated many of her novels and, later, all of her picture books. She reads widely and her interest in language is evident in the witty dialogue through which her characters reveal their personalities. A recurring theme throughout her novels and short stories is finding a sense of self. In *From the Mixed-up Files* Claudia leaves home to establish a sense of her own importance. Jennifer, of *Jennifer, Hecate . . .* , teaches Elizabeth how to find her sense of self. In *Throwing Shadows*, a collection of short stories that was nominated for an American Book Award, each story can be understood in light of the theme of self-discovery.

Konigsburg has experimented in her writing by exploring unusual settings and challenging characters. Her historical novels, about Eleanor of Aquitaine (*A Proud Taste for Scarlet and Miniver*) and Leonardo da Vinci (*The Second Mrs. Giaconda*), were developed after a great deal of research into the time periods and personalities of these historic figures. Her essays on children's literature, collected in *TalkTalk*, are also inventive and reflect her interests in art and science as she has brought those disciplines to bear on her perception of books and reading.

In more recent years, Konigsburg has been writing and illustrating picture books featuring her own grandchildren in *Samuel Todd's Book of Great Colors, Samuel Todd's Book of Great Inventions,* and *Amy Elizabeth Explores Bloomingdale's.* Her earlier novels have been adapted for television. In 1973 *Jennifer, Hecate, Macbeth, William McKinley, and Me, Elizabeth* was televised, retitled *Jennifer and Me. From the Mixed-up Files of Mrs. Basil E. Frankweiler* appeared in an adaptation in 1995, and the 1990 television adaptation of *Father's Arcane Daughter* was renamed *Caroline?*

In 1999 E. L. Konigsburg received the Distinguished Alumni Achievement Award from Carnegie Mellon University in Pittsburgh, Pennsylvania. She lives with her husband in Jacksonville, Florida.

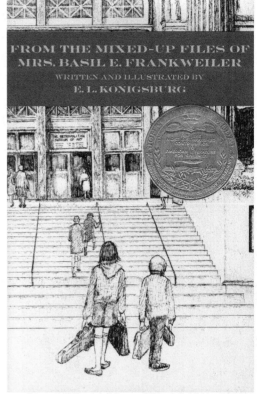

Courtesy of Simon & Schuster Children's Publishing Division

SELECTED WORKS: *Jennifer, Hecate, Macbeth, William McKinley, and Me, Elizabeth,* 1967; *From the Mixed-up Files of Mrs.Basil E. Frankweiler,* 1967; *About the B'Nai Bagels,* 1968; *(George),* 1970; *Altogether, One at a Time,* 1971; *A Proud Taste for Scarlet and Miniver,* 1974; *Dragon in the Ghetto Caper,* 1974; *The Second Mrs. Giaconda,* 1975; *Father's Arcane Daughter,* 1976; *Throwing Shadows,* 1979; *Journey to an 800 Number,* 1982; *Up from Jericho Tel,* 1986; *Samuel Todd's Book of Great Colors,* 1990; *Samuel Todd's Book of Great Inventions,* 1991; *Amy Elizabeth Explores Bloomingdale's,* 1992; *T-Backs, T-Shirts, COAT, and Suit,* 1993; *The View from Saturday,* 1996.

SUGGESTED READING: *Authors and Artists for Young Adults,* vol. 3, 1989; *Children's Literature Review,* vol. 1, 1976; vol. 47, 1998; *Contemporary Authors,* New Revision Series, vol. 59, 1998; *Dictionary of Literary Biography,* vol. 52, 1986; Gallo, Don, ed. *Speaking for Ourselves, Too,* 1993; Konigsburg, E. L. *TalkTalk,* 1995; *Major Twentieth Century Writers,* 1991; McElmeel, Sharon, *100 Most Popular Children's Writers,* 1999; Pendergast, Sara, ed. *St. James Guide to Children's Writers,* 5th ed., 1999; Silvey, Anita, ed. *Children's Books and Their Creators,* 1995; *Something About the Author,* vol. 4,

1973; vol. 48, 1987; vol. 94, 1998. Periodicals—Jones, Linda T., "Profile: Elaine Konigsburg," *Language Arts*, February 1986; Konigsburg, E. L., "Newbery Acceptance Speech," *The Horn Book*, August 1968, July/August 1997; Scales, Pat, "E. L. Konigsburg's *The Second Mrs. Giaconda*: An Update," *Book Links*, March 1996.

WEB SITE: *www.simonsayskids.com*

An earlier profile of E. L. Konigsburg appeared in *Third Book of Junior Authors* (1972).

Courtesy of Jan Cheripko

Virginia Kroll

Virginia Kroll

April 28, 1948–

"I've always wanted to be a writer and now that I am one, I always want to be a writer. To me, writing is like breathing. If I'm not doing it constantly, I feel like I'm suffocating. I write anything: poems, plays, puzzles, crafts, rebuses, short stories, nonfiction articles. I write anywhere: at home, in church while I'm waiting for mass to begin, outdoors, on school visits, during breaks, in check-out aisles, on buses, and in cars (if someone else is driving, of course).

"Most of my subjects are within easy reach. I have three sons, three daughters, and a granddaughter whose experiences and idiosyncrasies have given me a wealth of ideas. Same for my pets. I have dogs, cats, rabbits, birds, turtles, guinea pigs, hamsters, gerbils, a mouse, a hedgehog, a degu, and a goldfish. Then there's Nature, which has been a passion of mine since I was seven years old and awakened to the wildlife right in my own backyard.

"But what about my multicultural books? 'Why do you write about Africa, or South America, Japan, or Australia?' they ask. I've never traveled. A writer should 'write what she knows' after all, shouldn't she? The most honest answer I can give is that I don't know why. Maybe it's because at Christmas as a six-year-old I received a set of books about children of other countries. The fascination took hold of me then and has never let go. Maybe it's that simple. Or not so simple, since the experience was so profound. And I'm not sure I need to know, as long as my words are authentic and entertain, educate, enlighten, and enthrall my readers.

"If I'm happy, my stories are full of joy. If I'm sad or angry or anxious, my work reflects these emotions too. The cruel mental illness of two family members worries and unnerves me. After spending time with one of them at a family gathering, I wrote *My Sister, Then and Now* about a girl whose confusion and sorrow over her sibling's failing mental state are abated by the help of others and her own hope.

"My mother's Alzheimer's disease broke my heart, and I wrote *Fireflies, Peach Pies, and Lullabies* because I didn't know what else to do with my feelings. Years later I am thrilled to hear from others about how comforting my words have been to them.

"That's what writing is about for me: making a difference, even in a very small way. Borrowing the blessings around me, then giving them back as gifts to others, wrapped in meaningful words and tied up in memorable phrases."

* * *

Virginia Kroll was born in Buffalo, New York, and has lived most of her life there. She attended both Canisius College and the State University of New York in Buffalo. She has taught grade school, arts and crafts, and religion, as well as children's writing at Medaille College. A full-time author since 1984, she is a frequent speaker in schools and at conferences and workshops.

Kroll's work has received numerous awards and citations. In 1992, *Masai and I* was a Book of the Month Club Selection, named one of the Best Books of 1992 by *Publishers Weekly*, listed in the American Booksellers Association's Pick of the Lists, and commended by the Jane Addams Peace Association. *Wood-Hoopoe Willie* won the American Book Award in 1994. Kroll's book about Alzheimer's disease, *Fireflies, Peach Pies, and Lullabies*, was named a Notable Children's Trade Book in the Field of Social Studies. *Sweet Magnolia* won the *Skipping Stones* Multicultural Book Award and was named an Outstanding Science Trade Book for Children. It was also named the KIND Book of the Year by the Humane Society of the United States. *Butterfly Boy* was named the Language Arts Best Picture Book of the Year by the Society of School Librarians International and included on the ABA Pick of the Lists.

Under the pseudonym "Melrose Cooper," Kroll wrote *I Got a Family*, which was named a Notable Children's Trade Book in the Field of Social Studies in 1994, and *I Got Community*, which became a *Reading Rainbow* selection in 1995.

The author lives in Hamburg, New York, with her huband, David Haeick. They have six children and one grandchild.

> *"I have dogs, cats, rabbits, birds, turtles, guinea pigs, hamsters, gerbils, a mouse, a hedgehog, a degu, and a goldfish."*

SELECTED WORKS: *Masai and I*, illus. by Nancy Carpenter, 1992; *My Sister, Then and Now*, 1992; *Wood-Hoopoe Willie*, illus. by Katherine Roundtree, 1993; *Africa Brothers and Sisters*, illus. by Vanessa French, 1993; *Jaha and Jamil Went Down the Hill: An African Mother Goose*, illus. by Katherine Roundtree, 1994; *Sweet Magnolia*, illus. by Laura Jacques, 1995; *Shelter Folks*, illus. by Jan N. Jones, 1995; *Fireflies, Peach Pies, and Lullabies*, illus. by Nancy Cote, 1996; *Can You Dance, Dalila?*, illus. by Nancy Carpenter, 1996; *Butterfly Boy*, illus. by Gerardo Suzan, 1997; *Hands!*, illus. by Cathryn Falwell, 1997; *With Love, to Earth's Endangered Peoples*, 1998; *Faraway Drums*, illus. by Floyd Cooper, 1998. As "Melrose Cooper": *I Got a Family*, 1993; *Life Riddles*, 1994; *I Got Community*, 1995.

SUGGESTED READING: *Contemporary Authors*, vol. 143, 1994; *Something About the Author*, vol. 76, 1994. Periodicals— *Publishers Weekly*, December 28, 1992.

Jane Kurtz

April 17, 1952–

"When I was two years old, my parents left their home in Portland, Oregon, and headed off for language school to study Amharic, then the official language of Ethiopia. Less than a year later, our family moved to Ethiopia, where members of the Kurtz family would end up living for more than thirty years.

"I spent most of my childhood near Maji, a small town in southwestern Ethiopia. When I was in the fourth grade, I started boarding school in Addis Ababa. Before that, I was homeschooled. My memories are of whole days filled with wandering the paths around our home, making up stories and acting them out with my sisters.

"In many of the places I traveled when I was young, my sisters and I were the only white children the people who lived in those places had ever seen. Sometimes I didn't like being stared at or poked. But most of the time I was passionately in love with everything around me, including the flowers and the frogs and the waterfalls that spilled over the rocks high above me and filled my face with spray.

"We spent two years in the United States—when I was seven and when I was thirteen. Because of my experiences during those years, I became convinced that I would never be able to talk to people in the United States about Ethiopia. When I came back to the U.S. for college, I listed my grandmother's Des Moines, Iowa, address in the student directory so I wouldn't have to answer any 'dumb questions.'

"After I graduated from Monmouth College in Illinois, I taught in and was the director of an alternative school in southern Illinois; was a high school English teacher in Trinidad, Colorado; and worked as director of Trinidad Downtown Area Development, an arts and economic development project. During those years, I wrote poetry (and published a little of it in literary journals) and started my first novel—but for adults, not for children. I'd always loved to read, but I didn't know much about children's books because we didn't have many books with us in Ethiopia, only a few, like *Black Beauty* and *Caddie Woodlawn*, that I read over and over.

"But during those years when I was living in Illinois and Colorado, I was also having kids—three of them: David, Jonathan, and Rebekah. And I was reading children's books to them. Hundreds of books! I fell in love with children's books. I became

hungry, *hungry* to publish my own children's book. For one thing, I loved the way some of the picture books I read to my children were just like poetry, with spare language and vivid images. And I loved the hopefulness of children's books . . . the light that almost always seemed to shine out from those ending pages.

"When my children were young, it was hard for me to go away to conferences, so it felt like forever before I learned how to publish a book. I never even met any authors until I was in my thirties. But finally my first book was accepted—*I'm Calling Molly*, inspired by something that really happened to my oldest son. About the time the book came out, our family moved to North Dakota. Maybe it was because of the harsh winters here, but I began to be homesick for my own childhood and for Ethiopia. But I didn't think I could ever go back there. That's when I first realized I could write about Ethiopia. After twenty years of not talking about my childhood home, I finally found a way to show a little bit of Ethiopia to people here in the United States, something I had thought I could never, never do."

＊　＊　＊

Jane Kurtz has shown more than a "little bit" of Ethiopia to young American readers. She has brought the folklore, the human interest stories, and the geography and culture of that country alive through her picture books, fiction, and nonfiction. In addition to her B.A. from Monmouth College, Kurtz earned an

M.A. in 1995 from the University of North Dakota, where she is currently a senior lecturer in the English department. Married in 1979 to Leonard Goering, she has three children who have sometimes provided inspiration and sometimes an audience for her books.

Miro in the Kingdom of the Sun and *Only a Pigeon* were named to the annual *Children's Literature* Choice Lists. *Miro* was also cited on New York Public Library's annual list, 100 Titles for Reading and Sharing, as was *The Storyteller's Beads*. *Pulling the Lion's Tail* and *The Storyteller's Beads* were both named Notable Trade Books in the Field of Social Studies. A retelling of the Ethiopian legend "The Lion's Whiskers," *Pulling the Lion's Tail* relates the story of Almaz's attempts to win the love of her homesick stepmother, a futile effort until she learns the art of patience. *The Storyteller's Beads* is a gentle but powerful fictional story about the flight of Ethiopian refugees and the growing friendship between two girls from different ethnic backgrounds who discover they have similar legends in common. The stories lead them slowly and haltingly into a bond of trust. A fine complement to these stories is Kurtz's nonfiction book, *Ethiopia: The Roof of Africa*, which describes life in modern Ethiopia.

A trip to a school in Maine as a visiting author prompted Kurtz to collaborate with librarian Toni Buzzeo on a book about making the most of an author's or storyteller's school visit. The result was *Terrific Connections with Authors, Illustrators and Storytellers: Real Space and Virtual Links*.

Jane Kurtz lives in Grand Forks, North Dakota, with her family.

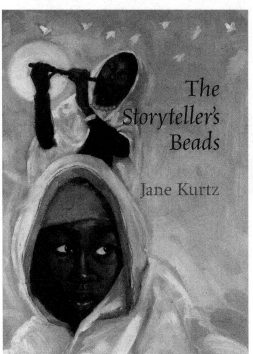

Courtesy of Harcourt Brace & Co.

SELECTED WORKS: *I'm Calling Molly*, illus. by Irene Trivas, 1990; *Ethiopia: The Roof of Africa*, 1991; *Fire on the Mountain*, illus. by E. B. Lewis, 1994; *Pulling the Lion's Tail*, illus. by Floyd Cooper, 1995; *Miro in the Kingdom of the Sun*, illus. by David Frampton, 1996; *The American Southwest Resource Book: The People*, 1999; *Only a Pigeon*, with Christopher Kurtz, illus. by E. B. Lewis, 1997; *Trouble*, illus. by Durga Bernhard, 1997; *The Storyteller's Beads*, 1998; *I'm Sorry, Almira Ann*, 1999; *Terrific Connections with Authors, Illustrators and Storytellers: Real Space and Virtual Links*, with Toni Buzzeo, 1999; *River*

Friendly, River Wild, illus. by Neil Brennan, 2000; *Faraway Home*, illus. by E. B. Lewis, 2000.

SUGGESTED READING: *Contemporary Authors*, vol. 155, 1997; *Something About the Author*, vol. 91, 1997. Articles authored by Jane Kurtz—"Connecting Children with Modern Urban Ethiopia," *Book Links*, March 1998; "Finding a Place to Call Home," *Writer's Digest*, April 1994; "The Finely Tuned Author Visit," with Tony Buzzeo, *Book Links*, March 1998; "Memoirs and the Teenage Reader," *Booklist*, September 1999; "Multicultural Children's Books: The Subtle Tug of War," *School Library Journal*, February 1996.

"I've loved hearing stories for as long as I can remember. As a child my parents read to me, and when I grew older, I read to myself. After visiting the children's room of my local library, I knew I'd found my favorite place in the world. I spent much of my childhood there, making friends with the librarians and losing myself in the books. We didn't have a lot of money, so my library card felt like a charge card to me. I loved the idea of being able to take home whichever book appealed to me at the moment.

"I began writing as a child and still haven't stopped. I've found this to be true of most writers. Few people who become authors at twenty-five begin writing when they are twenty-four. If writing is what you want to do, you usually know it at an early age. I know that I did.

"I've always written nonfiction and that's all I ever want to do. While it may not seem as glamorous as creating novels, I think in some ways it can be even more exciting. My first job after college was as a newspaper reporter, and that's where I learned the importance of bringing relevant issues to light. I still try to do that today in many of the books I write, and at times I've felt like a pioneer with a pen.

"Being a nonfiction writer allows me to travel a great deal and learn about countless topics I might not have otherwise had an opportunity to delve into. I've written on many diverse subjects through the years: cowboys, ghosts, teenage drinking, rabies, homelessness, near-death experiences, marine mammals, ESP,

Courtesy of Devon Cass

Elaine Landau (signature)

Elaine Landau

February 15, 1948–

state birds, planets, eating disorders, the white power movement, tuberculosis, child abuse, and much more.

"My favorite trip was to Scotland while writing a book on the Loch Ness monster. Although I didn't catch a glimpse of Nessie, I spoke with dozens of people who claimed to have done so. And who could forget digging for dinosaur bones in Utah while preparing for a series of books on dinosaurs and fossils? Writing nonfiction means that I'm never bored at work. Each topic introduces me to new ideas and experiences so I never feel that I am doing the 'same old thing' every day. It's a job that forces me to grow both personally and professionally.

"Creating books for young people is especially wonderful. My son Michael is my greatest fan, and he often suggests topics for me to tackle. He has spent hours studying the pictures in my animal books and has my planet book covers on the walls of his room. When I think of young people reading my work, I feel as though I've had a chance to talk with them—to share what I've learned or let them know my feelings on a particular issue. I don't know of any other profession where I'd be able to reach as many young people at such an important time in their lives.

Courtesy of Millbrook Press, Inc.

"There are those who feel that writing isn't the best profession to pursue—especially if you want to have a roof over your head and continue eating three meals a day. My family certainly wasn't thrilled with my decision to become an author. They warned me that writers sometimes spend more time looking for work than working. Admittedly, freelance writing isn't always as secure as a typical nine-to-five job. Yet I heartily encourage any 'wannabe' authors reading this to give it a try. Once you succeed, you'll see that it ranks among the most creative and fulfilling ways to earn a living. So, do what I did—start writing and don't stop."

Elaine Landau is a prolific writer of well-researched, topical nonfiction for children and young adults. Her range of topics is broad, including health, history, earth science, current events, biology, and the supernatural, as well as teen issues such as dating, drinking, and drugs.

Born and raised in New Jersey, Elaine Landau earned her B.A. from New York University in 1970 and her M.L.S from Pratt Institute in 1975. She was a reporter for a community newspaper, an editor for a New York publisher, and director of a public library while she attended school and published her first books. Landau is a member of the National Organization for Women, Women's Equity Action League, and the American Library Association.

A number of Landau's books, including *Death: Everyone's Heritage* and *Alzheimer's Disease*, have won awards from the New Jersey Institute of Technology, and others have been named Outstanding Science Trade Books for Children. *We Have AIDS* was a Notable Children's Trade Book in the Field of Social Studies and an ALA Quick Pick for Reluctant Young Adult Readers. *We Survived the Holocaust* was also a Notable Trade Book in the Field of Social Studies. *Neptune* was selected for the Best Children's Science Books list by the American Association for the Advancement of Science. *The White Power Movement* was named to the "Best of 1993" list by the Society of School Librarians. *Rabies* was included in Outstanding Science Trade Books for Children in 1994.

Elaine Laudau currently lives in Miami, Florida.

SELECTED WORKS: *Hidden Heroines: Women in American History*, 1975; *Occult Visions: A Mystical Gaze into the Future*, 1979; *The Teen Guide to Dating*, 1980; *Alzheimer's Disease*, 1987; *Teenagers Talk about School—and Open Their Hearts about Their Closest Concerns*, 1988; *Surrogate Mothers*, 1988; *We Have AIDS*, 1990; *We Survived the Holocaust*, 1991; *Neptune*, 1991; *The White Power Movement: America's Racist Hate Groups*, 1993; *The Right to Die*, 1993; *Rabies*, 1993; *The Beauty Trap*, 1994; *Mountain Mammals*, 1996; *The Sumerians*, 1997; *Tourette Syndrome*, 1998; *Parkinson's Disease*, 1999; *Mars*, 1999; *Air Disasters*, 1999.

SUGGESTED READING: *Contemporary Authors*, vol. 53–56, 1975; *Contemporary Authors*, New Revision Series, vol. 5, 1982; *Something About the Author*, vol. 10, 1976; vol. 94, 1998.

E-MAIL: *writersworld @webtv.net*

Nancy Larrick

December 28, 1910–

"I grew up in the small town of Winchester, Virginia, just two blocks from the public library, a magnificent Beaux Arts building, now listed as 'A National Treasure.' There was no children's room, and no children's librarian, but we flocked to that imposing building and happily clattered up the winding black iron stairway which we knew led to books for us. Every few days I would take home an armful of books, as did each of my friends.

"I am sure my addiction to that library and its treasures resulted from growing up in a reading family. There were always books and magazines in our house, plus two daily newspapers—the local *Star* of course, but also the *Baltimore Sun*, the city paper that blanketed our area and stimulated heated debate on social, economic, and political issues.

"Both my father and mother read to me—animal stories, folktales, and poetry, in particular. Grandmother had a beautifully illustrated book of Mother Goose songs from which we sang, evening after evening. I realize now that I got much of my love of books by ear. The rhythm of poetry and folk tales took over.

"This continued into high school, where our English teacher

Courtesy of Allan Richardson

Nancy Larrick

(undoubtedly the best teacher I have ever had) read aloud to us every day—rhythmically, dramatically, convincingly. Poetry was my love.

"I graduated from Goucher College in 1930 as the Great Depression was taking over and jobs were drying up. Although prospects looked bleak, I did get a job—teaching eighth-grade English in my hometown. Although I had almost no preparation, I plunged in with determination. By this time I realize that as a teacher I probably learned a great deal more than my pupils. Part of my new learning grew out of the requirement that each teacher make an early fall visit in the home of each of her pupils.

"I was shocked to see the hardships that prevailed in some of those homes, and I was impressed by the untiring efforts of parents to help their children in school. In time I recognized that the children who were doing well at school were those who had the support and encouragement of their parents. I soon realized that one of my big jobs was to help parents to be their children's teacher at home.

"In my early years as a classroom teacher, I enrolled in a graduate course in Modern American Poetry and was swept off my feet by such poets as Robert Frost, Carl Sandburg, Langston Hughes, and Edna St. Vincent Millay. Each Wednesday evening I came home from my poetry class practically singing their poetic lines. Often I would let my enthusiasm spill over to my eighth graders the next morning, and they quickly asked for more. I learned to respect their taste and their judgment, and became certain they were captivated by the sound of poetry.

"By the 1950s I had been drawn into editorial work—first magazines for children, then trade books for children. This meant living in New York, where I enrolled as a part-time graduate student at New York University to learn more about children's literature, children's reading, and how parents could help. Out of this came several books that I wrote for parents: *A Parent's Guide to Children's Reading*, *A Parent's Guide to Children's Education*, *Reading Begins at Home*, and *Encourage Your Child to Read*.

"By the mid-1960s, I was teaching in the Graduate School of Education of Lehigh University. As an adjunct professor I was encouraged to experiment and, not suprisingly, took flight with a workshop in Poetry for Children. Most of my students were very talented in-service teachers, each with a class of 25 to 30 six- to twelve-year-olds.

"This was a time when poetry for children and by children was on the upsurge. As one critic of the 1960s put it: 'Somebody turned on a tap in these kids, and the poetry just kept coming.' In our university workshops we sang and chanted poems, we moved to the rhythm of poetry, we dramatized poems, we wrote poems. We read and read and read. Out of these Lehigh Workshops came a book for parents and teachers: *Let's Do a Poem!*

"At about this time I was asked to compile an anthology of 'easy-to-read' poetry for second and third graders. I enlisted help from children in a neighborhood school. What poems could they read? Which poems did they like? What should go into 'our book'?

"The children were wonderful: very outspoken, and very sure of their judgment. Invariably the poems they rejected were 'too sweet,' as they put it. They preferred poems about the here and now (trucks, planes, city traffic) and about the rugged and wild—'not covered over with the beautiful,' as one boy put it.

"'And what should be the title?' I asked: '*The Easy-to-Read Poetry Book*, which teachers and publisher had suggested?' No way! One boy explained, 'If you do that, you'll have to put it in very small type.' So, with the children's approval, it was called *Piper, Pipe That Song Again*.

"Over the intervening years I have had nineteen poetry anthologies published, all compiled with the help of young readers and with titles they approved, such as *Room for Me and a Mountain Lion*, *On City Streets*, *I Heard a Scream in the Street*, *Cats Are Cats*, and *The Night of the Whippoorwill*. Several became mass-market paperbacks.

"And what am I doing now? Chairing the Friends of the Library Committee to raise $3,000,000 for more books for the three branches of that same public library of my childhood more than eighty years ago!"

"I enlisted help from children in a neighborhood school. What poems could they read? Which poems did they like? What should go into 'our book'?"

*   *   *

Nancy Larrick's roots in the region of her birthplace—Winchester, Virginia—date back to pre-Revolutionary times. She taught for twelve years in Winchester after her graduation from Goucher College and then spent three years in Washington, D.C., 1942–1945, as education director for the War Bonds Division of the U.S. Treasury. Moving to New York, Larrick pursued a career in publishing while earning an M.A. from Columbia University and a doctorate in Education from New York University in 1955. Out of her doctoral thesis and longstanding concern for parental education came her immensely popular *A Parent's Guide to Children's Reading*. First published in 1958, this book went through five editions and was often referred to as the "Dr. Spock" of children's reading. In 1959 it received the Edison Foundation Award.

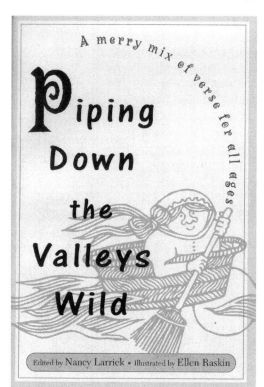

Courtesy of BDD Books

Married in 1958 to Alexander Crosby, a journalist, Larrick collaborated on several nonfiction books with her husband. Both became adjunct professors of Education at Lehigh University in the 1960s. Throughout her career, Larrick has been an advocate for children's reading. As one of the founding members and the second president of the International Reading Association, she spearheaded an organization that now has over 95,000 members in 73 countries. She was the first editor of *The Reading Teacher*, the journal of the IRA, and received the IRA Citation of Merit in 1977.

In 1965 Nancy Larrick published an article in the *Saturday Review* that has been called one of the most important articles on children's literature to appear in the twentieth century: "The All-White World of Children's Books." Calling attention to the absence of ethnically diverse characters in books for young people, she raised consciousness in the publishing field during the days of the civil rights movement and urged the inclusion of Black and other minority characters in children's books of the future. In that same year she published the first of her many fine poetry anthologies, all with titles that reflect the joyful exuberance of children's responses to good poetry when it is presented to them for pure delight. Many of her poetry volumes appeared in mass-market paperback or book-club editions, bringing poetry to a wider range of young readers.

In 1966 Larrick was at the University of Eastern Nigeria, teaching would-be writers of trade books for Nigerian children. In 1981 she was sent by the U.S. Department of State to deliver the keynote speech at the UNESCO seminar held in Singapore during the International Book Fair of Southeast Asia. In 1986 she had a similar assignment during the International Book Fair in New Delhi. At each of these meetings her topic was the importance of involving parents in children's reading.

Over the years Larrick has served as teacher and workshop director at numerous colleges and universities. Now retired, she lives in the town where she was born and raised.

SELECTED WORKS WRITTEN: *A Parent's Guide to Children's Reading*, 1958, fifth edition, 1983; *Color ABC*, 1959, reissued as *First ABC*, 1965; *Rockets into Space*, with Alexander L. Crosby, 1959; *A Teacher's Guide to Children's Books*, 1960; *Rivers: What They Can Do*, with Alexander L. Crosby, 1961; *Junior Science Book of Rain, Hail, Sleet, and Snow*, 1961; *A Parent's Guide to Children's Education*, 1963.

SELECTED WORKS EDITED: *You Come Too: Poetry of Robert Frost*, 1959; *Piper, Pipe That Song Again*, illus. by Kelly Oechsli, 1965; *Poetry for Holidays*, illus. by Kelly Oechsli, 1966; *Piping Down the Valleys Wild*, illus. by Ellen Raskin, 1967; *On City Streets*, photos by David Sagarin, 1968; *I Heard a Scream in the Street: Poems by Young People in the City*, illus. with photos by students, 1970; *The Wheels of the Bus Go Round and Round*, illus. by Gene Holtan, 1972; *More Poetry for Holidays*, illus. by Harold Berson, 1973; *Male and Female Under 18: Frank Comments from Young People about Their Sex Roles Today*, with Eve Merriam, 1973; *Room for Me and a Mountain Lion: Poetry of Open Space*, 1974; *Crazy to Be Alive in Such a Strange World: Poems About People*, photos by Alexander Crosby, 1977; *Bring Me All of Your Dreams*, photos by Larry Mulvehill, 1980; *Tambourines! Tambourines to Glory!: Prayers and Poems*, illus. by Geri Grienke, 1982; *When the Dark Comes Dancing: A Bedtime Poetry Book*, illus. by John Wallner, 1983; *Cats Are Cats*, illus. by Ed Young, 1988; *Songs of Mother Goose*, illus. by Robin Spowart, 1989; *Mice Are Nice*, illus. by Ed Young, 1990; *To Ride a Butterfly*, illus. by various artists, 1991; *The Night of the Whippoorwill*, illus. by David Ray, 1992.

SUGGESTED READING: *Contemporary Authors*, First Revision, vol. 1–4, 1967; *Contemporary Authors*, New Revision Series, vol. 1, 1981; *Dictionary of Literary Biography*, vol. 61, 1987; *Something About the Author*, vol. 4, 1973. Articles authored by Nancy Larrick—"The All-White World of Children's Books," *Saturday Review*, Sept. 11, 1965; "Poetry Becomes a Way of Life," *Top of the News*, January 1971; "Divorce,

Drugs, Desertion, the Draft: Facing up to Realities in Children's Literature," *Publishers Weekly*, Feb. 21, 1972; "Poetry in the Story Hour," *Top of the News*, January 1976; "The Changing Picture of Poetry Books for Children," *Wilson Library Bulletin*, October 1980; "From Tennyson to Silverstein: Poetry for Children 1910–1985," *Language Arts*, October 1986; "Give Us Books! . . . But Also . . . Give Us Wings!" *The New Advocate*, Spring 1991.

Courtesy of Keunhee Lee

Dom Lee

May 4, 1959–

"**I** was raised by an artist, and thus my home was always filled with art, like the smell of oil paint permeating the room. I often watched my father work meticulously through the days and nights. Those years of my childhood were a great influence on my life, and so were my parents. They started me on my long journey through the world of art.

"With an artist's hours and fluctuating pay, life was not easy for my family. We often traveled from place to place, finding shelter where we could. Therefore, I never really had the chance to make any friends. This lack of social interaction caused me to become more quiet and reserved with each passing day, but it also drew me closer to the arts.

"I first began to experiment in a rather unique way. There was not enough paper for me to use. So I drew on the walls of the temporary homes provided by our landlords. I was fortunate enough to have parents who encouraged me in art. They didn't prevent me from my hobbies. Instead, they painted over my work each time we left. During these early days, I learned for the very first time to observe various subjects carefully and burn the images into my memory.

"From my first year in elementary school, I participated in every art-related club and competition that I could find. My confidence in my abilities as an artist grew with every trophy and medal that I took home. However, with all of the awards I received, one stood out beyond the rest. While attending junior high school, I won a contest in which I was given a prize of $30. That was the peak of my artistic path up to that point, probably because it was the first time I earned money with my skill. When I look back on that glorious day, I now see it as a premonition heralding my eventual life as an artist.

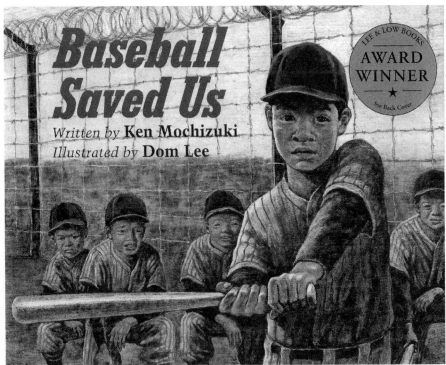

Courtesy of Lee & Low Books, Inc.

"Sometime during high school, my father told me something that would stay with me for the rest of my life. He said, 'Before you are being an artist or whoever, you must have a good personality. After being a good man, you can be anyone else.' His words inspired me in a way that nothing else had ever done before. After listening to him, I also realized that I needed more experience in order to become a 'good man' and an artist thereafter.

"It was during my years in college that my future as an illustrator began to take form. While translating a story of words into a tale told by art, I found that I preferred a series of images to any single portrayal. From such revelations, I have now established a place in the art world as a freelance artist dedicated to the field of illustrations.

"For my projects, I try to gather as many references as possible. Photographs, videos, old magazines, clothing, and hats were a few of the items that I collected. When I interpret the author's words into works of art, I do not merely represent a tale. I try to see the world through the eyes of the characters in the book and show the reader what they see. In this way, I hope to inspire children not only to have a good imagination, but a sense of reality as well.

"I was never very good when it came to carrying on a conversation with other people, but my art gave me the chance to express myself and show those around me how I felt. Art led me through my lonely childhood and sustained me through the rest of my life. It shaped me into who I am today and set my place in the world."

* * *

Dom Lee was born in Seoul, the capital of South Korea, and received his bachelor's degree from the College of Fine Arts at Seoul National University. For several years he was a drawing instructor at the Hyang-Lin Institute, an art school established by his father. In 1990 Lee, along with his wife and children, emigrated to the United States. He received his M.F.A. from Manhattan's School of Visual Arts. Several one-man and group exhibitions followed; a showing at the Art Directors' Club of New York City attracted the attention of a children's book editor and led to Dom Lee's entry into the field of picture books.

Baseball Saved Us, written by Ken Mochizuki, is the story of Japanese-American children interned during World War II. Lee illustrated the volume using his own encaustic method of melting beeswax onto paper and then scratching out images through the layer of wax. The book won a number of honors, including a Parents' Choice Award, the Washington Governor's Writers Award, a *Publishers Weekly* Cuffies Award for Best Multicultural Title, and inclusion on the American Booksellers Association's Pick of the Lists. The book has also been translated into Japanese and Spanish. *Heroes*, a second Mochizuki story with a Japanese-American theme, was a Children's Book of the Month Club Selection and a Notable Children's Trade Book in the Field of Social Studies.

A third collaboration between Mochizuki and Lee, *Passage to Freedom: The Sugihara Story*, celebrates the efforts of a Japanese consul in Lithuania to save the lives of thousands of Polish Jews during World War II. This multiple award winner was selected as an ALA Notable Children's Book and a *Bulletin of the Center for Children's Books* Blue Ribbon title and received a Children's Choice Award from the Association of Booksellers for Children.

Dom Lee's wife, Keunhee, is also an artist and teamed with her husband to illustrate *Fireworks*, which was displayed at the Bologna International Children's Book Fair, as well as a number of elementary school readers. Lee has also provided dust jacket illustrations for young adult novels and has contributed to *Cricket* magazine. He continues to exhibit his work in both the United States and Korea.

Dom Lee lives in New Jersey with his wife and their two children, a son and a daughter.

SELECTED WORKS ILLUSTRATED: *Baseball Saved Us*, by Ken Mochizuki, 1993; *Heroes*, by Ken Mochizuki, 1995; *Fireworks*, by Hae-sun Lee, 1996; *Passage to Freedom: The Sugihara Story*, 1997; *The Journey Home*, by Lawrence McKay, Jr., 1998; *The All-American Girls Professional Baseball League*, by Christopher Erickson, 1999; *Young Heroes of the Bible*, by Kirk Douglas, 1999.

SUGGESTED READING: *Something About the Author*, vol. 83, 1996; *Something About the Author Autobiography Series*, vol. 26, 1998. Periodicals—*Asian New Yorker*, August 1993; *People's Weekly World*, May 15, 1993; Wilde, Susie, "Coaching Kids on Conflict," *Learning*, October/November 1995.

"When I was eleven, my parents sent my brother and me away from war-torn Vietnam to study English. I had never left my family before. The Franciscan sisters in Macao, with whom I eventually boarded, understood my distress and my loneliness. They gave me colored chalks and said, 'You can draw.'

"There were twelve-inch slate boards along two walls of the classroom; on these boards I drew all the things that I missed from home. I drew trees and fruits of South Vietnam, I drew emerald rice fields that were on the way to my grandmother's, I drew my baby brother running among the rubber trees. I drew us children on the beach of Cap St. Jacques cheering the fishermen as they pulled their nets onto the sand with hundreds of small fishes.

"For months, I buried myself in these drawings. Time flew by without my realizing it. I went to classes. Then, suddenly, I discovered the English language, so much easier to learn than French. I found I could read English with a dictionary. I started with Bible stories the sisters gave me, the life of Jesus Christ, of Mary Magdalene, etc. Having been born into a Buddhist environment and gone to a secular French school, the Christian world fascinated me. I wrote to my father in English, to practice. I told him about the new things I was learning inside the high walls of the convent school. I was at last content enough.

Courtesy of Prof. Nakabka

Jeanne M. Lee

May 17, 1943–

THE SONG OF MU LAN

JEANNE M. LEE

Courtesy of Front Street Books, Inc.

"As I became a teenager, the walls of the school became claustrophobic. I resented the strict rules, but unlike the other boarders I could not go home, because of the war. At that time, I started keeping a notebook where I wrote about random things in private; sometimes I did line drawings in it. Most often I just read—I could thus lose myself in other worlds. Dickens was allowed, along with Jane Austen, Charlotte Brontë, Mark Twain, and one book from Steinbeck that made me wish to know America, *The Red Pony*.

"I finally went home when I graduated from high school, and left shortly after to go to college in the U.S. But those difficult six years in the convent school in Macao had molded me into the person I am today. Of course we rebelled against the harsh rule of the sisters, and some of my friends got into trouble, yet I did discover painting, journal-keeping, and reading during those turbulent years.

"I cannot describe the fantastic feeling that I can have when I am painting, writing, or reading. It is as if I am lost inside myself and yet I am reaching far beyond in all directions to other places. Doing children's books is a natural medium for me because it combines all these activities.

"One day, after I had children of my own, I painted out a story that I had heard over and over as a child and brought it to New York. Miriam Chaikin, who was with Henry Holt Publishers then, looked at my watercolors and showed me how to make a book, which became *The Legend of the Milky Way*. In it, I painted rice fields and water buffaloes. I was painting my childhood. I painted the orchards and our ancestral graves in *Bà-Năm*, Ankor Wat and the lotus ponds that I visited at age seven in *Silent Lotus*. Many places that I knew are nonexistent now, including the ancestral graves. I have to describe them to the children— these stories could be their fairy tales. Now, as I grow older, maybe it is time for me to tell the next set of stories about a world where we have to make choices every day. I think I will try to work on this for a while."

*   *   *

Jeanne M. Lee brings the culture of the Far East alive in the stories she writes, translates, and illustrates for children. Using varied but complementary media, she often combines the delicate artwork and traditional techniques of the East with the vibrant colors and surreal images of the contemporary West. The results are always true to the story being told.

Lee was born in Saigon, Vietnam. As a child she studied Chinese, French, and English; later she taught geometry and algebra before coming to the United States to go to college. She earned a B.F.A. from Sacred Heart College (now Boston College) in 1967. She then worked as a graphic artist before she began illustrating children's books. Lee's illustrations have been exhibited in libraries around the country as well as in the Delaware Museum and the Hawaii Academy of Arts. Many of her larger paintings are in private collections.

In *Silent Lotus* Lee's elegant watercolors tell the story of a deaf-mute Cambodian girl who becomes a story dancer in the Khmer court. In *The Song of Mu Lan*, traditional Chinese colors, pencil drawings, and calligraphy portray the courage and determination of a young woman who took her father's place in the emperor's army. For Laurence Yep's *The Butterfly Boy*, brightly colored forms and Chinese woodcuts convey the dreamlike story of a young boy's transformation. *Toad Is the Uncle of Heaven* won a Parents' Choice Honor Award for illustration in 1990. *Legend of the Milky Way*, *Toad Is the Uncle of Heaven*, and *Bà-Năm* were all named Notable Children's Books in the Field of Social Studies, and *Silent Lotus* was a featured *Reading Rainbow* book.

SELECTED WORKS WRITTEN AND ILLUSTRATED: *Legend of the Milky Way*, 1982; *Legend of the Li River: An Ancient Chinese Tale*, 1983; *Toad Is the Uncle of Heaven: A Vietnamese Folk Tale*, 1985; *Bà-Năm*, 1987; *Silent Lotus*, 1991; *The Song of Mu Lan*, 1995; *I Once Was a Monkey: Stories Buddha Told*, 1999.

SELECTED WORKS ILLUSTRATED: *Butterfly Boy*, by Laurence Yep, 1993; *The Ch'i-lin Purse: A Collection of Ancient Chinese Stories*, by Linda Fang, 1994.

Courtesy of Karl H. Jacoby

Marie G. Lee

April 25, 1964–

"I first knew I would become a writer at age nine, when I received an old portable typewriter from my brother. The first time I typed something out, I was thrilled by the way the letters looked, so neat and professional right off the bat that I decided then and there that I would be a writer. From that day on, I tried to write something every day.

"At the same time, I wanted to be like my father, who was a doctor, and become one myself. While other little kids had tea parties for their stuffed animals, I had a hospital for mine, where all sorts of surgeries and other miraculous cures were performed. When I grew older, another favorite toy was one my father had bought me, 'Visible Woman,' which was a clear plastic shell housing all the organs, bones, and circulatory system of a woman. I spent hours learning the different parts and where they belonged.

"But I still wanted to write, of course, and I did. In high school I had two marvelous English teachers, Mrs. Klatsbach and Mrs. Boreman. Mrs. Klatsbach was one of the first teachers to recognize I had some writing talent, and Mrs. Boreman actually let me skip out of her grammar class and spend that time writing in the library. Because of Mrs. Boreman, I wrote my first published piece, an essay on volunteer work, which was published by *Seventeen* magazine.

"After that early triumph, I thought writing would be easy. But even though I wrote and sent things out in college, I couldn't get anything published. Brown University has a great creative writing program, but I couldn't take too many classes because they didn't give you grades and I kept thinking I was going to go to medical school, when in reality, I had pretty much given that up freshman year. I really wanted to be like my father, but I had to face it: I hated the sight of blood. Years later, watching my best friend from college go through medical school, I realized that I would have hated it, and had I somehow been able to drag myself through, I would have been a terrible doctor.

"I knew I was meant to be a writer, although for many years no one seemed to agree with me. I was working on Wall Street in order to have the privilege of living in New York (land of writers!) and I didn't like my job very much. I started writing my first novel, *Finding My Voice*, right after I got out of college. In college, I had spent a lot of time trying to copy my favorite writers: Flannery O'Connor, J. D. Salinger, etc. I, however, was Korean American, but I didn't want to write about it because I'd never seen any books by Korean Americans and somehow thought that meant that topic wasn't important.

"Well, I'm not sure why, but *Finding My Voice* was a different book. For one thing, it had a Korean American as narrator. It wasn't me, but someone very much like me. Perhaps James Baldwin was right when he said that novelists always write their first novel about their own lives because they have years of accumulated gunk to get off their chest. Well, that's exactly what I did: I wrote my heart out. Of course, getting published was another story, but this one, luckily, has a happy ending. It took a very long time, but everything I had done— moving to New York, etc.—eventually paid off. I met a very famous and generous young adult writer who got me in touch with the person who became my agent and who sold my first book. But in case you think, like the *Seventeen* article, that the whole thing was a snap, let me tell you, I was overjoyed when the publisher took *both* my novels; it had taken so long to sell number one that number two was already written.

"Now I no longer work on Wall Street. I do some teaching, and I also write for adults. I'm married, and my husband is a history professor at Brown

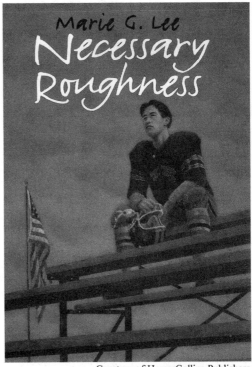

Courtesy of HarperCollins Publishers

University— yes, the place where I went to college, and also the place where he went . . . and the place where we had our first date. I spent a year in Korea as a Fulbright scholar researching my next book. I don't know what the next year will bring, but I'm looking forward to it."

* * *

Marie G. Lee was born on April 25, 1964, in Hibbing, Minnesota. Her parents had emigrated from Korea in 1953. The experience of growing up in a small town where hers was the only

Asian family had a strong influence on her later writing. Lee received her B.A. degree in 1986 from Brown University in Providence, Rhode Island. She worked at Standard and Poor's and Goldman Sachs & Co. on Wall Street before turning to writing full-time. She was an instructor of literature and creative writing at Yale University in 1996.

Marie Lee's first novel, *Finding My Voice*, received a Best Book Award from the Friends of American Writers. It was also selected as a Best Book for Reluctant Readers by the American Library Association and was named a Children's Choice book by a joint committee of the International Reading Association and the Children's Book Council in 1994. *Finding My Voice, If It Hadn't Been for Yoon Jun, Saying Goodbye*, and *Necessary Roughness* all received Books for the Teen Age citations from the New York Public Library. *Necessary Roughness* was also named an ALA Best Book for Young Adults. Lee's stories have been anthologized in *Matters of Fact*, published by Prentice-Hall in 1992, and *New Worlds of Literature*, published by Norton in 1994.

Lee and her husband, Karl Jacoby, were married in June 1997 and live in Providence, Rhode Island.

SELECTED WORKS: *Finding My Voice*, 1992; *If It Hadn't Been for Yoon Jun*, 1993; *Saying Goodbye*, 1994; *Necessary Roughness*, 1996; *F Is for Fabuloso*, 1999.

SUGGESTED READING: *Authors and Artists for Young Adults*, vol. 27, 1999; *Contemporary Authors*, vol. 149, 1996; *Contemporary Authors*, New Revision Series, vol. 71, 1998; *Lives of Famous Asian Americans: Literature*, 1995; *Something About the Author*, vol. 81, 1995; Unterberger, Amy L., ed. *Who's Who Among Asian Americans, 1994–95*, 1994. Periodicals— *Face*, July/August 1993; *Minnesota Monthly*, February 1993.

Frané Lessac

(fran-NAY le-SAK)

June 18, 1954

"I grew up in a small town on top of the Palisades in New Jersey. From my bedroom window I could see the famous skyscraper skyline of New York City. In the hot summer months I could hear the shrieks of people riding on the roller coaster at a nearby amusement park.

"I always wanted to be an artist or a veterinarian. By the time I was eight years old I had two cats, two dogs, fish, three snakes, and a pet monkey named Hercules that used to sit on my shoulder. Hercules stank and had fleas, and my mom finally said, 'Either you or that monkey has to go.'

"As a child, I spent many weekends in the city browsing through museums and galleries. I used to explore New York's Greenwich Village with my orange-tongued green snake entwined around my arm. I loved watching the painters in their berets smoking those long cigarettes and the poets reciting verse with the audience snapping their fingers in approval.

"I was surrounded by people of many different cultures. Our Thanksgiving dinners were like a United Nations meeting. I was always drawn towards people and places that were foreign and diverse.

"At eighteen, I headed for film school at the University of California in Los Angeles. My aim: to eventually make films about 'primitive' tribes before they were swamped by Western culture. I borrowed camera equipment and, given film, took off on the road in the American Southwest, documenting a rodeo team, a long distance trucker, and even the birth of a baby.

"Home was a beach house in Malibu furnished with the discarded furniture of the film and movie stars. We had Flip Wilson's lawn chairs and Barbra Streisand's settee. I worked hard to help finance my studies. My jobs included running the projector at the local Malibu cinema, chauffeuring the residents of Beverly Hills, and fertilizing cactus with a silver spoon at a desert nursery.

"I moved from California to the small Caribbean island of Montserrat in 1978. Stunned by its visual beauty, I concentrated on painting the old-style West Indian architecture and its people. I lived on the island during its music glory years when Sting, Elton John, Arrow, and others were recording at George Martin's Air Studio. Visiting rock stars and tourists began to buy my paintings.

Courtesy of Bron Sibree

"Wanting to publish a children's picture book about Montserrat, I moved to London in 1982 to be closer to publishers. I approached thirty publishers before one finally accepted the idea, and the book was released as *The Little Island* in 1984 in the United Kingdom. Six months later it was published in the United States as *My Little Island*. While waiting for the book to be published, I spent some time in France and Italy. In Paris I lived in a studio overlooking the city streets and spent lots of time romanticizing about the great artists who lived there before me. In the south of France and in Italy, I discovered the light of the 'golden hour,' which continues to influence my work.

"I met my Australian-born husband, a musician, in Bali while I was filming a documentary on Balinese painters. We moved to the enchanting port city of Fremantle, West Australia, where we

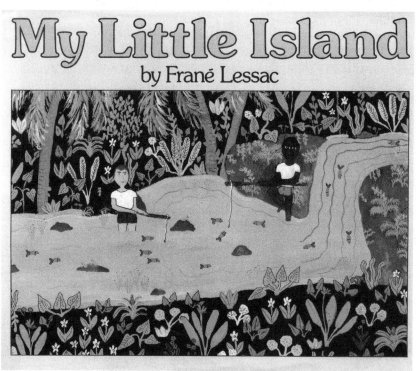

Courtesy of HarperCollins

now live with our two children, Luke and Cody, and many pets. I find the Australian landscape a brand new challenge. My canvas is inspired by the red ochre of the earth and the uniquely brilliant blue of the sky and sea.

"My work has led me on many adventures in numerous countries. Traveling continues to be a major source of inspiration for my work as I render my impression of a country and its way of life in oil and gouache paintings. My greatest ambition is to instill pride and self-esteem in children about their own unique heritage and their ability to capture in it pictures and words."

Frané Lessac was born in Jersey City, New Jersey. Her mother, Estelle, owns a travel agency, and Frané seems to have been born with wanderlust. Her father, Arthur, has also been an inspiration. He has a great appreciation of natural light, color, and the variety of life. He directed Frané's attention towards objects and scenes of beauty and diversity, thus enriching her visual outlook.

Lessac studied Ethnographic Film at the University of Southern California and UCLA. Besides illustrating over twenty books, she has exhibited her artwork on three continents; she has also produced greeting cards, CD covers, gift wrap, T-shirts, calendars, and posters.

My Little Island was selected as the St. Marteen Children's Book of the Year and included on the Library of Congress's 1985 Books for Children list. It was also a *Reading Rainbow* feature book, as was *The Wonderful Towers of Watts*. *Caribbean Canvas* received the American Institute of Graphic Arts' Book Show Award in 1990. Many of Lessac's books have been named to the annual lists of Notable Trade Books in the Field of Social Studies: *Caribbean Canvas, The Chalk Doll, The Bird Who Was an Elephant, Caribbean Alphabet, Caribbean Carnival, The Distant Talking Drum*, and *O Christmas Tree*. *Caribbean Carnival* was listed by the New York Public Library in 100 Titles for Reading and Sharing and by the Bank Street College of Education in Children's Books of the Year. The NCTE named *Not a Copper Penny* a Notable Children's Book in the Language Arts. *The Distant Talking Drum* was an ALA Notable Children's Book and an IRA Notable Book for a Global Society.

SELECTED WORKS WRITTEN AND ILLUSTRATED: *My Little Island*, 1985; *Caribbean Canvas*, 1987; *Caribbean Alphabet*, 1994.

SELECTED WORKS ILLUSTRATED: *The Dragon of Redonda*, by Jan Jackson, 1986; *The Chalk Doll*, by Charlotte Pomerantz, 1989; *The Bird Who Was an Elephant*, by Aleph Kamal, 1990; *Nine O'Clock Lullaby*, by Marilyn Singer, 1990; *Caribbean Carnival: Songs of the West Indies*, by Irving Burgie, 1992; *Not a Copper Penny*, by Monica Gunning, 1993; *The Fire Children*, by Eric Maddern, 1993; *The Wonderful Towers of Watts*, by Patricia Zelver, 1994; *Sleep Rhymes Around the World*, ed. by Jane Yolen, 1994; *The Distant Talking Drum*, by Isaac Olaleye,1994; *Good Rhymes, Good Times*, by Lee Bennett Hopkins, 1995; *O Christmas Tree*, by Vashanti Rahaman, 1996; *Queen Esther Saves Her People*, by Rita Gelman, 1998; *On the Same Day in March*, by Marilyn Singer, 2000.

SUGGESTED READING: *Contemporary Authors*, vol. 127, 1989; *Something About the Author*, vol. 61, 1990. Periodicals—*New York Times Book Review*, January 12, 1986.

E-MAIL: *artbeat@ozemail.com.au*

Alison Lester

November 17, 1952–

"I live on a little farm just south of Melbourne with my husband, Eddy; our three kids, Will, Clair, and Lachie; and the cats, dogs, and horses. We've got a big messy garden and a tennis court which is always being used for football, basketball, skateboarding, cricket, and bike-riding, as well as tennis. There's music going nearly all the time somewhere in the house, and apart from the odd scrap, we have a pretty good time. We are not a very serious-minded family. There's always too much driving the paddock bomb and shooting the air rifle and not enough study and quiet contemplation.

"The hardest thing about my work is actually finding time to do it. *Making* time is probably a more accurate term. It's the same for any mother, but squeezing work between kids, school, sport, elderly parents, the garden, the house, shopping, and travel can be tricky. I waste heaps of time riding. My head is always buzzing with ideas. I have stretches of time when I don't sleep much and I love lying awake at night nutting out stories. The days when I can get to my desk are great. The house is empty and quiet and I can look across the valley as a passage evolves.

Courtesy of Ross Bird

Harley the cat might smooch around my legs, and sometimes Eddy comes home for lunch. When Clair and Lachie get home on the school bus (Will is studying in Melbourne now), it seems like they've only been gone a couple of hours.

"I didn't ever plan to be a writer. I grew up on a beautiful farm overlooking the sea and I wanted to be a drover, then a vet, but instead took the safe girly option and trained to be a secondary art teacher. I was a hopeless teacher, always daydreaming and wishing I was somewhere else. I hated having to nag kids and tell them off.

"I started illustrating when Will was a baby. I didn't know what had hit me when I had him. We'd shifted from a shared house in Carlton (lots of friends, fun, eating out every night) to a rented farmhouse at Pakenham South. Talk about culture shock. No friends, no sleep, tragic body, cooking, cleaning—it was great to have some drawing to do. At first I worked while the baby slept, but by the time I had three kids I was so busy I had a full-time nanny. A series of full-time nannies. I hope my children will forgive me because there were some shockers amongst them.

"It's nearly twenty years since I started illustrating. Having started off doing drawing and no words, now I've finished my first novel, *The Quicksand Pony*, with words and no drawing. I hope the ideas keep coming."

* * *

Alison Lester grew up in Southeastern Australia on a cattle farm overlooking the sea. The youngest of four children, she grew up among animals. Every year she would raise a calf, and sometimes try to ride it, rodeo-style, before it was sold. Horses played an important part in Lester's growing years, and she still leaves her desk at any opportunity to go for a ride. She took her teaching degree at Melbourne State College in 1975 and taught high school art for several years.

In 1977 she married Edwin Hume and traveled in South America for a year. After the birth of her first child, Lester was looking for work she could do while raising her family. She took a folio of her drawings to a publishing house in Melbourne and very soon had a job illustrating *Big Dipper* by June Epstein. Her 1982 illustrations for Robin Klein's *Thing* won the Picture Book of the Year award from the Children's Book Council of Australia.

Clive Eats Alligators, the first book Lester wrote as well as illustrated, was a commended book for the Australian Picture Book of the Year award and is the first in a series of stories about a boisterous group of children. *My Farm*, in which Lester extols the joys of farm life for young children, was named a Blue Ribbon book by the *Bulletin of the Center for Children's Books*. Lester's stories and drawings are full of energy and detail; her books have now been translated into many languages and are enjoyed by children around the world. Today she spends much of her time traveling to schools to talk about her work and conduct writing and drawing workshops for students.

SELECTED WORKS WRITTEN: *The Quicksand Pony*, 1997.

SELECTED WORKS WRITTEN AND ILLUSTRATED: *Clive Eats Alligators*, 1985; *Ruby*, 1987; *Rosie Sips Spiders*, 1988; *Imagine*, 1989; *The Journey Home*, 1989; *Magic Beach*, 1990; *Tessa Snaps Snakes*, 1990; *Isabella's Bed*, 1991; *My Farm*, 1992; *I'm Green & I'm Grumpy*, 1993; *Yikes! In Seven Wild Adventures, Who Would You Be?*, 1993; *When Frank Was Four*, 1994; *Alice and Aldo*, 1996; *Celeste Sails to Spain*, 1997.

SELECTED WORKS ILLUSTRATED: *Big Dipper*, by June Epstein, 1980; *Big Dipper Rides Again*, by June Epstein, 1982; *Thing*, by Robin Klein, 1982; *Thingnapped*, by Robin Klein, 1984; *Ratbags and Rascals*, by Robin Klein, 1984; *Night-Night*, by Morris Lurie, 1986; *Summer*, by June Factor, 1987; *Thinglets* (collective title for *Thingitis*, *Thing Gets a Job*, *Thing's Concert*, *Thing's Birthday*), by Robin Klein, 1996.

Courtesy of Robin Lester

Helen Lester [signature]

Helen Lester

June 12, 1936–

"Sometime between the Age of Electricity and the Age of Television (actually it was in 1936) I was born in Evanston, Illinois. Most of my early writing was done in the form of thank-you notes at birthdays and Christmas and was not a voluntary activity. As I grew older, however, I began to appreciate the voluminous and clever letters my parents wrote to various friends and family members, and developed a sense of what fun could be had with the written word. Still, I had no dreams of becoming a writer, only of becoming a 'bride' (it was the '50s). Since no one wanted to turn me into a bride, I became a teacher.

"After ten years of teaching elementary school, during which time I did become a bride, I took temporary leave of that profession to spend time with our two young sons. It was during this domestic period that several factors came into play which ultimately influenced my writing career. First, in reading bedtime stories to my children, I remember being overjoyed every time I came across a story that would make me laugh, for often at 7:30 P.M. not much is funny. I decided the world needed more books that would amuse both adults and children. Secondly, my old second-graders came back to haunt me—more about them in a moment. And finally, I backed into writing thinking I was an illustrator. I'd always enjoyed drawing, and when a friend saw my work and casually suggested I should write children's books, I thought, 'Perhaps. Why not?'

"My early stories were just words written around my pictures, and finally, in 1979, after I'd suffered (*suffered* is the proper word here) many rejections, my first book was published. My husband, always the cheerleader, gave me a silver bowl with the book's title engraved on it. But it wasn't until a few years later, when my editor tactfully suggested that I might be a better writer than illustrator, that I really thought of myself as a writer. Since then, with a few exceptions, I've left the art in my books to the wonderful Lynn Munsinger, who draws what I would if I could.

"Back to my second-graders. They appear as Pinkerton the pushy pig in *Me First*, Buddy the oblivious rabbit in *Listen, Buddy*, and of course I never had a class without at least one Tacky (not to mention Goodly, Lovely, Angel, Neatly, and Perfect in the wings).

"After living in New York City, San Francisco, Chicago, and Minneapolis, we've settled in our favorite village, Pawling, New York, where my husband and I tend our writing, our dog, and our empty nest. In addition to writing I enjoy visiting schools all over the country encouraging children to write. Armed with messages such as 'My books don't jump out of the computer,' 'Not all of my stories get published,' and 'Being edited isn't fun but it's good for you,' I've found a new form of teaching. *Author: A True Story* comes directly from my school visits and is perhaps the book of which I'm most proud. How fortunate I am to have backed into this wonderful field."

* * *

Helen Lester earned an A.A.S from Bennett Junior College in 1956 and a B.S. from Wheelock College in 1959. She has worked as an elementary school teacher in Lexington, Massachusetts; Chicago, Illinois; and San Francisco, California. Lester's always humorous, often touching books have been well received by children and adults alike.

Tacky the Penguin has been the winner of statewide children's book awards in Colorado, California, and Nebraska. *Listen, Buddy* was a *FamilyFun* magazine Book of the Year winner in 1996. *Three Cheers for Tacky* was named an IRA/CBC Children's Choice book. *Author: A True Story* received a *Parenting* magazine Reading Magic Award in 1997. It was also selected for Capitol Choices by a committee of children's librarians and booksellers in the metropolitan Washington, D.C., area, was named a Notable Children's Book in the Language Arts by the NCTE, and was included in New York Public Library's 100 Titles for Reading and Sharing. *Hooway for Wodney Wat* was named an ALA Notable Book and a *School Library Journal* Best Book and won a Parents' Choice Gold Award in 1999.

> "I decided the world needed more books that would amuse both adults and children."

SELECTED WORKS WRITTEN: (all illus. by Lynn Munsinger): *A Porcupine Named Fluffy*, 1986; *Tacky the Penguin*, 1988; *The Revenge of the Magic Chicken*, 1990; *Three Cheers for Tacky*, 1994; *Listen, Buddy*, 1995; *The Four Getters and Arf*, 1995; *Princess Penelope's Parrot*, 1996; *Tacky in Trouble*, 1998; *Hooway for Wodney Wat*, 1999.

SELECTED WORKS WRITTEN AND ILLUSTRATED: *Cora Copycat*, 1979; *Author: A True Story*, 1997.

SUGGESTED READING: *Contemporary Authors*, vol. 115, 1985; *Contemporary Authors*, New Revision Series, vol. 38, 1993; vol. 58, 1997; *Something About the Author*, vol. 46, 1986; vol. 92, 1997.

Courtesy of Julius Lester

Julius Lester

January 27, 1939–

"I was born January 27, 1939 in St. Louis, Missouri. Moved to Kansas City, Kansas, at age two and to Nashville, Tennessee, at fourteen and finished Fisk University there with a B.A. in English in 1960.

"Perhaps the most important influence in my growing up was my father, a Methodist minister from the South and a good storyteller. From him I absorbed so much of Southern rural Black traditions, particularly music and stories. Equally important were the summers spent at my maternal grandmother's house in Arkansas as well as the adolescent years of my life in Nashville. The South is different in its way of life, and for me that was not wholly negative, despite segregation and discrimination.

"I guess I always wanted to be a writer, though I was drawn to music and art as careers. But I never doubted, I guess, that it would be writing. I'm not sure that one can even *want* to be a writer; you are one or you aren't, which is an innate knowledge. Of course, if one stops with that knowledge, he/she will never be a writer, because writing is, more than anything else, work, constant work.

"I never thought of writing for children until the editor of my first book said that she thought I could write for children. Amused, I asked her why. She couldn't explain, but she asked me if I'd be interested in meeting the children's book editor. I did and out of our conversation came the idea for *To Be a Slave*. Since then I have found writing for children of all ages more rewarding than writing for adults, primarily because I like the audience and the responses I get from children. I don't find it any easier to write for children, however, and in some ways it is more difficult. Children are a very critical audience.

"I have five children, three biological and two stepchildren. They range in ages from 34 to 19. When my own children were young, I wanted them to have books that I would have liked to read when I was growing up, and that was an important factor in my writing of children's books. Besides writing, I also teach at the University of Massachusetts, where I am a professor in the Department of Judaic Studies and an adjunct professor in the History and English Departments. I have taught at the university since 1971 and enjoy teaching enormously.

"I am the religious leader of Beth El Synagogue in St. Johnsbury, Vermont, where I go to conduct religious services once a month and for special religious observances. My hobbies are crossword puzzles, stamp collecting, and reading.

"I lead a rather solitary life, and with my wife, Milan Sabatini, live on a secluded twelve acres of woods and fields in western Massachusetts. We have one cat and about 15,000 books."

* * *

Julius Lester was actively involved in many aspects of the civil rights movement throughout the 1960s and early 1970s. He joined the Student Non-Violent Coordinating Committee (SNCC) in 1966 as head of the photography department and later became a field secretary. He traveled to North Vietnam in 1967 to photograph the effects of U.S. bombing there and later went to Cuba with Stokely Carmichael to attend the Organization of Latin American Solidarity Conference. As he wrote and spoke about his experiences and beliefs he became increasingly identified with Black radical politics, although he did not himself think he was a Black militant. The radio talk show on WBAI in New York which he hosted from 1968 to 1975 aired many controversial issues of the day.

An accomplished musician, Lester has recorded two albums of original songs and co-authored an instructional book with Pete Seeger called *The Twelve String Guitar as Played by Leadbelly*. His essays, reviews, and editorials on a variety of topics have appeared over the years in journals and newspapers, including the *Village Voice, New York Free Press*, the *Boston Globe*, the *New York Times Book Review*, and the *New Republic*. He has also edited poetry anthologies and published poems of his own.

Courtesy of Dial Books

Julius Lester's first book for young readers, *To Be a Slave*, a compelling collection of experiences narrated by ex-slaves, was named a Newbery Honor Book in 1969, won the Nancy Block Award for 1968, received a Lewis Carroll Shelf Award in 1970, and appeared on every major recommended list in its year of publication. Lester followed this book with *Black Folktales*, in which he retold stories from African and African American sources and became recognized as one of the most respected ex-

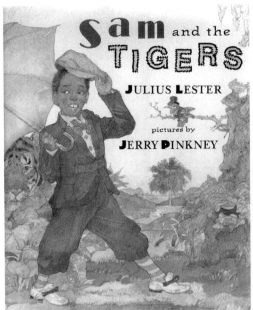

Courtesy of Dial Books

ponents of African American history and experience. *Black Folktales* was on the *New York Times* list of outstanding books of the year, as was *Long Journey Home*, which was nominated for a National Book Award in 1973.

A major contribution to children's literature is Lester's four-volume retelling of the Uncle Remus stories, originally collected in post–Civil War years by Atlanta newspaperman Joel Chandler Harris. In his versions of the stories, Harris attempted to re-create the speech patterns of the former slaves who told him the tales. These versions are virtually impossible to read today because of the heavy dialect, and they have become associated with the stereotyped image of a docile elderly slave, Uncle Remus. Lester breathed new life into these sparkling pieces of authentic American folklore by retelling them in what he termed "modified contemporary Southern Black English" with rollicking humor and contemporary references. The Uncle Remus character becomes only a voice, a storyteller relating the tales, rather than an actual person. Accompanied by the lively and witty watercolors of Jerry Pinkney, *The Tales of Uncle Remus* was named an ALA Notable Children's Book, along with many other citations; the subsequent three volumes were also published to great acclaim. In 1999 all four volumes were collected into one book and reissued as *Uncle Remus: The Complete Tales*.

Another retelling from African American tradition, a picture book version of the legend of John Henry, is also imbued with Lester's signature style of lively metaphor and upbeat narrative. With stunning illustrations by Jerry Pinkney, *John Henry* garnered a Caldecott Honor Book award and a *Boston Globe–Horn Book* Award in the picture book category. Listening in on a discussion among children's book specialists on the Internet about the much maligned storybook *Little Black Sambo*, Lester decided to write an updated version that would replace the old stereotyped characters with more positive images for all children. The result was *Sam and the Tigers*, also illustrated by Pinkney, which appeared on many of the "best" lists in 1996 and was named an ALA Notable Children's Book and a Notable Trade Book in the Field of Social Studies. Julius Lester continues to use his unique style and imagination to extend the folk tradition. *What a Truly Cool World!*, published in 1999, is an upbeat retelling of "How God Made the Butterflies," a story that first appeared in his *Black Folktales*.

Raised as the son of a Methodist minister, Lester discovered that his great-grandfather had been a German Jewish immigrant to the American South in the days before the Civil War. A musician in the Confederate Army Band, Adolph Altschul later married a woman who had been a slave. The story of Lester's decision to embrace this ancestor's religion is told in his autobiographical account, *Lovesong: Becoming a Jew.* In 1999 he published *When the Beginning Began*, his first book devoted entirely to the Jewish folk tradition. Here he uses traditional Jewish tales as well as original ones to retell the story of Creation from the beginning to the expulsion of Adam and Eve from the Garden of Eden.

Julius Lester's children from his first marriage are Jody, born in 1965, and Malcolm, 1967. He has a stepchild, Elena Grohmann, and a son, David, born in 1979, from his second marriage, and a stepchild, Lian Brennan, from his present marriage.

SELECTED WORKS: *To Be a Slave*, illus. by Tom Feelings, 1968; *Black Folktales*, illus. by Tom Feelings, 1969; *The Knee-High Man and Other Tales*, illus. by Ralph Pinto, 1972; *Long Journey Home: Stories from Black History*, 1972; *This Strange New Feeling*, 1982; *The Tales of Uncle Remus: The Adventures of Brer Rabbit*, illus. by Jerry Pinkney, 1987; *More Tales of Uncle Remus: Further Adventures of Brer Rabbit, His Friends, Enemies, and Others*, illus. by Jerry Pinkney, 1988; *How Many Spots Does a Leopard Have? and Other Tales*, illus. by David Shannon, 1989; *Further Tales of Uncle Remus: The Misadventures of Brer Rabbit, Brer Fox, Brer Wolf, the Doodang, and Other Creatures*, illus. by Jerry Pinkney, 1990; *The Last Tales of Uncle Remus*, illus. by Jerry Pinkney, 1994; *John Henry*, illus. by Jerry Pinkney, 1994; *The Man Who Knew Too Much: A Moral Tale from the Baila of Zambia*, illus. by Leonard Jenkins, 1994; *Othello: A Novel*, 1995; *Sam and the Tigers: A New Retelling of Little Black Sambo*, illus. by Jerry Pinkney, 1996; *From Slave Ship to Freedom Road*, illus. by Rod Brown, 1998; *Black Cowboy, Wild Horses: A True Story*, illus. by Jerry Pinkney, 1998; *What a Truly Cool World!*, illus. by Joe Cepeda, 1999; *When the Beginning Began: Stories about God, the Creatures, and Us*, illus. by Emily Lisker, 1999; *Uncle Remus: The Complete Tales*, illus. by Jerry Pinkney, 1999.

SUGGESTED READING: *Authors and Artists for Young Adults*, vol. 12, 1994; *Children's Literature Review*, vol. 2, 1976, vol. 41, 1997; Collier, Laurie and Joyce Nakamura, eds. *Major Authors and Illustrators for Children and Young Adults*, 1993; *Contemporary Authors*, New Revision Series, vol. 43, 1994; Lester, Julius. *All Is Well: An Autobiography*, 1976; Lester, Julius. *Lovesong: Becoming a Jew*, 1988; Silvey, Anita, ed. *Children's Books and Their Creators*, 1995; *Something About the Author*, vol. 12, 1977; vol. 74, 1993. Periodicals—Del Negro, Janice, "The *Booklist* Interview," *Booklist*, February 15, 1995; Nikola-Lisa, W., "John Henry: Then and Now," *African American Review*, Spring 1998; "Writing About Religion," *Book Links*, November 1999.

An earlier profile of Julius Lester appeared in *Fourth Book of Junior Authors and Illustrators* (Wilson, 1978).

Courtesy of David Levine

Gail Carson Levine

September 17, 1947–

"**I** was born on September 17, 1947, in New York City, where I grew up and lived until quite recently. My father was interested in writing, and my mother, a teacher, wrote full-length plays in verse for her students to perform. Both of them had a reverence for creativity and creative people, which they passed along to my sister and me. My older sister, Rani, is a wonderful painter of Jamaican (West Indies) subjects and a professor of fine arts.

"I didn't plan to be a writer, even though I started writing early. In elementary school I was a charter member of the Scribble Scrabble Club, and in high school my poems were published in an anthology of student poetry. But my ambition was to act or to be a painter like my sister. My interest in the theater led to my first writing experience as an adult. My husband, David, wrote the music and lyrics and I wrote the script for a children's musical, *Spacenapped*, that was produced by a neighborhood theater in Brooklyn.

"And painting brought me to writing for children in earnest. I took a class in writing and illustrating children's books and found that I much preferred the writing to the illustrating. Another writing class got me started on *Ella Enchanted*. I had to write something for class, and I couldn't think of a plot. The fairy tale 'Cinderella' already had a plot, so I decided to do a Cinderella story. Then, when I thought about Cinderella's character, I realized she was such a goody two-shoes that I would hate her before I finished ten pages. So I came up with the curse: she's only good because she has to be, and she's in constant rebellion.

"Before *Ella* I wrote several picture books, which are unpublished to this day, and a historical novel. My father grew up in the Hebrew Orphan Asylum in Harlem in New York City. I was always curious about the frightening childhood of my safe, happy-go-lucky dad. Since he wouldn't talk about it, I had to invent my own version of events. Seven years in the making, *Dave at Night* takes place in 1926. At night, the hero, Dave, slips out of the orphanage—where he is half-starved, half-frozen, and beaten—to have adventures in the Harlem Renaisssance.

"My career before I became a writer had to do with welfare, first helping people find work and then as an administrator. The earlier experience was more direct and satisfying, and I enjoy thinking that a bunch of people somewhere are doing well today because of my help. Most of the recipients I've known have been decent and good-natured under terrible circumstances. I haven't yet found a way to write about the subject, but I hope to someday.

"David and I and our Airedale, Jake, now live in a 200-year-old farmhouse in Brewster, New York. I left my job in November of 1997 to write full-time, except for my favorite afternoon every week. On that afternoon, I give a writing workshop for kids who've also been bitten by the writing bug. We all write together, working on thorny problems like beginnings or characterization or setting. And we read our work out loud and talk about it."

Courtesy of HarperCollins Publishers

* * *

A city girl, Gail Carson grew up in New York. Her father, David Carson, owned a commercial art studio, and her mother, Sylvia, was a teacher. She married David Levine, a software developer, in 1967 and completed her B.A. at the City College of the City University of New York in 1969. The author worked for twenty-seven years in state government departments concerned with labor and welfare, but she is now writing full-time.

Levine's first novel, *Ella Enchanted*, won instant notice for its humor and charm, a Cinderella tale with a flesh-and-blood heroine whose greatest desire is to be allowed to be herself and not so incurably nice. *Ella Enchanted* was selected as a 1998 Newbery Honor Book, an ALA Notable Children's Book, and an ALA Best Book for Young Adults and was cited on the list of Quick Picks for Young Adults. Clearly a favorite of young readers as well as reviewers, *Ella Enchanted* has also been the winner of statewide children's choice awards in Vermont and Arizona. *Dave at Night* was chosen as an ALA Notable Children's Book, an ALA Best Book for Young Adults, and a *School Library Journal* Best of the Year.

SELECTED WORKS: *Ella Enchanted*, 1997; *Dave at Night*, 1999; *The Fairy's Mistake*, 1999; *The Princess Test*, 1999; *Princess Sonora and the Long Sleep*, 1999; *The Wish*, 2000; *Cinderellis and the Glass Hill*, 2000.

SUGGESTED READING: *Contemporary Authors*, vol. 166, 1999; *Something About the Author*, vol. 98, 1998.

Courtesy of Ted Lewin

Betsy Lewin

May 12, 1937–

"**G**rowing up in Clearfield, Pennsylvania, a little town nestled in an Allegheny Mountain valley, was mostly wonderful. The woods nearby was my favorite place to be, a place that put a child's imagination to work and instilled in me a deep love for the natural world. Sometimes I felt restless and wondered what the rest of the world was like. My fantasies took me out west to live the life of a cowboy (at least the way that life was portrayed in Hollywood westerns), on African safaris and tiger hunts in India (without a gun), or to New York City, where there were more people in my view than I could count and the music from *My Friend Irma* or a Ginger Rogers and Fred Astaire movie would inspire the fantasy.

"My mother taught kindergarten in our house, where picture books numbered in the hundreds. I knew them all by heart. My father was Irish and a natural storyteller. Neither of my parents could 'draw a straight line,' as they put it, but their love of children and books, and quirky sense of humor, all have been stirred into my artistic efforts.

"I've always loved to draw and even my earliest pictures told stories. If I drew a tree, someone peeked out from behind it. If I drew a cat, it was stretching or leaping or stalking invisible prey. I never wanted to be anything but an artist. My elementary and junior high school art teachers encouraged me, and my private art teacher convinced my parents to send me to art school. So, in the fall of 1955, following graduation from high school, the first of many childhood fantasies came true. I was off to New York City and Pratt Institute, where I majored in Illustration. My first job after graduation from Pratt was assistant art director in a greeting card company. But my goal was to be a freelance illustrator. I accepted all sorts of assignments, mostly spot drawings for brochures and magazines. Once in a while, I wrote and illustrated a story or poem for a children's magazine called *Humpty Dumpty*. I didn't know it then, but one of those little poems would lead me into the world of picture books again, this time as an illustrator.

"A children's book editor saw my illustrated poem 'Cat Count' in a magazine and asked me to expand it into a picture book. I did and it was an altogether gratifying experience. The challenge of working in a picture book format, the excitement of holding that first copy in my hands, then imagining my book in the hands of a child, made me realize that this is what I wanted to do. Since *Cat Count* I've illustrated over thirty books, some of my own and some by other authors. I've found the latter to be no less challenging or interesting to me than illustrating my own stories. It offers opportunities to explore subjects I might never have chosen, to see things from another's point of view, and to interpret their words in pictures. Almost all of my books are of a humorous nature. I like stories that make you laugh, and I particularly love to draw animals.

"*I never wanted to be anything but an artist.*"

"Other childhood fantasies came true when my husband, Ted, also an author/illustrator of books for children, and I began traveling to exotic places around the world in search of stories. African safaris and tiger hunts in India (with cameras) became realities, as did travels to South America, Australia, Canada, and Alaska, and there are more stories waiting for us in other faraway places. These travels have added a new dimension to our lives and to our books. Although we travel together and share the same experience, we each find our own story to tell.

"I always look forward to the next book. Whether it's illustrating someone else's story or taking a child with me on a journey to a new place, one thing is for sure—I'm going to enjoy it."

* * *

Betsy Lewin is the daughter of an insurance salesman and a teacher. She received her B.F.A. from the Pratt Institute of Art in 1959 and married Ted B. Lewin in 1963. She and her husband make their home in an historic brownstone house in Brooklyn, New York, journeying out from there to exotic and wilderness areas in many parts of the world. A love of hiking, canoeing, and observing nature—from flowers to skunks to household pets—

BOOBY HATCH

Written and illustrated by **Betsy Lewin**

Courtesy of Houghton Mifflin

permeates her work. In the field she sketches animals as she sees them and paints flowers in watercolor, sometimes returning to the studio to finish the work.

Booby Hatch, a book that grew out of a Galapagos Islands adventure, shows the life of a blue-footed booby. It was cited as a Best Book in *School Library Journal*, as was *Walk a Green Path* with its large paintings of plants in their native environments in various parts of the world, each picture accompanied by one of Lewin's poems. Among books she has illustrated, *Araminta's Paintbox* and *Ho! Ho! Ho! The Complete Book of Christmas Words* were both among the American Booksellers Association Pick of the Lists. *Yo! Hungry Wolf* and *Somebody Catch My Homework* were 1994 IRA/CBC Children's Choices.

The first collaboration between Betsy and Ted Lewin, *Gorilla Walk*, recounted their journey to Uganda's Bwindi–Impenetrable Forest National Park to view the mountain gorillas. It was named an ALA Notable Children's Book in 2000.

SELECTED WORKS WRITTEN AND ILLUSTRATED: *Animal Snackers*, 1980; *Cat Count*, 1980; *Hip, Hippo, Hooray*, 1982; *Booby Hatch*, 1995; *Walk a Green Path*, 1995; *Chubbo's Pool*, 1996; *What's the Matter, Habibi?*, 1997; *Gorilla Walk*, with Ted Lewin, 1999.

SELECTED WORKS ILLUSTRATED: *Greens: Poems*, by Arnold Adoff, 1988; *Weird! The Complete Book of Halloween Words*, by Peter R. Limburg, 1989; *Araminta's Paintbox*, by Karen Ackerman, 1990; *What If the Shark Wears Tennis Shoes?*, by Winifred Morris, 1900; *Gobble: The Complete Book of Thanksgiving Words*, by Lynda Graham Barber, 1991; *The Hummingbirds' Day*, by Harry Allard, 1991; *Itchy, Itchy Chicken Pox*, by Grace Maccarone, 1992; *Jim Hedgehog and the Lonesome Tower*, by Russell Hoban, 1992; *Yo! Hungry Wolf: A Nursery Rap*, by David Vozar, 1993; *Ho! Ho! Ho! The Complete Book of Christmas Words*, by Lynda Graham-Barber, 1993; *The Boy Who Counted Stars: Poems*, by David L. Harrison, 1994; *What's Black and White and Came to Visit?*, by Evan Levine, 1994; *M.C. Turtle and the Hip Hop Hare: A Nursery Rap*, by David Vozar, 1995; *Somebody Catch My Homework*, by David L. Harrison, 1995; *Bug Boy*, by Carol Sonenklar, 1997; *Snake Alley Band*, by Elizabeth

Nygaard, 1998; *Aunt Minnie McGranahan*, by Mary Skillings Prigger, 1999; *Promises*, by Elizabeth Winthrop, 2000.

SUGGESTED READING: *Contemporary Authors*, vol. 104, 1982; *Contemporary Authors*, New Revision Series, vol. 58, 1997; *Something About the Author*, vol. 32, 1983; vol. 90, 1997; *Something About the Author Autobiography Series*, vol. 25, 1998.

An autobiographical sketch of Betsy's husband, Ted Lewin, appeared in *Seventh Book of Junior Authors and Illustrators* (Wilson 1996).

"When I was growing up, I was free to choose anything I wanted to be. My father had been a skilled fighter, but that wasn't what he chose to be. He became the most experienced art handler at the Philadelphia Museum of Art, the one they turned to for hanging their most valuable paintings. He was very happy with his work, but when he was young no one told him what he should do when he grew up.

"My first few years in school gave many people the wrong impression. I always strove to be the best at what I did, even as a child, but in school what I wanted to do was make everyone stop and look at me. I had a great need to hold other people's undivided attention, but being a kid, the only way I knew how to do that was to act up, to make such a commotion that everyone would look up to see what was the matter, who was making all that fuss. I was so good at this that no teacher wanted me in their class, no one who was serious wanted me to sit next to them because I would disrupt the whole room, I would break through any concentration, I would steal all the attention for myself. I was uncontrollable, and it often landed me in the principal's office. Every other day my parents had to come to school and hear what their son had done to disturb others. As upset as my parents were, I was gloating over the situation, because I was stage center.

"When I look back now, I can see that what disturbed me so much was the deep frustration I felt about my sister coming along and being the center of attention in my family. Before her,

Courtesy of E. B. Lewis

E. B. Lewis

December 16, 1956–

everyone had doted on me—my parents, grandparents, all my parents' brothers and sisters were my exclusive audience, my support group. When she was born, I was just shoved in the background, and I felt I had to compete for their attention.

"When sixth grade came, we had to prepare ourselves to go into junior high school, and they held Careers Day in the auditorium. A panel of six professionals sat on the stage and spoke about their work, taking questions at the end. A hush went out over the room; it was a very serious moment to ponder what you would do for the rest of your life. My mother always said, 'Earl, you're such a great liar, you'd make a great lawyer someday.' I raised my hand, and everyone turned and they must have thought, 'Well, here we go: one of Earl's famous wisecracks coming right on cue.' I said that I wanted to be a lawyer when I grew up. The room exploded. Everyone laughed at the picture of me being a lawyer. I had convinced them I was the class clown, and I was so good at it, it was inconceivable for them to take anything I said seriously. Even the teachers had a good laugh. Deeply embarrassed, I just sat there feeling stunned. The joke really was on me this time because I wasn't kidding. I suddenly realized that I didn't want to be the funniest kid in the room. I wanted them to pay attention and pay respect to me. It was a turning point in my life.

"I suddenly realized that I didn't want to be the funniest kid in the room. I wanted them to pay attention and pay respect to me."

"Now I was ready for the next step in my life, and that came when my uncle, who was an artist by profession, quietly began taking me to the Temple University School Art League every Saturday, where I drew and painted. For the first time, I forgot about the other children in the room and became so immersed in my work, I lost track of time. I began to look forward to these sessions, where the competition for attention was carried on with lines and colors—marks that represented emotions, ideas, things around me. As the teachers introduced new media, I was putting down my experiences, my family, animals, the world around me and feeling freer and freer with a power that could do more than make people laugh. I could make people think. I could make them feel things I wanted them to think about. I began to understand what a great tool for education art was, and how to use it effectively. Naturally, I became an artist, an illustrator, and a teacher. But I believe it also helped me to be a better father and a more responsible person. I want to share my gift with the world, to help children realize the powers they have, how to unlock them, how to use them. God bless the child who controls his own mind. Wadud said that. He is my best friend, and he is an artist."

* * *

E. B. (Earl Bradley) Lewis is an artist, a teacher, and a graphic designer who began illustrating children's books in 1994. Born in Philadelphia, Pennsylvania, he received his degree from the Temple University Tyler School of Art in 1979 and went directly into teaching. Lewis is an accomplished watercolorist whose original artwork is part of distinguished collections and is exhibited and sold in galleries across the country, including the prestigious Rosenfeld Gallery in Philadelphia. In addition to illustrating children's books and book jackets, he teaches illustration at the University of the Arts in Philadelphia, is a member of the Society of Illustrators in New York City, and visits schools across the country making presentations to students, parents, and educators.

Lewis's masterful watercolor illustrations create a sense of setting and place that conveys the rich cultural context integral to the stories being told. "I like the strong human-interest stories," Lewis has said, "the kind that evoke emotion . . . stories that touch the heart." Lewis has won numerous honors, including two Coretta Scott King Honor Book awards for *The Bat Boy and His Violin* and *My Rows and Piles of Coins*. *The New King* was listed on New York Public Library's annual list, 100 Titles for Reading and Sharing. Both *Only a Pigeon* and *The New King* received awards from the African Studies Association, and *Only a Pigeon* won a Parents' Choice Gold Award in 1997. *Down the Road* was an ALA Notable Children's Book and *The New King* and *I Love My Hair* were named Notable Trade Books in the Field of Social Studies.

SELECTED WORKS ILLUSTRATED: *Fire on the Mountain*, by Jane Kurtz, 1994; *Big Boy*, by Tololwa M. Mollel, 1994; *The New King: A Madagascan Legend*, adapt. by Doreen Rappaport, 1995; *Down the Road*, by Alice Schertle, 1995; *The Magic Moonberry Jump Ropes*, by Dakari Hru, 1996; *Magid Fasts for Ramadan*, by Mary Mathews, 1996; *Creativity*, by John Steptoe, 1997; *Only a Pigeon*, by Jane Kurtz and Christopher Kurtz, 1997; *The Bat Boy and His Violin*, by Gavin Curtis, 1998; *I Love My Hair*, by Natasha Tarplay, 1998; *The Jazz of Our Street*, by Fatima Shaik, 1998; *The Magic Tree: A Folktale from Nigeria*, by T. Obinkaram Echewa, 1999; *My Rows and Piles of Coins*, by Tololwa M. Mollel, 1999; *Faraway Home*, by Jane Kurtz, 2000; *Dirt on Their Skirts*, by Doreen Rappaport, 2000.

SUGGESTED READING: Cummins, Julie, ed. *Children's Book Illustration and Design*, vol. 2, 1998; *Something About the Author*, vol. 93, 1997. Periodicals—"Only a Pigeon," *Book Links*, March 1998.

WEB SITE: *www.eblewis.com*

Courtesy of Tom Thompson

Megan Lloyd

November 5, 1958–

"I love to read about how other illustrators became illustrators. Many of them seem to have known they were destined to become illustrators from the time they were little. I can't say that's true for me. I didn't realize I wanted to illustrate children's books until I was in college studying something else! I never even thought of illustration as a career possibility until my mother, a kindergarten teacher, suggested I might like to combine my love of reading stories with my ability to draw and paint. She showed me some of the wonderful picture books she used with her students so I could see what was being done with picture books at that time. I remember thinking how exciting the picture books looked and that it would be wonderful to work with books 'for a living'! So, although I did like to draw and paint when I was growing up, it wasn't until I was nineteen that I decided to be an illustrator.

"At that time I was attending Pennsylvania State University. I felt I needed stronger art training, so I transferred to Parsons School of Design in New York. After graduation I landed a job at a publishing house in New York. It was a great opportunity for me to learn about publishing and especially about how a picture book is made.

"I also began showing my portfolio of drawings to different publishing companies in an attempt to get work as an illustrator. I took my portfolio to many, many publishers before I got very, very lucky. An editor at Harper & Row saw a little book called 'Chicken Tricks' in my portfolio. This was actually a book I had written and illustrated for a school homework assignment. The editor liked it and she gave me a contract to publish it. I was amazed! And *then* she even gave me a contract to illustrate *another* book!!!

"With two book contracts in hand I decided to leave my job in New York City. I wanted to work full-time on my first two books. I also wanted to be out in the country, not in a city. I have always loved farm animals, and I wanted to see cows and pigs, chickens and sheep when I looked around, not cars and buses and skyscrapers! So, in 1982, I returned to Pennsylvania.

"Since then I have been very fortunate. Editors have given me stories to illustrate and I am surrounded by farm animals. My husband and I live on a small farm, where we have a flock of

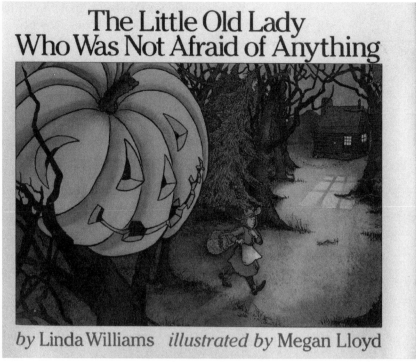

The Little Old Lady Who Was Not Afraid of Anything

by Linda Williams   *illustrated by* Megan Lloyd

Courtesy of HarperCollins Publishers

sheep, a wonderful milk cow named Fiona, her little calf Flannery, a flock of chickens, two great dogs, and three spunky cats. My day starts and ends with milking the cow (by hand, of course!) and feeding the sheep. Drawing, painting, and reading stories fill the time between morning and evening milkings, and I think I am very, very lucky!

"Many of the people, places, and animals around me wind up in my pictures. I have never been able to 'make up' pictures. I need to *see* what I want to draw. At times, this means I have to travel to see something, as I did when illustrating the book *Cactus Hotel*, by Brenda Guiberson. Tom (my husband) and I had to spend time in Arizona studying and photographing the saguaro cactus and other desert plants and animals in order for me to paint accurate pictures for the book.

"I enjoy the research I need to do in order to illustrate a story. Nonfiction books are particularly fun to illustrate because they demand that I put 'real' information in my pictures.

"Drawing, for me, is actually the least 'fun' part of illustrating a book. In fact, I often *hate* drawing because it can be quite a struggle for me to capture exactly what I want to capture on paper. Sometimes I'm lucky and the pictures flow easily—but many more times I have to try, and try, and try again to 'get it right.' I throw an awful lot of horrible pictures away. But as hard as drawing sometimes is, a good story makes it worthwhile.

Reading a story and 'seeing' all the different images an author's words create in my mind is so much fun that I'm willing to put up with the struggle and frustration of trying to get those images onto paper."

* * *

Megan Lloyd was born in Harrisburg, Pennsylvania, and attended Penn State University from 1976 to 1978. Transferring to Parsons School of Design in New York City, she earned her B.F.A. in 1981. She returned to Pennsylvania soon after graduation and married Tom Thompson in 1993. Lloyd is adept at illustrating both fiction and nonfiction books. Her very precise, detailed ink drawings and sometimes vivid, sometimes muted watercolors lend themselves to highlighting and explaining new concepts to readers, as in her Let's Read and Find Out About Science series and other nonfiction titles. In fiction Lloyd's illustrations can be spooky and scary or rollicking and humorous, depending on the type of story.

The Little Old Lady Who Was Not Afraid of Anything and *A Regular Flood of Mishap* were IRA/CBC Children's Choice books, and *How We Learned the Earth Was Round* and *Gingerbread Doll* were named Notable Children's Trade Books in the Field of Social Studies. *Cactus Hotel* won a Parent's Choice Picture Book Award. *Dance with Me*, a book of poems by Barbara Esbensen which Lloyd illustrated, won the NCTE Award for Excellence in Poetry in 1995. Both *Chirping Crickets* and *Lobster Boat* were cited as Outstanding Science Trade Books for Children.

Megan Lloyd lives with her husband on a farm near Carlisle, Pennsylvania. She spins yarn and makes felt from the wool of their own Cotswold and Shetland sheep, two rare breeds that they raise to help preserve genetic diversity in livestock. Lloyd also makes soap from various vegetable oils and surplus milk from their cow, Fiona, which she sells in small quantities under the brand name Cowdance.

SELECTED WORKS ILLUSTRATED: *Surprises*, by Lee Bennett Hopkins, 1984; *All Those Mothers at the Manger*, by Norma Farber, 1985; *The Little Old Lady Who Was Not Afraid of Anything*, by Linda Williams, 1986; *More Surprises*, by Lee Bennett Hopkins, 1987; *How We Learned the Earth Was Round*, by Patricia Lauber, 1990; *Cactus Hotel*, by Brenda Z. Guiberson, 1991; *Baba Yaga: A Russian Folktale*, by Eric Kimmel, 1991; *Look Out for Turtles!*, by Melvin Berger, 1992; *Lobster Boat*, by Brenda Z. Guiberson, 1993; *Gingerbread Doll*, by Susan Tews, 1993; *The Gingerbread Man*, by Eric Kimmel, 1993; *A Regular Flood of Mishap*, by Tom Birdseye, 1994; *Dance with Me*, by Barbara Juster

Esbensen, 1995; *Winter Wheat*, by Brenda Z. Guiberson, 1995; *What Color Is Camouflage?*, by Carolyn Otto, 1996; *Too Many Pumpkins*, by Linda White, 1996; *Chirping Crickets*, by Melvin Berger, 1998; *Seven at One Blow: A Tale from the Brothers Grimm*, by Eric Kimmel, 1998; *Pioneer Church*, by Carolyn Otto, 1999.

SUGGESTED READING: *Something About the Author*, vol. 77, 1994.

"I was a 'Navy brat' as a child, the son of an officer in the U.S. Navy. We moved every 1–3 years and lived all over the country—plus on the island of Puerto Rico. For a while, I wanted to become a career naval officer like my father. I also thought of becoming an archaeologist (I liked digging up things in the ground), an historian, and a pro baseball player. I never thought I would become a writer. Not until I was in college, anyway. In college, though I was studying history, I started to read poetry. I read the poems of the Beat poets: Allen Ginsberg, Gary Snyder, Jack Kerouac, and others. I also read the poems by the great Chilean poet Pablo Neruda and the Russian poet Yevgeny Yevtushenko. I even wrote Yevtushenko a letter. Reading these poets changed my life—they spoke directly to my heart. I started to write my own poems.

Courtesy Bhabti Smith

Jonathan London

March 11, 1947–

"And so when I completed my master's degree in Social Sciences I joined a dance company! But I continued to write poetry. Writing became my passion, and for the first time I dreamed of becoming a writer. If I didn't write at least one poem a day, I felt somehow incomplete. I sent my poems out and was published in over a hundred magazines and literary journals.

"I quit dancing after three years and spent most of ten years traveling around the world. I continued to write poems and started to write and publish short stories as well. I received almost no money for my writing—I wrote for the love of it. I remember well the first time I got paid for a poem. The *Malahat Review* at the University of Victoria sent me $10. I was so excited I took my wife out to a club for dinner and dancing. On my way there I got pulled over and fined for going 33 in a 25-mph speed zone. The next day at the bank I realized my $10 was in Canadian money. With the exchange rate and bank's fee I only received $4.80. Subtract the speeding ticket and the dinner, and my first paid poem cost me about $80! But do you think that stopped me from writing?

"My wife and I had kids late; I was thirty-six when my first son, Aaron, was born and thirty-nine when Sean was born. When they were little they asked me to tell them stories. Every night before bed I would read to them or tell them a story. If they liked a story, they'd say, 'Tell it again, Daddy.' One story—more like a lullaby—I told so many times that Aaron memorized it and would tell it to Sean. One day I thought, 'This would make a good picture book.' So I wrote it down and called it *The Owl Who Became the Moon*. I was reading *Winnie the Pooh* to the kids around this time and sent my story to the same publisher, E. P. Dutton. I didn't hear a word for several months. Then I got a call. They wanted to publish my book! I was so excited I walked around about thirteen inches above the ground.

"That call was it. I've been writing for children ever since. That was in 1989. That first story didn't come out as a book until 1993—after *Thirteen Moons on Turtle's Back*, which I co-authored with Joseph Bruchac, *The Lion Who Had Asthma* (for my son Sean, who has asthma), and *Froggy Gets Dressed*, which were all published in 1992.

"I've used all my travels and experience as a poet to write books I love to write and hope kids love to read. I couldn't ask for a better life."

> *"Writing became my passion . . . If I didn't write at least one poem a day, I felt somehow incomplete."*

*   *   *

Born on March 11, 1947, in Brooklyn, New York, son of Harry and Anne London, Jonathan London attended San Jose State University in California, receiving his B.A. in 1969 and M.A. in 1970. He married his second wife, a registered nurse named Maureen Weisenberger, in 1976, and they now have two children, Aaron and Sean. He received his K–12 teaching certificate in 1985 from Sonoma State University. Along with his poetry and writing he enjoys traveling, hiking, backpacking, kayaking, and cross-country skiing.

In 1979 London was awarded the Ina Coolbrith Circle Award for Poetry. In the field of children's literature, he has created texts that allow him to combine poetry, humor, insight into children's feelings, and a love of nature and the earth in varying ways. *Froggy Gets Dressed*, *The Owl Who Became the Moon*, *Into This Night We Are Rising*, and *Let's Go, Froggy!* were all main selections of the Children's Book of the Month Club. *Let's Go, Froggy!*, *Froggy Learns to Swim*, *Jackrabbit*, and *Baby Whale's Journey* were Junior Library Guild Selections. *Voices of the Wild* and all five Froggy titles have been cited as IRA/CBC Children's Choices, and both *Voices of the Wild* and *The Eyes of the Gray Wolf* were named Outstanding Science Trade Books for Children. *Thirteen Moons on Turtle's Back* and *Hip Cat* were chosen as *Reading Rainbow* books. *Ali, Child of the Desert* won a Parents' Choice Gold Award and was named a Notable Children's Trade Book in the Field of Social Studies, as was *The Village Basket Weaver*. *The Sugaring-off Party*, *Hurricane!*, *Like Butter on Pancakes*, and *Red Wolf Country* were all listed by *School Library Journal* as Best Books of the Year. London's novel *Where's Home?* was selected for New York Public Library's list, Best Books for the Teen Age.

Jonathan London lives with his family in Graton, California.

SELECTED WORKS: *Thirteen Moons on Turtle's Back: A Native American Year of Moons*, with Joseph Bruchac, illus. by Thomas Locker, 1992; *Froggy Gets Dressed*, illus. by Frank Remkiewicz, 1992; *The Lion Who Had Asthma*, illus. by Nadine Bernard Westcott, 1992; *Into This Night We Are Rising*, illus. by G. Brian Karas, 1993; *The Eyes of the Gray Wolf*, illus. by Jon Van Zyles, 1993; *Hip Cat*, illus. by Woodleigh Hubbard, 1993; *The Owl Who Became the Moon*, illus. by Ted Rand, 1993; *Fire Race*, illus. by Sylvia Long, 1993; *Voices of the Wild*, illus. by Wayne McCloughlin, 1993; *Let's Go, Froggy!* illus. by Frank Remkiewicz, 1994; *Where's Home?*, 1995; *Froggy Learns to Swim*, illus by Frank Remkiewicz, 1995; *Like Butter on Pancakes*, illus. by G. Brian Karas, 1995; *The Sugaring-off Party*, illus by Giles Pelletier, 1995; *Jackrabbit*, illus. by Deborah Kogan Ray, 1996; *Red Wolf Country*, illus. by Daniel San Souci, 1996; *Froggy Goes to School*, illus. by Frank Remkiewicz, 1996; *What Newt Could Do for Turtle*, illus. by Louise Voce, 1996; *The Village Basket Weaver*, illus. by George Crespo, 1996; *Ali, Child of the Desert*, illus. by Ted Lewin, 1997; *Let the Lynx Come In*, illus. by Patrick Benson, 1997; *Puddles*, illus. by G. Brian Karas, 1997; *At the Edge of the Forest*, illus. by Barbara Firth, 1998; *Froggy's First Kiss*, illus. by Frank Remkiewicz, 1998; *Dream Weaver*, illus. by Rocco Baviera, 1998; *Hurricane!*, illus. by Henri Sorensen, 1999; *Wiggle Waggle*, illus. by Michael Rex, 1999; *Froggy Plays Soccer*, illus. by Frank Remkiewicz, 1999; *Froggy's Halloween*, illus. by Frank Remkiewicz, 1999; *Shawn and Keeper and the Birthday Party*, illus. by Renee Williams-Andriani, 1999.

SUGGESTED READING: London, Jonathan. *Tell Me a Story*, 1998; *Something About the Author*, vol. 74, 1993. Periodicals— "Thirteen Moons on Turtle's Back: Bruchac, London, and Locker Connect," *School Library Media Activities Monthly*, December 1992.

Courtesy of Len Bordeaux

Nancy Luenn

December 28, 1954–

"When I was growing up in Los Angeles, I didn't know that I was going to be a writer. I did know I liked books. My family didn't have a television, so my mother read aloud to us each evening. Our house was full of books. There were floor-to-ceiling bookshelves in our living room and more books in the hall. Every few weeks we went to the library to check out even more. By the time I was eleven we had six library cards and could check out sixty books at a time. Usually we did!

"I was the oldest of six children. We often fought and argued, but we also played a lot of games together. Not computer games or video games but games where we made up the stories. Inside the house, we created worlds for our toys to inhabit—all over the living room floor. Outside, we had a big, untidy backyard where we could build forts and dig holes. We spied on the neighborhood kids from our treehouse and rowed across our small pond in a boat called Pooh.

"In summer we went camping. Both of my parents taught college. During their vacations we headed to the mountains or the desert. They shared their enthusiasm and knowledge of nature—teaching us the names of birds, plants, and animals. Books of mine like *Otter Play* and *Squish! A Wetland Walk* are rooted in those camping trips.

"All of this may sound like fun, but I was quite shy. I felt awkward at school, and I hated parties. Although I always had a few good friends, I spent a lot of time by myself: reading, drawing, and writing. In high school I started a journal. I wrote poems and romantic descriptions of people and places. But I still didn't think about being a writer.

"I thought about being an artist. When I was growing up, I loved to draw. I drew pictures of horses, rock stars and castles. In 1970, I started embroidering a tapestry of a unicorn in the woods. Years later, this image evolved into an unpublished story, which changed and evolved into two of my books: *Nessa's Fish* and *Nessa's Story*.

"After high school I headed north to study at Evergreen State College. I took classes in art and outdoor education. My friends were kayakers and climbers. We ran whitewater rivers; they taught me to ski. Few people realized that I was a bookworm.

"But I still was. One summer, I went to work for the U.S. Forest Service in southern Oregon. I didn't have any friends there, so I went to the library to find some familiar companions. While rereading some of my favorite picture books and fantasy novels, I discovered I had read all of the fantasy in the Medford Library. 'Somebody should write some more,' I thought. 'Maybe I will.' I started writing down ideas and sending out stories. Three years and many rejection letters later, *The Ugly Princess* was accepted.

"That was twenty years ago. I've written so many stories since then. Some have been published; a lot of them haven't. Writing is hard work. Not every idea grows into a story. And not every book succeeds in the market. For someone who loves ideas, art, and books, this is painful. But recently, I've realized I've accomplished a goal I've held in my heart since I was in my teens. With the help of some wonderful illustrators, editors, art directors, and designers, I've created something of beauty that may be remembered. I've created some beautiful books."

* * *

Born in Pasadena, California, Nancy Luenn is the daughter of Gilbert and Elizabeth Jones, both college professors. She graduated from Evergreen State College in 1978 and first worked as a bookkeeper/manager at White Water Sports in Seattle, Washington. Luenn also held jobs as a conservation coordinator and an educational assistant before deciding to combine work as a freelance writer with visits to schools and conferences, where she introduces the writing process as well as her own books. She is a member of the Yakima Valley Audubon Society, the Yakima Greenway Foundation, and the Cowiche Canyon Conservancy, as well as the Society of Children's Book Writers and Illustrators.

Starting with her first book, *The Ugly Princess*, a modern fairy tale with a thoroughly practical ending, Luenn has combined her interest in fantasy, myth, and mythic themes with a concern about environmental issues. *The Dragon Kite* won a 1982 Parents' Choice Award and received an American Institute of Graphic Arts award. *Arctic Unicorn* received a Grand Prize from the 1982 Pacific Northwest Writers Conference contest. *Nessa's Fish* won a Parents' Choice Award and was named a Notable Children's Trade Book in the Field of Social Studies; *Nessa's Story* was listed in Bank Street College's Children's Books of the Year. *Squish! A Wetland Walk* was voted an Outstanding Science Trade Book for Children and won a Washington Governor's Writers Award. *Voice of Youth Advocates* cited Luenn's young adult novel, *Goldclimbers*, on its Best Science Fiction, Fantasy, and Horror list. *A Gift for Abuelita* was named a 1999 Notable Book for a Global Society and a Notable Trade Book in the Field of Social Studies, and was selected as a commended

"I discovered I had read all of the fantasy in the Medford Library. 'Somebody should write some more,' I thought. 'Maybe I will.'"

title for the 1998 Américas Award for Children's and Young Adult Literature.

SELECTED WORKS WRITTEN: *The Ugly Princess*, illus. by David Wiesner, 1981; *The Dragon Kite,* illus. by Michael Hague, 1982; *Arctic Unicorn*, 1986; *Unicorn Crossing*, illus. by Peter Hanson, 1987; *Nessa's Fish*, illus. by Neil Waldman, 1990; *Goldclimbers*, 1991; *Mother Earth,* illus. by Neil Waldman, 1992; *Song for the Ancient Forest*, illus. by Jill Kastner, 1993; *Nessa's Story*, illus. by Neil Waldman, 1994; *Squish! A Wetland Walk*, illus. by Ronald Himler, 1994; *The Miser on the Mountain*, illus. by Pierr Morgan, 1997; *A Gift for Abuelita / Un Regalo para Abuelita: Celebrating the Day of the Dead*, 1998; *Otter Play,* illus. by Anna Vojtech, 1998; *Celebrations of Light: A Year of Holidays Around the World*, 1998.

SELECTED WORKS EDITED: *A Horse's Tale: Ten Adventures in One Hundred Years*, illus. by Connie J. Pope, 1989.

SUGGESTED READING: *Contemporary Authors*, vol. 116, 1986; *Contemporary Authors,* New Revision Series, vol. 39, 1992; *Something About the Author*, vol. 51, 1988; vol. 79, 1995.

P. J. Lynch

March 2, 1962–

"As a little boy, I was always drawing. I remember my mother telling me how wonderful my pictures were; she was telling my brothers and sister that their drawings were great too, but somehow I took her encouragement to heart, and I kept drawing and drawing. When I was a little older, I knew that I wanted to be an artist—not an illustrator particularly, but an artist like Leonardo da Vinci or Rembrandt. But on arriving at Art College I was profoundly disappointed by what was going on in the area of 'Fine Art.' At that time, figurative art was very much discouraged. So I got myself into an illustration course where the emphasis was on developing sound technique and constantly improving draftsmanship through life-drawing classes.

"One of the tutors at Brighton College of Art was Raymond Briggs (author/illustrator of *The Snowman*). His work and his huge success were a great inspiration to us, and several of the students chose to specialize in the field of children's books. On leaving college, though, it wasn't easy to get commissions, and for a time I was pretty convincing in the role of the penniless artist.

"Luckily, an editor named Enid Fairhead saw my work and decided to risk commissioning me to illustrate a book of fairy tales, *A Bag of Moonshine*, by Alan Garner. The book was to be illustrated mostly with ink line drawings, interspersed with a number of color plates, a rather old-fashioned format which suited me very well, given my fondness for the work of Arthur

Rackham and Edmund Dulac. I won the Mother Goose Award for my work on that book. The prize was a real goose egg, coated with copper and gold, which is still one of my most valued possessions. It was a wonderful start to my career in children's books.

"Since then I have illustrated an average of one book each year. The first few months of each project are spent researching the period, costumes, and settings. When it is possible I will visit the appropriate locations for the story. It is extremely important for me to achieve a kind of authenticity in each book, whether it be a medieval fantasy like *East o' the Sun and West o' the Moon* or a story set in the more recent past, such as *When Jessie Came Across the Sea*. My aim is always to bring the story to life for the reader. To this end I search long and hard for the right people to model as my characters and I take hundreds of photographs of them acting their particular roles. Some of these photographs are then used as reference when I embark on my paintings. The painting part of the process takes about nine months per book.

"I owe a great debt of gratitude to Susan Wojciechowski, as it was Susan who suggested I should illustrate her beautiful story, *The Christmas Miracle of Jonathan Toomey*. Previously my work had been very much in the realm of fantasy and fairy tale, and illustrating a story which is essentially an intimate drama about personalities and relationships was a considerable departure for me. Now I feel that the picture-book format is ideal for tackling the most complex issues and difficult subjects in a way that is accessible to children and adults alike.

"I have been extremely fortunate in the wonderful writers I have worked with so far, and I can only hope that in the future I will continue to have such inspirational stories to illustrate."

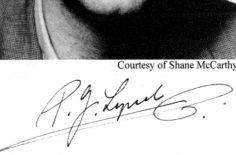

Courtesy of Shane McCarthy

*   *   *

Patrick James Lynch's vibrant illustrations have been delighting audiences on both sides of the Atlantic since the publication of *A Bag of Moonshine* in 1986. Born in Belfast, Ireland, the youngest of five children, he attended Brighton College of Art in England, graduating with a B.A. Honors degree in 1984. His

Courtesy of Candlewick Press

illustrations at first were mostly for folk tale collections and picture book fantasy stories. His illustrated edition of E. Nesbit's nineteenth-century fantasy, *Melisande*, was cited as an ALA Notable Children's Book in 1990. With the publication of *The Christmas Miracle of Jonathan Toomey*, Lynch demonstrated that he could depict a poignant realistic story with equal success, winning the Kate Greenaway Medal in 1995. In the United States, *The Christmas Miracle of Jonathan Toomey* was named to the ALA Notable Children's Books list and received a Christopher Award in 1996. *When Jessie Came Across the Sea*, the story of a young girl emigrating to the United States from Ireland, won a Christopher Award, was an ABBY Honor Book, and won a second Kate Greenaway Medal for the illustrator. *Jessie* was also cited as a Notable Children's Trade Book in the Field of Social Studies in 1998. Whether illustrating a fairy tale or a realistic story, P. J. Lynch's pictures illuminate character and setting with strong expression and luminous color.

In addition to his book illustration, Lynch was honored to be asked to design stamps for the Irish Post Office. He has done three sets of stamps: one on mythological subjects, one on Christmas themes, and a third to mark the centenary of Oscar Wilde in 2000. He has also worked on designs for an animated film about the legendary Irish hero Finn MacCool. In 1991, after eleven years in England, the artist returned to his home country.

He presently lives and works in Dublin, which he calls "possibly the liveliest city in Europe."

SELECTED WORKS ILLUSTRATED: *A Bag of Moonshine*, by Alan Garner, 1986; *Raggy Taggy Toys*, by Joyce Dunbar, 1988; *Melisande*, by E. Nesbit, 1989; *Fairy Tales of Ireland*, by W. B. Yeats, 1990; *Stories for Children*, by Oscar Wilde, 1990; *East o' the Sun and West o' the Moon*, by George Dasent, 1991; *The Steadfast Tin Soldier*, by H. C. Andersen, 1991; *The Candlewick Book of Fairy Tales*, ed. by Sarah Hayes, 1993; *The Snow Queen*, by Hans Christian Andersen, 1993; *Catkin*, by Antonia Barber, 1994; *The Christmas Miracle of Jonathan Toomey*, by Susan Wojciechowski, 1995; *The King of Ireland's Son*, by Brendan Behan, 1996; *When Jessie Came Across the Sea*, by Amy Hest, 1997; *Grandad's Prayers of the Earth*, by Douglas Wood, 1999.

SUGGESTED READING: *Something About the Author*, vol. 79, 1995. Periodicals—*Times Educational Supplement*, July 19, 1996.

E-MAIL: *peeejaay@tinet.ie*

Roger Lea MacBride

August 6, 1929–March 5, 1995

Roger Lea MacBride was born in New Rochelle, New York. He attended Phillips Exeter Academy in New Hampshire, Princeton University, from which he graduated with an A.B. in 1951, and Harvard University, where he received a law degree in 1954. During 1954–1955 he was a Fulbright Scholar.

It was while he was a student at Exeter that the sixteen-year-old MacBride first met Rose Wilder Lane, an established journalist and novelist, and "the person . . . who influenced me more than any other." He met her through his father, an editor at *Reader's Digest*, who was at the time condensing Lane's novel *Let the Hurricane Roar*. Much taken by her personality and her fascinating stories, MacBride continued to correspond with Rose Wilder Lane throughout his school years and beyond, visiting, doing chores, and listening to a wealth of stories of her youth. There was a 42-year age difference between the two, and they came to regard themselves as "honorary" grandmother and grandson.

As a young lawyer, MacBride became the agent and attorney for Lane. When her famous mother, Laura Ingalls Wilder, died in 1957, MacBride began to handle business affairs for the *Little House* books and became involved with many of the Wilder museums and foundations devoted to preserving the family legacy, eventually serving on the board of directors of the Laura Ingalls Wilder Home Association.

After Rose Wilder Lane's death in 1968, Roger Lea MacBride was named the executor of both the Wilder and Lane estates and controlled their literary properties. He became closely involved with ensuring that later developments remained authentic and true to both Wilder's and Lane's voices. He discovered the manuscript for the final chapter in Laura Ingalls Wilder's *Little House* series and developed it into a book entitled *The First Four Years*. He edited letters Wilder had written to her husband, Almanzo, during a visit with Rose and published them in the book *West from Home: Letters of Laura Ingalls Wilder, San Francisco 1915*. He also published a collection of Lane's letters, *The Lady and the Tycoon: The Best of Letters Between Rose Wilder Lane and Jasper Crane*, as well as a biography, *Rose Wilder Lane: Her Story*.

MacBride was involved in the launching of the *Little House on the Prairie* television series, begun in 1974, but eventually disassociated himself from the series, unhappy about liberties taken with Wilder's life and her stories. He also worked on the television miniseries *Young Pioneers*, based on Lane's novel *Let the Hurricane Roar*.

Courtesy of HarperCollins

In 1993, in response to children's overwhelming interest in learning more about Laura Ingalls Wilder and her family, MacBride penned the first of the well-received *Rocky Ridge* series, based on extensive research and recollection of the stories Rose Wilder Lane had shared with him about her childhood. He had completed three more books in the series and prepared notes and research materials for another four when he died of a heart attack at age sixty-five. His daughter, Abigail MacBride Allen, has now seen these through to completion.

In addition to his activities involving the Wilder family, MacBride worked as an attorney in New York, Vermont, and Virginia. Interested in politics, he served as a Vermont state representative from 1963 to 1965 and was the Libertarian Party candidate for president in 1976, receiving over 173,000 votes in 32 states. He also wrote books for adults, including *The American Electoral College* and *A New Dawn for America: The Libertarian Challenge*. However, he is best known and most remembered as the heir and protector of the beloved stories of Laura Ingalls Wilder and her daughter.

SELECTED WORKS WRITTEN: *Little House on Rocky Ridge*, illus. by David Gilleece, 1993; *Little Farm in the Ozarks*, illus. by David Gilleece, 1993; *In the Land of the Big Red Apple*, illus. by David Gilleece, 1995; *On the Other Side of the Hill*, illus.

by David Gilleece, 1995; *Little Town in the Ozarks*, illus. by David Gilleece, 1996; *New Dawn on Rocky Ridge*, illus. by David Gilleece, 1997; *On the Banks of the Bayou*, illus. by Dan Andreason, 1998; *Bachelor Girl*, illus. by Dan Andreason, 1999.

SELECTED WORKS EDITED: *The First Four Years*, by Laura Ingalls Wilder, 1971; *West from Home: Letters of Laura Ingalls Wilder, San Francisco 1915*, 1974.

SELECTED WORKS FOR ADULTS: *The Lady and the Tycoon: The Best of Letters Between Rose Wilder Lane and Jasper Crane*, 1972; *A New Dawn for America: The Libertarian Challenge*, 1976; *Rose Wilder Lane: Her Story*, 1978.

SUGGESTED READING: *Contemporary Authors*, vol. 147, 1995; *Contemporary Authors*, First Revision Series, vol. 81–84, 1979; *Something About the Author*, vol. 85, 1996. Periodicals—*New York Times*, March 8, 1995; *Publishers Weekly*, August 15, 1994; March 20, 1995; October 16, 1995.

Courtesy of HarperCollins Publishers

Amy MacDonald

June 14, 1951–

"When I was a child, I was constantly in trouble for being a bookworm. I remember being teased by my grandfather for reading books while I brushed my teeth. At school, I discovered how to keep an open book under my lift-top desk lid and read during math class.

"I was never without a book. As one of four children, all one year apart, I also learned to read in any environment, no matter how noisy. Books were my refuge.

"I grew up in a quiet, middle-class town north of Boston. My father was a pediatrician, my mother a full-time mom who went back to school and became a psychologist at age fifty. I am convinced that our family connection to books and love of reading is what made me into a children's author. My mother's family grew up next door to F. Scott Fitzgerald in St. Paul, and her family is immortalized in one of his books. My great aunt Susan Lesley is both the star of that classic children's book, *The Peterkin Papers* (she's the model for the wise Lady from Philadelphia), and had the book dedicated to her by author Lucretia Mott Hale, her friend.

"My mother read to us at the dinner table—perhaps a smart ploy to keep the four of us quiet, perhaps because she loved books. *Hurry Home, Candy. The Wheel on the School.* The E. Nesbit books. *The Peterkin Papers.* All the classics.

"I don't remember writing a great deal in school. I was not one of those children whom I meet today—and am amazed by—who write constantly. I probably didn't start until middle school, and only began writing for pleasure in high school. In college, at the University of Pennsylvania, I took writing classes with Jerre Mangione and John Edgar Wideman—both excellent teachers. I also took a course with Philip Roth, much to Mr. Roth's suprise. I sneaked my way into that class. I hadn't been at school when they were taking registrations for it (I was being a ski bum in Aspen), and students were supposed to submit writing samples and get approval by Mr. Roth to get into the class. Instead, when I went into the English office one day, I noticed a pile of pre-stamped registration cards on a counter and on an impulse stole one and filled it in for his class. It was a wonderful class, but Roth never could quite figure out who I was or how I got there.

"I was at college during the freewheeling sixties, and we invented something called the Free University at Penn in those days: it consisted of students teaching any course they wanted, to anyone who bothered to come. As a freshman, I offered to teach my favorite subject: children's literature. The course was memorable only for the fact that it showed how longstanding my obsession with children's books was.

"I think, in fact, I never outgrew children's books, but it wasn't until I was thrty-five, and a mother, that I stumbled upon the idea of writing for children. I had long been working as a jounalist and freelance writer. I had made stabs at writing fiction for adults but never had the discipline to finish anything.

"Then one day I was standing by the edge of a pond in New Hampshire, a pond where I spent summers as a child at our family camp. I was showing my eighteen-month-old son Alexander how the pond had an echo. We stood there yelling 'Hello' for a bit, and then he turned to me and asked, 'Mom, what *is* an echo?' Instead of trying to explain it to him (what two-year-old understands the laws of acoustics?), I went up to our little cabin, sat

Courtesy of T. Urquhart

down, and forty-five minutes later had written a story that I felt would enlighten him about echoes.

"Thus was *Little Beaver and the Echo* born—destined to sell half a million copies in over twenty languages.

"More important: I had finally found a genre in which it was impossible not to finish a project!"

* * *

Born in Beverly, Massachusetts, Amy MacDonald received her B.A. from the University of Pennsylvania in 1973. She has been employed in a number of positions related to writing and publishing. She worked as an editor of the *Harvard Post* and *Highwire Magazine* and as a copy editor at the Cambridge University Press in England. As a freelance journalist, she has been published in national and international magazines, from *Europ* to the *New Yorker*. She has also taught writing at Harvard University, the Stonecoast Writers Conference, and the University of Maine at Farmington.

Published by the Harvard Common Press under the pseudonym Del Tremens, MacDonald's first book, *A Very Young Housewife*, was an adult parody of a children's book. Her successive books have all been written specifically for a young audience. *Little Beaver and the Echo* appeared on the *Horn Book* Fanfare list and was cited as one of the year's top ten children's books by both the *New York Times* and *Parents* magazine. It won the Silver Stylus Award in the Netherlands and was shortlisted for Great Britain's Children's Book Award and the Kate Greenaway Medal. *Rachel Fister's Blister* was another *Horn Book* Fanfare selection, while a second book about the same characters, *Cousin Ruth's Tooth*, was an American Booksellers Association Pick of the Lists and an IRA/CBC Children's Choice. MacDonald's books have been published in over twenty languages.

Amy MacDonald is married to Thomas Urquhart, a conservationist, and lives with her husband and three children in Falmouth, Maine, where she is active in theater and environmental groups and is president of the Maine Writers and Publishers Alliance. She conducts workshops in schools across the eastern seaboard and has developed teacher training workshops on writing for the John F. Kennedy Center for the Performing Arts in Washington, D.C.

"I remember being teased by my grandfather for reading books while I brushed my teeth."

SELECTED WORKS: *Little Beaver and the Echo*, illus. by Sarah Fox-Davies, 1990; *Rachel Fister's Blister*, illus. by Marjorie Priceman, 1990; *Let's Do It*, illus. by Maureen Roffey, 1991; *Let's Make a Noise*, illus. by Maureen Roffey, 1991; *Let's Play*, illus. by Maureen Roffey, 1992; *Let's Try*, illus. by Maureen Roffey, 1992; *Let's Go*, illus. by Maureen Roffey, 1994; *Let's Pretend*, illus. by Maureen Roffey, 1994; *No More*

Nice, illus. by Cat Bowman Smith, 1996; *Cousin Ruth's Tooth*, illus. by Marjorie Priceman, 1996; *The Spider Who Created the World*, illus. by G. Brian Karas, 1996.

SUGGESTED READING: *Contemporary Authors*, vol. 135, 1992; *Something About the Author*, vol. 76, 1994.

Courtesy of Andy Newman

Gregory Maguire

June 9, 1954–

"When I was a kid in Albany, New York, I didn't play with computer games because there weren't any yet. Nobody had a computer at home. Our family had two kinds of things to play with:

1. Creative things: Crayons, paper, glue, blunt scissors. (Not to mention the hundreds of library books we read for inspiration.)
2. Friendly things: Each other. (There were seven kids in my family.)

"I liked to organize the friendly things with the creative things. I liked to boss my brothers and sisters around in making stuff up. We made newspapers. We produced a newspaper called 'The Maguire Daily.' The first two issues came out a month apart. (There wasn't a third.) We put on concerts and plays. Once we smeared my baby brother Joe with ketchup so he could play a baby killed by collapsing buildings in a drama called 'The Spectacular San Francisco Earthquake Disaster Catastrophe.' (Joe performed the role with gusto, except he cried when ketchup got in his eyes, which dead babies can't actually do.)

"We produced a movie called 'Passion, Pride, and a Place to Pray.' It wasn't a real movie, just a series of still photographs we noisily shot at the Woolworth's Five and Dime, in the booth where, for a quarter, you could pose for a strip of four tiny photos. (We were cordially invited by the staff of Woolworth's never to visit again.) And we made books, or I did, anyway. Since I loved to read, making books seemed a natural hobby. I wrote my first stories when I was about six. I drew pictures for them too, and loved doing pictures. (Pictures for books are like these off-hand remarks hunching inside their parentheses.)

"I wrote songs and poetry, learned to paint in watercolors and to draw with pen and ink. When I was in high school I had an idea for a story about a boy who meets a perfect identical twin. I didn't know the word *clone* then, but I suppose I was thinking of a clone. But what if your clone was a different age than you? Would you actually even recognize him? Without knowing it, I was hatching the idea for my first book for children, *The Lightning Time*. In the end, however, it wasn't the main character who was 'split' or 'cloned,' but his grandmother.

"I sold my first book when I had been out of college for a year, and I've continued to write for children ever since. I've done about ten novels for children so far, and a couple for adults. There are a few picture books as well. I'm middle-aged as I write this; my hair is a little gray at the sides, and I wear bifocals. But I still like two things:

1. Creative things: Computer keyboards and printers, a piano, a set of paints. (And other people's creative work: movies, plays, music, and books, books, books.)
2. Friendly things: My dear friends and my family. (You may never get more brothers and sisters, but you can always make more friends. And I always do. One of the ways I make friends is by writing books. I hope, in a distant way, even if you read this long after I'm dead and buried, that you're a kind of friend of mine.) (I also still like parentheses.)"

Courtesy of Clarion Books

Growing up in a large, blended family that encouraged learning and creativity, Gregory Maguire wrote his first book, *The Lightning Time*, while still a junior at the State University of New York at Albany. By the time he received his M.A. from Simmons College and a Ph.D. in children's literature from Tufts University, he was an established author with many notable books to his credit. *The Daughter of the Moon* was named to the New York Public Library's list, 100 Titles for Reading and Sharing. *The Dream Stealer*, a fantasy with its roots in Russian folklore, received a Children's Books of the Year citation from the Child Study Children's Books Committee and a Teacher's Choice Award from the National Council of Teachers of English. *I Feel like the Morning Star*, a futuristic novel, was an ALA Best Book for Young Adults. The author received another Children's Books of the Year citation in 1994, for his novel *Missing Sisters*, and his comic farce, *Seven Spiders Spinning*, was named an ALA Notable Children's Book. *The Good Liar* was named a *Booklist* Editors' Choice and selected as a Junior Library Guild book. Maguire has also written *Wicked*, an adult novel about the witch from *The Wizard of Oz*.

Most of Maguire's professional accomplishments are related to literature and education. Just out of college he returned to his own Catholic grade school as an English teacher. He has also taught and served as associate director at the Simmons College Center for the Study of Children's Literature and has been the director of Children's Literature New England. He has lectured widely on writing and children's books, both in the United States and in Great Britain, and has contributed book reviews to the *Horn Book*, *School Library Journal*, and the *New York Times Book Review*. Maguire lives in Concord, Massachusetts, with the painter Andy Newman and their son, Luke.

SELECTED WORKS: *The Lightning Time*, 1978; *The Daughter of the Moon*, 1980; *Lights on the Lake*, 1981; *The Dream Stealer*, 1983; *The Peace and Quiet Diner*, illus. by David Perry; 1988; *I Feel like the Morning Star*, 1989; *Missing Sisters*, 1994; *Seven Spiders Spinning*, 1994; *Oasis*, 1996; *Six Haunted Hairdos*, 1997; *Five Alien Elves*, 1998; *The Good Liar*, 1999; *Crabby Cratchitt*, illus. by Andrew Glass, 2000.

SELECTED WORKS FOR ADULTS: *Innocence and Experience: Essays and Conversations on Children's Literature*, ed. and comp. with Barbara Harrison, 1987; *Wicked: The Life and Times of the Wicked Witch of the West*, illus. by Douglas Smith, 1995; *Origins of Story: On Writing for Children*, ed. and comp. with Barbara Harrison, 1999; *Confessions of an Ugly Stepsister*, 1999.

SUGGESTED READING: *Authors and Artists for Young Adults*, vol. 22, 1997; *Contemporary Authors*, New Revision Series, vol. 53, 1997; Pendergast, Sara, ed. *St. James Guide to Children's Writers*, 5th ed., 1999; *Something About the Author*, vol. 28, 1982, vol. 84, 1996; *Something About the Author Autobiography Series*, vol. 22, 1996. Periodicals—*Wilson Library Bulletin*, December 1989.

"I was born in Chicago, Illinois, into a huge family; I have five brothers and sisters, and for the first ten years of my life I shared a bed with a younger sister. My father owned a used furniture store, and almost everything in our house was secondhand. We even had a 'used' bird, a parakeet named Burpy, who came with a house full of furniture that my father bought.

"I was an active kid, always outside. I loved running and getting dirty, and playing hide-and-seek and hopscotch, and roller-skating. I owned only one book, a Little Golden Book by Eloise Wilkins. I learned to read in first grade, with *Fun with Dick and Jane*. I especially remember how enchanted I was with the shape and sound of the word *cooky*. Today, I have a cat named Cooky and I love to say her name over and over.

"I graduated from Chicago Teachers College and came to New York City six months later. I lived in a wonderful Quaker boardinghouse and there I met Brinton Turkle, the Quaker author-illustrator of *Obadiah the Bold*, who introduced me to Ezra Jack Keats—an event that changed my life.

"Ezra and I became close friends, and when his editor at Harper & Row needed a new secretary, Ezra recommended me. I had no idea that I was stepping into a legendary publishing department! My boss was Ursula Nordstrom, editor of *Goodnight Moon*, *Charlotte's Web*, and *Where the Wild Things Are*, and my immediate supervisor was Charlotte Zolotow. One day after I'd worked at Harper & Row for about four years, I asked Charlotte what she wanted for Christmas. She said, 'Fran, write me a book.' I protested, 'No, I'm not a writer!' She insisted that I was, and so I went home and I wrote a story for her, called 'Beach Day.' Charlotte loved it, but Ursula told me, 'Fran, you can do better.' And she gave my story back to me.

I was heartbroken, and I thought, 'That's the only idea I'll ever have. I'll never write another story.' But six months later I wrote 'Baby,' which became my first book. *Baby* was translated into French, German, Swedish, Danish, Portuguese, Dutch, Norwegian, and Japanese. I get so much pleasure seeing these books lined up on my shelf! When it was published in paperback, *Baby* became *Baby Come Out!* I thought the title was livelier.

Courtesy of Fran Manushkin

Fran Manushkin

November 2, 1942–

"Although my family celebrated most of the Jewish holidays, I don't remember reading any books about them when I was a child. In the late 1980s, when I began to explore my Judaism more deeply, I wrote my first story with a Jewish holiday setting, *Latkes and Applesauce*. I followed this with *The Matzah That Papa Brought Home: A Passover Story*; *Starlight and Candles: The Joys of the Sabbath*; and *Miriam's Cup: A Passover Story*.

"When I was a child, I was never told that girls could excel at anything, let alone write a book that thousands of people would enjoy. That's why it is so important to me to talk to as many children as I can, telling them that they, too, have the power to write, to paint, to achieve their dreams. I wish someone had told this to me when I was six, seven, or eight!

"I live in New York City, on the third floor of an apartment house overlooking a courtyard with trees. My windowsills have flower pots on them, and believe it or not, it's quiet and peaceful and I'm often awakened in the morning by the songs of house finches, not honking cars. I still read like a maniac, and my apartment is filled with floor-to-ceiling bookcases. I own zillions of books, something I could never have imagined was possible as a child.

"I get ideas for books all the time: when I'm in the bathtub or gazing out a train window, or daydreaming. (Daydreaming is very serious work!) The secret to good writing is to write what you are excited about—then the book will be alive."

The Matzah That Papa Brought Home

by FRAN MANUSHKIN

Illustrated by NED BITTINGER

Courtesy of Scholastic, Inc.

* * *

Fran Manushkin attended the University of Illinois, Roosevelt University, and received her B.A. from Chicago Teachers College in 1964. She briefly taught elementary school before moving to New York to begin a career in publishing—first as a secretary, then as an editor, and finally as a full-time writer of children's books. Entertaining and heartwarming, Manushkin's books about religious holidays highlight the simple joys of family and community in both Jewish and Christian celebrations. Many of her books, including the novels in her Angel Corner series, illustrate that girls can be anything they want. She is a member of PEN, the Author's League of America, and the National Audubon Society.

The Matzah That Papa Brought Home was cited as an ALA Notable Children's Book and an American Booksellers Association Pick of the Lists. *Miriam's Cup* was a Children's Book of the Month Club selection, was selected by *Booklist* as one of the Top Ten Religious Books for Youth, and was cited as a Notable Trade Book in the Field of Social Studies.

SELECTED WORKS: *Baby*, illus. by Ronald Himler, 1972 (*Baby Come Out*, 1984); *Swinging and Swinging*, illus. by Thomas DiGrazia, 1976; *The Perfect Christmas Picture*, illus. by Karen A. Weinhaus, 1980; *Ketchup, Catch Up!*, illus. by Julie Durrell, 1987; *Latkes and Applesauce*, illus. by Robin Spowart, 1990; *The Best Toy of All*, illus. by Robin Ballard, 1992; *My Christmas Safari*, illus. by R. W. Alley, 1993; *Peeping and Sleeping*, illus. by Jennifer Plecas, 1994; *The Matzah That Papa Brought Home*, illus. by Ned Bittinger, 1995; *Rachel, Meet Your Angel*, 1995; *Starlight and Candles: The Joys of the Sabbath*, illus. by Jacqueline Chwast, 1995; *Miriam's Cup: A Passover Story*, illus. by Bob Dacey, 1998.

SUGGESTED READING: *Contemporary Authors*, New Revision Series, vol. 1, 1981; vol. 61, 1998; *Something About the Author*, vol. 7, 1975; vol. 54, 1988; vol. 93, 1997.

Ron Maris

May 16, 1932–

"As in all the best stories, I am the son of a shoemaker; born in Northampton, the center of England's shoemaking industry.

"When young I was always reading and queued outside the Public Library on the very first day I was allowed a borrower's ticket. The first books I borrowed were Henry Williamson's *Tarka the Otter* and *Just William* by Richmal Crompton. I can't remember a time when I didn't draw. All through grammar school my best subjects were Art, English, Science, and Mathematics.

"At Art School I studied Illustration and at the Royal College of Art I studied Printmaking, winning the Silver Medal in Etching and Engraving, a continuation year, and the British Institute Prize in Engraving. Already an Associate of the Royal College of Art, I was elected to the Royal Society of Painter-Etchers and Engravers.

"It seemed right then to become a teacher, and for thirty-two years I taught art students drawing, printmaking, and graphic design; meeting, teaching, and then marrying Margaret, my lovely wife (who has also written and illustrated children's books). We now have three children and, so far, five grandchildren.

"The most wonderful way of introducing children to ideas and encouraging their imagination is through writing and drawing children's books. In 1980, our great friend, Pat Hutchins, bullied me into producing a book idea. I based it on my observations of animals and birds. There were lots of frogs in the garden ponds, field mice and voles hiding in the garden walls, badgers up the hill, owls in the wood, and rabbits in the fields. I wondered if there might be a clash of interests among animals looking for a home, so *Better Move On, Frog* appeared.

"In writing for small children, it is important to use language well. I learned a lot by refining the text, cutting the number of words to the minimum, and making them complementary to the illustrations. Honesty and simplicity in communication; creating concepts accessible to the very youngest child; the ability to draw and design; knowledge of printmaking and printing techniques—all are important to the creator of children's books. But possibly the most important is a refusal to grow up—common among creative people working in the visual area.

"Artists need to look long and hard, with the intensity of children, and then communicate honestly and simply, not just show how clever they are technically.

"I work at home in an old house full of tin toys, top hats, musical instruments, puppets, pictures, enamel signs, books and clocks. This old farmhouse is on top of the Pennine hills in Yorkshire, England. Every morning is a joy—a fresh opportunity! If the weather is fine, we work outside, building dry stone walls, hanging gates, feeding our Highland cattle, taking the dogs for walks.

"If it rains or snows there is masses to do indoors in the big studio upstairs . . . Oh, and rain or shine, if I haven't a book to read I suffer withdrawal symptoms—irritability, faintness, disorientation, and general debility."

Courtesy of Margaret Maris

* * *

Before entering the field of children's books, Ron Maris had enjoyed a long career as a painter, etcher, and senior lecturer in Art and Design at Huddlesfield Polytechnic in West Yorkshire. The well-known illustrator Pat Hutchins is the wife of Maris's boyhood friend and suggested often that he consider doing a children's book. The idea for *Better Move On, Frog* came to him during a walk with his dog, but the preliminary sketches stayed in a drawer in his studio. When Maris and his wife went to visit their friends in London, Pat Hutchins urged him to bring the drawings along. On arrival Maris found that she had three appointments set up for him to meet editors: the first one bought his book, and since then there have been eighteen more books, translated into eight languages and appearing in twelve countries.

Maris's picture books for young children, which usually feature animal characters, have won acclaim for their colorful artwork and comforting storylines. *My Book* was a runner-up for England's Kate Greenaway Medal. This story of a cat giving a tour of its home features half-page panels that reveal items hidden inside the house. Maris has used this "lift the flap" technique in other titles, such as *Runaway Rabbit, Little Chick,* and *Is Anyone Home?* In recent years he has designed board books for the youngest readers, including *Ducks Quack* and *Frogs Jump.*

Ron Maris and his wife live at Old Upperhouse Farm in West Yorkshire, England.

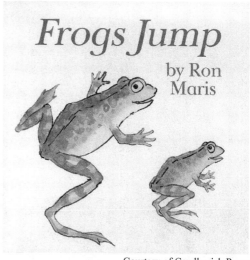

Courtesy of Candlewick Press

SELECTED WORKS WRITTEN AND ILLUSTRATED: *Better Move On, Frog,* 1982; *My Book,* 1983; *The Punch and Judy Book,* 1984; *Are You There, Bear?,* 1984; *Is Anyone Home?,* 1985; *I Wish I Could Fly,* 1987; *In My Garden,* 1987; *Runaway Rabbit,* 1989; *Hold Tight, Bear!,* 1988; *Bernard's Boring Day,* 1990; *Ducks Quack,* 1992; *Frogs Jump,* 1992; *Little Ginger,* 1994; *Little Chick,* 1995; *Buttercup's Breakfast,* 1999.

SELECTED WORKS ILLUSTRATED: *Humblepuppy and Other Stories for Telling,* compiled by Eileen Colwell, 1981.

SUGGESTED READING: *Something About the Author,* vol. 45, 1986; vol. 71, 1993.

" After my brother got a book published at fourteen, I yearned to do the same. Everything he did, I wanted to do. Unfortunately, I was very shy and timid, and not half as talented. The only place where I could make things happen was in my imagination, writing stories.

"Born in a London suburb on June 6, 1951, the third child of a fireman and a teacher, I lived rather in the shadow of my clever brother and sister. I was always writing, but as a way of escaping to other identities, other worlds. We did not have television at home until I was nine: it made a bigger impact on me than it did on the rest of the family, I think—on the way I imagine and the way I write.

Geraldine McCaughrean

(mik-KORK-ran)

June 6, 1951–

"When I grew up I went on writing—always and everywhere, writing—never really getting published. I did a succession of jobs—rather badly, if I'm honest. My first and favorite was a secretary at Thames Television, the Schools, Adult Education, and Religious programs department.

"Then something persuaded me to train as a teacher: my mother said it was a terrible idea, I was not cut out to teach. She was absolutely right. So next I went to work at a publishing company, as a secretary, then sub-editor on magazines about fishing, music, cooking . . . and stories for children. What a God-send! I ended up as 'Staff Writer,' writing stories to fill the pages left after the commissioned stuff (by proper authors) was all filled up.

Courtesy of Images Studio

"Meanwhile, of course, I went on writing as I traveled to and fro to work—just as a hobby. I went to church, in those days, with a children's publisher. One day he mentioned that he was planning a version of *The Arabian Nights*. 'Let me write it!' I pleaded. That was the start, but still it did not occur to me to earn my living by writing. It still seems almost wicked to do something so enjoyable for a living—like being a professional pool player. But about ten years ago I took the plunge. I gave up the day job, got married, and wrote full-time.

"Now I have a daughter to vet my stories and a husband to vet my spelling. Oh, and a dog to distract me. I usually have three or four projects on the go at any one time, as well as a novel I am mulling over for some future date. I have written five novels (and a radio play) for adults, and six novels for children . . . but about fifty other books, all for children. So I count myself a children's writer, first and foremost. Recently, I discovered a secret passion for myth. Perhaps it is because myths were never told 'for children' or 'for adults,' but to whole communities who understood the importance and magic of storytelling. I have retold a great many myths and legends, and naturally my love of them has influenced the way I tell and structure my other stories.

"I have also been given the chance to retell several classics of literature—such as Chaucer and Shakespeare and *Moby Dick*—which, despite having a plot and substance of interest to children, are too difficult for them to tackle in the original. I try never to adapt anything which children could perfectly well read in its original form.

"People often ask me how I discipline myself to write each day. My reply is that I have to discipline myself to be a decent mother and wife: writing is easy by comparison."

* * *

Geraldine McCaughrean was born Geraldine Jones in Enfield, a suburb of London, England. She attended Southgate Technical College and received her B.A. degree from Christ Church College, Oxford, in 1977. Since her writing career began in earnest, she has produced a remarkable variety of books—stories for young children and young adults, adult fiction, textbooks, myths and legends from around the world, translations and adaptations of classic novels. Her style is vigorous and immediate, breathing life into old tales and new stories alike.

McCaughrean's novels for teens have been especially well received in England, where she won the Whitbread Award in 1987 for her first novel, *A Little Lower Than the Angels*, a story set in the Middle Ages. *A Pack of Lies* was awarded the *Guardian* Children's Fiction Award and the Carnegie Medal, England's equivalent of the Newbery Award. *Gold Dust* was the recipient of the Beefeater Prize (formerly the Whitbread).

Best known in the United States for her retellings of age-old stories, especially in her Myths and Legends of the World series, McCaughrean has garnered many honors. *The Golden Hoard* was named to *School Library Journal's* Best Books of the Year and the New York Public Library's 100 Titles for Reading and Sharing. *The Silver Treasure*, *Stories from Shakespeare*, and *Greek Myths* were also named to New York Public Library's annual list, *Greek Myths* being a *Booklist* Editors' Choice as well. *The Bronze Cauldron* and *God's People* were both named Notable Trade Books in the Field of Social Studies, and *The Pirate's Son* was an ALA Notable Children's Book.

The author lives with her husband, John McCaughrean, and their daughter, Ailsa (named after the Scottish island of Ailsa Craig), in Berkshire, England.

> *"I went to church, in those days, with a children's publisher. One day he mentioned that he was planning a version of* The Arabian Nights. *'Let me write it!' I pleaded."*

SELECTED WORKS WRITTEN: *A Little Lower Than the Angels*, 1987; *A Pack of Lies*, 1988; *Gold Dust*, 1993; *Casting the Gold Adrift*, 1998; *The Pirate's Son*, 1998.

SELECTED WORKS RETOLD: *One Thousand and One Arabian Nights*, illus. by Stephen Lavis, 1982; *The Canterbury Tales*, illus by Victor Ambrus, 1985; *Saint George and the Dragon*, illus. by Nicki Palin, 1989; *El Cid*, 1989; *Greek Myths*, illus. by Emma Chichester Clark, 1993; *The Odyssey*, illus. by Victor Ambrus, 1993; *Stories from Shakespeare*, illus. by Anthony Maitland, 1994; *The Random House Book of Stories*

Courtesy of Simon & Schuster Children's Publishing Division

from the Ballet, illus. by Angela Barrett, 1995; *The Golden Hoard*, illus. by Bee Willey, 1996; *The Silver Treasure*, illus. by Bee Willey, 1997; *God's People: Stories from the Old Testament*, illus. by Anna Leplar, 1997; *Unicorns! Unicorns!*, illus. by Sophie Windham, 1997; *The Bronze Cauldron*, illus. by Bee Willey, 1998; *Greek Gods and Goddesses*, 1998; *Moby Dick*, 1998; *The Crystal Pool*, illus. by Bee Willey, 1999; *God's Kingdom: Stories from the New Testament*, illus by Anna Leplar, 2000.

SUGGESTED READING: *Authors and Artists for Young Adults*, vol. 23, 1998; *Children's Literature Review*, vol. 38, 1996; *Contemporary Authors*, vol. 117, 1986; *Contemporary Authors*, New Revision Series, vol. 52, 1996; *Something About the Author*, vol. 43, 1986; vol. 87, 1996. Periodicals— Philip, Neil, "Mining a Rich Seam," *Times Educational Supplement*, February 3, 1995.

Hilary McKay

June 12, 1959–

"I was born in 1959, in Boston, Lincolnshire, the eldest of four girls. My parents were (and are) great readers, and they provided us with books as naturally and casually as they provided us with food. They also shared with us books they were currently enjoying themselves, books from their childhood, and even books from my grandparents' childhood. We became addicts. We anesthetized ourselves against the big bad world with large doses of literature. The local library was as familiar to us as our own home. We dressed and ate and walked down the road reading books. It was all most antisocial . . . .

"I did not like school, and was an uncooperative child. I was never much good at writing essays and used to grind out the minimum three sides of exercise book with great agony of mind and as enormous a handwriting as I dared to use. I was very interested in natural history and so took up sciences, which led to the huge mistake of taking a B.Sc. instead of a B.A. degree. Not that it mattered very much in the end, because I kept on reading, and reading led quite naturally to writing.

"I wrote my first book, *The Exiles*, in 1989, and after it had been heavily knocked into shape by a most efficient editor it was published in 1991. I feel that I owe my writing career to that editor, who kick-started me into action, and to the Guardian Children's Fiction Award that I shared with Rachel Anderson the following year and which forced me to write a second book. Between the two I had a very, very lucky beginning.

"I do not consciously write to please anyone except myself. Of course, I have learnt certain tricks of the trade as I have gone along, the biggest being the danger of self-indulgent woffle, so useful for filling the page and so deadly to read afterwards. Filling the page is my greatest difficulty. I love the idea of being a writer. I believe very much in the power of books. I get an enormous kick out of making people laugh. This is my ideal career. And yet when it comes to actually filling the page I would rather do almost anything than begin.

Courtesy of Hilary McKay

"The question people ask most often is, 'Where do you get your ideas from?' I can never answer it properly because I do not know. I wish I did. I would rather discover the source of ideas than a gold mine in the garden. I generally begin a book with the characters and the location fixed, and the story comes from the characters themselves. Once they begin to speak to each other, once they begin to say, 'Do you remember . . . ?' then the plot can start to unfold.

"One of the best things about being a writer is the letters that arrive from people who have read my books. As a child I must have read hundreds and hundreds of books, and yet it never once occurred to me that I might contact their author. I wish now that I had. There are so many people I ought to have thanked."

* * *

Hilary McKay was living in coastal England and performing odd jobs directed at the tourist trade, including cleaning vacation cottages and selling paintings, when a friend suggested she try her hand at writing. Her first book, *The Exiles*, won England's prestigious Guardian Award in 1992. This humorous novel about four headstrong sisters spending the summer with their grandmother also received critical acclaim in the United States, where it appeared on the annual best-book lists of both the *Horn Book* and the *Bulletin of the Center for Children's Books*. After this early success, McKay moved to Derbyshire, where she worked as a chemist during the day and continued writing in the evenings. *The Exiles*

The EXILES

HILARY McKAY

Courtesy of Simon & Schuster Children's Publishing Division

at Home, a second volume about the Conroy sisters, received the 1994 Smarties Book Prize—winning the grand prize for all the categories. The third volume in the series, *The Exiles in Love*, was cited on the *Horn Book*'s Fanfare list.

Dog Friday, the beginning of another series, was named an ALA Notable Children's Book and was selected as a best book of the year by *School Library Journal*, *Booklist*, and the *Horn Book*. *The Amber Cat* and *Dolphin Luck* were named *School Library Journal* Best Books and *Booklist* Editors' Choices.

McKay's books have been released in audiotape versions and published in foreign-language editions. Some, including the four volume Paradise House series, have not yet been published in the United States. Now a full-time writer, Hilary McKay continues to live in Derbyshire with her husband and two children.

SELECTED WORKS: (British publication dates) *The Exiles*, 1991; *The Exiles at Home*, 1993; *Dog Friday*, 1994; *The Amber Cat*, 1995; *The Zoo in the Attic*, 1995; *The Treasure in the Garden*, 1995; *The Exiles in Love*, 1996; *The Echo in the Chimney*, 1996; *Happy and Glorious*, 1996; *The Magic in the Mirror*, 1996; *Practically Perfect*, 1996; *Why Didn't You Tell Me?*, 1996; *Dolphin Luck*, 1999.

SUGGESTED READING: *Contemporary Authors*, vol. 156, 1997; *Something About the Author*, vol. 92, 1997; *Something About the Author Autobiography Series*, vol. 23, 1997.

Patricia McMahon

(mick-MAN)

September 1, 1952–

"When I was young and somebody asked me, 'Little girl, what do you want to be when you grow up?' my most likely answer would have been 'a missionary nurse, and then President of the United States.' A children's book author? Not a likely answer, for I had not yet discovered that writers were real people. I assumed they lived on Park Avenue and rode in horse-drawn carriages through Central Park, a ride we could not afford.

"I was born in Pittsburgh, Pennsylvania, the second of five children. A scant six months after my birth my parents returned to New York City and the company of their large Irish American families. A few years later my family joined the new migration, not west but east, where the potato fields of Long Island were turned over to make row upon row of new houses. I grew up surrounded by children—thirty-eight on our short block, sixty in each class at the local Catholic school, the five McMahon kids in our small house. But for me, there was no life like the one to be found in books. Books were home to me, books were my friends. I read anything and everything off the shelves at the local public library. I discovered *Pippi Longstocking*. 'Ah,' I thought.

"I was always in love with words. The long litany of the names of the Blessed Mother transfixed me in the middle of a long High Mass as did the way my grandmother's Irish brogue changed ordinary words into something new. I was in love with stories—of my grandmother's farm in Ireland, of my mother's childhood in Brooklyn, of my father's adventures in World War II, of rebels and rebellions in the Irish music played constantly at our home. Once, in high school, a poet came to visit. An ordinary and unimpressive man, he taught me the astounding truth that writers were real people. In college one day, I simply decided: I will write children's books.

"Still, I had to make a living, and there was the life I wanted to lead as well. I *had* to see the world I'd discovered in the public library. I still had the list of 'The Ten Places I Have to See Before I Die,' written when I was ten in that library. So I took curious jobs, wrote poetry, and fell in love with a man named McCarthy who had gone to the same crowded school as me. I handed him my list. He suggested we go together. 'Ah,' I thought.

Courtesy of Allyn Dukes

Patricia McMahon

"We went to Boston, where I studied children's literature and wrote a bad book. We lived in Africa for three years, had swell adventures and I wrote a not-so-bad book. Then on to Korea, which was not on my original list, but now holds a piece of my heart, where I wrote a pretty good book. Back to Boston for the birth of my red-haired son who has my grandmother's name, then back to Korea. A time in Concord, Masachusetts, where I kept my eye on Louisa May Alcott's house. We live now in Houston, Texas, where the countryside has skies like my African home and owns another piece of my heart.

"And I've kept writing. I stumbled onto nonfiction when I cured my Korean homesickness by writing *Chi-Hoon: A Korean Girl*, my first published book. And I stumbled, as well, into the patented McMahon Method of Writing Nonfiction: pick a real child somewhere in the world, move into his or her life for a time, watch and learn while a photographer takes pictures of everything. Listen for the story that is there waiting to be told. For now I know that it matters not whether I'm writing fiction or nonfiction: I'm still trying to tell a story as best I can, to play with words, or fight with them, to tell this story I believe needs telling. So I have told the tale of an eight-year-old Korean girl who so wants to fit in, to win a prize, but who, because she is so wonderfully herself, may never win. And the tale of Conor Healy, and his frustration at being seen as his disability, as an extension of his wheelchair, instead of himself, in *Summer Tunes*. My newest book, *One Belfast Boy*, tells of Liam Leathem's desire to make something of himself and see the world beyond his troubled city.

"I have fallen in love with writing nonfiction, as the books are a wonderful collaboration between this writer, the photographers, and the real child who is always at the center of my story."

Courtesy of Boyds Mills Press

Patricia McMahon earned her B.A. from the State University of New York at Oswego. She was married to Joe McCarthy in 1976 and received a master's degree from the Center for the Study of Children's Literature at Simmons College in 1978. After living for three years in South Africa, where McCarthy was working on the world's largest construction site, the couple returned to the Boston area. McMahon joined the children's book marketing department of Little, Brown and Co. until once again her husband's work took them abroad. While living in Seoul, McMahon found herself drawn to the Korean culture in a way she never expected, and that fascination became the basis for her first published children's book years later.

Chi-Hoon: A Korean Girl was a *Booklist* Editors' Choice in 1993 and later listed by that journal as one of the best books of a five year period. *Listen for the Bus: David's Story*, chronicling a day in the life of a kindergartener who is blind, was a *Smithsonian* magazine Best Book of the Year and was named one of the top five books in an exhibit created for the Bologna Book Fair in 1997 by the International Board on Books for Young People; the exhibit later traveled to many other locations. McMahon has developed a knack for finding children whose stories are representative of a culture or a special way of life and then working collaboratively with photographers to develop picture/story profiles of her subjects.

In 1987 McMahon's son Conor was born, and in 1999 the family expanded to include Claire, a daughter adopted from Kunming in the southern part of China. Patricia McMahon continues to search out interesting subjects for her nonfiction picture books. Currently she is working on the story of a dance troupe in Cleveland, Ohio, that includes both able-bodied dancers and those with physical challenges.

SELECTED WORKS: *Chi-Hoon: A Korean Girl*, photos by Michael O'Brien, 1993; *Listen for the Bus: David's Story*, illus. by John Godt, 1995; *Summer Tunes: A Martha's Vineyard Vacation*, illus. by Peter Simon, 1996; *Six Words, Many Turtles & Three Days in Hong Kong*, illus. by Susan Drinker, 1997; *One Belfast Boy*, photos by Alan O'Connor, 1999.

SUGGESTED READING: "On Writing *Chi-Hoon*," *Book Links*, January 1995.

Colin McNaughton

May 18, 1951–

"**I** suppose I've made a virtue out of what most sensible, normal people would call a character flaw. You see, my brain doesn't work in an A-to-Z sort of way. I'm scatterbrained—lovely word, that. What I call 'messing around' is just the way my mind works anyway. It leaps, seemingly randomly, from one subject to another. So that pirates, aliens, pigs, dinosaurs, and monsters naturally interact in my world. I don't know why, but after twenty-odd years doing picture books, I've just come to accept it and go with the flow. It may seem like a crazy way of going about things, but it works for me. And, as Willie Nelson once said, 'If you ain't crazy, you must be mad.'

'The Trial'

Ladies and Gentlemen—
In court today,
Wearing a red nose
And Frenchman's beret,
A dangerous villain,
To whom you must say:
We accuse you of not growing up!

We've witnesses lined up,
Respectable men:

Accountants, solicitors,
Vicars, amen:
And their evidence proves it
Again and again—
We accuse you of not growing up!

Accounts of your crimes
Take up page after page,
Always playing the fool,
Never acting your age:
With behaviour like this

You should work on the stage.
We accuse you of not growing
up!

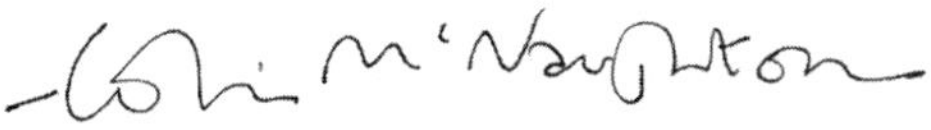

You draw silly pictures
And write silly verse:
We've found them in book-
shops,
But really, what's worse,
You should be maturing
But it's the reverse.
We accuse you of not growing
up!

You were seen on a skateboard
In Kensington Park,
And shouting at boaters,
'Behind you a shark!'
When asked why you did it
You said, 'For a lark.'
We accuse you of not growing
up!

Courtesy of The Herald & Weekly Times/Melbourne Australia

Members of the Jury,
There can be no doubt,
He cannot be serious,

Joking throughout:
When I asked him his job
He said, 'Messing about!'
We accuse you of not growing up!

Silence in court!
Are the Jury agreed?
We've evidence damning,
Much more than we need;
So, Mr. McNaughton,
How do you plead?

'Guilty, Your Honour, as charged.
Tra-la. Guilty, Your Honour,
As charged!'

"When I say I've never grown up, I suppose what I mean is
. . . I've never lost the ability to play. When I'm making a picture book, I'm doing exactly what I did when I was seven years old and playing with my toys—then a shoebox was a skyscraper, my kitten was Godzilla, and my lead soldiers were alive.

"I work project to project. I never think of it as a direct line. I'm obviously technically better than I was twenty-two years ago when I started and I'm not afraid of trying anything really— except horses and ballerinas. Can't draw those. My place in the world? It's not too important to me. I'm not really very ambitious. I always said that what I want to do is to create one really cracking book and that's what I'm still trying to do. Some of my books are pretty good but they all have flaws in them. And when I've created that one really great book? Well, then I'll try to do another one even better! (Mind you, I'd probably settle for a not-so-great book which sold ten million copies!)"

* * *

Colin McNaughton was born in Wallsend-upon-Tyne, Northumberland, England. He attended a foundation course in art in Newcastle, then moved to London in 1970 to study graphic design at the Central School of Art and Design. He received an M.A. in Illustration from the Royal College of Art, where he was still a student when the first of his many books was published. His work is noted for zany characters and hilarious situations, often accompanied by rhyming verse. Pirates, aliens, and monsters figure prominently, reflecting the influence of the comic books he loved in his youth. An early interest in acting is also reflected in the staging of many of his tales, which he refers to as 'little plays.' In 1970 he married, and his wife, Françoise, has become his business manager and agent. They live in London, England, with their two sons.

Colin McNaughton has written and illustrated over sixty picture books and collections of verse. He has collaborated with Russell Hoban, author of the Hungry Three books, and Allan Ahlberg, with whom he produced the Happy Families and Red Nose Readers series. He received the 1978 Letteratura Didàttica Prize in Bologna for the combined Italian edition of *Colin McNaughton's ABC and Things* and *Colin McNaughton's 1, 2, 3 and Things*. In 1996 he was awarded Britain's Smarties Book Prize Gold Award—age five and under category—for *Oops!*

Making Friends with Frankenstein was a *Booklist* Editors' Choice, an IRA/CBC Children's Choice, a Parents' Choice Award winner, and an American Booksellers Association Pick of

"When I say I've never grown up, I suppose what I mean is . . . I've never lost the ability to play."

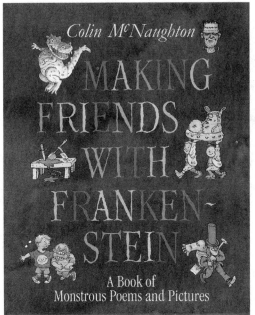

Courtesy of Candlewick Press

the Lists. *Suddenly!* received the Virginia State Reading Association Young Readers Award (Primary Level) and was named a Notable Children's Trade Book in the Language Arts. *Here Come the Aliens!* and *Dracula's Tomb* were also IRA/CBC Children's Choices.

SELECTED WORKS WRITTEN AND ILLUSTRATED: *Colin McNaughton's ABC & 1,2,3,* 1976; *The Rat Race,* 1978; *The Great Zoo Escape,* 1979; *Anton B. Stanton & the Pirats,* 1980; *Soccer Crazy,* 1981; *Crazy Bear,* 1983; *Seasons,* 1984; *Who's Been Sleeping in My Porridge? A Book of Silly Poems and Pictures,* 1990; *If Dinosaurs Were Cats & Dogs* (rev. ed.), 1991; *Walk Rabbit Walk* (with Elizabeth Attenborough; rev. ed), 1992; *Who's That Banging on the Ceiling?,* 1994; *Captain Abdul's Pirate School,* 1994; *Making Friends with Frankenstein: A Book of Monstrous Poems and Pictures,* 1994; *Jolly Roger and the Pirates of Captain Abdul,* 1995; *Suddenly!,* 1995; *Boo!,* 1996; *Oops!,* 1997; *Here Come the Aliens!,* 1995; *Dracula's Tomb,* 1998; *Preston's Goal!,* 1998; *Yum!,* 1999; *Wish You Were Here (And I Wasn't),* 2000.

SELECTED WORKS ILLUSTRATED: *They Came from Aargh!,* by Russell Hoban, 1981; *Miss Brick the Builder's Baby,* by Allan Ahlberg, 1982; *The Great Gumdrop Robbery,* by Russell Hoban, 1982; *The Pink Fairy Book,* by Andrew Lang, 1982; *The Flight of Bembel Rudzuk,* by Russell Hoban, 1982; *Big Bad Pig,* by Allan Ahlberg, 1985; *Happy Worm,* by Allan Ahlberg, 1985; *Fee Fi Fo Fum,* by Allan Ahlberg, 1985; *Help!,* by Allan Ahlberg, 1985; *Treasure Island,* by Robert Louis Stevenson, 1995.

SUGGESTED READING: *Children's Literature Review,* vol. 54, 1999; *Contemporary Authors,* vol. 112, 1985; *Contemporary Authors,* New Revision Series, vol. 47, 1995; Peppin, Brigid and Lucy Micklethwait. *Book Illustrators of the Twentieth Century,* 1984; *Something About the Author,* vol. 39, 1985; vol. 92, 1997.

"Many adult artists knew in an enlightened moment of childhood that they would grow up to be artists. I wasn't one of them. Drawing and painting and 'making stuff' are things I've always enjoyed and done. Happily, those things worked themselves into a career. Growing up 'to be' something is kind of a silly notion anyway, don't you think? The words 'to be' should not be a destination, and growing, hopefully, never stops. At least not in the ways that matter! Anyway, I guess what I'm trying to get at is that I was as much of an artist when I was five years old as I am now.

"Dressing up, exploring the out-of-doors, dancing, swimming, climbing beech trees, and making pictures were all activities I enjoyed when I was young, and, come to think of it, still do. I have a younger sister, Andrea; an older brother, Jeffrey; and parents, Russ and Joanne. Our home was in a small town north of Boston. We spent time during the summer in a cottage on a small lake in New Hampshire. The birch trees, the softness of the water, and the easy rhythm of the days shaped my sense of wonder.

Courtery of Orchard Books

Holly Meade

September 14, 1956–

"As I grew, my family, along with neighborhood friends and a string of animals, made for a full and fun life. Among those animals were the guinea pigs that star in *John Willy and Freddy McGee*. In that book they get into a tight squeeze in a pool table. In real life, they did spend time in our pool table. They'd scamper around inside and poke their heads up out of the holes occasionally to get their bearings. Sometimes they would leave their droppings in the tunnels, which stuck to the balls. This quite angered my brother when he reached for a ball to play a game. I used to laugh so hard over this scene that my stomach would ache! These many years later the memory struck me as the makings of an entertaining children's book, and so it's proven to be!

"One of my clearest memories is of my kindergarten teacher placing a new box of crayons on my desk that first day of school. A row of fat bright crayons, each one with a flat side to prevent it from rolling onto the floor. The top of the box lifted off like a present. Oh! The worlds that could be created with the contents of that box!

"Believe it or not, I somehow managed to fail art in my freshman year of high school. The next year there was a change of art teacher, and midway through my sophomore year I approached

Courtesy of Orchard Books

her with the earnest request to be let back into the art room. She not only welcomed me, but allowed me to join my classmates without having to make up the missed time or failed class. Her name is Wendy Newman, and I'll never forget her.

"Later I attended the Rhode Island School of Design and studied painting. Since then I've been an art teacher, graphic artist, flag designer, and most importantly, a mom to a son and daughter. Their names are Noah and Jenny, and now they're sixteen and nineteen years old.

"Making pictures for children's books is fun as well as hard work. Each book is challenging in new ways, and the learning never stops. Thinking about stories and how to picture them comes with a lifestyle I'm grateful for. Since I work at home, I can be drawing while the bread is rising, and be around for my high school daughter if she needs me. On snowy days I can rearrange my work to get in a cross-country ski. And if it's mild out, I can manage a bike ride when the day calls me.

"One of the difficult aspects of what I do is simply spending so much time alone. So it's extra meaningful and welcome when I hear from children about the pictures I make.

"So there it is, an autobiography of sorts. Now it's back to the drawing table, where I'm putting together pictures for *Steamboat!* by Judy Gilliland, the true story of steamboat captain Blanche Leathers and the Mississippi River."

* * *

New Englander Holly Meade was born in Boston, has lived in Amherst, New Hampshire, and now resides in Newburyport, Massachusetts.

Two of her early books, *Rata-Pata-Scata-Fata* and *Small Green Snake*, were selected as American Booksellers Association Pick of the Lists. *Small Green Snake* was also chosen for New York Public Library's list, 100 Titles for Reading and Sharing. Meade's illustrations for *Hush!: A Thai Lullaby*, by Minfong Ho, received a Caldecott Honor Award. This book was also named a *Hungry Mind Review* Children's Book of Distinction and an ALA Notable Children's Book, appeared on the *Horn Book*'s Fanfare list, won the Red Clover Award, and received a *Parenting* magazine Reading Magic Award. *Boss of the Plains* was a

Horn Book Fanfare title, an ALA Notable Children's Book, one of the New York Public Library's 100 Titles for Reading and Sharing, and a Notable Trade Book in the Field of Social Studies. It won the 1999 Regional Book Award from the Mountains and Plains Booksellers Association as well.

The first book that Meade both wrote and illustrated, *John Willy and Freddy McGee*, was named an Honor Book in the competition for the Charlotte Zolotow Award, which is presented for outstanding writing in a picture book. This story of two guinea pigs who escape from their cage was also cited as an IRA/CBC Children's Choice and was included on the New York Public Library's list, 100 Titles for Reading and Sharing.

Holly Meade's artwork has been exhibited at the De Cordova Museum in Lincoln, Massachusetts.

SELECTED WORKS WRITTEN AND ILLUSTRATED: *John Willy and Freddy McGee*, 1998.

SELECTED WORKS ILLUSTRATED: *This Is the Hat*, by Nancy Van Laan, 1992; *Rata-Pata-Scata-Fata: A Caribbean Story*, by Phillis Gershator, 1993; *Small Green Snake*, by Nancy Van Laan, 1994; *Sleep, Sleep, Sleep*, by Nancy Van Laan, 1995; *Pie's in the Oven*, by Betty G. Birney, 1996; *Hush!: A Thai Lullaby*, by Minfong Ho, 1996; *Cocoa Ice*, by Diana Applebaum, 1997; *Boss of the Plains: The Hat That Won the West*, by Laurie Carlson, 1998.

SUGGESTED READING: "Watching for Accidents," *The Horn Book*, March/April, 1998.

Angela Shelf Medearis

(muh-DARE-iss)

November 16, 1956–

"I love introducing children all over the world to all the different aspects of African American history, folklore, and culture. I love picture books because it's a challenge to convey complex ideas in a simple form for children. I really enjoy presenting history factually and vividly in a 32- or 48-page book. It's wonderful to be able to hold a child's attention and teach something important at the same time. Picture books are a child's first step into a lifetime of reading. That's why I feel that my job is important. I want to write in such an interesting and exciting way that the memory of reading my book and the information I've included about a particular event will linger with a young reader for a lifetime.

"I've always loved history and most of my books are historically based. I enjoy doing research on African-American history because I didn't have the opportunity to study it when I was in school. Many of my books are the result of some wonderful discovery I've made while doing research for something else.

"I remember my teachers commenting on how well I could write ever since I was in elementary school. I didn't think it was any big deal and I didn't realize that writing is a talent until I was thirty and started writing professionally. When I was growing up, authors didn't visit children in school. That's why I really enjoy visiting schools now. I know how important it is to tell young people that if they can write well, they are just as gifted as any other type of artist. If you want to be a writer, your first stop should be the library. Read as much as you can and check out books about writing.

"My father was a top recruiter in the Air Force and my mother was a housewife. We moved constantly. I used books and reading as a way of adjusting to new surroundings. I knew that my favorite books would be waiting for me at the library in whatever new place we were going. I also knew there would be a nice librarian there who would be friendly to me. Knowing this made it much easier to deal with a new school and new friends.

Courtesy of Back In A Flash

"I've always loved to read but I can't recall ever reading any books by or about African Americans when I was in elementary school. My favorite author then was Laura Ingalls Wilder. I also enjoyed biographies about famous people in history. My taste in books hasn't changed much since I was a child. I still love biographies, and ninety percent of the books I read are children's books!

"I've read thousands of books because I love to read; my favorite books are picture books. I also read all the time because I need special information when I write my own books. One day, I started counting all the books I own and I stopped at 500. I must have at least 2,500 or more books. I really don't have a favorite book—I just love to read any book that is well written.

"I love children and I really like to write books for them. I enjoy the wonderful feeling I get when I have a great idea and can't wait to get started working on it. I don't know where my ideas come from but if I sit quietly long enough, something pops into my head. I like thinking about all the children that have read my work; my books have been published in Africa, France, England, and other places I don't even know about. It's fun to think that someone, somewhere is reading one of my books or checking them out of the library.

"I've been writing since the second grade, and professionally (getting paid!) for the last seven years. I love writing but I didn't decide upon it as a career until I got fired from my job as a legal secretary (booorrrrinnnng). I like all types of poetry and I'm better at writing free verse. I enjoy writing poetry and I don't worry if anyone else likes it but me, although I'm pleased that so many people 'get' the poems in *Skin Deep*. My favorite poems are by Gwendolyn Brooks and Langston Hughes. I always wanted to be happily married and have a nice house and family and I've achieved that. I don't have any spare time anymore really but I do love going to the movies with my husband and writing partner, Michael, and having my daughter Deanna, her husband Joey, and my grandchild Anysa over for dinner.

"Most people think I'm funny. I like to make people laugh. I really, really like to make children laugh. It's one of the happiest sounds in the world."

* * *

Angela Shelf Medearis published her first book, *Picking Peas for a Penny*, in 1990. Since then she has written over seventy books; she has been called "one of the most influential writers of children's literature" in the state by *Texas Monthly Magazine*. Medearis was not always a Texan. She was born in Hampton, Virginia, and traveled all over the country with her family before settling in Austin, Texas, in 1975, after marrying Michael Medearis, who has collaborated with her on a number of books about Texas and African American arts.

"If you want to be a writer, your first stop should be the library. Read as much as you can. . . ."

Angela Medearis is the founder and past director of Book Boosters, a nonprofit, multicultural tutorial reading program. In addition to writing children's books, she has compiled three cookbooks celebrating the African American kitchen and Kwanzaa. She also produces story videos, visits classrooms all over the country, contributes to magazines, and is a writing consultant.

Medearis has served as the curator of two African American history exhibits for the George Washington Carver Museum in Austin. She is a member of the American Black Book Writers Association, the Society of Children's Book Writers and Illustrators, the Texas Library Association, the Texas State Reading Association, and the Texas Institute of Letters.

Picking Peas for a Penny was a Blue Ribbon Paperback Book Club selection. *Dancing with the Indians* and *The Singing Man* were named Notable Children's Trade Books in the Field of Social Studies. *The Singing Man* also received a Coretta Scott King Honor Book award for its illustrations by Terea Shaffer. *Zebra Riding Cowboy* appeared on the American Booksellers Association's Pick of the Lists. *Poppa's New Pants* won a Parents' Choice Gold Award, was nominated for the Tennessee Volunteer State Book Award for 1998–1999, and won the first annual Teddy

Award from the Austin Writers' League. A book of poems, *Skin Deep and Other Teenage Reflections*, also won a special citation of merit from the Austin Writers' League. *The Princess of the Press: The Story of Ida B. Wells-Barnett* was a Carter G. Woodson Honor Book award winner.

SELECTED WORKS: *Picking Peas for a Penny*, illus. by Charles G. Shaw, 1990; *Dancing with the Indians*, illus. by Samuel Byrd, 1991; *Zebra Riding Cowboy*, 1992; *Poppa's New Pants*, illus. by John Ward, 1993; *The Seven Days of Kwanzaa*, 1994; *The African-American Kitchen: Cooking from Our Heritage*, 1994; *The Singing Man*, illus. by Terea D. Shaffer, 1994; *Dare to Dream: Coretta Scott King and the Civil Rights Movement*, illus. by Anna Rich, 1994; *The Adventures of Sugar and Junior*, illus. by Nancy Poydar, 1995; *Treemonisha*, illus. by Michael Bryant, from the opera by Scott Joplin, 1995; *Haunts: Five Hair-Raising Tales*, illus. by Trina Schart Hyman, 1996; *Too Much Talk*, illus. by Stefano Vitale, 1996; *The Spray Paint Mystery*, 1996; *The Princess of the Press: The Story of Ida B. Wells-Barnett*, 1997; *Rum-a-Tum-Tum*, illus. by James Ransome, 1997; *Skin Deep and Other Teenage Reflections*, 1998.

SUGESTED READING: Rollock, Barbara. *Black Authors & Illustrators of Children's Books*, 2nd ed., 1992; *Something About the Author*, vol. 72, 1993. Periodicals—Berry, Mary Ann, "Who Is Angela Shelf Medearis?" *Emergency Librarian*, May/June 1998; *Texas Monthly*, September 1997.

Milton Meltzer

May 8, 1915–

"I did my growing up in Worcester, Massachusetts, where I was born. My parents came young from Europe and worked in factories until my father achieved a shaky independence hiring himself out to wash windows at fifteen cents apiece. Uneducated themselves, my mother and father had a great respect for learning. They felt the future was assured when they saw me reading—no matter what. It was more often a Nick Carter or a Tom Swift than something uplifting, but so long as it was words on paper, I loved them.

"My older brother took me crying to school the first day, but the tears soon stopped. For here were books, far more than I had seen in one place before, and adults who were paid to read to us. I think I must have decided that day to be a teacher. Then I discovered the public library and began reading from one wall to the other. Soon I found that I liked to make words on paper, too. By high school, I was working on student magazines.

"I went off to Columbia University in 1932, at the lowest point of the Great Depression, just making it on five dollars a week from home, a scholarship, and a waiter's job for my meals. I was preparing to teach school, a job that seemed doubly important because it was one of the few ways to survive those terrible times. But towards the end of college I knew teaching wasn't for me. I wanted instead what I thought of as the more active life of a journalist in the swiftly changing world outside. Apart from service in World War II, many years went into writing jobs of all kinds—for the WPA Federal Theater, for trade unions, for political campaigns, for community organizations, for public relations agencies, for industrial corporations, for a medical newspaper. Meanwhile, I married Hilda Balinky and helped raise our two daughters, Jane and Amy.

Not until the 1950s did I learn that what I liked most was digging into American history, and writing about it. The desire to write a book came out of the sad realization that nothing I had ever written would last, or would be worth keeping. Happily for me, Langston Hughes agreed to collaborate on my first idea, *A Pictorial History of the Negro in America*. Then came book after book, worked on in early morning hours before going off to the daily job. Finally, with some twenty books published, I was able to quit the job and give all my time to the books waiting to be written.

"Perhaps because of what I learned coming of age in the 1930s, I have found the greatest meaning and the greatest joy in telling of the struggle to win freedom and equality and justice for all. All my books are somehow connected to this theme. I hope they help readers to understand the truth about our past and to want to take part in making the life of man more human."

Courtesy of Catherine Noren

*   *   *

Milton Meltzer is one of the foremost writers of nonfiction for young readers, particularly in the fields of history and biography. His conviction and passion for social justice are evident throughout his work. His original collaboration with the Black poet and author Langston Hughes resulted in a landmark study that has to date seen six editions. Now titled *A Pictorial History of African Americans*, this volume remains a standard reference work in the field, and though it was written originally for adults, the illustrative nature of the work makes it equally accessible to younger students.

After his college years, Meltzer became a staff writer for the Works Progress Administration in New York City. He served in the U.S. Air Force during World War II, attaining the rank of sergeant, then worked briefly for CBS and for the Henry A. Wallace presidential campaign. In the 1950s and early 1960s he had a variety of jobs, including public relations at Pfizer, Inc. and editor for the Science and Medicine Publishing Company in New York. Since 1968 he has been a full-time writer and has also served as a consulting editor to several publishers of children's books. An adjunct professor at the University of Massachusetts in Amherst from 1977 to 1980, Meltzer has been a sought-after lecturer at universities in both the United States and England.

Meltzer's historical studies and biographies make creative use of original source material—letters, diaries, speeches, and documents—that allows readers to feel an immediacy about the era. Meltzer's strong narrative voice in each book puts this source material in context and creates a vivid picture of the times. Whether writing about poverty, slavery, the Holocaust, or the Depression, Meltzer makes his readers experience the lives of ordinary people as well as those who existed in the limelight. In *Rescue* he tells gripping true-life stories of non-Jews who risked their own lives to save their Jewish neighbors from Nazi death camps during the Holocaust. *Never to Forget: The Jews of the Holocaust*, one of his most honored books, received the Jane Addams Peace Association Children's Book Award and the National Jewish Book Award and was named to ALA's list "Best of the Best Books 1970–83." A spirited study of peace activism, *Ain't Gonna Study War No More*, also received the Jane Addams prize as well as an Olive Branch Award from the Writers' and Publishers' Alliance for Nuclear Disarmament.

> "I have found the greatest meaning and the greatest joy in telling of the struggle to win freedom and equality and justice for all."

Meltzer's biographies are admired for exploring the humanity of their subjects, bringing historical figures to life within the context of their times. He writes with insight and narrative skill about major figures—Washington, Franklin, Columbus—and social activists—Betty Friedan, Mary McLeod Bethune, Frederick Douglass. His first biography for young readers, *A Light in the Dark: The Life of Samuel Gridley Howe* (1964) depicted the life of a man who worked against slavery and risked his own safety to help others. This theme of self-sacrifice out of a passion for social justice runs through all Meltzer's work.

Many of Meltzer's books have been selected as Library of Congress Best Children's Books of the Year, Notable Children's Trade Books in the Field of Social Studies, ALA Notable Children's Books, and *New York Times* Outstanding Children's Books of the Year. Early in his writing career, Meltzer won the Thomas Alva Edison Mass Media Award for excellence in portraying America's past for *In Their Own Words: A History of the American Negro, vol. 2, 1865–1916*. He has been nominated for the National Book Award five times and won the Christopher

Medal twice, in 1970 for *Brother, Can You Spare a Dime?* and again in 1980 for *All Times, All Peoples.* The Golden Kite Award for Nonfiction in 1986 was awarded by the Society of Children's Book Writers and Illustrators to Meltzer's *Poverty in America.* In 1997 he received the honorary degree of Doctor of Humane Letters from Worcester State College in his own hometown, and in 2000 the Catholic Library Association awarded him its Regina Medal for lifetime achievement in children's literature.

Milton Meltzer lives with his wife in New York City.

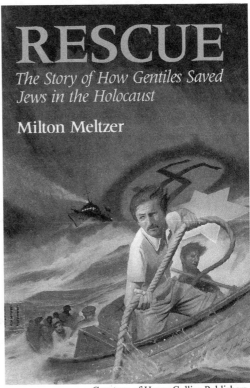

Courtesy of HarperCollins Publishers

SELECTED WORKS: *A Pictorial History of the Negro in America*, with Langston Hughes, 1956 (6th revised edition *A Pictorial History of African Americans*, with Langston Hughes, C. Eric Lincoln, and Jon Michael Spencer, 1995); *A Light in the Dark: The Life of Samuel Gridley Howe*, 1964, 1991; *In Their Own Words: A History of the American Negro*, vol. 1: 1619–1865, 1964; *vol. 2: 1865–1916*, 1965; *vol. 3: 1916–1966*, 1967 (revised edition: *The Black Americans: A History in Their Own Words, 1619–1983*, 1984); *Tongue of Flame: The Life of Lydia Maria Child*, 1965; *Bread—and Roses: The Struggle of American Labor, 1865–1915*, 1967, 1991; *Thaddeus Stevens and the Fight for Negro Rights*, 1967; *Langston Hughes: A Biography*, 1968, illus. by Stephen Alcorn, 1997; *Brother, Can You Spare a Dime? The Great Depression 1929–1933*, 1969, 1991; *Hunted like a Wolf: The Story of the Seminole War*, 1972; *The Right to Remain Silent*, 1972; *World of Our Fathers: The Jews of Eastern Europe*, 1974; *Bound for the Rio Grande: The Mexican Struggle, 1845–1850*, 1974; *Never to Forget: The Jews of the Holocaust*, 1976; *All Times, All Peoples: A World History of Slavery*, illus. by Leonard Everett Fisher, 1980; *The Truth About the Ku Klux Klan*, 1982; *The Terrorists*, 1983; *A Book About Names*, 1984; *Ain't Gonna Study War No More: The Story of America's Peacekeepers*, 1985; *Mark Twain: A Writer's Life*, 1985; *Betty Friedan: A Voice for Women's Rights*, 1985; *Dorothea Lange: Life Through the Camera*, 1985; *Poverty in America*, 1986; *Winnie Mandela: The Soul of South Africa*, 1986; *George Washington and the Birth of Our Nation*, 1986; *Mary McLeod Bethune:*

Voice of Black Hope, 1987; *The American Revolutionaries: A History in Their Own Words, 1750–1800*, 1987; *Rescue: The Story of How Gentiles Saved Jews in the Holocaust*, 1988; *Benjamin Franklin: The New American*, 1988; *Voices from the Civil War: A Documentary History of the Great American Conflict*, 1989; *The Bill of Rights: How We Got It and What It Means*, 1990; *Crime in America*, 1990; *Columbus and the World Around Him*, 1990; *Thomas Jefferson: The Revolutionary Aristocrat*, 1991; *The Amazing Potato*, 1992; *Andrew Jackson and His America*, 1993; *Gold: The True Story of Why People Search for It, Mine It, Trade It, Steal It, Mint It, Hoard It, Shape It, Wear It, Fight and Kill for It*, 1993; *Lincoln: In His Own Words*, 1993; *Cheap Raw Material: How Our Youngest Workers are Exploited and Abused*, 1994; *Who Cares? Millions Do: A Book About Altruism*, 1994; *Theodore Roosevelt and His America*, 1994; *Hold Your Horses: A Feedbag Full of Fact & Fable*, 1995; *Frederick Douglass: In His Own Words*, 1995; *Weapons and Warfare: From the Stone Age to the Space Age*, 1996; *Tom Paine: Voice of a Revolution*, 1996; *The Many Lives of Andrew Carnegie*, 1997; *Ten Queens: Portraits of Women of Power*, 1998; *Food: How We Hunt and Gather It, How We Grow and Eat It, How We Buy and Sell It, How We Preserve and Waste It—and—How Some Have Too Much and Others Have Too Little of It*, 1998; *Witches and Witch-hunts: A History of Persecution*, 1999; *Carl Sandburg*, 1999; *They Came in Chains: The Story of the Slave Ships*, 2000; *Driven from the Land: The Story of the Dust Bowl*, 2000.

SUGGESTED READING: Collier, Laurie and Joyce Nakamura, eds. *Major Authors and Illustrators for Children and Young Adults*, 1993; *Contemporary Authors*, New Revision Series, vol. 38, 1993; *Dictionary of Literary Biography*, vol. 61, 1987; *Directory of American Scholars*, vol. 1; Hipple, Ted, ed. *Writers for Young Adults*, 1997; Meltzer, Milton. *Starting from Home: A Writer's Beginnings*, 1988; Saul, Wendy, ed. *Nonfiction for the Classroom: Milton Meltzer on Writing, History and Social Responsibility*, 1994; Silvey, Anita, ed. *Children's Books and Their Creators*, 1995; *Something About the Author*, vol. 1, 1971; vol. 50, 1988; vol. 80, 1995; *Something About the Author Autobiography Series*, vol. 1, 1986. Periodicals—"Writing History: A Conversation with Milton Meltzer," *Cobblestone*, January 1990.

An earlier profile of Milton Meltzer appeared in *Third Book of Junior Authors* (1972).

"When I was growing up, my mother was the family photographer. We were all accustomed to her ever-present Rolleiflex, and I was introduced early to the wonders of a darkroom. Because of my mother, I grew up in a house filled with family photographs that were valued and enjoyed.

"As a child, I also spent many hours looking through two very powerful books: *The Family of Man,* edited by Edward Steichen, and *You Have Seen Their Faces,* by Erskine Caldwell and Margaret Bourke-White. Even when I was young, I was aware of the ability of a photograph both to evoke a strong emotional response and to create unique visual connections to the past.

"After college, I worked in children's book publishing for seven years, then took time off to be at home with our two children, Kate and Jacob. Like my mother, I became the self-appointed family photographer, and I quickly discovered how much I enjoyed taking pictures. I loved the pursuit of my subject, the tension of waiting to press the shutter, and the thrill of realizing that I had captured a special moment.

"When our children were both in school, I began looking for a new role that would give me the flexibility to be at home and to work. The combination of photography and children's books was the key, but I knew that I needed more experience. I went back into the darkroom with my mother, but this time as her student. I took courses and read about photography, but mostly I practiced with my camera, taking pictures everywhere—from family gatherings to grade-school portraits.

"When I start a new book project, it's both exciting and a little scary. Each book is an adventure in which I am the creator, the director, the casting agent, the location manager, and the camera person, all rolled into one. Unlike an illustrator, who can create whatever world he visualizes in his head, I have to find a piece of real life and take its picture.

"Because of my emotional connections to the family photograph, my special love is photographing people, especially children. Photographing children is both exhilarating and exhausting. When I'm faced with a toddler's classic meltdown, I wonder why I base my livelihood and sense of personal success on the whims of two- and three-year-olds. I wonder how I can capture

Courtesy of David Reuther

Margaret Miller

March 3, 1945–

Courtesy of William Morrow & Co., Inc.

natural, appealing photos in spite of runny noses, low blood sugar, and brief attention spans.

"None of the kids in my books is a model. They are children of friends, friends of friends, or strangers whom I approach in the grocery store or the park. Sometimes I have never laid eyes on the child until I show up with my camera and lighting equipment in tow.

"When I walk through the front door, I'm hunting for an emotional bond with the child, the joy of newfound friends that animates a photograph. In my ideal picture, the child is comfortable and relaxed and, at the same time, radiates an appealing energy. Overcoming the basic discomfort of the situation—the common anxiety of being photographed, the flashing strobes, the need to take not just one photograph but many—is a continual challenge.

"I always arrive with a wish-list of photos, based on careful planning of the layout of a book. But I have learned to go with the flow of the child and to improvise quickly. I will use every device from silly animal noises to playing hide-and-seek to sharing crackers in order to create my personal hybrid: a photo play date.

"As I pack up my equipment and say good-bye, I may be tired but I'm also high with excitement because I love taking photographs; I love the challenge and the hard work; and I am supremely complimented when the three-year-old says. 'That was fun. I want to do it again!'"

* * *

Margaret Miller is a freelance photographer whose striking photographs of babies and children tell wonderful stories that both entertain and teach developing minds. Her photo-essays are engaging and appealing to both adults and children because her subjects are perfectly matched to the concepts she is illustrating. And who can resist looking at pictures of babies and children discovering change, growth, functions, colors, shapes, and relationships while having a wonderful time?

Miller is an author-photographer of more than forty-five popular books for children. Her concept books *Can You Guess?* and *Whose Shoe?* won the *Parenting* Reading Magic Award. *Guess Who?* was an American Booksellers Association Pick of the Lists; *Where Does It Go?* was a Pick of the Lists and a *New York Times* Best Illustrated Book of the Year, and also won the *Parenting* Reading Magic Award. In addition, Miller has provided the photographs for numerous books by Joanna Cole, most notably *How You Were Born*, which was an ALA Notable Children's Book, a Golden Kite Honor Book, and a *Reading Rainbow* Review Book. *My Puppy Is Born*, also by Joanna Cole, was a *Reading Rainbow* Review Book. Miller has worked with children's author Elaine Scott to produce photo-documentaries about the Hubble telescope, twins, and careers in film, comic books, and television.

Margaret Miller is a lifetime New Yorker. She grew up in Rockland county north of New York City, graduated from Barnard College with a B.A. in American Studies, and has lived in New York City ever since. She is a member of the Authors Guild and the Society of Children's Book Writers and Illustrators.

SELECTED WORKS WRITTEN AND PHOTOGRAPHED: *Whose Hat?*, 1988; *Who Uses This?*, 1990; *Whose Shoe?*, 1991; *Where Does It Go?*, 1992; *Can You Guess?*, 1993; *Guess Who?*, 1994; *My Five Senses*, 1994; *Now I'm Big*, 1996; *Baby Faces*, 1998; *Big and Little*, 1998; *I Love Colors*, 1999; *Me & My Bear*, 1999.

SELECTED WORKS PHOTOGRAPHED: *Ramona: Behind the Scenes of a Television Show*, by Elaine Scott, 1988; *My Puppy Is Born*, by Joanna Cole, 1991; *How You Were Born*, by Joanna Cole, 1993; *Adventure in Space: The Flight to Fix the Hubble*, by Elaine Scott, 1995; *Riding Silver Star*, by Joanna Cole, 1996; *The New Baby at Your House*, by Joanna Cole, 1998; *Twins*, by Elaine Scott, 1998; *Friends*, by Elaine Scott, 2000.

SUGGESTED READING: "Family Albums," *The Horn Book*, March/April 1998; Phelan, Carolyn, "Elaine Scott and Margaret Miller's 'Adventure in Space,'" *Book Links*, March 1996.

Courtesy of Judith Petrovich

Wendell Minor

March 17, 1944–

"I can remember watching a mother robin feed her young in a tree just outside my schoolroom window when I was in first grade. At the time, I was seated in a circle of chairs with my classmates and we were supposed to be reading from our *Fun with Dick and Jane* readers. Miss Cottington reminded me that I should not daydream, but pay attention to my reading! My world has always been visual. Reading appreciation came to me later in life.

"By the time I was in fourth grade, I knew I would be an artist someday. I was praised for my drawing ability, and that gave me a sense of self-esteem that nurtured my desire to excel. Thanks to my father, who was an avid outdoorsman, I learned to be a keen observer of nature. We would sit for hours waiting for the fish to bite or a squirrel to appear on a high branch in an oak tree.

"My sixth-grade teacher, Mr. Gilkey, brought the art of the written word to me by reading aloud to our class the works of some of America's great writers. Jack London was my favorite. I will never forget *The Call of the Wild.* Mr. Gilkey's deep voice made the words come alive with vivid pictures of the Far North. It was at that moment that my visual world and reading came together. In retrospect, it was that particular experience that forged my future as an illustrator of books! It was therefore a great pleasure for me to paint full-color pictures for a new edition of *The Call of the Wild*, published as a Scribner's Modern Classic in the fall of 1999, and to dedicate these illustrations to his memory. Life has come full circle.

"I believe I was very fortunate to have grown up in the midwest in the 1950s and to have experienced the rural landscape near my hometown of Aurora, Illinois. My mother and father both grew up on farms, and their sensibilities were well rooted in the Illinois soil. They taught me to appreciate the simple joys of everyday life: the sweet smell of a freshly plowed field after a rainstorm; tending the large birdhouse for a purple martin community that would return faithfully to our backyard every spring; the smell of burning leaves in autumn and the celebration of harvest-time at the county fair. These images are indelibly etched in my memory forever. It has taken me a lifetime to realize how much those early experiences in nature have defined my identity as a mature artist.

"In 1986, I was asked to read a poem by Diane Siebert entitled 'Mojave.' I remember that day very well and knew immediately that I wanted to paint pictures for Diane's visually rich and beautifully descriptive text. We clearly shared a love of nature and passion for a sense of place. From that day forward I knew that my mission as an artist was to communicate to future generations of children that love of nature and sense of place. My interest in reading, natural history, science, landscape painting, and America would be brought together in one place to create children's picture books celebrating all manner of natural environments from every corner of our great land."

* * *

Wendell Minor was born and raised in the town of Aurora, Illinois, the son of Gordon and Marjorie Sebby Minor. In high school he was art editor of the school newspaper and editor-in-chief of the yearbook. He attended the Ringling School of Art and Design, the Kansas City Art Institute, and the Art Students League in New York City. While at Ringling, he was recruited by Hallmark Cards and spent one and a half years there. He moved back to Aurora for a short time to work for a design firm, then went on to New York City. For two years he worked for the Paul Bacon Studio before becoming a freelance illustrator and designer in 1970.

Courtesy of HarperCollins Publishers

Minor is well known in the publishing industry for designing and painting the jackets of hundreds of bestselling novels and biographies for adults, including Pat Conroy's *Beach Music*, David McCullough's Pulitzer Prize–winning *Truman*, and Woodward and Bernstein's *All the President's Men*. This aspect of his work is explored fully in *Wendell Minor: Art for the Written Word*, a retrospective of twenty-five years of his book-cover art, published in 1995. Minor has received over 250 awards in major graphics competitions and had many solo exhibitions. Examples of his work can be found in museums throughout the country. As President of the Society of Illustrators from 1989 to 1991, Minor was responsible for the organization of an international exhibition entitled *Art for Survival: The Illustrator and the Environment* as well as the publication of a book by the same title.

Wendell Minor's children's books have consistently exhibited his love for the land and environment. Illustrating books for naturalist authors Jean Craighead George and Diane Siebert, among others, he approaches his art by researching and experiencing each environment he illustrates. His books have consistently been named on the annual lists for Notable Trade Books in the Field of Social Studies, Outstanding Science Trade Books, and IRA Teachers' Choices. *Sierra* won the John and Patricia Beatty Award from the California Library Association. In addition to picture books, Minor has created cover art and interior illustrations for novels for young people, including Jean Craighead George's *Julie* and *Julie's Wolf Pack*, and redesigned the cover for the twenty-fifth anniversary edition of the Newbery award–winning *Julie of the Wolves*. Wendell Minor and his wife, Florence, live in Washington, Connecticut, where he also has his studio.

SELECTED WORKS WRITTEN AND ILLUSTRATED: *Grand Canyon*, 1998.

SELECTED WORKS ILLUSTRATED: *Mojave*, by Diane Siebert, 1988; *Heartland*, by Diane Siebert, 1989; *Sierra*, by Diane Siebert, 1991; *The Seashore Book*, by Charlotte Zolotow, 1992; *Red Fox Running*, by Eve Bunting, 1993; *The Moon of the Owls*, by Jean Craighead George, 1993; *Julie*, by Jean Craighead George, 1994; *Everglades*, by Jean Craighead George, 1995; *Arctic Son*, by Jean Craighead George, 1997; *Shaker Hearts*, by Ann Turner, 1997; *Grassroots*, by Carl Sandburg, 1998; *The Call of the Wild*, by Jack London, 1999; *A Lucky Thing*, by Alice Schertle, 1999; *Morning, Noon, and Night*, by Jean Craighead George, 1999; *Snow Bear*, by Jean Craighead George, 1999; *Sky Memories*, by Pat Brisson, 1999.

SUGGESTED READING: Minor, Wendell. *Wendell Minor: Art for the Written Word*, 1995; *Something About the Author*, vol. 78, 1994. Periodicals—*American Artist*, January 1987; October 1987; *The Country and Abroad*, December 1998; *Modern Maturity*, January/February 1998; *Publishers Weekly*, October 9, 1995; *U.S. Airways Attaché Magazine*, December 1998; *Watercolor: An American Artist Publication*, December 1998.

WEB SITE: *www.minorart.com*

Ken Mochizuki

May 18, 1954–

"During camping trips when I was young, I was the one who liked telling scary stories. For me, the challenge was to see if I could draw my listeners totally into the story—and deliver the good scare at the end.

"I was born and raised in Seattle, Washington, and a good story always enthralled me. As much as I encourage young people to read rather than watch TV, I have to admit that I learned a lot about good storytelling from TV shows during the '60s, such as the original *Star Trek* series.

"My appearance would also affect the rest of my life and ultimately lead to a career as a writer with something to say. My grandparents were from Japan, my parents (born in Seattle) have visited the country once, and I have never been there. Yet, even today, many people assume I must be from Japan and treat me like I am new to America, or can never be a part of America. While growing up, I've had my share of being called derogatory names.

"My first enriching encounter with creative writing happened during ninth grade when I had to keep a journal. To receive an A for the week, I had to write fifteen pages on any subject. However, if I wrote something creative, I only had to write five pages. Five pages of making something up? Piece of cake, I thought, as I wrote a lot of science fiction and scary stories.

"Throughout high school and college I didn't think about being a writer because music and movies were my main interests. Being a film director fascinated me the most. After college, I headed to Los Angeles and spent five years there as a professional actor. Actors spend a lot of time being unemployed, so I spent much of that time reading. That was when I decided to become a writer.

"And there's only one way to become a writer: write. I returned to Seattle and became a print journalist and freelance writer. Learning how to use the least amount of words to say the most and having done so many different types of writing would later help me immensely to become a writer for young readers.

Courtesy of Steve Uyeno

"I had always planned on writing adult novels, but in 1991 a publisher starting his own children's picture book company invited me to write a story. Drawing on information and stories I had heard during my years as a journalist, I wrote my first book, *Baseball Saved Us*, which was published in 1993. This story, about a young Japanese-American boy playing baseball in an American prison camp for Japanese-Americans during World War II, went on to become a tremendous success.

"Having experienced prejudice and being stereotyped often during my life, those subjects are so much a part of me that they often work their way into my books. And I also feel that it is my

Courtesy of Lee & Low Books, Inc.

job, and mission, to tell as much of America as possible that those of Asian descent are a part of this country, and have been for a long time.

"A lot of adults are jealous of me because I make a living as a writer. It took a long time to get here, but yes, I do now have the luxury of doing what I love and what I believe in. And I also create my own movies all by myself. Only they are at a bookstore instead of at a movie theater near you."

*   *   *

Ken Mochizuki has lived most of his life in Seattle, Washington. After earning a B.A. degree from the University of Washington, he worked as an actor for five years in Los Angeles before returning to Seattle and becoming a staff writer for *The International Examiner,* a Seattle newspaper. He has also worked as an assistant editor for the *Northwest Nikkei.* Before he turned his hand from newspaper writing to children's book writing, there were very few books for children that described the Japanese-American experience.

Mochizuki's books do more than entertain and teach history—their focus on social problems provides opportunities for young readers to develop and test their own value systems. His first book, *Baseball Saved Us*, introduced children to the little-taught subject of the Japanese-American internment during World War II. His next book, *Heroes*, explored the theme of racial stereotyping and its effect on a young boy. In his third book, *Passage to Freedom*, Mochizuki told the true story of a Japanese diplomat who, prompted by his young son, helped thousands of Jews escape the Holocaust.

Baseball Saved Us won a Parents' Choice Award and a Washington State Governor's Writers Award; it was also an American Booksellers Association Pick of the Lists and winner of the *Publishers Weekly* Cuffies Award for Best Multicultural Title. *Heroes* was a Notable Children's Trade Book in the Field of Social Studies, a Children's Book-of-the-Month Club selection, an IRA Teachers' Choice, and a Smithsonian Notable Children's Book. *Passage to Freedom* was an ALA Notable Children's Book, a Smithsonian Notable Children's Book, a Notable Children's Trade Book in the Field of Social Studies, an IRA Notable Book for a Global Society, an NCTE Notable Book in Language Arts, and an ABA Pick of the Lists. It also won *Parenting* magazine's Reading Magic Award and was named the Best Book in the Social Studies K–6 category for 1997–1998 by the Society of School Librarians International.

SELECTED WORKS: *Baseball Saved Us*, illus. by Dom Lee, 1993; *Heroes*, illus. by Dom Lee, 1995; *Passage to Freedom: The Sugihara Story*, illus. by Dom Lee, 1997.

SUGGESTED READING: *Contemporary Authors*, vol. 149, 1996; *Something About the Author*, vol. 81, 1995; *Something About the Author Autobiography Series*, vol. 22, 1996. Periodicals— Wilde, Susie, "Coaching Kids on Conflict," *Learning*, October/November 1995.

"My love of books was spurred, ironically, by my lack of them. As a child in Tanzania, I didn't own my first book until I started school. But even before I knew my alphabet, as I saw people read from books I remember thinking, with intense fascination and awe, what an absolutely magical phenomenon it was. How could anyone, I wondered, give voice to strange-looking markings on paper? I couldn't wait to go to school so I, too, could learn this magic.

"The next year, 1958, not only did I go to school, but I also got to own my very first book—a glossy new alphabet book that the teacher gave me on my first day in Grade One. That book was special to me, I couldn't get my eyes and hands off it. I ran my fingers across the colors on its shiny surface. I touched the letters. I smelled the paper. It smelled of a faraway magical place, where I thought books came from. Thereafter, all through my primary school years, whenever I got a new book, I went

Tololwa M. Mollel

(tuh-LOHL-lah moh-LELL)

June 25, 1952–

through the same ritual of savoring everything about it, including its magical smell.

"The middle school I went to was one of the very few schools to have a library, consisting of books donated from abroad through American missionaries in Tanzania. There was a curious assortment of books—encyclopedias, textbooks, children's books, travelogues, magazines. We read indiscriminately. A friend of mine and I cheerfully sank our teeth into the encyclopedias, from the beginning. We knew the life histories of all the American presidents. What good this would do us we never stopped to wonder.

"In the secondary school I went to from 1967 to 1972, one of

Courtesy of Richard Woolner

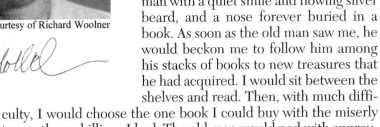

my favorite haunts was the library, a musty narrow room at the head of a steep flight of stairs. To me there was no smell sweeter than that of the old hardbound books, mostly classics, in that library. I looked forward to Tuesday and Thursday afternoons, the library's only opening hours. Since one could only borrow one book at a time, I would try to read a whole book in the library itself and borrow one when I left. On Tuesdays, I borrowed a book that I could finish by Thursday, when I could borrow a thick one that would get me through the weekend. God forbid that I finish the book before Tuesday!

"My other favorite place was a secondhand bookstore not far from the school. It was owned by a stooped old man with a quiet smile and flowing silver beard, and a nose forever buried in a book. As soon as the old man saw me, he would beckon me to follow him among his stacks of books to new treasures that he had acquired. I would sit between the shelves and read. Then, with much difficulty, I would choose the one book I could buy with the miserly two or three shillings I had. The old man would nod with approval when I made a good choice. Sometimes he would throw in an extra book free, much to my delight.

"As with many writers, it was my love of reading that led to my love of writing. Many times in school, after reading an inspiring story, I found myself with a pen in hand trying to write a story of my own. I wrote many half-finished stories this way—adventure, detective, fantasy, romantic stories. In grade six, I wrote the only story that I ever finished, a true story of a time I ran away and went missing for a whole week. I still remember the relish with which I threw myself into the story. I made a little notebook and broke up the story into as many chapters as there were pages, just so I could have the pleasure of thinking up a new chapter title every day. Even now I remember the thrill I experienced in discovering the dozens of alternative chapter titles I could come up with, and the endless ways I could embellish the story.

"I still get the same thrill when I write a story, the thrill of discovering something worthy of a story from my life experience; of discovering and exploring a story worth sharing; and discovering the little things that make a story work for children and for me. It's the thrill of a treasure hunt—finding and shaping a story idea, struggling for a nifty, enchanting beginning, and searching for the words that marry action to character, setting, and theme.

"My favorite story, out of my own stories, is any story that I happen to be working on. Embarking on a new story is like being on the threshold of an adventure. I look forward to the discoveries to be made, to challenging questions regarding plot and character leaping out at me, and to answers to the questions springing out at me when I least expect. I look forward to the beautiful nuggets to be mined out of the story and my creative imagination.

"Nothing makes my day like suddenly alighting on a word, a phrase, a description, an image that jolts a story to life, brings clarity to an awkward sentence, and tightens a slack scene or plot. Writing picture-book stories has taught me a lot and made me learn the microscopic aspects of writing fiction. It has taught me the power of language. In a short story, every word is worth its weight in gold. I like the process of rewriting and rewriting, which to me is what writing, especially for children, is all about. And I like the challenge of expressing big or complicated ideas and concepts simply, clearly, engagingly, and memorably, in terms relevant to a child."

"It's the thrill of a treasure hunt—finding and shaping a story idea . . ."

✳   ✳   ✳

Tololwa Marti Mollel was raised by his paternal grandparents on a coffee farm in Tanzania, not far from Mount Kilimanjaro. His family heritage is Arusha Maasai, and he grew up in a culture of traditional storytelling. After receiving his B.A. degree in Literature and Theatre at the University of Dar es Salaam in 1975, Mollel moved to Canada to take an M.A. in Drama at the University of Alberta. From 1979 to 1986 he was a university lecturer, actor, and co-director of a children's theatrical group in Tanzania. From 1986 to 1999 he lived in Edmonton, Alberta, but traveled extensively across Canada and the United States, conducting writing workshops and storytelling sessions and presenting readings and talks, in and out of schools. He served as a Writer-in-Residence for the Edmonton Public Library and has conducted drama and storytelling workshops in Winchester College, England.

It wasn't until his first son was born that Mollel decided to try his hand at writing for children and began producing the picture book treatments of African folklore and contemporary African life that have brought him so many honors. *The Orphan Boy: A Maasai Story* was designated an ALA Notable Children's Book and won the Canadian Governer General's Award. It was also an ABA Pick of the Lists, a Notable Trade Book in the Field of Social Studies, and a Parents' Choice Award book. *Rhinos for Lunch and Elephants for Supper!* won a Florida Reading Association award and *The King and the Tortoise* was cited as a Notable Trade Book in the Field of Social Studies. *Big Boy* was a Canadian Library Association Honor Book and won the R. Ross Annett Award from the Writers Guild of Alberta. In *My Rows and Piles of Coins*, an ALA Notable Children's Book, Mollel relates an incident remembered from his own boyhood in Tanzania. Most of his books have been cited on the annual Choice lists of the Canadian Children's Book Center.

Tololwa Mollel currently lives in Minneapolis, Minnesota, with his wife, Obianuju, and their two teenage boys, Lese and Emeka.

SELECTED WORKS: *The Orphan Boy: A Maasai Story*, illus. by Paul Morin, 1991; *Rhinos for Lunch and Elephants for Supper! A Maasai Tale*, illus. by Barbara Spurll, 1992; *A Promise to the Sun: An African Story*, illus. by Beatriz Vidal, 1992; *The King and the Tortoise*, illus. by Kathy Blankley, 1993; *The Princess Who Lost Her Hair*, illus. by Charles Reasoner, 1993; *The Flying Tortoise: An Igbo Tale*, illus. by Barbara Spurll, 1993; *Big Boy*, illus. by E. B. Lewis, 1995; *Kele's Secret*, illus. by Catherine Stock, 1997; *Ananse's Feast: An Ashanti Tale*, illus. by Andrew Glass, 1997; *Shadow Dance*, illus. by Donna Perrone, 1998; *Kitoto the Mighty*, illus. by Kristi Frost, 1998; *Song Bird*, illus. by Rosanne Litzinger, 1999; *My Rows and Piles of Coins*, illus. by E. B. Lewis, 1999; *Subira Subira*, illus by Linda Saport, 2000.

SUGGESTED READING: *Canadian Who's Who*, vol. 33, 1998; *Contemporary Authors*, vol. 137, 1992; Pendergast, Sara, ed. *St. James Guide to Children's Writers*, 5th ed., 1999; *Something About the Author*, vol. 88, 1997. Periodicals—Saldanha, Louise, "Bordering the Mainstream: The Writing of Tololwa Mollel," *Canadian Children's Literature*, Spring 1996.

"During the Mexican Revolution of 1910, my grandparents and my father, who was then a little boy, traveled to the north, to *el norte*, across the Rio Grande River to settle in El Paso, Texas. My mother was born there, as was I on January 19, 1942. I'm the eldest of four children. When we were growing up we all enjoyed driving across the bridge to Mexico to buy good *pan dulce*, sweet bread, and to visit the market and see women making tortillas and piñatas. We'd stroll the aisles speaking English and Spanish, listening to mariachi music and smelling the ripe tomatoes and limes and mangoes. Those markets and the El Paso desert are part of many of my books, such as *Uno, Dos, Tres / One, Two, Three* and *This Big Sky*.

Courtesy of Cynthia Farah

Pat Mora

January 19, 1942–

"My grandmother and aunt lived with us. This aunt, Ignacia Delgado, the star of my first children's book, *A Birthday Basket for Tía*, was a wonderful storyteller. She'd sit on the edge of our beds and in Spanish tell us about when she was a little girl in Mexico, about the time she was punished and ate all the candy that was cooling in the room next to the classroom. Her voice, like a magic Spanish carpet, carried me back with her.

"I'm a reader because of my mother. When she was little, she'd hide under the covers with a flashlight to finish her books. She always bought books for us and took us to the library until we were old enough to go by bus. I joined the library summer reading clubs and read biographies, the Pollyanna books, and Laura Ingalls Wilder. My mother would always read my papers and speeches and give me good suggestions.

"I liked school and didn't like to be absent, but when I was sick, I enjoyed listening to soap operas on the radio and reading an orange set of books called *Childcraft*. My favorites were the book of poems and the stories of long ago, with carriages and women in long dresses and fringed shawls.

"My parents gave me a gray portable typewriter when I graduated from eighth grade and a box of stationery with gold scalloped edges. I sat and typed rhyming poems and still remember how good the keys felt under my fingers, the way they feel now when I work at my computer. When I was growing up, I never met or saw a writer, and don't think I ever considered being one until I was an adult. I was too busy planning to be a nun! But

Courtesy of Random House

after college, I taught, raised three children, and then became a university administrator.

"When I was little, I liked sinking into the world of a book. That pleasure has only deepened, and that is why I'm a writer. Writing is a kind of magic. It means taking a blank page and creating music without violins or pianos, creating colors without paints or oils, creating scents without flowers or herbs.

"I feel very lucky to spend my days writing or visiting schools and campuses. Whether I'm writing for adults or children, whether I'm writing poetry or prose, writing is how I discover and play. Maybe it's like visiting the Mexican market. I smell the words and hear their colors and their music, feel their thorns and their smooth roundness. I'm trying to take all those possibilities and create something that has never quite existed before—to take you, the reader, with me into the desert or Mexico or the border or into a bilingual family. I don't know where our journey will take us next. But me . . . I'm full of curiosity!"

* * *

Pat Mora, a frequent speaker at conferences and universities, promotes diversity, ecological and cultural. Mexican–American culture is an important theme in Mora's writing, as well as in her life. One of her goals is to establish pride in their Mexican heritage for young Chicanos. Pat Mora has been a consultant to the Kellogg Foundation on U.S.-Mexico youth exchanges.

Mora received a B.A. from Texas Western College in 1963 and an M.A. in 1967 from the University of Texas at El Paso, where she later served as an administrator and museum director. She has taught English at all levels. She is the mother of three grown children and divides her time between the Cincinnati area and the Southwest. During the fall of 1999 she was the Carruthers Chair Distinguished Visiting Professor at the University of New Mexico. She speaks and writes in both Spanish and English. She is currently involved in a project to celebrate April 30th as Día de los Niños / Día de los Libros, an effort to make the nation aware that we must open the world of books to all children.

In 1998, she received the Tomás Rivera Mexican American Children's Book Award from Southwest Texas State University for *Tomás and the Library Lady*, which was also an IRA/CBC Teachers' Choice and received the Multicultural Honor Award from *Skipping Stones* magazine. *Confetti: Poems for Children* was named a Notable Book for a Global Society by the International Reading Association, and *The Desert Is My Mother / El Desierto Es Mi Madre* won the Nature and Ecology Honor Award from *Skipping Stones* magazine. The University of Wisconsin-Milwaukee gave Mora the Américas Award for Children's and Young Adult Literature from the Consortium of Latin American Studies Programs for *Tomás and the Library Lady* and *Pablo's Tree*. *A Birthday Basket for Tía* won the Southwest Book Award from the Border Regional Library Association. The author has also been honored with a 1994 Poetry Fellowship from the National Endowment for the Arts and a 1986–1989 Kellogg National Leadership Fellowship.

SELECTED WORKS: *A Birthday Basket for Tía*, illus. by Cecily Lang, 1992; *Agua, Agua, Agua*, illus. by José Ortega, 1994; *Listen to the Desert / Oye al Desierto*, illus. by Francisco Mora, 1994; *The Desert Is My Mother / El Desierto Es Mi Madre*, illus. by Daniel Lechon, 1994; *Pablo's Tree*, illus. by Cecily Lang, 1994; *The Gift of the Poinsettia / El Regalo de la Flor de Nochebuena*, with Charles Ramirez Berg, 1995; *The Race of Toad and Deer*, 1995; *Uno, Dos, Tres / One, Two, Three*, illus. by Barbara Lavallee, 1996; *Confetti: Poems for Children*, illus. by Enrique Sanchez, 1996; *Tomás and the Library Lady*, illus. by Raúl Colón, 1997; *Delicious Hullabaloo / Pachanga Deliciosa*, 1998; *This Big Sky*, illus. by Steve Jenkins, 1998; *The Rainbow Tulip*, illus. by Elizabeth Sayles, 1999.

SUGGESTED READING: Balassi, William, John F. Crawford, and Annie O. Eysturoy, eds. *This Is About Vision: Interviews with Southwestern Writers*, 1990; *Children's Literature Review*, vol. 58, 2000; *Contemporary Authors*, vol. 129, 1990; *Contemporary Authors*, New Revision Series, vol. 57, 1997; Day, Frances Ann. *Latina and Latino Voices in Literature for Children and Teenagers*, 1997; Krstovic, J. O., ed. *Hispanic Literature Criticism*, vol. 2, 1994; Nagel, Rob, and Sharon Rose, eds. *Hispanic American Biography*, 1995; *Something About the Author*, vol. 92, 1998. Peridocials—*Children's Literature in Education*, September 1997; *Language Arts*, March 1998; *New Advocate*, Fall 1998; *Publishers Weekly*, December 5, 1994; *School Library Journal*, October 1994; "Talking with Pat Mora," *Book Links*, September 1997.

WEB SITE: *www.patmora.com*

Courtesy of Ken Heyman

Ann Morris

October 1, 1930–

"I think my work as a children's book writer can be directly and indirectly attributed to my own early years and early schooling. I had the good fortune to attend the Hunter Elementary School, where we had unlimited access to a wonderful library, excellent teachers who encouraged reading and storytelling and book illustration. Professors from Hunter College came into our classroom and regaled us with stories about their trips to Egyptian tombs and desert expeditions. And then there was something called 'audio-visual enrichment.' I loved it. All those slides and sounds and different sorts of exposure to worlds near and far. We had poetry readings and book fairs and spelling bees and 'free time' to read whatever we wanted. And of course, all the book reports and then—getting my own library card! I think of that as a major event. All those books could be mine! I couldn't believe it. I lived near the Museum of Natural History, where I spent many rainy Saturdays. There was a wonderful bookshop there where I poked around and planned what I would ask for when my birthday rolled around. Then there were the many summers at camp, which also contributed in their own way to my love of books. The endless volumes of the Bobbsey Twins and Nancy Drew, along with *Heidi, Mr. Popper's Penguins, The Wizard of Oz, Peter Pan*, Popeye, Superman, and Dick Tracy. What a world!

"When I finished college and became a teacher of young children I was able to transmit my love of books to my kindergartners. We read, and wrote, and made books and talked books. Then I taught older children and, with them, discovered a whole new bibliography: *The Hobbit, The Phantom Tollbooth, Island of the Blue Dolphins*, all of 'Alice.' The children made their own books and read them to each other. Then I taught teachers and I learned the many different ways they introduced children to books. All the while, I was discovering my own writing ability.

"Inadvertently, I became a children's book editor. I had gotten bogged down in completing my doctoral studies and had to leave the university after the initial three years. It was a blessing in disguise. I was offered a job in educational publishing, and it opened up a whole new world. All of a sudden all sorts of creative possibilities were available. I was asked to develop a complete early childhood program with books, recordings, slide pro-

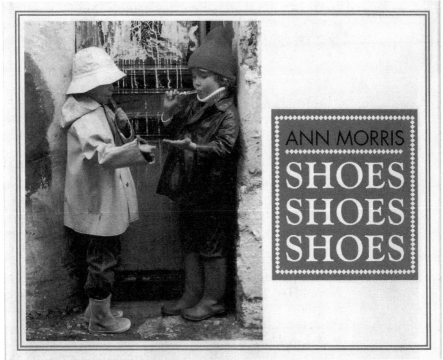

Courtesy of William Morrow & Co, Inc.

grams, teacher materials, using every available resource. It was all so challenging and stimulating, and what's more, I was good at it! Those years served to stimulate my imagination and intellect, and I am thankful for them. When I left that job I was ready to 'do my own thing.'

"I started writing all sorts of books and ultimately sold the beginning of what has become a most successful series to a well-known editor I had met at a conference at Vassar. She had made a speech there about how it was impossible to deal with unsolicited manuscripts and how important it was to get to know what each editor liked to publish before making any attempts at submission. It was all very discouraging. But I thought I really had something she would like. When I got back from the weekend I phoned her early in the morning, before the secretary would put me off. We briefly chatted, and she invited me to come down to see her with the dummies that very afternoon. I sold my first books to her on the spot! Doing the unexpected and of course believing in what I had written, led to my first publication.

"I have some wonderfully creative and supportive editors who have made my books more than I could make them myself. I've worked with some very talented illustrators and photographers. My work has taken me to a traveling circus, a ballet school, a teddy bear factory and a goat farm, to name a few of the interesting places. It has also taken me to Russia, Israel, Italy, England, Vermont, San Francisco, Boston, and New Orleans. My books have been translated into French, Spanish, Swedish, Finnish, and even Chinese! I've met wonderful people along the way. *Mr. Rogers* and *Reading Rainbow* highlight my books, too."

* * *

Having grown up in New York City amidst its cultural diversity, Ann Morris has a thirst for seeing the parts of the world from which her neighbors came. "I'm a gypsy by nature," she says. "I always have my suitcase packed." After graduating from college, she taught children in public and private schools in New York City and adults at Bank Street College, Columbia Teachers College, New York University and Queens College of the City of New York. Recently she has taught writing for children at the New School. She left teaching to become editorial director of Scholastic's early childhood department and eventually began writing books herself.

Now, twenty-five years later, she has published over sixty books. Her interest in travel and the arts took her to the famous Vaganova Academy in Russia, where children of the Kirov Ballet Company are instructed. This resulted in *On Their Toes*, followed by *Dancing to America*, a book about one of the Russian children and his family, who emigrated to New York, where he now attends the School of American Ballet. Another time, she and photographer Ken Heyman traveled across the United States documenting the lives of ten different families.

Ann Morris's books have won many awards. *Tools, Houses and Homes, On the Go,* and *Bread, Bread, Bread* have all been chosen Pick of the Lists by the American Booksellers Association. In 1989 *Bread, Bread, Bread* received the NCTE Orbis Pictus Award for Outstanding Nonfiction. *Houses and Homes, Loving, Dancing to America,* and *Bread, Bread, Bread* were all cited as Notable Children's Trade Books in the Field of Social Studies.

In addition to writing, Morris leads workshops and conducts classroom presentations throughout the United States. She enjoys taking her books into schools and getting suggestions and feedback from children.

SELECTED WORKS: *Bread, Bread, Bread,* illus. by Ken Heyman, 1989; *Hats, Hats, Hats*, illus. by Ken Heyman, 1989; *Loving,* illus. by Ken Heyman, 1990; *On the Go*, illus. by Ken Heyman, 1990; *Tools*, illus. by Ken Heyman, 1992; *Houses and Homes*, illus. by Ken Heyman, 1992; *Dancing to America*, illus. by Paul Kolnik, 1994; *How Teddy Bears Are Made*, illus. by Ken Heyman, 1994; *The Daddy Book*, illus. by Ken Heyman, 1995; *Weddings*, 1995; *Shoes, Shoes, Shoes*, illus. by Ken Heyman, 1995; *Karate Boy*, illus. by David Katzenstein, 1996; *Light the Candle! Bang the Drum!*, illus. by Peter Linenthal, 1997; *Work*, 1998; *Play*, 1998; *Teamwork*, 1999.

"When I was a child I was always preoccupied with making 'things' or drawing pictures. The 'things' were usually toy animals. I used all sorts of scraps of material found around the house—corks, seed pods, felt, fur, even babies' diapers for the first toy horses I made when aged seven. My grandmother taught me to sew while my mother encouraged creativity generally. At Christmas and Easter we always decorated the house—one Christmas I made an entire set of cardboard reindeer pulling Santa's sleigh, complete with bells and tinsel. They stretched the length of our stairway, pinned to the wall.

"I remember making simple picture books stapled down the spine, mainly depicting horses. When I was ten I wrote and illustrated a saga called *Freckles the Pony*. However, the thought of becoming an illustrator of picture books never occurred to me until I was a student at art school studying graphic design. I actually wanted to become a toy maker, but since there was no course in Melbourne on such a subject, my second choice was design and illustration. When I majored in Illustration in the early 1970s, I designed and made eight models of mythical creatures. Some of these appeared in the collage illustrations of my book *Fabulous Beasts*. In 1975, assisted by an Australia Council grant, I traveled from Asia to Europe and America looking at various types of puppetry from traditional to contemporary. A highlight was spending a day with Jim Henson on the Muppet sets in England. I made puppets in the U.K. and Australia for several years while continuing to illustrate picture books.

"The fabrics and textures I used for my puppets I began to incorporate into my illustration work. *Rummage* by Christobel Mattingley (1981) uses fur, beads, fabric, etc., in the illustrations, combined with watercolor and ink. The textures and effects achieved with paper also inspired me, and I began to use tissue-paper collage almost exclusively for my illustration work. From the early 1980s to the present, I have continued to explore paper collage and develop my technique, culminating in books such as *V for Vanishing*, *Dinosaur Encore*, and *One Horse Waiting for Me*. I like using real-life models wherever possible, and this means my family and pets often appear in the illustrations.

Courtesy of Geoffrey Kench

Patricia Mullins

September 19, 1952–

"My childhood love of horses has never left me, and somewhere over twenty-five years ago a passion for real horses shifted to an obsession with wooden equines, from those on rockers to the more elaborate carousel breed. I have restored old rocking horses for many years and in 1999 was involved in the heritage restoration of the wonderful 1913 American carousel at Luna Park, Melbourne. Between 1985 and 1991 I researched and wrote *The Rocking Horse: A History of Moving Toy Horses*, a 370-page reference book which has since become the definitive work on the subject. Researching this book took me to many obscure and amazing places, such as Ohrdruf in the Thuringian forest in Germany. Similarly, research for my book illustration leads to all sorts of unexpected places and people. It's one of the most interesting parts of being an illustrator and writer."

* * *

Patricia Mullins's distinctive, bold illustrations are appreciated by children and adults in America as well as her native Australia. She received a Diploma of Graphic Design in 1971 and a Fellowship of Illustration in 1974, both from the Royal Melbourne Institute of Technology. She traveled widely overseas studying puppetry and spent 1975–1976 living in England and working as a puppetmaker for BBC television. On returning to her native country, she designed and made puppets for Australian puppet theaters in the late 1970s. Mullins's first picture book was published in 1972, but it wasn't until the 1980s that her books began to appear internationally. She has held several exhibitions, and her work is found in private and public art collections in Australia.

Courtesy of HarperCollins Publishers

Rummage won the Children's Book Council of Australia's Junior Book of the Year Award in 1982, and *The Magic Saddle* was shortlisted for the Picture Book of the Year Award in 1984. *Hattie and the Fox,* written by Mem Fox, has been a favorite for group storytelling in libraries and preschools since it first appeared in 1986 and has now been translated into German, Chinese, Indonesian, and Japanese; it was designated a Parents' Choice Award book in the United States. *Shoes from Grandpa,* a second collaboration with Fox, garnered starred reviews for its cumulative text and bright collage illustrations.

Of the books both written and illustrated by Mullins, *Dinosaur Encore* was shortlisted for the Eve Pownell Information Book Award given by the Children's Book Council of Australia, and *V for Vanishing* won that award the following year. These well-researched and vividly illustrated volumes were also both listed as Fanfare titles by the *Horn Book* magazine. *V for Vanishing* received "best" awards from the Australian Book Publishers' Association and the Wilderness Society of Australia, as well as a Gold Award in the paper collage category at the Dimensional Illustrators Awards Show, 1994, in New York. *One Horse Waiting for Me* won a Bronze Award in the paper collage category at the same show in 1997.

Patricia Mullins lives in Melbourne, Australia.

SELECTED WORKS WRITTEN AND ILLUSTRATED: *Fabulous Beasts,* 1976; *Dinosaur Encore,* 1992 (U.S. edition, 1993); *V for Vanishing: An Alphabet of Endangered Animals,* 1993 (U.S. edition, 1994); *One Horse Waiting for Me,* 1997 (U.S. edition, 1998).

SELECTED WORKS ILLUSTRATED: *The Happy Bush,* by Heather Larsen, 1972; *Dolphins Are Different,* by Letitia Parr, 1972; *All in Together,* by Vashti Farrer, 1974; *Flowers for Samantha,* by Letitia Parr, 1976; *All Sorts of Poems,* ed. by Ann Thwaite, 1977; *Pelican Point,* by Sue Couper, 1977; *Rummage,* by Christobel Mattingley, 1981 (U.S. edition, 1991); *Duck Boy,* by Christobel Mattingley, 1983 (U.S. edition, 1986); *The Magic Saddle,* by Christobel Mattingley, 1983, 1996 (US edition, 1996); *Hattie & the Fox,* by Mem Fox, 1986 (U.S. edition, 1987); *Crocodile Beat,* by Gail Jorgensen, 1988 (U.S. edition, 1989); *The Triantiwontigongolope,* by C. J. Dennis, 1989; *Shoes from Grandpa,* by Mem Fox, 1989 (U.S. edition, 1992); *The Sea-Breeze Hotel,* by Marcia Vaughan, 1991 (U.S. edition, 1992); *Iceflowers,* by Jutta Goetze, 1992; *The Dream of the Dusky Dolphin,* by Jonathan Harlen, 1995; *Who's Who at the Zoo,* by Celeste Walters, 1996.

SUGGESTED READING: Hamilton, Margaret. *The Picture Book People,* 1993; Lees, Stella and Pam MacIntyre, eds. *The Oxford Companion to Australian Children's Literature,* 1993; McVitty, Walter. *Authors and Illustrators of Australian Children's Books,* 1989; Muir, Marcie. *A History of Australian Children's Book Illustration,* 1982; Scobie, Sue, comp. *The Dromkeen Book of Australian Children's Illustrators,* 1997.

Courtesy of Robert Munsch

Robert Munsch

June 11, 1945–

"I was born on June 11, 1945, in Pittsburgh, Pennsylvania, the fourth of nine children. I was in the middle; a very bad position as it meant I was attacked by both the younger coalition and the older coalition. I did badly in elementary school—daydreamed all the time, never learned how to spell, graduated from eighth grade counting on my fingers to do simple addition.

"I did, however, all through elementary school, write poetry. Funny poems, silly poems, all sorts of poems. Nobody thought that was very important. When I went to a Catholic high school in Pittsburgh, Pennsylvania, I didn't get along with anybody, read lots of books, and decided to be a Catholic priest.

"I studied for seven years to be a Jesuit priest and finally gave that up. While I was studying with the Jesuits, I worked part-time at an orphanage to escape from deadly classes in philosophy. So I knew I liked working with kids; and when I left the Jesuits I decided to work in daycare for a year till I figured out what I wanted to do. What I figured out I wanted to do was to work in daycare.

"After I had been in daycare for a while I decided to learn something about what I was supposed to be doing, so I went back to school for a year at the Elliot Pearson School of Child Studies at Tufts University in Medford, Massachusetts. It was there that I made up my first story while on a student teaching placement at the Wellesley College Child Studies Preschool. I did it for a circle time. I did not know that it was going to be a book called *Mortimer*. It took it twelve years to get to be a book.

"Back in daycare I discovered that I could get the kids to shut up during naptime by telling them stories. For ten years I did this without thinking I had any special skill. After all, while I made the best stories in the daycare center, most of the other teachers made better Play-Doh. I eventually got a long list of stories I told, but I never wrote them down.

"Once when my wife (I met her over a diaper at Bromley Heath Infant Daycare in Jamaica Plain, MA) and I were both out of work because a daycare lost its funding, we decided to try to look for work in Canada. We both ended up at a lab preschool at the University of Guelph in Guelph, Ontario. The wife of my boss happened to be a children's librarian and she heard me telling stories. She told me to publish and I didn't listen. She told my boss to make me publish, and my boss told me to publish and I listened. In fact, he gave me two months off to do it. So I had a great two months off and on the last day, I wrote down ten stories and sent them off to ten different publishers. Nine said 'No,' and one said 'Yes' to a story called 'Mud Puddle.'

"So I became a writer. *Mud Puddle* sold 3,000 copies the first year. Oh *wow!* But Annick Press kept putting out my books, and they slowly sold better and better. (*Mud Puddle* had its best year ten years after it was published!) My next book was called *The Paper Bag Princess*. It sold really well. Finally I quit my job at the University and started just writing and telling stories.

"The telling sometimes got very big, since I was discovered by children's festivals in Canada and then by entertainment promoters. Sometimes I was telling stories to 3,000 kids at once in concert halls—and that is a lot different from a daycare naptime. But I still kept doing schools and daycares because I liked doing them. I also started to travel all over Canada and stay with families while telling stories. I first stayed with families because I did not have money for a hotel, but I soon found out that families were a great place to look for stories. A book called *Moira's Birthday* grew out of staying with Moira's family in Hay River, NWT, Canada.

"Along the way I became Canada's best-selling author, but I was not selling much in the USA. Then *Love You Forever* came out as a Canadian book in 1986. I had written it as a memorial for two stillborn babies we had in 1979 and 1980. The story actually started out as a song.

"I really wanted this story to be a book, and I had to change publishers since my regular publisher did not want to do it. I was worried that it would not sell. It was the best-selling Canadian children's book from 1986–1988, selling one million copies in 1988. The strange thing was that it was also the best-selling children's book in the United States, but nobody knew it, including me.

"The Canadian publisher had, at the time, no salespeople in the USA. *Love You Forever* did not get reviewed in any U.S. newspapers and received no publicity in the United States. It became the best-selling picture book in the United States with no publicity at all.

"I knew that it had sold millions of copies in the U.S. but assumed that there must be lots of books that were outselling it, because it was not on any lists. It never occurred to me that it could be an invisible bestseller. Then, in 1994, the *New York Times* did an update of their list of best-selling children's books. The last update of their list was in 1978, because the list was very stable. *Goodnight Moon* had been #1 since 1948! They found *Love You Forever* at the top of the list with 8,000,000 sold. This was a major embarrassment, as they had never reviewed it, did not know it existed, and it was a foreign title that did not even

> *"I discovered that I could get the kids to shut up during naptime by telling them stories."*

have a U.S. publisher or distributor. Somebody from the *Times* called me up and asked, 'Who *are* you?' That is how I found out that I had the #1 picture book in the United States. It took me eight years to find out!"

*   *   *

During the seven years that Robert Munsch studied for the Roman Catholic priesthood, he earned a bachelor's degree in history (1969) from Fordham University and a master's degree in anthropology from Boston University (1971). He later studied at Tufts University and earned a master's degree in education in 1973, focusing on child studies. Munsch married Ann Beeler, a university educator, on January 22, 1973. They have three children: Julie, Andrew, and Tyya. Robert Munsch is a member of the Association of Canadian Television and Radio Artists, the Canadian Association of Children's Authors, Illustrators and Performers, and the Writers Union of Canada. His hobbies are cycling and geology. He taught in the Bay Area Childcare in Coos Bay, Oregon, from 1973 to 1975; then he and his wife emigrated to Canada, where he taught at the Family Studies Laboratory Preschool at the University of Guelph in Ontario. He was an assistant professor there from 1975 to 1984. Since then he has focused on storytelling and writing children's books.

Munsch likes to capture the attention of his young audiences and challenge convention with words such as *underwear* and plots that reverse expectations, such as one about a princess who rescues a prince. He usually spends up to three years telling his stories to audiences before he finally submits them to a publisher. In 1985 Robert Munsch received the Ruth Schwartz Children's Book Award from the Ontario Arts Council for *Thomas' Snowsuit* and the Juno Award for the best Canadian children's record of the year for *Murmel, Murmel, Munsch*. He was named the Author of the Year by the Canadian Booksellers Association in 1991.

SELECTED WORKS: *Mud Puddle*, illus. by Sami Suomalainen, 1979, rev. ed. 1982; *The Paper Bag Princess*, illus. by Michael Martchenko, 1980; *Murmel, Murmel, Murmel*, illus. by Michael Martchenko, 1982; *The Fire Station*, illus. by Michael Martchenko, 1983; *50 Below Zero*, illus. by Michael Martchenko, 1985; *Love You Forever*, illus. by Sheila McGraw, 1986; *I Have to Go!*, illus. by Michael Martchenko, 1986; *Moira's Birthday*, illus. by Michael Martchenko, 1987; *A Promise Is a Promise*, with Michael Kusugak, illus. by Vladyana Krykorka, 1988; *Something Good*, illus. by Michael Martchenko, 1990; *Purple, Green and Yellow*, illus. by Helen Desputeaux, 1992; *Wait and See,* illus. by Michael Martchenko, 1993; *Where Is Gah-Ning?* illus. by Helene

Desputeaux, 1994; *Alligator Baby*, illus. by Michael Martchenko, 1997; *Get Out of Bed!*, illus. by Lea and Alan Daniel, 1998; *Andrew's Loose Tooth*, 1998; *Munschworks: The First Munsch Collection*, illus. by Michael Martchenko, 1998; *Ribbon Rescue*, illus. by Eugenie Fernandes, 1999. Recordings—*Munsch: Favorite Stories*, 1983; *Murmel, Murmel, Munsch*, 1985.

SUGGESTED READING: *Children's Literature Review*, vol. 19, 1989; Collier, Laurie and Joyce Nakamura, eds. *Major Authors and Illustrators for Children and Young Adults*, 1993; *Contemporary Authors*, vol. 121, 1987; *Contemporary Authors*, New Revision Series, vol. 37, 1992; Pendergast, Sara, ed. *St. James Guide to Children's Writers*, 5th ed, 1999; *Something About the Author*, vol. 48, 1987; vol. 50, 1988; vol. 83, 1996. Periodicals—*CM: Canadian Materials for Schools and Libraries*, March 1987; *Globe and Mail* (Toronto), November 5, 1983, and January 24, 1987; *The Horn Book*, May/June 1985; "Profile: Robert Munsch," *Language Arts*, October 1989; *Sun* (Vancouver), December 3, 1983.

Courtesy of Annick Press Ltd.

"I grew up in Connecticut. (I really hated math.) I went to the Rhode Island School of Design. (I loved to draw and make diagrams and maps, and to record things by making pictures of them.) After the Rhode Island School of Design, I worked in educational publishing in Boston. (That's when I learned more about how people learn. And that lots of people are visual learners and like to learn through images and storytelling).

"My next move was to Chicago. (Chicago is a wonderful city, filled with visual experiences and great learning opportunities.) Now, I live in Evanston, Illinois, with my wife, Nancy. We have two grown children, Randy and Kristin, a new grandson, Jack, and a dog, Blitzen, who arrived at Christmastime and was named after one of our favorite reindeer.

"There were a few more steps along the way, but this is the basic path that led to my interest in education—and, especially, visual learning. I think that most people understand things best when they can see them. It's often better to draw a map than to try to explain where you're going to meet someone. Family trees help to show how people are related to one another. And graphs

Stuart J. Murphy

April 25, 1942–

are usually the easiest way to demonstrate comparisons between two or more things.

"A number of years ago, I started working with a group of top mathematicians on a major new secondary school program. I found the same thing to be true—many of the concepts that students find difficult are easier for them to understand when they are presented visually. Because today's students have grown up in a highly visual environment—with TV, advertising, video games, and the Internet—I knew that I needed to communicate difficult math concepts with drawings, photos, and graphics whenever possible.

"When I was in school, the long lists of equations to solve didn't make any sense to me. If you knew how to do one of them, you could do them all; and if you didn't know how to do them, you couldn't do any of them. All the word problems seemed kind of weird, too. They didn't relate to any experiences that I was having in my life. I decided that I wanted to do something to make today's students like math.

"I began writing stories for young children that demonstrated mathematics in real-life situations and were entertaining too. I write stories about things kids are interested in: circuses, carnivals, vacations, birthdays, shopping, lost socks, pets, gymnastics, food, and face painting. Through these stories kids can see that math is everywhere.

Courtesy of Russ Berkman Photography

Stuart J. Murphy

"One of my favorite aspects of being an author is traveling all over the United States visiting kids at schools and libraries. On a recent visit a boy told me that he thought I had written more books about dogs than cats. His comment led to the idea for a story about the first year of a kitten's life. The story will help children learn about time and sequence, and how to read a calendar.

"I also get ideas from things that happened during my life as well as in the lives of my children. For example, the brother and sister in *Give Me Half* are based on my two children, Randy and Kristin, and the sibling rivalry that is so much a part of growing up. As is the case for many children, it wasn't so easy for them to split something right down the middle!

"The idea for *A Pair of Socks* came one day when I was hunting in my drawer for a pair of socks that matched. This happens to everyone, I thought. Why not write a story about patterns? Then I thought how much fun it would be to tell the story from

Courtesy of HarperCollins Publishers

the sock's point of view. MathStart is a series that teaches math by telling stories. After all, most real-life math occurs within real activities, within the stories of our lives."

Born on April 25, 1942, in Rockville, Connecticut, Stuart Murphy graduated from the Rhode Island School of Design in 1964 with a Bachelor of Fine Arts degree. He had spent his senior year in Rome, Italy, as a participant in the European Honors Program. Ten years later, in 1973, he would return to Italy, to Venice, where he would serve for the year as director of special projects for the International Fund for Monuments.

Positions that Murphy has held during his accomplished career include: art director of the *Art Gallery* magazine (1964–1967), art director for Ginn and Company, educational publishers (1967–1980), and co-founder and president of Ligature, Inc., a research-and-development firm dedicated to working with publishers to conceptualize and prepare high-quality books for American schools (1980–1992). The demands of the latter position led him to enter the Owner-President Management Program at the Harvard Business School, from which he graduated in 1986. In 1992 he began working as an author and consultant in the field of visual learning. He is part of the authorship team of two major textbooks in the field of mathematics; his own series, MathStart, is designed to help children become more fluent in the language of mathematics and more comfortable with its concepts, while at the same time improving their reading and language-arts skills.

Murphy was the 1992 recipient of the Chicago Book Clinic's Mary Alexander Award for service to the Chicago area book publishing community. He also received the W. A. Dwiggins Award, Bookbuilders of Boston in 1993, for his contributions to quality book publishing. He is a member of the Arts in Education Advisory Council for Harvard University's Graduate School of Education, the Board of Trustees for the Rhode Island School of Design, Northwestern University's Library Council's Board of Governors, and the Art Institute of Chicago's Committee on Museum Education.

SELECTED WORKS: *The Best Bug Parade*, illus. by Holly Keller, 1996; *A Pair of Socks*, illus. by Lois Ehlert, 1996; *Give Me Half*, illus. by G. Brian Karas, 1996; *Ready, Set, Hop*, illus. by Jon Buller, 1996; *Get Up and Go*, illus. by Diane Greenseid, 1996; *Betcha!*, illus. by S. D. Schindler, 1997; *Divide and Ride*, illus. by George Ulrich, 1997; *Elevator Magic*, illus. by G. Brian Karas, 1997; *The Best Vacation Ever*, illus. by Nadine B. Westcott, 1997; *Circus Shapes* (MathStart: Recognizing Shapes), illus. by Edward Miller, 1998; *A Fair Bear Share*, illus. by John Spiers, 1998; *Lemonade for Sale*, illus. by Tricia Tusa, 1998; *Henry the Fourth*, illus. by Scott Nash, 1999; *Jump, Kangaroo, Jump*, illus. by Kevin O'Malley, 1999; *Super Sand Castle Saturday*, illus. by Julia Gorton, 1999; *Pepper's Journal: A Kitten's First Year*, illus. by Marsha Winborn, 2000.

SUGGESTED READING: "Learning Math Through Stories," *School Library Journal*, March 1999; "MathStart in the Making," *Book Links*, July 1996; *Teaching Children Mathematics*, October 1998; *Teaching PreK–8*, January 1998, January 1999.

WEB SITE: *www.harperchildrens.com/schoolhouse*

Donna Jo Napoli

February 28, 1948–

"'You should be a writer,' said the voice of my college instructor. He telephoned to say that, after reading a fiction piece I wrote for a required freshman writing course. That was the first time I thought about being a writer, and I thought about it for all of two seconds. Writers live in financial jeopardy. I grew up financially insecure and, while I never wanted to be rich, I absolutely wanted a secure career. Writing wasn't it. Besides, I loved math and languages. So I became a linguistics professor.

"As a child I read a lot. Libraries were my favorite places. And empty lots. I grew up around Miami, Florida, at a time when that area wasn't very populated. So there were many open spaces, and I used to wander. I'd read a book about surviving in the wild and then I'd fashion bows and arrows out of palm fronds and pretend to be living alone in the wilderness. I also loved animals, and I was constantly imprisoning lizards in jars and luring home stray cats. I made up adventures in which the animals played dramatic roles.

"In 1974 my first child, Elena, was born. During that pregnancy, I sang and read poetry aloud (some of which I wrote). From her first day of life, I told her stories. By the time she was two, she was telling stories. Before she went to bed each night, we'd read for at least an hour. Then we'd turn off the light and tell stories in the dark. The whole family, including my husband, Barry, read together and then took turns telling stories.

"Between the births of Elena and Michael, I had a miscarriage. I fell into a depression and wrote letters daily to my friend, Thad Guyer, about everything that was bothering me. He once handed me a box of those letters and said, 'You've written a novel.' Around that time another friend, Alice Galenson, listened to our family bedtime stories and said I should be a writer. So I wrote down some of my stories. Soon I submitted them to publishing houses. And eventually my first book came out.

"I write about anything that comes into my head, and I write in many styles. Sometimes the stories are based on events in my life or in the lives of people I love, and sometimes I have no idea where the stories come from. So when

Courtesy of Barry Furrow

Donna Jo Napoli

children ask me how I got the idea for a certain book, I often don't know.

"But I know why I write. My family world in childhood was often happy, but also filled with problems that I had no control over. Books allowed me to be someplace else—to live in a different world. Books were my best friends and they supplied me with the details I needed to create the adventures in my head as I played alone. I write because I have an irrepressible urge to create worlds. I want my books to be the best friends of children and to help them step into different worlds from the ones they live in, because we all need that.

"Right now I am still a professor and, because it costs so much to send five children to college, I will probably continue to teach for several years. But now, finally, I can see that that instructor who telephoned me my freshman year was right: I hope to be a full-time writer some day."

*   *   *

Attending Harvard on a full scholarship, Donna Jo Napoli received her B.A. in mathematics and a Ph.D. in Romance linguistics. She has taught linguistics at Smith College, Georgetown University, the University of Michigan, and Swarthmore College, and has published and edited academic volumes in this field. Her first book for children, *The Hero of Barletta*, was an Italian folklore adaptation, and she has since published works in a variety of genres, including realistic novels for middle-grade readers, historical fiction, and sophisticated fairy-tale adaptations for young adults.

> *"I'd read a book about surviving in the wild and then I'd fashion bows and arrows out of palm fronds and pretend to be living alone in the wilderness."*

The Magic Circle was an ALA Best Book for Young Adults and a Recommended Book for Reluctant Young Adult Readers. In addition, it made the best-of-year lists in the *Bulletin of the Center for Children's Books*, *Publishers Weekly*, and *Booklist*. *Zel* was chosen as a *Publishers Weekly* Best Book, received a *Bulletin of the Center for Children's Books* Blue Ribbon, and was a *School Library Journal* Best Book. *Song of the Magdalene* was an ALA Best Book for Young Adults and was cited as a Notable Trade Book in the Field of Social Studies. *Stones in Water* was an ALA Best Book for Young Adults and an ALA Notable Children's Book; it also received the 1997 Golden Kite Award from the Society of Children's Book Writers and Illustrators and the 1999 Sydney Taylor Book Award from the National Jewish Librarians Association.

Three of Napoli's books have been chosen as Children's Books of the Year by the Bank Street Child Study Children's Book Committee: *The Prince of the Pond*, *When the Water Closes over My Head*, and *Jimmy, the Pickpocket of the Palace*. A number of her books have been nominated for regional awards and, fittingly for a linguistics professor, many have been published in foreign-language editions—German, Dutch, Danish, and Chinese.

SELECTED WORKS: *The Hero of Barletta*, illus. by Dana Gustafson, 1988; *Soccer Shock*, illus. by Meredith Johnson, 1991; *The Prince of the Pond*, illus. by Judith Byron Schachner, 1992; *The Magic Circle*, 1993; *When the Water Closes over My Head*, illus by Nancy Poydar, 1994; *Jimmy, the Pickpocket of the Palace*, illus. by Judith Byron Schachner, 1995; *Zel*, 1996; *The Song of the Magdalene*, 1996; *On Guard*, 1997; *Stones in Water*, 1997; *Changing Tunes*, 1998; *Sirena*,

1998; *For the Love of Venice*, 1998; *Spinners*, with Richard Tchen, 1999; *Crazy Jack*, 1999; Angel Wings series, illus. by Lauren Klementz-Harte: *Friends Everywhere, Little Creatures, On Her Own, One Leap Forward*, 1999; *Albert*, illus. by Jim LaMarche, 2000.

SUGGESTED READING: *Authors and Artists for Young Adults*, vol. 25, 1998; *Children's Literature Review*, vol. 51, 1999; *Contemporary Authors*, vol. 156, 1997; *Something About the Author*, vol. 92, 1997; *Something About the Author Autobiography Series*, vol. 23, 1997. Periodicals—"Fairy Tales, Myths, and Religious Stories," *ALAN Review*, Fall 1997.

"**I** was born in Chicago and grew up in Des Moines, Iowa. We had a home full of books. My mother had been an English teacher and believed in reading, in reading out loud, in reading anything one wanted. What mattered most to her was that we wanted to read. There was no censorship, and a great deal of discussion at the dinner table.

"Des Moines was, and is, a green, lovely community in which to grow. So many of the tensions of present-day life were nonexistent then, or so I recall. I don't think that my growing up period was in any way unusual, or really very interesting. I don't think I'm terrifically unusual, either, and when, after years of hearing how special I was—a parental mantra for millions of kids—I learned that I wasn't, I was hugely relieved. Also learning that helped my work: if something made me angry, or made me sad, chances were—if I could write well enough—my readers would feel the same way.

"I always wanted to be a writer. Not necessarily a writer of children's books, but of plays, novels, musicals, films. Happily, writing for children has not limited those other goals. When *Edgar Allan* was published, it carried the designation 'For All Ages.' I thought that was appropriate because it is about a family and its problems, not just the children in it. In thirty years, however, the story has come to be considered reading for children from nine up—times change. Once labeled, not easily reborn. So that, after *Lisa, Bright and Dark* was published, almost everything I've done has carried the message 'By

Courtesy of John Neufeld

John Neufeld

December 14, 1938–

the author of . . .' I argue and scream that I've done other books, for grown-ups, for children. But I'm always 'the author of *Lisa, Bright and Dark.*'

"I'm truly grateful for all of the above, and pleased that so many young readers take time to write and share their thoughts about my work. If I grumble a bit, it's really only happy grumbling.

"I was a lucky kid: fortunate in my parents and my schooling. After the Army, I worked in the publishing industry for seven years before deciding to gamble and become a full-time writer. While I missed the camaraderie of an office, I've never regretted that decision. I've also been fortunate in finding wonderful stories to tell. I try never to do the same sort of story, just as when I go out on the road to promote a book I never deliver the same speech.

"I have a rule of thumb: if I can't sit down and work on a new book for four days in a row happily, then I'm writing the wrong book.

"In this age of computers, I'm somewhat at a disadvantage because I write fiction rather than nonfiction. Other authors design a Web page and fill it with fascinating data about their own specialty. My specialty is too general: growing up. And I think my readers probably know as much about that as I do. What I can do is tell stories that allow a reader facing new problems as he/she grows to understand that nothing he experiences is as unique and terrifying as he imagines, that there are solutions at the end of the day, and hope.

"If I feel a sense of mission about this, what matters is that the mission is accomplished. I believe that often it has been, and I hope in the coming years with new books, it will be again."

> "If I can't sit down and work on a new book for four days in a row happily, then I'm writing the wrong book."

* * *

After attending Phillips Exeter Academy and Yale University, John Neufeld entered the publishing world as an editor, copywriter, and publicist. Seven years later, he left publishing to pursue a writing career and quickly established a reputation as an author unafraid of tackling controversial issues. His first book, *Edgar Allan*, concerned the topic of interracial adoption. It was named an ALA Notable Children's Book and appeared on the annual "best" lists of both *Time* magazine and the *New York Times*. *Lisa, Bright and Dark* was one of the first young adult novels to portray teenage mental illness. It too was an ALA Notable Children's Book, and was televised as a Hallmark Hall of Fame production, for which Neufeld wrote the script. He has since written other teleplays, as well as several adult novels.

Neufeld has worked as an English teacher and done volunteer work at a daycare center for homeless children—an experience that generated the young adult book *Almost a Hero*. He moved into new literary directions with his first historical novel, *Gaps in Stone Walls*. This mystery, set in Martha's Vineyard during the late nineteenth century, garnered a nomination for the 1997 Edgar Allan Poe Award in the juvenile category.

The author currently lives and works in Connecticut.

SELECTED WORKS: *Edgar Allan*, 1968; *Lisa, Bright and Dark*, 1969; *Touching*, 1971; *Sleep, Two, Three, Four!*, 1971; *Freddy's Book*, 1973; *Sharelle*, 1983; *Almost a Hero*, 1995; *Gaps in Stone Walls*, 1996; *Boys Lie*, 1999.

SUGGESTED READING: *Authors and Artists for Young Adults*, vol. 11, 1993; *Children's Literature Review*, vol. 52, 1999; Collier, Laurie and Joyce Nakamura, eds. *Major Authors and Illustrators for Children and Young Adults*, 1993; *Contemporary Authors*, New Revision Series, vol. 11, 1984; vol. 37, 1992; vol. 56, 1997; *Contemporary Literary Criticism*, vol. 17, 1981; *Something About the Author*, vol. 6, 1974; vol. 81, 1995; *Something About the Author Autobiography Series*, vol. 3, 1987.

Matt Novak

October 23, 1962–

"When I was growing up in the small coal-mining town of Sheppton, Pennsylvania, I knew at a very early age that I wanted to be an artist. I loved to watch all the cartoons on television and create my own primitive animated films on the corners of my school notebooks. We did not have many books in our house, and our town did not have a library. We did have a bookmobile that visited my elementary school every week. I would search through all the shelves full of magic and excitement and inevitably walk out with *Harold and the Purple Crayon* week after week. I guess I always felt a kinship with Harold because he could use his crayon and his imagination to escape from his everyday surroundings.

"My teachers were all very supportive of my artistic endeavors. Miss Krensevage, my fourth-grade teacher, in particular allowed me to do all sorts of out-of-the-ordinary things. When I wanted to put on a puppet show for the class, she made time in our schedule and allowed me to put on an elaborate Christmas extravaganza. I remember thinking, as I was making all the puppets and building the stage, that maybe I had bit off a little more than I could chew. That was how I generally approached things, though. I think I am still that way. I don't remember if the show was a success or a flop, but to me the fun has always been in the process of creation.

"When I went to high school, another teacher, Mrs. Jamelli, had a profound influence on my life. I was the small skinny kid in the class and to top it all off I had lots of red curly hair. At this new school I became a target for teasing by many of the other boys. It got to the point where I really dreaded going to school. Mrs. Jamelli stopped me in the hallway one day and asked if I would like to audition for the school production of *Bye Bye Birdie*. I had never performed in a musical, but I auditioned and got the part. I'm not sure if it was because the other boys now respected me or that I had more self-confidence, but the teasing stopped. This made me realize that the gifts I had inside were a lot more important than what was on the outside. This is definitely a recurring theme in many of my books. I continued acting throughout high school. I performed in a nationally distributed radio program called *Willow Crossing*, and during the summers my best friend and I created and performed puppet shows at local amusement parks, farmer's markets, and those

kinds of places. I think all of these experiences helped to develop my creative abilities and my love for writing.

"Throughout all this I never wavered from my desire to grow up one day to be a Disney animator. When I graduated from high school I went off to Kutztown State University and then to the School of Visual Arts in New York City. I had many wonderful instructors there, but perhaps the one who changed things most for me was Jane Zalben, well-known children's book writer and illustrator. Her class on writing and illustrating children's books opened my eyes to a world of possibilities that I had never imagined. I learned how to put together a book dummy and present it for publication. My first book, *Rolling*, was accepted for publication in 1985, which was my final year at S.V.A.

Courtesy of Victoria W. Novak

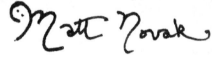

"Since then I have done some teaching and actually fulfilled my dream of working as a Disney artist. Unfortunately, by that time my heart had been stolen by my love for children's books, so I left Disney after only a few years. I did meet my beautiful wife, Victoria, while working there, so I feel it was meant to be.

"When I look at my past I become more and more thankful to all those wonderful people who helped me grow in so many ways and who influenced the way I write and the subjects I write about. I hope that someday one of my books will inspire someone like *Harold and the Purple Crayon* inspired me."

* * *

Courtesy of Orchard Books

Matt Novak was born on October 23, 1962, in Trenton, New Jersey. He earned a B.F.A. from the School of Visual Arts, New York City, in 1985. He worked as a puppeteer with the Pegasus Players in Sheppton, Pennsylvania, and later as an art teacher at St. Benedict's Preparatory School in Newark, N.J., and an instructor at Parsons School of Design in New York City. In 1989 he moved to Orlando, Florida, and worked as an artist for Walt Disney Studios, where he met his wife, Victoria. They married in 1991. Victoria still works in animation at Disney, but Matt writes children's books full-time. He concentrates on humor, often with an underlying message. He just "likes telling a good story." When he's not writing, Novak spends his time gardening, bicycling, and hiking.

Mouse TV was included on New York Public Library's annual list, 100 Titles for Reading and Sharing, in 1994.

SELECTED WORKS WRITTEN AND ILLUSTRATED: *Rolling*, 1986; *Elmer Blunt's Open House*, 1992; *The Last Christmas Present*, 1993; *Mouse TV*, 1994; *Gertie and Gumbo*, 1995; *Newt*, 1996; *The Pillow War*, 1998; *The Robobots*, 1999; *Jazzbo Goes to School*, 1999; *Jazzbo and Googy*, 2000.

SELECTED WORKS ILLUSTRATED: *Ghost and Pete*, by Dayle Ann Dobbs, 1995; *Twelve Snails to One Lizard: A Tale of Mischief and Measurement*, by Susan Hightower, 1997.

SUGGESTED READING: Blount, R. Howard, Jr. and Martha Venning Webb. *Art Projects Plus*, 1997; *Contemporary Authors*, vol. 125, 1988; Cummins, Julie, ed. *Children's Book Illustration and Design*, vol. 2, 1998; *Something About the Author*, vol. 52, 1988; vol. 60, 1990; vol. 104, 1999.

Courtesy of Valentine Hart

Anne Sibley O'Brien

July 10, 1952–

"I was born in Chicago where my father was in medical school, but on my first birthday my family moved to a farm in the hills of New Hampshire. My brothers and sister and I spent most of our time outside, running through meadows full of wildflowers, building fairy moss houses under the big maple trees, playing in our tree house in the woods, and digging forts and tunnels in the deep snow. I also loved drawing pictures, and I loved books. By the time I was seven I was informing people that I was going to be an artist when I grew up. What I loved to draw best was people.

"That same year brought an enormous change to my life. My parents got accepted as medical missionaries, and our family moved halfway around the world to South Korea. When I went to the market, I gathered a crowd of curious people, like a visiting celebrity. People exclaimed over my light brown hair, saying it looked like gold, my big eyes, my big nose, and my height. And when I greeted people in Korean, they responded with amazed delight, as if I'd done something really special. This experience of being the one who was different, and at the same time, highly privileged, has been the defining one of my life.

"I came back to the States for college, and majored in studio art at Mount Holyoke College, returning to Korea for my junior year to study Korean arts at Ewha Women's University in Seoul. Illustration was always something that appealed to me, but it was a course in writing and illustrating children's books taught by Eric Carle that finally decided me. I put some of my sketches into a portfolio and started visiting publishers in New York and Boston.

"Seven years later (October 28, 1984!) I got my first contract to write and illustrate four board books. I was so excited! Doing the rough sketches was wonderful, but when it came to the final paintings, I got scared. I had no idea if I could really do this or

not! Right after finishing those books, I began the illustrations
for the first Jamaica book. In 1991, I met Margy Burns Knight
and editor Mark Melnicove at Tilbury House in Maine and we
formed the team which has collaboratively created the *Talking
Walls* books and others. Making multiracial and multicultural
picture books has been an important way of exploring my own
worldview as a person with two languages, two cultures, and two
countries. One of my favorite projects was retelling a Korean
folktale, *The Princess and the Beggar*. Painting the pictures felt
magical, like going home to Korea again.

"For the past nineteen years, my home has been on Peaks Island, a real island two miles out in the harbor of Portland, Maine.
I live here with my husband O.B., our son Perry, our daughter
Yunhee, Pavlov the dog, and Molly the cat. We live in a winter-
ized summer cottage, next to a smaller cottage which is my studio. Since I often use real people as models, both of my children
appear in many of my books.

"These days I'm learning to find my own individual voice,
whatever medium I'm working in. I'm discovering that it comes
out in many unexpected ways. I'm doing a lot of writing, including a novel set in my high school in Korea, and lots of acting and
singing, including a one-woman performance piece called
'White Lies,' which I wrote. Next I'm planning to experiment
with my painting and see what new places that may take me."

> *"These days I'm learning to find my own individual voice, whatever medium I'm working in."*

*   *   *

Growing up in a family that loved and valued books, Anne Sibley O'Brien entered the field of children's literature with a series
of board books based on the experiences of her toddler son.
These realistic volumes demonstrate the benefits of sharing, doing chores, and napping. Several of the titles, including *Come
Play with Us, I'm Not Tired, Where's My Truck?*, and *I Want
That!* were named Children's Books of the Year by the Child
Study Association of America. O'Brien has provided watercolor
illustrations for a series of picture books by Juanita Havill featuring Jamaica, a spirited African American girl. *Jamaica's Find* was
named a Children's Book of the Year by the Child Study Association of America and an IRA/CBC Children's Choice. The nonfiction *Talking Walls* books have also garnered numerous honors,
winning a Human and Civil Rights Award from the National Education Association in 1997 and receiving honors from the *Hungry Mind Review* and the *Boston Globe*. *Talking Walls: The Stories Continue* was cited as a Notable Children's Trade Book in
the Field of Social Studies. These books have also been packaged
with related CD-ROMs and videos.

Prior to her career in children's books, O'Brien worked in the
area of humanitarian public service. She designed educational
aids for the Kojedo Community Health Project in Korea, served

as a teacher and administrator of a Massachusetts community resource center, and was the director of an organization providing free entertainment to shut-ins. For several years, she was also the chair of the Commission on Religion and Race for the Maine Annual Conference of the United Methodist Church. She continues to write and illustrate children's books while exploring a variety of artistic forms.

SELECTED WORKS WRITTEN AND ILLUSTRATED: *Come Play with Us*, 1985; *I'm Not Tired*, 1985; *Where's My Truck?*, 1985; *I Want That!*, 1985; *I Don't Want to Go*, 1986; *It Hurts*, 1986; *It's Hard to Wait*, 1986; *Don't Say No*, 1986; *The Princess and the Beggar*, 1993.

SELECTED WORKS ILLUSTRATED: *Jamaica's Find*, by Juanita Havill, 1986; *The Mystery of the Haunted Cabin*, by Judy Delton, 1986; *Jamaica Tag-Along*, by Juanita Havill, 1989; *Talking Walls*, by Margy Burns Knight, 1992; *Who Belongs Here?: An American Story*, by Margy Burns Knight, 1993; *Jamaica and Brianna*, by Juanita Havill, 1993; *Jamaica's Blue Marker*, by Juanita Havill, 1995; *Jouanah: A Hmong Cinderella*, by Jewell Reinhart Coburn and Tzexa Lee, 1996; *Talking Walls: The Stories Continue*, by Margy Burns Knight, 1996; *Welcoming Babies*, by Margy Burns Knight, 1996; *Jamaica and the Substitute Teacher*, by Juanita Havill, 1999; *Africa Is Not a Country*, by Margy Burns Knight, 2000.

SUGGESTED READING: *Contemporary Authors*, vol. 122, 1988; *Something About the Author*, vol. 48, 1987; vol. 53, 1988; vol. 80, 1995.

Kevin O'Malley

September 8, 1961–

"Years ago, on a sunny afternoon, I found myself trapped in my elementary school library instead of playing kickball outside at recess. There I was, being punished for not keeping my trap shut in class, stuck with a bunch of fluffy kids' books and boring biographies about long-dead inventors while my friends were having good fun cracking wise and creating chaos without me.

"Resigned to my fate, I grudgingly started to leaf through a pile of picture books. There were pictures of cute little ponies, cute little puppies, and cute little children with smiling parents beaming behind them. Yuck, yuck, and double yuck! Then, just when I thought I would fall off my chair and die of cuteness, I came upon a picture of a boy in a wolf suit who was threatening to eat his mother. In another picture he was chasing his dog with a fork. This was somebody I could relate to. I kept reading as the boy cavorted through the forest with big, hairy monsters. I loved it! The book was, of course, *Where the Wild Things Are* by Maurice Sendak.

"My mother tells me that I drew a lot as a little kid, and while I was certainly not the 'best' artist in my class, I could hold my own when it came to drawing an army scene or the Green Lantern. I didn't see that art was much use anyway, as my aptitude test said I was going to be a park ranger when I grew up. But that was before I discovered that little heathen in the wolf suit. From then on, I wanted to illustrate children's books. Not cute children's books, but books for kids like me.

"It wasn't quite that easy. My father's reaction was, 'What! Maybe we can work on his math a bit.' Even after he came around, I faced years of studying art and about a million rejection letters on the road to getting published. But I learned a lot along the way. I learned how to load a restaurant dishwasher and how to create 'exciting and dynamic seasonal displays for the retail shopping industry.' I learned that gallery shows do not a fortune make and that when you draw a Snidely Whiplash mustache on the portrait of George Washington you've created for a Smithsonian audiovisual production, the curators are not amused.

"Having been Mr. Mom for years now, I've learned the most valuable lessons of all: Junior will not play quietly for five hours while Daddy does a little work, and you should never work with colored pencils around a white couch.

"I live in Baltimore, Maryland, with my very patient wife, Dara, and our two wild things, Connor and Noah. My studio is in the attic, which provides an inspirational view of the alley below."

Courtesy of Robert J. Smith, Jr.

*   *   *

Kevin O'Malley was born in Lansdale, Pennsylvania, the second of six children. He was in fourth grade when he fell in love with *Where the Wild Things Are*, an event that foretold his future career. By twelfth grade he had written and submitted four books to publishers without any positive response. In 1983 he graduated from the Maryland Institute College of Art with a B.F.A. in Illustration. A variety of art-related jobs followed, including developing 2,500 illustrations for a sixty-slide show, creating displays for the Museum of American History at the Smithsonian Institute, and designing and building Christmas displays for the retail industry.

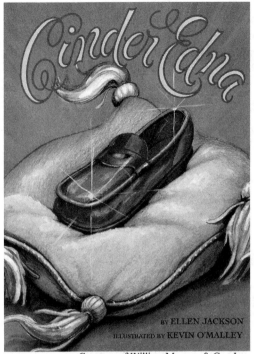

By ELLEN JACKSON
ILLUSTRATED BY KEVIN O'MALLEY

Courtesy of William Morrow & Co., Inc.

Since 1990 O'Malley has been a free-lance illustrator. His first solo effort, *Froggy Went A-Courtin'*, was published in 1991, and the following year he began visiting schools with his presentation "Boring Old Books . . . I Don't Think So," to share with students his love of writing and illustrating books. In these visits he calls on the imagination of the audience, illustrating kids' suggestions on the spot as they create stories together.

Roller Coaster received a *Parenting* magazine Reading Magic Award. *Rosie's Fiddle*, written by Phyllis Root and illustrated by O'Malley and Margot Apple, was named a *Child* magazine Best Book and appeared on the New York Public Library's list, 100 Titles for Reading and Sharing. *What's for Lunch?* with text by John Schindel was an American Booksellers Association Pick of the Lists. In 1989 O'Malley's artwork was exhibited at the Cordish, Charles Street, and Coop galleries in Baltimore. He has received awards from the Society of Illustrators, *Print* magazine, and *Communication Arts*.

SELECTED WORKS WRITTEN AND ILLUSTRATED: *Froggy Went A-Courtin'*, 1991; *The Box*, 1992; *Bruno, You're Late for School*, 1992; *Who Killed Cock Robin?*, 1993; *Roller Coaster*, 1995; *There Was a Crooked Man*, 1995; *Carl Caught a Flying Fish*, 1996; *Velcome*, 1998; *Leo Cockroach, Toy Tester*, 1999; *My Lucky Hat*, 1999.

SELECTED WORKS ILLUSTRATED: *Cinder Edna*, by Ellen Jackson, 1994; *What's for Lunch?*, by John Schindel, 1994; *Miss Malarkey Doesn't Live in Room 10*, by Judy Finchler, 1995; *Big Squeak, Little Squeak*, by Robert Kraus, 1996; *Too Many Kangaroo Things to Do!*, by Stuart Murphy; *Chanukah in Chelm*, by David Adler, 1997; *Colliding with Chris*, by Dan Harder, 1998; *The Planets in Our Solar System*, by Franklyn Branley, 1998; *Halloween Pie*, by Michael Tunnell, 1999.

SUGGESTED READING: "Talking with . . . Kevin O'Malley," *Book Links*, July 1999.

"I grew up in the military. By the time I was fifteen, I had lived in Oklahoma, Austria, Florida, and four different army posts in Virginia and North Carolina. Moving was never traumatic for me, partly, I think, because I had very close and loving relationships with my parents, my twin brother, my younger brother, and my older sister.

"But if moving was not traumatic, staying in one place was. When my dad finally retired to a small town in North Carolina, I nearly went crazy with boredom. I craved the adventure and changing scenery of our military life. Miraculously, one day I found these things, literally only a block away—at the local community theater. From then on, I spent nearly every waking hour after school there, either acting or working backstage. When I stepped from the sunny street into that musty-smelling, dark little theater, all things seemed possible.

"I went on to study drama at the University of North Carolina at Chapel Hill. In my junior year, I discovered an even greater realm of adventure and changing scenery: the world of mythology and comparative religion. So I became a religion major, and learned as much as I could about other cultures.

"After graduating from college, I lived an intensely varied life. For a while I camped in a cave on the island of Crete. Then I joined up with a small band of European young people heading to 'The East.' We traveled overland in a caravan of rickety vans through sixteen Asian countries, including Iraq, Iran, Afghanistan, Pakistan, India, and Nepal. We nearly lost our lives, first in an earthquake in northern Afghanistan and then in a riot in Kabul. My trip came to an abrupt end in Kathmandu when I got blood poisoning. During the two weeks I spent in a missionary hospital there, I read all of the Tolkien trilogy—*The Fellowship of the Ring*, *The Two Towers*, and *The Return of the King*. I would sleep, read, and look out the windows at the Himalayas. To this day my journey to 'The East' is tangled up in my mind with Frodo's adventures.

"After I returned home and recovered from my illness, I promptly headed back into the 'real world.' While working as a Russian travel consultant in Washington, D.C., I attended the opening of a musical play about Jesse James. From the balcony, I fell in love with Will Osborne, the actor/musician playing Jesse.

Courtesy of Norma Klein

Mary Pope Osborne

May 20, 1949–

A year later, in New York City, we were married. After that I worked at a number of different jobs when I wasn't on the road with Will, traveling with a theatrical production.

"One day, out of the blue, I began writing a story about an eleven-year-old girl in the South. The girl was a lot like me, and many of the incidents in the story were similar to the happenings in my childhood. The first draft was crudely written, but it must have communicated something to an editor, because it became a young adult novel called *Run, Run as Fast as You Can*. Finally I knew what I wanted to be when I grew up.

"Now twenty years and forty books later, I feel I'm one of the most fortunate people on earth. I've journeyed through Greek mythology, Norse mythology, medieval stories, and American tall tales. I've 'met' George Washington and Ben Franklin, and without even leaving my home I've traveled around the globe, learning about the religions of the world.

"Most recently, I've taken journeys through the Magic Tree House, visiting the times of dinosaurs, knights, mummies, pirates, and ninjas. The Magic Tree House has also whisked me to schools all over the country, and the contact I now have with children has brought overwhelming joy into my life. I love the letters I get from them and I love reading the countless Magic Tree House stories *they've* written. I feel as if these kids and I are all exploring the creative process together, using our imaginations plus our reading and writing skills to take us wherever we want to go. This is *true* magic."

"The Magic Tree House has also whisked me to schools all over the country, and the contact I now have with children has brought overwhelming joy into my life."

* * *

Mary Pope was born at Fort Sill, Oklahoma, the daughter of a U.S. Army Colonel and a mother whose maiden name was Dickens, a foreshadowing of Mary's eventual career choice. She received a B.A. degree from the University of North Carolina at Chapel Hill in 1971. Married in 1976 to actor Will Osborne, she worked variously as a window-dresser, medical assistant, waitress, and acting teacher before turning to writing full-time.

Osborne's first novel, *Run, Run As Fast As You Can*, was cited as an IRA/CBC Children's Choice. Since then she has written many highly acclaimed books for children and young adults in a wide variety of genres— picture books, early chapter books, biographies, historical fiction, mysteries, and retellings of fairy tales, myths, and legends. Her novel *Spider Kane and the Mystery Under the May-Apple* received a Parents' Choice Honor Award and was one of Bank Street College's Best Books of the Year. *Spider Kane and the Mystery at Jumbo Nightcrawler's* was an Edgar Award Nominee for Best Juvenile Mystery in 1993. *One World, Many Religions* won an Orbis Pictus Honor Award from the National Council of Teachers of English.

American Tall Tales was cited as a Best Book of the Year by *School Library Journal* and the *Bulletin of the Center for Children's Books*, was named a Notable Trade Book in the Field of Social Studies, and won the Utah Children's Book Award. *Mermaid Tales; Favorite Greek Myths; One World, Many Religions;* and *Standing in the Light* were also named Notable Trade Books in the Field of Social Studies. In addition *Standing in the Light* was an IRA/CBC Children's Choice book. *Dinosaurs Before Dark*, the first in Osborne's popular Magic Tree House series, was one of Bank Street College's Best Books of the Year in 1992 and received the Diamond State (Delaware) Reading Association Award. *Dolphins at Daybreak* and *Midnight on the Moon* both received Children's Choice awards from the Association of Booksellers for Children.

Mary Pope Osborne served two terms as the president of the Authors Guild, the second children's author in the Guild's long history to hold that position. In 1994 she received a Distinguished Alumnus Award from the University of North Carolina at Chapel Hill, N.C. At present the author and her husband, Will, are working together on a series of nonfiction books related to The Magic Tree House. They live in New York City.

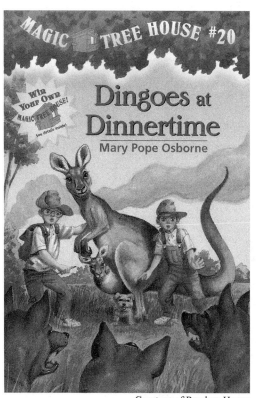

Courtesy of Random House

SELECTED WORKS: *Run, Run as Fast as You Can*, 1982; *Favorite Greek Myths*, illus. by Troy Howell, 1989; *American Tall Tales*, illus. by Michael McCurdy, 1991; *The Story of Christopher Columbus: Admiral of the Ocean Sea*, 1987, reissued 1997; *The Many Lives of Benjamin Franklin*, 1990; *Moonhorse*, illus. by S. M. Saelig, 1991; *George Washington: Leader of a New Nation*, 1991; *Spider Kane and the Mystery Under the May-Apple*, illus. by Victoria Chess, 1992; *Spider Kane and the Mystery at Jumbo Nightcrawler's*, illus. by Victoria Chess, 1993; *Mermaid Tales from Around the World*, illus. by Troy Howell, 1993; *Molly and the Prince*, illus. by Elizabeth Sayles, 1994; *One World, Many Religions: The Ways We Worship*, 1996; *Haunted Waters*, 1994; *Favorite Norse Myths*, illus. by Troy Howell, 1996; *Rocking Horse Christmas*, illus. by Ned Bittinger, 1997; *Standing in the Light: The Captive Diary of Catherine Carey Logan,*

Delaware Valley, Pennsylvania, 1763, 1998; *Favorite Medieval Tales*, illus. by Troy Howell, 1998; *Adaline Falling Star*, 2000.

SELECTED WORKS: Magic Tree House Series (all illus. by Sal Murdocca)—*Dinosaurs Before Dark*, 1992; *The Knight at Dawn*, 1993; *Mummies in the Morning*, 1993; *Pirates past Noon*, 1994; *Night of the Ninjas*, 1995; *Afternoon on the Amazon*, 1995; *Sunset of the Sabertooth*, 1996; *Midnight on the Moon*, 1996; *Dolphins at Daybreak*, 1997; *Ghost Town at Sundown*, 1997; *Lions at Lunchtime*, 1998; *Polar Bears past Bedtime*, 1998; *Vacation Under the Volcano*, 1998; *Day of the Dragon King*, 1998; *Viking Ships at Sunrise*, 1998; *Hour of the Olympics*, 1998; *Tonight on the Titanic*, 1999; *Buffalo before Breakfast*, 1999; *Tigers at Twilight*, 1999; *Dingoes at Dinnertime*, 2000.

SUGGESTED READING: *Contemporary Authors*, vol. 111, 1984; *Contemporary Authors*, New Revision Series, vol. 62, 1998; Ehrlich, Amy, ed. *When I Was Your Age: Original Stories About Growing Up*, 1996; *Something About the Author*, vol. 41, 1985; vol. 55, 1989; vol. 98, 1998. Periodicals—Raymond, Allen, "Mary Pope Osborne: 'Free Spirit' Finds Home," *Teaching PreK–8*, November/December 1993.

WEB SITE: *www.randomhouse.com/magictreehouse*

Steven Otfinoski

(OTT-fin-AH-skee)

January 11, 1949–

"One of the first people to take note of my writing was my seventh-grade history teacher, Mr. Wilderman. I had written a paper for his class about an important battle in American history. After he read it, he told the class, 'I got so wrapped up in Steve's paper, that I wanted to run in there and join the fight myself.' It was a great compliment, and I realized, perhaps for the first time, how writing about history and real people could be just as exciting as telling a fictional story. I say *fictional* story because good nonfiction involves telling a story too. It's just a story that actually happened.

"As I grew older, I continued to be attracted to history and nonfiction, but I also turned to other kinds of writing. In high school I discovered poetry and wrote a long, pretentious poem patterned after T. S. Eliot's *The Wasteland* for the literary magazine. In college, I was drawn to the stage and in my junior year became a theater major. Although I soon switched to major in literature, I began writing plays and to date have written over forty of them, a number of which have been staged in various venues. (Broadway, alas, continues to elude me.)

"After college, I worked as a newspaper reporter, then an editor for a children's language arts magazine published by Weekly Reader. Laid off from my job, I began freelancing, writing fiction and nonfiction readers for students. I moved to New York

City to pursue the theater, met my wife, and started writing for textbooks.

"I moved back to my native Connecticut eight years later, and after numerous fictional novels and stories for young readers, I got my first assignment for a full-length biography through an agent. My subject was Soviet leader Mikhail Gorbachev. Although this was nonfiction, my editor encouraged me to write an opening and closing chapter that involved fictional characters that would help American children better understand Russian society and culture. Thus I was able to combine my talents as a fiction and factual writer. Since that book, with the exception of a few stories and novels, I have written nonfiction almost exclusively.

"As a nonfiction writer I find myself in the lucky position of being able to write about pretty much anything that interests me. Sometimes, however, the assignment comes first and as I do my research I fall in love with the subject. For example, I had long been interested in the fascinating life of ragtime composer Scott Joplin. But only after I began writing a biography of him did I discover the joys of ragtime music, and now I'm hooked.

"Sometimes a project has led me down new and unexpected paths. In 1989, my town of Stratford, Connecticut, was looking for a way to celebrate its 350th anniversary. Being keenly interested in local history, I volunteered to write a play about the town's most famous, and infamous, residents. The result, *Stratford Characters*, was performed locally to some acclaim. With the proceeds from the production, the entire company traveled to Stratford-on-Avon in England, our sister city, and performed the play in Shakespeare's hometown. That was a thrilling experience. This play led me to form my own little theater company, History Alive!, devoted to bringing American history to life for students throught dramatic monologues delivered by actors playing the part of people from the past. Somehow I think my old history teacher Mr. Wilderman would approve."

Courtesy of Michael Lachiema

* * *

Steven Otfinoski was born in Queens, a borough of New York City, and raised in Farmingdale, Long Island, with his two younger brothers. When Steve was ten, the family moved to Middletown, Connecticut, his father's hometown. He attended Boston University for several years and received his B.A. degree from Antioch College in 1972. A year spent studying in London, England, during his college career helped Otfinoski discover the joys of writing, as he kept a journal of his experiences and observations during that time. After college he worked as a news reporter on a daily paper in Hartford, Connecticut, and for a while was an assistant editor for *Read* magazine, published by Xerox Educational Publications. Since 1975 he has been a freelance writer.

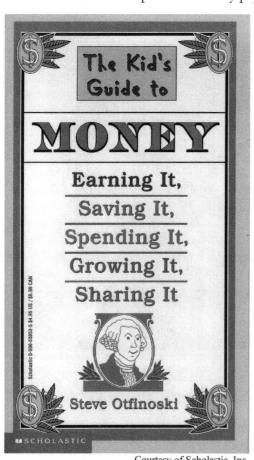

Courtesy of Scholastic, Inc.

Otfinoski's children's books cover a variety of genres. He likes to write stories of adventure, mystery, and the supernatural—all the kinds of stories he enjoyed reading himself when he was young, and still enjoys. His nonfiction has covered many topics, from history to how-to books, from biography to rock music; his work also appeals to a wide range of ages, from beginning readers to young adults. Otfinoski has written books in a number of popular series: Makers of Modern Science, When Disaster Strikes, Nations in Transition, Library of Famous Women, Issues of Our Time, and Here We Go!, among others. Two of his nonfiction titles, *Triumph and Terror: The French Revolution* and *Poland*, have been selected for New York Public Library's Books for the Teen Age list. In 1997, he published his first nonfiction title specifically for the adult market: *The Golden Age of Rock Instrumentals*. Many of his children's and young adult titles can serve as effective introductions to their topics for readers of any age.

Playwriting has long been a vital part of Otfinoski's career, and he has published over a hundred plays for classroom use, as well as more than forty for the professional stage, which have been produced in small theaters in and around New York. Married in 1981 to Beverly Larson, a children's book editor and harpist, Steven Otfinoski lives with his wife and their children, Daniel and Martha, in Stratford, Connecticut.

SELECTED WORKS: *The Monster That Wouldn't Die and Other Strange but True Stories*, 1976; *Plays About Strange Happenings*, 1976; *The World's Darkest Days: Stories of Great Tragedies of the Past*, 1977; *Midnight at Monster Mansion*, 1984; *Master of the Past*, 1987; *Mikhail Gorbachev: The Soviet Innovator*, 1989; *Nineteenth Century Writers*, 1991; *Marian Wright Edelman: Defender of Children's Rights*, 1991; *Nelson Mandela: The Fight Against Apartheid*, 1992; *Putting It in Writing*, 1993; *Triumph and Terror: The French Revolution*, 1993; *Joseph Stalin: Russia's Last Czar*, 1993; *Oprah Winfrey: Television Star*, 1993; *Great Black Writers*, 1994; *Whodunit?: Science Solves the Crime*, 1995; *Scott Joplin: A Life in Ragtime*, 1995; *Boris Yeltsin and the Rebirth of Russia*, 1995; *Poland*, 1995; *The Kid's Guide to Money: Earning It, Saving It, Spending It, Growing It, Sharing It*, 1996; *The Czech Republic*, 1996; *Behind the Wheel: Cars Then and Now*, 1997; *Speaking Up, Speaking Out: A Kid's Guide to Making Speeches, Oral Reports and Conversation*, 1996; *The Golden Age of Rock Instrumentals*, 1997; *John Wilkes Booth and the Civil War*, 1999; *The Golden Age of Novelty Songs*, 2000.

SUGGESTED READING: *Something About the Author*, vol. 56, 1989.

Steve Parker

December 7, 1952–

"It was a long time ago. I was twelve years old, and it was my first biology lesson at senior school. In those days we learned about animals by cutting them up. This is called *dissection*. We killed the animals first, of course.

"My creature for the day was an earthworm. I pinned it onto the wax base of a shallow tray, and half-filled the tray with water. Worms are long but thin, so I looked through a dissecting microscope that resembled a pair of binoculars on a stand, to make the view bigger. Then I took a very sharp knife called a scalpel and carefully slit the worm all along its body. The worm's skin pulled back. Inside were its intestines, its many hearts, its nerves and blood vessels—in fact, all of its body parts, exactly as shown in my biology dissection guidebook. But they were not in different bright colors, as color-coded in the book. They were mostly reddish-brown.

"Great! I had never seen anything so fascinating as all those bits and pieces inside the worm. They worked together to make the worm into a slimy, wriggling, soil-munching thing that was *alive*. And what is more important than life itself? At that moment I knew that I wanted to have a job that involved animals. But I also felt sad for the worm, and I knew that I didn't want to cut up animals for a living. I would not make a very good butcher or a laboratory worker who tested drugs on animals. Luckily, times have changed. Now very few people cut up animals at school.

"I went on to college and passed my B.Sc. (Bachelor of Science) degree in Zoology. This is the scientific study of animals and how they live, move about, hunt, feed, breed, behave, and of course reproduce. Then I was fortunate enough to work at the world-famous Natural History Museum in London, as a member of the team that creates exciting new exhibitions on topics such as dinosaurs, African wildlife, and the world of bugs. For each new exhibition at the museum, there was a souvenir guidebook. No one else on the team seemed bothered about writing them, so I had a go. I found out that people seemed to like reading my words. I also liked working mainly on my own, rather than in a busy office or factory. This was how I began my career as an author.

Courtesy of Steve Parker

"That was nearly twenty years ago. I've now written more than 170 books, all nonfiction, and all fully illustrated in color (but not by me). I've branched out from animals into general science. My books mostly explain biology, zoology, ecology, technology, lots of other -ologies; also animal behavior, conservation and other aspects of the life sciences, and general sciences, including geology, prehistory, transport, astronomy and even cosmology. They are translated into many languages and sold all over the world by many different publishers. I've got copies of my books translated into Hungarian, Chinese, Greek, and Catalan.

"Between writing books, I've found time to get married and raise a family. I live in the country farming area of East Anglia, with my wife and two sons. We all love animals, and our family has had many fantastic pets. At the moment they include two dogs, two cats, a rabbit, lots of tropical fish, a ferret named Elmo, and a Fell pony called Merrol.

"I write books and work on CD-ROMs because I'm keen to help people find out about how things work and what makes them tick. It may be a space shuttle, a micro-robot, a dinosaur, or blue whale. But the more we know and understand, the better we can care for each other, for our animals and plants, and for our whole world.

"I owe a lot to that worm."

*　　*　　*

Born in Warrington, England, Steve Parker grew up in the small village of Bagshot, about thirty miles southwest of London. He graduated from Bangor, the University College of North Wales. In addition to working at the Natural History Museum, he was an editor of the medical magazine *General Practitioner* and spent three years as an editor at Dorling Kindersley Publishers.

Parker is a Scientific Fellow of the Zoological Society of London and researches many of his books at the Wolfson Library, located at the London Zoo. He also maintains a large personal library, subscribes to scientific journals, and consults scientists and other experts. The Internet plays a growing role in his research.

Of his nearly two hundred published books, many have been released in series, including the What If...? series, the Factfinder series, Science Discoveries, 20th Century Inventions, and many of the popular Eyewitness books. Several of his titles have been singled out for recognition. *The Body Atlas* was shortlisted for the Rhone Poulenc Junior Science Book of the Year award. *Inside the Whale and Other Animals* won the *Times Educational Supplement* Junior Information Book of the Year award in England; in the United States it was chosen as a Recommended Book for Reluctant Young Adult Readers by the American Library Association and cited in the New York Public Library's list, 100 Titles for Reading and Sharing. One of Parker's entries in the Eyewitness series was chosen as an Honor Book in the Secondary Science category by the Society of School Librarians International in 1995. *The Human Body* was shortlisted for the *Times Educational Supplement* Award in 1997.

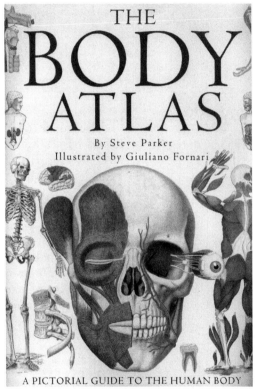

A PICTORIAL GUIDE TO THE HUMAN BODY
Courtesy of DK Publishing, Inc.

Parker has served as a writer-in-residence in British schools and regularly visits libraries, book festivals, and science fairs. In his leisure time, he plays bass guitar and sings harmony with a local rock band and runs a mobile disco available for weddings, birthdays, and special events. Other hobbies include attending local soccer and cricket games, horseback riding, and traveling with his family.

SELECTED WORKS: *Life Begins*, 1986; *Mighty Mammals of the Past*, 1986; *The Day of the Dinosaurs*, 1987; *Skeleton*, 1988; *Living with Blindness*, 1989; *Mammal*, 1989; *The Lungs and Breathing*, 1990; *Camouflage*, 1991; *Catching a Cold*, 1991; *Dinosaurs and How They Lived*, 1991; *Charles Darwin and Evolution*, 1992; *The Body Atlas*, illus. by Guiliano Fornari, 1993; *Flight and Flying Machines*, 1993; *Inside the Whale and Other Animals*, illus. by Ted Dewan, 1993; *Inside Dinosaurs and Other Prehistoric Creatures*, illus. by Ted Dewan, 1994; *Medicine*, 1995; *Brain Surgery for Beginners and Other Major Operations for Minors*, illus. by David West, 1995; *The Human Body: An Amazing Inside Look at You*, illus. by Tim Wootton, 1996; *Shocking Science: 5000 Years of Mishaps and Misunderstandings*, illus. by John Kelly, 1996; *The Beginner's Guide to Animal Autopsy: The Hands-In Approach to Zoology*, 1997; *High in the Sky: Flying Machines*, 1997; *Fuels for the Future*, 1998.

Tom Paxton

October 31, 1937–

" Although I was born in and spent my first ten years in Chicago (a town where they played no major league baseball), I have always considered Oklahoma to be my home state. We moved to Bristow, Oklahoma, in early June of 1948, and I went through junior and senior high schools there and then attended the University of Oklahoma, taking a bachelor of fine arts degree in 1959.

"I was always drawn to the arts. I made my debut as Uncle Sam in (I think) the first or second grade, and in Oklahoma played trumpet in the high school marching and concert bands and—a born ham—acted in all the school plays. When I went down to Norman to enroll as a freshman at OU, I somehow switched my major from journalism to drama without remembering when I changed my mind. I was to appear in some forty plays over my four years there, playing everything from butlers to leads.

"An all-summer acting job in a melodrama in Cripple Creek, Colorado, just after graduation convinced me I was not meant to be an actor. This was not a painful realization as I had by then developed a love of playing and singing folk songs. It was while I was studing at OU that I also began to write songs in the folksong tradition, heavily influenced by such writers as Woody Guthrie, Pete Seeger, and Tom Lehrer. To date I've written a few thousand songs and will admit to liking a couple hundred of them to one degree or another.

"From a hitch in the army right after college I went immediately into the coffehouses of Greewich Village in New York City to begin a career as a folk singer. To my gratified amazement, it worked out, and I've now spent some thirty-eight years traveling the world with my wife, Midge, singing my songs in Australia,

Japan, England, Scotland, Ireland, etc. and have recorded some thirty-five albums of my songs.

"Writing prose seriously was something I dreamed of doing, but apart from writing liner notes for some of my recordings, I shied away from it for years. Finally David Reuther, then editor-in-chief of Morrow Junior Books, called me unexpectedly and asked me if I would like to have my children's song 'Jennifer's Rabbit' —written for my daughter when she was three years old—done as a picture book. Of course I would.

"Meeting with David for the first time opened some kind of floodgate for me, and I asked him if he'd like a book of Aesop's fables done in verse. He told me to try one and when that one worked he asked for more. We did four of them and I began to get more ideas. Sometimes we did books based on my children's songs, which required very little of me, but other ideas arose from whole cloth; my first prose tale was *The Story of Santa Claus*, and when that was well received, I attempted *The Story of the Tooth Fairy*.

"For me, writing of any kind is an arduous pleasure—what I tell my songwriting students we should think of as 'serious fun.' I find that the ideas come indiscriminately; I might find myself beginning a serious song about the search for a just society or a lampoon of yet another political malefactor, a children's song or a children's book, a love song or an elegy for a friend no longer living. It's never easy, but there is still no thrill for me like that of having just completed a piece of work that I consider worthy."

Courtesy of Senor McGuire

* * *

Tom Paxton's singing and songwriting have delighted audiences of adults and children since the early 1960s. He has been a leader in the folk music world throughout that time, writing songs that comment on contemporary issues and human relationships as well as his rollicking children's music. While Paxton's songs for adults are often humorously satirical ("Yuppies in the Sky") or poignantly romantic ("Last Thing on My Mind"), his children's songs are purely for fun, and range from nonsense ("Engelbert the Elephant") to family interaction ("Marvelous Toy") to special occasions ("Going to the Zoo"). He has made more than thirty-five recordings of his songs over the years, and his music has often been recorded by other major folk, country, pop, and classical artists.

Paxton's children's books grew naturally out of his songs, his first publication being a picture book version of the imaginative song he wrote for his older daughter, "Jennifer's Rabbit." In the four volumes of *Aesop's Fables*, Paxton retells the age-old tales with a breezy wit that is matched perfectly by the sly humor of Robert Rayevsky's illustrations.

Paxton has been married to Margaret ("Midge") Cummings since 1963, and they have two grown daughters, Jennifer and Kate. He is a member of the American Society of Composers, Authors and Publishers. After many years of living in New York City, the Paxtons now reside in Alexandria, Virginia, and Tom continues to perform in folk festivals and concert halls all over the world.

SELECTED WORKS: *Jennifer's Rabbit*, illus. by Wallace Tripp, 1970, (reissued 1988, illus. by Donna Ayers); *Aesop's Fables: Retold in Verse*, illus. by Robert Rayevsky, 1988; *Belling the Cat and Other Aesop's Fables*, illus. by Robert Rayevsky, 1990; *Tom Paxton Children's Songbook*, illus. by Kerstin Fairbend, 1990; *Engelbert the Elephant*, illus. by Steven Kellogg, 1990; *Androcles and the Lion and Other Aesop's Fables*, illus. by Robert Rayevsky, 1991; *Birds of a Feather and Other Aesop's Fables*, illus. by Robert Rayevsky, 1993; *Where's the Baby?*, illus. by Mark Graham, 1993; *Engelbert Moves the House*, illus. by Don Vanderbeek, 1995; *The Story of Santa Claus*, illus. by Michael Dooling, 1995; *The Story of the Tooth Fairy*, illus. by Robert Sauber, 1996; *Going to the Zoo*, illus. by Karen Schmidt, 1996; *The Marvelous Toy*, illus. by Elizabeth Sayles, 1996; *Engelbert Joins the Circus*, illus. by Steven Kellogg, 1997; *The Jungle Baseball Game*, illus. by Karen Schmidt, 1999.

SUGGESTED READING: *Meet Tom Paxton* (Let Me Read series), 1996; Okun, Milton. *Something to Sing About*, 1968; *Something About the Author*, vol. 70, 1993; Stambler, Irwin and Grelun Landon. *Encyclopedia of Folk, Country and Western Music*, 2nd ed., 1983. Periodicals—*The New York Times*, November 25, 1994, p. C1.

> *"Meeting with David for the first time opened some kind of floodgate for me . . ."*

Marcus Pfister

(FISS-ter)

July 30, 1960–

"I was born July 30th, 1960, in Bern. Today I still live and work here in Switzerland. I don't remember much about children's books from my childhood. What I remember are the stories my father told us. These were stories that he made up, and often they would continue the next day. There were short adventure stories about children or animals that had us hanging onto every word. His stories were so good that it was no wonder we were always begging for more.

"This is also one of the motivating forces in my own life. What could be better than sitting with children, telling them stories, watching their eyes open in wonder, and their expressions change from extreme tension to pure happiness?

"Even when I was in the first and second grades, I loved to draw. But back then, it wasn't picture books and animal stories, but sports cars and airplanes—typical boy things. I would usually make these drawings during math class, and then I would sell them for a few cents to enthusiastic classmates during recess. After the obligatory nine years of schooling, I studied at the art school in Bern for five years and became a graphic artist.

"After getting my degree, I moved to Zurich, Switzerland's business capital. I worked there for two years as a graphic artist in an advertising agency and made posters, advertisements, and ad campaigns for clients from all sorts of industries.

"In 1983 I decided to apply for a work permit to come to the United States for six months, because many graphic designers from Europe found it helpful to their careers to get job experience in the United States. Unfortunately, the work permit was denied, since I couldn't get a firm offer from any American company. In retrospect, it was a stroke of luck for me, that instead of spending half a year at an ad agency in California, I was only able to get a tourist visa for six months to travel across the United States.

Courtesy of Marcus Pfister

"It was really great to be able to spend that time traveling around with my wife doing what we wanted every day. The only problem was having to go back to my earlier lifestyle with a full-time job. So, after returning to Switzerland, I decided to make some changes in my life. Instead of working full-time, I took a job working three days a week as a graphic artist.

"Having the luxury of some free time, in 1984 I had the idea of creating a children's book. My wife, who was working as a kindergarten teacher, was very knowledgeable about children's books and gave me lots of inspiration.

"Hand in hand, the art and the text for my first book, *The Sleepy Owl*, were created. By the middle of 1984, I had finished the book. But instead of sitting on the desk of an enthusiastic editor, it sat in my studio. It would take two years and many rejections before the book was published by Nord-Süd Verlag (North-South Books in the United States) in 1986.

"In this first book, my love of technical and formal details is obvious. I love abstract art—leaving out unnecessary details and limiting things to what is absolutely necessary. Perhaps this is something I've carried over from my days as a graphic artist, where a message must be given to the public in a clear and simple form. This thought line has also made me create very simple backgrounds. This way the observer immediately sees the focus of the picture without getting sidetracked. Of course, during the years my style has gotten better, the technique has been perfected, and above all, my writing has improved. But sometimes I think back nostalgically at the ease with which I created *The Sleepy Owl*.

"Today the writing and inventing of new stories is my favorite part of the work. I enjoy developing book concepts, including all the questions of production, like the use of holographic foil stamping in *The Rainbow Fish*, or books with alternate endings, like *Milo and the Magical Stones*."

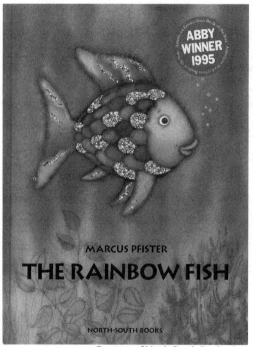

Courtesy of North-South Books, Inc.

* * *

Marcus Pfister's signature style of soft watercolors, often highlighted by holographic foil stamping, and the gentle messages of his picture book stories have earned him an enthusiastic following among young readers. *The Rainbow Fish* alone has sold over five million copies worldwide, has been translated into more than thirty languages, and has remained on bestseller lists across the United States since its American publication in 1992. It has also garnered many awards, including the Bologna Book Fair *Critici in Erba* Prize, a 1993 Christopher Award, and the 1995 American Booksellers Book of the Year (ABBY) award.

Many of Pfister's titles have appeared in the American Booksellers Association Pick of the Lists. *The Rainbow Fish, Rainbow Fish to the Rescue!, How Leo Learned to Be King*, and *Rainbow Fish and the Big Blue Whale* were all IRA/CBC Children's Choices, and *Rainbow Fish to the Rescue!* was also named a Notable Trade Book in the Field of Social Studies. *Milo and the Magical Stones* won Pfister his second Christopher Award, in 1998, and was also cited for a *Storytelling World* Award and a *Learning Magazine* Teachers' Choice Award.

The popularity of Pfister's books has led to a marketing blitz of items to accompany the books: card games, puppets, mobiles, calendars, mugs, foil-stamped buttons, and postcards.

Marcus Pfister lives with his wife and sometime collaborator, Kathrin Siegenthaler, and their three children in Bern, Switzerland.

SELECTED WORKS WRITTEN AND ILLUSTRATED: *The Sleepy Owl*, tr. by J. J. Curle, 1986; *Penguin Pete*, tr. by Anthea Bell, 1987; *Penguin Pete's New Friends*, tr. by Anthea Bell, 1988; *Penguin Pete & Pat*, tr. by Anthea Bell, 1989; *Sun & Moon*, tr. by Rosemary Lanning, 1990; *Shaggy*, tr. by Lenny Hort, 1990; *Hopper*; tr. by Rosemary Lanning, 1991; *The Rainbow Fish*, tr. by J. Alison James, 1992; *Hopper Hunts for Spring*, tr. by Rosemary Lanning, 1992; *Hopper's Easter Suprise*, tr. by Rosemary Lanning, 1993; *The Christmas Star*, tr. by J. Alison James, 1993; *Pengiun Pete, Ahoy!*, tr. by Rosemary Lanning, 1993; *Dazzle the Dinosaur*; tr. by J. Alison James, 1994; *Penguin Pete & Little Tim*, tr. by Rosemary Lanning, 1994; *Rainbow Fish to the Rescue!*, tr. by J. Alison James, 1995; *Hang On, Hopper!*, tr. by Rosemary Lanning, 1995; *Wake Up, Santa Claus!*, tr. by J. Alison James, 1996; *Milo & the Magical Stones*, tr. by Marianne Martens, 1997; *How Leo Learned to Be King*, tr. by J. Alison James, 1998; *Rainbow Fish and the Big Blue Whale*, tr. by J. Alison James, 1998; *Make a Wish, Honey Bear*, 1999.

SELECTED WORKS ILLUSTRATED: *Four Candles for Simon*, by Gerda Marie Scheidl, tr. by Anthea Bell, 1987; *Santa Claus and the Woodcutter*, by Kathrin Siegenthaler, tr. by Elizabeth Crawford, 1988; *Miriam's Gift: A Christmas Story*, by Gerda Marie Scheidl, tr. by Rosemary Lanning, 1989.

SUGGESTED READING: *Children's Literature Review*, vol. 42, 1997; *Something About the Author*, vol. 83, 1996; Ward, Martha. *Authors of Books for Young People*, 1990. Periodicals—"Marcus Pfister's Shimmering Success," *Teaching PreK–8*, March 1999; "The Winner's Circle," *Booklist*, May 1, 1993.

Andrea Davis Pinkney

September 25, 1963–

"I get asked the same question a lot: 'So, how did you decide to become a writer?' I never quite know how to answer that question, because I don't think I *decided* to become a writer. A writer is just who and what I am. I've always loved to tell, listen to, and read stories. This probably has something to do with the fact that my mother was a schoolteacher who always read books like crazy, and my father was—and still is—a master storyteller.

"As a child, I didn't watch much television (I mostly read books) but, ironically, there were two TV shows that encouraged me to pursue a writing career. One was *The Waltons.* The eldest Walton son, John Boy, was an aspiring novelist. Each episode of *The Waltons* ended with John Boy's voice reading a lovely narrative from his journal. Every time I watched the show, I thought, 'What a great way to live your life—by writing it all down.'

"*The Mary Tyler Moore Show*, about a broadcast journalist who lived in Minneapolis, was another favorite. The main character, Mary Richards, wasn't a writer per se, but she was a career woman who lived in a big city. I liked that. So when I graduated from Syracuse University with a journalism degree, I moved to New York City and worked as a gardening editor for a small home decorating magazine. That's where I met illustrator Brian Pinkney (he worked in the art department at the magazine across the hall), who, years later, became my husband.

Courtesy of Dwight Carter

"While working at the magazine, I spent nights and weekends writing for fun. I wrote short stories, essays, children's poems, whatever came to mind. One weekend I wrote an essay about my experiences as an African American girl growing up in Wilton, Connecticut, where my family moved when I was twelve. Wilton was a suburb where there were few black families. On a whim, I sent the piece to the *New York Times*—and they published it! It was then that I started to think of myself as a real writer.

"Eventually I left the magazine to write full-time. As a freelance writer, I wrote articles for *American Visions*, *Highlights for Children*, *Executive Female*, and *Essence* magazines. I also collaborated with my husband on several picture books. Then, years after the *Times* essay came out, I used it as the basis for my first young adult novel, *Hold Fast to Dreams.*

"For me, writing for children is like dancing—it lets my imagination whirl and encourages me to play with rhythm."

*　　*　　*

After receiving her B.A. in Journalism from Syracuse University in 1985, Andrea Davis began her career as a gardening editor for a small home decorating magazine. Across the hall was the

office of *Field and Stream*, where Brian
Pinkney worked in the art department.
Brian was taking his portfolio to children's book editors on his lunch hour,
and when he received his first contract,
Andrea helped him with photo shoots.
They were married in 1991 and soon after began the first of their many collaborations in writing and illustrating award-
winning children's books.

One of their early joint projects—a
biography of the legendary dancer Alvin
Ailey—won an NAACP Image Award,
was chosen as a *Reading Rainbow* book,
and was named to the *Horn Book*'s Fanfare list. *Dear Benjamin Banneker* received a Carter G. Woodson Honor
Award and was listed by the Child Study
Association as one of the best books of
the year. *Dear Benjamin Banneker*,
Duke Ellington and *Bill Pickett* were all
named Notable Trade Books in the
Field of Social Studies, and the latter
two were both ALA Notable Children's

Courtesy of Hyperion Books

Books as well. *Duke Ellington* garnered both a Caldecott Honor
Award and a Coretta Scott King Honor Book citation. Andrea
Pinkney's first novel, *Hold Fast to Dreams,* was an American
Booksellers Association Pick of the Lists, and *Raven in a Dove
House* was selected for the New York Public Library's Books for
the Teen Age.

Andrea Davis Pinkney held positions as a children's book editor at several publishing houses before moving to Hyperion and
becoming the editorial force behind Jump at the Sun, an imprint
that celebrates the uniqueness of African American life and culture. She lives in New York City with her husband and their two
small children.

SELECTED WORKS: *Seven Candles of Kwanzaa,* illus. by Brian
Pinkney, 1993; *Alvin Ailey,* illus. by Brian Pinkney, 1993;
Dear Benjamin Banneker, illus. by Brian Pinkney, 1994; *Hold
Fast to Dreams,* 1995; *Bill Pickett—Rodeo Ridin' Cowboy,*
illus. by Brian Pinkney, 1996; *Solo Girl,* illus. by Nneka
Bennett, 1997; *I Smell Honey,* illus. by Brian Pinkney, 1997;
Shake, Shake, Shake, illus. by Brian Pinkney, 1997; *Watch Me
Dance,* illus. by Brian Pinkney, 1997; *Pretty Brown Face,* illus.
by Brian Pinkney, 1997; *Raven in a Dove House,* 1998; *Duke
Ellington,* illus. by Brian Pinkney, 1998; *Silent Thunder: A
Civil War Story,* 1999.

SUGGESTED READING: "The Booklist Interview," *Booklist,* February 2, 1999; "Hyperion Launches African American Children's Imprint," *Publishers Weekly,* July 6, 1998; Winarski, Diane, "The Rhythm of Writing and Art," *Teaching PreK–8,* October 1997.

A profile of Andrea Pinkney's husband, Brian, appears in *Seventh Book of Junior Authors and Illustrators* (1996).

Courtesy of Myles C. Pinkney

Gloria Jean Pinkney

September 5, 1941–

"I was born on September 5, 1941, in Lumberton, North Carolina, and raised in Philadelphia, Pennsylvania.

"I became curiously fascinated by people and their stories at an early age. At four, I could figure out sentences the grown-ups were spelling by watching their gestures while listening to their tone of voice. It was 1945. This peculiar skill was not understood, nor was it appreciated. So my mother, her friends, and other family members kept me well supplied with delightful picture books. This, they hoped, would 'keep Miss Jones,' as they nicknamed me, 'out of grown-folks conversation.'

"My first books inclued *Little Red Riding Hood* and *Mother Goose Nursery Rhymes.* Later, *The Wonder Clock,* *Grimm's Fairy Tales,* *Aesop's Fables,* *Hans Christian Andersen Tales,* *Little Women,* and *Heidi.* I never owned an African-American storybook. I read this latter grouping over and over again. Also, my stepfather bought me a small rolltop desk. It had in it an endless supply of tools to create my own storybooks.

"One month after my eighth birthday, childhood was permanently changed by the sudden loss of my mother. My stepfather remarried. Great-aunt was appointed legal guardian. It was often difficult those earlier years, being raised without other children about. Great-aunt had to become a dayworker. She usually returned home late and tired; 1949 was a time when children were expected to be seen and not heard. So I'd often retreat into a beautiful fantasy world of books. Or I'd spend hours recording my innermost feelings in a diary.

"I was a good writer in grade school. My stories were often singled out for creativity and imagination. However, I was very weak in the area of punctuation. Regrettably, I took the easy way out by creating simple sentences which became dull, boring compositions. I became an oral storyteller to avoid imperfect papers. It was a cowardly decision (one I encourage children not to make).

"A wonderful thing happened in sixth grade. My favorite teacher encouraged me to acquire a library card. Many joy-filled hours were spent at the Lehigh Branch Public Library in North Philadelphia. I had a teacher and librarian that cared. Both encouraged weekly visits there.

"Because of these two ladies, my childhood as a 'latch-key kid' became intermingled with my storybook friends. We had exciting adventures and conquests.

"As an adult, I never dreamed of being published. During the 1970s and 1980s, I began working along with my husband, illustrator Jerry Pinkney, as a production assistant. I knew I could tell a good story. But I thought writing was beyond my talent.

"Then an unexpected blessing arrived in our mailbox. We were invited to a family reunion in Lumberton, North Carolina. It was a gathering of my mother's people. The occasion ignited a need to put my life journey on paper. With much difficulty I wrote *Back Home*. *The Sunday Outing* was easier because I was a little more experienced. In writing these two books, I established a voice (my own way/style of linking words and thoughts).

"Imagine, I'm using words from my childhood, voices of southern relatives and friends that were living in my aunt's house in those early years. Now their voices are heard in my stories. They, and I, love sharing them."

*"I became
curiously
fascinated by
people and
their stories at
an early age."*

*　*　*

Gloria Pinkney met her husband-to-be, Jerry Pinkney, when she was in high school in Philadelphia. They have been married almost forty years and have four children, who are all involved in the arts. Their son Brian and his wife, Andrea, illustrate and write children's books; their photographer son Myles has also illustrated several books for young readers; Scott is an art director for an advertising agency; and daughter Troy is an art therapist. In the 1980s Gloria ran a boutique for which she designed and made jewelry, hats, and clothes. She still designs clothes for her own family.

Gloria has always worked closely with her husband, hiring models, assembling costumes, photographing sets, and helping with his research on various projects, including a series of four Black History Calendars for which she also did some of the writing. A family reunion in 1989 in Lumberton, North Carolina, sparked Gloria's memories of a previous visit there at the age of eight. Her two books were born out of the experience, and her collaboration with her husband took on a new dimension when he illustrated both *Back Home* and *The Sunday Outing*. Gloria

Pinkney is currently working on her third book. When she is not writing she speaks at schools, universities, and churches all over the country. She is active in the Women's Ministry and a member of the Gospel Chorus of the Star of Bethlehem Baptist Church in Ossining, New York.

Back Home won a Parents' Choice Award, was named an ALA Notable Children's Book, was included in New York Public Library's 100 Titles for Reading and Sharing, was cited as a Notable Children's Trade Book in the Field of Social Studies, and was a *Booklist* Editors' Choice for 1992. *The Sunday Outing* was a Society of Writers at the United Nations' President's Recommended Selection for Children's Literature. It was cited as a Children's Book of the Year by the Child Study Children's Book Committee and was an ABA/CBC selection for their list Children's Books Mean Business. The *New York Times* selected it as one of the Ten Best Illustrated Books of the Year.

SELECTED WORKS: *Back Home*, illus. by Jerry Pinkney, 1992; *The Sunday Outing*, illus. by Jerry Pinkney, 1994.

SUGGESTED READING: Murphy, Barbara Thrash. *Black Authors and Illustrators of Books for Children and Young Adults*, 3rd ed., 1999; *Something About the Author*, vol. 85, 1996. Periodicals—Bishop, Rudine Sims, "The Pinkney Family: In the Tradition," *The Horn Book*, January/February 1996; *Teaching Tolerance*, Fall 1996.

A profile of Gloria Pinkney's husband, Jerry, appears in *Sixth Book of Junior Authors and Illustrators* (1989).

Connie Porter

July 29, 1959–

"I did not always know that I wanted to write. I liked science a lot when I was in school, and I still do. If I were not a writer, I would like to be an oceanographer or a marine biologist. It may not seem that writing and science have much in common, but one thing you must do in both is observe. And both require a kind of silence. As a writer I watch people and—most important—I listen.

"I am the second youngest of nine children, and I think because of that I learned to listen. My parents and older brothers and sisters always had stories to tell, and I would listen to them. I didn't listen just to what they said, but to how they said it. I believe that listening is as much a skill as writing. It is especially important for a writer.

"I like being from a large family. Having four brothers and four sisters, I always had someone to play with when I was growing up. We didn't have much money. Actually, we were quite poor, but I don't think I noticed it much. My family lived in a very crowded apartment in a housing project, the Baker Homes in Lackawanna, New York, which is a small city near Buffalo. My mother made clothes that my sisters and I wore. I especially looked forward to Christmas and Easter, when my mother made us wonderful dresses. My mother was also a fantastic cook, and no matter what we ate for dinner—chicken, beans, or even biscuits and syrup—it tasted good.

"On Sundays, our family went to Saint Mark's A.M.E. Zion Church. Church was important to my family. Our father always gave each of us money to put in the collection plate and some to spend. It was usually a nickel or dime, and before we came home, we would stop and buy penny candy. The licorice, peach stones, fire balls, and peanut butter cups were a real treat.

"When I was a little girl I was very quiet, partly because I listened so much. I also got hurt when I was four. I fell on some broken glass and nearly cut off my hand. The accident left me scared about going outside, so until I was about seven years old, I mostly stayed in the house with my mother and baby sister.

"It was in that quiet time after my accident that I became really interested in reading. Before my younger sister, Brenda, was born, I remember being the only one in the whole house who couldn't read. I recall being angry about it. But I was so happy when my brothers would spread out the Saturday color comics to read to me. Lying on our stomachs, one of them would read all the comics to me—I made sure we didn't miss any. I thought reading was a kind of magic since it could unlock the funny and colorful world on those pages.

"I learned to read after I began attending Roosevelt Elementary School. It was a neighborhood school, only a few blocks from where we lived. We walked to school and went home for lunch. I liked going home at lunchtime, especially glad my mother was home on those blustery afternoons. The windows would be all steamed up from the hot soup and cocoa she made to go with our peanut butter and jelly sandwiches.

Courtesy of Connie Porter

Connie Porter

"My interest in writing developed while I was in high school. When I was in the tenth grade my parents gave me a typewriter for Christmas, and I started to write poetry. Later a *real* poet came to visit my school. I attended his special classes for students interested in writing. I don't think my poetry was very good, but it was the first time I had met someone who was doing what I wanted to do.

"When I went to college I still knew I wanted to be a writer, but I was afraid to admit it to myself. It was not a very practical thing to want to do—like being a teacher or a marine biologist was. But I stuck with my love of writing. I like to think that my writing does something very important. It gives a voice to people who might otherwise be voiceless. It allows characters like Addy to speak."

* * *

Connie Rose Porter received her B. A. degree from the State University of New York at Albany in 1981 and her M. F. A. degree from Louisiana State University in 1987. She has taught creative writing at Milton Academy, Emerson College, and Southern Illinois University at Carbondale. Her first adult novel, *All-Bright Court*, was selected by the American Library Association as one of the Best Books of 1991 and by the *New York Times* as one of its Notable Books of 1991.

Courtesy of Pleasant Company

Porter's stories about Addy Walker, a character in the American Girls series, show the determination of a young African American girl who escapes from slavery during the Civil War era. "I wanted children to see African American people as part of strong, loving families, caught up in slavery, doing what they had to do to survive," she has said. Booksellers around the country voted the Addy books the Best Children's Series of 1993 in the annual Cuffie Awards sponsored by *Publishers Weekly*. Porter's first novel for teens, *Imani All Mine*, was named one of the Top Ten Best Books for Young Adults by the American Library Association in 2000.

In 1995 Porter was named a Regional Winner in *Granta* magazine's contest, Best Writers in America under 40. She writes five or six days a week in her Virginia home, usually between 7 P.M. and 1 A.M. She claims that the phone doesn't ring as much during those hours as it does in the morning.

SELECTED WORKS: *All-Bright Court*, 1991 (for adults); *Meet Addy*, 1993; *Addy Learns a Lesson*, 1993; *Addy's Surprise*, 1993; *Addy Saves the Day*, 1994; *Changes for Addy*, 1994;

Happy Birthday, Addy, 1994; *Imani All Mine*, 1999; *High Hopes for Addy*, 1999.

SUGGESTED READING: *Contemporary Authors*, vol. 132, 1991; *Contemporary Literary Criticism*, vol. 70, 1992; Perlman, Mickey. *Listen to Their Voices*, 1993; *Something About the Author*, vol. 81, 1995. *Periodicals—American Libraries*, February 1992; *Booklist*, August 1993; "Connie Porter: Telling It the Way It Was," *Teaching PreK–8*, October 1994; "Connie Porter: Writing About Home," *Essence*, September 1991; Porter, Connie, "The Faces of Friendship," *Glamour*, April 1994.

"**I** was born during the blizzard of '58, January 8th to be exact—which makes my birthday the same day as Elvis Presley's, though that is where the similarity ends. As far as I know, there are no singers—or writers, for that matter—in my family, nor anyone particularly famous, although my great-great-grandmother, who I never knew, was famous in our family for climbing apple trees when she was 101 years old and for growing a third set of teeth. Or so the story goes.

"My father was famous for fixing things and reading two-ton novels. My mother was known for a dish we affectionately called 'soggy chicken' and for being the one mother on the block who could cut bangs straight and for being an artist. For one entire year, it seemed, her subject was pineapples. Later she moved on to nudes. But this was the 1960s and these nudes were orange or green or black-and-white checks, which gave them the effect of being more or less dressed. Still, it was shocking to the neighborhood kids.

Courtesy of Marjorie Priceman

Marjorie Priceman

January 8, 1958–

"I myself was known for drawing people from the feet up. The reason, and I'm sure there was one, is lost forever. I dabbled in all the arts, never serious about any one. At twelve I attempted a film about my Yorkshire terrier, Daphne, complete with handwritten subtitles but abandoned it after one reel. It was all fur and character with no plot to speak of. After that I began work on a novel called *The Mystery of the Emerald Cave*, also abandoned, with the heroines, Molly and Polly, in the wood-paneled station wagon heading for an adventure . . . and never getting there. Three decades later, still stuck in chapter one.

"I cannot mine the past of a single event or influence that led me to my current career. But writing and drawing are things I have always done, in one form or another. I recall adding details in green pen to an alphabet book, an enhancement or defacement depending on your point of view. Then there was the time my sister and I tried to make cupcakes with purple and green frosting, but our color-mixing resulted in frosting the color of dryer lint and army fatigues. (Where there is risk, there is the possibility of failure.) I remember a plaster-of-paris map of Italy I had made sliding soundlessly off its wooden board and shattering on the ground as the third grade watched. I remember making magic wands out of empty bead containers filled with water and sparkles and selling them at a table on the sidewalk. Somewhere there is a maple tree with my initials carved in it (sorry). And a square of sidewalk with my palm print. I no longer work with tree bark and concrete; these days I prefer paper and paint.

Courtesy of Simon & Schuster Children's Publishing Division

"After high school I attended the Rhode Island School of Design, where I majored in illustration. I took classes in drawing and painting and metalsmithing and graphics. I took a class called 'The Flower,' where students drew the same flower every day for weeks until it shriveled and died, which was really very interesting. I took a class called 'Color,' where each week we sat on the floor and painted a bunch of oranges placed there by the teacher. We were instructed to 'paint the space *between* the oranges.' Most of us stubbornly insisted on painting the actual oranges, myself included, much to the teacher's dismay. I also took a class called 'Picture and Word,' which was a children's book writing and illustrating class. I received a B for the picture part and a D (!) for the word part. Sometimes I think it must have been a mistake, but I never looked into it so I'll never know.

"What I do know is this. Writing and illustrating books is about the best job imaginable. As a movie buff it strikes me sometimes that creating a picture book is a little like making a movie (but without the million-dollar budget). Like a screenwriter, you write the story. Like a casting agent, you decide if a character will be played by a short man or a large dog. Like a cinematographer, you choose the camera angles—long shot or close up from behind the potted plant. Like a director, you give directions to the actors—'smile, look this way, sit down.' You design the costumes, the hairstyles, scout the locations. You create your own unique world between the covers of the book: the alternate universe of the story. The only thing missing is sound and motion. But the unlimited imagination of the reader can supply those details. I have no doubt."

*   *   *

Marjorie Priceman was born and grew up on Long Island, near famous Jones Beach. After receiving her degree from the Rhode Island School of Design, she worked at a variety of jobs in and around New York City. She did illustrating for *Newsday* on Long Island, fashion sketches for several companies, and fabric designs for Gapkids clothing. One of the drawbacks of fabric designing is that you never know whether or not your work will be used, and Priceman was surprised once to see a design of hers on a tie worn by a celebrity on television. Looking for a career that was more satisfying, Priceman received help and encouragement in creating her first picture book from her former professor at the Rhode Island School of Design, David Macaulay.

Marjorie Priceman's picture book art is characterized by bright watercolors and free-flowing lines. Her Caldecott Honor Award–winning illustrations for Lloyd Moss's *Zin! Zin! Zin! A Violin* exhibit a bouyancy and flow that mirror the chamber music described in the text, while all of the musicians remarkably resemble their instruments of choice. The animals that chase each other through the pages were inspired by Priceman's own cats. In addition to the Caldecott Honor, *Zin! Zin! Zin!* was an ALA Notable Children's Book, a *School Library Journal* Best Book of the Year, a *New York Times* Best Illustrated Book, and a *Reading Rainbow* feature title. *How to Make an Apple Pie and See the World* and *What Zeesie Saw on Delancey Street* were also named ALA Notable Children's Books and appeared as well on the Blue Ribbon list of the *Bulletin of the Center for Children's Books. Rachel Fister's Blister* and *A. Nonny Mouse Writes Again!* were both cited in the *Horn Book*'s Fanfare, and *For Laughing Out Loud* and *One of Each* were among *School Library Journal*'s Best Books of the Year. *Emeline at the Circus* was a *New York Times* Best Illustrated Book and an ALA Notable Children's Book.

Whether she is illustrating her own stories, the works of other writers, or a poetry anthology, Priceman's art typically exhibits a rollicking humor and an expressive exuberance. After living in New York through most of the 1980s, she moved to Lewisburg, Pennsylvania, where she enjoys a more rural lifestyle.

SELECTED WORKS WRITTEN AND ILLUSTRATED: *Friend or Frog*, 1989; *How to Make an Apple Pie and See the World*, 1994; *My Nine Lives, by Clio*, 1998; *Emeline at the Circus*, 1999; *Froggie Went A-Courting: An Old Tale with a New Twist*, 2000.

SELECTED WORKS ILLUSTRATED: *Rachel Fister's Blister*, by Amy MacDonald, 1990; *A Mouse in My House*, by Nancy Van Laan, 1990; *For Laughing Out Loud: Poems to Tickle Your Funnybone*, comp. by Jack Prelutsky, 1991; *A. Nonny Mouse Writes Again!*, by Jack Prelutsky, 1993; *For Laughing Out Louder: More Poems to Tickle Your Funnybone*, comp. by Jack Prelutsky, 1995; *Zin! Zin! Zin! A Violin*, by Lloyd Moss, 1995; *How Emily Blair Got Her Fabulous Hair*, by Susan Garrison, 1995; *Cousin Ruth's Tooth*, by Amy MacDonald, 1996; *What Zeesie Saw on Delancey Street*, by Elsa Okon Rael, 1996; *One of Each*, by Mary Ann Hoberman, 1997; *When Zaydeh Danced on Eldridge Street*, by Elsa Okon Rael, 1997; *Dancin' in the Kitchen*, by Frank P. Christian and Wendy Gelsanliter, 1998; *Serafina Under the Circumstances*, by Phyllis Theroux, 1999.

SUGGESTED READING: Cummins, Julie, *Children's Book Illustration and Design*, vol. 2, 1998; *Something About the Author*, vol. 81, 1995. Periodicals—Allen, Tammy, "The Apple Pie Tour," *Teaching PreK–8*, February 1998; Mitchell, Kathryn, "Journeying Through Books," *Reading Teacher*, May 1995.

Bonnie Pryor

December 22, 1942–

"I fought all my life to avoid being a writer. In addition to an active imagination I was also blessed with a hard practical side. It was this side of me that kept me from pursuing what seemed to be an impossible dream. And yet, almost every happy memory I have in life is connected in some way or another with books and storytelling.

"I was born in California. When I was five I was adopted by an aunt and uncle and moved to Washington State. My new parents were an older couple, highly educated, but not readers. They did not know what to make of this shy, quiet little girl who wanted to do nothing but read. They saw this as a problem and actually did everything they could to keep me away from books. I never went to a public library or bookstore until I was an adult. School was not much different. I made good grades and I was so quiet I was mostly overlooked, except when the teachers confiscated the school library book hidden inside my math book.

"My new parents adopted another baby who had serious health problems. My adoptive mother had a bad heart, and it took all her energy to care for the new baby. As a result I spent most of my childhood by myself. I told stories to entertain myself, long exciting tales where I was the heroine who saved everyone. These stories were like a soap opera, continuing day after day. I had to hurry and get my chores done so I could get out to my huge plum tree where I told most of my stories. This plum tree served me later when I wrote *The Plum Tree War*.

"I briefly attended college with the idea of becoming a nurse, but it didn't take long to realize that was not for me. I married, raised six children, and worked at a variety of jobs, none of them having anything to do with books. All this time I continued to read everything I could find. I especially enjoyed the books I read to my children. Every week I would bring home a stack of books from the library. I devoured all those beautiful books I had yearned for as a child.

"For Christmas in 1983 my husband bought me a typewriter and challenged me to make my dream come true. I wrote several magazine articles, but I soon realized that what I really wanted was to write for children. My first book was published in 1985. Although my stories are made up, they are peppered with incidents from my childhood or that of my children. *The House on Maple Street* came about when my daughter Chrissy found an arrowhead, *Porcupine Mouse* when a son left home.

"I think a good book for children teaches some subtle lesson. I hope mine say that life is easier with a sense of humor and some love. Sometimes when I visit schools children ask how long I want to keep writing. 'As long as I can totter to my computer,' I tell them. 'I have so many more stories in me I want to share.'"

Courtesy of Robert Pryor

Bonnie Pryor.

* * *

A resident of Gambier, Ohio, Bonnie Pryor owns children's bookstores in Mount Vernon and Newark, Ohio. Working in the stores during the day, she can keep up with what's currently being published for young people. Late in the evening at home, she makes her own contributions to the field by writing popular, award-winning books. The Child Study Children's Book Committee of Bank Street College of Education included *Mr. Z and the Time Clock* and *The Dream Jar* in its list of Children's Books of the Year. *The House on Maple Street* was named an Outstanding Science Trade Book and also an American Booksellers Association Pick of the Lists. *The House* on *Maple Street*, *Seth of the Lion People*, and *The Dream Jar* were all named Notable Trade Books in the Field of Social Studies. *The Dream Jar* was also chosen as an outstanding book by the Smithsonian Institute. *Porcupine Mouse* received the Irma Simonton Black Award from the Bank Street College of Education in 1989. *Marvelous Marvin and the Pioneer Ghost* was nominated for the 1996 Edgar Allan Poe Award for the year's best juvenile mystery.

Books in Pryor's series about Marvin Snodgrass have been nominated for numerous state children's choice awards. *Vinegar Pancakes and Vanishing Cream* has appeared on the ballots of the Kansas, Kentucky, and Ohio state awards. *Poison Ivy and Eyebrow Wigs* won the 1998 Maryland state award. In 1995,

by Bonnie Pryor
illustrated by Mark Graham

Courtesy of William Morrow & Co., Inc.

Bonnie Pryor received the Ohioana Award for the body of her work. She is especially excited about her new series of historical novels featuring boys. Known as the American Adventures series, it has to date featured Thomas, who lives during the Revolutionary War; Joseph, a boy of the Civil War era; and Luke, who takes part in the California Gold Rush.

SELECTED WORKS: *Grandpa Bear*, illus. by Bruce Degen, 1985; *Grandpa Bear's Christmas*, illus. by Bruce Degen, 1986; *Mr. Z and the Time Clock*, 1986; *The House on Maple Street*, illus. by Beth Peck, 1987; *Vinegar Pancakes and Vanishing Cream*, illus. by Gail Owens, 1987; *Seth of the Lion People*, illus. by Dennis Nolan, 1988; *Porcupine Mouse*, illus. by Maryjane Begin, 1988; *Poison Ivy and Eyebrow Wigs*, illus. by Gail Owens, 1993; *Marvelous Marvin and the Wolfman Mystery*, illus. by Melissa Sweet, 1994; *Marvelous Marvin and the Pioneer Ghost*, illus. by Melissa Sweet, 1995; *The Dream Jar*, illus. by Mark Graham, 1996; *Toenails, Tonsils, and Tornadoes*, illus. by Helen Cogancherry, 1997; *Thomas* (American Adventures, No. 1), illus. by Bert Dodson, 1998; *Joseph: A Rumble of War, 1861* (American Adventures, No. 2), illus. by Bert Dodson, 1999; *Luke: On the Golden Trail, 1849* (American Adventures, No. 3), illus. by Bert Dodson, 1999; *Louie and Dan Are Friends*, illus. by Elizabeth Miles, 1999.

SUGGESTED READING: *Contemporary Authors*, vol. 130, 1990; *Something About the Author*, vol. 69, 1992; Ward, Martha, ed. *Authors of Books for Young People*, 1990.

WEB SITE: *www.Bergenstein.com/SCBWI/pryor/pryor.htm*

E-MAIL: *chrissy@ecr.com*

"**O**ur family vacations, when I was young, were spent at the ocean. We shared a rental beach house at Grayland, Washington, with another family who were close friends. There were four of us kids, two in my family, two in the other family. On sunny days we dug in the sand, played in the surf, and pestered our parents to let us walk to the nearby country store by ourselves to 'just look' at the candy. On rainy days we hung out on the sleeping porch where we played Chinese Checkers, put jigsaw puzzles together, and read. We all were good readers, which wasn't unusual in those days. Most everyone was a good reader. We didn't have the distraction of television.

"Our mothers watched over what we read. Although they would have preferred we read the classics, a good comic book on vacation was O.K. A movie magazine, the forerunner of today's supermarket tabloid, certainly was not. One rainy day Doris, the other family's daughter, found dozens of movie magazines stored under a bed out on the sleeping porch. What a find. We each grabbed a stack and dove right into reading the forbidden. Our concentration created absolute quiet, and this quiet, unfortunately, alerted our mothers. The movie magazines were immediately taken away.

"I will never forget how happy I was reading those magazines our mothers thought so unfit, or forget some of the information featured in the articles. For instance, did you know there once was a famous actress who died of liver failure caused by the bleach she used to lighten her hair? You didn't?

"Although reading was an important part of my growing up, I did not dream of becoming a writer. It never entered my mind. I dreamed instead of becoming a dancer, a dream my parents did not care to encourage. Instead of being sent to dancing school I was given piano lessons. This led to my playing the piano

Courtesy of Walmsley Studio

Gloria Rand

Gloria Rand

November 8, 1925–

at a dancing school in exchange for ballet instruction. I soon discovered that playing for hours for a raggedy line of little ballerinas left me too exhausted to even think about taking a lesson myself.

"I began writing seriously during World War II, not articles or manuscripts for books, but writing letters. I wrote hundreds of what I hoped were newsy pieces of mail. I wrote to my friends in the service, my father's friends in the service, and every relative who joined the armed forces. At the end of the war my writing shifted from letters to writing copy for fashion advertising. The fashion illustrator in the office where I worked was a recently returned Navy Air Force navigator named Ted Rand. I created fashion copy until I became Mrs. Ted Rand, some fifty years ago. Ted's career changed from doing advertising art to illustrating children's books.

"A friend of ours heard a wonderful story about a dog that rode a ferryboat and suggested to Ted that he should write a story about that little dog. Ted turned to me and asked, 'Why don't you write it?' I couldn't think of why not, and so began my writing of children's picture books with the publication of *Salty Dog*.

"Writing for children has greatly enhanced my life. It has brought me in contact, through researching, publishing, and lecturing, with a wide assortment of wonderful people. It has given me friends that I would otherwise never have had. If asked to list my good luck in life I would list my happy marriage to Ted, having a terrific daughter and a terrific son, being the grandmother of three equally terrific grandchildren, and, of course, having the good fortune of being a writer. What more could anyone ask?"

"Ted turned to me and asked, 'Why don't you write it?' I couldn't think of why not."

*　*　*

Gloria Kistler Rand was born in San Francisco, California, on November 8, 1925, to Roy and Mini Kistler. While she was still an infant her family moved to Seattle, Washington, where she later graduated from Roosevelt High School. She attended the University of Washington in Seattle and Madame Chaunard's Art Institute in Los Angeles. While working as a copywriter she met Ted Rand on April Fool's Day 1946. This was no April Fool, though; the couple married on May 1, 1948, and raised two children, Martin and Theresa. While the children were still young, Gloria and a friend wrote a manuscript and sent it off to publishers. After about six rejection slips, Gloria decided that she didn't like those rejection slips, so she took up figure-skating.

Fortunately, her husband urged her to collaborate with him on *Salty Dog* some years later. The book was included on the *Parents* magazine Best Kids Books list and was chosen as an American Booksellers Association Pick of the Lists title in 1989. Further adventures of the canine hero were described in *Salty*

Sails North, Salty Takes Off, and *Aloha, Salty!. Prince William,* about the rescue of an injured baby seal, was also chosen as an ABA Pick of the Lists title and was cited as a Notable Children's Trade Book in the Field of Social Studies.

Always athletic, Gloria Rand still loves to swim, play tennis, and dance. The Rands begin their days early with exercise. After breakfast, they repair to studios at opposite ends of their home on Mercer Island. Gloria's study is small and cozy and looks out on the Rands' lovely wooded gardens. Although the Rands work separately, they consult each other often and frequently do research together.

SELECTED WORKS: (All illus. by Ted Rand) *Salty Dog,* 1989; *Salty Sails North,* 1990; *Salty Takes Off,* 1991; *Prince William,* 1992; *The Cabin Key,* 1994; *Aloha, Salty,* 1996; *Willie Takes a Hike,* 1996; *Baby in a Basket,* 1997; *A Home for Spooky,* 1998; *Fighting for the Forest,* 1999.

SUGGESTED READING: *Contemporary Authors,* vol. 168, 1999; *Something About the Author,* vol. 101, 1999.

A profile of Ted Rand appears in *Sixth Book of Junior Authors and Illustrators* (1989).

Peggy Rathmann

March 4, 1953–

"I grew up in a suburb of St. Paul, Minnesota, with two brothers and two sisters. Every night before bed we would pile onto the couch while my mom or dad read to us. We loved *Mike Mulligan and His Steam Shovel, Winnie the Pooh,* and the Dr. Seuss books. And even though there was a ten-year spread in our ages, we all found something entertaining about those books. Now when I'm working on a book, I picture my brothers and sisters on the couch and I try to figure out ways to keep all of them amused.

"But I didn't start writing and illustrating children's books until I was thirty-six years old. My dad was a scientist, so I figured that's what I would be too. When I was nine, my dream was to be an anthropologist. My mother said that Margaret Mead practiced being an anthropologist by taking notes about her younger siblings, so I started writing about my little brother. I had a hard time sticking to the truth, though. Every journal entry was pure fantasy—some of them were in the form of limericks. I knew I wasn't going to cut it as a scientist and I was concerned about my future.

"In elementary school, it took awhile for me to get with the program. I was tall, so I was assigned a seat in the back of the room, but no one knew how nearsighted I was, not even me. I remember hearing the teacher talk about the alphabet and thinking, 'What alphabet?' Finally, in the fifth grade, I was fitted for glasses. After that, school was a lot easier. I liked art class the best.

"Back at home, I was the babysitter for my little brother and sister. I entertained them by drawing their portraits, telling them stories, and putting on puppet shows. By the time I graduated from high school, I was considering a career in art, so I attended a summer workshop at a local art school. On the first day, the instructor said 'We just want you to know that *no one* is making a living doing art right now except Picasso.' I went home thinking I'd better find a job in a different field. So I decided to go into psychology. . . then medicine. . . and finally, after seven years of college, *commercial* art. I remember the day it hit me that an *artist* had been paid to create the anatomical models we used in biology class. So off I went to a commercial art school, eventually switching to a fine art school specializing in portraiture.

Courtesy of Brooke Forsythe

Peggy Rathmann

"It had been years since I'd looked after my little brother and sister, and I'd forgotten how much I enjoyed entertaining children. It wasn't until my nieces were born that I remembered. In fact, it was during a car trip with my brother's kids that I began writing and illustrating. My nieces had been battling over a spot in the front seat of the car, and the loser was sent howling to the back seat to sit with me. In desperation, I pulled out my sketch book and began drawing a story starring my unhappy niece as an extremely attractive person with a good personality and a high IQ. She stopped crying and I knew I was in business.

"The book that came out of that car trip was never published, but having it rejected by lots of editors drove me to take a class in writing and illustrating children's books. The teacher of the class said that the first job of a picture book was to *entertain*. She also said that a good way to create an entertaining story was to give the main character one of our own embarrassing secrets. I hate admitting I have embarrassing secrets, but I've used them in every book I've written since taking that class, and the teacher was right, it turns out to be a good way to entertain a couchful of kids."

* * *

Margaret Crosby (Peggy) Rathmann has fond memories of her childhood as one of five children growing up near St. Paul, Minnesota. After graduating from Mounds View High School in

New Brighton, Minn., she attended several colleges before earning her B.A. degree in psychology from the University of Minnesota. Rathmann has said that after college she wanted to teach sign language to gorillas, but after taking a class in signing, she realized that she'd rather draw pictures of gorillas. She pursued courses in commercial art at the American Academy in Chicago and then fine art at the Atelier Lack in Minneapolis before trying a course in children's book writing and illustration at the Otis Parsons School of Design in Los Angeles.

Ruby the Copycat came out of that class, based on Rathmann's own embarrassing secret—she was tempted to copy ideas from the other students. *Ruby* won her a Cuffie Award from *Publishers Weekly* in 1991 as "Most Promising New Author." *Bootsie Barker Bites,* which Rath-

mann illustrated the following year, was written by her teacher at Otis Parsons, Barbara Bottner. *Good Night, Gorilla*, a nearly wordless picture book and bedtime story, was named an ALA Notable Children's Book in 1995 and listed in the *Horn Book*'s Fanfare. *Officer Buckle and Gloria,* the humorous story of a school safety officer upstaged by his canine partner, appeared on all the "best" lists of 1995 and won the Caldecott Award in 1996. In 1999 *10 Minutes till Bedtime* was cited as an ALA Notable Children's Book; a full-page illustration from this humorous look at bedtime rituals was featured in the *New Yorker* magazine's children's book round-up in December 1998.

Peggy Rathmann and her husband, John Wick, were married on February 29, 1996—a date that would help them remember their anniversary and give them four years to be newlyweds. They live in San Francisco, where Peggy con-

Courtesy of Penguin Putnam

tinues to write and illustrate books that keep her—and all of us—laughing.

SELECTED WORKS WRITTEN AND ILLUSTRATED: *Ruby the Copycat,* 1991; *Good Night, Gorilla,* 1994; *Officer Buckle and Gloria,* 1995; *10 Minutes till Bedtime,* 1998.

SELECTED WORKS ILLUSTRATED: *Bootsie Barker Bites,* by Barbara Bottner, 1992.

SUGGESTED READING: *Contemporary Authors*, vol. 159, 1998; Cummins, Julie, ed. *Children's Book Illustration and Design*, vol. 2, 1998; Pendergast, Sara, ed. *St. James Guide to Children's Writers*, 5th ed., 1999; *Something About the Author*, vol. 94, 1998. Periodicals—"About Our Cover Artist," *Publishers Weekly*, February 20, 1995; Peck, Jackie, "Meet 'Officer Buckle and Gloria' Through Their Creator's Own Story," *Reading Teacher*, February 1997; "Peggy Rathmann: Opening Doors with Pictures," *Publishers Weekly*, July 20, 1998; Rathmann, Peggy, "Caldecott Acceptance Speech," *The Horn Book*, July/August 1996.

WEB SITE: *www.peggyrathmann.com*

Courtesy of Mara Lavitt

Lynn Reiser

Lynn Reiser

(RYE-zer)

July 28, 1944–

"When I was five, I made my first book. I called it 'Animal Houses.' Since I could draw but I did not know how to read or write, my book had illustrations but no words. Like my later picture books, this book began with ideas from my life. The houses looked like those in Charlotte, North Carolina, the town where I spent my childhood. Its animals looked like those I knew as a child. My family lived at the edge of town with fields and pastures and a creek and woods just beyond our backyard. We watched wild animals in the woods and horses and cows in the nearby fields. We had almost every pet we wanted—dogs and cats and rabbits and canaries and turtles and snakes and chickens and ducks.

"I could walk easily to the public library and to the ice cream store beside it. I liked to eat ice cream; I liked to read; I liked to draw; and I liked to play with the children who lived on our street, friends from school, and always my younger brother and my even younger sister. And I liked to make up stories and games. Every summer my family went on vacations to the beach or to the mountains, some summers to both.

"After I started school I did not make picture books for many years. During these years I kept reading, drawing, and learning about nature. I discovered in science classes that the best way to understand something, and then remember it, was to draw it.

"I stayed in North Carolina until I graduated from Duke University. Then I moved to Connecticut to study medicine and psychiatry at Yale Medical School. For many years I practiced psychiatry and taught and wrote scientific articles. Eventually I became a clinical professor at Yale Medical School.

"All this time I still liked animals and to read and play. I still liked to draw and to make up stories, but the stories were in my mind. Finally, in 1991, I decided to make a picture book again. So I did. It told a story in pictures like my first book, 'Animal Houses.' My editor, Susan Hirschman, told me that if I knew what the words were, I should write them down. This story became my first published book—*Bedtime Cat*.

"Since *Bedtime Cat,* I have written and illustrated one or two children's books each year. All begin with something I remember. I get more ideas as I write and draw, solving the problems and answering the questions that making the books present—questions like 'What happens between the beginning and the end?' or problems like 'Where did this little boy get the eggs to give his little hen?'

Courtesy of William Morrow & Co.

"I live with my husband, our black dog named Loki, and our striped cat named Carmel, in a house in a garden in a wood in a town near the university and the office where I practice psychiatry. I write my stories on a computer against the wall, and I draw on a table in front of a window. I look out and see deer, wild turkeys, raccoons, rabbits, chipmunks, and birds. Sometimes I see foxes and woodchucks. Here winters are cold and snowy and summers are hot. We like to go to the beach in the winter and to the mountains in the summer.

"I always carry a sketchbook with me. I draw or solve 'book problems' when I have a few minutes waiting in line or when I am riding on an airplane or train. I still make up stories and games, but now I write them and draw them and share them in picture books."

* * *

Lynn Reiser, the daughter of a Charlotte, North Carolina, businessman and a college professor, always loved nature and always loved to draw. She graduated from Duke University with a B.S. degree in 1966 and received her M.D. from Yale Medical

School in 1970. In 1975 she completed five years of a psychiatric residency at the Yale Department of Psychiatry and in 1985 completed her psychoanalytic training at the Western New England Institute for Psychoanalysis. Much of her time is spent practicing and teaching at Yale Medical School; her children's books provide a creative outlet of a different sort.

Reiser's *Dog and Cat* was selected for the Child Study Children's Book Committee's annual list, Children's Books of the Year. *Any Kind of Dog* received a Parents' Choice Award and was a PBS *Storytime* title. *The Surprise Family*, a Junior Library Guild selection, was designated an ALA Notable Children's Book in 1995. Four of her books have been named American Booksellers Association Pick of the Lists. *Tomorrow on Rocky Pond* was an IRA/CBC Children's Choice in 1993.

Reiser has been the recipient of awards in the fields of medicine and psychiatry, including the Lustman Research Prize, Yale University Department of Psychiatry, in 1974 and the Nancy C. A. Roeske, M.D., Certificate of Recognition for Excellence in Medical Student Education, American Psychiatric Association, in 1992.

Reiser feels that her two careers are similar. As a physician she helps others to express themselves, to discover their own stories, and to fit them together to make more sense of their lives. As an author/illustrator she creates stories to help children express their feelings and understand themselves and the world around them. In a unique cross-cultural venture, she created a companion book to her own four-generation family story, *Cherry Pies and Lullabies*. Using paintings from a women's group in Costa Rica known collectively as Corazones Valientes, *Tortillas and Lullabies / Tortillas y Cancioncitas* describes family activities shared by mothers and daughters through four generations in that country.

SELECTED WORKS WRITTEN: *Tortillas and Lullabies / Tortillas y Cancioncitas*, pictures by "Corazones Valientes," coordinated and translated by Rebecca Hart, 1998.

SELECTED WORKS WRITTEN AND ILLUSTRATED: *Bedtime Cat,* 1991; *Dog and Cat,* 1991; *Any Kind of Dog,* 1992; *Christmas Counting,* 1992; *Tomorrow on Rocky Pond,* 1993; *Margaret and Margarita / Margarita y Margaret,* 1993; *The Surprise Family,* 1994; *Two Mice in Three Fables,* 1995; *Night Thunder and the Queen of the Wild Horses,* 1995; *Beach Feet,* 1996; *Best Friends Think Alike,* 1997; *Cherry Pies and Lullabies,* 1998; *Little Clam,* 1998; *Earthdance,* 1999.

SUGGESTED READING: *Something About the Author,* vol. 81, 1995. Periodicals—"Going from *But* to *And*: Challenges in Creating a Pair of Picture Books from Different Cultures," *The Horn Book*, September/October 1998; "Sharpie Markers to the

Rescue," *The Horn Book*, March/April 1998; Winarski, Diane, "Lynn Reiser: Exploring the Edges of Her Mind," *Teaching PreK–8*, January 1996.

"I was born in Riverside, Illinois, in 1957, and grew up in another Chicago suburb, Downers Grove. I have an older brother, Mike, and a younger sister, Gail. We had dogs in our family when I was growing up—German shepherds, a Shetland sheepdog, a poodle, and a Newfoundland, named Cinders.

"I played Little League baseball for six years: I was a good fielder, smart on the bases, but had no power. I was known for clean singles up the middle. I was a lousy student but was very interested in biology and ecology. I had large collections of rocks and minerals, insects, leaves, and animal skulls (collected in the field and got from taxidermists). In high school I was a volunteer keeper at the Brookfield Zoo. I spent every weekend at the children's zoo, cleaning enclosures, feeding, caring for, and observing the animals.

"My first story was a comic: 'The Adventures of Steve Star,' who each week would make the galaxy safe from evil masterminds bent on enslaving all living things. My first published writing was an article in the *Lapidary Journal* entitled 'A Short History of the Industrial Diamond.' I was fifteen. In high school, with my sister and two friends, I wrote and published a neighborhood newspaper, 'The Deer Creek Express.'

"I started my advanced education as a biology major at the College of DuPage (a junior college—my grades were too bad to get into a four-year school), then transferred to Illinois State University, where I studied commercial art, biology, and anthropology. I received my M.F.A. from Arizona State University with a concentration in printmaking and fine bookmaking.

"My books begin with pictures. An idea comes to me, sparked by what I see in the world or by a memory, and it's always a picture. When I imagine stories they're also sequences of pictures, sometimes like a movie, sometimes a series of related images like a picture book. I think children see the world this way as well. Before children speak and write they observe their surroundings and, through seeing, begin learning the world. I began to draw

Courtesy of Eric Rohmann

Eric Rohmann

October 26, 1957–

as a way to better see the world. Like any curious child, when I encountered something strange and interesting I discovered that I could get closer to it, know more about the thing, by looking deliberately and carefully trying to see with my full attention. I felt that no matter how unusual, I would know the thing better if I could draw it. This is what drawing is—deep, attentive seeing.

"My interest in observing the world, then drawing what I see, has never wavered. Now I travel as much as I can because the unfamiliar always causes me to hesitate, linger, and look closely. I like to walk, visit museums and keep a sketchbook. I try to travel overseas at least once a year, and take four or five smaller holidays throughout the year. Unfamiliar surroundings force me away from habit, and like a young child I have to rely on my senses and not what I've always known. It all starts with seeing. Seeing leads to pictures and pictures lead to stories—the stories and pictures lead to books.

"My favorite part of the bookmaking process is the beginning: exploration, discovery, daydreaming and sketching. This is where ideas come alive, when thoughts are put to paper and made tangible. At first I have only an inkling of what I want the book to look like and I'll put those first rudimentary ideas down in pencil sketches or a rough dummy. This is a point of departure. From there I can see my choices and move ahead. And the pictures I make always seem like images from a larger story. As a boy, I drew battle scenes, farms, city streets, and fanciful machines after Rube Goldberg. I drew monsters, knights, soldiers, rockets, and dinosaurs. After a while I strung these pictures together and made stories.

"This is what drawing is— deep, attentive seeing."

"I make books I want to see, that no one has made yet. I speak at schools and libraries and I have some experience with children (and I was one once), but I'm the audience I understand best, and I think I make books that will interest and delight me—and in the end, I'm blessed that children seem to like what I do. I make books for children because they are the best audience: children are curious, enthusiastic, impulsive, generous, and pleased by simple joys. They laugh easily at the ridiculous and are willing to believe the absurd. Children are not ironic, disillusioned, or indifferent, but hopeful, open-minded, and open-hearted, with a voracious hunger for pictures.

"I live in LaGrange, Illinois, in a third-floor walk-up. The view is nice, the stairs aren't. Each year I talk at libraries, schools, conferences, and conventions. This is one of my favorite parts of working in children's books."

* * *

Eric Rohmann's love of the outdoors and nature in his growing years is reflected in the books he illustrates today. He received his B.S. in Art in 1980 and his M.S. in Studio Art in 1985, both from Illinois State University. His position as coordinator of galleries at the McLean County Arts Center in Bloomington, Illinois, from 1986 to 1988 gave him the opportunity to see many kinds of art and to appreciate the importance of detail in knowing one's craft, as well as in framing and hanging works of art. In 1990 he received his M.F.A. in Printmaking and Fine Bookmaking with a secondary emphasis on painting and drawing from Arizona State University, where he was presented with the Jacob Kenneth Heller Award as Outstanding Printmaker in the School of Art.

During his years in Arizona, Rohmann was a graduate teaching assistant and research assistant. He still enjoys teaching college students as well as those of elementary and high school age. From 1991 through 1994 he worked with children aged eight to seventeen at a performing and visual arts camp in Massachusetts.

In 1993 Rohmann put together a portfolio of work and made appointments to meet editors in New York. Illustrating books was something that had been in his mind since high school. The portfolio included illustrations for his first book, *Time Flies*, which was bought by Crown Publishers on that trip. *Time Flies*, the imaginative juxtaposition of a modern-day museum and a prehistoric scene, was named a Caldecott Honor Book and an ALA Notable Children's Book. It was also a *New York Times* Notable Book of the Year and the winner of a Golden Duck Foundation Award for Excellence in Science Fiction for Children. *The Cinder-Eyed Cats* was listed as one of the best books of 1997 by the *Chicago Tribune*, *Child Magazine*, and the *New York Times* as well as being cited on New York Public Library's list of 100 Titles for Reading and Sharing.

In addition to picture books, Rohmann has designed book-jacket art for the American editions of Philip Pullman's His Dark Materials trilogy, beginning with *The Golden Compass* in 1995. He has had solo exhibitions of his watercolors, oils, and illustration art in Columbus, Ohio; Monmouth and Galesburg, Illinois; and Northfield, Minnesota. His work has been shown in group shows at the Society of Illustrators in New York, the Art Institute of Chicago, and the State University of New York at Purchase.

SELECTED WORKS WRITTEN AND ILLUSTRATED: *Time Flies*, 1994; *The Cinder-Eyed Cats*, 1997.

SELECTED WORKS ILLUSTRATED: *King Crow*, by Jennifer Armstrong, 1995; *The Prairie Train*, by Antoine O'Flatharta, 1999.

Courtesy of Sterling Roop

**Peter and
Connie Roop**

*Peter Roop:
March 8, 1951–
Connie Roop:
June 18, 1951–*

"Peter was born with a pencil in his hand and Connie with a book in hers. At least, that's the story we like to tell.

"Connie says, 'I was really born in Elkhorn, Wisconsin, and grew up in nearby Delavan, once home of many circuses. My mother, a longtime journal-keeper and birdwatcher, read to me often and still does, especially when we travel. There is nothing like hearing *Huckleberry Finn* read aloud while driving along the Mississippi. I frequented my local library where I read fiction, biographies, and nonfiction. More than once, my parents had to chase me outside to play instead of exploring the world through books. I still visit the library and even belong to two book discussion groups. Now our children have to chase me out to play!

"'My love of stories comes from my father, who still tells the best stories around. He told us tales of growing up on an Illinois farm, of rounding up wild horses in South Dakota, of getting his first pony at Christmas when he was only six, and of playing practical jokes on friends and family. Whenever our family gets together, there are stories galore. But I never thought I would grow up and see my own stories in the card catalog of the Aram Public Library in Delavan.'

"Peter teases, 'My first words were, Where is the pencil sharpener? Since then, I have written on paper, birch bark, walls, computers, my arms, and just about any place I can scribble words or a story idea.

"'As a child, I treasured Saturdays because my mother took my three sisters and me to the library to replenish our stock of books. My school in Memphis did not have a library, so we made the best use of the local public library, always getting our limit of six books each. However, I can still remember being frustrated that the library did not carry *The Hardy Boys* books, my favorites for a while. But, through trading with friends and family, I was able to read most of them. My interests in reading have branched out considerably as I now devour nonfiction, biographies, historical fiction, joke and riddle books, history books, and occasionally a good mystery. Funny thing is, these are the kind of books we like to write!

"'My love of stories came from the books I read, but also from the tall tales and spooky stories my father told around campfires while camping on trips from Memphis to Maine. He would take a famous scary story and retell it, setting it near to where we were camping and adding details of what we had seen or done that very day. There's nothing like hearing the thump-thump, thump-thump of the telltale heart beneath your tent or learning that Paul Bunyan's campfires made the Smoky Mountains smoky.

"'I never planned to become an author as I grew up, but I loved to write. I wrote stories, poems, and articles. My happiest days were when my writing was published in the school newspaper. My saddest writing day ever was when I found my poems in a garbage can, rejected by a school editor. But I stuck with it and wrote through college and wrote stories with other students. We wrote plays and even had a mime group that performed in our area. Telling a story without any words is a real challenge!'

"When we got married, Peter was writing by himself. But one day, while watching the ocean tide rise, we got the idea for a joke book and have since written all of our books as a team. We share ideas, read drafts out loud, laugh (and argue) as we create our books together.

"There are three parts of writing we truly enjoy. The first is doing the research for a book, whether it be flying over Matinicus Rock in Maine for *Keep the Lights Burning, Abbie* or standing in the room where Grace Bedell wrote her famous letter to Mr. Lincoln in *Grace's Letter to Lincoln*. Our trips have taken us to rain forests in Belize, buffalo jumps in Montana, coral reefs in the Caribbean, down the Missouri River in a canoe, observing rare whooping cranes in Texas, whale-watching in the Pacific, and to museums of every size in all fifty states and on four continents.

"Our second favorite part is the actual writing of the book. Here we get to take the pieces of a story puzzle and put them together into a book. Sometimes, the pieces don't fit the way we want them to so we must be creative problem solvers and find a way to make the puzzle complete.

"Then comes sharing the story through the book or, as often as we can, in person. This is the moment we wait for, when someone else joins in the stories we are telling.

"Today we both write and teach. Connie teaches high school science and Peter teaches first and second grade in Appleton, Wisconsin. We have taught in England and Peter even taught in China! But, whenever and wherever you find us, we will both have pencils and books in our hands. Or at least nearby!"

> *"We share ideas, read drafts out loud, laugh (and argue) as we create our books together."*

* * *

Peter Roop was born in Winchester, Massachusetts, and Connie Roop in Elkhorn, Wisconsin. They each earned a B.A. from Lawrence University in Appleton, Wisconsin, in 1973, and were married in August of that year. Peter went on to receive an M.A. from Simmons College, while Connie earned an M.S.T. from Boston College, both in 1980. For a year they taught in Kingston, England, as Fulbright exchange teachers.

Peter began his writing career with stories and articles for *Cricket* and *Cobblestone* magazines. He had published several books before he and Connie collaborated on six joke/riddle books and two historical novels; as a team they have now written over fifty books on topics ranging from Columbus to dinosaurs to life among the Cherokee. They have authored series on holiday celebrations in the United States and on visiting distant countries. They have also developed a variety of writing and story programs, including one on teaching science using fiction, and they travel all over the United States presenting writing workshops for both teachers and students.

Keep the Lights Burning, Abbie, based on the true story of Abbie Burgess, who singlehandedly kept two lighthouses going during a month-long siege of bad weather in 1856, was named a Children's Book of the Year by the Child Study Association and *School Library Journal* and was an Irma Simonton Black Honor Book. Seven of the Roops' books have been chosen as *Reading Rainbow* books; *Keep the Lights Burning, Abbie* was a feature selection. *I, Columbus* was named a Library of Congress Book of the Year. *Ahyoka and the Talking Leaves*, *Off the Map*, and *Pilgrim Voices* have all been cited as Notable Children's Trade Books in the Field of Social Studies. *Seasons of the Crane* and *Capturing Nature* were named Outstanding Science Trade Books. Of the Roops' popular joke books, *Out to Lunch!* and *Space Out!* were named IRA/CBC Children's Choices.

In addition to receiving awards and recognition for their writing, the Roops have been honored for excellence in teaching. Peter was Wisconsin State Teacher of the Year in 1986, while Connie was honored with the Women Leaders in Education Award from the American Association of University Women in 1988. Both have received Kohl Educational Foundation Awards for Exceptional Teaching. The Roops live in Appleton, Wisconsin, with their children, Sterling and Heidi.

SELECTED WORKS: By Peter Roop—*Who Buries the Funeral Director?*, 1979; *The Cry of the Conch*, 1984; *The Buffalo Jump*, illus. by Bill Farnsworth, 1996.

SELECTED WORKS: By Peter and Connie Roop—*Out to Lunch!*, 1985; *Space Out!: Jokes About Outer Space*, illus. by Joan Hanson, 1985; *Buttons for General Washington*, illus. by Peter E. Hanson, 1986; *Keep the Lights Burning, Abbie*, illus. by Peter E. Hanson, 1985; *Seasons of the Cranes*, 1989; *I,*

Columbus, 1990; *Capturing Nature: James John Audubon*, 1993; *Ahyoka and the Talking Leaves*, illus. by Yoshi Miyake, 1994; *Westward Ho, Ho, Ho!*, illus. by Anne C. Green, 1996; *Pilgrim Voices: Our First Year in the New World*, illus. by Shelley Pritchett, 1997; *Susan B. Anthony*, 1997; *Martin Luther King, Jr.*, 1998; *Grace's Letter to Lincoln*, illus. by Stacey Schuett, 1998; *Let's Celebrate Christmas!*, 1998; *Let's Celebrate Halloween!*, 1998; *Off the Map; The Journals of Lewis and Clark*, illus. by Tim Tanner, 1998; *If You Lived with the Cherokee*, illus. by Kevin Smith, 1998; *Let's Celebrate Thanksgiving!*, 1999; *Let's Celebrate Valentine's Day!*, 1999; *An Eye for an Eye: A Revolutionary War Story*, 1999; *Sacagawea: The Girl from the Shining Mountains*, 1999.

SUGGESTED READING: *Contemporary Authors*, vol. 122, 1988; *Contemporary Authors*, New Revision Series, vol. 48–49, 1995; *Something About the Author*, vol. 49, 1987; vol. 54, 1988.

WEB SITE: *www.author-illustr-source.com*

E-MAIL: *peterroop@aol.com*

Courtesy of Millbrook Press, Inc.

Barry Root

June 27, 1954–

"I was born in Huntsville, Alabama, but grew up mostly in Decatur, Georgia, in the suburbs of Atlanta. I was the middle child of three boys, and we all ended up pursuing art in some way (Tom, four years younger, is now a painter and married to a painter; Steve, who was five years older, was studying art when he died at age nineteen). I don't think our parents intentionally set out to produce only artists, but the conditions of our growing-up were perfect for it—lots of free time, paper and pencils available, plenty of praise and encouragement, no TV, and no one rushing us off for art lessons at the first sign of talent. I remember a lot of lying around on the floor, drawing and showing our pictures to each other. Drawing was a group activity for us.

"We read a lot too, and some of my favorite books also had great pictures, like *Winnie the Pooh* (before the abominable Disneyization) with Ernest Shepard's spare, suggestive drawings that left so much room for imagination, and *Stuart Little*, with Garth Williams's wonderful pictures. When I was thirteen I discovered James Thurber in a big way, and by extension (via *The Thirteen Clocks* and *The Wonderful O*), Marc Simont. These artists made a big impression on me, but they didn't make me want to become a children's book illustrator. They were like figures out of legend to me, and besides, I never thought about the future back then.

"But by the time I was eighteen, art school seemed like a natural step; afterward I moved back to Atlanta and scratched out a living providing spot illustrations for the local magazines. It was exciting to be published. Usually the articles were on local topics and I couldn't resist a little editorializing—some poor soul wrote about joining an assertiveness training course, and I drew him as a dog, biting people's ankles. The local library had started loaning out garden tools; remembering some perceived ill-treatment at their hands, I pictured the elderly librarians glaring at a man holding an implement who was saying, 'I'd like to check out this old bat—I mean rake.' Of course now that my livelihood depends substantially on the goodwill of librarians (they're a great bunch o' folks!), I am filled with remorse about that, but at the time I was young, restless, and stuck in my hometown; it made me irritable.

Courtesy of Barry Root

"I moved to New York in 1980 and was soon doing illustrations for a lot of computer magazines and business magazines. No more silly cartoons; conceptual was the way to be. Conceptual means things hanging in the sky, like in the paintings of the artist Magritte. Computers in the sky, business people in the sky, floppy discs, briefcases in the sky. I had an excellent rep; work came in from all over the country. They all wanted those deeply symbolic computers floating in the conceptual sky. I began having headaches.

"One very good thing happened: I met Kim. First I admired her work, then we became friends and I started following her around everywhere. We married in 1984, and moved out to Lancaster County, Pennsylvania, in 1987.

"Some of the assignments were actually enjoyable, especially the posters I did for Let's Find Out at Scholastic, with Jean Marzollo and Carol Carson. Still, I was trying to spend more time painting, hoping to get out of illustrating altogether. When I was offered the manuscript for *The Araboolies of Liberty Street* from Clarkson Potter, I hesitated at first. I knew it would take months to do (it took five), and did I really want to get into all that? Of course I took it—how could I say no to all those animals and kids running around? And there wasn't a computer or business person in it anywhere, nor in any of the twenty or so books that I have done since (well, maybe one or two, but they were not in the sky, and there was nothing conceptual about them). For this, and for many other things these days, I am profoundly grateful."

* * *

Barrett Voorhees Root attended DeKalb College in Georgia before transferring to the Ringling School of Art in Sarasota, Florida, from which he graduated in 1977. After moving to New York in 1980, he took additional classes at the Art Students League and New York Academy. Before his career in children's books, Root supplied illustrations for a wide variety of publications, including the *New York Times*, *Forbes*, *Newsday*, *Sports Illustrated*, and *Publishers Weekly*, among others. He has also designed posters for the U.S. Postal Service.

Root's first picture book, *The Araboolies of Liberty Street,* won Maryland's Black-Eyed Susan Award for best picture book in 1993. *Pumpkins* received an Honorable Mention for illustration at the Bologna Book Fair in 1994. *Chinook!* and *Two Cool Cows* were chosen as American Booksellers Association Pick of the Lists titles, and *Two Cool Cows* was an IRA/CBC Children's Choice book as well. *Someplace Else* was one of the *New York Times* Best Illustrated Books of the Year and a *Reading Rainbow* feature selection.

Courtesy of Simon & Schuster Children's Publishing Division

Barry Root's other interests include music; he once played electric bass for an instrumental group called The Ordinaires in New York and now sings in his church choir. He is also fascinated by cars, and anything else with wheels. At one time he volunteered as corner crew for sports car races at Road Atlanta, but he gave up thoughts of a racing career when he started art school. Today he lives in rural Lancaster County, Pennsylvania, with his wife, the illustrator Kimberly Bulcken Root, their children Janna, Sam, and Benjamin, and three dogs.

SELECTED WORKS ILLUSTRATED: *The Araboolies of Liberty Street*, by Sam Swope, 1989; *The Saint and the Circus*, by Robert Piumini, 1991; *The Christmas Box*, by Jeanne Stewart Wetzel, 1992; *The Singing Fir Tree*, by Marti Stone, 1992; *Pumpkins: A Story for a Field*, by Mary Lyn Ray, 1992; *Chinook!*, by Michael O. Tunnell, 1993; *Old Devil Wind*, by Bill Martin, Jr., 1993; *April Bubbles Chocolate: An ABC of Poetry*, by Lee Bennett Hopkins, 1994; *Alvah and Arvilla*, by Mary Lyn Ray, 1994; *Wan Hu Is in the Stars*, by Jennifer Armstrong, 1995; *Two Cool Cows*, by Toby Speed, 1995; *Someplace Else*, by Carol P. Saul, 1995; *Fishing Sunday*, by Tony Johnston, 1996; *Whoosh! Went the Wish*, by Toby Speed, 1997; *Grandpa Takes Me to the Moon*, by Timothy Gaffney, 1996; *Nobody's Dog*, by Charlotte Graeber, 1998; *The Giant Carrot*, by Jan Peck, 1998; *Cowboy Dreams*, by Kathi Appelt, 1999; *Messenger, Messenger*, by Robert Burleigh, 2000.

SUGGESTED READING: Cummins, Julie, ed. *Children's Book Illustration and Design*, vol. 2, 1998.

Kimberly Bulcken Root

May 19, 1957–

"There was a thick but not completely repellent odor in the room. My father placed my three-year-old brother and four-year-old me on the open window sill. We sat facing in and could see several wooden painting easels. On each was a very different picture of my brother, me, and a red and blue ball with a white star. We had been models for the painting class my father, an architectural student, was taking. That atmosphere and those early paint fumes are, perhaps, why I happily sit long hours at a drawing board trying to make pictures of typescript.

"My mother liked to read to us, often from books she had as a child. There were her books of foreign lands and my father's art and architecture volumes on low shelves. No one said no, so I sat and looked, before I could read, at pictures of Chinese in colored silks, Arabian nomads, legionnaires and elephants etched and engraved, and Egyptian tombs robbed centuries before. Around this time my father brought in a box with the great Sphinx printed on the lid. It was full of yellow legal pads. No tomb robbers could have been happier with this spoil than my brother and me. I think my father was actually a little disappointed at how fast we drew our way through it.

"My father became an architect. We moved. More brothers came along. Drawing pictures was a safe, reassuring thing to do with each change of neighborhood and school. I could rely on drawing in school to give me identity and get through the tedium of writing assignments. I found science and math could even benefit from decoration. Never did I think of myself as the 'best artist'; someone else usually had a formula for a kitten or comic book character that was crowd-pleasing. I had draftsmen heroes:

Howard Pyle and his pirates; Milo Winter, whose contorted ink Scrooges and ghosts graced an old copy of Dickens; E. H. Shepard and his kings, dairymaids, and wild, only-in-England trees. They were among those who could draw with detail but still leave much room for my imagination to get lost in.

"Life, in the family I grew up in, seemed somewhat adrift in my teenage years. We lived on an island off the South Carolina coast. I left drawing for awhile my last year of high school. There was not much encouragement at home or in school. So, at the end of the semester, I found myself enrolled in pre–veterinary medicine at a large southern university. That summer I worked three jobs, including a veterinary clinic, tried to draw occasionally and felt great misgivings. Then, in what was a most illuminating answer to many furtive prayers, I got a phone call.

"Joe Bowler, portrait painter and father of a high school friend, asked me to gather up whatever art work I had about and bring it to his studio. A successful magazine illustrator of the 1950s and '60s, Joe also had taught at the Parsons School of Design. Unbeknownst to me he had seen some things I'd drawn and arranged for me to meet his houseguest, Murray Tinkelman, who was then the dean of the Parsons Illustration Department. They convinced me to do what I already deeply wanted but had not acknowledged—to draw. I went to Parsons, giving up the other scholarship and scraping by for four years.

"In New York I found much-needed independence and grew to love the subways, buses, and museum steps full of characters. I stayed away from children's book classes, but took as many life and costume drawing classes as possible. At the advice of a teacher, I worked only in black and white and mostly in pen my last two years of school. After graduation I carried my heavy black portfolio full of heavy black and white drawings around New York from one editorial office to another. For some reason I was hoping to become a heavy black and white cross-hatch Eastern European emigré conceptual illustrator like my new heros who did brilliant drawings for the Op-Ed page. Although I was given some work from the *Times*, the *Nation*, the *Boston Globe*, and the *Village Voice*, I was not an emigré, particularly European, or a heavy conceptual illustrator. Many art directors leafing through my portfolio

Courtesy of Barry Root

were saying 'children's books' (but children's book people kept saying 'editorial').

"In all of this I met Barry. We had been given introduction by a mutual friend who happened to be an art director. The black and white person fell in love with an amazing colorist. We married, and at his encouragement I began the color portfolio that would lead to my first children's book.

I love New York and expected to end my days there, but before that happened Barry felt the need for some room to paint and we moved to rural Pennsylvania. It has been a good thing; children and animals running around prove this.

I feel deeply indebted to the patient art directors, editors, and authors who wait as I try to make the characters have the right expressions and attempt to find the odd detail that will help make the book a rich place for a young imagination."

GULLIVER
IN
LILLIPUT

retold by Margaret Hodges
from Gulliver's Travels by
Jonathan Swift

illustrated by Kimberly Bulcken Root

Courtesy of Holiday House, Inc.

* * *

Kimberly Bulcken Root was born in York, Pennsylvania, and grew up in Connecticut and South Carolina. She graduated from the Parsons School of Design in 1979. Many of her children's books reflect the beginnings of her career in editorial illustration; they often feature small detailed drawings and paintings inset within the text and extending the visual story beyond her full-page watercolors.

In 1993 *Papa's Bedtime Story* won a Silver Medal in the Children's Book Original Art Exhibition sponsored by the Society of Illustrators. *When the Whippoorwill Calls* was designated one of the Best Illustrated Books of the Year by the *New York Times. The Toll-Bridge Troll* won an honor award in Language Arts from the Society of School Librarians International. *Hugh Can Do* and *The Toll-Bridge Troll* were both named ALA Notable Children's Books. *Birdie's Lighthouse* won a Parents' Choice honor award and was listed as a Blue Ribbon book by the *Bulletin of the Center for Children's Books. Parenting* magazine presented a Reading Magic Award to *The True Story of Johnny Appleseed; Year of the Ranch* was cited as a Notable Trade Book in the Field of Social Studies; and *Gulliver in Lilliput* was named a *School Library Journal* Best Book of the Year.

In 1999 Kimberly Root returned to black-and-white illustration when she created twelve interior pieces and eleven chapter headings for a new edition of Dorothy Canfield Fisher's *Understood Betsy*, but she has many more picture book manuscripts in the works in full color. Root lives with her husband, the illustrator Barry Root, and their children, Janna, Samuel, and Benjamin, in Lancaster County, Pennsylvania.

SELECTED WORKS ILLUSTRATED: *Granny, Will Your Dog Bite, and Other Mountain Rhymes*, by Gerald Milnes, 1990; *Hugh Can Do*, by Jennifer Armstrong, 1992; *Papa's Bedtime Story*, by Mary Lee Donovan, 1993; *The Palace of Stars*, by Patricia Lakin, 1993; *When the Whippoorwill Calls*, by Candice F. Ransom, 1995; *The Toll-Bridge Troll*, by Patricia Rae Wolff, 1995; *Gulliver in Lilliput*, retold by Margaret Hodges, 1995; *Billy Beg and His Bull: An Irish Tale*, retold by Ellin Greene, 1994; *Junk Pile*, by Lady Borton, 1997; *The True Story of Johnny Appleseed*, by Margaret Hodges, 1997; *Birdie's Lighthouse*, by Deborah Hopkinson, 1997; *Bronco Busters*, by Alison Herzig, 1998; *The Peddler's Gift*, by Maxine Rose Schur, 1999; *Understood Betsy*, by Dorothy Canfield Fisher, 1999.

SUGGESTED READING: Cummins, Julie, ed. *Children's Book Illustration and Design*, vol. 2, 1998. Periodicals—"*Birdie's Lighthouse*," *Book Links*, November 1997; "Talking with Kimberly Bulcken Root," *Children's Book Review*, Summer/Early Fall 1996.

Phyllis Root

February 14, 1949–

"I was born in Fort Wayne, Indiana, and grew up among green grass, gardens, trees, open fields, and books, books, books. My father says he remembers me reading in my high chair. I used to make up stories in bed at night when I couldn't sleep and my parents had caught me with my book and flashlight. My cousins loved the ghost stories I would tell them. In second grade I was one of three students in our class who won a basket for writing a story about Africa. By fifth grade I knew I wanted to be a writer, but I did not start writing books until I was thirty, when I took a class that taught me all those tools of writing I had never encountered before, things like character, setting, plot, tension, dialogue, and so on. I have been writing for twenty years now and still love messing around with stories.

"In those years I have published fifteen or so books, starting with *Moon Tiger*. In 1997 *Aunt Nancy and Old Man Trouble* won the Minnesota Picture Book text award. Aunt Nancy began to live in my mind when I realized that of all the trickster tales I had read, none had a female trickster. Well, said I, I will just have to write one then. Old Man Trouble got his start from a song the church ladies sang in church one morning. Since then

Aunt Nancy has managed to inhabit three more stories, *Aunt Nancy and Cousin Lazybones*, *Aunt Nancy and Old Woman Woeful*, and *Aunt Nancy and Mr. Death*. She is one of my favorite characters, and I hope to be a lot like her some day.

"One thing I love about writing is that I never know what story will happen next. A remark from a friend became *Sam Who Was Swallowed by a Shark*. A story my parents used to tell about thunder became *Soup for Supper*. A road sign that said 'Crazy Woman Creek' turned into *Rosie's Fiddle*. Numerous muddy, mucky portages canoeing in the Boundary Waters became part of *One Duck Stuck*. And on a particularly bad day when all I wanted was someone to take care of me, I started the story that became *What Baby Wants*. I particularly love playing around with the sounds of words and with the rhythm of the language in a story.

"Now I live in Minneapolis, Minnesota, with my children, two cats, and assorted butterflies in season amid green grass, trees, lakes, and more books, books, books. When I am not writing or teaching in the M.F.A. program in Writing for Children at Vermont College, my family and I love to camp, canoe, sail, bike, travel, garden, and, of course, read."

Courtesy of Kelly Pouo

* * *

Phyllis Root grew up in Fort Wayne, Indiana. She attended Valparaiso University, moved to Chicago, and now lives in Minneapolis. She worked as an architectural drafter, costume maker, bicycle repair person, and administrative assistant before becoming a full-time writer and writing instructor.

Root's first book, *Moon Tiger*, was named a Children's Book of the Year by the Child Study Association of America and was cited at the 1985 Bologna International Children's Book Fair. In 1997, her first trickster tale, *Aunt Nancy and Old Man Trouble*, was the recipient of the Minnesota Picture Book Award. *Moon Tiger*, *Aunt Nancy and Old Man Trouble*, and *Rosie's Fiddle* were all chosen for inclusion on the New York Public Library's annual list, 100 Titles for Reading and Sharing. *What Baby Wants* was cited as a *School Library Journal* Best Book of the Year in 1998.

Courtesy of Candlewick Press

SELECTED WORKS: *Gretchen's Grandma*, with Carol A. Marron, illus. by Deborah K. Ray, 1983; *No Place for a Pig*, with Carol A. Marron, illus. by Nathan Y. Jarvis, 1985; *Moon Tiger*, illus. by Ed Young, 1985; *Soup for Supper*, illus. by Sue Truesdell, 1986; *The Listening Silence*, illus. by Dennis McDermott, 1992; *The Old Red Rocking Chair*, illus. by John Sanford, 1992; *Coyote and the Magic Words*, illus. by Sandra Speidel, 1993; *Sam Who Was Swallowed by a Shark*, illus. by Axel Scheffler, 1994; *Contrary Bear*, illus. by Laura Cornell, 1996; *Mrs. Potter's Pig*, illus. by Russell Ayto, 1996; *Aunt Nancy and Old Man Trouble*, illus. by David Parkins, 1996; *One Windy Wednesday*, illus. by Helen Craig, 1997; *The Hungry Monster*, illus. by Sue Heap, 1997; *Rosie's Fiddle*, illus. by Kevin O'Malley and Margot Apple, 1997; *One Duck Stuck*, illus. by Jane Chapman, 1998; *What Baby Wants*, illus. by Jill Barton, 1998; *Aunt Nancy and Cousin Lazybones*, illus. by David Parkins, 1998; *Grandmother Winter*, illus. by Beth Krommes, 1999.

SUGGESTED READING: *Contemporary Authors*, vol. 123, 1988; *Contemporary Authors*, New Revision Series, vol. 50, 1996; *Something About the Author*, vol. 48, 1987; vol. 55, 1989; vol. 94, 1998.

Courtesy of Will Shively

Michael J. Rosen

September 20, 1954–

"I was the first of three children, the one featured in most of our home movies. (Actually, I was preceded by Freckles, the first of many dogs to share my life.) Recently, when my parents prepared to move, they unearthed a year-end evaluation from my preschool teacher. Besides the fact that nobody calls me 'Mike' now, nothing has changed: my interests in building and dabbling with things; my talkativeness and inquisitiveness; my need to be engaged with duties and other people; even my need to be reminded, occasionally, to hang up my coat.

"My parents built my childhood house in a new development situated amid a former pasture. For years, I explored those construction sites and fields, hunting entries for my nature center: cocoons, milkweed pods, chrysalises, along with the catch from fishing trips that would swim in our washtub. Every Sunday we enjoyed country drives: gathering buckeyes, feeding roadside horses, fishing. From age four to twenty-six, I rode a bus along those country roads to summer camp, and when I turned fourteen, I joined its staff and worked year-round at the community center that sponsored the camp. Many years later, I moved to ninety forested acres only thirty minutes from that camp. Each morning, walking dogs or mushroom-hunting, I still feel the calming yet exciting sensations of being at camp, although now I'm better at avoiding poison ivy.

"At camp, sailing, canoeing, and horseback riding made me feel at home (though we had no horses, canoes, or sailboats at home). Later I understood that, besides being fun, these activities spared me the uneasiness I felt when playing team sports like Little League or spending phys ed classtime waiting to be chosen, wishing to be elsewhere. That dread of being singled out lingered through middle school. I never realized that almost everyone there harbored some reason to feel uncomfortable. The art room became my haven, where I spent every elective class, volunteered during study hall, and even made artwork during lunch period. At that time, I took Hebrew and guitar lessons, collected comics, practiced magic, pretended to wrestle like Flying Fred Curry on TV, listened to the Supremes and Temptations, spent Saturdays at my best friend's father's advertising agency (dazzled by the fancy art supplies and machines), and filled many notebooks with drawings and ramblings.

"My parents attended everything I did, encouraged all my interests. Our house was a place where friends congregated, and my father entertained with his perfect joke-telling. In college, I first realized how exceptional my parents' love and happiness were.

"Luckily, several teachers found something in me worth encouraging (that is, besides hanging up my coat). I was invited into a special reading seminar and an honors biology class. My American literature teacher challenged me personally with higher expectations. Most influential, I found a mentor in my neighbor, Mimi Chenfeld, who was becoming one of our country's most creative educators. She read everything I composed (and still does today). Her passion suggested doors where before I had imagined walls.

"I studied pre-med at Ohio State University. Family practice seemed a way to combine working with children (my year-round job since ninth grade) and my fascination with natural history. I majored in animal behavior, sneaked in a few writing and ceramics classes, and briefly attended medical school before earning a master's degree in poetry at Columbia University.

"Today I support my family creating books, collaborating with other artists and writers, and visiting schools. Every day I realize how fortunate I am that my occupation includes so many things I want to better understand, and hope my readers might, too."

* * *

Born and reared in Columbus, Ohio, Michael J. Rosen received a B.S. degree in zoology from Ohio State University in 1976, went on to do postgraduate work in pre-med areas, and eventually spent half a year at St. George's School of Medicine in Grenada, West Indies. During his college days, he took three ceramics classes, his only art training beyond high school, as well as poetry classes. He attended three Bread Loaf Writers' Conferences prior to enrolling in Columbia University's M.F.A. program in poetry from 1979 to 1981. While in New York City, Rosen began creating spot illustrations for the *New Yorker* and *Gourmet*, expanding his work as an editorial illustrator for other magazines and businesses while preparing his first books for publication. He taught in the continuing education program at Ohio State University for many years and also enjoyed brief appointments to that university's creative writing department. In 1982 Rosen helped to establish Thurber House, a cultural center for readers and writers in the restored home of the great humorist James Thurber; Rosen has served as its literary director ever since. He administers the Thurber Prize for American Humor and edits *The Thurber Bi-annual of American Humor*. His teaching over the last twenty years consists primarily of workshops, conferences, and short residencies.

> "The art room
> became my
> haven . . ."

Rosen's books for adult readers include three collections of his own poetry and five compilations of stories by others; he has also edited three volumes of James Thurber's work. In 1990 he founded a small granting program, The Company of Animals Fund, which offers grants to animal welfare agencies through profits from the books Rosen has created with the help of about 250 like-minded artists and writers. Other philanthropic efforts include the four children's books Rosen has written, illustrated, and/or edited for Share Our Strength, one of the nation's largest anti-hunger agencies. Much of his time is spent as an advocate and advisor for those groups.

Rosen's children's books include nonfiction, fiction, and poetry for a wide range of ages. *Elijah's Angel* has received many distinctions, including the National Jewish Book Award, and premiered as a family operetta in 1998. *A School for Pompey Walker* received the inaugural Simon Wiesenthal Museum of Tolerance Once Upon a World Book Award. *The Heart Is Big Enough* was chosen for New York Public Library's annual list, 100 Titles for Reading and Sharing. The Ohiana Library presented Rosen with its career award for children's literature in 1997.

SELECTED WORKS: *The Kids' Book of Fishing, Complete with Hook, Line, and Sinker*, 1991; *Elijah's Angel*, illus. by Aminah B. Robinson, 1992; *Kids' Best Dog Book*, 1993; *Kids' Field Guide to Neighborhood Dogs*, 1993; *Speak! Children's Book Illustrators Brag About Their Favorite Dogs*, editor, 1993; *All Eyes on the Pond*, illus. by Tom Leonard, 1994; *The Greatest Table*, author and editor, 1994; *A School for Pompey Walker*, illus. by Aminah B. Robinson, 1995; *Bonesy and Isabel*, illus. by James E. Ransome, 1995; *Purr . . . Children's Book Illustrators Brag About Their Cats*, editor, 1996; *Fishing with Dad*, illus. by Will Shively, 1996; *Food Fight: Poets Join the Fight Against Hunger with Poems About Their Favorite Foods*, editor, 1996; *The Heart Is Big Enough: Five Stories*, illus. by Matthew Valiquette, 1997; *Down to Earth*, editor, 1998; *The Dog Who Walked with God*, 1998; *Avalanche*, 1998; *A Thanksgiving Wish*, illus. by John Thompson, 1999.

SUGGESTED READING: *Contemporary Authors*, vol. 132, 1991; *Contemporary Authors*, New Revision Series, vol. 49, 1995; *Something About the Author*, vol. 86, 1996. Periodicals—"Live It Once, Revise It a Dozen Times," *Book Links*, July 1999; *New Advocate*, Winter 1995; *Ohio Journal of the English Language Arts*, Winter 1988; *Oxford Review*, Spring/Summer 1998; *Reading Today*, August/September, 1999; "Talking with Michael J. Rosen," *Book Links*, January 1997.

WEB SITE: *www.michaeljrosen.com*

"I grew up in a large rambling house on a hilltop overlooking Lake Grapevine outside the small town of Lewisville, Texas. My father, who is an enrolled member of the Cherokee Nation of Oklahoma, was a pilot for Braniff Airlines, and my mother had her hands full with four children and the assorted animals we kept for pets. We had horses, cats, dogs, hamsters, and snakes, along with an occassional orphaned wild possum or raccoon! My brother and sisters and I had acres of woods, fields, and lakeshore to ramble, and most of our fun involved being outdoors. We didn't realize it at the time, but our lives were being shaped by the seasons and the land, and even today I am happiest when I am at home in my house on the Pedernales River in Central Texas, far from the clutter of cities and towns.

"My Cherokee grandmother lived with us and we were brought up with the stories of our Cherokee family and the histories of our nation. One of my ancestors was John Ross, Principal Chief of the Cherokee Nation during the tragic time of the Trail of Tears. I heard many stories of that time in 1838 when the majority of the Cherokee people were forced from our ancestral homeland in the Smoky Mountains of the southeastern United States and made to walk all the way to what is now Oklahoma. Over 4,000 Cherokees perished on that long walk, which is how it came to be called the Trail of Tears.

"Grandmother Anne was a wonderful storyteller and writer and I know that I inherited my love of traditional stories from her. In school, I did well in any course that involved reading and writing: English, History, Social Studies, and, of course, Language Arts. I also had a flair for the dramatic, which meant that I loved Theater and Music courses as well. In college, I majored in Theater with a minor in Radio, Television, and Film. While still attending the University of Texas at Arlington, I answered an ad for an intern position at a Dallas radio station, and that simple ad changed my life!

"Working at the radio station was so absorbing and challenging that I soon found myself spending all my time there, and my school work was suffering. When the station offered me a full-time position, I happily accepted and was soon launched on a very exciting career. I became the first woman on-air news reporter for the station, which led to a job offer from a television

Courtesy of Gayle Ross

Gayle Ross

Gayle Ross

October 3, 1951–

station in Austin, Texas. For the next several years, I had several positions in media and they all involved writing and speaking. Though I couldn't have put my finger on it at the time, I was not truly satisfied with the work I was doing. I didn't know it then, but another big life-change was on the way.

"I had always loved music, and many of my friends were folk musicians and songwriters. Another friend who felt this way was a children's librarian for Dallas Public Library named Elizabeth Ellis. In 1978, Elizabeth invited me to take a trip to her home state of Tennessee to see the National Storytelling Festival. We were so inspired by the storytellers we met in Jonesborough, Tennessee, that we began to tell stories ourselves—the Appalachian mountain tales that Elizabeth had grown up with and the stories of my Cherokee heritage. We traveled the country in a Volkswagen van, appearing at schools, libraries, folk clubs, and the many storytelling festivals that began to pop up around the country. After four years performing as a duo, we made the decision to concentrate on careers as solo tellers, but we are still close friends today and we still know the stories we used to tell together.

"Working alone, I found that I could focus completely on the stories of Native American heritage which were the legacy of my grandmother. More and more opportunities to work in 'Indian Country' were coming my way and this brought me in contact with some wonderful people who were great teachers for me. Most important of these is a Chippewa-Cree storyteller named Ron Evans. Our relationship became so close that we formally adopted one another as brother and sister. In 1993 I was asked to record some of my Cherokee stories for a Native American storytape series produced by *Parabola* magazine. HarperCollins Children's Audio division bought the distribution rights to the tape and asked if I wanted to write some stories down for a children's book. This has led to possibly the most satisfying part of my work as a storyteller. Over the years, I had learned how to shape a story so that it sounds good to the ears, and now I enjoyed equally learning how to craft it for the eyes. It is a wonderful challenge to try to set a story down so that it reads well and yet still has the feel of the storyteller's voice.

"Today I feel that all the experiences I had as a child and in my early career in media have come together in work that I truly feel blessed to be able to do. Eighteen years ago, while I was performing in Minneapolis, I met my wonderful husband, Reed Holt, and we have two children, Alan and Sarah. We live in a house several miles outside the small town of Fredericksburg, Texas, and my children have grown up roaming the woods and fishing in the river just as I did. I stay active in the Indian community, and I take my children to Oklahoma as often as I can to visit with relatives and to learn about their Cherokee heritage. In Native American culture, storytelling is still a powerful force

"We didn't realize it at the time, but our lives were being shaped by the seasons and the land . . ."

for teaching and passing on pride in Indian heritage. As long as our stories continue, so will the people. And family stories are perhaps the greatest gift one can pass down. This has certainly been true for me."

*　*　*

Gayle Ross entered the field of storytelling at a time when this ageless art form was in the midst of a renaissance in America, spearheaded by the newly formed National Association for the Preservation and Perpetuation of Storytelling in Jonesborough, Tennessee. Now known as the National Storytelling Network, the organization sponsors a festival every October that attracts people from all over the nation. Ross has appeared five times at this prestigious event, telling the tales of her Cherokee heritage and other Native American stories. In 1989 she received an award from the TEJAS Storytelling Association for her contribution to the art of storytelling in Texas. In 1995 she made her debut at the Kennedy Center in Washington, D.C., as part of the cast for *Tall Tales—White Lies*, and she performed for the diplomatic corps in an event called "A Taste of Tennessee" at the home of Vice President and Mrs. Al Gore.

Ross has established an international reputation as well, appearing in festivals in Denmark, Ireland, England, and Wales. The National Storytelling Association honored her with its Circle of Excellence Award in 1997. Her books *The Girl Who Married the Moon* and *The Story of the Milky Way*, both co-authored with noted Abenaki writer Joseph Bruchac, were named Notable Trade Books in the Field of Social Studies. *How Rabbit Tricked Otter* received an Anne Izard Storyteller's Choice Award as well as the American Folklore Society's Aesop Award; *How Turtle's Back Was Cracked* also captured an Aesop Award.

Gayle Ross presents her programs of Native stories in schools and festivals throughout the country and abroad, balancing her touring schedule with time to write and stay active in Native American heritage groups and projects.

SELECTED WORKS: *The Girl Who Married the Moon: Tales from Native North America*, with Joseph Bruchac, illus. by S. S. Burrus, 1994; *How Rabbit Tricked Otter, and Other Cherokee Trickster Stories*, illus. by Murv Jacob, 1994; *The Story of the Milky Way: A Cherokee Tale*, with Joseph Bruchac, illus. by Virginia Stroud, 1995; *How Turtle's Back Was Cracked*, illus. by Murv Jacob, 1995; *The Legend of the Windigo: A Tale from Native North America*, illus. by Murv Jacob, 1996.

Courtesy of C. Little Agency

J. K. Rowling

(ROLL-ing)

July 31, 1965–

Joanne Kathleen Rowling entered the world in Chipping Sodbury General Hospital in Bristol, England, a fitting beginning for someone who would later enjoy making up strange names for people, places, and games played on flying broomsticks. Her younger sister Di was born just under two years later.

Rowling remembers that she always wanted to write and that the first story she actually wrote down, when she was five or six, was a story about a rabbit called Rabbit. Many of her favorite memories center around reading—hearing *The Wind in the Willows* read aloud by her father when she had the measles, enjoying the fantastic adventure stories of E. Nesbit, reveling in the magical world of C. S. Lewis's Narnia, and reading and rereading her favorite story of all, *The Little White Horse* by Elizabeth Goudge.

The family moved twice while she was growing up. The first move was across Bristol to Winterbourne, where she and her sister played with a group of children in the neighborhood. Two of the children had the surname Potter, a name she remembers liking very much. Her own name, pronounced "rolling," led to annoying jokes about rolling pins from the other children in school. When Joanne was nine the family moved again, this time to Tutshill near Chepstow in the Forest of Dean. Her parents were both Londoners and had a dream of living in the country. Wandering across the fields and along the River Wye with her sister was very pleasant to Joanne, but her new school was small and old-fashioned and the teacher was strict and frightening to the quiet, imaginative young girl.

Her high school years were spent at Wyedean Comprehensive, where her favorite subject was English and she did not excel in sports; she actually broke her arm playing net ball. Her favorite activity was telling stories to her studious and serious friends over lunchtime—serial stories, in which they all performed heroic feats and good deeds. She was made Head Girl in her final year.

At Exeter University Rowling took her degree in French and spent one year studying in Paris. After college she moved to London to work for Amnesty International as a researcher and bilingual secretary. The best thing about working in an office, she has said, was typing up stories on the computer when no one was watching. During this time, on a particularly long train ride from Manchester to London in the summer of 1990, the idea came to her of a boy who is a wizard and doesn't know it. He attends a school for wizardry—she could see him very plainly in her mind. By the time the train pulled into King's Cross Station four hours later, many of the characters and the early stages of the plot were fully formed in her head. The story took further shape as she continued working on it in pubs and cafés over her lunch hours. Rowling had been writing short stories and working on two unpublished novels for adults, but now the idea of Harry Potter took over her writing time.

In 1992 Rowling left working in offices and moved to Portugal to teach English as a second language. In spite of her students making jokes about her name (this time they called her "Rolling Stone"), she enjoyed teaching. She worked afternoons and evenings, leaving mornings free for writing. Several years later Rowling returned to Britain with her infant daughter and a suitcase full of Harry Potter notes and chapters. She settled in Edinburgh to be near her sister and set out to finish the book before looking for a teaching job. Wheeling her daughter's carriage around the city to escape their tiny, cold apartment, she would duck into coffee shops to write when the baby fell asleep. In this way she finished the book and started sending it to publishers. It was rejected several times before she found an London agent, chosen because she liked his name—Christopher Little, who sold the manuscript to Bloomsbury Children's Books.

Courtesy of Scholastic, Inc.

Rowling was working as a French teacher (with students who serenaded her with the theme song from *Rawhide*—"Rolling, rolling, rolling, keep those wagons rolling . . .") when she heard that her book about the boy wizard had been accepted for publication. *Harry Potter and the Philosopher's Stone* was published in June 1997 and achieved almost instant success. It won the Smarties Book Prize Gold Medal for ages 9–11 and was named the British Book Awards' Children's Book of the Year. It was also shortlisted for the Guardian Fiction Award and Carnegie Medal (for which it received a "Commended" citation). At the Bologna Book Fair, Arthur Levine, an editorial director for Scholastic Books, bought the American rights for $105,000, an unprecedented figure for a first-time children's author. The advance for the American edition made it possible for Rowling to quit her teaching job and write full-time. She had always conceived of the stories as a seven-book saga and now had the luxury to concentrate on writing the sequels to the first installment.

With the publication of the American edition, retitled *Harry Potter and the Sorcerer's Stone*, in 1998, Rowling's books continued to make publishing history. *Harry Potter* climbed to the top of all the bestseller lists for children's and adult books. Indeed, the story of the boy wizard, his Cinderlad childhood, and his adventures at Hogwarts School of Witchcraft and Wizardry caught the imagination of readers of all ages. In Britain a separate edition of the first book appeared with a more "adult" dust jacket so that grown-ups reading it on trains and subways would not have to hide their copy behind a newspaper. In the United States, those eager for the second book started ordering it from Amazon.uk, prompting Scholastic to move up the publication date from September to June of 1999 for *Harry Potter and the Chamber of Secrets*. And when *Harry Potter and the Prisoner of Azkaban* was released in September of 1999, all three titles captured the first, second, and third slots on the *New York Times* Bestseller List, remaining there for months afterwards. In Britain Rowling has won the Smarties Book Prize three years in a row, the first author to do so, and has requested that future Harry Potter titles not be considered for the award.

The books have been critically acclaimed in the United States as well as Britain. Named to the best-of-the-year lists in 1998 by *School Library Journal*, *Booklist*, *Publishers Weekly*, *Parenting* magazine, and the Cooperative Children's Book Center, *Harry Potter and the Sorcerer's Stone* was also cited as an ALA Notable Children's Book and ranked number one on the top ten list of ALA's Best Books for Young Adults. The two sequels that have appeared so far are also accumulating awards and enjoying worldwide popularity. To date the books have been translated into approximately thirty languages and have been issued in highly praised audio recordings as well as print; a major motion picture is scheduled for release in 2001.

What is the secret of Rowling's remarkable success? Many articles in journals, interviews on television, and discussions on the Internet have tried to analyze the ingredients that make the Harry Potter books irresistible to readers of all ages—the fast-paced cliffhanger action, the sparkling humor, the Dickensian names. But perhaps the true secret lies in what Rowling herself said in an interview published in *Book Links* magazine: "The book is really about the power of the imagination. What Harry is learning to do is to develop his full potential. Wizardry is just the analogy I use." While magic and wizardry inform many plot elements, the books are ultimately about the innate human desire to be unique and special, to form lasting friendships and connections with others, and to see forces for good triumph over forces for evil.

Jo Rowling lives in Edinburgh, Scotland, with her daughter, Jessica, and continues to work on writing the seven-book saga of Harry Potter.

SELECTED WORKS: *Harry Potter and the Philosopher's Stone*, 1997 (U.S. edition retitled *Harry Potter and the Sorcerer's Stone*, illus. by Mary Grandpré, 1998); *Harry Potter and the Chamber of Secrets*, 1998 (U.S. edition, illus. by Mary Grandpré, 1999); *Harry Potter and the Prisoner of Azkaban*, 1999 (U.S. edition, illus. by Mary Grandpré, 1999); *Harry Potter and the Doomspell Tournament*, illus. by Mary Grandpré, 2000

SUGGESTED READING: "Flying Starts," *Publishers Weekly*, December 21, 1998; "Keeping Up with Harry," *Publishers Weekly*, November 1, 1999; "Not for Muggles," *New York Review of Books*, December 16, 1999; "Talking with . . . J. K. Rowling," *Book Links*, July 1999; "The Truth About Harry," *School Library Journal*, September, 1999; "Wild About Harry," *Time*, September 20, 1999.

WEB SITES: *www.okukbooks.com* and *www.scholastic.com/harrypotter/index.htm*

Robert Sabuda

March 8, 1965–

"Sometimes kids really do know what they want to be when they grow up. Sometimes kids just quietly know, in a deep-down place where very few adults ever go. I suppose I was always like that. From the beginning I loved to draw. My mother, who worked as a secretary for Ford Motor Company, would sneak home reams of white letterhead paper since we couldn't really afford anything like artist's paper. The refrigerator soon began to look like a gallery exhibit 'sponsored in part' by Ford. If I wanted to build things in three dimensions (hence an early love for pop-ups) she would swipe manila filing folders. But never new ones, only used. 'Mr. Nisonger—Accts. Dept.' had no idea his old file was about to become a towering castle with pipe-cleaner supports and glitter brickwork.

"In school things were even better. Whenever it came time for my teacher to put up a new bulletin board she (sorry to sound sexist, but in Pinckney, Michigan, population: not enough black-top to not be 'the sticks,' it was *she*) would turn to me. I always considered it a great honor to Magic-Marker and construction-paper the bulletin board into oblivion. As a child it made me feel very special, although I'm sure my teacher was just relieved that she didn't have to do it. Of all the adults in my boyhood life (except for my parents) every one of my teachers fully supported my desire to be an artist. They could see into my deep-down place even when I sometimes couldn't.

"It is said (I don't remember who, I just remember somebody said it, so trust me) that all humans draw at the same level until they are twelve. After that, the majority of humans continue right on drawing at the age-twelve level. But sometimes a few sneak by and continue to get better and better. This has been the *biggest* luck of the draw I have ever received (if I don't get any more, fine). During high school it became apparent that I could really make a go out of this. I had a terrific art teacher (although she would blow her nose on a tissue that she kept hidden up her sleeve, which kind of freaked us out) who gave me that extra push. My final year I applied to Pratt Institute, an art school in New York City, where she *insisted* that I go. Lo and behold, I received a scholarship to attend, much to my parents' relief (no one in my family had ever gone to college and art schools are very expensive).

Courtesy of Ron Reeves

"For four years I served my sentence until the day of release (sometimes excitedly called 'graduation' by students from non-art colleges who don't spend every single minute of every single day, including weekends, slaving over projects). My whole family came up to the Big House to see the warden, I mean president, hand us the piece of paper with that centuries-old implicit message: *You got this far, don't screw it up now. And don't get anything on that gown, we have to rent it again next year.*

"Fortunately I had no plans for screwing up. During my senior year at Pratt I had fallen into an internship at Dial Books for Young Readers. I was pretty much a go-fer, which I used to think was a 'gopher' but really means 'go fer this' or 'go fer that' (although trust me, NO ONE in New York says 'fer'). On occasion I did a little bit of design work. But the really big treat was that I got to unpack incoming original children's book art that would arrive at the office. Especially if the art came in a wooden crate. And if people in NY don't say 'fer,' they *certainly* don't dirty their hands opening wood crates. The artwork was truly a revelation for me—from Barbara Cooney to James Marshall, I saw it all. And oftentimes I was the very first to see it. I was determined to become a children's book artist.

"Pounding the pavement sounds like something the Fuller Brush Man does (and exactly what is a Fuller Brush?), but that's what I did. I took my portfolio everywhere and eventually was given a manuscript to illustrate by an editor at Dial who had moved to another publishing house. In 1992 I began to write my own books. I never really understood the importance of the word 'edit' in 'editor' before I began to write. Now I look at the words on my grocery list, wondering and worrying whether a seven-year-old can read, pronounce, and understand 'arugula' or if I should just say 'lettuce.'

"Most of my picture books deal with historical figures or are in some way nonfiction. I find that people or events that actually existed are often more interesting than fiction. I'm a real 'tell-it-like-it-is' kind of guy, anyway. At least that's what my boyfriend says.

"In 1994 I revisited my early love for pop-up books after I saw a simple, white paper dove on the front of a card (and the fact that I had been aching to do a Christmas book didn't hurt). Now I spend half my time working on picture books and the other half on pop-ups. People often comment that 'surely I must just *love* kids' since I create children's books for them. But that's not completely true. I do like kids, but mostly I make books for the child in me—the one in that deep-down place that never has to grow up."

Courtesy of Simon & Schuster Children's Publishing Division

*   *   *

Robert Sabuda was born and raised "a typical overachieving middle child" with an older brother and younger sister in Pinckney, Michigan, a small town surrounded by lakes. Water and the outdoors were a big part of his childhood and had a lasting impact on his work. Sabuda received a bachelor of fine arts degree from Pratt Institute in 1987. He has lived in New York City ever since and is now an associate professor at Pratt.

Although most of his time is spent creating books, Sabuda is a movie buff and reads widely, from Stephen King to histories, memoirs, and biographies. In addition he is studying the art of stained glass. He personally supervises the production of his pop-up books, which are manufactured in Colombia and Equador. With each new picture book Sabuda challenges himself with a new technique—mosaic, cut-paper, faux stained glass and batik, among others.

Sabuda's illustrations for *The Paper Dragon* by Marguerite Davol in 1997 won the Golden Kite Award. *The Paper Dragon* was also an ALA Notable Children's Book and a Notable Children's Trade Book in the Field of Social Studies. *The Christmas Alphabet* was a Golden Kite Honor Book and named an ALA Notable Children's Book. *Tutankhamen's Gift* was placed on the *New York Times*'s list, Notable Books of the Year for 1994. *Walden*, a selection of writings by Henry David Thoreau, edited by Steve Lowe and illustrated by Sabuda, was named in 1990 a Notable Children's Trade Book in the Field of Social Studies and one of the New York Public Library's 100 Titles for Reading and Sharing. Sabuda illustrated Constance Levy's *A Tree Place*, which was named a *Boston Globe–Horn Book* Honor Book for Nonfiction. *The Blizzard's Robe* was chosen as a Junior Library Guild selection.

SELECTED WORKS WRITTEN AND ILLUSTRATED: *Saint Valentine*, 1992; *Tutankhamen's Gift*, 1994; *The Christmas Alphabet*, 1994; *Arthur and the Sword*, 1995; *The Twelve Days of Christmas: A Pop-Up Celebration*, 1996; *Cookie Count*, 1997; *ABC Disney*, 1998; *The Blizzard's Robe*, 1999; *The Movable Mother Goose*, 1999.

SELECTED WORKS ILLUSTRATED: *Walden*, by Henry David Thoreau, selections by Steve Lowe, 1990; *Earth Verses and Water Rhymes*, by J. Patrick Lewis, 1991; *I Hear America Singing*, by Walt Whitman, 1991; *The Ibis and the Egret*, by Roy Owen, 1993; *A Tree Place: and Other Poems*, by Constance Levy, 1994; *A Kwanzaa Celebration Pop-Up Book*, by Nancy Williams, 1995; *The Paper Dragon*, by Marguerite W. Davol, 1997

SUGGESTED READING: *Contemporary Authors*, vol. 149, 1996; Cummins, Julie, ed. *Children's Book Illustration and Design*, vol. 2, 1998; *Something about the Author*, vol. 81, 1995. Periodicals—"Paperies and Trash Cans," *The Horn Book*, March/April, 1998; *Publishers Weekly*, November 25, 1996, November 16, 1998.

WEB SITE: *www.scbwi.org/goldkitespeech97.htm*

Marilyn Sadler

November 17, 1950–

"I was born in Pittsburgh, Pennsylvania, in 1950. A child of the '50s, I grew up listening to my older brother's rock-and-roll music. About the time I was ready for school, my family moved to a postwar bungalow neighborhood in Cleveland, Ohio. My younger brother was born soon after, and I became the middle child with a brother on either end. Unbeknownst to me, they were to become the models for some of my future book characters.

"As a child, the books I enjoyed reading most were the Nancy Drew mysteries. I read every one written. I even created my own plots, which I acted out with the help of my younger brother. He played the part of Ned, Nancy's boyfriend, and, of course, I was Nancy. My own writing at that time was mostly humorous. No sad, sappy stories for me. I liked to make myself laugh. My characters had funny names, were goofy, and usually ended up looking pretty silly for one reason or another.

"When I was in the fourth grade my family moved to Coshocton, a small town in southern Ohio, where I lived until college. I had a rather typical childhood: wholesome, safe, and nurturing. We lived farther out from town and it took some time to adjust to the isolation. Fortunately, I had my brother, who was more than willing to play Nancy Drew with me. In no time at all, however, I was sixteen and driving down the hill into town.

"I left for Ohio State University after high school. I chose a degree in art and lugged my art supplies back and forth to Hayes Hall. It was a frustrating time personally to be an art student, because the training was not commercially oriented but, rather, geared for everything abstract. When I graduated, I searched unsuccessfully for a job in the art field, settling instead for a position as an assistant buyer for a department store in Pittsburgh. A few years later, I moved to Cleveland to work as the registrar at the Cleveland Institute of Art and returned to school, earning a master's degree in Special Education from Case Western Reserve University.

Courtesy of Marilyn Sadler

"In 1976, I met my future husband, Roger Bollen, a hard-working cartoonist with three comic strips. When he asked me to team up with him on a project for a large Cleveland-based company, I could hardly say no. We began our partnership creating an annual report for the children of the company's stockholders. In writing and illustrating a funny fictional tale about how the first business was started, we realized we had collaborated on our first children's book.

"That following year we sold our first commercially published children's book to Hamish Hamilton Ltd. while vacationing in London, England. It was the lead title in a series of five books featuring a fastidious little English boy named Alistair Grittle, who had bigger-than-life adventures. Having created a boy with such perfect behavior, we turned our attention to a not so perfectly behaved boy. His name was P. J. Funnybunny, and he exists in a series of books published by Random House.

"Many characters and books later, Roger and I became more involved with children's television. P. J. Funnybunny appeared in three ABC weekend specials. Several Alistair books were featured on PBS's *Reading Rainbow*. And our most recent character, Zenon Kar, appeared in a full-length feature film on the Disney Channel in 1999. Because Zenon lives in the year 2045 on a space station, her adventures have been incredibly interesting to write. Her issues in life are not dissimilar from those of any twelve-year-old today. The difference is that Zenon lives in a world of greatly advanced technology. The best part is . . . I get to make it all up, and much of it is pretty silly."

✳ ✳ ✳

Marilyn Sadler's varied professional background includes teaching high school, working as a freelance copywriter and illustrator, and creating greeting cards. Her husband, Roger Bollen, is best known for his syndicated comic strip "Animal Crackers." Together, the author/artist duo have produced children's books in a variety of genres, including illustrated stories (*Elizabeth and Larry*), board books (*Bedtime for Bunnies*), beginning readers (*Parakeet Girl*), and concept books on such subjects as counting (*Blue Barry Bear Counts from One to Twenty*), matching objects (*Match This, P. J. Funnybunny*), and sequencing (*What's Next, P. J. Funnybunny?*.)

> *"No sad, sappy stories for me. I liked to make myself laugh."*

Sadler's work has spread beyond the pages of books into other media. *Alistair's Elephant* was featured on the PBS children's series *Storytime*, while *Alistair in Outer Space* and *Alistair's Time Machine* were featured on *Reading Rainbow*. *Elizabeth and Larry* was broadcast on *Shelley Duvall's Bedtime Stories*. *The P. J. Funnybunny Christmas Special* shown on ABC-TV was one of several animated programs featuring this character. Sadler and Bollen's book *Zenon: Girl of the 21st Century* was made into a television movie for the Disney Channel, and Sadler created an original Alistair story for the British Broadcasting Corporation.

It's Not Easy Being a Bunny won an International Classroom Children's Award, and *Elizabeth and Larry* received a Parents' Choice Award and won an Honorable Mention in the category of picture books in the California Children's Book Awards.

Sadler lives with her husband in Cleveland, Ohio, and enjoys travel and gardening in addition to writing.

SELECTED WORKS: (all illus. by Roger Bollen) *Ump's Fwat*, 1980; *Alistair's Elephant*, 1983; *It's Not Easy Being a Bunny*, 1983; *Alistair in Outer Space*, 1984; *The Very Bad Bunny*, 1984;

Alistair's Time Machine, 1986; *P. J., the Spoiled Bunny*, 1986;
Chuck Wood and the Woodchucks in the Big Game, 1989;
Faces in Places, 1989; *Elizabeth and Larry*, 1990; *Nanny Goat
and the Lucky Kid*, 1991; *Blue Barry Bear Counts from One
to Twenty*, 1991; *Elizabeth, Larry, and Ed*, 1992; *P. J. Bunny
Camps Out*, 1994; *Alistair and the Alien Invasion*, 1994;
Bedtime for Bunnies, 1994; *Zenon: Girl of the 21st Century*,
1996; *P. J. Funnybunny and His Very Cool Birthday Party*,
1996; *Honey Bunny Funnybunny*, 1997; *Parakeet Girl*, 1997;
Match This, P. J. Funnybunny, 1998; *What's Next, P. J.
Funnybunny?*, 1999.

SUGGESTED READING: *Something About the Author*, vol. 79, 1995.

"I was born in Philadelphia, Pennsylvania, the son of a Navy fighter pilot and an art student from the Hawaiian Islands. When I was two months old, Mom and I were shipped back to Hawaii on an appropriated luxury liner protected by a convoy of Navy destroyers. I lived, for that time crossing the Pacific Ocean, in a cardboard box under a sink.

"I spent my entire childhood on the islands of Oahu and Hawaii, the most glorious of days in the most remote, most beautiful place in the world. In my teens I skippered a small glass-bottom boat and worked as a deckhand on a deep-sea charter fishing boat. I also surfed my brains out. My friends were of every imaginable race, mostly all mixed up—haole, Japanese, Chinese, Hawaiian, Filipino, Portuguese, and many more. My stories mostly come from those guys and those times.

"The most significant element of my life is the fact that I was raised, essentially, without a father. Although I had three of them, I knew none of them. My real father was killed in World War II; my first stepfather died when I was ten; my second stepfather was inaccessible. My stories often explore friendship, loyalty, courage, honor, and the relationship between fathers and sons. That last part is for me; it's what I do to fill the fatherless void in my life.

"My stories come from the far corners of my mind, and if I'm lucky, from my deepest heart. *Blue Skin of the Sea* captured pieces of my adolescence on the Big Island of Hawaii. *Under the*

Courtesy of Ray Warren

**Graham
Salisbury**

April 11, 1944–

Blood-Red Sun explored a question I'd grown up with: what was it like in Honolulu on the day Pearl Harbor was bombed? *Shark Bait* was based on a good friend of mine, a kid who loved to fight, something I wanted no part of. But he had this magnetic pull on me. I really liked the guy.

"*Jungle Dogs* grew out of a phrase that came to me one day as I was driving to the gym: 'My hero is my dog.' Weird, how that phrase just popped up like that. But it made me think of heroes, the people we look up to in our lives. What makes them stand out? What makes them such extraordinary human beings? What is a hero? The story began (quite unexpectedly, actually) as I was working on something else. That weird phrase wouldn't let go: my hero is my dog.

Courtesy of BDD Books

"I day-dreamed. I considered possibilities.

"I began to write: 'Far out on the ocean a small reef of clouds . . . .'

"And I was gone. Slipped away into another world. (I *love* that part, that entering into new worlds.)

"I drew on my experiences delivering the morning paper in Kailua with the bats swooshing just overhead. I drew on friendships I had, on places I explored. I drew on my respect for strong father-son and strong sibling relationships. I drew on my gut feelings, looking for a heartbeat, which is where all good stories must begin.

"When it comes to writing, I believe in magic. Generally, I have in mind a glimpse of where I want to go when I begin a novel. I try to sketch out a premise and possible storyline before I begin. It's all extremely nebulous at this point, trying to create something out of nothing. The magic comes, really, in the writing. Something happens between my fingertips and the keyboard. I don't understand it, but it's absolutely the most fabulous and surely the most mysterious part of the writing process: write, and things happen.

"Of all my novels, *Jungle Dogs* is truly a result of that magic. This story just presented itself. And I am pleased that it did. It speaks to me in many ways.

Magic.

From the universe.

A window, open to the Great Unknown.

Wow.

"I love being a writer, a daydreamer. Life is good, if we allow it to be."

*   *   *

Graham Salisbury was born in 1944 on a naval base in Philadelphia, the son of Lieutenant Commander Henry Graham and Barbara Twigg-Smith. His mother's family had been in Hawaii since 1820, and he spent his early childhood on Oahu. His father was shot down in a fighter plane over southern Japan on the day Graham turned one year old. Graham was two when his mother married Guy Salisbury, another Navy man, and ten when Guy died of cancer. By then he had three sisters, and they all went to Kailua-Kona on the Big Island of Hawaii to live with their mother and her third husband, a deep-sea charter-boat fisherman.

Salisbury went to the mainland for college but soon dropped out to join a rock band as a bass player. Later he joined Millenium, a seven-man studio band, as a singer and songwriter. Though the band was successful, he found he didn't want to stay in the music business and went back to school, this time graduating magna cum laude from California State University, Northridge. Having decided he would be a teacher, he went to Italy to study the Montessori method and taught for two years in a small, struggling Montessori school in Utah until it closed. From there he tried out graphic design and became a production manager at Brigham Young University. In 1984 he moved to Portland, Oregon, where he still lives, with his wife, Robyn, and their three children.

Salisbury came late both to reading for pleasure and to writing, crediting Alex Haley's *Roots* as his inspiration. After some work on his own, he enrolled in the writing program run by Vermont College of Norwich University, and earned an M.F.A. in 1990. Now he is a member of the faculty of their Writing for Children Program, which meets twice a year in Montpelier, Vermont. He won the PEN/Norma Klein Award for an emerging voice among American writers of children's fiction when his first novel, *Blue Skin of the Sea*, was published in 1992. This novel was listed as a *School Library Journal* Best Book of the Year, an NCTE Notable Trade Book in the Language Arts, and an ALA Best Book for Young Adults and received the Bank Street Child Study Book Award for 1992. Salisbury's second book, *Under the Blood-Red Sun*, received the 1994 Scott O'Dell Award for Historical Fiction and appeared on many "best books of the year" lists; it was nominated for many state award lists and won the Nene Award in Hawaii and the California Young Readers Medal. *Jungle Dogs* was named an ALA Best Book for Young Adults. Salisbury's first three novels have all won Parents' Choice Awards and the Oregon Book Award.

Salisbury's writing is rooted in his early years in Hawaii, expressing his deep love and respect for the islands and their natural beauty, the intensities of boyhood friendships, the impact of the war, and life near and on (or in) the sea.

SELECTED WORKS: *Blue Skin of the Sea*, 1992; *Under the Blood-Red Sun*, 1994; *Shark Bait*, 1997; *Jungle Dogs*, 1998.

SUGGESTED READING: *Authors and Artists for Young Adults*, vol. 26, 1997; *Contemporary Authors*, vol. 143, 1994; Graham, Paula. *Speaking of Journals*, 1998; Hipple, Ted, ed. *Writers for Young Adults*, 1997; Kutzer, Daphne M. *Writers of Multicultural Fiction for Young Adults*, 1996; *Something About the Author*, vol. 76, 1994; *Something About the Author Autobiography Series*, vol. 7, 1988. Periodicals—Benton, Janet, "Writing My Way Home: An Interview with Graham Salisbury," *ALAN Review*, Winter 1997; "A Leaf on the Sea," *ALAN Review*, Fall 1994; Winarski, Diana L., "Graham Salisbury's Newfound Career," *Teaching PreK–8*, March 1998.

Courtesy of Ray Hunold

Steve Sanfield

August 3, 1937–

"I remember the exact moment I decided I was going to be a writer. I often went to the old stone library about a mile from my house in Lynn, Massachusetts. My local librarian, Elsie Grubb, loved two things above all else— books and children—and it was her goal in life to bring them together. She would sometimes recommend particular books, and when I returned them I would tell her my thoughts about them. After reading *The Adventures of Tom Sawyer* I told her it was the best book ever. She then handed me another, saying, 'If you liked that I think you'll like this one also.' The book, of course, was *The Adventures of Huckleberry Finn*. She was right. I devoured it, and in the process wore out the batteries in my father's flashlight reading it under the covers. I told Miss Grubb I'd been wrong before. This was undoubtedly the greatest book ever written. 'Well, you know,' she said, 'the same man, Mark Twain, wrote them both.'

"That simple statement was like being hit by lightning. Up until then I never connected writers with the books on the shelves. I'm not sure what I thought before, but this was the first time I understood that it was people who wrote books. And I blurted out, 'That's what I'm going to be, a writer, and I'll write a better book than *Huckleberry Finn*.' I was eight years old, and I've been at it ever since, still trying to fulfill my promise to the librarian who changed my life.

"The first book I wrote back then was, not surprisingly, called 'A Boy on a Raft', only the boy was named Steve, not Huck, and the river was the Merrimack, not the Mississippi. It would take many journeys and almost forty years before I would begin to publish books for children.

"After college, I headed for Hollywood with dreams of a career in show business. I worked as a gossip columnist, a publicist (one of my clients was an actor named Ronald Reagan), a news editor for CBS Radio, a TV scriptwriter, and, having decided show biz wasn't for me, a bookstore manager, which was a far more pleasant occupation. A few years later I went off to the Greek islands to write a novel (completed and

Courtesy of Philomel Books

deservedly unpublished). I lived and worked at odd jobs around the Mediterranean, North Africa, and the Middle East, all the time darkening pages with ink and scribbling poems. Upon my return to the United States, I lived as a Zen Buddhist monk for three years before I got married.

"With my wife and young son, I moved to the foothills of California's Sierra Nevada mountains, where I've lived ever since. At first we tried to create a self-sufficient life. We built our own home, grew a huge garden, and planted an orchard of fruit trees. After a few years we decided that although we could be full-time farmers, it wasn't what we really wanted to do. My wife returned to her painting, I to my poetry.

"I began to work in the Poetry-in-the-Schools Program. Instead of trying to convince children they could write 'great' poetry, I wanted to introduce them to the joys of reading and listening to it. I immediately discovered the poems they enjoyed most were narrative poems which told a good story. I soon discovered that what they really wanted and needed were the stories themselves. I started telling more and more stories until the administrators of the poetry program suggested I leave.

"Thanks to the California Arts Council, I was appointed the first full-time Storyteller-in-Residence in the United States. For four years I told hundreds and hundreds of tales to the children in my local school district and then continued to do so at schools and festivals all across the country.

"The first two children's books I published, *A Natural Man* and *The Adventures of High John the Conqueror*, grew out of stories I was telling orally, stories that seemed to be favorites of both children and adults. Now, after ten books for young people, I'm not sure which comes first—the written story or the oral one. Sometimes it happens one way, sometimes the other. Sometimes they grow together, but there are also times when they never meet. It doesn't seem to matter. What matters is the story itself. If the story, whether read or heard, whether on the page or on the breath, touches the reader/listener and makes her/him laugh or cry or think or remember, then I've done my job as a storyteller.

"And for me there is no better job. All my life I've loved words and poems and stories, and I feel blessed that I've been able to raise my family and pay the grocer and the cobbler by bringing them to others."

* * *

Born in Cambridge, Massachusetts, Steve Sanfield is the son of Harold and Rose Sanfield. He attended the University of Massachusetts at Amherst, graduating in 1958, and married Jacqueline Bellon, an artist, in 1969. Divorced in 1977, he married Sarah Ruth Sparks, a teacher, on September 6, 1985. He has one son, Aaron, by his first marriage.

Sanfield published his first book of poems, *Water Before and Water After*, in 1974 and has followed that with eleven more volumes of poetry to date. He became the associate editor of *Kuksu: A Journal of Backcountry Writing* and a founding and later contributing editor to *Zero: A Journal of Contemporary Buddhist Life and Thought*. Affiliated with the California Poets in the Schools Program, 1975–1977, he went on to become a storyteller-in-residence through the California Arts Council, 1977–1980. He is the artistic director of the Sierra Storytelling Festival, which he founded in 1985.

Sanfield is a member of the Authors Guild, the Society of Children's Book Writers and Illustrators, and the National Storytelling Association. *The Adventures of High John the Conqueror* garnered many honors, including being named an ALA Notable Children's Book, an IRA Young Adult Choice, and a 1990 Notable Trade Book in the Field of Social Studies. *The Feather Merchants and Other Tales of the Fools of Chelm*, was a 1991 American Booksellers Association Pick of the Lists and a Parents' Choice Honor Book. In 1996 *The Great Turtle Drive* was an Association of Children's Libraries Distinguished Book of the Year; *Bit by Bit* was the 1997 Arizona Picture Book of the Year. In 1996 Sanfield was presented with the National Storytelling Association Service and Leadership Award.

SELECTED WORKS: *A Natural Man: The True Story of John Henry*, illus. by Peter J. Thornton, 1986; *The Adventures of High John the Conqueror*, illus. by John Ward, 1989; *The Feather Merchants and Other Tales of the Fools of Chelm*, illus. by Mikhail Magaril, 1991; *Bit by Bit*, illus. by Susan Gaber,1995; *Strudel, Strudel, Strudel*, illus. by Emily Lisker, 1995; *Snow*, illus. by Jeanette Winters, 1995; *The Girl Who Wanted a Song*, illus. by Stephen T. Johnson, 1996; *The Great Turtle Drive*, illus. by Dirk Zimmer, 1996; *Just Rewards, or Who Is That Man in the Moon & What's He Doing Up There Anyway?*, illus. by Emily Lisker, 1996.

SUGGESTED READING: *Contemporary Authors*, vol. 124, 1988.

"I lived in a number of houses when I was growing up; my father bought and sold real estate in and around Los Angeles, and my family would move into whatever place he had purchased—until he sold it again. Sometimes I'd drive out into the California foothills with my parents to look at farms and ranches and orange groves that my father had seen advertised in the newspaper. I always hoped there would be animals—chickens or geese or sheep or, if I was really lucky, a horse to ride. Years later, I began writing *A Lucky Thing* as a series of poems about animals I loved as a child—creatures of meadow and pond and barnyard—but soon another theme developed and it became a book about the actual process of writing those poems. Many of the poems I have written about animals are really ways of saying something about human nature.

"When I was five I got my first cat. I won it in a school contest and brought it home in a paper bag. My parents were not nearly as enthusiastic as I had anticipated, and spoke firmly, and often, about 'getting rid of it.' Nevertheless, Muggins was the first of a series of cats who came to stay. I've almost always had a cat since then and find them vain, superior, contrary, unpredictable—perfectly irresistible subjects for fiction or poetry. One of the poems I wrote for *I Am the Cat* tells of the first cat, who drank the moon. When I was developing that poem and had written a number of revised and rejected sections, I suddenly wrote the opening lines: 'In the beginning /

Courtesy of Susan Pearson

Alice Schertle

April 7, 1941–

when the cat could fly . . . .' That was when I realized that I was actually writing a feline version of the fall from grace in the Garden of Eden. I have no idea why that idea came into my head, but it illustrates what, for me, is one of the wonders and joys of writing: stories and poems can happen right on the page.

"I began writing in the first grade and never stopped. During much of my childhood I favored wild flights of fancy, writing first of fairies and elves, then of space aliens; later there were stories of intrigue and espionage, murder and mayhem. When I was in high school a wonderful teacher, who thought there might be a writer in me, helped me to see the drama and beauty in the ordinary, real, familiar things of life. Though I still like to write Halloween stories and other picture-book fantasies, my writing now is often grounded in observation of people and things in the real world—family stories such as *Down the Road* or collections of poems such as *Keepers*.

"I continued writing during my college years at the University of Southern California and sold a couple of short pieces to *Reader's Digest*. That was the first time I ever saw my work in print, and the small checks that came in the mail were the first money I ever made as a writer. Both experiences felt awfully good!

"After college I taught fourth and fifth grades and then took time off to marry and have three children of my own. I read to them from the time they were tiny babies, and loved their picture books as much as they did. Soon I was writing picture-book stories of my own, and after two years of submissions and rejections sold my first manuscript. I had written and published twenty-five picture books when I took a poetry class at U.C.L.A. taught by Myra Cohn Livingston. It felt like coming home. The things I learned and the friends I made in Myra's class have enriched my life. I'll always love writing fiction, but often when I sit down at the keyboard a poem is what happens. Poetry is where my heart is."

> "When I was in high school a wonderful teacher, who thought there might be a writer in me, helped me to see the drama and beauty in the ordinary, real, familiar things of life."

* * *

Alice Schertle was born in Los Angeles, California, the youngest of four children of Floyd and Marguerite Sanger. She received her B.A. degree in fine arts from the University of Southern California in 1963 and married Richard Schertle in December of that year. After two years of teaching at Highland Elementary School in Inglewood, California, Schertle turned her attention to raising a family. Her first picture book, with illustrations by Paul Galdone, was published in 1977; she has been publishing steadily ever since.

Many of Schertle's picture books and poetry collections have been recognized for their excellence and appeal. She received a Christopher Award and a Parents' Choice Picture Book Award for *William and Grandpa*, the gentle story of a connection between generations. *Witch Hazel*, with its evocative illustrations by Margot Tomes, garnered another Parents' Choice Award, as well as a *School Library Journal* Best Book citation and a *Bulletin of the Center for Children's Books* Blue Ribbon. *Advice for a Frog and Other Poems* was cited as a *School Library Journal* Best Book of the Year and was named to NCTE's Notable Trade Books in the Language Arts. *Advice for a Frog*, *Down the Road*, and *How Now, Brown Cow?* were all named ALA Notable Children's Books within a two-year period. In 1999 *I Am the Cat* was included on New York Public Library's list of 100 Titles for Reading and Sharing, and *A Lucky Thing*, a collection of poems about the creative process, became an American Booksellers Association Pick of the Lists as well as a Children's Book-of-the-Month Club selection.

After living most of her life in California, Alice Schertle now resides in Yorktown Heights, New York. She has two grandchildren, Spencer and Dylan, and divides her time between writing, gardening, and visiting schools to discuss the writing process.

SELECTED WORKS: *The Gorilla in the Hall*, illus. by Paul Galdone, 1977; *The April Fool*, illus. by Emily Arnold McCully, 1981; *Hob Goblin and the Skeleton*, illus. by Katherine Coville, 1982; *Goodnight, Hattie, My Dearie, My Dove*, illus. by Linda Strauss Edwards, 1985; *Jeremy Bean's St. Patrick's Day*, illus. by Linda Shute, 1987; *William and Grandpa*, illus. by Lydia Dabcovich, 1989; *Witch Hazel*, illus. by Margot Tomes, 1991; *Little Frog's Song*, illus. by Leonard Everett Fisher, 1992; *How Now, Brown Cow? Poems*, illus. by Amanda Schaffer, 1994; *Down the Road*, illus. by E. B. Lewis, 1995; *Maisie*, illus. by Lydia Dabcovich, 1995; *Advice for a Frog and Other Poems*, illus. by Norman Green, 1995; *Keepers*, illus. by Ted Rand, 1996; *A Lucky Thing*, illus. by Wendell Minor, 1999; *I Am the Cat*, illus. by Mark Buehner, 1999.

SUGGESTED READING *Contemporary Authors*, New Revision Series, vol. 59, 1998; *Something About the Author*, vol. 36, 1984; vol. 90, 1997. Periodicals—Schertle, Alice, "Up the Bookcase to Poetry," *The Horn Book*, July/August 1996.

Steven Schnur

(shner)

April 8, 1952–

"The summer I turned eight, my family moved from the suburban town I had lived in all my life to a neighboring community six miles away. For my parents, who had spent their childhoods fleeing Hitler, the change meant little more than an additional bedroom or two for their growing family of four sons. But for me, the sudden loss of neighborhood and friends seemed an upheaval as great as any they had endured during the 1930s. In an instant I became an outsider, a stranger, the new kid on the block. The shock awakened me from the cozy sleep of infancy and thrust me overnight into the great world of newspapers and radios and books, a world full of mystery and menace and wonder.

"It was a fascinating and fearsome time to wake up: John Kennedy was about to be elected president, the threat of nuclear war hung in the air, and the first cautious explorations of outer space coincided with the first tentative revelations of the horrors of the Holocaust.

"With the Cold War providing the persistent background hum of impending annihilation, a hum that filled the ears of every child of the 1950s, I began to learn the Holocaust's terrible lessons of man's limitless capacity for evil. The more I read about those awful years, the more I realized that events played out on the world stage had enormous impact on my own life. Though my immediate family had escaped unscathed from the flames of Europe, many distant relatives had not. And had it not been for the war, I would have grown up not as an American in a suburb of New York City, but, like my parents, as a German citizen of Berlin or Dresden.

Courtesy of Nancie Schnur

"There was one other central constellation in the firmament of my youth: love. I was blessed to fall in love early in life and remain that way. Within days of meeting my future wife I knew we would one day marry. Eight years later, after high school, college, and postgraduate studies, we did. A long period of infertility followed, but then, with the swiftness of a miracle, three children were born: a daughter and boy/girl twins. Ever since I have thought of myself as a father first; everything else has become secondary.

"Writing for me has always been an expression of gratitude, an outgrowth of the impulse to give thanks for love received, for children born, for the miraculous existence of the imagination. When I write for adults I often do so in a state of wonder, transfixed by blessings. When I write for children I try to recapture the eight-year-old boy I once was, a boy filled with a passionate interest in the unfolding world around him. And finally I write in the hope of leaving behind a legacy of thought and feeling that my children might one day mine, if not for answers at least for solace, in the recognition that we traveled the same road of doubt and discovery."

* * *

After obtaining his bachelor's degree from Sarah Lawrence College and a master's degree from Hunter College, Steven Schnur embarked on a career in literature and education. He has taught writing on the college level and has served as an editor at *Reform Judaism Magazine* and with the Union of American Hebrew Congregations. The UAHC published his first children's books, *The Narrowest Bar Mitzvah* and *The Return of Morris Schumsky*. Subsequent novels and picture book texts have explored the themes of Judaism and the wonders of nature.

The Shadow Children received the Sydney Taylor Award from the Association of Jewish Libraries. It was also named an ALA Notable Children's Book and a Notable Trade Book in the Field of Social Studies, and received the 1996 Best Children's Book Award from the Women's International Zionist Organization. *The Tie Man's Miracle*, Schnur's picture book about a modern-day peddler and his effect on a family's holiday observance, was named a Notable Trade Book in the Field of Social Studies and received the Washington Irving Award from the Westchester (N.Y.) Library Association. *Autumn: An Alphabet Acrostic* was an American Booksellers Association Pick of the Lists, as was *The Koufax Dilemma*, a novel about the concerns of a contemporary Jewish boy. Schnur's young adult novel *Beyond Providence* was a Washington Irving Honor Book in 1998.

Steven Schnur's work has also appeared in periodicals ranging from the *New York Times* and the *Christian Science Monitor* to *People* and *Woman's Day*. He teaches at Sarah Lawrence College and lives with his family in Scarsdale, New York.

Courtesy of William Morrow & Co., Inc.

SELECTED WORKS: *The Narrowest Bar Mitzvah,* 1986; *The Return of Morris Schumsky,* 1987; *Hannah and Cyclops,* 1990; *The Shadow Children,* 1994; *The Tie Man's Miracle: A Chanukah Tale,* illus. by Stephen T. Johnson, 1995; *Beyond Providence,* 1996; *The Koufax Dilemma,* 1997; *Autumn: An Alphabet Acrostic,* illus. by Leslie Evans, 1997; *Spring: An Alphabet Acrostic,* illus. by Leslie Evans, 1999; *Spring Thaw,* illus. by Stacey Schuett, 2000.

SUGGESTED READING: *Contemporary Authors,* vol. 140, 1993; *Something About the Author,* vol. 95, 1998.

Courtesy of Alan Schroeder

Alan Schroeder

Alan Schroeder

January 18, 1961–

"When I was young I loved reading Dr. Seuss's *Green Eggs and Ham* and I was fascinated by the weird characters in *The Wind in the Willows* (especially Mr. Toad, who liked to drive a fast car). However, my warmest memories are of the nights that I spent at my grandparents' house. After dinner my grandfather, Otto, would get out his collection of Danish fairy tales and read me a Hans Christian Andersen story. The one I remember best was 'The Little Match Girl.' The image of that poor girl freezing to death in the snow, clutching a handful of burnt matches, has stayed with me always. There's a realism to Andersen's stories that I love—a truthfulness about human character—as well as a deep melancholy. Even as a child, I was aware that his stories weren't like anyone else's, and to some degree he has influenced me as a writer.

"Another source of inspiration was Jack London, the California author who wrote *The Call of the Wild*, which remains one of my all-time favorite books. For years now, I've been trying to think of some way to introduce picture book readers to the brutal and beautiful world of Jack London, but I haven't yet figured out how. Give me time!

"Over the years, I've written several different kinds of books for young readers, including biographies and folktales, but the stories that give me the deepest satisfaction tend to be realistic. More often than not, they're taken from the life of someone I admire. I've written about the childhoods of dancer Josephine Baker, musician Louis Armstrong, and abolitionist Harriet Tubman.

"Kids often ask me which of my books I like the most. That's a hard question to answer, because each book is a reflection of some aspect of myself. For instance, I love listening to ragtime music, so *Ragtime Tumpie* was a delightful project (but also a difficult one—it was my first picture book, and I had a lot to learn about how to put a book together.) Travel is another one of my interests. I've always wanted to visit the country of Japan, so *Lily and the Wooden Bowl* gave me a wonderful opportunity to immerse myself for six months in Japanese research. I'll always have a special fondness for that book, because it was the first and only time I got to meet my illustrator beforehand.

"Another book I enjoyed writing was *Carolina Shout!* It's one of my shortest and least complicated books: a portrait of a girl named Delia who lives in Charleston, South Carolina. Delia is a very musical child. In the book, she tells the reader about the wonderful 'music' she hears on the streets of Charleston—work songs, vendors calling out their wares in the market, the waffle man's shout, the cry of the hot pepper sauce man, etc.

"My favorite shout in the book is the final one—the song the charcoal man sings while he's making his rounds. There's a melancholy feel to the whole scene that I like (shades, maybe, of Hans Christian Andersen?). *Carolina Shout!* was an enjoyable project from beginning to end. The only real problem was coming up with enough authentic shouts. I had to search for nearly a year, looking through old novels, diaries, magazines, cookbooks, and reproductions of billboards. As an author, you never know where your research will take you, and that's part of the fun of being a writer.

"There's one thing I don't like about writing: the rough draft. You start off with a wonderful idea. You rush to your computer, sit down, and start typing—and little by little, you feel the enthusiasm begin to dwindle, and you watch, horrified, as the sentences fall flat on the screen. By the time I finish one of my books, I've revised it at least 25 or 30 times. Naturally, I wish the story would come out perfectly the first time around, but it never does. Good writing, I've learned, is the result of hard work and plenty of it. Sure, it's frustrating when things don't go well, but I also get a real feeling of satisfaction when I finish a book and know that I've done a good job."

> *". . . the stories that give me the deepest satisfaction tend to be realistic."*

*　*　*

Alan Schroeder has always loved to read and was fortunate to grow up in the San Francisco Bay Area, where there are dozens of wonderful libraries. He was even luckier to have a godmother who was a teacher. Maggie always made sure that he had a book in his hands. He attended public schools in Alameda, California, and graduated from the University of California at Santa Cruz, where he received the prestigious Chancellor's Award for creative writing.

Schroeder can spend as much as two years on a picture book. It is extremely important to him to tell the story with accuracy and make it so compelling that students and teachers will enjoy reading it. He thinks that doing the best work you can and hoping that someone likes it is what being a real writer is all about.

He enjoys jigsaw puzzles (the bigger, the better!), pizza, shrimp curry, chicken pot pie, risotto, and fresh-baked bread. His favorite color is cobalt blue and, although his house is too small for pets now, he wanted a pig when he was little.

In 1992 the New York Public Library chose *Josephine Baker* as a Best Book for the Teen Age. *Ragtime Tumpie* was an ALA Notable Children's Book, and a *Booklist* Editors' Choice. *Carolina Shout!* was named an ALA Notable Children's Book and also a Children's Book of the Year by the Bank Street College Child Study Children's Book Committee. *Minty: A Story of Young Harriet Tubman* received a Coretta Scott King Award for Illustration, a 1996 Christopher Award, and the 1998 Bluegrass Award and was an ALA Notable Children's Book. *Satchmo's Blues* was a 1997 IRA Teachers' Choice and an ABA Pick of the Lists. *Smoky Mountain Rose: An Appalachian Cinderella* was also chosen as an ABA Pick of the Lists.

SELECTED WORKS: *Ragtime Tumpie*, illus. by Bernie Fuchs, 1989; *Josephine Baker: Entertainer*, illus. by Nathan I. Huggins, 1991; *Jack London*, 1992; *Booker T. Washington*, 1992; *James Dean*, 1994; *The Stone Lion*, illus. by Todd L. W. Doney, 1994; *Lily and the Wooden Bowl*, illus. by Yoriko Ito, 1994; *Carolina Shout!*, illus. by Bernie Fuchs, 1995; *Minty: A Story of Young Harriet Tubman*, illus. by Jerry Pinkney, 1996; *Satchmo's Blues*, illus. by Floyd Cooper, 1996; *Charlie Chaplin: The Beauty of Silence*, 1997; *Smoky Mountain Rose: An Appalachian Cinderella*, illus. by Brad Sneed, 1997; *The Tale of Willie Monroe*, illus. by Andrew Glass, 1999.

SUGGESTED READING: *Contemporary Authors,* vol. 133, 1991; *Something About the Author*, vol. 66, 1991; vol. 98, 1998; Westley, Joan and Holly Melton, *Across America—Windows on Social Studies: Multicultural Adventures Through Literature*, 1994. Periodicals— *Denver Post*, February 8, 1998; *New York Times*, December 8, 1996; *Smithsonian*, November 1996; *Time*, December 9, 1996.

WEB SITE: *www.randomhouse.com/teachersbdd/schr.html*

Tres Seymour

(trace SEE-more)

December 30, 1966–

"**I** was born looking at the world a little differently than most people. I grew up thinking a little too hard about everything and worrying more than most of the kids around me. When the world got a bit too intense, I went and lived for a while in a book—lots of them, in fact. I wasn't a writer then, and had no intention of ever becoming one. In those days, I was thinking of becoming an astronaut—until I realized how bad I was at math.

"I rediscovered children's books as a college freshman. It was like meeting an old friend from whom I had drifted away. The rediscovery began as a tickle in my mind, a memory of a book with a green cover, about some children and a coin, in our old public library in Morristown, Tennessee. I went back and found the book by sight, having no idea of title or author. It was Edward Eager's *Half Magic*. Next I found again my favorite book of all time, Carol Kendall's *The Gammage Cup*. My studies in Shakespeare and Faulkner tumbled downhill. There was no time. I made weekly visits to one of the best children's bookstores in the nation and came away laden with Nesbit, Alexander, LeGuin, Cooper, Babbitt, Jacques, Aiken, Christopher, E. B. White, T. H. White, and so many others. I haven't stopped reading them yet. I have no notion why suddenly, as a college freshman, I decided to start writing books, except perhaps that I couldn't imagine anyone paying me to read for a living. Reading had taught my eye and ear how words work together, so when I at last decided to try writing, I was ready.

"I wrote a dreadful first novel (don't even ask to see it), followed by three mediocre ones before I veered into the world of picture books, which I had never dreamed of writing. Then I sidestepped into young adult novels. I have never written what I wanted to write. I want to write fantasies for fourth-graders, and I really have tried, but every story either condenses into a picture book or becomes long-winded and self-aware and ends up as a novel for young adults. I read somewhere that A. A. Milne really wanted to write mysteries, but instead became famous for *Winnie-the-Pooh*. I hope that's not the way it is with me; and yet, in the same breath, I have to say, 'Thy will be done,' in acknowledgement of where this gift comes from.

Courtesy of Tres Seymour

"The biblical parable tells us that we must take our talents and grow them, not hide or bury them so that they are unproductive. I see the sharpening of my writing as a responsibility. Luckily for me, I don't have to try very hard at it. The stories come when it's time. I sit down and listen, and tell them on paper, and then wait for the next one. People often say, 'Look at all your books! Aren't you proud?' I never know how to answer. I didn't invent these stories any more than a farmer invents pumpkins. He may grow a good crop, but the existence of the pumpkins is due to a higher author. My writing is like this too. The stories come to me, often suddenly and unexpectedly, and I simply accept them and use my ability to tell them.

"Sometimes I worry that there won't be any more. This usually happens after I finish one and don't have another really good idea to work on. But another has always come and, as long as it suits the Lord's purpose, I suppose they always will."

* * *

Tres Seymour was born in Glasgow, Kentucky, and raised in Tennessee. After receiving a B.A. in both English and journalism from Southern Methodist University, he obtained a master's degree in library science from the University of Kentucky. He did graduate work in children's literature at Simmons College in Boston and worked toward a master's in English at the University of Tennessee. While attending college he was employed as a seasonal park ranger at Mammoth Cave National Park in Kentucky, and continues to work there as a visual information specialist for the Park's Division of External Programs. He is also a graphic designer.

Early in his writing career, Seymour received critical acclaim for his work. *Life in the Desert* was selected as an ALA Recommended Book for Reluctant Young Adult Readers in 1993. *Hunting the White Cow* was a *School Library Journal* Best Book of the Year, an ALA Notable Children's Book, and a Marion Vannet Ridgway Memorial Award Honor Book, and was selected for the NCTE Notable Children's Books in the Language Arts list as well as the New York Public Library's annual list, 100 Titles for Reading and Sharing. An "admirer and student" of C. S. Lewis, Seymour's other interests include fencing, travel, and music; he plays a number of instruments, including the bodhran (a drum-like Celtic instrument, pronounced "bow-rawn"), banjo, dulcimer, Celtic harp, and fife. Tres Seymour lives with his wife and young children in Munfordville, Kentucky.

Courtesy of Orchard Books

SELECTED WORKS WRITTEN: *Life in the Desert*, 1992; *Pole Dog*, illus. by David Soman, 1993; *Hunting the White Cow*, illus. by Wendy Anderson Halperin, 1993; *I Love My Buzzard*, illus. by S. D. Schindler, 1994; *The Smash-up, Crash-up Derby*, illus. by S. D. Schindler, 1995; *Black Sky River*, illus. by Dan Andreasen, 1996; *Too Quiet for These Old Bones*, illus. by Paul Brett Johnson, 1997; *We Played Marbles*, illus. by Dan Andreasen, 1998; *The Revelation of Saint Bruce*, 1998; *Our*

Neighbor Is a Strange, Strange Man, illus. by Walter Krudop, 1999.

SELECTED WORKS WRITTEN AND ILLUSTRATED: *The Gulls of the Edmund Fitzgerald*, 1996.

SUGGESTED READING: *Contemporary Authors*, vol. 149, 1996; *Something About the Author*, vol. 82, 1995.

"I've always liked to draw pictures, but it wasn't until I had completed a number of children's books that I realized that storytelling is what really interested me from the start. As a kid growing up in Spokane, Washington, I drew lots of pirates, knights, Indians, and especially baseball players—most of them inspired by books I was reading. One book that made a big impression on me was *The Boy's King Arthur*, illustrated by N. C. Wyeth, who is still a big influence on my work.

"For some reason, it never occurred to me that I could illustrate books like that too. And by the time I attended art school at Art Center College of Design in Pasadena, California, my main focus was on political illustration for newspapers and magazines. After graduation, I moved to New York City to see if anyone would actually pay me to paint pictures. At first no one did, and I had to eat rats and cockroaches just to survive. Not really—I did eat a lot of canned soup, though! It was very frustrating, but I kept at it and eventually I got plenty of work.

Courtesy of Richard Trimarchi

David Shannon

October 5, 1959–

"One day, I got a call from Scholastic, a children's book publisher. They had seen one of my paintings in the *New York Times* and wondered if I wanted to illustrate a children's book. They sent me a story by Julius Lester called *How Many Spots Does a Leopard Have?* It was a wonderful story, and I thought it would be fun to illustrate it, so I said yes. I had no idea it would open up a whole new world for me.

"I planned on doing just the one book, but after it was published, people sent me more wonderful stories to illustrate, and the next thing I knew, all I was doing was illustrating books. And I was having a really good time! It was about then that I noticed I was drawing the same things I drew as a kid—pirates, knights,

Indians, and baseball players. I also started writing my own stories.

"A few years ago, my mother sent me a book I made when I was a little kid. It was called 'No, David!,' and it was illustrated with drawings of David doing all sorts of things he wasn't supposed to do. The text consisted entirely of the words 'no' and 'David.' (They were the only words I knew how to spell at the time.) I decided to make a new version of the story, only this time David's mom also says things like, 'Don't play with your food!' and 'Stop that this instant!' I tried to make the illustrations look like the ones in the original version because I thought they had a lot of personality. So now, not only was I drawing the same things I drew as a kid, I was drawing them the same way I drew as a kid. Life can be pretty weird sometimes.

Courtesy of Scholastic, Inc.

"So that's how I found out what, deep down, I knew all along. I love storytelling. And I'm really lucky that I get to do it for a living!"

The book that David Shannon re-created from his childhood masterpiece, *No, David!*, was named a 1999 Caldecott Honor Book. A sequel, *David Goes to School*, followed soon after. Shannon says he particularly enjoyed doing the illustrations for these books because, in keeping with their style and content, he could "color outside the lines."

David Shannon was born in Washington, D.C., and grew up in Spokane, Washington. He attended the Art Center College of Design in Pasadena, California, where he earned a B.F.A. in 1983. He then moved to New York City and began his career as an illustrator. His editorial illustrations have appeared in the *New York Times*, *Time* magazine, and *Rolling Stone*, and his artwork has appeared on a number of book jackets. Currently he lives in Los Angeles, California, with his wife and daughter.

Shannon tells his stories with vibrant, imaginative pictures. Working with acrylic paints, he creates characters and settings that both illustrate and expand the story being told. His artwork is richly colored, and the results can be funny, mischievous, ironic, sensational, spooky, serious, even epic. His first illustrated book, *How Many Spots Does a Leopard Have?*, was an ALA Notable Children's Book.

The Boy Who Lived with the Seals and *Sacred Places* were both named Notable Trade Books in the Field of Social Studies. *How Georgie Radbourn Saved Baseball* was chosen by the *New York Times* as one of the Ten Best Illustrated Books of 1994. *The Bunyans* was included in New York Public Library's list, 100 Titles for Reading and Sharing. *The Ballad of the Pirate Queens* was cited as an ALA Notable Children's Book and received a Blue Ribbon award from the *Bulletin of the Center for Children's Books. No, David!*, in addition to receiving the Caldecott Honor Award, was named an ALA Notable Children's Book, a *School Library Journal* Best Book of the Year, and a *Bulletin of the Center for Children's Books* Blue Ribbon title and was also included in New York Public Library's 100 Titles for Reading and Sharing.

SELECTED WORKS WRITTEN AND ILLUSTRATED: *How Georgie Radbourn Saved Baseball*, 1994; *The Amazing Christmas Extravaganza*, 1995; *A Bad Case of Stripes*, 1998; *No, David!*, 1998; *David Goes to School*, 1999.

SELECTED WORKS ILLUSTRATED: *How Many Spots Does a Leopard Have?*, by Julius Lester, 1989; *Encounter*, by Jane Yolen, 1992; *The Boy Who Lived with the Seals*, by Rafe Martin, 1993; *Gawain and the Green Knight*, by Mark Shannon, 1994; *The Ballad of the Pirate Queens*, by Jane Yolen, 1995; *The Bunyans*, by Audrey Wood, 1996; *Sacred Places*, by Jane Yolen, 1996; *Nicholas Pipe*, by Robert D. San Souci, 1997; *The Acrobat and the Angel*, by Mark Shannon, 1999.

SUGGESTED READING: Cummins, Julie, ed. *Children's Book Illustration and Design*, vol. 2, 1998; *Something About the Author*, vol. 107, 2000. Periodicals—Bolle, Sonja, "David Shannon: A Merry Prankster," *Publishers Weekly*, July 19, 1999.

Anne Shelby

September 25, 1948–

"Once long ago, in a small town in Kentucky, there lived a girl. The girl, whose name was Anne, lived in a soft green world of hills and creeks and trees, a world inhabited by gentle people who grew gardens, sang songs, and painted pictures. Sometimes the girl went to see her grandmother and grandfather on her father's side. They lived in a big old house in the country called the homeplace, where there were dozens of cousins to play with.

"Sometimes she went to see her grandmother and grandfather on her mother's side. They lived in a big old house in the country too. And they ran a country store, where there were many interesting things to see and do, and many interesting stories to hear.

"On Sundays the girl and her mother and father and sister got all cleaned up and went to church. At church they learned what to do—to love and care for other people and the earth. Sometimes after church there was a big potluck dinner, with tables spread under the trees. Everybody brought their favorite foods to share with everybody else. The girl liked the church and the potluck dinners. She liked her parents' house and her grandparents' houses. But she dreamed of a house of her own someday, with dogs and cats in the yard, a huge tree to climb, and a big swing on the front porch.

"Sometimes grownups asked the girl her name or how old she was. She knew the answers to those questions. But sometimes they asked her what she would be when she grew up. She did not know the answer to that. The girl's parents were teachers. She did not want to be a teacher. For a time she thought she would be a doctor. Then she fainted at the sight of blood. She thought she would be an interior decorator. But she did not really know what that was. She thought it would be pleasant to be a movie star. But she did not know how to get a job like that.

Courtesy of Anne Shelby

"The girl liked songs and poems and stories. She loved the ABCs. But she did not think about becoming a writer. She did not know any writers. She thought they must all be very rich men who lived very far away, in Hollywood, New York, England, or Spain. Sometimes the girl wanted to grow up, and sometimes she did not want to grow up. But of course she grew up anyway, whether she wanted to or not. The girl went to college and graduate school. She read many books and wrote many papers. She learned many interesting things. She learned that there were many writers who were women. She learned that there were many writers from Kentucky. And she thought that if she tried very, very hard, maybe she could be a writer, too. And so she began.

"The woman wrote poems and stories and plays. She wrote books for children. She wrote about the homeplace and the store and the potluck dinners. She wrote about what to do and about the someday house. She liked being a writer. And she liked living in a big old house in the country, with dogs and cats and trees in the yard and a big swing on the front porch.

"And she lived happy. Not ever after. Not all the time. But happy."

* * *

Anne Shelby was born in Berea, Kentucky. She spent her growing-up years in a number of small towns in eastern Kentucky. Her parents, Luther and Jessie Gabbard, were teachers in Jackson County. When her father took a job with the U.S. Department of Agriculture, the family moved to Burkesville and later to London, Kentucky, where Anne graduated from high school in 1966 as class valedictorian. She attended Kentucky Southern College in Louisville and received her B.A. in English from St. Andrews Presbyterian College in North Carolina in 1970.

After college she worked as a secretary, a junior high school English teacher, GED instructor, technical writer and editor, and editor of a literary quarterly of Appalachian writing and art. She earned an M.A. in English from the University of Kentucky in 1981 and began writing and publishing poetry, nonfiction, and children's books. Most of her writing comes from her own experiences.

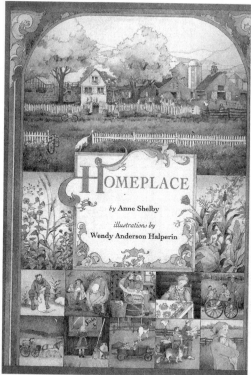

Courtesy of Orchard Books

Anne is married to a teacher, Edmund Shelby, and they have a son, Graham, who is also a writer. In addition to her writing, Anne performs folk tales from many cultures, specializing in stories from Kentucky.

We Keep a Store was an American Booksellers Association Pick of the Lists and was named a Notable Children's Trade Book in the Field of Social Studies. *Homeplace* was a Junior Library Guild selection, was chosen as one of *School Library Journal*'s Best Books of the Year, and was named to New York Public Library's annual list, 100 Titles for Reading and Sharing.

SELECTED WORKS: *We Keep a Store*, illus. by John Ward, 1990; *Potluck*, illus. by Irene Trivas, 1991; *What to Do About Pollution*, illus. by Irene Trivas, 1993; *Homeplace*, illus. by Wendy Anderson Halperin, 1995; *The Someday House*, illus. by Rosanne Litzinger, 1996.

SUGGESTED READING: *Contemporary Authors*, vol. 151, 1996; *Something About the Author*, vol. 85, 1996; *Something About the Author Autobiography Series*, vol. 26, 1998.

Courtesy of Bob Kaminski

Judy Sierra [signature]

Judy Sierra

June 8, 1945–

"I was born in Washington, D.C., and I grew up in Falls Church, Virginia. My father was a photographer and my mother was a librarian. Both of them loved books, music, and the theater. They read to me from a very early age and encouraged me to learn songs and poems. I am certain that my parents' fondness for T.S. Eliot, Lewis Carroll, Cole Porter, and Gilbert and Sullivan greatly influenced my writing.

"By the time I was six, I was creating stories, poems, songs and plays; my favorite toys were the typewriter and the tape recorder. I had my own puppet theater, and in the summer I would put on shows for the neighborhood. I was always writing plays and songs, and I wrote many of my school reports in rhyme, but I was only doing it for fun, and never dreamed my books would one day be published. In high school, I edited the literary magazine and drew cartoons for the school newspaper.

"I studied French literature at American University and planned to teach college, but I found that I needed a more creative profession. I worked for several years as a children's librarian, then set out on my own in a career that has included being a toy maker, a puppeteer, a storyteller, and now a writer. My first books were collections of tellable tales and of puppet plays for teachers and librarians.

"When I attended my first conference on writing for children, I heard a speech by the award-winning writer and illustrator Uri Shulevitz. He remarked that a picture book is a small theater for an adult and child to enjoy together. I had been a puppeteer and storyteller for ten years, and I thought to myself, 'I know a lot about small theaters and entertaining children. I think I'll write picture books.' My fourth attempt, *The Elephant's Wrestling Match*, was published by Lodestar Books in 1992.

"Some of my children's books are original poetry, while others are retellings of traditional oral tales. As a storyteller, I've always been fascinated by folktales: Why are the same stories told in far distant parts of the world, with so many variations? Why are folktales so much fun to tell and to improvise upon? Why do children love them so much? To answer these questions, I undertook graduate studies at UCLA, and received my Ph.D. in folklore and mythology studies in 1993.

"When I retell a folktale, I study the entire tradition of the source culture as thoroughly as I can, and I work with people from that culture to help me recapture the tale's spirit and meaning. Because traditional storytelling is nearly always participatory, I create texts that invite audience participation. All of my writing for children is meant to be read aloud. I'm very happy when parents tell me that they and their children have made up extra verses for my poems, or adapted my folktales to fit their way of seeing the world.

"Ideas for my poetry books come from looking at ordinary things in a new way. What if the house that *Jack* built was really the house that *Drac* built? What if penguins could talk and tell people about their lives? It takes an improbable but exciting idea to sustain me during the long writing process. I work on each poetry book for a year or more. Of course, I don't work on a particular book every day. I set a manuscript aside from time to time, so that I can see it with a fresh and critical eye.

"I now live in the San Francisco area with my husband, Bob Kaminski, a puppeteer and storyteller. We enjoy canoeing and hiking in the nearby mountains. We have a son, Chris, who is grown and lives in California."

Courtesy of Penguin Putnam

* * *

Judy Sierra always wanted to create her own books. Just writing them wasn't enough; she wanted to make the whole book. Today she actually publishes some of her own books. First she writes them, then edits and designs them on a computer, and finally she markets them herself. These books are published under the name of Folkprint. The most recent and most successful one is *Celtic Baby Names: Traditional First Names from Ireland, Scotland, Wales, Brittany, Cornwall & the Isle of Man*, published in 1997.

Sierra gets her ideas from everywhere—from friends, from reading, from going to new places. As a youngster, she hoped to travel and have lots of adventures when she grew up. She has traveled and actually lived in many places—Virginia, California, Massachusetts, Illinois, New Mexico, Switzerland, and Oregon. She likes the outdoors, especially in a canoe or when she's cross-country skiing, and she enjoys growing vegetables. She makes puppets, dolls, quilts, and clothes, and she plays in a traditional

Indonesian orchestra called a *gamelan*, made up mostly of bronze gongs and xylophones.

Sierra's book *The House That Drac Built* earned an IRA/CBC Children's Choice Award in 1995 and has been featured on PBS in the nationally syndicated *Storytime* series. In 1996 *Nursery Tales Around the World* was named an ALA Notable Children's Book and received the American Folklore Society's Aesop Award, as well as a Parents' Choice award. In the same year Sierra received a *Storytelling World* award for *Multicultural Folktales for the Feltboard and Readers' Theater*. In 1997, she won a *Storytelling World* award again for the second edition of *The Flannel Board Storytelling Book*. In 1998, Sierra received the Anne Izard Storytellers' Choice Award for *Storytellers' Research Guide: Folktales, Myths, and Legends*, and in 2000 *Tasty Baby Belly Buttons* was designated an ALA Notable Children's Book.

SELECTED WORKS WRITTEN: *The Flannel Board Storytelling Book*, 1987; 2nd ed., 1997; *Fantastic Theater: Puppets and Plays for Young Performers and Young Audiences*, 1991; *The Elephant's Wrestling Match*, illus. by Brian Pinkney, 1992; *The House That Drac Built*, illus. by Will Hillenbrand, 1995; *Wiley and the Hairy Man*, illus. by Brian Pinkney, 1996; *Storytellers' Research Guide: Folktales, Myths, and Legends*, 1996; *Counting Crocodiles*, illus. by Will Hillenbrand, 1997; *Antarctic Antics: A Book of Penguin Poems*, illus. by Jose Aruego and Ariane Dewey, 1998; *Tasty Baby Belly Buttons*, illus. by Meilo So, 1999; *The Dancing Pig*, illus. by Jesse Sweetwater, 1999; *The Beautiful Butterfly: A Folktale from Spain*, illus. by Victoria Chess, 2000.

SELECTED WORKS EDITED: *Cinderella* (The Oryx Multicultural Folktale series), 1992; *Nursery Tales Around the World*, illus. by Vitale Stefano, 1996; *Multicultural Folktales for the Feltboard and Readers' Theater*, 1996.

SUGGESTED READING: *Contemporary Authors*, vol. 128, 1990.

WEB SITE: *www.judysierra.com*

Erica Silverman

May 21, 1955–

"One of my earliest memories is reciting Mother Goose rhymes into a tape recorder with my father, thrilled to be getting such attention from him and delighted at the sound of my own voice and the delicious musical quality of the old poems. Nursery rhymes sparked my love of language. To this day, they influence my books—most obviously *The Halloween House*, which takes its structure from 'Over in the Meadow' and *On the Morn of Mayfest*, which is patterned after 'The House That Jack Built.'

"Folk and fairy tales nurtured my imagination. Life in those stories seemed exciting and romantic. I wanted to tromp loudly across the bridge and scare the troll, just like the biggest billy goat. I pretended to eat porridge like Goldilocks, even though I hated oatmeal. I imagined being tiny enough to sleep in a walnut shell. My grandmother read me a story about a gigantic turnip, and years later it inspired me to write *Big Pumpkin*.

"My grandmother was a profound influence on me in so many ways. My second picture book, *On Grandma's Roof*, is really a love song to her. She often told me about the little store she had before I was born and about the cat that lived there. That cat became the model for Shadow in *Mrs. Peachtree and the Eighth Avenue Cat*. I set the story one hundred years ago. While researching life back then, I discovered that women were not supposed to ride bicycles. People said it was unhealthy, dangerous, or unladylike. I knew that such prejudices wouldn't stop Mrs. Peachtree and so I wrote *Mrs. Peachtree's Bicycle*. When I wrote at the end of the story about not giving up, I realized I was talking about myself. It took persistence to get my first book published and, like Mrs. Peachtree, I sometimes felt like giving up. Persistence, too, I learned from my grandmother, who lived through very hard times and never lost her sense of humor.

"Two of my books—*Gittel's Hands* and *Raisel's Riddle*—celebrate life in the Jewish villages of Eastern Europe. This was where my grandmother grew up. Her apartment always had a feeling of the old country and she instilled the values of that culture in her family. Teachers have also been very important to me. My fourth-grade teacher praised my poems and stories. Two high school

Courtesy of Marilyn Sanders

Erica Silverman

English teachers and a college creative writing professor took my writing seriously. Accomplished children's book authors shared generously their knowledge of the craft of writing and gave me the honest feedback I needed to improve.

"For many years, I was a teacher. It was rewarding for me to nurture students as I had been nurtured. Although I don't teach now, I enjoy doing manuscript consultations, school visits, and speaking engagements. But I am always working on a book project. Writing, just like playing an instrument or excelling at sports, takes practice.

Courtesy of Farrar, Straus & Giroux

"As a child, I loved to play 'pretend' games. These days, I pretend to be my characters, to explore what they feel and how they might behave in different situations. I think about a story for months or even years. I write a first draft and then spend a long time rewriting. A picture book looks short and simple, but can take years to complete. Writing is hard but satisfying. When a reader tells me they enjoyed something I wrote, I feel very happy deep down inside."

* * *

Erica Silverman was born in Brooklyn and grew up in New York City. She attended the State University of New York at Albany but received her B.A. from the University of California at Los Angeles in 1982 and has been living in California ever since. In addition to writing books for children, she has been a Sunday School teacher, a health educator, a pre-school teacher, a teacher of English as a second language, a speaker, and a manuscript consultant. She is a member of the Society of Children's Book Writers and Illustrators, the YIVO Institute for Jewish Research, the National Yiddish Bookcenter, the National Writers Union, and the Southern California Council on Literature for Children and Young People.

Silverman credits both her grandmother, who told her humorous, ironic, and sometimes tragic stories of life in an Eastern European *shtetl*, and her father, who taught her about imagery, composition, and focus through his love of photography, with influencing how she writes. In *Gittel's Hands* Silverman recrafted the tale of "Rumpelstiltskin" into a Passover story, and in *Raisel's Riddle* she transformed "Cinderella" into Queen Esther, with the ball becoming the costumed celebration of Purim. Both these stories are set in Jewish villages in Poland, mirroring her grandmother's childhood memories.

Big Pumpkin, Silverman's retelling of the European folktale "The Turnip," was a Library of Congress Book of the Year and an IRA/CBC Children's Choice. *Don't Fidget a Feather* was an ALA Notable Children's Book and a Junior Library Guild selection, and won the California Young Readers Medal. *Big Pumpkin*, *Don't Fidget a Feather*, *Gittel's Hands*, *Mrs. Peachtree's Bicycle*, *On the Morn of Mayfest*, *Raisel's Riddle*, and *The Halloween House* have all been chosen for the ABA's Pick of the Lists. *The Halloween House* was an IRA/CBC Children's Choice and has been translated into Korean, French, German, and Dutch.

SELECTED WORKS: *Warm in Winter*, illus. by Michael J. Deraney, 1989; *On Grandma's Roof*, illus. by Deborah Kogan Ray, 1990; *Big Pumpkin*, illus. by S. D. Schindler, 1992; *Mrs. Peachtree and the Eighth Avenue Cat*, illus. by Ellen Beier, 1993; *Don't Fidget a Feather*, illus. by S. D. Schindler, 1994; *Fixing the Crack of Dawn*, illus. by Sandra Spiedel, 1994; *Mrs. Peachtree's Bicycle*, illus. by Ellen Beier, 1996; *Gittel's Hands*, illus. by Deborah N. Lattimore, 1996; *The Halloween House*, illus. by Jon Agee, 1997; *On the Morn of Mayfest*, illus. by Marla Frazee, 1998; *Raisel's Riddle*, illus. by Susan Gaber, 1999.

SUGGESTED READING: *Something About the Author*, vol. 78, 1994.

"'How do you pronounce your last name?' That is the most frequently asked question when people approach me. It is pronounced, soon-peet. 'What kind of name is that?' Well, my father is from Holland. 'Funny, you don't look Dutch.' Actually, I'm from South Korea.

"When I was six years old, my mother died of a brain hemorrhage. The following year my father was killed in an auto accident. That left me, my brother, and my four sisters orphans. Our orphanage tried to find us a family so that we would not be separated. But a year later, when I was eight, a family in Hawaii was willing to adopt the two youngest—me and my twelve-year-old sister. My teenaged brother and sisters were left to fend for themselves back in South Korea. That would be the last time I

Chris K. Soentpiet

(SOON-peet)

January 3, 1970–

would see them until I took on the illustration project of *Peace-bound Trains*.

"*Peacebound Trains* is my fourth book, published by Clarion. It is a survival story about a family's ordeal during the Korean War. When I was first approached about this project, I was a bit skeptical because my knowledge of Korea has faded since I left nineteen years ago. Nonetheless, my instinct said to agree.

"My first phase of illustrating is research. Extensive research. Of how the army men and tanks looked during the Korean War. How the Korean people dressed during that time, etc. I went to the Brooklyn Public Library and the Midtown Library in Manhattan. But the visual images were not enough for me to capture the reality of this historical event. So I went to the Korean embassy for help. They suggested I go to the Korean War Museum in South Korea.

Courtesy of Ted Lewin

"'South Korea,' I thought. Maybe I can go and research over there, and most importantly visit my brother and sisters with whom I had lost contact. I met up with my sister who was adopted with me. She lives in Oregon. We both agreed to meet in New York, and we flew to South Korea together. Suddenly, on the plane, all my memories of Korea and my Korean family flashed in front of me. When I got off the plane, I didn't know if I could recognize them. Suddenly I saw someone that resembled my birth mother. And she was crying. I knew that was my oldest sister. Behind her stood my brother and my other sisters. When they approached us, they bowed. I remembered laughing. So I just hugged them. The American way.

"To my surprise *Peacebound Trains* went on to win the 1996 gold medal at the Society of Illustrators in New York City.

"I didn't take drawing seriously until I was about seventeen years old in Portland, Oregon. My high school art teacher, Mr. Janson, encouraged me to draw and pursue a higher education specializing in the arts. During my senior year in high school, my class project was to work on five paintings. Unknown to me, Mr. Janson was taking slide photos of my paintings and sending them off to different art colleges throughout the United States. One of them was Pratt Institute in Brooklyn, New York. That is how I made my way to the Big Apple, which inspired me to write and illustrate my first book, *Around Town*.

"Along with Mr. Janson, I met several people who inspired me to become an illustrator. One is Caldecott honoree Ted Lewin. We met exercising at our local neighborhood gym, then started talking. I later showed him some of my artwork and he invited me to his home. Ted and his wife, Betsy Lewin, also a children's book illustrator and author, both supported and encouraged me to pursue children's book illustration.

"I am extremely blessed to be working passionately in a field I adore. My wife plays an active role in my work process. She performs general clerical duties, finds costumes, and most importantly, she's the one who keeps the children happy who come in to model for the characters in my books."

* * *

Born in Seoul, Korea, Chris Soentpiet was adopted, along with one of his sisters, by an American family living in Hawaii. A year later the family moved to Portland, Oregon, where Chris spent the rest of his childhood. He studied advertising, illustration, graphic design, and art education at the Pratt Institute in New York, receiving his B.F.A. in 1992. He married his wife, Rosanna, on May 22, 1995. They live in Flushing, N.Y.

Courtesy of Orchard Books

The luminous quality of Soentpiet's art creates an emotional impact in every book he illustrates. His meticulous research into historical time periods and events is evident in the books he has illustrated that have been named Notable Childen's Trade Books in the Field of Social Studies: *The Last Dragon, More Than Anything Else, Peacebound Trains, So Far from the Sea,* and *Something Beautiful. More Than Anything Else* and *Molly Bannaky* have both been designated as ALA Notable Children's Books and International Reading Association Books of the Year. *Peacebound Trains*, in addition to receiving a 1996 Society of Illustrators' Gold Medal, was named a *Smithsonian* magazine Notable Book and an International Reading Association Best Book of 1996.

SELECTED WORKS WRITTEN AND ILLUSTRATED: *Around Town*, 1994.

SELECTED WORKS ILLUSTRATED: *The Last Dragon*, by Susan Miiho Nunes, 1995; *More Than Anything Else*, by Marie Bradby, 1995; *Peacebound Trains*, by Haemi Balgassi, 1996; *Silver*

Packages, by Cynthia Rylant, 1997; *A Sign*, by George Ella Lyon, 1998; *So Far from the Sea*, by Eve Bunting, 1998; *Something Beautiful*, by Sharon Dennis Wyeth, 1998; *The Silence in the Mountains*, by Liz Rosenberg, 1999; *Molly Bannaky*, by Alice McGill, 1999; *Where Is Grandpa?* by T. A. Barron, 2000; *Momma, Where Are You From?*, 2000.

SUGGESTED READING: *Something About the Author*, vol. 97, 1998.

WEB SITE: *www.soentpiet.com*

Courtesy of Gary Spector

Javaka Steptoe

April 19, 1971–

"My mother's name is Stephanie Douglas. My father's name is John Steptoe. They were both artists and met in the lunchroom of Art and Design High School in New York. They started dating and not too long after that, my sister Bweela was born, and then me. I have two other siblings, my brother Orin, who is four years younger, and my sister Iman, who is nineteen years younger than me. Because my parents were separated, we moved around a lot—periodically going from the Bronx to Manhattan or the Bronx to Brooklyn, living with one parent, then the other.

"The creative ability of my parents influenced me greatly. Not just as artists, but as people. Through their artwork they taught me about life, creating the foundation of who I am today. My father started his children's book career in high school. I grew up watching him create these books and participated in his work as a model and, more importantly, as inspiration for his work. He used family members and people in the community in his books. We were the models and the characters in his stories. From his first book to his last, his artwork changed dramatically. Creating books was a means for him to grow as an artist and as a person. He was a great influence on my work ethic. I was taught to be accountable for the images I made, so that they will better represent the things in life I believe. He taught me I should do something I love for a living or I will never be happy. And that I should never let other people compromise my artwork. These are lessons that I try to incorporate in my life as well as my art.

Courtesy of Lee & Low Books, Inc.

"My mother likes to paint. She also uses collage in her work. She has never told me, but I think her favorite color is blue—a nice deep royal blue. She also loves clouds; they constantly show up in her work. It has a lot to do with spirituality. She has helped instill a sense of spirituality in me through her explorations. And because of her I love wheat bread and tofu. She has inspired me in more ways than I can count. I have seen her work progress, and I also know the sacrifices that she has made to make sure we had what we needed to grow and be healthy. I admire her strength and independence. I only hope that I measure up.

"Of all my brother and sisters, I was the one most interested in art. It was something I did every day and didn't really think about. I drew on everything in my possession—notebooks, school textbooks, flyers, candy wrappers, jeans . . . the list goes on. It's kind of funny, because that's what I get paid to do today. Cartoons and comic books took up a lot of my spare time, as well as reading science fiction, weird mystery stories, or books about sorcery, kings, and knights. They would motivate me to make up my own heroes and create stories that I would make into comic books.

"As an adult I find inspiration all over the place—from movies, conversations, current events, songs, or just looking at my surroundings. I carry a sketchpad with me all the time. It helps me keep a record of my life I can look back on and discover influences that have brought me where I am today. From there I can look to the future knowing the path I must walk. If you know who you are, you know where you need to go."

*   *   *

Javaka Steptoe entered the field of children's book illustration with *In Daddy's Arms I Am Tall: African Americans Celebrating Fathers*. Featuring thirteen poems by such authors as Angela Johnson and E. Ethelbert Miller, the volume is illustrated with collages that incorporate all kinds of materials—including buttons, coins, seashells, and sand. The original artworks, which took four years to produce, ranged in size from quite small to over ten feet wide. One of the entries in the book is "Seeds," a poem that Javaka Steptoe wrote in tribute to his late father, the children's book author and artist John Steptoe.

This debut work garnered critical praise and won several national honors. Steptoe received the 1998 Coretta Scott King Award for Illustration. In addition, the book was an ALA Notable Children's Book, received the Reading Magic Award from *Parenting* magazine, and was nominated for an NAACP Image Award in the category of Outstanding Children's Literary Work.

Like his parents, Javaka Steptoe attended the Art and Design High School. He is a graduate of Cooper Union in New York City. A resident of Brooklyn, he teaches art to children and continues working as an illustrator and fine artist.

SELECTED WORKS ILLUSTRATED: *In Daddy's Arms I Am Tall: African Americans Celebrating Fathers*, 1997; *Do You Know What I'll Do?*, by Charlotte Zolotow, 2000.

SUGGESTED READING: Bishop, Rudine Sims, "Following in Their Fathers' Paths," *The Horn Book*, March/April 1998.

A profile of John Steptoe, Javaka Steptoe's father, appears in *Fourth Book of Junior Authors and Illustrators* (1978).

Sarah Stewart

August 27, 1938–

"I was a skinny, nearsighted, and very shy child. Crowds of two overwhelmed me. When my mother would invite her bridge club to our house, I'd flee to my closet, armed with stuffed animals and favorite books, and stay there for hours.

"Besides the closet, there were two other safe places in my young life: our neighborhood library and my grandmother's garden. You wouldn't think that the two have much in common, but they do.

"Both a library and a garden are silent places, and I needed silence. From my earliest memory, there's been a committee of voices, my muses, carrying on serious, and sometimes silly, conversations in my head, so going to the library and daydreaming over a book was sheer bliss. And in my grandmother's garden—actually, gardens—I could dig in the earth or cut a bouquet or simply lie down between the rows and listen to the silence.

"Remembering those long afternoons spent looking up at the sky makes me think of another common vein running through the library and the garden. There is an order in each one—the systematic shelves of catalogued books, the regular rows of named vegetables and flowers—that calms me, reassures me. The chaos in my head, that ongoing conversation, is allowed to run its course without interruption.

"I carried a diary with me everywhere, even at a very young age, and, daydreaming in one of my safe places, I would write down my thoughts. They would read like gibberish today, but those early scribbles were the first tentative breaths of the writer's life I was to lead.

"And that statement takes me to hope: the third quality that the library and the gardens had in common for me as a girl. If you have ever finished a book and said to yourself, 'I can do that,' or 'I want to grow up and be just like that person,' then you understand my excitement, returning an armful of books to the library, anxious to check out more. And anyone who has ever planted seeds and watched them grow knows what I mean about the hope in gardens.

"And to this very day the library and the garden remain my favorite places. I have five gardens and an orchard in which I work, almost daily, from early May until the first frost. Then much of the late fall and winter is spent in my library, daydreaming and reading and writing, on the second floor of our home. Like a small animal in hibernation, I make a warm nest in the old wing

Courtesy of David Small

chair with my grandmother's quilt and the lamp and my beloved books. It is paradise.

"I don't own a computer. I know nothing about the Internet, e-mail, etc. I *do* own an ancient Olivetti typewriter and an extraordinary historic home. And, I'm married to a remarkable man who loves me just as I am. I am blessed indeed.

"Here are Sarah Stewart's Rules for Aspiring Writers:
1. Study Latin.
2. Read the great poetry written in your native language.
3. Find a quiet place and go there every day.

4. If there's no quiet place where you live, find that place *within* you for a few minutes each day.
5. Put your ambition into writing, never into making money."

* * *

Sarah Stewart was born in Corpus Christi and spent most of her early life in Texas. She attended Miss Porter's School in Farmington, Connecticut, and in English class fell in love with the poetry of William Blake, Emily Dickinson, and Walt Whitman. At Radcliffe, Austin College, and the University of Texas she studied Latin and philosophy, as well as engaging in Ph.D. studies in ethics at the University of Texas.

THE
Gardener
Sarah Stewart   Pictures by David Small
Courtesy of Farrar, Straus & Giroux

Stewart has held a variety of positions—she has been a teacher for Head Start and first grade, a copy editor for the *Texas Observer,* a speechwriter for a New York state politician, and an ombudsman for Syracuse University and the State University of New York at Fredonia. It was while working in Fredonia that she met her husband, David Small, who was an assistant professor in the art department. They were married in Kalamazoo, Michigan, where David had taken a position on the faculty at Kalamazoo College, and where Sarah has now taught courses in journal writing and "Ways of Seeing: The Use of the Arts in Everyday Life." The couple have five grown children between them, David having two and Sarah three from previous marriages.

Sarah Stewart is a lifelong diarist as well as a poet; more than a hundred of her poems have been published in academic and poetry journals and popular magazines. Her acclaimed children's books have all been illustrated by her husband, and each one represents a remarkably fine marriage of text and illustration. *The Money Tree* poses the question of what would happen if money grew on trees and concludes with the gentle message that money is less important than nature and the daily cycle of life. *The Library,* a witty rhymed text about Elizabeth Brown who wants nothing more than to read, was an ABBY Award Honor Book, an American Booksellers Association Pick of the Lists, a *Parenting* magazine Best Book of the Year, and a *New York Times* Outstanding Book of the Year. *The Gardener* was one of the most honored books of 1997, receiving a Caldecott Honor Award, a Christopher Award, and a first-place Juvenile Literary Award from the Friends of American Writers in Chicago. *The Gardener* appeared on most of the "best" lists of the year, was named an ALA Notable Children's Book, tied as first-place picture book for *Publishers Weekly*'s Cuffies, and received Vermont's 1998 Red Clover picture book award.

With the help of Amish neighbors, Sarah Stewart has restored the gardens, orchard, and grounds of the historic Michigan home on a bend of the St. Joseph River which she and her husband share with a dog named Simon and a cat (who is in charge) named Otis. They are currently working on another collaborative picture book.

SELECTED WORKS: (All illustrated by David Small) *The Money Tree*, 1991; *The Library*, 1995; *The Gardener*, 1997.

SUGGESTED READING: "A Gardener's Soul—A Loving Heart," *The School Librarian's Workshop*, April 1998; "Visual Links," *Book Links*, July 1997.

A profile of Sarah Stewart's husband, David Small, appeared in *Sixth Book of Junior Authors and Illustrators* (1989).

Janet Morgan Stoeke

April 30, 1957–

"**I** have had a lot of jobs. I've been a gymnastics instructor, a waitress, a baby photographer, a museum docent, a bookstore clerk, and an advertisement designer. While I was working at these jobs, I didn't think about being a children's book creator, because all along my goal was to paint. And I did paint, sometimes with happy results. The problem was, it didn't turn out to be a job. Like, when you get paid to do something. So I was doing the job, whatever it was, and painting. It worked for a while. I painted gymnasts and babies and copied the beautiful Degas at the Phillips Collection.

"Soon after I started working at the bookstore, I gravitated towards the children's section, and before long I was in charge of buying the stock. I saw some wonderful books and a lot of terrible books, some that treated children as though they were stupid, or not worth much trouble. I got very opinionated about 'my' book section. I cheered when a brilliant new book came in. And I complained loudly about having to stock copycat books with bad artwork, just because they would sell.

"Years later, when I became an ad designer, that seemed like a real job. I worked hard and spent long hours at the magazine. There wasn't much time to paint, but I did paint when I went on vacations with my family, a very artistic group of people. I was back from one of these vacations when my boss handed me an article about a children's book contest. It was almost like a dare, and I took it. I remembered an image from a recent dream: a chicken sitting on a windowsill. I tugged on the image, and pulled on the idea until Minerva (the name of the typeface I designed the book with) started to become a character. The deadline for the contest was only ten days after I had heard about it, so I was very rushed. I think that saved me from overworking the story, and throwing out my first sketches. They were all I had; I *had* to make them work!

"The chicken story was a hit. I won the contest, and have been thrilled with the chance to paint for a living! It has been terrific fun being the Mom of a famous chicken as well as three rambunctious boys who came a little later. I use my past job experiences more than I ever knew I would. It really helps to have known all those children that I photographed and taught back hip-circles to. I learned a lot about what was good or bad about books when I worked at the bookstore And there's nothing like seeing absolutely stunning artwork every day to learn what it is about: color and form that makes sense to your eyes. I'd never have guessed it then, but I've been heading here for a long time and I'm really happy to stay awhile."

Courtesy of Sandra Brennon

* * *

Janet Morgan Stoeke was born in Pittsfield, Massachusetts. She received her B.A. degree from Colgate University in 1979 and her M.F.A. degree in painting from George Washington University in 1987. She married Barrett Brooks in 1990, and is the mother of six-year-old twins Colin and Harrison and two-year-old Elliott. She speaks to local school groups about her life as an author/illustrator, and sometimes gets to paint things besides chickens with heavy black outlines (usually when she goes on vacation with her family).

Minerva Louise won first prize in the Dutton Picture Book Contest. *A Hat for Minerva Louise* was selected as a *Horn Book* Fanfare Picture Book, a *Parents* magazine Best Book of 1994, a *School Library Journal* Best Book of the Year, an ALA Notable Children's Book, and a Parents' Choice Silver Award winner of 1994, and was a PBS *Storytime* feature. *Minerva Louise at School* was chosen by the American Booksellers Association as a Pick of the Lists. *A Friend for Minerva Louise* won the Silver Medal from the Society of Illustrators for 1997. It also won the

Courtesy of Penguin Putnam

Parenting magazine Reading Magic Award and was on the *Children's Literature* Choice List for 1998.

SELECTED WORKS WRITTEN AND ILLUSTRATED: *Minerva Louise*, 1988; *Lawrence*, 1990; *A Hat for Minerva Louise*, 1992; *Minerva Louise at School*, 1996; *A Friend for Minerva Louise*, 1997; *One Little Puppy Dog*, 1998; *Five Little Kitty Cats*, 1998; *Rainy Day* (a Minerva Louise Board Book), 1999; *Hide and Seek* (a Minerva Louise Board Book), 1999.

SELECTED WORKS ILLUSTRATED: *Hunky Dory Ate It*, by Katie Evans, 1993; *Hunky Dory Found It*, by Katie Evans, 1994.

SUGGESTED READING: *Something About the Author*, vol. 90, 1997.

George Sullivan

August 11, 1927–

"When I speak to groups at schools or libraries, people always seem surprised when I tell them I've published over 150 books. To me, it doesn't seem like a big number. After all, I've been writing books for children and young adults for more than thirty years. Writing is more than a profession for me. I'm driven by it. Six days a week, I write for four or five hours beginning early in the morning, before five o'clock. I spend much of the rest of the day doing research, interviewing, or meeting with editors. (I do manage to play tennis two or three times a week.)

"When my wife, Midge, and I travel, you can be sure a book is involved. For example, we like to visit Key West in the winter. While there, I've researched several books about the great treasures to be found in the waters of the Keys. These include not only gold and silver coins and jewelry, but the structural remnants, shackles, and other artifacts from a seventeenth-century British slaver. My book *Slave Ship: The Story of the Henrietta Marie* resulted from that research. When I go to the West Coast, it's not to visit Disneyland but to take photographs of the Los Angeles Dodgers or the Oakland Raiders for a book that I'm working on.

Courtesy of Ann Hagen Griffith

George Sullivan

"Some people say you can live anywhere and be successful as a freelance writer, if you have a phone, fax, and computer. I don't think that's true. For me, living in New York City has been very important. I work with several different publishers and I speak with editors daily and see them frequently. (Some of them are my tennis partners.) I also take full advantage of the wonderful research facilities here. The excitement of the city and its great diversity help me to generate ideas for books. I'm sure I could write books if I lived in Keokuk, Iowa, or Nome, Alaska, but I don't think I could have accomplished all that I have as a writer if I lived somewhere other than New York City.

"From the first months I started freelancing in 1962, I was able to find markets for what I wanted to write. Fortunately, I had some experience writing. In the Navy from 1945 to 1948 I edited the Navy newspaper on Treasure Island in San Francisco. After college, I worked as a public relations manager for AMF, a manufacturer of golf, bowling, and tennis equipment. So the first books I wrote for kids were instruction books about sports. My agent at that time, Lurton Blassingame, steered me toward the children's book field.

"My books demanded specialized photographs, so I took courses in photography to be able to take the photos I needed. Through the years I've found other topics besides sports that trigger my curiosity and enthusiasm. In recent years, I've become more and more involved in photography, especially in making greater use of historic photographs. I've come to appreciate the photographic treasures in the Library of Congress, the National Portrait Gallery, and other such institutions. My books *Black Artists in Photography* and *Portraits of War: Civil War Photographers and Their Work* developed from this interest.

"When I was growing up, I always had some vague idea that I wanted to be a writer, but I never expected that I'd be writing nonfiction books for kids. It's made for an exciting life. I've stood on the deck of a work boat as divers returned from the ocean's depth with Spanish gold that had been on the ocean bottom for more than 300 years. I've been on private tours of the White House and seen where the President bowls and watches movies, and I've peeked into the Oval Office. (In the days before he moved in, President Clinton read my book *How the White House Really Works*.) I've taken photographs from the sidelines at the Super Bowl and chatted with players around the batting cage at Yankee Stadium before a World Series game.

"Writing nonfiction books for kids can be an exciting profession and I recommend it. But it helps to be a little bit obsessed with the topics you write about."

* * *

Born and raised in Massachusetts, George Sullivan has lived in New York City since moving there to attend college in 1949. He earned a B.S. from Fordham University in 1952 and then worked in public relations and publicity before beginning his freelance writing career in 1962. Sullivan is a member of PEN, the Authors Guild, and the American Society of Journalists & Authors. In addition to writing books for children and young adults, he is also a frequent contributor to children's and popular magazines, as well as to *The World Book Encyclopedia*.

Over the years, many of George Sullivan's books have been recognized for their excellence by the New York Public Library, the American Library Association, Bank Street College, and the Children's Book Council. *Slave Ship: The Story of the Henrietta Marie* was named a Best Book of 1994 by *Parents* magazine. *Mathew Brady, His Life and His Photographs* was named a Notable Children's Trade Book in the Field of Social Studies in 1995 and cited on the New York Public Library's list, 100 Titles for Reading and Sharing. A number of his books have been Junior Library Guild selections.

> *"Writing is more than a profession for me. I'm driven by it."*

SELECTED WORKS: *Treasure Hunt: The Sixteen-Year Search for the Lost Treasure Ship Atocha*, 1987; *How the White House Really Works*, 1988; *Great Lives: Sports*, 1988; *All About Baseball*, 1989; *All About Football*, 1990; *Mikhail Gorbachev*, 1990; *All About Basketball*, 1991; *Here Come the Monster Trucks*, 1992; *In-Line Skating: A Complete Guide for Beginners*, 1993; *Slave Ship: The Story of the Henrietta*

Marie, 1994; *Pitchers, Twenty-seven of Baseball's Greatest*, 1994; *Mathew Brady, His Life and His Photographs*, 1994; *Presidents at Play*, 1995; *Black Artists in Photography: 1840–1940*, 1996; *Portraits of War: Civil War Photographers and Their Work*, 1998; *All About Hockey*, 1998; *Burnin' Rubber: Behind the Scenes in Stock Car Racing*, 1998; *Snowboarding*, 1999; *100 Years in Photographs*, 1999; *To the Bottom of the Sea*, 1999.

SUGGESTED READING: *Contemporary Authors*, New Revision Series, vol. 44, 1994; *Something About the Author*, vol. 4, 1973; vol. 89, 1997; Wyatt, Flora, et. al. *Popular Nonfiction Authors for Children*, 1998.

Courtesy of Penguin Putnam

Simms Taback

(TAY-bak)

February 13, 1932–

"I grew up in a working class neighborhood in the Bronx made up mostly of socially aware Eastern European Jews who built their own cooperative housing project. It was like a Utopia for me, complete with a community center, science and sports clubs, art classes, and its own library. I also spent my summers at a progressive secular Jewish summer camp. In later years I would draw from this experience in creating *Joseph Had a Little Overcoat*.

"My mother was especially supportive of my artistic talent, and I attended the High School of Music and Art, graduating in 1950, and the Cooper Union, graduating in 1953. I began my career in the applied arts as a graphic designer at the *New York Times*, Columbia (CBS) Records, and as an art director at a pharmaceutical advertising agency. As a freelance illustrator, I shared a studio with fellow Cooper alumnus Reynold Ruffins for over thirty years. We were partners in a design/illustration office for seven years. Along with illustration assignments for major advertising clients, I illustrated posters for Scholastic's *Let's Find Out* magazine and editorial assignments for *Sesame Street* magazine. Many of these commissions garnered awards from the Society of Illustrators, Art Directors Club, and the American Institute of Graphic Arts.

"I produced my own line of greeting cards—designing, manufacturing, and wholesaling them to greeting card stores throughout the U.S. I designed and illustrated the first McDonald's

Happy Meal box in 1977. Over the years I have also illustrated about thirty-five picture books for children.

"My background in design has greatly influenced how I create a picture book. It's very important to me to control every element of the book, including layout, typography or lettering, and the visual narrative (how the story unfolds). I incorporate design elements, like collage, and often introduce novelty aspects like flaps and die-cuts. Though I experimented with several styles in my illustration work, I soon settled on a naive approach to making pictures. My interest and influences have been art created by children and "outsider art," the folk art of unschooled artists like the work of Reverend Harold Finster. I have been inspired by Paul Klee, Saul Steinberg, early animated films, and the circus figures of Alexander Calder.

"I don't remember any picture books when I was growing up, but I enjoyed reading Dr. Seuss to my own children and, of course, Sendak's classic *Where the Wild Things Are*. I was struck by the simple beauty of *Goodnight Moon* with its almost perfect integration of picture and text, and I have been inspired by Ezra Jack Keats's *Snowy Day* and the early books of Tomi Ungerer, whose *Emile* is one of my favorites.

"I have taught design and illustration at the School of Visual Arts and in the Master's Program at Syracuse University. I served as president of the Graphic Artists Guild and received its Lifetime Achievement Award in 1997."

Courtesy of Penguin Putnam

* * *

After graduating from Cooper Union in 1953, Simms Taback spent two years in the U.S. Army before starting his career in the arts. He worked as a graphic designer for various companies before starting his own freelance business. His first children's book was published in 1964; entitled *Jabberwocky and Other Frabjous Nonsense*, it contained illustrated poems of Lewis Carroll. His second book, *Please Share That Peanut!*, written by Sesyle Joslin, was named a *New York Times* Best Illustrated Book of 1965. Many more titles followed including riddle books, cookbooks, nonfiction, and easy readers. Several of these were cited as Children's Books of the Year by the American Institute of Graphic Arts: *There's Motion Everywhere* in 1970, *Joseph Had a Little Overcoat* in 1979, and *Laughing Together* in 1980. Taback has received the greatest accolades for his own adaptations of traditional folk stories and rhymes. *There Was an Old Lady Who Swallowed a Fly* was named a *New York Times* Best Illustrated Book in 1997, an ALA Notable Children's Book, and a Caldecott Honor Book in 1998. A revised edition of his earlier title, *Joseph Had a Little Overcoat*, received the Caldecott Award in 2000. Both of these titles incorporate die-cuts to reveal elements of the story on the next page. Both are based on folk songs and are illustrated with a childlike exuberance that perfectly matches the tone of the story. Bold colors, imaginative patterns, playful details, and a highly original use of mixed-media combine to make Taback's style truly unique. Simms Taback was married in 1980 to Gail Kuenstler, a writer. He has three grown children—Lisa, Jason, and Emily—and several grandchildren. The Tabacks make their home in rural New York State and spend the winter months in Florida.

SELECTED WORKS WRITTEN AND ILLUSTRATED: *Joseph Had a Little Overcoat*, 1977; *There Was an Old Lady Who Swallowed a Fly*, 1997; *Joseph Had a Little Overcoat*, rev. ed., 1999.

SELECTED WORKS ILLUSTRATED: *Jabberwocky and Other Frabjous Nonsense*, by Lewis Carroll, 1964, 1967; *Please Share That Peanut!*, by Sesyle Joslin, 1965; *Too Much Noise*, by Ann McGovern, 1967; *There's Motion Everywhere*, by John Travers Moore, 1970; *Euphonia and the Flood*, by Mary Calhoun, 1976; *Laughing Together: Giggles and Grins from Around the Globe*, by Barbara K. Walker, 1977; *Fishy Riddles*, by Katy Hall and Lisa Eisenberg, 1983; *Where Is My House?*, *Where Is My Dinner?*, *Where Is My Friend?*, by Harriet Ziefert, 1984; *Buggy Riddles*, by Katy Hall and Lisa Eisenberg, 1986; *Jason's Bus Ride*, by Harriet Ziefert, 1987; *Snakey Riddles*, by Katy Hall and Lisa Eisenberg, 1990; *Noisy Barn*, by Harriet Ziefert, 1990; *Zoo Parade*, by Harriet Ziefert, 1990; *The Book of Cards for Kids*, by Gail MacColl, 1992; *Road Builders*, by B. G. Hennessy, 1994; *Where Is My Baby?*, by Harriet Ziefert, 1994; *Sam's Wild West Show*, by Nancy Antle, 1995; *Who Said Moo?*, by Harriet Ziefert, 1996; *Two Little Witches: A Halloween Counting Story*, by Harriet Ziefert, 1996; *When I First Came to This Land*, retold by Harriet Ziefert, 1998.

SUGGESTED READING: *Something About the Author*, vol. 36, 1984; vol. 40, 1985; vol. 104, 1999; *Contemporary Authors*, vol. 171. Peridocals—Wilson, Gahan, "Perhaps She'll Die," *New York Times Book Review*, November 16, 1997.

"**B**efore I learned how to write I used to dictate my stories to my mother. She would type these rambling adventures onto leftover stationery from my father's office, and afterwards I would draw in the illustrations. She must have had enormous patience; the stories were long, and not very good. But I loved making them, and always felt proud when they were done.

"My favorite books growing up were *Where the Wild Things Are*, anything by Dr. Seuss or Bill Peet, and later, the Narnia books by C. S. Lewis. Somehow, I never considered writing and illustrating children's books as a possible career. But the career ideas I did have were all from the books I read. I wanted to be a cowboy or an Arctic explorer or a clipper ship captain. Practicality was never my strong suit.

"By the time I reached college I was thoroughly confused. I studied history because I was genuinely interested in it (nearly fifteen years after graduating from U.C.S.C. I'm still not sure what I can do with my degree). My best thought in 1986 was that I should see the world and gather up experiences for a possible writing career. After three months my money was gone and I was in New York City wondering what to do next.

"Luck was with me. I'd been drawing in a sketchbook to kill time in various cheap motels. Those drawings helped me land a job working in the (now defunct) display department at Barnes and Noble's corporate office in Manhattan. That job became the art training I'd never had. For two years I worked every day learning art and design techniques while essentially copying book jackets for display signs. And I became reacquainted with children's books, which I hadn't really looked at since I was a kid. In the intervening years a revolution of sorts had taken place. The one- and two-color line drawings I remembered from my childhood had been replaced by elaborate full-color artwork. I stared at books by Chris Van Allsburg and William Joyce and finally knew what I wanted to do. In a few months I had my first book written and illustrated. Luck was with me again. Scholastic was actually looking for promising new writers and illustrators. In 1989 they published *The Trouble with the Johnsons*. The book was a modest success and I was on my way.

Courtesy of Laura Teague

Mark Teague

(teeg)

February 10, 1963–

Courtesy of Scholastic, Inc.

"Ten years later I still can't believe my good fortune. My job is so enjoyable I really don't think of it as 'work' at all. And it's so goofy I can't take myself too seriously—which is a good thing in itself. Still, I've come to feel a deep sense of responsibility to the children who are my audience. I want to open doors for them in the same way they opened for me as a child reading all kinds of books, from *Green Eggs and Ham* to *A Wrinkle in Time*. Those early reading experiences ushered me into a vast world of literature and art, of ideas. My life would have been much poorer without them. It troubles me that so many children never fall in love with books, and that, as a result, so many adults no longer read at all. My goal as a writer and illustrator is to give children books they can fall in love with."

* * *

Born in La Mesa, California, Mark Teague is the son of John and Joan Teague. He received a B.A. from the University of California, Santa Cruz, in 1985. Having no definite plan for what he wanted to do after college, Teague drove to New York where he eventually found his way into writing and illustrating children's books. He married Laura Quinlan in 1988. They now live in Coxsackie, New York, a small town on the Hudson River.

Teague's picture books are characterized by an exuberance that is appealing to young children. *The Secret Shortcut* was a Junior Library Guild Selection and *Pigsty* was named to the Association of Booksellers for Children's annual Choices list in 1995. Teague supplied the illustrations for Dick King-Smith's *Three Terrible Trins*, which was designated an ALA Notable Children's Book in 1995. His illustrations for Cynthia Rylant's Poppleton series are perfectly in keeping with the character of the gentle hero of these easy reading books.

SELECTED WORKS WRITTEN AND ILLUSTRATED: *The Trouble with the Johnsons*, 1989; *Moog-Moog, Space Barber*, 1990; *Frog Medicine*, 1991; *Pigsty*, 1994; *How I Spent My Summer Vacation*, 1995; *The Secret Shortcut*, 1996; *The Lost and Found*, 1998.

SELECTED WORKS ILLUSTRATED: *The Iguana Brothers: A Tale of Two Lizards*, by Tony Johnston, 1995; *Flying Dragon Room*, by Audrey Wood, 1996; *Poppleton,* by Cynthia Rylant, 1997; *Poppleton Forever,* by Cynthia Rylant, 1998; *Sweet Dream Pie*, by Audrey Wood, 1998; *How Do Dinosaurs Say Goodnight?* by Jane Yolen, 2000.

SUGGESTED READING: *Contemporary Authors*, vol. 136, 1992; Cummins, Julie, ed. *Children's Book Illustration and Design*, vol. 2, 1998; *Something About the Author*, vol. 68, 1992; vol. 99, 1999.

Jane Resh Thomas

August 15, 1936–

"The second of four children, I grew up in Kalamazoo, Michigan, during the 1940s and 1950s, when women's choices were very limited. The only professional women I ever met in my youth were teachers and nurses; all of the others were homemakers. Had I understood that real people like me could read and write as their lifework, I always would have planned to study literature and become a writer, but such plans would have seemed as foolish as my intending to be a chimpanzee. So I studied nursing.

"One of the great joys in my life was literature. After a few years as an emergency room nurse, I returned to college and earned a master's degree in English literature. I had always written for my own pleasure, but not until my little boy was two years old did I hope I might publish stories for children. Even then I didn't realize my experience was worthy, and I could draw stories from the well of my own life, my own childhood in Michigan. I tried original fairy tales and fables, but only when I wrote a story about a girl fishing with her father, as I had done, was I able to interest an editor in my work. From that day to this one I have been mining my own life for stories.

"Even *Behind the Mask: The Life of Queen Elizabeth I*, a biography, is close to my bone. My younger sister and I used to play Queen Elizabeth when we were children. Once we dressed up our brother, Dick, in our outgrown baby bonnets and smocked dresses and introduced him to our cousin Betty. We had exchanged Dick, we said, for this new little sister, Elizabeth. When Betty went home for lunch she begged Aunt Mary to turn in Betty's baby brother, Dale, for a girl, as we had done. The main character of my novel, *The Princess in the Pigpen*, named Elizabeth, is the daughter of a nobleman in the ancient court of the first Queen Elizabeth. As I wrote that book, I wondered how the queen might have felt husbandless and childless, without equals in her realm, alone and lonely. And the great queen haunted me until I had spent five years studying her life and times, trying to tell the complicated story clearly enough for young people to understand.

"During those years of reading and writing, I became so emotionally involved with my subject that, when people asked what I was writing, I frequently said, with an unintentional slip of the tongue, 'the autobiography of Elizabeth I.' Once when a stranger on a plane asked where I was from, I mistakenly answered, 'England,' although at the time I had never left the United States except for a childhood vacation at a fishing camp in the wilds of Canada.

"The seed for my next book, *The Snoop*, was in a visit when I was ten at the farm of my grandmother's friend Wilma. I learned to play 'Chopsticks' on the piano in the barn. I found a dead baby rabbit and was scolded for trying to keep it. And I snooped. Wilma heard me in her bedroom. When she called up the stairs to see what I was doing, I tried to throw my voice across the hall to the bathroom as I thought the ventriloquists did, hoping to fool her. The trick didn't work. Wilma came upstairs and caught me snooping in her dresser drawers. That kind old lady didn't even scold me. Instead, she showed me all the rest of her drawers until my curiosity was satisfied, invited me to make an apple pie with her, and promised never to tell my grandmother. She never did.

"I have learned in nearly thirty years of writing that every book I pour myself into, whether it be fiction or nonfiction, deeply involves my own self—who I am, what I care about, the

Courtesy of Dominick Cermele

Jane Resh Thomas

people and places I know, and the events of my life. Rumpelstiltskin spun gold, not out of thin air, but out of straw, the most ordinary substance in the world. The Crane Wife wove her miraculous fabric from feathers she plucked from her own body. Like them, writers use the common stuff of themselves and their everyday experience to spin stories.

"Anyone who visits the imagined people and worlds in my books knows me better than my neighbor does."

* * *

Most of Jane Resh Thomas's childhood was spent in Kalamazoo, Michigan, at her grandparents' peach orchard and tree nursery near Lake Michigan, and at a cottage on Big Cedar Lake. She loved to explore the natural surroundings and to go fishing with her father. Thomas also loved the Washington Square Library with its stone entranceway, its fireplace, leaded windows, and books. Her mother always found time to read to her four children, and Jane learned to love literature at her side.

Jane Resh Thomas graduated from the Bronson School of Nursing in 1957 and attended Michigan State University in 1959–1960. She graduated summa cum laude from the University of Minnesota in 1967 and earned her M.A. there in 1971. She has one adult son, Jason. Her career has included working as a registered nurse, teaching English composition, and editing books for children and adults. She has been a writing instructor at the University of Minnesota's Split Rock Arts Program, the Loft, and private workshops. For more than twenty years she wrote the Children's Books column for the *Star Tribune* newspaper. She teaches on the faculty of the MFA program in Writing for Children at Vermont College in Montpelier.

"From that day to this one I have been mining my own life for stories."

Courage at Indian Deep earned a Parents' Choice Award for fiction in 1984. *Wheels* and *Fox in a Trap* were named American Booksellers Association Pick of the Lists in 1986 and 1987, respectively. In 1989 *Saying Good-bye to Grandma* earned the Joan Fassler Award and was an ALA Notable Children's Book. *Behind the Mask: The Life of Queen Elizabeth I* won the Minnesota Book Award and was named an ALA list Best Book for Young Adults. Jane Resh Thomas's books have also earned international recognition. *The Princess in the Pigpen* was a Children's Book Award runner-up in England in 1989, and *Lights on the River* was commended for the Américas Award of the Consortium of Latin American Studies Programs in 1994. Thomas's sensitivity and emotional realism continue to make her books appealing to readers.

SELECTED WORKS: *Elizabeth Catches a Fish*, illus. by Joseph Duffy, 1977; *The Comeback Dog*, illus. by Troy Howell, 1981; *Courage at Indian Deep*, 1984; *Wheels*, illus. by Emily

McCully, 1986; *Fox in a Trap*, illus. by Troy Howell, 1987; *Saying Good-bye to Grandma*, illus. by Marcia Sewall, 1988; *The Princess in the Pigpen*, 1989; *Lights on the River*, illus. by Michael Dooling, 1994; *Daddy Doesn't Have to Be a Giant Anymore*, illus. by Marcia Sewall, 1996; *Scaredy Dog*, illus. by Marilyn Mets, 1996; *Celebration!*, illus. by Raul Colon, 1997; *Behind the Mask: The Life of Queen Elizabeth I*, 1998; *The Snoop*, illus. by Ronald Himler, 1999.

SUGGESTED READING: *Contemporary Authors,* vol. 106, 1982; *Contemporary Authors*, New Revision Series, vol. 59, 1998; *Something About the Author,* vol. 38, 1985; vol. 90, 1997; Thomas, Jane Resh. "Across the Marsh" in *The Most Wonderful Books: Writers on Discovering the Pleasures of Reading*, edited by Michael Dorris and Emilie Buchwald, 1997. Periodicals—*Booklist*, August 1994; *Five Owls*, December 1994.

Courtesy of Steve Anderson

Joyce Carol Thomas

May 25, 1938–

"When I look back on the turns my life has taken, I find that words are always on stage or waiting in the wings. I began scribbling little poems before I started grade school. Later, my studies in college focused on language. I loved to hear the dips, the twists, the flips! of language. In all its beautiful shifting sounds. The language of Standard English. The cadence of foreign language. Mama language, which is what I call the playful and serious expressions I hear from elder Black women. Brother language, the car language of my six brothers, who could take a car apart and put it back together again in a matter of minutes, and brother language in the sports talk of my sons, who play at football and bicycle and fish. I celebrate the word in all its various glories.

"My travels have taken me to other countries: to Guadalajara, Mexico, to see if I could speak Spanish fluently and understand what the native speakers were saying. To Lagos, Nigeria, as a poet in the International Festival of Arts representing North America for the State Department. To Saipan to teach English to the Amariana Island educators so they could qualify for their teaching credentials. To Hong Kong, China, on vacation. To Rome,

Italy, to take my teenaged son, gifted at drawing, on a tour of Michelangelo's masterpieces. To Australia and New Zealand on a writing cruise, and to Ecuador, again on a writing excursion. In all these countries, I was enthralled by the exotic, shimmering dance of language. The world is a fascinating place, with many cultures, accents, foods, smells, colors. Today I sometimes travel to conferences where I meet other writers, to schools and universities where I talk with students, librarians, and teachers. I return home energized.

"Children, teenagers, family members, and people in general have always inspired me, and so I continued to write during my twenty-five years of teaching students (from middle school to university).

"I now write full-time at home in Berkeley, California. Here I see my children and grandchildren on a daily basis. Keeping the balance between family and creative work is an on-going series of life-affirming discoveries. I dedicate my books to my children and grandchildren and by extension to all children who live on this planet. The seventh angel, my newest grandchild, was born this summer, and I'm sure she'll have a book dedicated to her. The two older granddaughters are bound for college and grad school, and, I think (hope!), writing careers.

As a mother of four, I used to cook a lot. Big Thanksgiving, Christmas, birthday dinners for my family and friends. Now I find that my children and grandchildren are competent cooks who have discovered the special secret of food. They understand that mealtime can be a time of communicating, of sharing love in a careful preparation of the dishes. I'm delighted when one of them calls me to the welcome table. Nowadays I eat lots of fruits and vegetables. I sometimes include fish and poultry in my diet. The tasty presence of food is faithfully stirred with love someplace in every book I write.

> "When the words begin to dance in my mind, I pick up my pen and joyously join in."

"My writing day ordinarily includes exercise. A few years ago I would drive up to Inspiration Point and walk four miles. Now that I am older, my journey is shorter. I walk up to the Rose Garden and back, approximately two miles.

"I believe in listening to my body. If I'm tired, I take a nap. To handle stress, I meditate. I believe the body and the imagination dance best when in rhythm with each other. I'm a morning person, so my best work is done at dawn, while everyone else in the house is asleep. Some mornings only the birds are up, chirping outside my study window. Sometimes I write in my garden, near the waterfall between the corkscrew willow and the corkscrew birch trees. Sometimes I follow the sun from room to room. I like to bask in its light. In all these places, I search for spiritual space.

"Writing is a constant source of surprise. I wait for the muse to visit and stay awhile. When the words begin to dance in my mind, I pick up my pen and joyously join in."

* * *

Poet, novelist, and playwright Joyce Carol Thomas was born on May 25, 1938, in Ponca City, Oklahoma (the setting for several of her novels), and moved with her large family to Tracy, California, in the San Joaquin Valley when she was ten years old. A migrant farmworker through most of her childhood, she developed a deep love for the language and storytelling of her Mexican co-workers, as well as a profound regard for music and for the natural poetry of those who testified at church services. Thomas loved school, in spite of starting late most Septembers in order to finish the harvest, and went on to major in Spanish and French in college, working her way through as a telephone operator, then completing a master's degree at Stanford University. She taught foreign languages in public schools, then creative writing at various universities while working on her own manuscripts.

Throughout the 1970s Thomas wrote poetry and plays for adults, then entered the world of young adult literature with her first novel, *Marked by Fire*. A powerful, poetic tale about a young black woman, Abyssinia Jackson, growing up in Oklahoma, *Marked by Fire* won the American Book Award in 1982 and the National Book Award in 1983, was named an Outstanding Book of the Year by the *New York Times*, and was cited as an ALA Best Book for Young Adults. Three more novels, *Bright Shadow*, *The Golden Pasture*, and *Water Girl*, involve Abyssinia, her love, Carl Lee, and a child of that love, Amber. *Bright Shadow* was a 1984 Coretta Scott King Honor Book. *Brown Honey in Broomwheat Tea*, which *Booklist* said created a "tangible sense of place and family," was cited as a Notable Children's Trade Book in the Field of Social Studies and named a Coretta Scott King Honor Book. *I Have Heard of a Land*, illustrated by Floyd Cooper, was an ALA Notable Children's Book, a Coretta Scott King Honor Book, a Notable Trade Book in the Field of Social Studies, and an IRA Teachers' Choice.

SELECTED WORKS: As author—*Marked by Fire*, 1982; *Bright Shadow*, 1983; *The Golden Pasture*, 1986; *Water Girl*, 1986; *Journey*, 1988; *When the Nightingale Sings*, 1992; *Brown Honey in Broomwheat Tea*, illus. by Floyd Cooper, 1993; *Gingerbread Days*, illus. by Floyd Cooper, 1995; *Cherish Me*, 1998; *I Have Heard of a Land*, illus. by Floyd Cooper, 1998; *The Blacker the Berry: Poems*, illus. by Brenda Joysmith, 1999; *Crowning Glory: Poems*, illus. by Brenda Joysmith, 1999; *You Are My Perfect Baby*, illus. by Nneka Bennett, 1999. As editor—*A Gathering of Flowers: Stories About Being Young in America*, 1992.

SUGGESTED READING: *Authors and Artists for Young Adults*, vol. 12, 1994; *Children's Literature Review*, vol. 19, 1989; Collier, Laurie and Joyce Nakamura, eds. *Major Authors and Illustrators for Children and Young Adults*, 1995;

Courtesy of HarperCollins Publishers

Contemporary Authors, vol. 116, 1986; *Contemporary Authors*, New Revision Series, vol. 48, 1995; *Dictionary of Literary Biography*, vol. 33, 1984; Drew, Bernard A. *The 100 Most Popular Young Adult Authors*, 1st ed., rev., 1997; Gallo, Don, ed. *Speaking for Ourselves*, 1990; Hipple, Ted, ed. *Writers for Young Adults*, 1997; Nelson, Emmanuel S., ed. *Contemporary African American Novelists*, 1999; *Something About the Author*, vol. 40, 1985; vol. 78, 1994; *Something About the Author Autobiographical Series*, vol. 7, 1988. Periodicals—Henderson, Darwin L. and Anthony L. Manna, "Evoking the 'Holy and the Horrible': Conversations with Joyce Carol Thomas," *African American Review*, Spring 1998.

WEB SITE: *www.joycecarolthomas.com*

Rob Thomas

August 15, 1965–

"I've always wanted to be a writer, though the sort of writer I've aspired to be has changed several times. I told my junior high counselor that I was going to be a novelist, but that was when I was bright-eyed and naive. By the time I began college, I had relegated 'novelist' to pipe-dream status. I didn't know anyone making his living writing books. I did, on the other hand, know several working journalists, and I decided that's what I would become. At the time I was both a college football player and an aspiring rock musician. I alternately told people I was going to write for *Rolling Stone* and *Sports Illustrated*. (I'm still a magazine junkie. My friends joke that I've written more novels than I've read, but I'm a voracious reader—it's just that most of my reading is pop culture–related.)

"All of my journalistic aspirations ended the night of my twenty-first birthday. My rock band was on tour, and we were playing a club in Knoxville, Tennessee. Apparently the local college radio station and the club had been playing my band's self-released record quite a bit. I was on stage. Packed house. I looked out in the crowd, and the audience was singing along. Singing words I had written in my bedroom 1,500 miles away in Texas. They had these words memorized!

"I had an epiphany. My life goals changed on the spot. No one had ever memorized any of my journalistic pieces. I spent the next seven years of my life attempting to be Elvis Costello or Pete Townshend. My success in this endeavor can most accurately be summarized as 'limited.' I was having a great time, but I knew rock and roll wasn't taking me anywhere.

"That's why I quit playing . . . seven years later. My final show was on my twenty-eighth birthday. Left with no outlet for my surplus creative energy, I returned to my junior high ambition—to be a novelist. I began writing one page a day. Ten months later I completed the first draft of *Rats Saw God*. Apparently, I had built up a lot of karma in my nine years of beating my head against a wall playing rock music in front of Bob Seger–demanding softball teams, because once I completed *Rats*, things happened quickly. Within eight weeks I had an agent. In another twelve, I had a book deal. Over the next three years, I wrote three other novels and a collection of short stories. To make ends meet, I also ghosted several books under my dogs' names. My move into screenwriting stemmed directly from the books. Teenagers became very hot in Hollywood. The then co-president of Sony Entertainment read my first novel and asked whether I would be interested in writing for *My So-Called Life*. I was extremely interested. Unfortunately, the show didn't get picked up for a new season, and it was another year before he recommended me to the producers of *Dawson's Creek*. In the interim, I wrote my first screenplay, a romantic comedy called *Fortune Cookie*. The

Courtesy of Rob Thomas

screenplay became the genesis of *Cupid,* a show I created for ABC."

* * *

Rob Thomas was born in Sunnyside, Washington, and moved to Texas at the age of ten. He graduated from San Marcos High School in 1983 and received a B.A. in history from the University of Texas at Austin in 1987. He has since alternated between Texas and Los Angeles, working as a high school journalism teacher, as a musician, at Channel One—a news program for students— and as a staff writer for television's *Dawson's Creek.* He was the executive producer of *Cupid,* a show he created and wrote for the 1998–1999 television season, and he has written screenplays for a number of upcoming films. It was while working at Channel One that Thomas began his first novel for young adults, which was published by Simon and Schuster to great critical and popular acclaim.

Rats Saw God was named one of the top ten ALA Best Books for Young Adults in 1997 and was also selected for the Quick Picks list for reluctant readers. It was included on most of the "best" lists of 1997 as well as the 1997–1998 Texas TAYSHAS High School Recommended Reading List for Teens, and received the 1998–1999 South Carolina Young Adult Book Award. *Doing Time: Notes from the Undergrad* was also named a Best Book for Young Adults and a Quick Pick and was included on the New York Public Library's list of Books for the Teen Age. Thomas's newest book represents a departure from his realistic books for older teens. *Green Thumb* is a science fiction adventure story for middle grade readers in which the thirteen-year-old protagonist outwits bullies in his Los Angeles school, then takes on deadlier foes during a trip to the Amazon rain forest.

> *"Left with no outlet for my surplus creative energy, I returned to my junior high ambition—to be a novelist."*

SELECTED WORKS: *Rats Saw God,* 1996; *Slave Day,* 1997; *Doing Time: Notes from the Undergrad,* 1997; *Satellite Down,* 1998; *Green Thumb,* 1999.

SUGGESTED READING:*Authors and Artists for Young Adults,* vol. 25, 1998; *Contemporary Authors,* vol. 164, 1998; *Something About the Author,* vol. 97, 1998. Periodicals—Shoemaker, Joel, "Rats Saw Rob: An Interview with Rob Thomas," *Voice of Youth Advocates,* June 1997.

WEB SITE: *www.mediacomp.com/robt*

Courtesy of D. Brown

Valerie Tripp

September 12, 1951–

"I love reading and I love stories. My mother and father were both great readers. Our house was full of books and magazines and newspapers. I can remember my parents reading parts of stories and articles aloud to each other and they would laugh together. Even before I could read, my parents showed me what a pleasure reading could be.

"My father read aloud to my sisters and my brother and me at night, before we went to sleep. He'd stretch out on the bed, and we'd surround him as he read *Charlotte's Web*, *Madeline*, *Beezus and Ramona*, *The Secret Garden*, 'Cinderella' and hundreds of other wonderful stories. Sometimes he would get so caught up in the language and humor of the story he'd read chapter after chapter, forgetting to stop. We'd all keep still so he'd keep reading. Now when I read to my daughter the same stories he read to me, I remember how his low, slow voice sounded. He enjoyed the stories as much as we did.

"We were a big, noisy, rambunctious, rag-taggle bunch. We were always up to something, usually outdoors. In winter there was sledding or ice-skating, or making angels in the snow, as Molly and Jill do in *Molly's Surprise*. And in the summer we squirted each other with the hose, put on plays in our front yard, or went for bike rides. We enjoyed picnics like the one Josefina and her sisters have in *Josefina Learns a Lesson*. We had a lot of fun together. And we all spent a lot of time reading.

"I grew up in Mt. Kisco, New York, which is not far from New York City. Sometimes my whole family would go into the city to see a Broadway show, or go to a museum or a concert or the ballet. When I was writing *Happy Birthday, Samantha!*, I remembered the feeling of exhilaration of being in the busy, fast-moving, enormous city. I knew just how Samantha felt. Every summer, the whole family would pile into the station wagon and we'd set forth on a vacation to the ocean or the mountains, or to a lake or an historic place. I remember our trip to Williamsburg very well. I was ten, and my sisters and I went to an evening concert at the Governor's Palace. It was one of the most elegant evenings of my life, just as Felicity's dance lesson at the Palace in the story *Felicity's Surprise* is one of the most elegant evenings of her life.

"I liked school, especially reading. I was like Molly in that I loved the teachers, and always wanted to be the star of the school play, to write the best story, and to win the spelling bee. Also, unfortunately, just like Molly, I was terrible at multiplication! I used to feel awkward because I was always the tallest one in my class. And my hair never looked exactly the way I wanted it to, so I fussed with it, just as Molly fusses with her hair in *Changes for Molly*.

"When I went to college, I studied about how children learn and grow. I worked with young children every day. I used to ask them to tell me the stories of their lives, and I would write the stories down for them. Their stories were always partly true and partly made up. Now when I visit schools and talk to children I always say, 'Pay close attention to your hopes and daydreams. Remember your experiences—both real and imaginary. Everything that is happening to you right now and everything you are thinking about is important. You must be especially observant and thoughtful if you would like to be a writer, because your memories and your imagination will be your best source of ideas.'"

* * *

One of the first women to be admitted to Yale University, Valerie Tripp graduated with honors in 1973. After college she worked in publishing, first for Little, Brown, and Co. and later at Addison-Wesley, where she wrote educational materials.

In 1981 Tripp received her master of education degree from Harvard University, where she focused on writing for children and ways of teaching reading.

FELICITY LEARNS A LESSON

A SCHOOL STORY ~BOOK TWO~

THE AMERICAN GIRLS COLLECTION®

Courtesy of Pleasant Company

Since then she has helped develop educational materials for major publishers, including the Just One More Poem books for beginning readers. Several of these texts have been translated into Spanish and used in bilingual reading programs.

Valerie Tripp is best known for her contributions to the American Girls collection, a series that focuses on young women living during various periods in American history. So far, she has written about four girls: Molly, who lives during World War II; Samantha, who lives in the early 1900s in New York City; Felicity, who lives in Colonial Williamsburg, and Josefina, an Hispanic girl who lives in New Mexico in the 1820s.

Meet Molly was chosen as an IRA/CBC Children's Choice, and *Felicity Learns a Lesson* received a Recognition of Excellence in Juvenile Trade Books from the Chicago Women in Publishing. *Meet Josefina* received the Washington EdPress' Excellence in Print Gold Award and was nominated for the Colorado Children's Book Award in 1998. The Josefina books have all been translated into Spanish.

Valerie Tripp is married to Michael Petty, a teacher. They have a daughter, Katherine, and live in Silver Spring, Maryland.

SELECTED WORKS: *Meet Molly: An American Girl*, 1986; *Molly Learns a Lesson*, 1986; *Molly's Surprise: A Christmas Story*, 1986; *Happy Birthday, Molly!: A Springtime Story*, 1987; *Molly Saves the Day: A Summer Story*, 1987; *Changes for Molly: A Winter Story*, 1987; *Baby Koala Finds a Home*, 1987; *Happy Birthday, Samantha!: A Springtime Story*, 1987; *Samantha Saves the Day: A Summer Story*, 1988; *Changes for Samantha: A Winter Story*, 1988; *Actions Speak Louder than Words*, 1990; *Meet Felicity: An American Girl*, 1991; *Felicity Learns a Lesson: A School Story*, 1991; *Felicity's Surprise: A Christmas Story*, 1991; *Happy Birthday, Felicity!*, 1992; *Felicity Saves the Day*, 1992; *Changes for Felicity*, 1992; *Meet Josefina: An American Girl*, 1997; *Josefina Learns a Lesson: A School Story*, 1997; *Josefina's Surprise: A Christmas Story*, 1997; *Happy Birthday, Josefina!: A Springtime Story*, 1998; *Josefina Saves the Day: A Summer Story*, 1998; *Changes for Josefina: A Winter Story*, 1998.

SUGGESTED READING: *Contemporary Authors*, vol. 146, 1995; *Something About the Author*, vol. 78, 1994.

WEB SITE: *www.americangirl.com*

Eugene Trivizas

(tri-VEE-zahs)

September 8, 1946–

"I remember that as a child, every time that I'd been told a bedtime story or had finished reading a book, I found it difficult to part with its heroes. Instead I'd imagine myself striding over the window and leaping into the darkness in order to join them. At times I'd challenge to a duel the prince who had married Snow White and after having defeated him, I would rightfully take her for a walk in the woods. Or I would rush into the gloomy cave of the defeated dragon to treat his wounds and feed him candied cherries. And if the fancy took me, I'd sow pumpkin seeds which would grow into magic pumpkin plants, or I'd hide in the hold of pirate ships moments before they set sail for the seven seas.

"These stories made me realize that within every little thing as ordinary and insignificant as it may seem, waits a tale yet to be told. Orange juice straws, ice cream sticks, cherry pits, sugared almonds, blue balloons and shiny candy wrappings, burned-out matches, bubbles, sugar cubes and velvet ribbons—all and each one of them hide the promise of thousands of stories.

"*The Chimney Pirates* (the story of two pirates who on a New Year's Eve kidnap Santa and take his place) was not only the first story I wrote, but would also prove to be indirectly the reason for deciding to continue to write for children. Upon its publication in a magazine, it earned me my first fan mail: a letter from a young girl telling me that '. . . it's funny how the Chimney Pirates feel so familiar, as if they lay hidden in my imagination all along and have now suddenly awakened. . . .' I chanced upon this letter at a later time, when I was considering ceasing all literary activity and devoting myself to my law studies. Re-reading it made me realize how eagerly kids longed for these stories and freed me of any doubts.

"My next book was a novel about a girl who makes a snowman and begs him to promise that he will never, ever melt. The snowman, bound by his promise, decides to head for the North Pole. The journey is long and dangerous, but the snowman is determined to keep his promise.

"This snowman is the first of a series of heroes in my books whose main characteristic is their determination to challenge the restraints of their existence and dare the impossible. Sometimes they succeed, sometimes they fail. What matters is that they have tried. In *Ignatious and the Cat* a mouse, after eating the picture of a cat in a library, sets his mind upon eating a real cat—with comic consequences. In *Fruitopia* fruits refuse to become soft drinks or preserves. And in the play *The Dream of the Scarecrow*, the scarecrow refuses to scare the birds away and instead befriends them and attempts to learn to fly.

Courtesy of Myrto-Athena

Eugene Trivizas

"This is one aspect of myself. I must, however, confess to another. The child I was never had much interest in the way things actually work, what makes a car engine run or why the lights come on at the click of a switch. What truly fascinated me was a desire to comprehend that which marks some people as good and sane while others as evil or mad. Consequently I read law, specialized in criminal law and later became a criminologist.

"Often my various aspects tend to get in each other's way. A few years ago I was expected to forward to the British Home Office a report on a criminological research project. Due to a mix-up what I actually submitted was a manuscript of *The Tunnel-Dragon*, the story of a dragon with a huge mouth conveniently pretending to be a tunnel in order to gulp down trains.

"There is a third aspect of myself. My readers believe that I am an explorer living in the Island of Fireworks with my white elephant, my parrot, and a green invisible kangaroo. But this is another story. . . ."

*   *   *

Born on September 8, 1946, in Athens, Greece, Eugene Trivizas is the son of Nicolaos and Sophia Trivizas. He was educated at Athens University, receiving his LL.B. in 1969 and B.Sc. in 1973, then went to England to complete his LL.M. at the University of London in comparative criminal law and his Ph.D. at the London School of Economics and Political Science in 1979. He makes his home in London, where he is a barrister at law. He lectures in international and comparative criminology and serves as director of Criminal Justice Studies at the University of Reading, England, and is also a visiting professor in criminology and penology at Pantion University in Athens.

A popular and prolific author of books for children in Greece, he has produced more than a hundred books and has received over twenty national and international literary awards. Many of his books have been turned into plays, musicals, or operas, or have been adapted for television and radio. His play *The Dream of the Scarecrow* was on the International Board on Books for Young People's Honour List. His first book for children to be published in the English language was *The Three Little Wolves and the Big Bad Pig*, which was an ALA Notable Children's Book and a *School Library Journal* Best Book of the Year. This twist on the classic folktale has been translated into twelve languages and has been a best-selling picture book in the United States.

In 1997 Trivizas won the first stage of a legal battle against the Coca-Cola company to prevent them from registering *Fruitopia* as a trademark name for soft drinks in his native Greece. *Fruitopia* is a word that Trivizas has used as the overall title for a series of TV programs and comic-strip books composed for Greek children. His fourteenth Fruitopia book has just been published, but these volumes are not available in the United States. Currently Eugene Trivizas is working on having more of his work translated into English.

"What truly fascinated me was a desire to comprehend that which marks some people as good and sane while others as evil or mad."

SELECTED WORKS: Published in the United States—*The Three Little Wolves and the Big Bad Pig*, illus. by Helen Oxenbury, 1993.

SELECTED WORKS: Published in Greece— *Emmanuel's Amazing Circus*, 1984; *The Crocodile's Loose Tooth*, 1985; *The Island Without Any Cats*, 1985; *The Tunnel-Dragon That Ate Trains*, 1985; *Fruitopia: The Mystery of the Disappearing Greengrocer*, 1988; *Fruitopia: The Dreadful Fruit-Monster*, 1989; *Lisa and the Sunflower*, 1990; *Fruitopia: The Sneezing Tenor*, 1991; *The Magic Pillows*, 1992; *The Lucky Two-Leafed Clover*, 1994; *The Hundred Lost Umbrellas*, 1994; *Something for You*, 1997; *Never Tickle a Gorilla!*, 1998; *The Robbery of the Strawberry*, 1998; *Who Made Pipi in the Mississippi?*, 1999.

SUGGESTED READING: *Contemporary Authors*, vol. 150, 1996; Kanatsouli, M. *Humour in Children's Literature*, Publications Ekfrasi, Athens, 1993 (in Greek); Moudatsakis, T. "Greek Theatre for Children: The Case of Eugene Trivizas," in *A Theory of Drama*, Publications Kardamitsa, Athens, 1994 (in Greek); *Something About the Author*, vol. 84, 1996.

E-MAIL: *E.Trivizas@reading.ac.uk*

EUGENE TRIVIZAS   HELEN OXENBURY

The
Three Little Wolves
and the
Big Bad Pig

Courtesy of Simon & Schuster Children's Publishing Division

"My love affair with books began when I was small. My grandmother who raised me would read to me every day. I soon discovered that books were the world's best teachers and entertainers, and I harbored the wish to create my own stories. For a number of years, I channeled my writing efforts into professional educational books and journal articles. Then in the early 1990s I wrote the picture book manuscript for *Chinook!*, which was accepted by Tambourine Books.

"Because I teach children's literature courses at a university, people sometimes ask if my teaching helps me to be a better writer. After all, I teach my students about children's books— what makes some 'better' than others—and I have critiqued books for review journals. However, when I began writing my own books I discovered critiquing someone else's work is an entirely different process than creating your own stories. Perhaps I was simply too close to my own work, which made applying

Michael O. Tunnell

June 14, 1950–

what I thought I knew about quality literature difficult. In any case, I had a lot to learn about the creative process.

"Historical themes seem to have worked their way into most of my books so far. I especially like to write about 'little people' in history rather than the famous ones—May Pierstorff in my picture book *Mailing May*, for instance. Parcel post was brand new in 1914, and May's financially strapped parents saw the new postal regulations as a way to afford sending their five-year-old daughter to visit her grandmother—for 53 cents they mailed her! This may seem an insignificant bit of Americana to many people, but to me it is the marvelous story of ordinary people using creative means to solve a difficult problem. By the same token, I was privileged to run on to the story of Lillian 'Anne' Yamauchi Hori and her third-grade class, who were interned during World War II in the Japanese-American relocation camp at Topaz, Utah. These children and their young teacher appear by name in no history textbooks, yet they are the ones who experienced firsthand the fallout of decisions made by well-known personalities such as Franklin Delano Roosevelt. Their class diary, an intergral part of *The Children of Topaz*, helps us see and feel the effects of war hysteria and prejudice on a personal level.

Courtesy of Michael O. Tunnell

"The research for *The Children of Topaz* and *Mailing May* was extensive—a lot of library research and, more importantly, a lot of searching for primary source materials. The most rewarding part of historical research is locating and interviewing people who have direct connections to the story I'm trying to tell. In the case of *The Children of Topaz*, this meant finding students, now in their sixties, and finding their teacher too. A few of the boys surfaced (girls were harder to find because their names changed with marriage), as well as Mrs. Hori's husband. But after the book was published, I received a letter from Mae Yanagi, a little girl on the front row of the class photograph. At her request, I provided addresses for a few of her classmates; then she went to work finding the rest. In October 1996, we all met in Berkeley, California, for a Children of Topaz Reunion. Fifteen of those twenty-three Japanese-American students attended. It was one of the most moving experiences of my life.

Courtesy of William Morrow & Co., Inc.

"With *Mailing May*, the quest for firsthand experience took me on the steep and winding railroad on which May traveled in the U.S. Post Office mail car. I also found and interviewed May's son, and I located in the possession of another relative a two-page, typed account of May's adventure written by Leonard Mochel, the mail-car postal clerk in charge of May on that cold February day in 1914.

"Even for a ghost story like *School Spirits*, I spent plenty of time researching the setting—1958 in a small town. I used the town where I grew up in Alberta, Canada, as the model for Waskasoo City in the story, so I read pictorial histories of the place, plus books about the 1950s, in order to refresh my memory. At one point, I even had to find a locksmith who could explain the particulars about locks and keys, circa 1900. And I contacted Nabisco to find out if Oreos were around in 1958 because I didn't remember eating them. They actually were created in 1912.

"I enjoy trying my hand at the various genres and formats of literature. The economy required by the picture book format makes that sort of writing a challenge. Naturally, nonfiction books demand careful attention to factual detail, and it is a big challenge to write nonfiction with flair. The novel, however, I find the most challenging. Writing novels requires sustained imaginative output unlike picture or informational books. Creating and developing believable characters who are doing things worth reading about for 100 pages or more is a difficult yet extremely fulfilling business."

* * *

Michael O'Grady Tunnell was born in Texas but raised in Alberta, Canada, after being legally adopted by his maternal grandparents, Grady and Trudy Chupp. He received his B.A. from the University of Utah, an M.Ed. from Utah State, and his doctor of education degree from Brigham Young University, where he has now been a professor of children's literature since 1992. Tunnell taught at the elementary and secondary levels and was also a school library media coordinator before turning to university teaching in 1985. He and his wife, Glenna Maurine Henry, a librarian, have four children.

Tunnell has contributed chapters to various professional books and has published numerous articles in educational journals, as well as several stories in the children's magazines *Cricket* and *Spider*. He has made an extensive study of Lloyd Alexander's books and has published a highly readable guide to the Prydain Chronicles as well as a bio-bibliography of the author, written with James Jacobs. Jacobs was also his collaborator on a textbook for children's literature courses, first published in 1996 and entitled *Children's Literature, Briefly*.

Tunnell's first and third picture books—*Chinook!* and *Beauty and the Beastly Children*—were both American Booksellers Association Pick of the Lists. *The Children of Topaz* and *Mailing May* both won Parents' Choice Awards and were named Notable Trade Books in the Field of Social Studies and Notable Books in the Language Arts. *The Children of Topaz* was also cited as a Notable Book for a Global Society and was a Carter G. Woodson Honor Book. *Mailing May* was named an ALA Notable Children's Book, won a *Storytelling World* award, and was cited on the International Reading Association's Teachers' Choices list.

SELECTED WORKS: *Chinook!*, illus. by Barry Root, 1993; *The Joke's on George*, illus. by Kathy Osborn, 1993; *Beauty and the Beastly Children*, illus. by John Emil Cymerman, 1993; *The Children of Topaz: The Story of a Japanese-American Internment Camp Based on a Classroom Diary*, with George W. Chilcoat, 1996; *Mailing May*, illus. by Ted Rand, 1997; *School Spirits*, 1997; *Halloween Pie*, illus. by Kevin O'Malley, 1999.

SELECTED WORKS FOR ADULTS: *The Prydain Companion: A Reference Guide to Lloyd Alexander's Prydain Chronicles*, 1989; *Lloyd Alexander: A Bio-Bibliography*, with James S. Jacobs, 1991; *The Story of Ourselves: Teaching History Through Children's Literature*, ed. with Richard Ammon,

1993; *Children's Literature, Briefly,* with James S. Jacobs, 2nd ed., 2000.

SUGGESTED READING: *Something About the Author,* vol. 103, 1999. Periodicals—Robb, Laura, "Talking with . . . Michael O. Tunnell," *Book Links,* November 1998.

" At an early age, I got quite good at making up whopper tales. It helped me pass the time during endless drives cross-country from California to Canada to Alabama and every which way we went. Since my dad was an Air Force Colonel, we moved constantly. I used to joke that he robbed banks for a living so we never stayed in one place too long. Off and on, I lived with my grandparents in Alabama. I loved spending time there. I would sit out on the porch and listen to tales told by whoever happened to stop by and pay a visit. So writing stories came pretty naturally to me, I suspect.

"Before I went into first grade, I wrote backwards and read upside down. Back then, there was no name for this kind of disorder. I was just a little weird, that's all. So I went to a special private school for extra help. I can still write backwards and read upside down if I want to, but now find it a bit easier to do these things the 'correct' way. My grades were never much to brag about before I somehow got into college. The only high scores I consistently made were in art, English, and science. Guess what? Those were my favorite classes! So I paid attention and learned.

"From the time I could walk, I was dancing on my tippy toes. This was my favorite pastime, next to making up stories. I can still see myself dressed in my mama's clothes, prancing around my grandparents' living room and singing up a storm. I entertained anybody who was visiting that day and would gladly do it even when I wasn't asked to. My goal was to become the finest prima ballerina in the world.

"This might have happened if I hadn't done something really stupid my first year in college. By then I already had a weekly TV show featuring my dance company performing ballets for children. I was majoring in dance and hoped to go on to New York after that. But I did a dumb thing. The mountains around

Courtesy of David Metzger

Nancy Van Laan

November 18, 1939–

my college in Virginia were covered in snow. This called for getting the whole dorm outdoors and sliding down the big hill on trays from the cafeteria. It was great fun, until I went over a big bump. It broke the tail-end of my spine and kept me from dancing for the rest of the year.

Then, just before finals, I begged the school nurse to let me sleep in the infirmary so I could get a good night's sleep before my French exam. As I turned over to turn off the alarm clock the next morning, I somehow dislocated my neck. And you know, that nurse didn't believe me? She thought I was just making up another whopper to get excused from my test. Well, this incident, coupled with the damage I did during the tray slide episode, put an abrupt halt to any hope of a dance career. So I changed schools and majors, ending up in radio and television. After college, I did go on to New York, but worked with ABC as a network censor, not at Radio City Music Hall as a Rockette.

"Around this same time, I began to write plays, short stories, and poetry. My continued interest in the fine arts kept me busy, with classes in drawing and painting squeezed in at nights or on weekends. In my early twenties, I wrote my first picture book and also did the illustrations for it. It was about a worm who lived in Central Park and, oddly enough, could spin plaid silk. A number of publishers expressed interest, but nobody bought it. Looking at it now, I can see why they didn't. It wasn't very good.

"Years later, when my third child was in kindergarten, I wrote another book about a worm. This one did not spin silk at all. *The Big Fat Worm* got my foot in the door of a new, unexpected career. When I wrote this story, I was teaching English full-time at a small private boarding school in Pennsylvania. Having taught for over ten years, I was getting a little worn out, so I was happy when my editor suggested writing full-time.

"Working at home took some getting used to, and I had to do a lot of creative juggling with overdue bills until I learned how to keep a tight budget. My children were always telling me to get a *real* job. Other parents got all dressed up in the morning and went off to an office. I stayed home comfortably content in an old pair of jeans. To me, this was the best kind of job in the world.

"Working at home allows me to enjoy my cat and dog, take long walks, bike, kayak, and, most importantly, work any time of the day I feel like doing it. I have never been a disciplined writer who sits down at a certain time each day to work. When I get an idea, I get busy and don't stop until it is finished. I always write the story in longhand first. When it is finally in good shape, that is when I type it into my computer. Some stories write themselves. *Possum Come A-Knockin'* was completed in three days. Others take much longer. It took me three months just to come up with the last line of *Rainbow Crow*. Of course, the big collections, such as *In a Circle Long Ago* and *With a Whoop and*

> *"I have never been a disciplined writer who sits down at a certain time each day to work. When I get an idea, I get busy and don't stop until it is finished."*

a Holler took several years of research before a rough draft was begun.

"One of the nicest things about creating books for a living is not ever having to retire. I can keep doing this any time, any place, for as long as I like. I don't plan to stop until I run out of ideas. Sure hope that doesn't happen any time soon!"

* * *

Nancy Van Laan grew up listening to stories in her grandparents' Alabama home, so it is no surprise that she became a storyteller too. Van Laan enjoys making up her own stories as well as retelling stories that have been in native cultures for hundreds of generations. Her stories are full of sound effects, rhythmic verse, singsong conversation, tongue twisters, and riddles.

Van Laan was born in Baton Rouge, Louisiana, and lived in Canada, England, Alabama, California, Kansas, and New Jersey while growing up. She graduated from the University of Alabama in 1961 with a B.A. in radio and TV broadcasting. During this time she began writing short stories and television scripts, and later she studied art and painted murals in private homes and schools. She also taught drama to children and directed community theater. After earning an M.F.A. from the Mason Gross School of the Arts at Rutgers University, she wrote two plays that were produced in regional theaters throughout New Jersey and won the state's Best Play of the Year Award.

Van Laan has been living in eastern Pennsylvania since the late 1970s, when she became the head of the English Department at a private boarding school. In 1989 she left teaching to write children's books full-time. She has written more than twenty books, many of them retelling tales and legends from Native America, Latin America, Scotland, or the American South. *Possum Come A-Knockin'* was a Junior Library Guild selection and won a Parents' Choice Award. *In a Circle Long Ago* was an ALA Notable Children's Book as well as a Children's Book-of-the-Month Club selection in 1995. *Shingebiss* won a Pennsylvania Library Association Carolyn Field Honor Award. *So Say the Little Monkeys* was an American Booksellers Association Pick of the Lists and was also cited as a Blue Ribbon Book by the *Bulletin of the Center for Children's Books*. *With a Whoop and a Hol-*

Courtesy of Alfred A. Knopf Books

ler was named an ALA Notable Children's Book and a *Booklist Editors' Choice*. Both *Possum Come A-Knockin'* and *Rainbow Crow* received various state book awards, and *Rainbow Crow* was a *Reading Rainbow* selection.

SELECTED WORKS: *The Big Fat Worm*, 1987; *Rainbow Crow*, illus. by Beatriz Vidal, 1989; *Possum Come A-Knockin'*, illus. by George Booth, 1990; *A Mouse in My House*, illus. by Marjorie Priceman, 1990; *This Is the Hat*, illus. by Holly Meade, 1992; *People, People Everywhere*, illus. by Nadine Bernard Westcott, 1992; *Buffalo Dance: A Blackfoot Legend*, illus. by Beatriz Vidal, 1993; *The Tiny Tiny Boy and the Big Big Crow*, illus. by Marjorie Priceman, 1993; *In a Circle Long Ago: A Treasury of Native Lore from North America*, illus. by Lisa Desimini, 1995; *Mama Rocks, Papa Sings*, illus. by Roberta Smith, 1995; *La Boda: A Mexican Wedding Celebration*, illus. by Andrea Arroyo, 1996; *Shingebiss: An Ojibwe Legend*, illus. by Betsy Bowen, 1997; *Little Fish, Lost*, illus. by Jane Conteh-Morgan, 1998; *The Magic Bean Tree*, illus. by Beatriz Vidal, 1998; *With a Whoop and a Holler: A Bushel of Lore from Way Down South*, illus. by Scott Cook, 1998; *So Say the Little Monkeys*, illus. by Yumi Heo, 1998; *Moose Tales*, illus. by Amy Rusch, 1999; *When Winter Comes: A Lullaby*, illus. by Susan Gaber, 1999.

SUGGESTED READING: *Something About the Author*, vol. 105, 1999.

E-MAIL: *nvanlaan@aol.com*

Janice VanCleave

January 27, 1942–

"I was born in Houston, Texas, and spent most of my childhood there. But Houston was a much smaller city then. Our house was on a dirt road. Most of the roads in the area were dirt. There were many wooded areas and I, along with my younger twin brother and sister, spent hours climbing trees and catching toads, lizards, and turtles. One of my most memorable specimen collections was of turtles. I had managed to collect about twenty turtles of different sizes and species. At my mother's suggestion, I painted names on their shells with bright red fingernail polish. Thinking the turtles needed a bit of exercise, I turned them loose on the lawn. But, as often happened then, as well as now, I got interested in something else and forgot about the wandering turtles. By the time I returned, they were gone. Specks of red polish allowed me to later identify my lost specimens. My interest in living things led me to volunteer at a local hospital. My job was primarily washing lab equipment, but the technician spent lots of time explaining to me the different tests he performed.

"My memories of high school are not my best. I found school a bit boring. Later I realized my problem was lack of participation in school activities—clubs, band, etc. I attended summer school, which allowed me to graduate at the age of sixteen. I was too young to get a good job, so I entered college. I majored in science with the desire to become a medical laboratory technician. A year later I married and dropped out of college to become a homemaker. At twenty, and the mother of three children, I returned to college, majoring in science education. It was a good choice for me and I taught for twenty-six years.

"I was never content to just use a textbook in my classes and constantly searched for ideas to make topics fun. School budgets have always been small, so I redesigned many experiments in order to use inexpensive around-the-house supplies. These experiments took the science concept out of the formal laboratory setting and put it on a plane of everyday life. Over the years, I collected hundreds of ideas which I adapted for use in the different science courses I taught.

"While teaching high school physics and chemistry, I was asked by a local community college to design and present an after-school enrichment class for elementary children. This class was called 'The Magic of Science.' The college catalog describing the class was seen by a book publisher, and I was asked to write a book based on the content of the enrichment program. *Write a book? Who, me?*

"The first book offer came in 1983. I now have more than forty books in print and contracts for others. I continued to teach until 1992. Today I am a full-time writer and work on many different books at the same time. My day is spent reading about science and testing ways of performing an experiment so that it's fun and requires inexpensive household supplies. My office is filled with live specimens. In fact, recently one of the tobacco hornworms escaped. It was found a day later crawling out from beneath my desk with lots of dust bunnies attached to it. It doesn't sound like much has changed in my life since I started observing and discovering for myself as a child. The only major difference is that I spend many

Courtesy of Janice VanCleave

Janice VanCleave

more hours making observations and have many more specimen collections.

"My advice to my six grandchildren and to all children is to saturate your mind with as much knowledge as possible. You may or may not see the value now but store it all away for future use. Do get involved in school activities. I encourage everyone, young and old, to explore and appreciate the scientific wonders staged by God for our enjoyment."

* * *

Janice Pratt VanCleave received her B.S. from the University of Houston in 1962 and a master's degree from Stephen F. Austin State University in 1978. During her teaching career, she taught a variety of science courses for grades six through twelve in several states, as well as in Germany, and won the Phi Delta Kappa Outstanding Teacher Award in 1983.

Since the publication of her first book, *Teaching the Fun of Physics*, she has created several series of titles all designed to convince children that science is fun. These include Janice Van-Cleave's Science for Every Kid, which features astronomy, biology, math, geography and other subjects; Janice VanCleave's Spectactular Science Projects, which provides ideas and instructions for projects involving gravity, magnets, weather, etc.; the Play and Find Out series for younger children; and Janice Van-Cleave's A+ Projects for Young Adults. Her books have been translated into thirteen languages. *A+ Projects in Biology* and *A+ Projects in Chemistry* have been included in the New York Public Library's Books for the Teen Age.

Janice VanCleave is in demand as a public speaker, visiting classrooms, conducting staff development workshops for science teachers, and lecturing at corporations, such as IBM, that seek to form links between children and science. In 1997 she traveled to Antarctica to perform experiments as a representative of the University of Chicago's Center for Astrophysical Research (CARA). Children from classrooms around the world were invited to participate in this exploration via the Internet.

The author and her husband live in Riesel, Texas.

SELECTED WORKS: *Teaching the Fun of Physics*, 1987; [The following titles all begin with *Janice VanCleave's. . .*] *Chemistry for Every Kid*, 1989; *Astronomy for Every Kid*, 1991; *Math for Every Kid*, 1991; *Animals*, 1992; *200 Gooey, Slippery, Slimy, Weird and Fun Experiments*, 1992; *A+ Projects in Biology*, 1993; *Microscopes & Magnifying Lenses: Mind-Boggling Chemistry and Biology Experiments*, 1993; *Dinosaurs for Every Kid*, 1994; *201 Awesome, Magical, Bizarre & Incredible Experiments*, 1994; *Ecology for Every Kid*, 1995; *Play and Find Out About Science*, 1996; *Guide to*

"I was never content to just use a textbook in my classes and constantly searched for ideas to make topics fun."

the *Best Science Fair Projects*, 1996; *202 Oozing, Bubbling, Dripping & Bouncing Experiments*, 1996; *Play and Find Out About Nature*, 1997; *Science Experiment Sourcebook*, 1997; *Play and Find Out About the Human Body*, 1998; *Insects and Spiders*, 1998; *Play and Find Out About Bugs*, 1999; *203 Icy, Freezing, Frosty, Cool & Wild Experiments*, 1999; *Guide to More of the Best Science Fair Projects*, 2000.

SUGGESTED READING: *Contemporary Authors*, vol. 142, 1994; *Something About the Author*, vol. 75, 1994. Periodicals— Winarski, Diana, "The Magic of Janice VanCleave," *Teaching PreK–8*, February 1995.

WEB SITE: *members.aol.com/Janvancle/Index3.html*

"**I** was born in Baltimore, the second of ten children. I loved being big sister to so many trusting little ones. While my family was still small, my mother used to gather two or three of us together on her bed and tell us stories. I did the same with my little brothers and sisters and later with my son Ben. We have always loved stories in my family.

"I grew up in a wonderful place. There was a stream with salamanders and crayfish, a pond with frogs, fields full of grasshoppers and other creatures, and woods big enough to get lost in. I spent much of my childhood by myself in those quiet places. I especially loved the woods, and the stream that ran through it. When I was young, I decided to grow up to be an Indian. First I had to kiss my elbow and turn into a boy. I would join a peaceful tribe and live in the woods on nuts and berries and venison. We would sit around the campfire and tell stories. I had it all worked out.

"I loved to read. I could sit through chaos if I had a good book, and with all those kids around, I often did. I played lots of games like jacks and hopscotch and jump rope. I was trying to jump to 1,000 on my pogo stick when a neighbor told me to stop because I was making too much noise. There were long, warm summer evenings when the neighborhood kids met outside after dinner to play kick the can. Afterwards, everyone went to my house because we had the only TV.

Courtesy of Robin Pulver

Ellen Stoll Walsh

Ellen Stoll Walsh

September 2, 1942–

"By the time I was thirteen, I had eight younger sisters and brothers. My father died just after my baby brother was born. My mother left for work when I got home from school, and my sister and I were in charge. It wasn't easy taking on so much responsibility.

"My favorite subject in school was art. When I graduated from high school, I went to an art school in Baltimore, the Maryland Institute. I was going to be a painter. Actually, I was going to be a great painter. Instead I married an art historian and spent a lot of time in Europe studying other people's paintings.

"Just after the birth of our son, we began the first of thirteen summers on an archaeological dig in England at Bordesley Abbey. It was founded in 1138 by Cistercian monks and destroyed in 1538 by Henry VIII. I loved to dig. I even got to dig my own skeleton. I also drew finds, especially floor tiles decorated with coats of arms, among other things, and bits of fourteenth- and fifteenth-century stained glass.

"Bordesley Abbey sits in one of several connected meadows with sheep, a river, a stream and fish ponds. When Ben was little, we would explore the meadows hand in hand. There were ducks on the fish ponds and swans on the mill pond. We stood on the bridge over the stream and played 'Pooh sticks.' As he got older, Ben spent more and more of his time with his friends, but we never stopped taking walks together.

"I could sit through chaos if I had a good book, and with all those kids around, I often did."

"I began reading to Ben when he was very small. For his third birthday, he was given *Alexander and the Wind-up Mouse* by Leo Lionni. Halfway through reading it for the first time I realized that I wanted to write and illustrate children's books too. I started by studying other people's books. I am always learning. With each new book I learn how to write and illustrate all over again. Making books is never easy for me. I spend a year or more on each one. There are always problems to solve and decisions to make, choosing the right words or finding the right paper to make a flamingo. But I love making children's books, especially on days when everything goes right.

"It is fun meeting kids and teachers and librarians. Last year, I even got to do school visits in China. As a children's writer I never know what will happen next."

*   *   *

Ellen Stoll Walsh's trademark cut-paper collages and colored ink drawings are striking in their simplicity. Her cut-paper mice, frogs, alligators, flamingos, and salamanders delight children while teaching them about colors, counting, jealousy, childhood fears, finding courage, and fitting in while remaining unique. Walsh balances her vibrant, full-color illustrations with sparse text against a white background, producing an appealing and captivating world for both children and the adults who read to them.

Ellen Stoll Walsh earned a B.F.A. in 1964 from the Maryland Institute of Art and then took courses at the University of Minnesota in the late 1960s. Extensive travel and archaeology work continue to inform her creativity. Walsh's artistic contributions were recognized in 1980 when she won both the Merit Award from the Art Directors Club at its 59th Annual Exhibition and an Award of Excellence from the American Institute of Graphic Arts for *Brunus and the New Bear*.

Theodore All Grown Up was an IRA/CBC Children's Choice Book. Both *Hop Jump* and *Mouse Count* were named ALA Notable Children's Books. *Mouse Paint* was an IRA/CBC Children's Choice Book, named by both *Redbook* and *Parenting* magazine as one of the Ten Best Picture Books of 1989, and chosen as an American Booksellers Association Pick of the Lists. *Mouse Paint*, *Mouse Count*, and *For Pete's Sake* have all been selected for New York Public Library's annual list, 100 Titles for Reading and Sharing. *Pip's Magic* was also an ABA Pick of the Lists. Walsh was the Ezra Jack Keats Fellow at the Kerlan Collection, University of Minnesota, in 1986. A number of her books have been translated into other languages, including Spanish, French, Dutch, Swedish, Japanese, Africaans, and Xhosa.

SELECTED WORKS WRITTEN AND ILLUSTRATED: *Brunus and the New Bear*, 1979; *Theodore All Grown Up*, 1981; *Mouse Paint*, 1989; *Mouse Count*, 1991; *You Silly Goose*, 1992; *Hop Jump*, 1993; *Pip's Magic*, 1994; *Samantha*, 1996; *Jack's Tale*, 1997; *For Pete's Sake*, 1998; *Mouse Magic*, 2000.

SUGGESTED READING: *Contemporary Authors*, vol. 104, 1982; Cummins, Julie, ed. *Children's Book Illustration and Design*, 1992; *Something About the Author*, vol. 49, 1987; vol. 99, 1999.

Kate Waters

September 4, 1951–

"I was born in Rochester, New York, in 1951 and grew up in many towns in New England in a very large family. I am the oldest of six children. My three brothers and two sisters and I were, and are, very close. When I was young, the two most important things in my life were books and our dress-up box. Books gave me privacy. The first time I heard my mother say, 'Hush. Leave Katie alone. She's reading,' I realized that reading would not only take me to other worlds and into other lives, it would also give me some peace and quiet for a few minutes!

"Our dress-up box was filled with lacy dresses, fancy hats, old ties and coats, and pieces of cloth that we made into turbans and masks and capes. We had enough children in our family to put on plays with many characters. The six Waters children spent a lot of time making up stories about people who lived in other times and places.

"My mother read to us every day. She made the magic worlds of Narnia and the Borrowers come alive. We were also often packed up for outings to New England mountains or the ocean. I learned about storytelling from my father, a children's heart doctor, who explained the constellations, the causes of fog and dew, how sap changes into maple syrup, and what a starfish is.

"I started writing stories and poems and keeping a diary in second grade. I think it helps all writers to keep a journal, to keep track of the questions and the wonderings they have, and to experiment with words.

"In high school, I acted in quite a few plays and played field hockey. In college, I studied the medieval world, especially early poetry about knights and ladies and monsters. After college I decided to go to graduate school to learn to be a librarian. I was following the example of my great Aunt Esther who worked at the New York Public Library.

"I was a children's and young adult librarian at the Boston Public Library for ten years. I learned what books people liked to read and what kinds of illustrations people liked to look at in books. I loved acting out books with children during story hours and giving booktalks to get children excited about my favorite books. Eventually I moved to New York City. While I was working on a children's magazine, I began thinking about a new way to celebrate Thanksgiving. I remembered visiting Plimoth Plantation when I lived in Boston and suggested that we take photographs there for an article about how the early settlers really lived. That was how my first book, *Sarah Morton's Day*, began.

Courtesy of Marjory Pressler

Kate Waters

"Making books involves many people. I have an editor who shares my belief that telling stories in the first person and using photographs helps people understand history. People at the museums where the photographs for my books have been taken are extremely helpful. They even make special clothes for the actors who play the parts of the children!

"My writing process involves about six months of research and two months of writing a first draft. I read all the primary source material I can find. I try to answer the questions: What was life like then? What were the child's hopes and dreams? How was this child like children today? When the story is finished, after several revisions, I make a list of the photographs we need to take. Then the photographer and I spend about one week at the museum working with the actors. For *The Story of the White House*, I collected photographs of the White House that had already been taken. And for *Lion Dancer*, the family was a real family, not actors.

"My big family has gotten even bigger in the last ten years. I now have twelve nieces and nephews to read to and take on journeys to see special places. We all trade books back and forth, sharing our favorites.

"I love writing. It combines the things that were so important to me growing up—storytelling and immersing myself in another time and place. I learn about writing from reading, reading, reading and practice, practice, practice."

* * *

Kate Waters tasted the delights of travel and exploration early in life. With her parents, Richard and Mary Ellen Waters, and a growing number of brothers and sisters, she moved all around the Northeast, living in Maryland, Connecticut, and New Hampshire. She spent her college years in Boston, graduating from Newton College of the Sacred Heart in 1973 and the Simmons College Graduate School of Library and Information Science in 1975, then became a children's librarian at the Boston Public Library for eleven years.

Moving to New York in 1986, Waters went to work for the Scholastic publishing company, using her knowledge of children's literature and its use in the classroom to become the editor of *Scholastic News* for the primary grades. She continues to work as an editor for Scho-

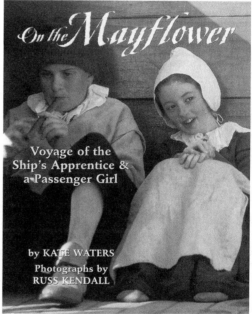

Courtesy of Scholastic, Inc.

lastic at present, editing nonfiction books for children. She usually works on her own books very early in the morning at a huge desk in her study.

Kate Waters's books on life in early America present a unique blend of a child's narrative with Russ Kendall's crisp photographs of authentically costumed participants at historic restoration sites. The result is a realistic look at a particular period in American history from the perspective of a child living in that time. *Sarah Morton's Day* was named an IRA Teachers' Choice in 1989. *Sarah Morton's Day* and *Tapenum's Day* were both designated Notable Children's Trade Books in the Field of Social

Studies. *Samuel Eaton's Day* and *On the Mayflower* were both cited as American Booksellers Association Pick of the Lists.

SELECTED WORKS: *Sarah Morton's Day: A Day in the Life of a Pilgrim Girl*, photos by Russ Kendall, 1989; *Lion Dancer: Ernie Wan's Chinese New Year*, with Madeline Slovenz-Low, photos by Martha Cooper, 1990; *The Story of the White House*, 1992; *Samuel Eaton's Day: A Day in the Life of a Pilgrim Boy*, photos by Russ Kendall, 1993; *On the Mayflower: The Voyage of the Ship's Apprentice and a Passenger Girl*, photos by Russ Kendall, 1996; *Tapenum's Day: A Wampanoag Boy in Pilgrim Times*, photos by Russ Kendall, 1996; *Mary Geddy's Day: A Colonial Girl in Williamsburg*, photos by Russ Kendall, 1999.

Courtesy of Joseph Whelan

Gloria Whelan

November 23, 1923–

"Many of my books take place in the summer; that's because I do a lot of my writing during northern Michigan blizzards. While the snow and sleet are beating against my window, I'm safe inside, lost in a world of sun and green grass, all of my own making. I tell children that one of the perks of being an author is that all the while you are writing your book, you can be anyone and anyplace you wish. Would you like to live in the days of the pioneers? Race sled dogs in Alaska? Sail across the China Sea? Live on Mackinac Island in 1812? You can. Just write a book about it. That's what I did.

"Telling stories has been a part of my life as long as I can remember. Before I could read or write, I used to dictate stories to my babysitter, who would type them out. The stories were always about a brother or sister. Since I was an only child, I must have learned early in life how imagination can fulfill wishes. When I was about nine I had an illness that kept me in bed for a whole year. I missed two semesters of school. The window in my bedroom looked out onto a red brick wall. The only way I could escape that bedroom and that red brick wall was to use my imagination. I made up stories in my head, and the bedroom and wall disappeared.

"But you need something besides your imagination. You must have convincing details. Poet Marianne Moore once said that you can write about imaginary gardens, but they must have real toads in them. My real toad is often the wonderful world of nature.

"Several years ago my husband and I moved north from Detroit to settle by a little lake in the woods. When I turn away from my work (and I often do) to look out of my study window, I see Canada geese and ducks on our lake. Early in the morning, or in the evening, a beaver swims by, a branch from one of our trees in its mouth. I see deer in the lake. (Deer have fleas and the cold water helps the itching.) There is even a pair of eagles that fish our lake (and sometimes help themselves to an occasional duckling).

"When I walk to our mail box in the afternoon, I walk a half-mile through the woods. Although I have walked that mile hundreds of times, I never walk it without seeing something new and interesting. Once I saw hundreds of sleepy bees hanging onto spikes of goldenrod. I like to wander in the woods, or like Thoreau, down the middle of a stream. What I see finds its way into my books. They are my real toads.

"I've never forgotten the books I read when I was young. They were as much a part of my childhood as my family and my home. Some of them changed my life. Every time I take up a pencil I think hard about that and about the responsibility of writing for young people."

✳ ✳ ✳

Gloria Whelan was born in Detroit and attended the University of Michigan. After obtaining a master's degree in social work, she was employed with the Minneapolis Family and Children's Service and the Children's Center of Wayne County, Michigan. She has also taught American literature at Michigan's Spring Arbor College. She has written an adult novel and her short stories have appeared in the *Michigan Quarterly*, the *Ontario Review*, and several anthologies.

Whelan's titles have been nominated for children's choice awards in Indiana, Florida, Texas, Georgia, and Iowa. *Hannah* was named an International Reading Association Teachers' Choice and a Notable Children's Trade Book in the Field of Social Studies. *A Clearing in the Forest* won the Friends of American Writers Award. *Night of the Full Moon* received the Society of Midland Authors Book Award. *Goodbye, Vietnam* was an IRA Teachers' Choice, an American Booksellers Association Pick of the Lists, an ALA Quick Pick for Reluctant Young Adult Readers and a *Bulletin of the Center for Children's Books* Blue Ribbon title. *The Secret Keeper* was nominated for the Edgar Allan Poe Award for best young adult mystery.

In 1998, Gloria Whelan was named Michigan Author of the Year. The parents of two children, she and her physician husband have lived in Mancelona, Michigan, since 1973.

SELECTED WORKS: *A Clearing in the Forest*, 1978; *A Time to Keep Silent*, 1979; *The Secret Keeper*, 1990; *Hannah*, 1991; *Goodbye, Vietnam*, 1992; *Night of the Full Moon*, 1993; *Once on This Island*, 1995; *The Indian School*, 1996; *The Pathless Woods*, 1998; *Farewell to the Island*, 1998; *Homeless Bird*, 2000.

SUGGESTED READING: *Contemporary Authors*, vol. 101, 1981; *Something About the Author*, vol. 85, 1996.

Courtersy of Scholastic, Inc.

Walter Wick

February 23, 1953–

"**M**y mother says that when I was a child, I walked with a bounce. This must be true because I remember having a very happy childhood. I grew up in a rural part of Connecticut with three older brothers and a younger sister. We loved exploring the nearby woods. Sometimes I would find objects I could use for homemade projects. I walked the neighborhood on stilts I made from tree limbs. I made them for other kids too. I also made skateboards out of old roller skates that I took apart and fastened to pieces of plywood. I loved to tinker and build.

"My father had a lot of junk in the basement that my mother was always embarrassed about, but it was there for the taking. I made a pogo stick from a large spring I found there. It would have worked, but I couldn't make it strong enough to support me. I also made a unicycle out of an old tricycle, and that did work.

"My first serious interest in art began with drawing and painting in high school. It was then that my brother Robert, who worked part-time in a camera store, introduced me to the magic of photography.

"I studied photography at Paier College of Art in Hamden, Connecticut. I could have chosen to study drawing and painting, but I was lured by the gadgetry of cameras and the promise of long walks through the woods in search of the perfect landscape. After graduating in 1973, I worked as a lab technician and assistant to a commercial photographer in Hartford. Besides film processing, my responsibilities included copying old photos and photographing tools and hardware for manufacturers. Most of the objects were not very interesting to look at, but I was fascinated with the technical challenges of making the shiny surfaces, shadows, and highlights look exactly right in the photographs.

"In my free time, I began to experiment with photographic puzzles. With a camera clamped to a rafter, I took an overall view of the studio, enlarged the photograph, and cut it into small squares. (Over the course of a year I sent the pieces, a few at a time, to a friend. Eventually my friend realized the squares were related, and reassembled the original photograph.) For another experiment, I photographed a street scene at night, and then the exact same scene in daylight. I then spliced the two scenes together merging different events into one picture. I have always been drawn to this kind of playful manipulation of the photographic image.

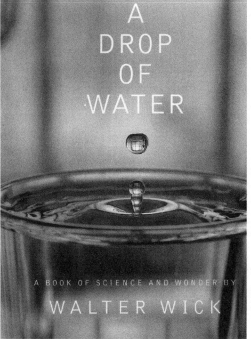

Courtesy of Scholastic, Inc.

"Before long I moved to New York City. After assisting a photographer for one year, I started my own studio in the fall of 1979. At first it was hard to find clients. The lack of work gave me time to explore new ideas and techniques, which resulted in a small but effective portfolio of seven images. Most of the pictures were carefully planned and executed special effects. One image, however, came about almost by accident. I was organizing screws, paper clips, springs, and other odds and ends that I had in a drawer. As I began sorting, I liked the way the objects looked spread out on my light box. After several hours of careful arranging, I took a picture. I could not have known it at the time, but this photograph of odds and ends was the spark that helped inspire the first *I Spy* book! But that would take another ten years.

"*Games* magazine was one of the first clients to respond to this new portfolio; other clients included *Psychology Today* and *Discover*. It never occurred to me to do a children's book, but the life of a freelance photographer is like a journey without a map. You never know where you'll end up! The 'odds and ends' photograph caught the eye of Carol Devine Carson, the art director, and Jean Marzollo, the editor of *Let's Find Out*, a kindergarten magazine published by Scholastic, Inc. They asked me to photograph colorful fasteners for an activity poster. The poster, in turn, caught the eye of editors in the Scholastic book division.

In the summer of 1991, Jean Marzollo and I collaborated on *I Spy: A Book of Picture Riddles*. After talking with Jean about picture concepts, I assembled a large selection of toys and props from stores, flea markets, and friends. I set up each photograph, working closely with Jean, as she wrote the riddles. The *I Spy* series and my collaboration with Jean have been among the most rewarding experiences of my creative life.

"Looking back, I'm grateful for the freedom I had as a child—the freedom to explore, invent, and discover. Those days provided the foundation for the work I do now—the work of making pictures that keep those childhood memories alive."

* * *

Walter Wick was born in Hartford, Connecticut, and grew up in the surrounding countryside. After graduating in 1973 from Paier College and working for several years in Connecticut, he moved New York City where there were more opportunities to explore his field. Wick opened his own studio a year after his move to New York and his first jobs were primarily magazine covers and book jackets, which led directly to his work with Scholastic.

Walter Wick was married in 1980. In 1991 he and his wife moved back to Connecticut, where his chief form of exercise is walking the dog and his leisure time is spent pursuing his interests in science, games, and puzzles. Among his other hobbies, he collects nineteenth-century books about science. In addition to his work on the *I Spy* books themselves, Wick serves as a consultant for the CD-ROM versions.

Of the volumes in this very popular series, *I Spy: A Book of Picture Riddles* and *I Spy School Days* were named to New York Public Library's list, 100 Titles for Reading and Sharing. *I Spy Fun House*, *I Spy Mystery*, and *I Spy School Days* were all chosen as ABA Pick of the Lists. *A Drop of Water* received the *Boston Globe–Horn Book* Award for Nonfiction in 1997 and was cited both as an Orbis Pictus Honor Book by the National Council of Teachers of English and as an Outstanding Science Trade Book for Children; named an ALA Notable Book, it appeared on all the other "best of the year" lists as well. *Walter Wick's Optical Tricks* was an ALA Notable Children's Book, a *Bulletin for the Center of Children's Books* Blue Ribbon title, one of *School Library Journal's* Best Books of the Year, a *Horn Book* Fanfare title, and one of the *New York Times's* Ten Best Illustrated Books of 1998.

SELECTED WORKS WRITTEN AND PHOTOGRAPHED: *A Drop of Water*, 1997; *Walter Wick's Optical Tricks*, 1998.

SELECTED WORKS PHOTOGRAPHED: (all written by Jean Marzollo) *I Spy: A Book of Picture Riddles*, 1992; *I Spy Christmas*, 1992; *I Spy Mystery*, 1993; *I Spy Fun House*, 1993; *I Spy Fantasy*, 1994; *I Spy School Days*, 1995; *I Spy Spooky Night*, 1996; *I Spy Super Challenger*, 1997; *I Spy Little Book*, 1997; *I Spy Gold Challenger!*, 1998; *I Spy Little Animals*, 1998; *I Spy Little Wheels*, 1998; *I Spy Little Christmas*, 1999; *I Spy Little Numbers*, 1999; *I Spy Treasure Hunt*, 1999; *I Spy Little Letters*, 2000.

SUGGESTED READING: *Interior Decoration*, August 1990; *Photo District News*, June 1997; *Popular Photography*, February 1999; Wick, Walter, *"Boston Globe–Horn Book* Award Acceptance," *The Horn Book*, January/February 1998.

WEB SITE: *www.scholastic.com*

"I seem to have inherited my love for drawing and painting from my mother. During World War II, while others around her were packing food and valuables on the way to the concentration camp, she picked up and clung to her painting box. I was told this story when I was very young and agree with her choice as wholeheartedly now as I did then.

"I grew up surrounded by the paraphernalia of painting. I soon developed a love affair with blank paper, pencils, and paint. However, during childhood, I was never considered one of the 'gifted' artists in my peer group. Although I would eventually produce satisfactory results, they were, and still are, more the product of a naive zeal than a wealth of natural talent. Fortunately, it is the struggle I enjoy, and over the years things do become easier. With this background, my decision to make my living from painting must not have seemed like the soundest one but, like my mother, I felt it the most important one. This is what I wanted to do above all else.

"My earliest breakthrough happened when my mother 'helped me out' with a school poster assignment. I received a lot of praise for it, which, not being academically inclined, I hungrily lapped up. On the other hand, I now also had a reputation to maintain as the class artist. This carrot and stick combination

Courtesy of Sharon Berman

Juan Wijngaard

September 22, 1951–

paved the way for me to take on increasingly ambitious projects and, so doing, live into and up to my own reputation.

"It took me a long time to find out that illustrations in books were photographically reduced versions of much larger paintings. By the time I discovered this, I had already developed a comfortable miniaturist style. Until recently, all my illustrations were the same size as they appear in the books. These days, however, my eyesight requires me to work bigger or to use magnifying lenses.

"I work mainly in water-based paints like watercolors and gouache for my book illustrations, and it takes me about six months to finish a book. Some can take over a year. Although I usually illustrate other authors' stories, I have recently started writing my own.

Courtesy of Candlewick Press

"Unlike the illustrators who prefer a recognizable look, I have not tied myself to any particular style. As soon as I read a new manuscript, I have a visual idea of how I would like to illustrate it, and more often than not it is nothing like my previous book. Trying out new approaches, techniques and materials keeps an edge on things, and I end up learning something new and broadening my range of experience. Similarly, I don't have a set way to tackle a new project. Every book is a new puzzle to solve. I have guidelines but no formulas. Sometimes I do painstaking research to get every detail correct, seek out models, take stacks of photographs, even enlist the help of computer-buff friends. Preparation sometimes takes many times longer than the actual painting. Other times I make a few sketches from my imagination and go straight to the finished artwork.

"My influences range from, among others, the historical illustrations in my school textbooks to Art Nouveau and surrealist painting, to the pre-Raphaelite and Flemish primitives of the fifteenth century, to Mughal and Persian miniatures. I paint for my own pleasure with oils, pastels, charcoal, and other materials. I also sculpt and occasionally make the odd stringed musical instrument. I play music of various kinds; my instrument of choice is the hurdy-gurdy."

Born of Dutch descent in Buenos Aires, Argentina, Juan Wijngaard was educated in England, began his professional career in Great Britain, and now lives in Inglewood, California. His books have been published in the United States, Great Britain, France, Germany, Switzerland, Japan, and Italy, among other places, and his art has been exhibited in both group and solo shows around the globe.

Wijngaard received a bachelor of fine arts in graphic design from Kingston Polytechnic College and a master of arts in illustration from London's Royal College of Art. Early professional experiences include working at CBS Records and Thames Television, and doing animation work for Grampian Television in Scotland.

Green Finger House earned the artist a Mother Goose Award as the most exciting newcomer to British illustration. He has also received "outstanding illustration" recognition from the Southern California Council on Literature for Children and Young People for *Going to Sleep on the Farm* and an Aesop Accolade from the American Folklore Society for *Esther's Story*. The Society of Illustrators of Los Angeles cited *Tales of Wonder and Magic* for a certificate of merit, and their national organization gave a 1994 gold medal to *Emma Bean*. Perhaps his most honored work is *Sir Gawain and the Loathly Lady*, which won the 1985 Kate Greenaway Medal as well as two European prizes— the Luchs 6 Award and Die Eule des Monats. The four "Baby Animal Board Books" that Wijngaard both wrote and illustrated—*Bear, Cat, Dog,* and *Duck*—were cited in the Top Ten Children's Books by *Parenting* magazine. *Thunderstorm!* was named an Outstanding Science Trade Book for Children.

Wijngaard also sculpts and has created artwork for stationery, cards, posters, and British postage stamps.

SELECTED BOOKS WRITTEN AND ILLUSTRATED: *Dog*, 1990; *Bear*, 1990; *Cat*, 1990; *Duck*, 1990.

SELECTED WORKS ILLUSTRATED: *Green Finger House*, by Rosemary Harris, 1979; *There Was an Old Man*, by Edward Lear, 1979; *Sir Gawain and the Green Knight*, by Selina Hastings, 1981; *Sir Gawain and the Loathly Lady*, by Selina Hastings, 1985; *The Blemyth Stories*, by William Mayne, 1986; *The Faber Book of Favorite Fairy Tales*, edited by Sarah and Stephen Corrin, 1988; (contributor) *Tail Feathers from Mother Goose*, edited by Iona Opie, 1988; *Going to Sleep on the Farm*, by Wendy Cheyette Lewison, 1992; *Emma Bean*, by Jean Van Leeuwen, 1993; *Thunderstorm!*, by Nathaniel Tripp, 1994; *Esther's Story*, by Diane Wolkstein, 1996; *Tales of Wonder and Magic*, by Berlie Doherty, 1997; *The Midas Touch*, by Jan Mark, 1999; *The King of the Golden River*, by John Ruskin, 2000.

Courtesy of Strem-Lauren Studio

Karen Lynn Williams

March 22, 1952–

"I was born in Hamden, Connecticut, on March 22, 1952. My mother, Lenora (Yohans) Howard, was a housewife and my father, Russell Howard, an optometrist. I have two younger brothers. The best parts of who I am come from my childhood. I was shy and sensitive and my mother's chronic illness and periods of hospitalization left lasting impressions, but I was happy.

"One of the reasons I became a writer is that my parents and grandparents were storytellers. My mother told the story of the birthday party she never had. It always made me cry, but I wanted to hear it over and over. My father told about the bear at the bottom of the bed, and my grandmother made up stories about me. We always read out loud as a family even after we could all read for ourselves. A family outing was to go to secondhand bookstores and browse for treasures. I also enjoyed looking at my mother's collection of antique children's books.

"I always wanted to be a part of books. I like stories and sharing ideas, communicating and playing with words. When I was eleven I had a writing club with neighborhood friends. My goal was to become the youngest published author ever. I knew Anne Frank was about twelve when she wrote her diary, so when I didn't publish by that time I gave up. I decided only famous people were writers. But I was always reading and still loved books. I read *The Secret Garden, Girl of the Limberlost*, and Nancy Drew books. I also enjoyed *Huckleberry Finn, Little Women*, and *Gone with the Wind*.

"I didn't begin writing seriously until after I had become a teacher of the deaf, gotten married and had two children. By then I was living in Malawi, Africa, where my husband and I were Peace Corps volunteers. I taught English at a high school and Steve was a doctor in a district hospital. Peter was a year old when we went to Africa and Christopher was born there. When I finished the course with the Institute of Children's Literature in 1982, I published a number of stories and articles in magazines such as *Highlights for Children* and *Junior Medical Detective*.

"I continued to write after we moved back to Pittsburgh, Pennsylvania, and several of my books are based on my experiences in Malawi. I was impressed with the simplicity of life there and the creativity of the children. These ideas are reflected in my books. After Rachel and Jonathan were born we moved to Haiti so our children could experience some of the qualities of life we had appreciated in Malawi, and two more books grew out of that experience.

"Making something from nothing is a theme in several of my books. *Applebaum's Garage* was inspired by my grandfather and his wonderful garage filled with junk that provided interesting building and play materials when I was growing up.

"Many of the ideas for my books come from the lives of my children as well as my own childhood. *A Real Christmas This Year* is about a boy I taught in my class for the hearing-impaired, but it is also about me when I was growing up. *One Thing I'm Good At* is about my daughter, Rachel, but some of the ideas for that story also come from something I heard on the news.

"As a writer I am always looking for ideas and people are always trying to give them to me. When my children ask what I want for Christmas or my birthday, I always want to say, 'Just give me a new story.' But I know that my stories have to come from me, from my heart and the things I care about most."

* * *

Karen Lynn Williams received her B.S. in speech pathology in 1974 from the University of Connecticut and an M.A. in deaf education in 1977 from Southern Connecticut State University. After graduation she worked as a teacher of the deaf for Area Cities Educational Services in a school in North Haven, Connecticut.

After her marriage in 1977 Karen Williams lived briefly in Pittsburgh, Pennsylvania. In 1980 she and her husband, Steve, traveled as Peace Corps volunteers to Malawi, in southeast Africa. *When Africa Was Home*, a *Booklist* Editors' Choice, reflects her young son's longings for his exotic home after they returned to America. *Galimoto*, the story of a young boy's creativity, also came from Williams's experience in Africa. *Galimoto* was a *Reading Rainbow* selection and a Parents' Choice Honor Book and received the 1992 Living the Dream Book Award given by the Manhattan School and P.S. 151 in New York City.

After the Williams family returned to Pittsburgh in 1983, two more children were born. They all moved to Haiti in 1990 for two years, while Steve served as a doctor at the Hospital Albert Schweitzer. From the experience of living in Haiti came two more picture books: *Tap-Tap*, a Junior Library Guild selection and one of three picture books to receive the 1995 *Hungry Mind Review* Children's Books of Distinction Award, and *Painted Dreams*, another story about the creative resourcefulness of children with few material goods; this was named one of the Smithsonian's 1998 Notable Books for Children. Karen Williams has also written middle grade novels and early chapter books for be-

"One of the reasons I became a writer is that my parents and grandparents were storytellers."

ginning readers. *A Real Christmas This Year* was a 1997 nominee for Missouri's Mark Twain Award.

Williams enjoys traveling, jogging, bicycling, gardening and quilting in her free time. She often designs her own quilts, which she considers another form of storytelling; in Haiti she taught quilting to a group of women who used their new skill to start a cottage industry in the village of Des Chapelles. Williams explores Pittsburgh on her bicycle and participates in the annual "Great Ride," a fifty-mile tour of the city.

SELECTED WORKS: *Galimoto*, illus. by Catherine Stock, 1990; *When Africa Was Home*, illus. by Floyd Cooper, 1991; *First Grade King*, illus. by Lena Shiffman, 1992; *Applebaum's Garage*, 1993; *Tap-Tap*, illus. by Catherine Stock, 1994; *A Real Christmas This Year*, 1995; *Painted Dreams*, illus. by Catherine Stock, 1998; *One Thing I'm Good At*, 1999.

SUGGESTED READING: *Contemporary Authors*, vol. 133, 1991; *Something About the Author*, vol. 66, 1991; vol. 99, 1999.

Rita Williams-Garcia

April 13, 1957–

"I owe every aspect of my creativity to my mother. My sister, brother, and I grew up thinking our mother, 'Miss Essie,' discovered Pop Art. When she wasn't cleaning, working, or in school, Miss Essie painted every little thing that needed color. Now, Miss Essie didn't paint the conventional floral or butterfly designs on ashtrays. She'd mix colors and paint angry motifs and declare 'I'm painting my mind!' One day my sister, brother, and I came home from school and found our garage door set ablaze with psychedelic orange, red, hot pink, and aqua birds or helicopters in some flight pattern. 'Vandals!' I cried, all the while knowing Miss Essie had been painting her mind.

"That wasn't the start of my inventive mind, but it explains it. Thanks to my mother, nothing was ever as interesting as how you could imagine it. Even though we—straightlaced Negro children that we were—thought Miss Essie was crazy, my sister, brother, and I were all infected by her need to make things.

"My mother discovered I could read when we went to the Red Cross for our shots. I knew all of the letters on the eye chart and could produce their sounds. When I figured out the sounds made words and the words made pictures—well, at two and a half, I was hooked. I began reading cereal boxes and billboards and moved on to books. By age twelve I was reading everything from Beverly Cleary to Eldridge Cleaver.

"Since kindergarten, I don't think a day has passed that I haven't written for my own pleasure. I made my first sale to *Highlights* magazine at fourteen and collected mounds of rejection letters before and after. In college, real life seemed to displace my need to 'make stories,' so I didn't write for nearly three years. (Real life was running my dance company and being political.)

It wasn't until my senior year when I took fiction workshops with Richard Price and Sonia Pilcer that I began to write once more.

"I wrote *Blue Tights* in my senior year of college out of necessity. I was working with a remedial reading group that needed materials from their point of view. Such a book did not exist, so I wrote out scenes, mostly taken from my reading group's lives, and we'd read them. My plan was to rewrite the manuscript after graduation, sell it, make a zillion dollars and retreat to my island and write the serious tome. How totally naive!

"After *Blue Tights* was published, nearly ten years later, I promised my editor that that was my last young adult novel. I didn't feel particularly encouraged by the glut of soulless teen novels that seemed to comprise young adult books at the time. I didn't want to make true experience palatable for ten-year-olds, didn't want to construct the NAACP poster child in hopes of winning some award, didn't want to kill the wonderful strangeness of fiction for the reader by explaining every little thing. No sooner had I vowed never to do another young adult novel than I ran smack into a figure from college. When I was in college, he was a major political and social force on campus who had the administration and student body waiting on his next move. When he left without collecting his degree many of us told ourselves it was for something really big. Yet there he was, fifteen years later, showing a kid how to flip burgers at a fast-food place. This made me think about the men I went to school with and how the B and C students hung on while the A students dropped out due to the 'conspiracy to fail black men.' I was inspired to write my second novel, *Fast Talk on a Slow Track*, for those bright young men who couldn't accept failure as a part of learning.

Courtesy of Rita Williams-Garcia

"Although my stories are contemporary and realistic, I don't write specifically about issues. I write about my characters' lives . . . where they must go or what they must do, given who they are. My characters are typically adolescent in that they have a long way to go before becoming the person they're supposed to be. When I tell people my third novel, *Like Sisters on the Homefront*, is about a twice-pregnant fourteen-year-old, they immediately conclude that it's about the abortion issue and the plight of the teen mother. *Like Sisters . . .* is about Gayle and her journey. My fourth novel, *Every Time . . . . a Rainbow Dies*, opens with the rape of a major character. The story is not about rape. Unlike my other work, my fifth novel, *No Laughter Here*, will be centered on an issue—female circumcision. I break my own rules when necessary.

"The best part about writing is anticipating reading my stories to kids. I love to meet the ones who have read my stories. Their faces, both doubtful and enthused, stay with me through the plotting of my next story."

* * *

Rita Williams-Garcia's father was in the army, and the family left the Queens neighborhood where she was born to move to Arizona when Rita was small. They settled in Seaside, California, where Rita and her siblings, Russell and Rosalind, spent much of their childhood playing outdoors. Born at the end of the 1950s, Rita was exposed early to racial issues. She remembers discussing the race riots of 1968, Martin Luther King Jr.'s assassination, and the political views of the militant Black Panthers when she was a young student. At age twelve, she left California, spent six months in Georgia, and settled in Jamaica, New York. From an early age, Williams-Garcia began looking for books with young black protagonists, but she found only a few. Encouraged by her teachers, she began writing the books she wanted to read.

Williams-Garcia's first novel, *Blue Tights*, was listed as a CCBC Choice and received a Parents' Choice Award. *Like Sisters on the Homefront* was included in all the "best" lists of 1995 as well as being named a Coretta Scott King Honor Book and an ALA Best Book for Young Adults. Her first three young adult novels were all named to ALA's annual list of books for reluctant readers and listed in the New York Public Library's Books for the Teen Age.

Rita Williams-Garcia graduated from Hofstra University and received an M.A. in English from Queens College. She has studied dance under Alvin Ailey and Phil Black. She lives in Jamaica, New York, with her daughters, Michelle and Stephanie, and works as a manager at a marketing services company.

> "I wrote Blue Tights *in my senior year of college out of necessity. I was working with a remedial reading group that needed materials from their point of view. Such a book did not exist . . ."*

SELECTED WORKS: *Blue Tights*, 1988; *Fast Talk on a Slow Track*, 1992; *Like Sisters on the Homefront*, 1995; *Catching the Wild Waiyuuzee*, illus. by Mike Reed, 2000.

SELECTED WORKS IN ANTHOLOGIES: "Into the Game," *Join In*, ed. by Donald Gallo, 1993; "Wishing It Away," *No Easy Answers*, ed. by Donald Gallo, 1997; "Chalkman," *Twelve Shots*, ed. by Harry Mazer, 1997; "Cross Over," *Trapped*, ed. by Lois Duncan, 1998; "Crazy as a Daisy," *Stories for Strong Girls*, ed. by Marilyn Singer, 1998; "About Russell," *Family Secrets*, ed. by Lisa Fraustino, 1999; "Food from the Outside," *When I Was Young*, ed. by Amy Erlich, 1999.

SUGGESTED READING: *Authors and Artists for Young Adults*, vol. 22, 1997; *Children's Literature Review*, vol. 36, 1995; *Contemporary Authors*, vol. 159, 1998; Jordan, Shirley Marie, ed. *Broken Silences*, 1993; *Something About the Author*, vol. 98, 1998. Periodicals—Rochman, Hazel, "The *Booklist* Interview: Rita Williams-Garcia," *Booklist*, February 15, 1993.

"Life doesn't always come with a map. We aren't all born with recognizable gifts that automatically direct our lives. This doesn't have to be a bad thing. Sometimes we can define our gifts and strengthen them by leaving ourselves open to new experiences. That's what happened to me.

"I didn't discover my gift for writing until I was pretty much an old woman of thirty-five! Even though I loved creative writing in elementary school and on into high school, I never imagined it as a career for myself. When I graduated from high school I didn't have a clue about a profession I should pursue. I thought it must be wonderful to be born with a gift for music, or art, for example, or to just know that you wanted to be a doctor.

"As happy as I was, I didn't see that I had any outstanding gifts. My parents were very understanding and supportive and never pressured me to be anything more than who I was. That was a gift. It allowed me to follow my heart and be comfortable with myself. I didn't need to be a doctor or an artist, or anything else to gain their approval.

"I went to college for two years and majored in English literature, still clueless about how I was going to make a living. At nineteen I was too restless to sit in a classroom any longer. I remember just wanting to get out and live my life. So I quit school and returned home to New Jersey, married my high school sweetheart, and took a job as a janitor in an office building.

"That was the beginning of a long road that finally led to writing. Over the next fifteen years I worked as a gardener, receptionist, ice-cream-truck driver, window-dresser, store owner, and storyteller in a library. I do believe having experienced so many different jobs and meeting all kinds of people has broadened my writing and the subjects I'm interested in. My last job, working in the library, took me back to my love of books and

Courtesy of Elvira Woodruff

Elvira Woodruff

June 19, 1951–

writing. My cousin, the author/illustrator Frank Asch, had been in the business of children's books for many years, and he was instrumental in showing me the ropes.

"I was lucky to sell my first story, but still didn't see myself as a writer. If I hadn't gotten divorced at about this time, I very well could have stayed at the library forever. But I needed a job that paid a bit more. I knew writing books was risky business, but I liked the challenge and wanted to try. So for the next four or five years I was writing three and four books a year! I began with picture books and moved on to novels and then to historical fiction. I've been writing for the last eleven years. About eight years ago I began speaking in schools, talking about creative writing.

"My restlessness doesn't get out of control due to my two very different jobs. As a speaker I must be very social and extroverted and bounce about the country. As a writer I must close in and be very introverted and remain for long hours holed up in my study. I enjoy both experiences and feel grateful I can divide my time that way.

"Even if I weren't doing a lot of public speaking, this business of writing could never be boring because each story that I slip myself into is a new adventure. I'm traveling to wherever my passion takes me, traveling in my imagination as well as physically, to do the research.

"I don't know of a greater pleasure than researching a subject you're passionate about. It's also an experience you can share with your family and friends. I often took my boys on research jaunts as they were growing up. That way we all learned together.

"I'm grateful my life didn't come with a map. I've been only too happy to map out the adventure myself."

> *"I do believe having experienced so many different jobs and meeting all kinds of people has broadened my writing and the subjects I'm interested in."*

* * *

Born and raised in New Jersey, Elvira Woodruff left in 1970 to attend Adelphi University and the next year went to Boston University. Her parents, John and Frances Pirozzi, understood her nature and supported her thirst for adventure. They weren't surprised when she returned home to work in a variety of jobs before she discovered that writing was her life's work. She thought the sale of her first manuscript was merely a piece of good fortune, but when she sold her second, she realized that she could be a writer. To do so, though, she would have to discipline herself. So she converted her sewing table into a writing desk, took down all the thread that lined the shelves of the wall and replaced it with papers and books. Her sewing machine went into the cellar and was replaced by a computer.

Woodruff was asked once, "Who do you write for? For kids, or for yourself?" The answer came quickly: "I write for the kid in me." She claims that "what you have to do as a writer is to feel, look, and listen. Your stories then become a celebration of those observations. And, most important, a writer needs to fall in love." She claims that she is constantly "falling in love—with colors, with flowers, with wings, with bubbles—and when you're writing under the influence of love, there's a power that will weave your words into magic."

Woodruff's books have been popular with young readers, and appear regularly on voting lists for readers' choice awards. *Ghosts Don't Get Goose Bumps* and *The Summer I Shrank My Grandmother* were both Florida Sunshine State Award winners, in 1998 and 1994, respectively. *The Summer I Shrank My Grandmother* was a 1997 Maud Hart Lovelace Award winner for the state of Minnesota, while *Ghosts Don't Get Goose Bumps* won the Blackeyed Susan Award in the state of Maryland in 1996. *Dear Napoleon, I Know You're Dead, But . . .* received a 1995 Crown Award, and *The Secret Funeral of Slim Jim the Snake* was a 1996 Charlie May Simon Award winner in Arkansas.

SELECTED WORKS: *Awfully Short for the Fourth Grade*, 1989; *The Summer I Shrank My Grandmother*, 1990; *The Wing Shop*, illus. by Stephen Gammell, 1991; *Dear Napoleon, I Know You're Dead, But . . .* , 1992; *The Disappearing Bike Shop*, 1992; *The Secret Funeral of Slim Jim the Snake*, 1993; *Ghosts Don't Get Goose Bumps*, 1993; *Dear Levi: Letters from the Overland Trail*, illus. by Beth Peck, 1994; *The Orphan of Ellis Island: A Time Travel Adventure*, 1997; *Can You Guess Where We're Going?*, 1998; *Dear Austin: Letters from the Underground Railroad*, illus. by Nancy Carpenter, 1998; *The Memory Coat*, 1999; *The Ghost of Lizard Light*, 1999.

SUGGESTED READING: *Contemporary Authors*, vol. 138, 1993; *Something About the Author*, vol. 70, 1993; vol. 106, 1999.

"I was born the same day as Lincoln, and for many years my birthday was a legal holiday. Then things got changed around and it was decided that we'd celebrate Presidents' Day instead of giving Lincoln and Washington their own individual holidays, and suddenly libraries and schools and banks were open on my birthday.

"I grew up in a religious family in which birthdays and holidays weren't celebrated. If we were celebrating someone's birthday in class, I had to excuse myself and go spend time in another classroom until the celebration was over. My family didn't vote or pledge to the flag or curse. Nor were we allowed to participate in any war. I have relatives who served time in prison because they didn't go to war. Some dancing was allowed but not much. Of course, I was always finding ways to do what I wasn't allowed to do. (Except go to war, which I still don't believe in.) I have

Jacqueline Woodson

February 12, 1963–

this memory of being in the park across the street from my house. I was about eleven or twelve and I was standing up on a swing, pumping my knees hard so that the swing went high into the air and I was singing 'America the Beautiful' at the top of my lungs. I loved that song! And I loved 'The Star-Spangled Banner.' Maybe I loved them so much because I wasn't allowed to sing either of these songs.

"There are a lot of roads by which one arrives at being the person they are. But I think that the person we are becoming is already somewhere inside of us, waiting to be born. I think of myself as a writer that way. I knew I wanted to be a writer as early as fifth grade. I knew there were stories I wanted to tell, things I wanted to say. I wanted clarity. I wanted to be able to create a world in which I had the answers, in which I could make up my own endings. I see myself as that little girl leaving the classroom as the teacher placed chocolate cupcakes with rainbow sprinkles on each of her classmates' desks, and I rewrite her into a girl who turns back into the classroom and says, 'No, I want to be a part of this!'

Courtesy of Anna Grace

Jacqueline Woodson

"For a long time, my writing stayed close to my real life. Like Margaret in *Last Summer with Maizon*, I too won a poetry contest for a poem I wrote in the fifth grade. My poem was about Martin Luther King Jr. I think it was the first time I received an award for something. I got to read the poem in the auditorium and everyone cheered. I still remember the way that felt. Years later, when I walked into a bookstore and saw my name on the cover of my first book, it was that same feeling—a combination of standing in front of that auditorium mixed with the feeling of standing in that swing and singing 'America the Beautiful.' Later on, I started moving away from my life a bit. When I wrote *From the Notebooks of Melanin Sun*, it was the first time I wrote from the point of view of a boy. It meant doing some hard work—the work of being a writer—stepping into another's shoes and seeing the world through their eyes. True, there is a lot of me in Melanin Sun, just as there is a lot of me in Lena and Marie and Staggerlee. But at the core of all of it is my desire to tell a good story, a story I would have enjoyed reading when I was a kid, a story that will give someone else the strength to stand up in that swing or go back into that classroom and have a cupcake. Heck, it's only a birthday!"

* * *

Born in Columbus, Ohio, Jacqueline Woodson lived on and off in Greenville, South Carolina, until she was seven and then settled in Brooklyn, New York, where she lives currently. She was raised as a strict Jehovah's Witness, which distanced her from her classmates in school. An interested seventh-grade teacher encouraged her to pursue writing as a career. In 1985 Woodson graduated from college with a B.A. in English. She worked as a drama therapist with runaway and homeless children in New York City in 1988 and 1989. A writing fellowship in 1990–1991 took her to the Fine Arts Work Center in Provincetown, Massachusetts. She has taught in the M.F.A. program at Goddard College and been a fellow at the MacDowell Colony in Peterborough, New Hampshire. Since 1996 she has spent part of each summer at a writing camp for underprivileged young people fourteen and older sponsored by the National Book Foundation.

Woodson's work has been widely recognized for its excellence. In 1992 she received the *Kenyon Review* Award for Literary Excellence in Fiction. *I Hadn't Meant to Tell You This* was named an ALA Best Book for Young Adults, an ALA Notable Children's Book, a Coretta Scott King Honor Book, and a Jane Addams Peace Award Honor Book. *From the Notebooks of Melanin Sun* was also a Coretta Scott King Honor Book and a Jane Addams Peace Award Honor Book. Both of these titles were cited as Notable Trade Books in the Field of Social Studies. *The House You Pass on the Way* received the Lambda Award for Young Adult fiction, and *If You Come Softly* was cited as one of the Top Ten of ALA's Best Books for Young Adults and awarded a *Bulletin of the Center for Children's Books* Blue Ribbon. *We Had a Picnic This Sunday Past* was named a Notable Trade Book in the Field of Social Studies; *Lena* and *If You Come Softly* were chosen as Junior Library Guild selections.

Courtesy of Scholastic, Inc.

SELECTED WORKS: *Last Summer with Maizon*, 1990; *Maizon at Blue Hill*, 1992; *Between Madison and Palmetto*, 1993; *I Hadn't Meant to Tell You This*, 1994; *A Way Out of No Way: Writings About Growing Up Black in America*, (editor), 1996;

From the Notebooks of Melanin Sun, 1997; *The House You Pass on the Way*, 1997; *If You Come Softly*, 1998; *We Had a Picnic This Sunday Past*, 1998; *Lena*, 1999; *Miracle's Boys*, 2000.

SUGGESTED READING: *Children's Literature Review*, vol. 49, 1998; *Contemporary Authors*, vol. 159, 1998; Graham, Paula W. *Speaking of Journals: Children's Book Writers Talk About Their Diaries, Notebooks, and Sketchbooks*, 1999; Murphy, Barbara Thrash. *Black Authors and Illustrators of Books for Children and Young Adults*, 3rd ed., 1999; Nelson, Emmanuel S. *Contemporary African American Novelists*, 1999; *Something About the Author*, vol. 94, 1998. Periodicals—Paylor, Diane, "Bold Type: Jacqueline Woodson's 'Girl Stories,'" *Ms*, November/December 1994; Woodson, Jacqueline, "Common Ground," *Essence*, May 1999; Woodson, Jacqueline, "A Stolen Childhood," *Essence*, May 1993.

Tim Wynne-Jones

August 12, 1948–

"When I was four, I ran away from home with a tea cozy on my head. I'm not sure if this contributed to my becoming a writer, but the tea cozy did keep my head warm. It is important when you are a writer to keep your head warm.

"That was in England. But we moved to the New World when I was four and found that some of the rocks and trees looked suspiciously old. And the Indians around Kitimat, British Columbia, where we settled, way up near the Alaska panhandle, seemed to think that the land had been around a long time. And so had they.

"My dad and I went hunting with the Indians. I remember playing soldiers with shotgun shells under a tarp stretched between trees to keep off the rain. It rains a lot in northern British Columbia. Maybe that's why we moved to Vancouver. It rains a lot there, too, so we moved again, east to Ottawa, Ontario, Canada's capital. It's pretty dry.

"It was in Ottawa, at about one o'clock in the afternoon of an otherwise average day in October, that I decided to become an architect when I grew up. I was eleven.

"I drew lots of houses and skyscrapers and read architectural magazines. I did lots of math and science in high school as well. I failed English. I liked it all right, but I wasn't very good at answering questions about the stories we studied. When I read, I feel like I am inside a story. It's hard to answer questions from inside a story. It is sort of like asking a character in a story what he thinks the author was trying to do. You know what he is going to say? 'What author?'

"Anyway, I wouldn't need English if I was going to be an architect, would I? So I went off to university and, after three years, failed out of architecture. Big time. Straight F's. That's when I joined a rock band. And then I really needed English, because I started writing songs. And since people heard the songs, I wanted to get the words right. I guess that was when I started writing seriously. Luckily, I didn't take it too seriously, because I wasn't very good at it.

"So I went back to school and studied visual art. I ended up with a master's degree and the promise of a teaching job in the fall, which is when I did the only sensible thing to do in such a situation. I ran away from home with a tea cozy on my head. No, just kidding. I rented a typewriter and spent the summer writing my first novel.

"The thing is, I had always been writing. Did I say that? Well, it's true. Ever since I was a kid I had been doing this fun thing of making things up and imagining 'What if this' and 'What if that,' and suddenly it was time to do something about it. Otherwise, I was going to be a teacher that fall!

"The novel was a thriller called *Odd's End*. It won a first-novel award.

"That was twenty years and twenty-two books ago. What else do you need to know? Okay, here goes. I've got three kids, a wife who's an artist, and four cats. I live in the country, which I love, in a house I designed, and I still sing in a rock band. Not the same one. But I'm still trying to get the words right."

Courtesy of Larry Ostrom

*   *   *

Born August 12, 1948, in Bromborough, Cheshire, England, Tim Wynne-Jones attended the University of Waterloo, Ontario, where he received his B.F.A. in 1974. He went on to complete his M.F.A. at York University in 1979. He married Amanda West Lewis, a writer and teacher, in 1980. They have three children—Alexander, Magdalene, and Lewis. Early in his career, Tim Wynne-Jones worked as a designer at a publishing company, as a graphic designer, and as a teacher of visual arts at both Waterloo and York universities. His first children's book, a fantasy called *Madeline and Ermadello*, was published in 1977, but it was his 1980 adult thriller, *Odd's End*, that earned him

Canada's Seal First Novel Award, with a cash prize of $50,000, and wide recognition as a promising new writer.

He wrote several more books for adults and then composed a gently humorous story for young children, *Zoom at Sea*, introducing an adventurous cat with a love for water and travel. An immediate favorite (and the first of a series), *Zoom at Sea* received the Amelia Frances Howard-Gibbons Award in 1983 and the Ruth Schwartz Children's Award in 1984. For older children, Wynne-Jones wrote *Some of the Kinder Planets*, a collection of nine stories about young people encountering new worlds. It won the 1993 Canadian Library Association Children's Book of the Year Award, the 1993 Governor-General's Award for Children's Literature, and the 1995 *Boston Globe–Horn Book* Award for fiction. *The Book of Changes*, another collection of short stories, was a 1994 ALA Notable Children's Book.

Courtesy of Orchard Books

The Maestro, Wynne-Jones's first young adult novel, won the 1995 Governor-General's Award for Children's Literature, was named the 1995 Young Adult Book of the Year by the Canadian Library Association, and was cited in the 1997 New York Public Library's Books for the Teen Age list. Wynne-Jones won the Vicky Metcalf Award from the Canadian Authors Association in 1997 for the body of his work. The following year *Stephen Fair* earned him another Book of the Year Award from the Canadian Library Association. He continues to range between adult, young adult, and children's books, always bringing a sense of wonder and unusual perspectives to his work. Wynne-Jones has also written a number of radio plays, as well as lyrics for the television program *Fraggle Rock*.

SELECTED WORKS: *Madeline and Ermadello*, illus. by Lindsey Hallam, 1977; *Zoom at Sea*, illus. by Ken Nutt, 1983, and illus. by Eric Beddows, 1993; *Zoom Away*, illus. by Ken Nutt, 1985, and illus. by Eric Beddows,1993; *I'll Make You Small*, illus. by Maryann Kovalski, 1986; *Architect of the Moon* (US: *Builder of the Moon*), illus. by Ian Wallace, 1988; *Zoom Upstream*, illus. by Eric Beddows, 1992; *Some of the Kinder Planets*, 1993; *The Book of Changes*, 1994; *The Maestro*, 1995; *Stephen Fair*, 1998; *Lord of the Fries*, 1999.

SUGGESTED READING: *Children's Literature Review*, vol. 21, 1990; vol. 57, 2000; *Contemporary Authors*, vol. 105, 1982; *Contemporary Authors*, New Revision Series, vol. 39, 1992; Pendergast, Sara, ed. *St. James Guide to Children's Writers*, 5th ed., 1999; Silvey, Anita, ed. *Children's Books and Their Creators*, 1995; *Something About the Author*, vol. 67, 1992; vol. 96, 1998. Periodicals—"Short Tempered," *The Horn Book*, May/June 1999; "Some of the Kinder Planets," *The Horn Book*, January/February 1996.

"I was born in Norfolk, Virginia, and learned to read before I went to school. I loved reading and loved drawing and did both constantly. When grownups asked what I wanted to do when I grew up, I always said I wanted to write books and draw my own pictures for them.

"I went to the University of Wisconsin on a writing scholarship, but for some reason did not study art at all and have never really done so. This would be a great regret for me except that I have been most fortunate to have gifted illustrators for the picture books I have written—such artists as H. A. Rey, Leonard Weisgard, Margaret Bloy Graham, Roger Duvoisin, Maurice Sendak, Garth Williams, Hilary Knight, Erik Blegvad, and Wendell Minor.

"After the University of Wisconsin, I married Maurice Zolotow, whom I met there. After we moved to New York, I worked for Ursula Nordstrom, editor of Harper's children's book department, as her editorial assistant. This brought me into contact not only with her own original and fascinating mind and approach to children's books, but with the books and illustrations as well. I loved it all.

Courtesy of Andrew Kilgore

Charlotte Zolotow

June 26, 1915–

"My first book, *The Park Book*, grew out of a memo to Ursula Nordstrom suggesting a book about Washington Square Park. She encouraged me to try it myself and the book was published in 1944, just before my son, Stephen, was born. Later books took form from bedtime stories I told him and experiences I had with him and the revelation his own very individual way of surveying experience was to me. My daughter, Ellen, eight years younger than Stephen, had a fresh and poetic way of seeing the world when she was young that opened up for me not only the universe in her own terms but—the past recalled—memories of my own childhood that I might have otherwise lost. It was really out of my contact with Steve and Ellen, with their friends, with the deepened perceptions and awareness children bring to people involved with them, as well as out of my earlier feeling for the spoken and written word, that my children's books have come.

"Stephen has grown up to be a tournament bridge player with a wonderful sense of humor and great skill as a consultant that endears him to people. Ellen is now known as Crescent Dragonwagon, and she has published some remarkable books for children, two novels, magazine articles, and several best-selling cookbooks—all of which give exceptional delight.

"I left Harper to raise my children but returned after a number of years to work in the Junior Books Department. In 1981 I was appointed associate publisher of Harper Junior Books and a vice president in Harper & Row, but six years later I relinquished these positions to become editorial consultant to Harper Junior Books and editorial director of my own imprint, 'Charlotte Zolotow Books.' Since 1991, I have been 'retired,' but still serve as an editorial consultant. My own writing continues, for I love to explore the life and feelings from remembered childhood on through my present eighty-three years in books that sometimes reach people of all ages.

"I was especially honored in 1998 when the University of Wisconsin together with the Cooperative Children's Book Center established what will be an annual Charlotte Zolotow Award for a book judged by teachers, librarians, and educators in the children's book field to have the most distinguished *text* in a picture book."

> *"My own writing continues, for I love to explore the life and feelings from remembered childhood on through my present eighty-three years."*

*   *   *

Charlotte Shapiro Zolotow attended the University of Wisconsin from 1933 to 1936 before joining the children's book department of Harper and Brothers (now HarperCollins). She served as senior editor from 1938 to 1944, left to raise her children, and returned to publishing in 1962. Her marriage to Maurice Zolotow ended in divorce in 1969. Throughout her career at Harper, she continued to write and is the author of over seventy books for children.

Charlotte Zolotow is known for the poetic quality of her writing, her ability to tune in to children's perceptions of their world, and the exploration of feelings and relationships in her picture-book texts. Her books are notable for their candor, simplicity, and gentle humor. It is an indication of the enduring quality of her stories that many of her picture books have been reissued, some more than once, often with new illustrations. The list of those who have illustrated her stories over a period of more than fifty years reads like a "Who's Who" of twentieth-century chil-

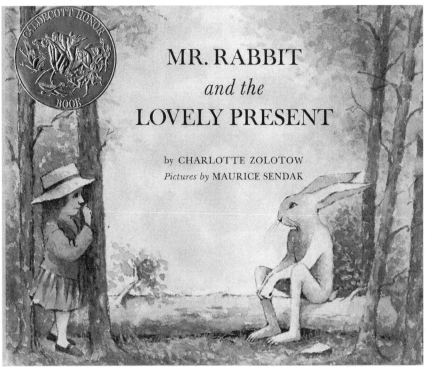

MR. RABBIT
and the
LOVELY PRESENT

by CHARLOTTE ZOLOTOW
Pictures by MAURICE SENDAK

Courtesy of HarperCollins Publishers

dren's book artists. Two of them won Caldecott Honor Book Awards for their illustrations: Maurice Sendak for *Mr. Rabbit and the Lovely Present* and Margaret Bloy Graham for *The Storm Book*.

Zolotow has kept a watchful and sensitive eye on how children's environments and private sensory worlds have changed along with the larger society since the 1940s, when she first began writing. She has addressed real-world emotional problems in such books as *My Friend John*, *The Hating Book*, *Big Sister and Little Sister*, and *The New Friend*. In 1974, she revised her earlier book, *The Night When Mother Was Away*, about a father caring for a child while the mother traveled; the new version, *The Summer Night*, showed a single father taking care of his child, reflecting a social reality increasingly familiar to her readers. In 1972, she published the groundbreaking *William's Doll*, about a boy who wants to play with a doll; William's grandmother helps his father understand that playing with a doll is a normal activity for a vigorous young boy. *William's Doll* was named an ALA Notable Children's Book, a *New York Times* Outstanding Book of the Year, and a *School Library Journal* Best Book. The story also brought Zolotow much acclaim from feminist critics and was subsequently produced as a film in 1981. Many of her other stories have also appeared in film adaptations.

In 1974 Charlotte Zolotow received a Christopher Award and an ALA Notable Children's Book citation for *My Grandson Lew*, a story that deals gently and sensitively with a boy's feelings about the death of his grandfather. One of the first picture books to tackle the subject of the death of a loved one, *My Grandson Lew* was also named an IRA/CBC Children's Choice. Over the years a number of Zolotow's books have been designated IRA/CBC Children's Choices, among them *It's Not Fair*, *May I Visit?*, and *Some Things Go Together*. She has not limited her work to the very young, but has also selected and edited two collections of stories for teenagers. *Early Sorrow: Ten Stories of Youth* was named an ALA Best Book for Young Adults in 1986.

Equally important to the children's book field is Zolotow's work as an editor, nurturing and developing new authors and illustrators and publishing award-winning titles. In 1974, for her contribution to books for children and teenagers, Zolotow was presented the Harper Gold Medal Award for editorial excellence. In 1986 she received the University of Minnesota's Kerlan Award for "her singular attainments in the creation of children's literature." The University of Southern Mississippi presented her its Silver Medallion in 1990 for "her distinguished contribution to children's literature," and in 1991 the American Library Association adopted a resolution expressing librarians' gratitude for her work on behalf of books for young people.

Charlotte Zolotow lives in Hastings-on-Hudson, New York.

SELECTED WORKS: *The Park Book*, illus. by H. A. Rey, 1944; *But Not Billy*, 1947, rev. ed. illus. by Kay Chorao, 1983; *The Storm Book*, illus. by Margaret Bloy Graham, 1952; *The Quiet Mother and the Noisy Little Boy*, 1953, rev. ed. illus. by Marc Simont, 1989; *One Step, Two . . .* , 1955, illus. by Roger Duvoisin, rev. ed. illus. by Cindy Wheeler, 1981; *Not a Little Monkey*, illus. by Roger Duvoisin, 1957, rev. ed. illus. by Michele Chessare, 1989; *Do You Know What I'll Do?*, illus. by Garth Williams, 1958; *The Sleepy Book*, illus. by Vladimir Bobri, 1958, rev. ed. illus. by Ilse Plume, 1988; *Mr. Rabbit and the Lovely Present*, illus. by Maurice Sendak, 1962; *When the Wind Stops*, illus. by Joe Lasker, 1962, rev.

My Grandson Lew

by
CHARLOTTE
ZOLOTOW

pictures by
WILLIAM
PÈNE DU BOIS

Courtesy of HarperCollins

ed. illus. by Stefano Vitale, 1995; *The Quarreling Book*, illus. by Arnold Lobel, 1963; *a rose, a bridge, and a wild black horse*, illus. by Uri Shulevitz, 1964, rev. ed. illus. by Robin Spowart, 1987; *A Tiger Called Thomas*, illus. by Kurth Werth, 1963, rev. ed. illus. by Catherine Stock, 1988; *Someday*, illus. by Arnold Lobel, 1965; *When I Have a Little Girl*, illus. by Hilary Knight, 1965; *Big Sister and Little Sister*, illus. by Martha Alexander, 1966; *When I Have a Little Boy*, illus. by Hilary Knight, 1967; *My Friend John*, illus. by Ben Shecter, 1968, rev. ed. illus. by Amanda Harvey, 2000; *The New Friend*, illus. by Emily Arnold McCully, 1968, rev. ed. 1981; *The Hating Book*, illus. by Ben Shecter, 1969; *Wake Up and Goodnight*, illus. by Leonard Weisgard, 1971, rev. ed. illus. by Pamela Paparone, 1998; *William's Doll*, illus. by William Pène du Bois, 1972; *The Beautiful Christmas Tree*, illus. by Ruth Robbins, 1972; *The Old Dog*, illus. by George Mocniak, rev. ed. illus. by James Ransome, 1995; *Janey*, illus. by Ronald Himler, 1973; *My Grandson Lew*, illus. by William Pène du Bois, 1974; *The Unfriendly Book*, illus. by William Pène du Bois, 1975; *It's Not Fair*, illus. by William Pène du Bois, 1976; *May I Visit?*, illus. by Erik Blegvad, 1976; *Someone New*, illus. by Erik Blegvad, 1978; *Say It!*, illus. by James Stevenson, 1980; *If You Listen*, illus. by Marc Simont, 1980; *The Song*, illus. by Nancy Tafuri, 1982; *Some Things Go Together*, illus. by Karen Gundersheimer, 1983; rev. ed. illus by Ashley Wolff, 1999; *I Know a Lady*, illus. by James Stevenson, 1984; *Timothy Too!*, illus. by Ruth Robbins, 1986; *I Like to Be Little*, illus. by Erik Blegvad, 1987; *Something Is Going to Happen*, illus. by Catherine Stock, 1988; *Everything Glistens and Everything Sings: New and Selected Poems*, illus. by Margot Tomes, 1987; *This Quiet Lady*, illus. by Anita Lobel, 1992; *The Seashore Book*, illus. by Wendell Minor, 1992; *The Moon Was the Best*, photos. by Tana Hoban, 1993; *Snippets: A Gathering of Poems, Pictures, and Possibilities . . .* , illus. by Melissa Sweet, 1993; *Peter and the Pigeons*, illus. by Martine Gourbault, 1993; *Who Is Ben?*, illus. by Kathryn Jacobi, 1997. As editor—*An Overpraised Season: 10 Stories of Youth*, 1973; *Early Sorrow: Ten Stories of Youth*, 1986.

SUGGESTED READING: *Children's Literature Review*, vol. 2, 1976; Collier, Laurie and Joyce Nakamura, eds. *Major Authors and Illustrators for Children and Young Adults*, 1993; *Contemporary Authors*, New Revision Series, vol. 38, 1993; *Dictionary of Literary Biography*, vol. 52, 1986; Pendergast, Sara, ed. *St. James Guide to Children's Writers*, 5th edition, 1999; Silvey, Anita, ed. *Children's Books and Their Creators*, 1995; *Something About the Author*, vol. 1, 1971; vol. 35, 1984; vol. 78, 1994. Periodicals—Cart, Michael, "Carte Blanche,"

Booklist, November 15, 1998; Novelli, Joan, "Author Study: Charlotte Zolotow," *Instructor-Intermediate*, April 1998; "Profile: Charlotte Zolotow," *Ladybug*, March 1994; "Refreshment for over 50 Years: Zolotow Receives USM's Silver Medallion," *Publishers Weekly*, April 27, 1990.

WEB SITE: *www.ipl.org/youth/AskAuthor/Zolotow.html*

An earlier profile of Charlotte Zolotow appeared in *More Junior Authors* (1963).

Awards and Honors
(cited in this volume)

American Booksellers Association Pick of the Lists
Chosen twice a year, from publishers' spring and fall offerings, these are the books that booksellers feel will be most popular with their customers. Pick of the Lists appears in the Spring and Fall issues of *Bookselling This Week*, the ABA magazine.

ALA Notable Children's Books
This annual list of distinguished books for children from infancy through age 14 is compiled by a committee of the Association for Library Service to Children, a division of the American Library Association. Available on the ALA Web site: *www.ala.org*.

Booklist Editors' Choice List
Cited each January in ALA *Booklist*, a reviewing journal of the American Library Association, these are the outstanding titles of the previous year, as chosen by the journal's youth editors from among the hundreds of books reviewed. The list usually runs from 40 to 60 titles.

Boston Globe–Horn Book Awards
These awards for the year's best fiction/poetry, nonfiction, and picture books are announced in *The Horn Book* magazine every fall and are formally presented at the annual conference of the New England Library Association. The awards were initiated in 1967.

Bulletin of the Center for Children's Books Blue Ribbon List
Published annually in January, this list comprises about 40 books chosen by the journal's editors and reviewers as exemplifying the best qualities to be found in children's literature in the preceding year.

Caldecott Medal and Caldecott Honor Awards
Announced annually at the Midwinter Conference of the American Library Association, the Caldecott Medal is presented by the Association for Library Service to Children to the illustrator of the most distinguished picture book for children (from infancy through age 14) published in the United States in the preceding year. Other books worthy of notice may also be cited. In 1971 the term "runners-up" was officially changed to "honor books" for these additional titles. Acceptance speeches are made by the Medal winners at a banquet at the Annual Conference of the ALA and printed in *The Horn Book* magazine and *The Journal of Youth Services*. The award was established in 1938.

Children's Book Committee at Bank Street College of Education
The Bank Street College of Education in New York City publishes a list of The Best Children's Books for each year, compiled by a committee that includes educators, librarians, authors, parents, and psychologists and also solicits comments from young reviewers across the country. Books are chosen for liter-

ary quality, excellence of presentation, and potential emotional impact on young readers. In addition to compiling the list of titles, the committee presents three annual awards: for fiction, for nonfiction, and for poetry. For further information, see the Web site at *www.bankstreet.edu/bookcom.*

Children's Book Council (CBC)
The Children's Book Council is a not-for-profit organization of publishers and packagers of trade books for children and young adults, located in New York City. Its goals include enhancing public perception of the importance of children's reading and working with other professional groups to increase awareness of children's books. For further information, see the CBC Web site at *www.cbcbooks.org.*

CCBC Choices
The Cooperative Children's Book Center (CCBC) at the University of Wisconsin, Madison, a children's and young adult literature reference library, publishes an annual list of about 250 outstanding books, annotated and arranged by subject area and genre. For more information, see the CCBC Web site at *www.soemadison.wisc.edu/ccbc/.*

Christopher Awards
The Christopher Awards are presented to writers, directors, and producers of books, motion pictures, and television specials that affirm the highest values of the human spirit. Presented by The Christophers, a lay religious organization headquartered in New York City, the most recent awards can be found listed at *www.christophers.org.* The awards were established in 1949.

Coretta Scott King Awards
Since 1970 this annual award, sponsored by the Social Responsibilities Roundtable of the American Library Association, has recognized the creative work of African American authors whose books are deemed outstanding, educational, and inspirational. In 1974 a parallel award was established for African American illustrators. The awards are announced at the Midwinter Conference and presented at the Annual Conference of the ALA.

Golden Kite Awards
Presented annually by the Society of Children's Book Writers and Illustrators, these four awards for children's fiction, nonfiction, picture book text, and picture book illustration are the only ones chosen for authors and artists by their peers. The awards are announced in April of every year, and lists of winners are available at the Society's Web site, *www.scbwi.org.*

Horn Book Fanfare
This annual compilation of 20–30 titles recognizes outstanding books of the previous year. The titles are chosen by the review staff of *The Horn Book* magazine, which publishes the list in an early issue in the new year.

IRA/CBC Children's Choices
A joint project of the International Reading Association and the Children's

Book Council, these books are the favorites of children polled in schools around the country. The list appears in a fall issue of *The Reading Teacher*, a publication of the International Reading Association.

IRA Teachers' Choices
This list identifies trade books that teachers have found outstanding and exceptionally useful in the classroom. The winning titles are selected by teams of teachers throughout the country and published in the November issue of *The Reading Teacher*, with annotations and suggestions for use in the curriculum.

Junior Library Guild
This subscription-service book club reviews books prior to publication and selects twelve a year for each of nine reading levels. Subscribers receive the books at a reduced price. The JLG editorial staff consistently choose books that later win awards and appear on "Best" lists. Once known as the Junior Literary Guild, the Junior Library Guild has its headquarters in Worthington, Ohio.

Newbery Medal and Newbery Honor Awards
Announced annually at the Midwinter Conference of the American Library Association, the Newbery Medal is presented by the Association for Library Service to Children for the most distinguished contribution to literature for children (up to age 14) published in the United States in the preceding year. Other books worthy of notice may also be cited. In 1971 the term "runners-up" was officially changed to "honor books" for these additional titles. Acceptance speeches are made by the Medal winners at a banquet at the Annual Conference of ALA and printed in *The Horn Book* magazine and *The Journal of Youth Services*. The award was established in 1921.

New York Public Library: 100 Titles for Reading and Sharing
This annual list of distinguished books of the year is published in an attractive pamphlet by the Office of Children's Services of the New York Public Library every November. Copies are available for a fee from the Office of Branch Services, New York Public Library, 455 Fifth Avenue, New York, NY 10016.

New York Public Library: Books for the Teen Age
A comprehensive and retrospective list of titles for teens, Books for the Teen Age is published each year by the NYPL Office of Young Adult Services. It is available for a fee from the Office of Branch Services, New York Public Library, 455 Fifth Avenue, New York, NY 10016.

Notable Children's Trade Books in the Field of Social Studies
This list, compiled and fully annotated by a committee of the National Council for the Social Studies in cooperation with the Children's Book Council, includes books intended for grades K–8 published in the previous calendar year. To qualify, books must emphasize human relations, represent a diversity of groups and display sensitivity to a broad range of cultural experiences. The list is published in the April/May issue of *Social Education* and is available in a brochure from the CBC.

Orbis Pictus Award for Outstanding Nonfiction

The National Council of Teachers of English makes this award every year to an informational children's book published in the preceding year. Established in 1990, the award is named for the book *Orbis Pictus*, published by Johan Amos Comenius in 1659 and generally considered the first book created specifically for children.

Outstanding Science Trade Books for Children

A fully annotated list compiled by a committee of the National Science Teachers Association in cooperation with the Children's Book Council, this focuses on books for grades K–8 published during the previous calendar year. The committee uses rigorous guidelines for content and presentation, accuracy and appropriateness for age level. The list is published in *Science and Children* in the spring and is available in a brochure from the CBC.

Parents' Choice Awards

These awards are given to books, toys, videos, computer programs, magazines, audio recordings, and television programs that are judged to be the best and most appealing products in their genre and to have a unique, individual quality. Awards are announced on the Web site *www.parents-choice.org*.

Pura Belpré Awards

Co-sponsored by the Association for Library Service to Children and the National Association to Promote Library Services to the Spanish Speaking, these awards are made biennially to a writer and an illustrator who are Latino/ Latina and whose works affirm and celebrate the Latino experience. First presented in 1996, the Pura Belpré Awards are named for the first Latina librarian in the New York Public Library.

School Library Journal Best Books of the Year

Published annually in the December issue, this list of 50–60 outstanding titles is compiled by the editors of *School Library Journal* from over 4,000 books reviewed throughout that year.

State Awards

Most of the fifty states now sponsor annual children's choice awards through a state library association or educational media association. The winners are typically chosen by children's votes, from a list of 10–20 titles recommended by librarians and teachers.

Note: This is a sampling of the awards and lists that are cited most frequently in this volume. Today children's book authors and illustrators are honored in many ways, an indication of the phenomenal growth of the field and its increasing reputation for excellence and variety. For a complete list of awards in children's literature, consult *Children's Books: Awards and Prizes*, published by the Children's Book Council.

Authors and Illustrators Included in This Series

The following list indicates the volume in which each
person may be found:

J—*The Junior Book of Authors*, second edition (1951)
M—*More Junior Authors* (1963)
3—*Third Book of Junior Authors* (1972)
4—*Fourth Book of Junior Authors and Illustrators* (1978)
5—*Fifth Book of Junior Authors and Illustrators* (1983)
6—*Sixth Book of Junior Authors and Illustrators* (1989)
7—*Seventh Book of Junior Authors and Illustrators* (1996)
8—*Eighth Book of Junior Authors and Illustrators* (2000)

Aruego, José—**4**
Arundel, Honor—**4**
Asch, Frank—**4**
Ashabranner, Brent—**6**
Asher, Sandy—**7**
Ashmun, Margaret—**J**
Asimov, Isaac—**3**
Atwater, Florence Hasseltine Carroll—**M**
Atwater, Montgomery Meigs —**M**
Atwater, Richard Tupper—**M**
Atwood, Ann—**4**
Auch, Mary Jane—**8**
Aulaire, Edgar Parin d'—**J**
Aulaire, Ingri Parin d'—**J**
Austin, Margot—**M**
Averill, Esther—**J**
Avery, Gillian—**4**
Avi—**5**
Ayer, Jacqueline—**3**
Ayer, Margaret—**M**
Aylesworth, Jim—**7**
Azarian, Mary—**8**

"Babbis, Eleanor"
    See Friis-Baastad, Babbis —**3**
Babbitt, Natalie—**4**
Bach, Alice—**5**
Bagnold, Enid—**4**
Bailey, Carolyn Sherwin—**J**
Baity, Elizabeth Chesley—**M**
Baker, Alan—**8**
Baker, Betty—**3**
Baker, Jeannie—**7**
Baker, Keith—**7**
Baker, Leslie—**7**
Baker, Margaret J.—**M**
Baker, Margaret—**J**
Baker, Mary—**J**
Baker, Nina Brown—**J**
Baker, Olaf—**J**
Baker, Rachel—**M**
Balch, Glenn—**M**
Balderson, Margaret—**4**
Baldwin, James—**J**
Balet, Jan—**3**
Balian, Lorna—**5**

"Ball, Zachary"—**4**
"Bancroft, Laura"
    See Baum, L. Frank—**3**
Bang, Betsy Garrett—**5**
Bang, Molly Garrett—**5**
Banks, Lynne Reid—**6**
Bannerman, Helen—**J**
Bannon, Laura—**M**
Barbour, Ralph Henry—**J**
Barne, Kitty—**J**
Barracca, Debra—**7**
Barracca, Sal—**7**
Barrett, Judi—**6**
Barrett, Ron—**6**
Barron, T.A.—**8**
Barton, Byron—**5**
Bartos-Höppner, Barbara—**4**
Base, Graeme Rowland—**7**
Bash, Barbara—**7**
Baskin, Leonard—**5**
Baudouy, Michel-Aimé—**3**
Bauer, Joan—**8**
Bauer, Marion Dane—**5**
Baum, L. Frank—**3**
Baumann, Hans—**3**
Bawden, Nina—**4**
Bayley, Nicola—**6**
Baylor, Byrd—**4**
Baynes, Ernest Harold—**J**
Baynes, Pauline—**3**
"BB"—**3**
"Beach, Webb"
    See Butterworth, W. E.—**5**
Beatty, Hetty Burlingame—**M**
Beatty, John—**3**
Beatty, Patricia—**3**
Becerra de Jenkins, Lyll
    See Jenkins, Lyll Becerra de—**7**
Beckman, Gunnel—**4**
Bedard, Michael—**7**
"Beddows, Eric"—**7**
Beeler, Nelson F.—**M**
Begay, Shonto—**7**
Behn, Harry—**M**
Behrens, June—**8**
Beim, Jarrold—**J**
Beim, Lorraine—**J**
Beisner, Monika—**6**

Bell, Anthea—**7**
Bell, Corydon—**3**
Bell, Margaret E.—**M**
Bell, Thelma—**3**
Bellairs, John—**5**
Belpré, Pura—**4**
Belting, Natalia Maree—**3**
Bemelmans, Ludwig—**M**
Benary-Isbert, Margot—**M**
Benchley, Nathaniel—**4**
Bendick, Jeanne—**M**
Bendick, Robert—**M**
Benét, Laura—**J**
Bennett, Jay—**6**
Bennett, John—**J**
Bennett, Rainey—**4**
Bennett, Richard—**J**
Berenstain, Jan—**5**
Berenstain, Stan—**5**
Berg, Björn—**4**
Berger, Barbara Helen—**6**
Berger, Melvin—**5**
Berna, Paul—**3**
"Bernadette"
    See Watts, Bernadette—**7**
"Berry, Erick"—**J**
Berry, James—**7**
Berson, Harold—**4**
Beskow, Elsa—**J**
Bess, Clayton—**6**
Best, Herbert—**J**
Beston, Henry—**J**
Bethancourt, T. Ernesto—**5**
"Bettina"—**M**
Betz, Betty—**M**
Bial, Raymond—**8**
Bialk, Elisa—**M**
Bianco, Margery Williams—**J**
Bianco, Pamela
    See Bianco, Margery Williams—**J**
Bierhorst, John—**5**
Bileck, Marvin—**4**
Bill, Alfred H.—**J**
Billings, Henry—**M**
Binch, Caroline—**7**
Birch, Reginald—**J**
Birdseye, Tom—**8**
Bischoff, Ilse—**M**

Bishop, Claire Huchet—**J**
Bishop, Elizabeth—**4**
Björk, Christina—**8**
"Blacklin, Malcolm"
   See Chambers, Aidan—**6**
"Blair, Shannon"
   See Kaye, Marilyn—**7**
Blake, Quentin—**5**
"Blake, Walker E."
   See Butterworth, W. E.—**5**
Bleeker, Sonia—**M**
Blegvad, Erik—**3**
Blegvad, Lenore—**3**
Bloch, Marie Halun—**4**
Block, Francesca Lia—**7**
Bloom, Lloyd—**6**
Blos, Joan W—**5**
Blough, Glenn O.—**M**
"Blue, Zachary"
   See Stine, R. L.—**7**
Blumberg, Rhoda—**6**
Blume, Judy—**4, 8**
Bock, Vera—**M**
Bodecker, N. M.—**6**
Bødker, Cecil—**5**
Bois, William Pène du
   See du Bois, William
   Pène—**J**
Bolliger, Max—**4**
Bolognese, Don—**4**
"Bolton, Elizabeth"
   See Johnston, Norma—**5**
"Bolton, Evelyn"
   See "Bunting, Eve"—**5**
Bond, Felicia—**6**
Bond, Michael—**3**
Bond, Nancy—**5**
Bonham, Frank—**3**
Bonners, Susan—**6**
Bonsall, Crosby Newell—**3**
Bontemps, Arna—**J**
Bonzon, Paul-Jacques—**4**
Borton, Elizabeth
   See Treviño, Elizabeth Borton de—**3**
Bosse, Malcolm J.—**5**
Boston, Lucy—**3**
Bothwell, Jean—**J**
Bottner, Barbara—**6**

Bourliaguet, Léonce—**4**
Boutet de Monvel—**J**
Bova, Ben—**5**
"Bowler, Jan Brett"
   See Brett, Jan—**6**
Bowman, James Cloyd—**J**
Boyd, Candy Dawson—**7**
Boylston, Helen—**J**
Bradbury, Bianca—**4**
Brady, Irene—**6**
Bragg, Mabel Caroline—**4**
Brancato, Robin F.—**5**
Brandenberg, Franz—**5**
Branley, Franklyn M.—**M**
Brann, Esther—**J**
Branscum, Robbie—**5**
Bransom, Paul—**M**
"Breck, Vivian"—**M**
Brenner, Barbara—**4**
Brenner, Fred—**4**
Brett, Jan—**6**
Bridgers, Sue Ellen—**5**
Bridwell, Norman R.—**7**
Brier, Howard, M.—**M**
Briggs, K. M.—**5**
Briggs, Raymond—**3**
Bright, Robert—**M**
Brimner, Larry—**8**
Brindze, Ruth—**M**
Brink, Carol Ryrie—**J**
Brinsmead, Hesba Fay—**4**
Brittain, Bill—**5**
Bro, Margueritte—**M**
Brock, C. E.—**J**
Brock, Emma L.—**J**
Brock, H. M.
   See Brock, C. E.—**J**
Brodsky, Beverly—**5**
Bromhall, Winifred—**M**
"Bronson, Lynn"
   See Lampman, Evelyn Sibley—**M**
Bronson, Wilfrid S.—**J**
Brooke, L. Leslie—**J**
Brooke, William J.—**8**
Brooks, Bruce—**6**
Brooks, Gwendolyn—**4**
Brooks, Martha—**7**
Brooks, Polly Schoyer—**7**

Brooks, Walter R.—**J**
Broster, D. K.—**J**
Brown, Don—**8**
Brown, Edna A.—**J**
Brown, Marc—**5**
Brown, Marcia—**M**
Brown, Margaret Wise—**J**
Brown, Palmer—**5**
Brown, Paul—**J**
Brown, Roy—**4**
Browne, Anthony—**6**
Bruchac, Joseph—**8**
Bruckner, Karl—**4**
Bruna, Dick—**5**
Brunhoff, Jean de—**J**
Brunhoff, Laurent de—**M**
Bryan, Ashley—**5**
Bryson, Bernarda—**3**
Buehr, Walter—**3**
Buehner, Caralyn—**8**
Buehner, Mark—**8**
Buff, Conrad—**J**
Buff, Mary Marsh—**J**
Bulla, Clyde Robert—**M, 8**
"Bunting, A. E."
   See "Bunting, Eve"—**5**
"Bunting, Eve"—**5**
Burbank, Addison
   See Newcomb, Covelle—**J**
Burch, Robert—**3**
Burchard, Peter—**3**
Burgess, Thornton W.—**J**
Burglon, Nora—**J**
Burkert, Nancy Ekholm—**3**
"Burnford, S. D."
   See Burnford, Sheila—**4**
Burleigh, Robert—**7**
Burnford, Sheila—**4**
Burningham, John—**3**
Burton, Hester—**3**
Burton, Virginia Lee—**J**
Busoni, Rafaello—**J**
Butler, Beverly—**6**
Butterworth, Oliver—**4**
Butterworth, W. E.—**5**
"Buxton, Ralph."
   See Silverstein, Virginia B.—**5**
Byard, Carole—**7**

Byars, Betsy—**3**

Caduto, Michael—**8**
Cain, Errol Le
  See Le Cain, Errol—**6**
Caldecott, Randolph—**J**
"Calder, Lyn"
  See Calmenson,
  Stephanie—**8**
Calhoun, Mary—**3**
Callen, Larry—**5**
Calmenson, Stephanie—**8**
Calvert, Patricia—**6**
Cameron, Ann—**7**
Cameron, Eleanor—**3**
Cameron, Polly—**4**
Camp, Walter—**J**
"Campbell, Bruce"
  See Epstein, Samuel—**M**
Cannon, Janell—**8**
Carigiet, Alois—**3**
Carle, Eric—**4, 8**
Carlson, Nancy—**8**
Carlson, Natalie Savage—**M**
Carlstrom, Nancy White—**6**
Carpenter, Frances—**M**
Carr, Harriett H.—**M**
Carr, Mary Jane—**J**
Carrick, Carol—**4**
Carrick, Donald—**4**
Carrick, Valery—**J**
Carris, Joan—**7**
Carroll, Latrobe—**M**
Carroll, Ruth—**M**
Carter, Alden—**7**
Carter, Helene—**M**
Caseley, Judith—**7**
Cassedy, Sylvia—**6**
Casserley, Anne—**J**
Catalanotto, Peter—**7**
Caudill, Rebecca—**M**
Cauley, Lorinda Bryan—**6**
Cavanah, Frances—**M**
Cavanna, Betty—**M**
Cazet, Denys—**7**
Chaikin, Miriam—**6**
Chalmers, Mary—**3**
Chambers, Aidan—**6**

"Chambers, Catherine E."
  See Johnston, Norma—**5**
"Chance, Stephen"
  See Turner, Philip—**4**
"Chapman, Walker"
  See Silverberg, Robert—**3**
Chappell, Warren—**3**
"Charles, Nicholas"
  See Kuskin, Karla—**3**
Charlip, Remy—**3**
Charlot, Jean—**M**
"Chase, Alice Elizabeth"
  See McHargue, Georgess
  —**5**
Chase, Mary Ellen—**4**
Chase, Richard—**M**
Chastain, Madye Lee—**M**
Chauncy, Nan—**3**
Chen, Tony—**5**
Cherry, Lynne—**7**
Chess, Victoria—**6**
Chetwin, Grace—**7**
Chew, Ruth—**6**
Childress, Alice—**5**
Chipperfield, Joseph E.—**M**
Chocolate, Debbi—**8**
Choi, Sook Nyul—**8**
Chönz, Selina—**4**
Chorao, Kay—**4**
Chrisman, Arthur Bowie—**J**
Christelow, Eileen—**7**
"Christopher, John"—**4**
Christopher, Matt—**5**
Church, Alfred J.—**J**
Church, Richard—**M**
Chute, B. J.—**M**
Chute, Marchette—**M**
Chwast, Jacqueline—**4**
Chwast, Seymour—**4**
Ciardi, John—**3**
Clapp, Patricia—**5**
"Clare, Helen"
  See Clarke, Pauline—**3**
Clark, Ann Nolan—**J**
Clark, Emma Chichester—**7**
Clark, Mavis Thorpe—**4**
Clarke, Arthur C.—**4**
Clarke, Pauline—**3**
Cleary, Beverly—**M, 8**

Cleaver, Bill—**4**
Cleaver, Elizabeth—**4**
Cleaver, Vera—**4**
Clements, Andrew—**8**
Clements, Bruce—**5**
Clifford, Eth—**6**
Clifton, Lucille—**5**
Climo, Shirley—**7**
Clymer, Eleanor—**4**
Coatsworth, Elizabeth—**J**
Cobb, Vicki—**5**
Cober, Alan E.—**4**
Coblentz, Catherine Cate—**J**
Coerr, Eleanor—**6**
Coggins, Jack—**M**
Cohen, Barbara—**5**
Cohen, Daniel—**6**
Cohen, Miriam—**5**
Colby, Carroll B.—**M**
Cole, Babette—**7**
Cole, Brock—**6**
Cole, Joanna—**5**
Cole, William—**4**
"Colin, Ann"
  See Ure, Jean—**6**
Collier, Christopher—**5**
Collier, James Lincoln—**5**
"Collodi, Carlo"—**J**
Collington, Peter—**7**
Colman, Hila—**3**
Colum, Padraic—**J**
Coman, Carolyn—**8**
Cone, Molly —**3**
Conford, Ellen—**5**
Conklin, Gladys—**4**
Conly, Jane Leslie—**7**
Conover, Chris—**6**
Conrad, Pam—**6**
Conroy, Robert
  See Goldston, Robert Con-
  roy—**4**
"Cook, John Estes"
  See Baum, L. Frank—**3**
Coolidge, Olivia E.—**M**
Coombs, Patricia—**5**
Cooney, Barbara—**M**
Cooney, Caroline B.—**8**
Cooper, Elizabeth K.—**4**
Cooper, Floyd—**7**

Cooper, Ilene—**8**
"Cooper, Melrose"
    See Kroll, Virginia—**8**
Cooper, Susan—**4, 8**
Corbett, Scott—**4**
Corbin, William—**M**
Corcoran, Barbara—**5**
Cormack, Maribelle—**J**
Cormier, Robert—**5**
Cosgrave, John O'Hara, II—**M**
Cosgrove, Margaret—**4**
Cottrell, Leonard—**4**
Courlander, Harold—**M**
Cousins, Lucy—**8**
Coville, Bruce—**7**
Cowcher, Helen—**7**
Craft, Ruth—**5**
Craig, Helen—**8**
Craig, M. Jean—**4**
Craig, Margaret Maze—**M**
Crane, Walter—**J**
Crawford, Phyllis—**J**
"Crayder, Teresa"
    See Colman, Hila—**3**
Credle, Ellis—**J**
Creech, Sharon—**7**
Cresswell, Helen—**4**
Crew, Fleming H.
    See Gall, Alice Crew—**J**
Crew, Helén Coale—**J**
Crew, Linda—**7**
Crews, Donald—**5**
Crichlow, Ernest—**4**
Cross, Gillian—**6**
Crossley-Holland, Kevin—**4**
Crowell, Pers—**M**
Crownfield, Gertrude—**J**
Crump, Irving—**J**
Crutcher, Chris—**7**
Ctvrtek, Václav—**4**
Cuffari, Richard—**5**
Cullen, Countée—**4**
Cummings, Betty Sue—**5**
Cummings, Pat—**6**
Cunningham, Julia—**3**
Curry, Jane Louise—**4**
Curtis, Christopher Paul—**8**
Cushman, Doug—**8**
Cushman, Karen—**7**

Culter, Jane—**8**
Cuyler, Margery—**7**

Dabcovich, Lydia—**6**
Dadey, Debbie—**8**
Dahl, Borghild—**3**
Dahl, Roald—**3**
Dalgliesh, Alice—**J**
Daly, Maureen—**M**
Daly, Niki—**6**
Dana, Barbara—**7**
Daniel, Hawthorne—**J**
Danziger, Paula—**5**
Daringer, Helen Fern—**M**
Darling, Louis—**M**
Daugherty, James—**J**
d'Aulaire, Edgar & Ingri
    Parin
    See Aulaire, Edgar & Ingri
    Parin d'—**J**
"David, Jonathan"
    See Ames, Lee Judah—**6**
Davies, Andrew—**5**
Davis, Jenny—**7**
Davis, Julia—**J**
Davis, Lavinia R.—**J**
Davis, Mary Gould—**J**
Davis, Robert—**J**
Davol, Marguerite—**8**
"Day, Alexandra"—**7**
de Angeli, Marguerite—**J**
de Brunhoff, Jean
    See Brunhoff, Jean de—**J**
de Brunhoff, Laurent
    See Brunhoff, Laurent de
    —**M**
de Groat, Diane—**5**
de Jong, Dola—**M**
de Jenkins, Lyll Becerra
    See Jenkins, Lyll Becerra
    de—**7**
De La Mare, Walter—**J**
de Leeuw, Adèle—**J**
de Leeuw, Cateau
    See de Leeuw, Adèle—**J**
de Regniers, Beatrice Schenk
    —**M**
de Saint-Exupéry, Antoine
    See Saint-Exupéry, Anto-
    ine de—**4**

de Treviño, Elizabeth Borton
    See Treviño, Elizabeth Bor-
    ton de—**3**
De Veaux, Alexis—**7**
DeClements, Barthe—**6**
DeFelice, Cynthia—**7**
Degen, Bruce—**6**
Degens, T.—**5**
DeJong, Meindert—**M**
del Rey, Lester—**3**
Delacre, Lulu—**8**
Delessert, Etienne—**6**
"Delmar, Roy"
    See Wexler, Jerome—**7**
Delton, Judy—**5**
"Delving, Michael"
    See Williams, Jay—**4**
Demi—**6**
Dennis, Morgan—**M**
Dennis, Wesley—**M**
Denslow, W. W.—**4**
dePaola, Tomie—**5**
Desimini, Lisa—**7**
Deucher, Sybil—**M**
Deutsch, Babette—**M**
Dewey, Ariane—**4**
Diamond, Donna—**5**
Diaz, David—**7**
Dickinson, Peter—**4**
Dickson, Marguerite—**M**
Dillon, Eilís—**3**
Dillon, Leo & Diane—**5**
Ditmars, Raymond L.—**J**
Dix, Beulah Marie—**J**
"Dixon, Page"
    See Corcoran, Barbara—**5**
Doane, Pelagie—**M**
Doherty, Berlie—**7**
Dolan, Edward—**8**
Dolbier, Maurice—**M**
Domanska, Janina—**3**
Donovan, John—**5**
Dorris, Michael—**7**
Dorros, Arthur—**7**
Doty, Roy—**8**
"Douglas, James McM."
    See Butterworth, W. E.—**5**
Dowden, Anne Ophelia—**5**
Dragonwagon, Crescent—**6**

Draper, Sharon M.—**8**
Drescher, Henrik—**6**
Drummond, V. H.—**3**
"Drummond, Walter"
    See Silverberg, Robert—**3**
"Dryden, Pamela"
    See Johnston, Norma—**5**
du Bois, William Pène—**J**
du Jardin, Rosamond—**M**
Du Soe, Robert C.—**M**
Duder, Tessa—**7**
Duff, Maggie—**6**
Duffey, Betsy—**8**
Duggan, Alfred—**4**
Duke, Kate—**8**
Dulac, Edmund—**J**
Duncan, Norman—**J**
"Duncan, Lois"—**5**
Dunlop, Eileen—**6**
Dunrea, Olivier—**7**
Duvoisin, Roger—**J**
Dyer, Jane—**7**
Dygard, Thomas J.—**6**

Eager, Edward—**M**
Earle, Olive L.—**M**
Eastman, Charles A.—**J**
Eaton, Jeanette—**J**
Eberle, Irmengarde—**J**
Eckert, Allan W.—**4**
Edmonds, Walter Dumaux
    —**M**
Egielski, Richard—**6**
Ehlert, Lois—**7**
Ehrlich, Amy—**7**
Eichenberg, Fritz—**M**
Eipper, Paul—**J**
Elkin, Benjamin—**4**
Ellis, Ella—**5**
Ellis, Sarah—**7**
Ellsberg, Commander
    Edward —**J**
Els, Betty Vander
    See Vander Els, Betty—**6**
Elting, Mary—**M**
Emberley, Barbara—**3**
Emberley, Ed—**3**
Emberley, Rebecca—**8**
Emery, Ann—**M**

Engdahl, Sylvia Louise—**4**
Enright, Elizabeth—**J**
Epstein, Beryl Williams—**M**
Epstein, Samuel—**M**
Erdman, Loula Grace—**M**
Ernst, Lisa Campbell—**7**
Esbensen, Barbara Juster—**8**
Estes, Eleanor—**J**
"Estoril, Jean"
    See Allen, Mabel Esther
    —**6**
Ets, Marie Hall—**J**
Evans, Eva Knox—**M**
"Every, Philip Cochrane"
    See Burnford, Sheila—**4**
Eyerly, Jeannette—**5**
Eyre, Katherine Wigmore
    —**M**

Fabre, Jean-Henri—**J**
Facklam, Margery—**8**
"Fall, Thomas"—**4**
Falls, C. B.—**J**
Farber, Norma—**5**
Farjeon, Eleanor—**J**
Farley, Carol—**5**
Farley, Walter—**J**
Farmer, Nancy—**7**
Farmer, Penelope—**4**
Fatio, Louise—**M**
"Faulkner, Anne Irvin"
    See Faulkner, Nancy—**4**
Faulkner, Nancy—**4**
Feagles, Anita MacRae—**4**
Feelings, Muriel—**4**
Feelings, Tom—**3, 8**
Felsen, Gregor—**J**
Felton, Harold W.—**M**
Fenner, Carol—**8**
Fenton, Carroll Lane—**M**
Fenton, Edward—**3**
Fenton, Mildred Adams—**M**
Ferris, Helen—**J**
Feydy, Anne Lindbergh
    See Lindbergh, Anne—**6**
Field, Rachel—**J**
Fife, Dale—**4**
Fillmore, Parker—**J**
Fine, Anne—**7**

Fischer, Hans Erich—**M**
Fisher, Aileen—**M**
Fisher, Leonard Everett—**3, 8**
Fitch, Florence Mary—**M**
"Fitzgerald, Captain Hugh"
    See Baum, L. Frank—**3**
Fitzgerald, John D.—**5**
Fitzhugh, Louise—**3**
Flack, Marjorie—**J**
Fleischman, Paul—**5**
Fleischman, Sid—**3**
Fleming, Denise—**7**
Fleming, Ian—**5**
Fletcher, Ralph—**8**
Floethe, Richard—**M**
Floherty, John J.—**J**
Flora, James—**3**
Florian, Douglas—**6**
Forberg, Ati—**4**
Forbes, Esther—**M**
Foreman, Michael—**6**
Forman, James—**3**
Fortnum, Peggy—**4**
Foster, Genevieve—**J**
Fox, Mem—**6**
Fox, Paula—**4**
Fradin, Dennis Brindell—**8**
"Francis, Dee"
    See Haas, Dorothy—**6**
François, André—**3**
"Françoise"—**M**
Franchere, Ruth—**4**
Franklin, George Cory—**M**
Frascino, Edward—**5**
Frasconi, Antonio—**3**
Fraser, Claud Lovat—**J**
Freedman, Russell—**6**
"Freedman, Peter J."
    See Calvert, Patricia—**6**
Freeman, Don—**M**
Freeman, Ira Maximilian—**M**
Freeman, Lydia—**M**
Freeman, Mae Blacker—**M**
Freeman, Suzanne—**8**
French, Allen—**J**
French, Fiona—**7**
"French, Paul"
    See Asimov, Isaac—**3**
Freschet, Berniece—**4**

Friedman, Frieda—**M**
Friermood, Elisabeth Hamilton —**M**
"Friis, Babbis"
See Friis-Baastad, Babbis —**3**
Friis-Baastad, Babbis—**3**
Fritz, Jean—**3, 8**
Froman, Robert—**4**
Frost, Frances—**M**
Fry, Rosalie K.—**3**
Fuchs, Erich—**4**
Fujikawa, Gyo—**4**
Fyleman, Rose—**J**

Gackenbach, Dick—**5**
Gaer, Joseph—**M**
Gág, Flavia—**M**
Gág, Wanda—**J**
"Gage, Wilson"—**3**
Galdone, Paul—**3**
Gall, Alice Crew—**J**
Gallant, Roy A.—**5**
Galt, Tom—**M**
Gammell, Stephen—**5**
Gannett, Ruth Chrisman—**M**
Gannett, Ruth Stiles—**4**
Gans, Roma—**5**
Gantos, John—**5**
Garcia, Rita Williams-
See Williams-Garcia, Rita—**8**
Gardam, Jane—**5**
Garden, Nancy—**5**
Gardiner, John Reynolds—**6**
Gardner, Beau—**6**
Gardner, John—**5**
Garfield, Leon—**4**
Garland, Sherry—**7**
Garner, Alan—**3**
Garnett, Eve—**5**
Garrett, Randall
See Silverberg, Robert—**3**
Garrigue, Sheila—**6**
Garst, Shannon—**J**
Garza, Carmen Lomas—**8**
Gates, Doris—**J**
Gatti, Attilio—**J**
Gauch, Patricia Lee—**5**

Gay, Kathlyn—**8**
Gay, Zhenya—**M**
Geisel, Theodor Seuss
See "Seuss, Dr."—**M**
Geisert, Arthur—**7**
Gekiere, Madeleine—**3**
George, Jean Craighead —**M, 8**
Geras, Ad`ele—**8**
Gerrard, Roy—**7**
Gerstein, Mordicai—**6**
Gibbons, Gail—**6**
Giblin, James Cross—**6**
"Gibson, Josephine"
See Hine, Al & Joslin, Sesyle—**3**
Gibson, Katharine—**J**
Giff, Patricia Reilly—**5**
Gilchrist, Jan Spivey—**7**
Gill, Margery—**4**
Gilson, Jamie—**6**
Ginsburg, Mirra—**6**
Giovanni, Nikki—**5**
Giovanopoulos, Paul—**4**
Gipson, Fred—**3**
Girion, Barbara—**6**
Girvan, Helen—**M**
Glaser, Milton—**4**
Glass, Andrew—**6**
Glenn, Mel—**7**
Glubok, Shirley—**3**
Goble, Dorothy
See Goble, Paul—**4**
Goble, Paul—**4**
Godden, Rumer—**M**
Goffstein, M. B.—**4**
Goldsmith, Diane Hoyt-
See Hoyt-Goldsmith, Diane—**7**
Goldston, Robert Conroy—**4**
Gollomb, Joseph—**J**
González, Lucía M.—**8**
Goodall, John S.—**4**
Goode, Diane—**5**
Goor, Nancy—**7**
Goor, Ron—**7**
Gordon, Sheila—**7**
Gorey, Edward—**4**
Gorog, Judith—**7**

Goudey, Alice E.—**3**
Goudge, Elizabeth—**3**
Grabianski, Janusz—**3**
Graham, Lorenz—**3**
Graham, Margaret Bloy—**M**
Graham, Shirley—**M**
Gramatky, Hardie—**J**
Gray, Elizabeth Janet—**J**
Gray, Libba Moore—**8**
Green, Roger Lancelyn—**3**
Greenaway, Kate—**J**
Greenberg, Jan—**6**
Greene, Bette—**5**
Greene, Constance C.—**4**
Greenfeld, Howard—**7**
Greenfield, Eloise—**5**
"Greenwald, Sheila"—**5**
Greenwood, Ted—**4**
"Gregory, Jean"
See Ure, Jean—**6**
Grierson, Elizabeth W.—**J**
Grifalconi, Ann—**3**
Griffin, Adele—**8**
Griffith, Helen V.—**7**
"Griffith, Jeannette"
See Eyerly, Jeannette—**5**
Griffiths, Helen—**4**
Grimes, Nikki—**8**
Grinnell, George Bird—**J**
Gripe, Harald
See Gripe, Maria—**3**
Gripe, Maria—**3**
Groat, Diane de
See de Groat, Diane—**5**
Guevara, Susan—**8**
Guillot, René—**M**
Guin, Ursula K. Le
See Le Guin, Ursula K.—**4**
Gundersheimer, Karen—**6**
Gurko, Leo—**3**
Gurko, Miriam—**3**
Guy, Rosa—**5**

Haar, Jaap ter—**4**
Haas, Dorothy—**6**
Haas, Irene—**3**
Haas, Jessie—**8**
Haddix, Margaret Peterson —**8**

Hader, Berta—**J**
Hader, Elmer—**J**
"Hadith, Mwenye"—**7**
Hadley, Lee
   See "Irwin, Hadley"—**6**
Hafner, Marylin—**6**
"Hagon, Priscilla"
   See Allen, Mabel Esther
   —**6**
Hague, Michael—**5**
Hahn, Mary Downing—**6**
Halacy, D. S. Jr.—**5**
Haley, Gail E.—**3**
Hall, Donald Jr.—**5**
Hall, Lynn—**5**
Hall, Rosalyn Haskell—**M**
Halperin, Wendy Ander-
   son—**8**
"Hamilton, Gail"
   See Corcoran, Barbara—**5**
Hamilton, Virginia—**4**
Hamre, Leif—**4**
Handford, Martin—**7**
Handforth, Thomas—**J**
Hanlon, Emily—**6**
Hansen, Joyce—**8**
Harkins, Philip—**M**
Harness, Cheryl—**8**
Harnett, Cynthia—**3**
Harris, Christie—**4**
"Harris, Lavinia"
   See Johnston, Norma—**5**
Harris, Rosemary—**4**
Harrison, Ted—**8**
Hartman, Gertrude—**J**
Harvey, Brett—**6**
Haseley, Dennis—**7**
Haskell, Helen Eggleston—**J**
Haskins, James
   See Haskins, Jim—**6**
Haskins, Jim—**6**
Hastings, Selina—**8**
Haugaard, Erik Christian—**3**
Hautzig, Deborah—**5**
Hautzig, Esther—**3**
Havighurst, Marion—**M**
Havighurst, Walter—**M**
Haviland, Virginia—**4**
Havill, Juanita—**7**

Hawkes, Kevin—**7**
Hawkinson, John—**4**
Hawthorne, Hildegarde—**J**
Hays, Michael—**8**
Hays, Wilma Pitchford—**3**
Haywood, Carolyn—**J**
Hazen, Barbara Shook—**6**
Headley, Elizabeth
   See Cavanna, Betty—**M**
Hearne, Betsy—**6**
Heide, Florence Parry—**4**
Heine, Helme—**6**
Heinlein, Robert A.—**M**
Heller, Ruth—**7**
Hendershot, Judith—**6**
Henderson, Le Grand
   See "Le Grand"—**J**
Henkes, Kevin—**6**
Hennessy, B. G.—**7**
Henry, Marguerite—**J**
Henstra, Friso—**4**
Hentoff, Nat—**3**
Herald, Kathleen
   See Peyton, K. M.—**3**
Herman, Charlotte—**7**
Hermes, Patricia—**6**
Hess, Fjeril—**J**
Hess, Lilo—**5**
Hesse, Karen—**8**
Hest, Amy—**7**
Hewes, Agnes Danforth—**J**
Heyliger, William—**J**
Hightower, Florence—**3**
Highwater, Jamake—**5**
Hildick, E. W.—**4**
Hill, Douglas—**6**
Hill, Eric—**6**
Hillenbrand, Will—**8**
"Hillman, Martin"
   See Hill, Douglas—**6**
Hillyer, V. M.—**J**
Himler, Ronald—**6**
Hine, Al—**3**
Hines, Anna Grossnickle—**6**
Hinton, S. E.—**4**
"Hippopotamus, Eugene H."
   See Kraus, Robert—**3**
Hirsch, S. Carl—**3**
Hirschi, Ron—**8**

Hirsh, Marilyn—**5**
"Hitz, Demi"
   See Demi—**6**
Ho, Minfong—**7**
Hoban, Lillian—**3**
Hoban, Russell—**3**
Hoban, Tana—**4**
Hobbs, Will—**7**
Hoberman, Mary Ann—**6**
Hodges, C. Walter—**3**
Hodges, Margaret Moore—**4**
Hoff, Syd—**3**
Hoffman, Mary—**7**
Hoffman, Rosekrans—**7**
Hoffmann, Felix—**3**
Hofsinde, Robert—**3**
Hogan, Inez—**M**
Hogner, Dorothy—**J**
Hogner, Nils—**J**
Hogrogian, Nonny—**3**
Holabird, Katharine—**8**
Holberg, Richard A.—**J**
Holberg, Ruth—**J**
Holbrook, Stewart—**3**
Holland, Isabelle—**5**
Holland, Kevin Crossley-
   See Crossley-Holland,
   Kevin—**4**
Holland, Rupert Sargent—**J**
Holling, H. C.—**J**
Holling, Lucille W.
   See Holling, H. C.—**J**
Holm, Anne—**4**
Holman, Felice—**4**
Höppner, Barbara Bartos-
   See Bartos-Höppner, Bar-
   bara—**5**
Hoobler, Thomas & Dor-
   othy—**8**
Hooks, William H.—**6**
Hoover, Helen M.—**5**
Hopkins, Lee Bennett—**5**
Hosford, Dorothy—**M**
Hotze, Sollace—**7**
Houston, Gloria—**7**
Houston, James A.—**4**
Howard, Elizabeth Fitzger-
   ald—**7**
Howard, Elizabeth—**M**

Howard, Ellen—**7**
Howe, Deborah—**6**
Howe, James—**6**
Howker, Janni—**6**
Hoyt-Goldsmith, Diane—**7**
Hudson, Cheryl Willis—**8**
Hudson, Jan—**7**
Hudson, Wade—**8**
Hughes, Dean—**6**
"Hughes, Eden"
   See Butterworth, W. E.—**5**
Hughes, Langston—**4**
Hughes, Monica—**6**
Hughes, Shirley—**5**
Hunt, Clara Whitehill—**J**
Hunt, Irene—**3**
Hunt, Mabel Leigh—**J**
Hunter, Kristin—**4**
Hunter, Mollie—**3**
Huntington, Harriet E.—**M**
Hurd, Clement—**M**
Hurd, Edith Thacher—**M**
Hurd, Thacher—**6**
Hürlimann, Bettina—**3**
Hurmence, Belinda—**6**
Hurwitz, Johanna—**6**
Hutchins, Pat—**4**
Hutchins, Ross E.—**3**
Hutton, Warwick—**6**
Hyde, Margaret O.—**3**
Hyman, Trina Schart—**4, 8**

Ichikawa, Satomi—**7**
"Ilin, M."—**J**
Ingpen, Robert—**7**
Ipcar, Dahlov—**3**
"Irving, Robert"
   See Adler, Irving—**3**
Irwin, Annabelle Bowen
   See "Irwin, Hadley"—**6**
"Irwin, Hadley"—**6**
Isaacs, Anne—**8**
Isadora, Rachel—**5**
Isbert, Margot Benary-
   See Benary-Isbert, Mar-
   got—**M**
Ish-Kishor, Sulamith—**5**
Iterson, S. R. van—**4**

"J Marks"
   See Highwater, Jamake—**5**
Jackson, Jacqueline—**4**
Jacques, Brian—**7**
Jacques, Robin—**3**
Jaffe, Nina—**8**
Jagendorf, Moritz Adolf—**M**
"James, Dynely"
   See Mayne, William—**3**
James, Will—**J**
Janeczko, Paul B.—**6**
"Janosch"—**4**
Jansson, Tove—**3**
Jardin, Rosamond du
   See du Jardin,
   Rosamond—**M**
Jarrell, Randall—**3**
Jasperson, Willliam—**7**
Jauss, Anne Marie—**4**
Jeffers, Susan—**4**
Jenkins, Lyll Becerra de—**7**
Jenkins, Steve—**8**
Jeschke, Susan—**5**
Jewett, Eleanore M.—**M**
Johnson, Angela—**7**
Johnson, Annabel—**3**
"Johnson, Crockett"—**3**
Johnson, Dolores—**8**
Johnson, Edgar—**3**
Johnson, Gerald W.—**3**
Johnson, J. Rosamond
   See Johnson, James Wel-
   don—**4**
Johnson, James Weldon—**4**
Johnson, Margaret Sweet—**J**
Johnson, Siddie Joe—**J**
Johnson, Steven T.—**8**
Johnston, Johanna—**4**
Johnston, Norma—**5**
Johnston, Tony—**6**
Jonas, Ann—**7**
Jones, Adrienne—**5**
Jones, Diana Wynne—**5**
Jones, Elizabeth Orton—**J**
Jones, Harold—**3**
Jones, Jessie Orton—**5**
Jones, Marcia Thornton—**8**
Jones, Mary Alice—**M**
Jones, Rebecca C.—**7**

Jones, Tim Wynne-
   See Wynne-Jones, Tim—**8**
Jones, Weyman B.—**4**
Jong, Dola de
   See de Jong, Dola—**M**
Joose, Barbara M.—**7**
Jordan, June—**4**
"Jorgenson, Ivar"
   See Silverberg, Robert—**3**
Joslin, Sesyle—**3**
Joyce, William—**6**
Judson, Clara Ingram—**J**
Jukes, Mavis—**6**
Juster, Norton—**4**
Justus, May—**J**

Kahl, Virginia—**M**
Kalashnikoff, Nicholas—**M**
Kalman, Maira—**7**
Karas, G. Brian—**8**
Karl, Jean E—**5**
Kästner, Erich—**3**
Kasza, Keiko—**7**
Kaye, Marilyn—**7**
Keats, Ezra Jack—**M**
Keeping, Charles—**3**
Kehret, Peg—**8**
Keith, Eros—**4**
Keith, Harold—**M**
Keller, Beverly—**7**
Kelley, True—**8**
Kellogg, Steven—**4**
Kelly, Eric P.—**J**
Kelsey, Alice Geer—**M**
Kendall, Carol—**3**
"Kendall, Lace"
   See Stoutenburg, Adrien
   —**3**
Kennaway, Adrienne—**7**
Kennedy, Richard—**5**
Kennedy, X. J.—**6**
Kent, Jack—**5**
Kent, Louise Andrews—**J**
Kepes, Juliet—**3**
Ker Wilson, Barbara—**4**
Kerr, Judith—**5**
"Kerr, M. E."—**4**
"Kerry, Lois"
   See "Duncan, Lois"—**5**

Kessler, Ethel—**5**
Kessler, Leonard—**5**
Kettelkamp, Larry—**3**
Khalsa, Dayal Kaur—**7**
Kherdian, David—**5**
Kimmel, Eric A.—**7**
Kindl, Patrice—**8**
King-Smith, Dick—**6**
"Kinsey, Elizabeth"
　See Clymer, Eleanor—**4**
Kinsey-Warnock, Natalie—**8**
"Kirtland, G. B."
　See Hine, Al & Joslin,
　Sesyle—**3**
Kingman, Lee—**M**
Kitamura, Satoshi—**8**
Kitchen, Bert—**7**
Kjelgaard, Jim—**J**
Klass, Sheila Solomon—**8**
Klause, Annette Curtis—**7**
Klein, Norma—**5**
Kleven, Elisa—**7**
Kline, Suzy—**7**
Knight, Eric—**4**
Knight, Hilary—**4**
Knight, Kathryn Lasky
　See Lasky, Kathryn—**6**
Knight, Ruth Adams—**M**
Knipe, Alden Arthur—**J**
Knipe, Emilie Benson—**J**
"Knox, Calvin M."
　See Silverberg, Robert—**3**
Knox, Rose B.—**J**
Knudson, R. R.—**6**
Koehn, Ilse—**5**
Koering, Ursula—**M**
Koertge, Ron—**7**
Komaiko, Leah—**8**
Konigsburg, E. L.—**3, 8**
Korman, Gordon—**7**
Krahn, Fernando—**4**
Krasilovsky, Phyllis—**M**
Kraus, Robert—**3**
Krauss, Ruth—**M**
Kredel, Fritz—**M**
Krementz, Jill—**5**
Krensky, Stephen—**6**
Kroll, Steven—**5**
Kroll, Virginia—**8**

Krull, Kathleen—**7**
Krumgold, Joseph—**M**
Krush, Beth—**M**
Krush, Joe—**M**
Krüss, James—**3**
Kuklin, Susan—**7**
Kullman, Harry—**5**
Kurelek, William—**5**
Kurtz, Jane—**8**
Kuskin, Karla—**3**
Kyle, Anne D.—**J**
"Kyle, Elisabeth"—**M**

Laan, Nancy Van
　See Van Laan, Nancy—**8**
Laboulaye, Édouard—**J**
La Mare, Walter De
　See De La Mare, Walter—**J**
Lamb, Harold—**J**
Lambert, Janet—**3**
Lamorisse, Albert—**4**
Lampman, Evelyn Sibley—**M**
Lamprey, Louise—**J**
Landau, Elaine—**8**
Langstaff, John—**3**
Langton, Jane—**5**
Lansing, Marion Florence—**J**
Larrick, Nancy—**8**
Lasker, Joe—**5**
Laskowski, Jerzy—**3**
Lasky, Kathryn—**6**
Latham, Jean Lee—**M**
Lathrop, Dorothy P.—**J**
Lattimore, Deborah Nourse
　—**7**
Lattimore, Eleanor Frances
　—**J**
Lauber, Patricia—**3**
Laut, Agnes C.—**J**
Lavies, Bianca—**7**
Lawrence, Jacob—**4**
Lawrence, Louise—**6**
Lawrence, Mildred—**M**
Lawson, Don—**6**
Lawson, Marie Abrams
　See Lawson, Robert—**J**
Lawson, Robert—**J**
Le Cain, Errol—**6**
Le Guin, Ursula K.—**4**

Le Sueur, Meridel—**M**
Le Tord, Bijou—**6**
Leach, Maria—**4**
Leaf, Munro—**J**
Lee, Dennis—**7**
Lee, Dom—**8**
Lee, Jeanne M.—**8**
Lee, Manning de V.—**M**
Lee, Marie G.—**8**
Lee, Mildred—**3**
Lee, Tina—**M**
Leedy, Loreen—**7**
Leeming, Joseph—**J**
Leeuw, Adèle de
　See de Leeuw, Adèle—**J**
Leeuwen, Jean Van
　See Van Leeuwen, Jean—**5**
"Le Grand"—**J**
Leighton, Margaret—**M**
"L'Engle, Madeleine"—**M**
Lenski, Lois—**J**
Lent, Blair—**3**
Lent, Henry B.—**J**
"Leodhas, Sorche Nic"
　See "Nic Leodhas,
　Sorche"—**3**
Lerner, Carol—**6**
Leroe, Ellen W.—**7**
Lessac, Frané—**8**
Lester, Alison—**8**
Lester, Helen—**8**
Lester, Julius—**4, 8**
Levin, Betty—**6**
Levine, Ellen—**7**
Levine, Gail Carson—**8**
Levinson, Riki—**6**
Levitin, Sonia—**5**
Levoy, Myron—**5**
Levy, Elizabeth—**5**
Lewellen, John—**M**
Lewin, Betsy—**8**
Lewin, Ted—**7**
Lewis, C. S.—**M**
Lewis, E. B.—**8**
Lewis, Elizabeth Foreman—**J**
Lewis, J. Patrick—**7**
Lewis, Richard—**7**
Lewiton, Mina—**M**
Lexau, Joan M.—**4**

Ley, Willy—**3**
Lifton, Betty Jean—**3**
Lindbergh, Anne—**6**
Lindbergh, Reeve—**7**
Linde, Gunnel—**4**
Lindenbaum, Pija—**7**
Linderman, Frank B.—**J**
Lindgren, Astrid—**M**
Lindgren, Barbro—**6**
Lindman, Maj—**J**
Lindquist, Jennie D.—**M**
Lindquist, Willis—**M**
Lingard, Joan—**5**
Lionni, Leo—**3**
Lipkind, William—**M**
Lippincott, Joseph Wharton—**M**
Lipsyte, Robert—**5**
Lisle, Janet Taylor—**6**
Little, Jean—**4**
Lively, Penelope—**4**
Livingston, Myra Cohn—**4**
Lloyd, Megan—**8**
Lobel, Anita—**3**
Lobel, Arnold—**3**
Locke, Robert
  See Bess, Clayton—**6**
Locker, Thomas—**6**
Löfgren, Ulf—**4**
Lofting, Hugh—**J**
London, Jonathan—**8**
Longstreth, T. Morris—**M**
Lord, Beman—**4**
Lord, Bette Bao—**6**
"Lord, Nancy"
  See Titus, Eve —**3**
Lorraine, Walter—**4**
Lovelace, Maud Hart—**J**
Low, Alice—**6**
Low, Joseph—**3**
Lownsbery, Eloise—**J**
Lowry, Lois—**5**
Lubell, Cecil—**4**
Lubell, Winifred—**4**
Lucas, Jannette May—**J**
Luenn, Nancy—**8**
Lunn, Janet—**6**
Lynch, Chris—**7**
Lynch, P. J.—**8**

Lyon, George Ella—**7**
Lyons, Mary E.—**7**

Macaulay, David—**5**
MacBride, Roger Lea—**8**
MacDonald, Amy—**8**
"MacDonald, Golden"
  See Brown, Margaret Wise—**J**
MacDonald, Suse—**6**
MacGregor, Ellen—**M**
Machotka, Hana—**7**
Mack, Stan—**4**
Mackay, Constance D'Arcy—**J**
MacKinstry, Elizabeth—**M**
MacLachlan, Patricia—**6**
MacPherson, Margaret—**4**
Maestro, Betsy—**6**
Maestro, Giulio—**6**
Magorian, Michelle—**6**
Maguire, Gregory—**8**
Mahy, Margaret—**4**
Maitland, Antony—**4**
Malcolmson, Anne—**M**
Malkus, Alida Sims—**J**
Malvern, Corinne
  See Malvern, Gladys—**J**
Malvern, Gladys—**J**
Manes, Stephen—**7**
Manning-Sanders, Ruth—**3**
Manushkin, Fran—**8**
Marcellino, Fred—**7**
Mare, Walter De La
  See De La Mare, Walter—**J**
"Mariana"—**3**
Marino, Jan—**7**
Maris, Ron—**8**
Mark, Jan—**5**
Marrin, Albert—**7**
Mars, W. T.—**4**
Marshall, James—**4**
Martin, Ann M.—**7**
Martin, Bill, Jr.—**6**
"Martin, Fredric."
  See Christopher, Matt—**5**
Martin, Patricia Miles
  See "Miles, Miska"—**4**
Martin, Rafe—**7**

Maruki, Toshi—**6**
Marzollo, Jean—**6**
Mason, Miriam E.—**M**
Matas, Carol—**7**
Mathers, Petra—**7**
Mathis, Sharon Bell—**4**
Matsuno, Masako—**4**
Mayer, Marianna—**4**
Mayer, Mercer—**4**
Mayne, William—**3**
Mays, Victor—**4**
Mazer, Harry—**5**
Mazer, Norma Fox—**5**
McCaffrey, Anne—**5**
McCaughrean, Geraldine—**8**
McCloskey, Robert—**J**
"McClune, Dan"
  See Haas, Dorothy—**6**
McClung, Robert M.—**M**
McCord, David—**3**
McCracken, Harold—**J**
"McCulloch, Sarah"
  See Ure, Jean—**6**
McCully, Emily Arnold—**4**
McCurdy, Michael—**7**
McDermott, Beverly Brodsky
  See Brodsky, Beverly—**5**
McDermott, Gerald—**5**
"McDole, Carol"
  See Farley, Carol—**5**
"McDonald, Jamie"
  See Heide, Florence Parry—**4**
McDonald, Megan—**7**
McDonnell, Christine—**6**
McGinley, Phyllis—**J**
McGovern, Ann—**4**
McGraw, Eloise Jarvis—**M**
McHargue, Georgess—**5**
McKay, Hilary—**8**
McKillip, Patricia A.—**5**
McKinley, Robin—**5**
McKissack, Fredrick L.—**7**
McKissack, Patricia—**7**
McKown, Robin—**3**
McLean, Allan Campbell—**4**
"McLennan, Will"
  See Wisler, G. Clifton—**7**
McMahon, Patricia—**8**

McMeekin, Isabel McLennan —**M**
McMillan, Bruce—**6**
McNaughton, Colin—**8**
McNeely, Marian Hurd—**J**
McNeer, May—**J**
McNeill, Janet—**4**
McPhail, David—**5**
McSwigan, Marie—**M**
Meade, Holly—**8**
Meader, Stephen W.—**J**
Meadowcroft, Enid—**J**
Meaker, Marijane
　　See "Kerr, M. E."—**4**
Means, Florence Crannell—**J**
Medary, Marjorie—**J**
Meddaugh, Susan—**7**
Medearis, Angela Shelf—**8**
Mehdevi, Anne Sinclair—**4**
Meigs, Cornelia—**J**
Meltzer, Milton—**3, 8**
Mendoza, George—**3**
Merriam, Eve—**3**
Merrill, Jean—**3**
"Metcalf, Suzanne"
　　See Baum, L. Frank—**3**
Meyer, Carolyn—**5**
"Michael, Manfred"
　　See Winterfeld, Henry—**3**
Miers, Earl Schenck—**3**
Miklowitz, Gloria D.—**6**
Mikolaycak, Charles—**5**
Miles, Betty—**5**
"Miles, Miska"—**4**
Milhous, Katherine—**J**
Miller, Edna—**6**
Miller, Elizabeth Cleveland—**J**
Miller, Margaret—**8**
Miller, Mitchell—**4**
Mills, Claudia—**7**
Milne, A. A.—**J**
Minarik, Else—**3**
"Minier, Nelson"
　　See Stoutenburg, Adrien —**3**
Minor, Wendell—**8**
Mizumura, Kazue—**3**
Mochizuki, Ken—**8**

Modell, Frank—**5**
Moeri, Louise—**5**
Mohr, Nicholasa—**5**
Mollel, Tololwa M.—**8**
Monjo, F. N.—**5**
Montgomery, Rutherford—**M**
Montresor, Beni—**3**
Monvel, Boutet de
　　See Boutet de Monvel—**J**
Moon, Carl—**J**
Moon, Grace—**J**
Moore, Anne Carroll—**J**
Moore, Lilian—**4**
Moore, Patrick—**4**
Mora, Pat—**8**
Moray Williams, Ursula—**4**
Mordvinoff, Nicolas—**M**
"More, Caroline"
　　See Cone, Molly—**3**
Morey, Walt—**3**
Morgan, Alfred P.—**M**
Morris, Ann—**8**
Morrison, Lillian—**6**
Mosel, Arlene—**5**
Moser, Barry—**6**
Most, Bernard—**7**
Mowat, Farley—**3**
Müller, Jörg—**6**
Mullins, Patricia—**8**
Munari, Bruno—**3**
Munro, Roxie—**6**
Munsch, Robert—**8**
Munsinger, Lynn—**7**
Murphy, Jill—**6**
Murphy, Jim—**7**
Murphy, Robert W.—**4**
Murphy, Shirley Rousseau —**6**
Murphy, Stuart J.—**8**
Myers, Walter Dean—**5**

Naidoo, Beverly—**7**
Namioka, Lensey—**7**
Napoli, Donna Jo—**8**
Nash, Ogden—**4**
Naylor, Phyllis Reynolds—**5**
Nelson, Theresa—**7**
Nesbit, E.—**M**
Ness, Evaline—**3**

Neufeld, John—**8**
Neville, Emily—**3**
Newberry, Clare—**J**
Newcomb, Covell—**J**
Newell, Crosby
　　See Bonsall, Crosby Newell—**3**
Newell, Hope—**M**
Newman, Robert—**6**
Newton, Suzanne—**6**
Ney, John—**5**
"Nic Leodhas, Sorche"—**3**
Nichols, Ruth—**4**
Nicolay, Helen—**J**
Nixon, Joan Lowery—**5**
Noble, Trinka Hakes—**6**
"Nodset, Joan L."
　　See Lexau, Joan M.—**4**
Nolan, Jeannette Covert—**J**
North, Sterling—**3**
"Norton, Andre"—**M**
Norton, Mary—**3**
Nöstlinger, Christine—**5**
Novak, Matt—**8**
Numeroff, Laura (Joffe)—**7**
Nutt, Ken
　　See "Beddows, Eric"—**7**
Nye, Naomi Shihab—**7**

O'Brien, Anne Sibley—**8**
O'Brien, Jack—**M**
"O'Brien, Robert C."—**4**
O'Dell, Scott—**M**
O'Kelly, Mattie Lou—**7**
O'Malley, Kevin—**8**
O'Neill, Mary—**3**
Oakley, Graham—**5**
Olcott, Frances Jenkins—**J**
Olcott, Virginia—**J**
Olsen, Ib Spang—**3**
"Oneal, Zibby"—**6**
Orgel, Doris—**4**
Orlev, Uri—**7**
Ormerod, Jan—**6**
Ormondroyd, Edward—**3**
Orton, Helen Fuller—**J**
"Osborne, David"
　　See Silverberg, Robert—**3**
Osborne, Mary Pope—**8**

Otfinoski, Steven—**8**
"Otis, James"—**J**
Ottley, Reginald—**4**
Owens, Gail—**6**
Oxenbury, Helen—**3**

"Page, Eleanor"
    See Coerr, Eleanor—**6**
"Paisley, Tom"
    See Bethancourt, T.
    Ernesto—**5**
Palazzo, Tony—**3**
Paola, Tomie de-
    See de Paola, Tomie—**5**
Paradis, Adrian A.—**M**
Parish, Peggy—**4**
Park, Barbara—**6**
Park, Ruth—**6**
Parker, Bertha M.—**M**
Parker, Dorothy D.—**4**
Parker, Edgar—**3**
Parker, Nancy Winslow—**5**
Parker, Robert Andrew—**4**
Parker, Steve—**8**
Parnall, Peter—**3**
Parrish, Maxfield—**J**
Parton, Ethel—**J**
Pascal, Francine—**5**
Patch, Edith M.—**J**
Patent, Dorothy Hinshaw—**6**
Paterson, Diane—**6**
Paterson, Katherine—**5**
Paton Walsh, Jill—**4**
Paull, Grace A.—**J**
Paulsen, Gary—**6**
Paxton,Tom—**8**
Pearce, Philippa—**3**
Peare, Catherine Owens—**M**
Pearson, Kit—**7**
Pearson, Susan—**7**
Pearson, Tracey Campbell
    —**7**
Pease, Howard—**J**
Peck, Anne Merriman—**J**
Peck, Richard—**5**
Peck, Robert Newton—**5**
Peet, Bill—**3**
Pellowski, Anne—**5**

Pène du Bois, William
    See du Bois, William
    Pène—**J**
"Penn, Ruth Bonn"
    See Clifford, Eth—**6**
Peppé, Rodney—**5**
Perkins, Lucy Fitch—**J**
Perl, Lila—**6**
Petersen, P. J.—**6**
Petersham, Maud—**J**
Petersham, Miska—**J**
Peterson, Hans—**4**
Petry, Ann—**3**
Pevsner, Stella—**5**
Peyton, K. M.—**3**
Peyton, Michael
    See Peyton, K. M.—**3**
Pfeffer, Susan Beth—**6**
Pfister, Marcus—**8**
Phillips, Ethel Calvert—**J**
"Phipson, Joan"—**3**
Piatti, Celestino—**3**
Picard, Barbara Leonie—**3**
Pienkowski, Jan—**4**
Pier, Arthur Stanwood—**J**
Pierce, Meredith Ann—**6**
Pierce, Tamora—**7**
"Pilgrim, Anne"
    See Allen, Mabel Esther
    —**6**
Pilkey, Dav—**7**
Pincus, Harriet—**4**
Pinkney, Andrea Davis—**8**
Pinkney, Brian—**7**
Pinkney, Gloria Jean—**8**
Pinkney, J. Brian
    See Pinkney, Brian—**7**
Pinkney, Jerry—**6**
Pinkwater, Daniel Manus—**5**
"Piper, Watty"
    See Bragg, Mabel Caro-
    line—**4**
Pitz, Henry C.—**M**
Platt, Kin—**5**
Plotz, Helen—**6**
Plume, Ilse—**5**
Pogány, Willy—**J**
Polacco, Patricia—**7**
Politi, Leo—**J**

Polland, Madeleine—**3**
Polushkin, Maria—**6**
Pomerantz, Charlotte—**6**
Poole, Lynn—**M**
Pope, Elizabeth Marie—**5**
Portal, Colette—**4**
Porte, Barbara Ann—**6**
Porter, Connie—**8**
Porter, Sheena—**3**
Potter, Beatrix—**J**
Poulsson, Emilie—**J**
Prelutsky, Jack—**5**
Preussler, Otfried—**4**
Price, Christine—**M**
Price, Edith Ballinger—**J**
Price, Susan—**7**
Priceman, Marjorie—**8**
Primavera, Elise—**6**
Pringle, Laurence—**4**
Proudfit, Isabel—**M**
Provensen, Alice—**3**
Provensen, Martin—**3**
Pryor, Bonnie—**8**
Pullman, Philip—**6**
Pyle, Katharine—**J**

Quackenbush, Robert—**4**
Quennell, Charles Henry
    Bourne—**M**
Quennell, Marjorie—**M**

Rabe, Berniece—**5**
Rackham, Arthur—**J**
Raffi—**6**
Rahn, Joan Elma—**6**
Rand, Anne (or Ann)—**3**
Rand, Gloria—**8**
Rand, Paul—**3**
Rand, Ted—**6**
Randall, Florence Engel—**6**
"Randall, Robert"
    See Silverberg, Robert—**3**
Rankin, Louise S.—**M**
Ransome, Arthur—**J**
Ransome, James E.—**7**
Raphael, Elaine
    See Bolognese, Don &
    Elaine Raphael—**4**
Rappaport, Doreen—**7**

Raschka, Chris—**7**
Raskin, Ellen—**3**
Rathmann, Peggy—**8**
Ravielli, Anthony—**3**
Rawlings, Marjorie Kinnan
—**3**
Rawls, Wilson—**6**
Ray, Deborah Kogan—**6**
Ray, Jane—**7**
Raynor, Mary—**5**
Reed, Philip—**3**
Reed, W. Maxwell—**J**
Reeder, Carolyn—**7**
Rees, David—**5**
Reeves, James—**3**
Regniers, Beatrice Schenk de
See de Regniers, Beatrice
Schenk—**M**
Reiser, Lynn—**8**
Reiss, Johanna—**5**
Rendina, Laura Cooper—**M**
Renick, Marion—**M**
Rey, H. A.—**J**
Rey, Lester del
See del Rey, Lester—**3**
"Rhine, Richard"
See Silverstein, Virginia
B.—**5**
"Rhue, Morton"
See Strasser, Todd—**6**
Ribbons, Ian—**4**
Rice, Eve—**5**
Richard, Adrienne—**5**
Richter, Hans Peter—**4**
"Rigg, Sharon"
See Creech, Sharon—**7**
Ringgold, Faith—**7**
Ringi, Kjell—**4**
Robbins, Ruth—**3**
Roberts, Willo Davis—**5**
Robertson, Keith—**M**
Robinson, Barbara—**5**
Robinson, Charles—**6**
Robinson, Irene B.—**J**
Robinson, Mabel Louise—**J**
Robinson, Tom—**J**
Robinson, W. W.—**J**
Rochman, Hazel—**7**
Rockwell, Anne F.—**5**

Rockwell, Harlow—**5**
Rockwell, Thomas—**5**
Rodgers, Mary—**5**
Rodowsky, Colby—**6**
Rogers, Fred McFeeley
See "Rogers, Mister"—**7**
"Rogers, Mister"—**7**
Rohmann, Eric—**8**
Rojankovsky, Feodor—**J**
Rolt-Wheeler, Francis—**J**
Roop, Peter & Connie—**8**
Roos, Ann—**M**
Roos, Stephen—**6**
Root, Barry—**8**
Root, Kimberly Bulcken—**8**
Root, Phyllis—**8**
Rose, Elizabeth—**3**
Rose, Gerald—**3**
Rosen, Michael J.—**8**
"Rosenberg, Ethel"
See Clifford, Eth—**6**
Ross, Gayle—**8**
Ross, Pat—**7**
Ross, Tony—**6**
Rostkowski, Margaret—**6**
Roth, Susan L.—**7**
Rounds, Glen—**J**
Rourke, Constance—**M**
Rowe, Dorothy—**J**
Rowling, J. K.—**8**
Rubel, Nicole—**5**
Ruby, Lois—**6**
Ruckman, Ivy—**6**
Ruffins, Reynold
See Sarnoff, Jane & Rey-
nold Ruffins—**5**
Rugh, Belle Dorman—**3**
Russo, Marisabina—**7**
Ryan, Cheli Durán—**5**
Ryder, Joanne—**6**
Rylant, Cynthia—**6**

S., Svend Otto—**6**
Sabin, Edwin L.—**J**
Sabuda, Robert—**8**
Sachar, Louis—**7**
Sachs, Marilyn—**4**
Sadler, Marilyn—**8**

Saint-Exupéry, Antoine de
—**4**
Salassi, Otto R.—**6**
Salisbury, Graham—**8**
Samuels, Barbara—**7**
San Souci, Daniel—**7**
San Souci, Robert D.—**7**
Sánchez-Silva, José—**3**
Sandberg, Inger—**3**
Sandberg, Lasse—**3**
Sandburg, Helga—**3**
Sanders, Scott Russell—**7**
Sandin, Joan—**6**
Sandoz, Mari—**3**
Sanfield, Steve—**8**
Sarg, Tony—**J**
Sargent, Pamela—**6**
Sargent, Sarah—**6**
Sarnoff, Jane—**5**
Sasek, Miroslav—**3**
Sattler, Helen Roney—**6**
Sauer, Julia L.—**M**
Savage, Deborah—**7**
Savage, Katharine—**4**
Savery, Constance—**J**
Savitz, Harriet May—**5**
Sawyer, Ruth—**J**
Say, Allen—**6**
Sayers, Frances Clarke—**J**
Scarry, Richard—**3**
Schaefer, Jack—**3**
Schami, Rafik—**7**
Schechter, Betty—**4**
Scheele, William E.—**3**
Schertle, Alice—**8**
Schick, Eleanor—**5**
Schindelman, Joseph—**3**
Schindler, S. D.—**7**
Schlee, Ann—**5**
Schlein, Miriam—**M**
Schmid, Eleonore—**4**
"Schneider, Elisa"
See Kleven, Elisa—**7**
Schneider, Herman—**M**
Schneider, Nina—**M**
Schnur, Steven—**8**
Schoenherr, John—**4**
"Scholefield, Edmund O."
See Butterworth, W. E.—**5**

Scholz, Jackson V.—**M**
Schoonover, Frank—**M**
Schroeder, Alan—**8**
Schultz, James Willard—**J**
Schulz, Charles—**3**
Schwartz, Alvin—**5**
Schwartz, Amy—**6**
Schwartz, David M.—**6**
Schweninger, Ann—**7**
Scieszka, Jon—**7**
Scoppettone, Sandra—**5**
Scott, Ann Herbert—**4**
Scott, Jack Denton—**6**
Scoville, Samuel Jr.—**J**
Seabrooke, Brenda—**7**
Seaman, Augusta Huiell—**J**
"Sebastian, Lee"
    See Silverberg, Robert—**3**
Sebestyen, Ouida—**5**
"Sefton, Catherine"
    See Waddell, Martin—**7**
Segal, Lore—**4**
Segawa, Yasuo—**4**
Seidler, Tor—**6**
Selden, George—**4**
Selsam, Millicent E.—**M**
Sendak, Maurice—**M**
Seredy, Kate—**J**
Serraillier, Ian—**3**
Service, Pamela F.—**7**
"Seuss, Dr."—**M**
Sewell, Helen—**J**
Sewell, Marcia—**5**
Seymour, Tres—**8**
Shannon, David—**8**
Shannon, George—**6**
Shannon, Monica—**J**
Shapiro, Irwin—**J**
Sharmat, Marjorie Wein-
    man—**5**
Sharmat, Mitchell—**6**
Sharp, Margery—**3**
Shaw, Nancy—**7**
Shecter, Ben—**3**
Shelby, Anne—**8**
Shepard, Ernest—**M**
Sherburne, Zoa Morin—**4**
Shimin, Symeon—**3**

Shippen, Katherine B.—**M**
Shotwell, Louisa R.—**3**
Showers, Paul C.—**4**
Shreve, Susan—**6**
Shub, Elizabeth—**5**
Shulevitz, Uri—**3**
Shura, Mary Francis—**3**
Shusterman, Neal—**7**
Shuttlesworth, Dorothy E.
    —**5**
Sidjakov, Nicolas—**M**
Siebert, Diane—**7**
Siegal, Aranka—**5**
Sierra, Judy—**8**
Silva, José Sánchez-
    See Sánchez-Silva, José—**3**
Silverberg, Robert—**3**
Silverman, Erica—**8**
Silverstein, Alvin—**5**
Silverstein, Shel—**5**
Silverstein, Virginia B.—**5**
Simon, Charlie May—**J**
Simon, Hilda—**4**
Simon, Howard—**M**
Simon, Seymour—**5**
Simont, Marc—**M**
Singer, Isaac Bashevis—**3**
Singer, Marilyn—**6**
Sis, Peter—**6**
Skinner, Constance Lind-
    say—**M**
Skurzynski, Gloria—**5**
Sleator, William—**5**
Slepian, Jan—**5**
Slobodkin, Louis—**J**
Slobodkina, Esphyr—**3**
Slote, Alfred—**5**
Small, David—**6**
"Small, Ernest"
    See Lent, Blair —**3**
Smith, Dick King-
    See King-Smith, Dick—**6**
Smith, Doris Buchanan—**5**
Smith, Janice Lee—**7**
Smith, Jessie Willcox—**J**
Smith, Lane—**7**
Smith, Robert Kimmel—**6**
Smith, William Jay—**5**
Snedeker, Caroline Dale—**J**

Sneve, Virginia Driving
    Hawk—**7**
Snyder, Zilpha Keatley—**3**
Sobol, Donald J.—**4**
Soe, Robert C. Du
    See Du Soe, Robert C.—**M**
Soentpiet, Chris K.—**8**
Sommerfelt, Aimée—**3**
Sorensen, Virginia—**M**
Soto, Gary—**7**
Souci, Daniel San
    See San Souci, Daniel—**7**
Souci, Robert D. San
    See San Souci, Robert D.
    —**7**
Southall, Ivan—**3**
Spanfeller, Jim—**4**
Speare, Elizabeth George—**M**
"Spencer, Cornelia"—**J**
Sperry, Armstrong—**J**
Spier, Peter—**3**
Spilka, Arnold—**3**
Spinelli, Jerry—**6**
Spirin, Gennady—**7**
Springstubb, Tricia—**6**
Spykman, Elizabeth C.—**M**
Spyri, Johanna—**J**
St. George, Judith—**6**
"St. John, Nicole"
    See Johnston, Norma—**5**
Stanley, Diane—**6**
"Stanton, Schuyler"
    See Baum, L. Frank—**3**
Stanley, Jerry—**7**
Staples, Suzanne Fisher—**7**
Stapp, Arthur D.—**M**
"Stark, James"
    See Goldston, Robert Con-
    roy—**4**
Steel, Mary Q.
    See "Gage, Wilson"—**3**
Steele, William O.—**M**
Steig, William—**3**
Stein, Evaleen—**J**
Steptoe, Javaka—**8**
Steptoe, John—**4**
Sterling, Dorothy—**3**
Sterne, Emma Gelders—**M**
Stevens, Janet—**6**

Stevenson, Augusta—**M**
Stevenson, James—**5**
Stewart, Sarah—**8**
Stine, R. L.—**7**
Stobbs, William—**3**
Stock, Catherine—**7**
Stockum, Hilda van
  See van Stockum, Hilda—**J**
Stoddard, Sandol—**4**
Stoeke, Janet Morgan—**8**
Stolz, Mary—**M**
Stone, Helen—**M**
Stong, Phil—**M**
Stoutenburg, Adrien—**3**
Strasser, Todd—**6**
Streatfeild, Noel—**J**
Suba, Susanne—**M**
Sublette, C. M.—**J**
Sueur, Meridel Le
  See Le Sueur, Meridel—**M**
Sullivan, George—**8**
Summers, James L.—**M**
Sutcliff, Rosemary—**M**
Swarthout, Glendon—**4**
Swarthout, Kathryn—**4**
Sweat, Lynn—**7**
Sweet, Ozzie—**6**
Swift, Hildegarde Hoyt—**J**
Syme, Ronald—**M**

Taback, Simms—**8**
Tafuri, Nancy—**6**
Talbert, Marc—**7**
Tamarin, Alfred H.—**5**
Tashjian, Virginia A.—**5**
"Tatham, Campbell"
  See Elting, Mary—**M**
Tate, Eleanora E.—**7**
Taylor, Mildred D.—**5**
Taylor, Sydney—**M**
Taylor, Theodore—**4**
Taylor, William—**7**
Teague, Mark—**8**
Teale, Edwin Way—**3**
Tejima, Keizaburo—**7**
Temple, Frances—**7**
Tenggren, Gustaf—**M**
Tenniel, Sir John—**J**

ter Haar, Jaap
  See Haar, Jaap ter—**4**
Terris, Susan—**5**
Testa, Fulvio—**7**
Tharp, Louise Hall—**M**
"Thayer, Jane"
  See Woolley, Catherine—**M**
"Thayer, Peter."
  See Ames, Rose Wyler—**3**
Thesman, Jean—**7**
Thiele, Colin—**5**
Thomas, Jane Resh—**8**
Thomas, Joyce Carol—**8**
Thomas, Rob—**8**
Thompson, Kay—**4**
Thomsen, Gudrun Thorne-
  See Thorne-Thomsen,
  Gudrun—**J**
Thomson, Peggy—**6**
Thorne-Thomsen, Gudrun
  —**J**
Thrasher, Crystal—**6**
Thurber, James—**M**
Thurman, Judith—**6**
Tiegreen, Alan—**5**
Titherington, Jeanne—**6**
Titus, Eve—**3**
Todd, Ruthven—**M**
Tolan, Stephanie S.—**6**
Tolkien, J. R. R.—**M**
Tomes, Margot—**5**
Tompert, Ann—**6**
Tord, Bijou Le
  See Le Tord, Bijou—**6**
Torrey, Marjorie—**M**
Tousey, Sanford—**J**
Townsend, John Rowe—**4**
Travers, Pamela—**J**
Trease, Geoffrey—**M**
Treece, Henry—**M**
Tresselt, Alvin—**M**
Treviño, Elizabeth Borton
  de—**3**
"Trez, Alain"—**3**
"Trez, Denise"—**3**
Tripp, Valerie—**8**
Tripp, Wallace—**5**
Trivizas, Eugene—**8**
Trnka, Jirí—**3**

Tudor, Tasha—**J**
Tunis, Edwin—**M**
Tunis, John R.—**M**
Tunnell, Michael O.—**8**
Turkle, Brinton—**3**
Turner, Ann—**6**
Turner, Philip—**4**
Turngren, Annette—**M**

Uchida, Yoshiko—**M**
Uden, Grant—**4**
Udry, Janice—**3**
Ullman, James Ramsey—**4**
"Uncle Shelby"
  See Silverstein, Shel—**5**
Ungerer, Tomi—**3**
Unnerstad, Edith—**3**
Unwin, Nora S.—**M**
Ure, Jean—**6**
Urmston, Mary—**M**
"Usher, Margo Scegge"
  See McHargue, Georgess
  —**5**

Vail, Rachel—**7**
Van Allsburg, Chris—**5**
"Van Dyne, Edith"
  See Baum, L. Frank—**3**
van Iterson, S. R.
  See Iterson, S. R. van—**4**
Van Laan, Nancy—**8**
Van Leeuwen, Jean—**5**
van Stockum, Hilda—**J**
Van Woerkom, Dorothy—**5**
Vance, Marguerite—**M**
VanCleave, Janice—**8**
Vander Els, Betty—**6**
Veaux, Alexis De
  See De Veaux, Alexis—**7**
Ventura, Piero—**7**
Verne, Jules—**J**
"Victor, Kathleen"
  See Butler, Beverly—**6**
Vigna, Judith—**7**
Vincent, Gabrielle—**6**
Vining, Elizabeth Gray
  See Gray, Elizabeth Janet
  —**J**
Viorst, Judith—**4**

Vivas, Julie—**7**
"Vivier, Colette"—**4**
Voake, Charlotte—**7**
Voight, Virginia Frances—**M**
Voigt, Cynthia—**5**

Waber, Bernard—**3**
Waddell, Martin—**7**
Wahl, Jan—**3**
Waldeck, Jo Besse
  McElveen—**J**
Waldeck, Theodore, J.—**J**
Walden, Amelia Elizabeth
  —**M**
Wallace, Barbara Brooks—**6**
Wallace, Bill—**7**
"Wallace, Daisy"
  See Cuyler, Margery—**7**
Wallace, Dillon—**J**
Wallace, Ian—**6**
Wallner, John C.—**5**
Walsh, Ellen Stoll—**8**
Walsh, Jill Paton
  See Paton Walsh, Jill—**4**
Walter, Mildred Pitts—**6**
Ward, Lynd—**4**
Warnock, Natalie Kinsey-
  See Kinsey-Warnock,
  Natalie—**8**
Watanabe, Shigeo—**6**
Waters, Kate—**8**
Watson, Clyde—**4**
Watson, Sally Lou—**4**
Watson, Wendy—**4**
Watts, Bernadette—**7**
Weber, Lenora Mattingly—**M**
Weil, Lisl—**4**
Weisgard, Leonard—**J**
Weiss, Ann E.—**6**
Weiss, Harvey—**3**
Weiss, Nicki—**6**
Wellman, Manly Wade—**M**
Wells, Rhea—**J**
Wells, Rosemary—**4**
Wersba, Barbara—**3**
Werstein, Irving—**4**
Werth, Kurt—**M**
Westall, Robert—**5**
Westcott, Nadine Bernard—**6**

Wexler, Jerome—**7**
Wheeler, Francis Rolt-
  See Rolt-Wheeler, Fran-
  cis—**J**
Wheeler, Opal—**M**
Whelan, Gloria—**8**
White, Anne Hitchcock—**4**
White, Anne Terry—**M**
White, E. B.—**M**
White, Eliza Orne—**J**
White, Robb—**J**
White, Ruth—**7**
Whitney, Elinor—**J**
Whitney, Phyllis A.—**J**
Wibberley, Leonard—**M**
Wick, Walter—**8**
Wier, Ester—**3**
Wiese, Kurt—**J**
Wiesner, David—**7**
Wijngaard, Juan—**8**
Wikland, Ilon—**4**
Wilder, Laura Ingalls—**J**
Wildsmith, Brian—**3**
Wilkinson, Barry—**4**
Wilkinson, Brenda—**5**
Willard, Barbara—**4**
Willard, Nancy—**5**
Willey, Margaret—**7**
"William, Kate"
  See Armstrong, Jennifer—**8**
Williams, Barbara—**6**
"Williams, Charles"
  See Collier, James Lin-
  coln—**5**
Williams, Garth—**M**
Williams, Jay—**4**
Williams, Karen Lynn—**8**
"Williams, Patrick J."
  See Butterworth, W. E.—**5**
Williams, Sherley Anne—**7**
Williams, Ursula Moray
  See Moray Williams,
  Ursula—**4**
Williams, Vera B.—**5**
Williams-Garcia, Rita—**8**
Williamson, Joanne S.—**3**
Wilson, Barbara Ker
  See Ker Wilson, Barbara
  —**4**

Wilson, Budge—**7**
Windsor, Patricia—**5**
"Winfield, Julia"
  See Armstrong, Jennifer—**8**
Winter, Jeannette—**7**
Winter, Paula—**6**
Winterfeld, Henry—**3**
Winthrop, Elizabeth—**5**
Wiseman, David—**5**
Wisler, G. Clifton—**7**
Wisniewski, David—**7**
Woerkom, Dorothy Van
  See Van Woerkom, Dor-
  othy—**5**
Wojciechowska, Maia—**3**
Wolf, Bernard—**5**
Wolff, Ashley—**6**
"Wolff, Sonia"
  See Levitin, Sonia—**5**
Wolff, Virginia Euwer—**7**
Wolitzer, Hilma—**5**
Wolkstein, Diane—**5**
"Wolny, P."
  See Janeczko, Paul B.—**6**
Wondriska, William—**3**
Wood, Audrey—**6**
Wood, Don—**6**
Wood, Esther—**J**
Wood, James Playsted—**4**
Woodruff, Elvira—**8**
Woodson, Jacqueline—**8**
Woody, Regina J.—**M**
Woolley, Catherine—**M**
Worth, Kathryn—**J**
Worth, Valerie—**5**
Wrede, Patricia C.—**7**
Wright, Betty Ren—**6**
Wrightson, Patricia—**4**
Wuorio, Eva-Lis—**3**
Wyeth, N. C.—**J**
Wyler, Rose
  See Ames, Gerald & Rose
  Wyler—**3**
Wyndham, Lee—**M**
Wynne-Jones, Tim—**8**

Yamaguchi, Marianne—**3**
Yamaguchi, Tohr—**3**
Yarbrough, Camille—**7**

Yashima, Taro—**M**
Yates, Elizabeth—**J**
Yates, Raymond F.—**M**
Yee, Paul Richard—**7**
Yep, Laurence—**5**
"Ylla"—**M**
Yolen, Jane—**4**
Yorinks, Arthur—**6**
York, Carol Beach—**5**
Youd, Samuel
  See "Christopher, John"—**4**

Young, Ed—**3**
Young, Ella—**J**
Zalben, Jane Breskin—**5**
Zarchy, Harry—**M**
Zei, Alki—**4**
Zelinsky, Paul O.—**6**
Zemach, Harve & Margot—**3**
Ziefert, Harriet—**7**
Zim, Herbert S.—**J**
Zimmer, Dirk—**6**

Zimnik, Reiner—**3**
Zindel, Paul—**5**
Zion, Gene—**M**
Zollinger, Gulielma—**J**
Zolotow, Charlotte—**M, 8**
Zwerger, Lisbeth—**6**
Zwilgmeyer, Dikken—**J**